ARIEL WORKSHOP MANUAL

for

Leader and Arrow
Two-stroke Motorcycles

ARIEL MOTORS LTD., BIRMINGHAM

7th Edition - 1965

A Floyd Clymer Publication by www.VelocePress.com 2023

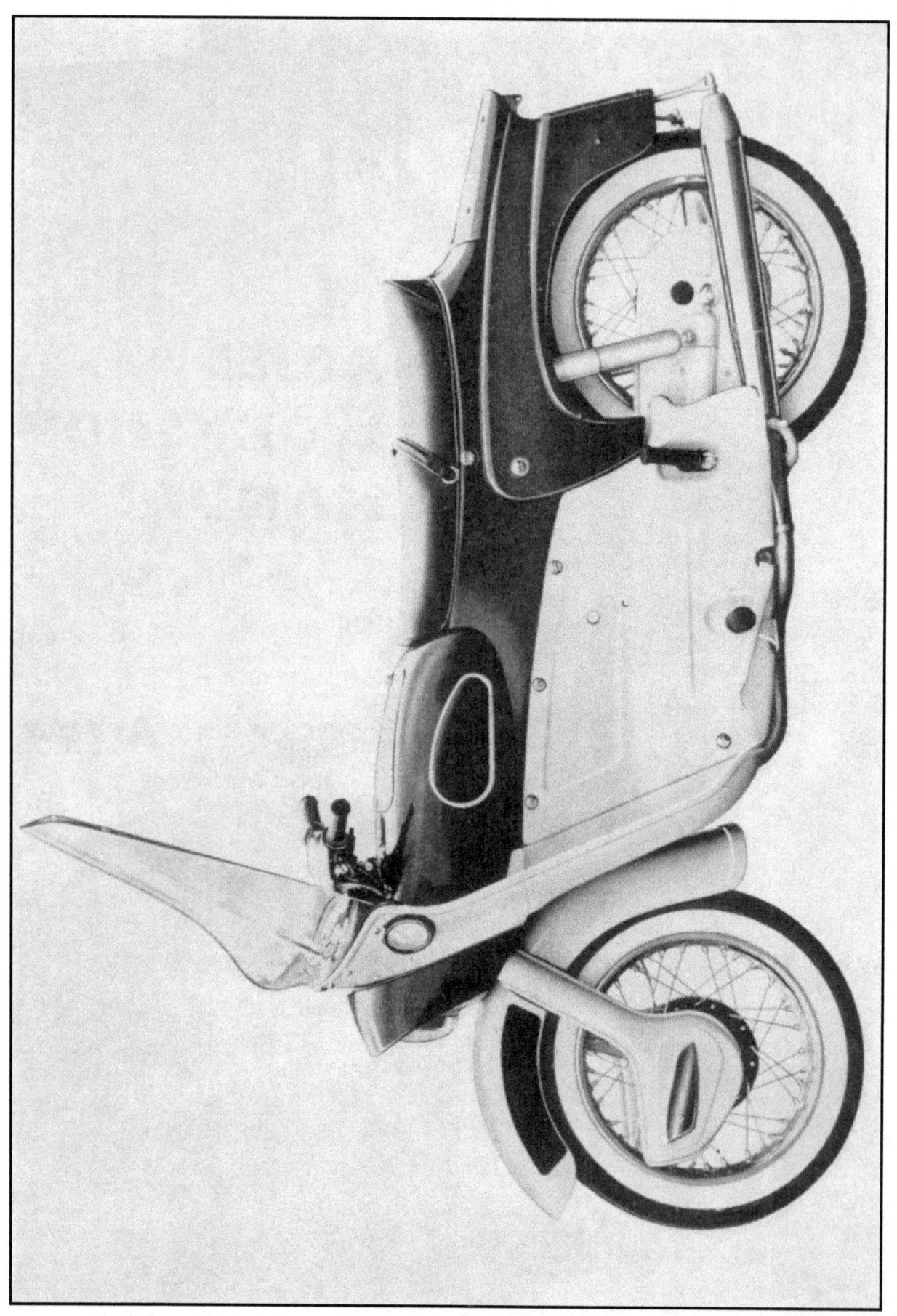

The Leader

The Arrow

FOREWORD

This manual has been written with the object of producing in one volume comprehensive service and maintenance instructions for both the ARIEL LEADER and ARROW two-stroke Motor Cycles. It has been compiled by our trained technical staff who are themselves keen motor cyclists. Whilst this book has been mainly produced for the Ariel service mechanic to assist him in every way to acquire a full knowledge of these motor cycles, the manner in which it has been written is also to offer to the keen owner with little mechanical knowledge the essential principles as clearly as possible, therefore every endeavour has been made to explain all details in the simplest way avoiding where possible the use of technical terms.

Whilst part of the descriptive matter may appear too simplified to the trained mechanic we trust he will bear with us and appreciate that everyone who uses a motor vehicle is not an engineer, and may find this book helpful, in any case the experienced man need only refer to the essential sections. The Leader and Arrow machines are similar in many respects, both using the same basic chassis but differing with regard to appearance and requirements. Many sections in this manual refer to both models, where a difference occurs there is a separate section, therefore care should be exercised to ensure that the instructions being used are relevant to your machine.

The best advice we can offer is to read all the relevant instructions concerned, prior to commencing work, so that spare parts or special service tools that may be required can be obtained beforehand and so avoiding unnecessary delay, also in your own interests always use genuine Ariel spares. Finally, whilst every endeavour has been made to cover the servicing of these machines as accurately and as clearly as possible, it must be appreciated that we cannot accept responsibility for any damage caused by errors or inexperience, it is therefore strongly recommended that all work of a serious nature be entrusted to a competent Ariel dealer.

CONTENTS

	PAGE
SECTIONAL INDEX	6
TECHNICAL DATA	8
LUBRICATION CHARTS	10
WORKSHOP MANUAL FOR LEADER AND ARROW	14
WIRING DIAGRAM	212, 215 & 240
TRACING TROUBLES	227
SERVICE TOOLS	231
OPTIONAL EXTRAS	232
PROPRIETARY MANUFACTURERS	233
ALPHABETICAL INDEX	236
SPORTS ARROW—SUPPLEMENTARY INSTRUCTIONS	239
SUPPLEMENTARY INSTRUCTIONS FOR THE 200 c.c. ENGINE, MODEL 1964	239

SECTION INDEX

	Leader	Arrow
ENGINE	14	14
LUBRICATION	10	10
SPARKING PLUGS	18	18
CONTACT BREAKER AND IGNITION TIMING	58	58
CARBURETTER	19	19
AIR CLEANER	24	24
PRIMARY CHAIN AND CASE	24	24
CLUTCH	35	35
DECARBONISING	36	36
CYLINDER BARRELS AND PISTONS	43	43
SMALL END BUSHES	44	44
CRANKSHAFT ASSEMBLY	46	46
REMOVAL OF ENGINE FROM MOTOR CYCLE	15	15
GEARBOX	61	61
LUBRICATION	10 & 61	10 & 61
KICK STARTER CASE COVER	61	61
DISMANTLING	65	65
RE-ASSEMBLING	72	72
FRONT WHEEL	76	76
LUBRICATION	10 & 88	10 & 88
REMOVAL	76	76
RE-FITTING	85	85
BRAKE ADJUSTMENT	86	86
BRAKE ANCHOR PLATE	90	90
BRAKE LININGS	88 & 92	88 & 92
HUB AND BEARINGS	93	93
WHEEL BUILDING	97	97
TYRES	97	97
REAR WHEEL	98	98
LUBRICATION	10 & 109	10 & 109
REMOVAL	98	105
RE-FITTING	105	105
BRAKE ADJUSTMENT	107	107
BRAKE PEDAL	108	108
BRAKE PLATE	110	110
BRAKE LININGS	111	111
CHAIN WHEEL AND CHAIN CASE	111	111
HUB AND BEARINGS	113	113
CHAIN ADJUSTMENT	118	118
CHAIN	120	120
WHEEL ALIGNMENT	122	122
WHEEL BUILDING	123	123
TYRES	124	124
HANDLEBAR	124	124 & 129
COVER	124	—
CONTROL LEVERS	124	124 & 129
CLUTCH CABLE	126	131
THROTTLE CABLE	127	130
FRONT BRAKE CABLE	126	130
REMOVAL	185	129

	Leader	Arrow
FRONT FORK	132	132
LUBRICATION	132	132
STEERING HEAD ADJUSTMENT	133	145
REMOVAL	141	146
DISMANTLING FORK LEGS	135	135
RE-FITTING FRONT FORKS	142	146
STEERING HEAD BEARINGS	147	147
FRONT MUDGUARD	153	153
SIDE PANELS	154	—
REMOVAL	154	—
RE-FITTING	154	—
ENGINE COVER	—	155
LEG SHIELDS	155	—
REMOVAL	155	—
RE-FITTING	155	—
WINDSCREEN	155	211
REMOVAL	155	—
RE-FITTING	156	—
EXTENSION	157	—
CLEANING	226	—
INSTRUMENT PANEL	157	—
REMOVAL	166	—
RE-FITTING	166	—
SPEEDOMETER	157	163
AMMETER	159	162
WARNING LIGHTS	160	—
EIGHT-DAY CLOCK	164	—
PARKING LAMP	165	—
LIGHTING AND IGNITION SWITCHES	160	160
HEADLAMP COWL AND SHELL	167	—
FITTINGS	167	—
FRONT SHIELD	167	—
FITTINGS	167	—
LICENCE HOLDER	167	—
BODY	168	—
FITTINGS	168	—
GLOVE COMPARTMENT LID	168	—
LIFTING HANDLE	168	—
FRONT SHELL	—	170
TOOL BOX	—	170
SPORTS ARROW	—	239

	Leader	Arrow
DUAL SEAT	169	169
FITTINGS	169	169
REMOVAL	169	169
WATERPROOF COVER	169	169
TAIL SECTION	172	173
REMOVAL	172	173
RE-FITTING	172	173
TAIL LAMP	172	173
SILENCER SUPPORT STAY	172	173
PETROL TANK	174	175
FITTINGS	174	175
REMOVAL	174	175
RE-FITTING	174	175
REAR FORK	176	179
REMOVAL	176	179
RE-FITTING	179	179
PIVOT BUSHES	177	177
REAR HYDRAULIC UNITS	180	180
SUPPLEMENTARY SPRINGS	182	182
FOOTRESTS	182	182
CENTRE STAND	183	183
PROP STAND	184	184
FRONT STAND	183	183
EXHAUST PIPES and SILENCERS		
REMOVAL	37	37
RE-FITTING	43	43
DECARBONISING	42	42
GENERAL DISMANTLING	185	201
RE-ASSEMBLING	193	203
PANNIERS	208	—
FITTING	208	—
LOCK—PANNIER LID	210	—
REAR LUGGAGE CARRIER	210	210
REAR FENDER	211	—
REAR VIEW MIRRORS	211	—
ELECTRICAL EQUIPMENT		
BATTERY	212	212
HEADLAMP UNIT	213	214
STOP AND TAIL LAMP	172	173
STOP LAMP SWITCH	219	219
ELECTRIC HORN	214	216
AMMETER	159	162
IGNITION COILS	216	216
RECTIFIER	217	217
INSPECTION LAMP	162	—
ALTERNATOR	218	218
DIP SWITCH	220	220
LIGHTING AND IGNITION SWITCHES	160	160
FLASHING INDICATORS	220	—
NEUTRAL INDICATOR	225	—
CLEANING and POLISHING	225	225

TECHNICAL DATA

Ariel Engine	Leader	Arrow
Bore	54 mm. = 2.125 inches.	54 mm. = 2.125 inches.
Stroke	54 mm. = 2.125 inches.	54 mm. = 2.125 inches.
Number of Cylinders	Two	Two
Capacity	247 cc. = 15 cubic inches.	247 cc. = 15 cubic inches.
Compression Ratio	8.25 : 1. or 10 : 1.	8.25 : 1. or 10 : 1
B.H.P.	16 at 6,400 r.p.m. or 17.5 at 7,000 r.p.m.	16 at 6,400 r.p.m. or 17.5 at 7,000 r.p.m.
Ignition Timing	20° B.T.D.C. = 2 mm. = 0.080 inch.	20° B.T.D.C. = 2 mm. = 0.080 inch.
Piston Clearance	.002 inch—.0035 inch measured at front or rear of piston at bottom of cylinder barrel.	.002 inch—.0035 inch measured at front or rear of piston at bottom of cylinder barrel.
Piston Ring Gap	.070 inch—.073 inch allowing for peg in ring groove.	.070 inch—.073 inch allowing for peg in ring groove.
Lubrication	Petroil. See page 10.	Petroil. See page 10.
Carburetter	Amal Monobloc Type No. 375/33. Fitted with 'Cold' Start device, Air filter and Silencer. Choke size, 7/8 inch. Main Jet 140 (see page 23). Pilot Jet 30. Needle Jet 105. Needle Position 3. Throttle size 3½.	Amal Monobloc Type No. 375/33. Fitted with 'Cold' Start device. Air filter and Silencer. Choke size 7/8 inch. Main Jet 140. Pilot Jet 30. Needle Jet 105. Needle Position 3. Throttle size 3½.
Gear Box	Four speed.	Four speed.
Gear Ratios	First: 19.0 : 1. Second: 11.0 : 1. Third: 7.8 : 1. Fourth: 5.9 : 1.	First: 19.0 : 1. Second: 11.0 : 1. Third: 7.8 : 1. Fourth: 5.9 : 1.
Gear Box Lubrication	S.A.E. 30 oil. See page 10.	S.A.E. 30 oil. See page 10.
Clutch	Wet type, three friction plates, with transmission shock absorber in clutch centre.	Wet type, three friction plates, with transmission shock absorber in clutch centre.
Primary Drive	Endless roller chain 3/8 inch pitch .225 inch wide; 70 links; enclosed in oil bath chaincase. Oil capacity 3/4 pint S.A.E. 20.	Endless roller chain 3/8 inch pitch .225 inch wide; 70 links; enclosed in oil bath chaincase. Oil capacity 3/4 pint S.A.E. 20.
Secondary Drive	Roller chain ½ inch pitch .305 inch wide, 113 links. Enclosed in chaincase, automatically lubricated.	Roller chain ½ inch pitch .305 inch wide, 113 links. Enclosed in chaincase, automatically lubricated.
Sprocket sizes	Engine shaft: 22 teeth. Clutch chain wheel: 50 teeth. Gear Box: 18 teeth. Rear Wheel: 47. 1,000 r.p.m. in top gear = 11.0 m.p.h. = 17.7 k.p.h.	Engine shaft: 22 teeth. Clutch chain wheel: 50 teeth. Gear Box: 18 teeth. Rear Wheel: 47. 1,000 r.p.m. in top gear = 11.0 m.p.h. = 17.7 k.p.h.
Electrical Equipment	Lucas.	Lucas.
A/C Generator	50 watt type R.M. 13/15. or type R.M. 18.	50 watt type R.M. 13/15. or type R.M. 18.

Ariel Engine	Leader	Arrow
Battery	13 amp type MLZ.9E 6 volt.	13 amp type MLZ9E, 6 volt.
Rectifier	Type F.S.X. 1849, F.S.X. 1501, or 2 D.S. 506. See page 218.	Type F.S.X. 1849, F.S.X. 1501, or 2 D.S. 506. See page 218.
Headlamp	6 inch diameter Prefocus light unit. Main bulb 24/30 watt double filament. Pilot bulb 3 watt.	6 inch diameter Prefocus light unit. Main bulb 24/30 watt double filament. Pilot bulb 3 watt.
Rear Lamp	Stop and Tail bulb, 18-3 watt double filament.	Stop and tail bulb 18-3 watt double filament.
Electric Horn	Type H.F. 1849 or 8H.	Type H.F. 1849 or 8H.
Ignition	Coils, two separate, oil filled Type M.A. 6.	Coils, two separate, oil filled Type M.A. 6.
Contact Breaker	Gap 0.014 inch—0.016 inch.	Gap 0.014 inch—0.016 inch.
Sparking Plugs	Lodge, Type 2HLN or Champion N4. Electrode gap 0.030 inch.	Lodge, Type 2HLN or Champion N4. Electrode gap 0.030 inch.
Front Wheel	Rim size WM2—16. Number of spokes: 36. Tyre size 3.25 inch × 16 inch Ribbed tread. Hub, full width. Brake size 6 inch dia. × 1⅛ inch wide.	Rim size WM2—16. Number of spokes: 36. Tyre size 3.25 inch × 16 inch Ribbed tread. Hub, full width. Brake size 6 inch dia. × 1⅛ inch wide.
Rear Wheel	Rim size WM2—16. Number of spokes: 36. Tyre size 3.25 inch × 16 inch Studded tread. Hub, full width. Brake size 6 inch dia. × 1⅛ inch wide. Quickly detachable, pull out spindle.	Rim size WM2—16. Number of spokes: 36. Tyre size 3.25 inch × 16 inch Studded tread. Hub, full width. Brake size 6 inch dia. × 1⅛ inch wide. Quickly detachable, pull out spindle.
Wheel Base	51 inches = 130 cm.	51 inches = 130 cm.
Overall length	76½ inches = 194 cm.	78 inches = 198 cm.
Overall width	27¼ inches = 69 cm.	25¼ inches = 64 cm.
Dual seat height	30½ inches = 77 cm.	28½ inches = 73 cm.
Ground clearance	5 inches = 13 cm.	5 inches = 13 cm.
Weight (dry)	310 lbs. = 141 kg.	285 lbs. = 129 kg.
Weight (fully equipped with all extras)	340 lbs. = 154 kg.	—
Fuel Tank capacity	2.3 gallons = 10.46 litres, or 3 gallons = 13.6 litres.	2.3 gallons = 10.46 litres, or 3 gallons = 13.6 litres
Oil measure	Integral part of fuel tank cap. See recommended lubricants for quantity.	Integral part of fuel tank cap. See recommended lubricants for quantity.
Tyre pressures	Front: 18 lb. per square inch. Rear: 25 lb. per square inch. Increase pressure as recommended on page 124 when carrying a pillion passenger or extra load.	Front: 18 lb. per square inch. Rear: 22 lb. per square inch. Increase pressure as recommended on page 124 when carrying a pillion passenger or extra load.
Maximum speed	Approximately 70 m.p.h. = 113 k.p.h.	Approximately 70 m.p.h. = 113 k.p.h.
Petrol consumption (with Premium grade fuel)	Approximately 80-90 m.p.g. at 40 m.p.h. = 28-32 k.p.l. at 64.5 k.p.h.	Approximately 80-90 m.p.g. at 40 m.p.h. = 28-32 k.p.l. at 64.5 k.p.h.

RECOMMENDED MAINTENANCE PERIODS

Key	ITEM	WEEKLY	Every 1000 mls. 1600 km.	Every 2500 mls. 4000 km.	Every 10,000 mls. 16,000 km.
A	Control Levers, Cables, etc.	A few drops of cycle oil	—	—	—
B	Petrol Tank See chart below	—	—	—	—
C	Battery	Check Electrolyte level and top up if necessary	—	Clean and check Terminals	—
D	Front and Rear Hubs and Front Anchor Bar	—	Check Wheel Spindle Nuts	—	Remove existing grease, clean and repack See pages 88 & 109
E	Front and Rear Brake Cam Spindle	—	—	Grease sparingly	—
F	Brake Pedal Spindle and Centre Stand	—	—	Grease	—
G	Gear Box	Check level and top up if necessary	—	—	Drain, flush and refill
H	Contact Breaker Wick	—	—	A few drops of engine oil on felt pad	—
J	Primary Chain Case	—	Check level and top up if necessary	—	Drain, flush and refill
K	Brake Plate Bush, Nipple in Front Spindle	—	Oil (SAE30) Sparingly	—	—
L	Front Links	—	—	Grease	—

RECOMMENDED LUBRICANTS

	Quantity	WAKEFIELD	ESSO	MOBIL	SHELL	B.P.
Engine	* See Below	Castrol Two Stroke Oil	Esso Two Stroke Motor Oil	Mobilmix TT	2T Mixture or 2T Two Stroke Oil	B.P. Zoom or Energol Two Stroke Oil
Gear Box	1 Pint	Castrol XL	Essolube 30	Mobiloil A	Shell X100—30	Energol 30
Primary Chaincase	¾ pint	Castrolite	Esso Extra 20 W 30	Mobil Oil Arctic	Shell X100 20/20 W	Energol S.A.E. 20 W
Front and Rear Hubs	See Page 88 & 109	Castrolease L.M.	Esso Multipurpose Grease H.	Mobil Grease M.P.	Retinax A.	Energrease L.2
Grease Points		do.	do.	do.	do.	do.

Use Premium Grade Petrol for Best Performance.

When using:—Castrol Two Stroke oil, Esso Two Stroke Motor oil or Mobil Mix T.T., which are blended for quick and easy mixing, the Petrol/Oil ratio is 24 : 1, i.e. one gallon of petrol to three Tank Cap measures of oil or half a pint of oil to one and a half gallon of petrol.

With Shell 2T Two Stroke oil or Energol Two Stroke oil, the Petrol/Oil ratio is 32 : 1, i.e. one gallon of petrol to two and a half Tank Cap measures of oil or quarter of a pint of oil to one gallon of Petrol.

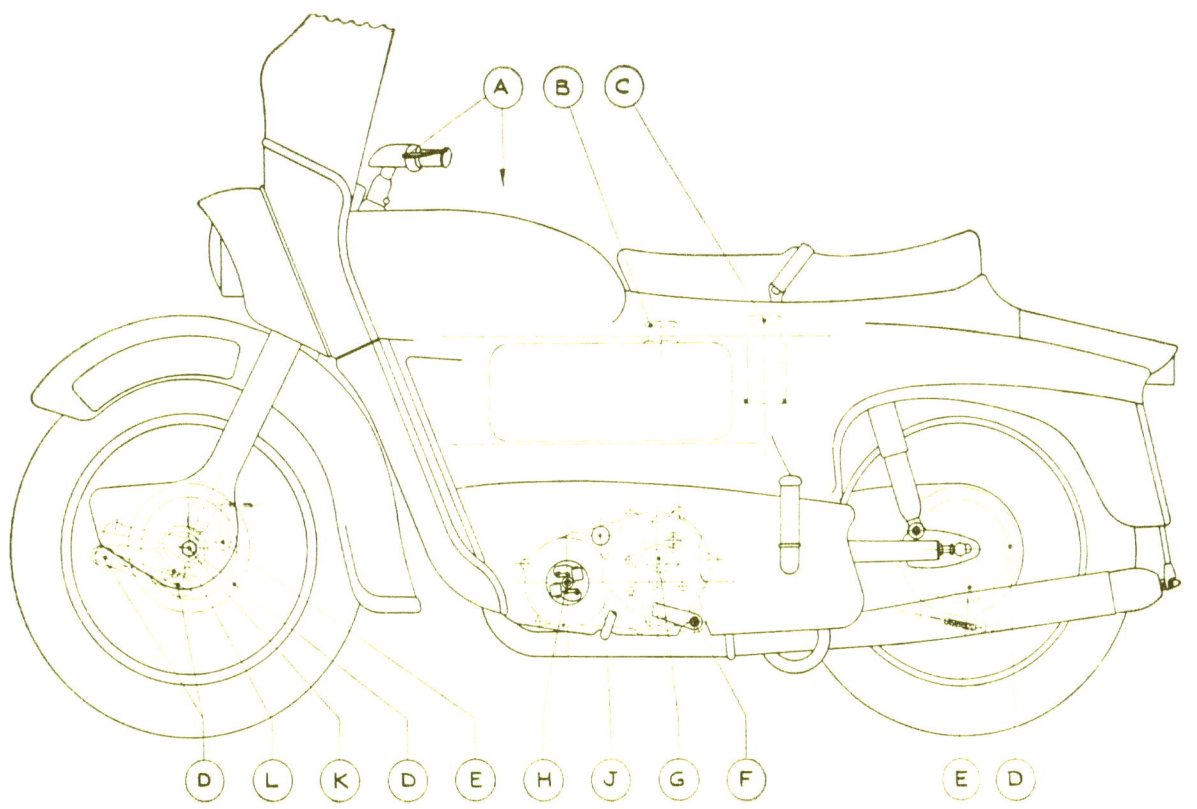

Lubrication Diagram for the Ariel "Leader"

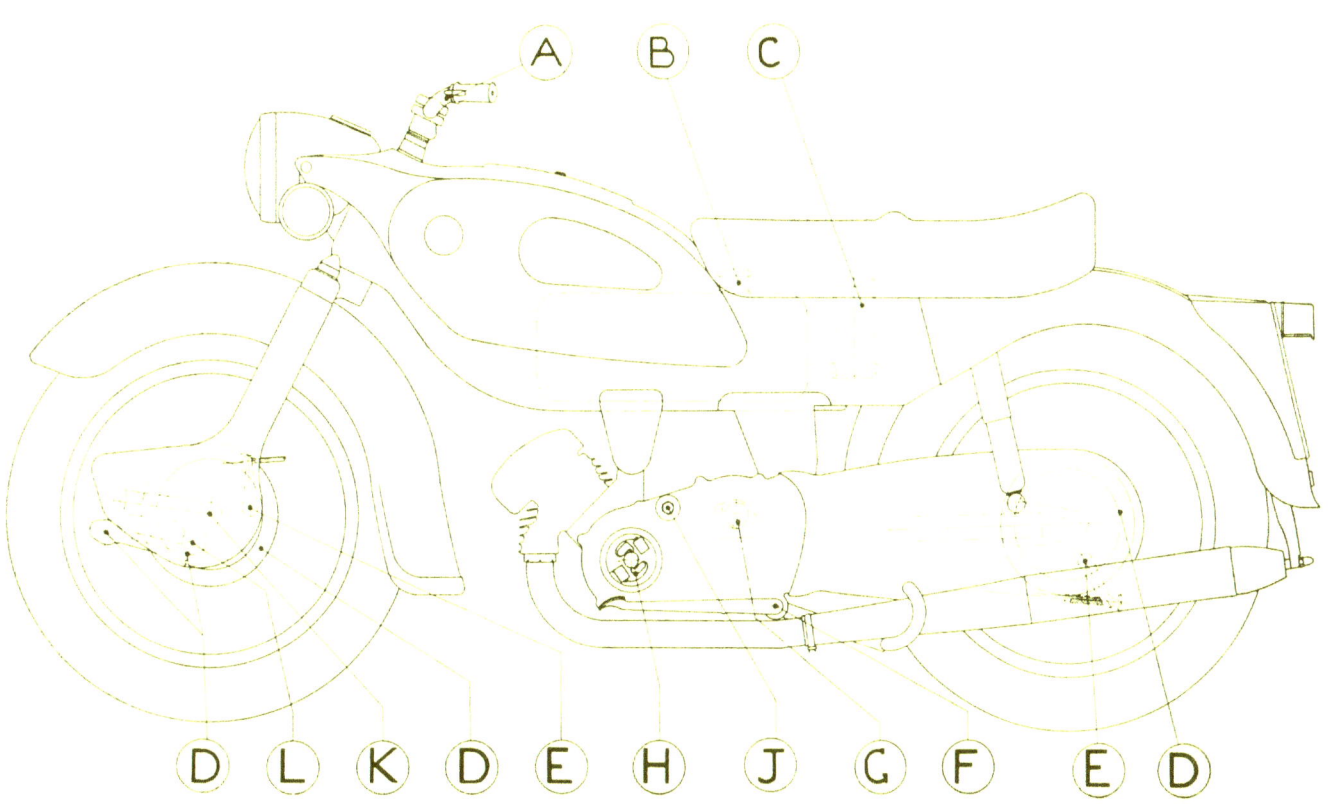

Lubrication Diagram for the Ariel "Arrow"

IMPORTANT DATA ON SCREWS AND THREADS, etc.

Whenever parts of the motor cycle have been dismantled: on re-assembling make quite certain that the correct bolts, nuts and washers are refitted. Many of the bolts are made of special material so that they are extra strong, to carry greater loadings at important points, and they must not be replaced with any other type. Also special locking nuts are fitted in a number of places, these nuts are used at vital points where it is most important that they do not work loose, and they must only be replaced with nuts of the same type.

The plain, shake-proof and spring washers have a definite purpose. The plain washers are used to distribute the load exerted by the bolts and nuts over a larger area. The shake-proof washers have a number of sharp ears which have a locking effect, and help to prevent nuts working loose. The spring washers do a similar job.

With the exception of the carburetter, electrical equipment and some of the handlebar fittings, all studs, bolts, screws and nuts have unified threads. Unified coarse threads are used for studs, bolts and screws which screw into aluminium castings, all others have unified fine thread.

When replacing lost or damaged bolts and nuts, etc., make quite certain that the new ones have the correct thread.

Important: Normal open-ended and tube S.A.E. or unified A/F spanners are suitable for all unified nuts and bolts. If, however, it is desired to use ring spanners, whilst these are admirable tools, extra care must be taken due to their increased leverage to avoid bolt breakage.

Whenever work is to be carried out necessitating disconnecting electrical circuit wires, it is essential always to disconnect the battery first to eliminate a potential fire risk.

Note: Where reference is made to the sides of the motorcycle, the offside is the righthand, and the nearside the lefthand, when viewed from the seated position.

IMPORTANT INFORMATION

PAGE NUMBERS: This manual consists of two separate factory publications – a 240 page workshop manual and a 42 page illustrated parts list. The parts list starts immediately after the workshop manual at page 241.

NOTE FROM THE PUBLISHER: The information presented is true and complete to the best of our knowledge. All recommendations are made without any guarantees on the part of the author or the publisher, who also disclaim all liability incurred with the use of this information.

TRADEMARKS: We recognize that some words, model names and designations, for example, mentioned herein are the property of the trademark holder. We use them for identification purposes only. This is not an official publication.

INFORMATION ON THE USE OF THIS PUBLICATION: This manual is an invaluable resource for those interested in performing their own maintenance. However, in today's information age we are constantly subject to changes in common practice, new technology, availability of improved materials and increased awareness of chemical toxicity. As such, it is advised that the user consult with an experienced professional prior to undertaking any procedure described herein. While every care has been taken to ensure correctness of information, it is obviously not possible to guarantee complete freedom from errors or omissions or to accept liability arising from such errors or omissions. Therefore, any individual that uses the information contained within, or elects to perform or participate in do-it-yourself repairs or modifications acknowledges that there is a risk factor involved and that the publisher or its associates cannot be held responsible for personal injury or property damage resulting from the use of the information or the outcome of such procedures.

WARNING! One final word of advice, this publication is intended to be used as a reference guide, and when in doubt the reader should consult with a qualified technician.

ENGINE

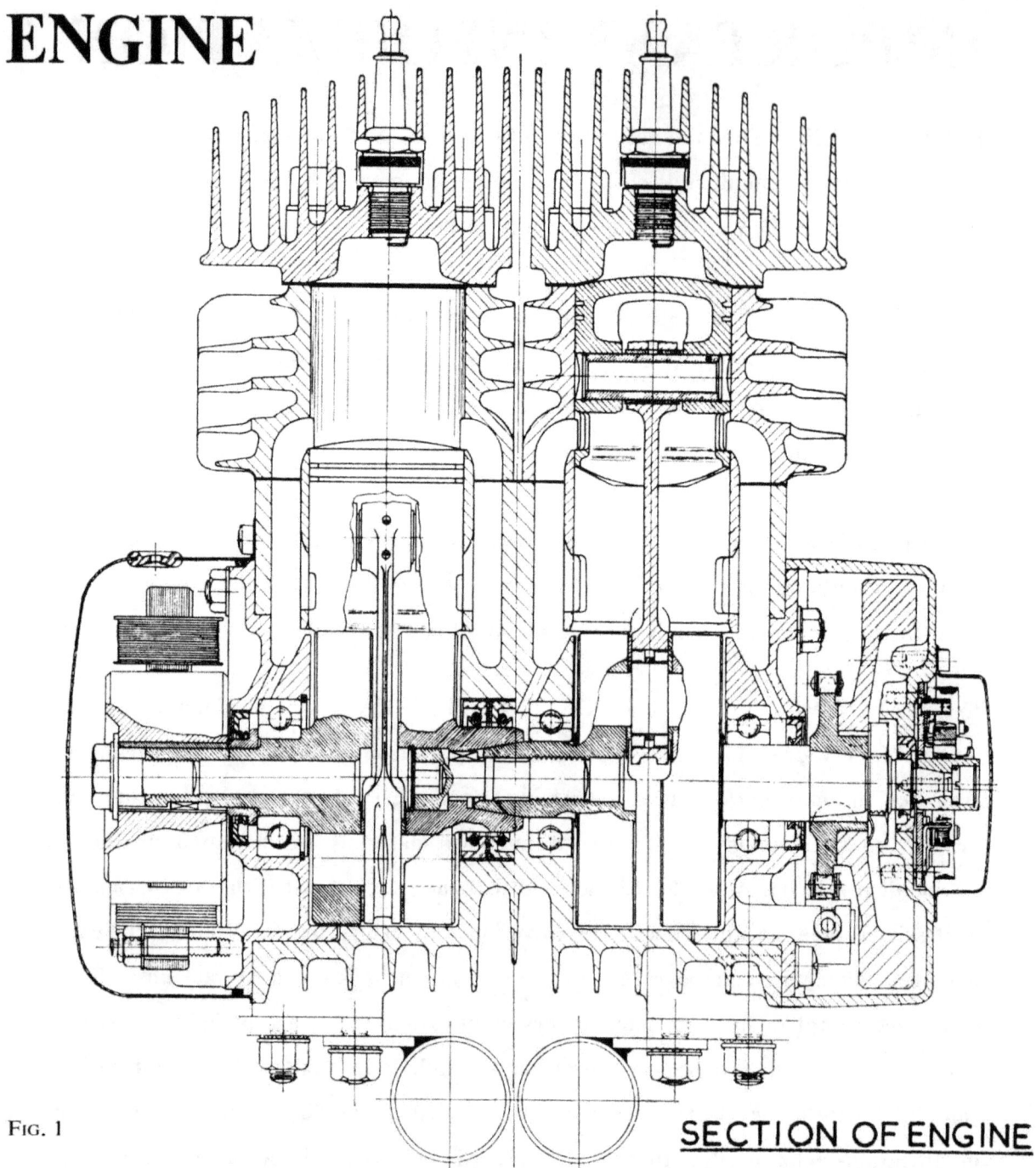

Fig. 1 **SECTION OF ENGINE**

THE ENGINE UNIT—LEADER AND ARROW

The 247 c.c. twin two-stroke engine unit incorporates a Lucas A/C generator, which supplies the electric current for ignition and lighting, etc., a four-speed gear box, providing a series of reduction gears in order to use the engine's power effectively to drive the motor cycle, and an Amal carburetter to supply fuel and air for the engine.

Due to the overall design it is possible not only to carry out normal routine maintenance, but also to completely overhaul the engine unit without removing it from the motor cycle. If, however, it is desired to remove the engine unit from the motor cycle, see page 15. For instructions on dismantling and overhauling the engine unit, see page 46.

In order to obtain the best results from the engine unit, it is essential that all adjustments, etc., are maintained correctly, and with this in view regular checks should be made of the following items:

Sparking plugs, page 18
Contact breaker, page 58
Oil level—Primary chaincase, page 25
Oil level—gear box, page 61
Primary chain, page 25
Clutch, pages 126 and 131
Decarbonising, page 36
Carburetter, page 19
Air cleaner, page 24.

ENGINE REMOVAL—LEADER AND ARROW

If it should be required to remove the engine unit from the motor cycle proceed as follows. Begin with the machine on the centre stand, and with a front stand also fitted, then remove the following parts as described on the pages mentioned.

	Leader	Arrow
Side Panels	154	—
Legshields	155	—
Engine Cover	—	155
Exhaust Pipes	37	37
Rear Brake Pedal	108	108
Rear Fork	176	179
Throttle Cable	127	130
Clutch Cable	126	131
Speedometer Cable	158	163
Cold-start Control Rod	22	22

Then disconnect the petrol pipe by undoing the union nut below the petrol tap, lift the high tension leads off the sparking plugs, separate the snap connectors in the two leads from the contact breaker, and the three leads from the alternator. Next remove one of the nuts from the front engine securing stud, and withdraw the stud from the machine. The motor cycle can then be lifted clear, leaving the engine unit complete on the stands.

When re-fitting the engine unit to the motor cycle begin with the engine on the centre and front stands, then slacken the two socket head set screws which are situated in the two engine lugs at the top rear of the gear box on the offside of the engine. A special key spanner will be required to slacken these screws, and this can be obtained from most good tool dealers. The key required is Unbrako W $5\frac{5}{32}$ inches across flats. When the screws have been slackened, the distance tubes which fit in each lug will be loose, but they must not be removed. Then lift the motor cycle into position on to the engine, with the brackets on the underside of the frame located on to the lugs on the top of the engine and gear box. The front engine securing stud must be fitted first, it can be passed through the frame brackets and engine lug from either side, and when fitted the stud must have a cable clip, a plain washer, a shake-proof washer and a nut at both ends. The cable clip is only fitted on the Leader and is shaped like a large washer with a long tag attached; with a rubber sleeve covering the tag. Do not fully tighten the nuts on the front engine stud at this stage.

Next, locate the frame correctly on the lugs at the top and rear of the gear box, and pass the top securing bolt partially through the engine lug and the frame bracket. This bolt should only be pushed in loosely in order to hold and locate the frame in position whilst fitting the rear fork. Next check to make certain there is a washer fitted to the lug on the nearside of the gear box where the rear fork pivot bolt screws in. This washer is not loose, but retained in a recess in the lug and is secured in position by punching over the metal surrounding the washer in a number of places. Then fit the distance washer on to the rear fork pivot bolt. This washer is $1\frac{1}{2}$ inches in diameter and has a spigot in the centre, and when fitted to the pivot bolt the spigot must face away from the head of the bolt. Next, place one of the nylon thrust washers on the pivot bolt and locate it on the spigot in the centre of the distance washer. The pivot bolt is then ready for securing the rear fork in position, and it should be placed somewhere convenient whilst the fork is located in position at the rear of the gear box. The fork must be placed with the pivot lugs in line with the two engine lugs at the rear of the gear box, and the offside fork pivot lug must be outside the offside engine lug. Also, at the same time as the fork is being placed in position, the second nylon thrust washer must be placed between the offside fork pivot lug and the offside engine lug, so that the rear fork and the nylon thrust washer are located into position together. It will be found that the fork will not push straight into position, therefore, it will be necessary to push the fork at a slight angle with a twisting action to locate it correctly (see Fig. 2). Then pass the pivot bolt through the fork and engine lugs from the offside of the machine. Carefully locate the threaded portion of the pivot bolt into the nearside engine lug and securely tighten. But make sure the rear fork hydraulic unit securing studs are approximately $12\frac{1}{4}$ inches from the underside of the suspension bracket in the frame when tightening the pivot bolt. Failure to do this can substantially reduce the life of the fork pivot bushes. Note the cranked locking plate which locks the pivot bolt to the top engine bolt. This must be fitted over the hexagon head of the pivot bolt in a position whereby the plain hole in the other end of the locking plate is in line with the hole in the engine lug where the top engine bolt is fitted. At this point the top engine bolt which had previously been loosely fitted, should be removed in order to line up the cranked locking plate with the top bolt hole. Also, a shake-proof washer must be fitted under the head of the bolt, when it can then be passed through the hole in the cranked locking plate and the engine lug and frame bracket (see Fig. 3), but before the threaded portion of the bolt is located into the nearside engine lug, the special spacing washer must be fitted between the frame bracket and the nearside engine lug and located on to the bolt as it is passed into the nearside engine lug. The top engine bolt can then be securely tightened. The two socket headed set screws in the two offside engine lugs can now be securely tightened. Then fit the long screw into the rear edge of the primary chaincase, and tighten the two nuts on the front engine stud.

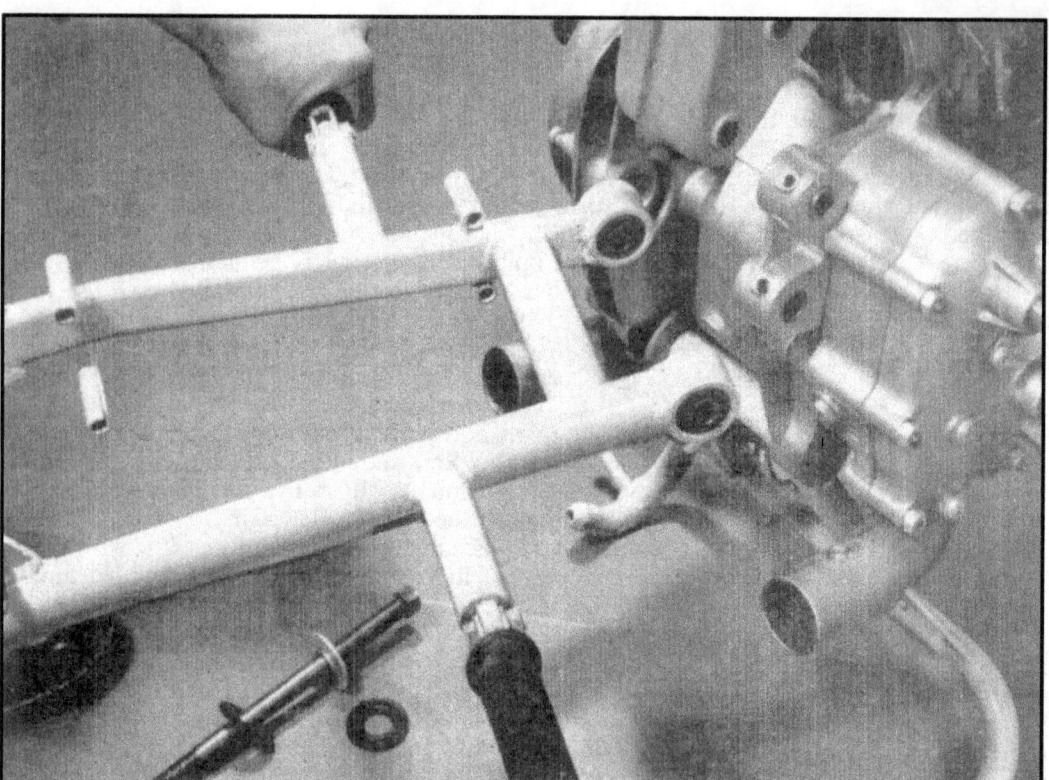

Fig. 2

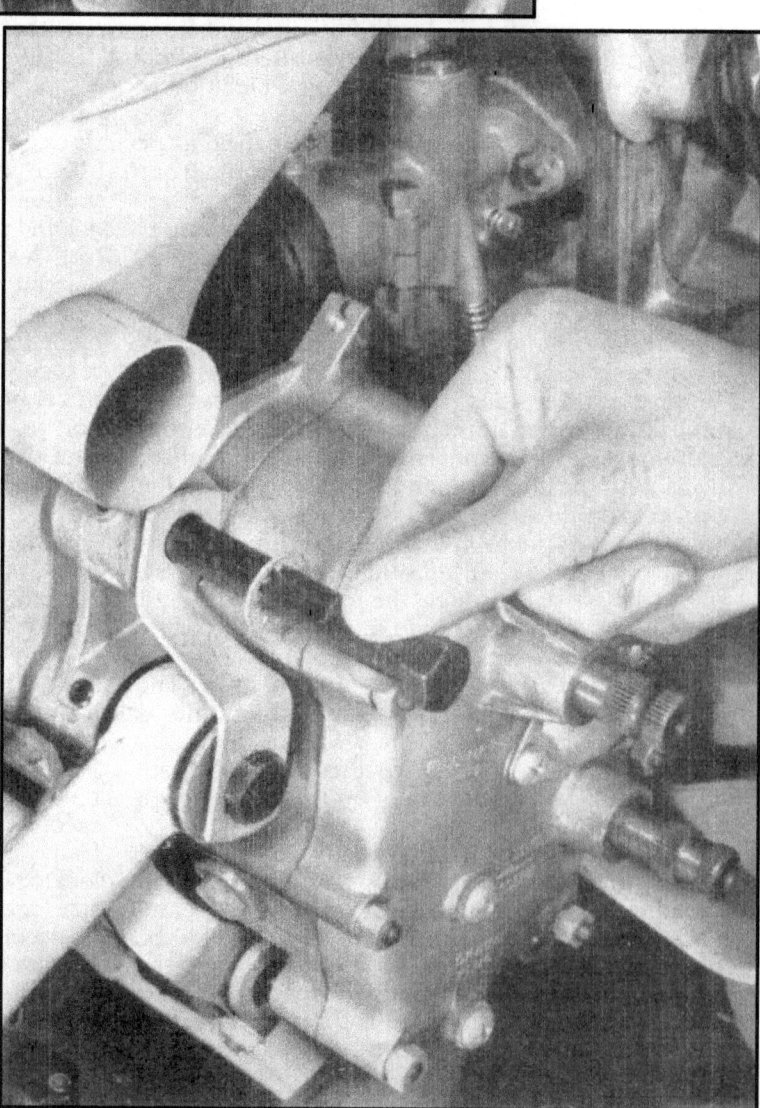

Fig. 3

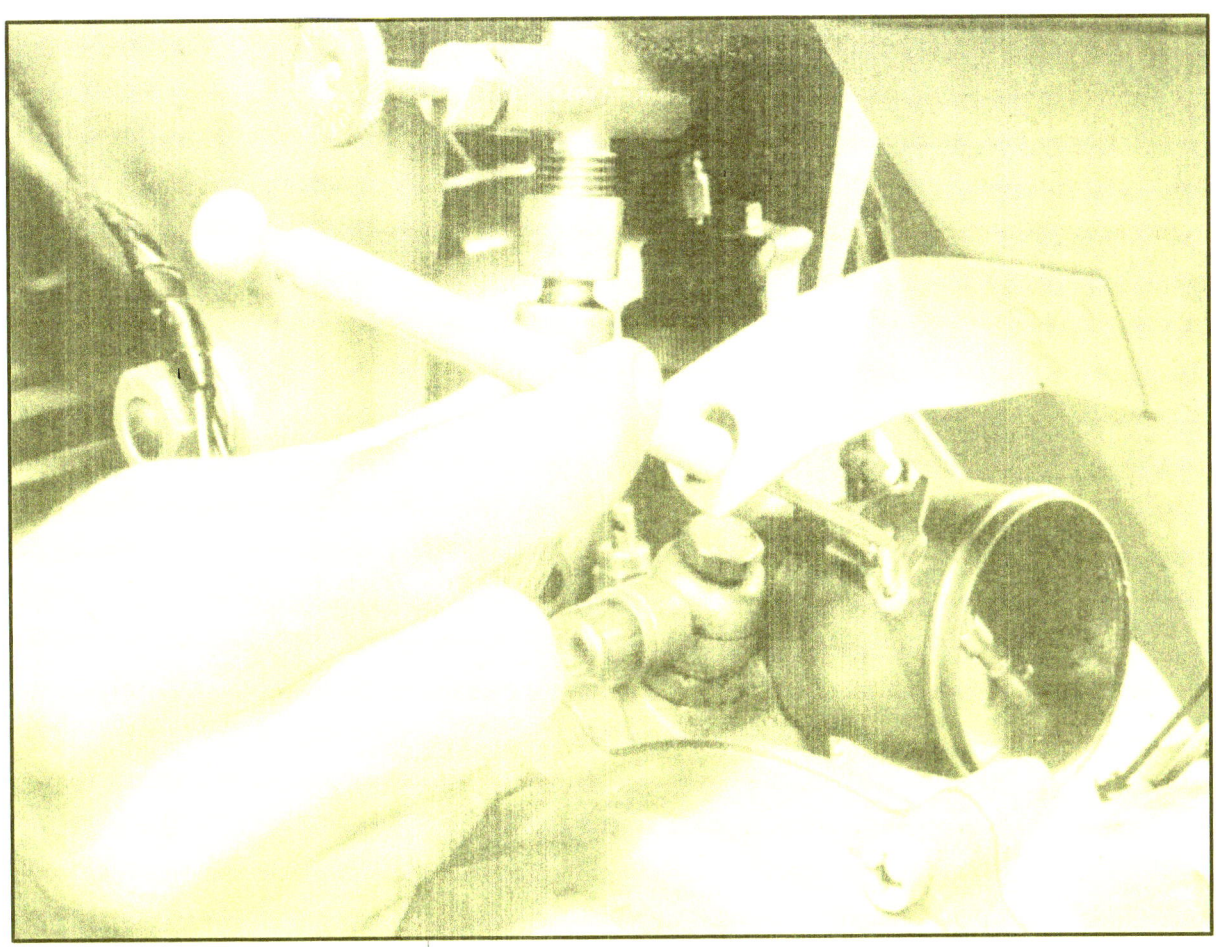

Fig. 4

Fit the cold start operating rod into the bracket on the frame, and slip the cranked end of the rod through the small hole in the end of the lever on the cold start device (see Fig. 4). When the operating rod was removed, the cold start device was rotated in an anti-clockwise direction in order to facilitate removal of the rod, and the cold start device must be in this same position to refit the rod. It can then be rotated clockwise until the lever is uppermost and horizontal, then the clamp bolt on the offside of the cold start device can be securely tightened. Fit the rubber connector between the cold start device and the rear frame bracket, but first liberally wet the rubber connector with petrol or petroil mixture. This will greatly facilitate assembly and in this particular instance the petrol will not harm the rubber as it is special petrol- and oil-proof material. The oval-shaped end of the connector has a channel moulded around the outer edge, and this end of the connector fits into the oval-shaped hole in the frame bracket; note that the end of the connector is also shaped to suit the angle of the frame bracket. The seam along the top of the connector must be central and the edge of the hole in the frame bracket must be located in the moulded channel. It is then an easy matter to slip the other end of the connector over the end of the cold start unit, but afterwards check to make certain that the connector is correctly located at both ends.

The air cleaner is fitted next to the tube incorporated in the offside of the rear frame to engine bracket. Begin by clamping the ends of the air cleaner spring clip together with a pair of pliers in order to increase the internal diameter of the clip. Then pass the clip only over the tube on the frame bracket, and keep it clamped between the pliers while the air cleaner is fitted over the frame bracket tube and inside the clip, release the clip from the pliers when it will secure the air cleaner in position. Next fit the petrol pipe from the carburetter to the petrol tap by locating the pipe on the tap and tightening the union nut firmly but not excessively.

Refit the rear mudguard as described on page 196 for the Leader, and page 206 for the Arrow. Refit the rear hydraulic units, page 197 and 206. Refit the rear chain, page 197 and 206. Refit the rear chaincase, page 197 and 206.

The rear stop switch leads should be fitted next, together with the neutral gear indicator leads, if an indicator is fitted, see page 225 for full instructions. The rear wheel can then be fitted as described on page 105 for the Leader, and page 105 for the Arrow, and the exhaust pipes and silencers, as described on page 43. Next clip the high tension leads on to the sparking plugs, and reconnect the two contact breaker leads to the leads from the nearside of the frame, which have corresponding colours. Also reconnect the three alternator leads to the leads from the offside of the frame, which have corresponding colours.

		Leader	*Arrow*
Re-fit the rear brake pedal as described on	page	108	108
Re-fit the throttle cable	page	127	130
Re-fit the clutch cable	page	126	132
Re-fit the speedometer cable	page	158	164
Re-fit the leg shields	page	155	—
Re-fit the side panels	page	154	—
Re-fit the engine cover	page	—	155

SPARKING PLUGS—LEADER AND ARROW

Use only the recommended sparking plugs, either Lodge 2HLN or Champion N4, which after intensive tests have been proved to be the most suitable. The sparking plugs should be removed and inspected during routine maintenance, as they require occasional adjustment and cleaning.

If the engine is performing satisfactorily, the sparking plugs should be left until a convenient time when other routine maintenance work is being attended to. If, however, any trouble is experienced with difficult starting, poor performance, misfiring or excessive petrol consumption, the sparking plugs should be removed and their condition examined, as it may well be that cleaning and adjustment of the sparking plugs will overcome the trouble. In addition to this, it is strongly recommended that spare sparking plugs of the correct type and in good condition, are carried on the motor cycle, so that in the event of an emergency a spare one can be fitted.

There are two sparking plugs fitted to the engine, one to each cylinder head, and they are easily accessible without removing any other parts of the motor cycle. To remove the sparking plugs, first lift off the black plastic covers which attach the high tension leads to the sparking plugs. Then, dealing with each sparking plug separately, fit a suitably sized tube spanner over the sparking plug, and using a tommy bar in conjunction with the tube spanner, turn the tube spanner in an anti-clockwise direction, after initially loosening it should be possible to remove the tommy bar and continue turning the tube spanner by hand until the sparking plug is free and can be lifted clear. *Note:* There is a special washer fitted between the sparking plug and the cylinder head, and upon removing a sparking plug the washer may be lodged on the threaded portion of it. Otherwise, the washer will remain on the cylinder head. The important point is that a sparking plug must not be fitted to the engine unless the washer is in place.

With the sparking plugs removed, it will be seen that at the lower ends there is a projection from the side of the plug facing inwards. This projection is the earthing point, and inside the lower end of the plug the centre portion tapers to a point just above the end of the earthing point. The tapered portion is the centre electrode and the gap between the earthing point and the centre electrode is really the most important part of the sparking plug, because the electric current from the high tension lead passes through the sparking plug and a spark occurs as the current crosses from the centre electrode to the earthing point, but if the gap is too wide or too narrow, the engine performance and the petrol consumption will deteriorate.

Whenever the sparking plugs are removed, the gap between the earthing point and the centre electrode should be checked, and it must be not less than .030 inch, and not more than .035 inch. The width of the gap should be checked with a .030 inch feeler gauge. These gauges are available in sets from most motor cycle agents or tool dealers. The .030 inch feeler gauge should just pass through the gap.

If upon checking the gap between the earthing point and the centre electrode, it is found to be too narrow or too wide, the gap must be adjusted by very carefully bending the earthing point. Under no circumstances must the centre electrode be touched. The best method of bending the earthing point is to use a special gap setting tool which is produced by the sparking plug manufacturers, and available from most motor cycle agents. The tool fits on to the earthing point and can be used to lever it either closer to, or further away from the centre electrode, whichever is required to adjust the gap to the correct width.

If trouble has been experienced with a sparking plug, it can be tested to find out whether it is still sparking by removing both plugs from the engine and with the high tension leads fitted, place the sparking plugs so that the threaded portion is in contact with the fins of the cylinder head, and with the earthing point and centre electrode visible. Then, with the ignition switched on, depress the kick starter lever with the free hand, when a spark should occur across the gap between the earthing point and the centre electrode each time the engine completes a revolution. This is a task which is easily accomplished if tackled from the offside of the motor cycle, and by removing both sparking plugs, it is much easier to depress the kick starter lever. If the kick starter can be depressed sharply the engine will revolve several times, and a number of sparks should occur, and if the plug does spark satisfactorily it is very doubtful if there is an electrical fault, and the carburetter should be investigated.

If a plug does not spark when tested, first make certain that the gap between the earthing point and the centre electrode is clear, as occasionally this gap may become bridged by carbon. This is commonly called "whiskering." The remedy in this event is to remove the carbon, which can be done by passing the .030 inch feeler gauge through the gap. Also make quite sure that the gap between the earthing point and the centre electrode is correctly adjusted. If after this the plug still fails to spark, a spare plug should be fitted. Then later if the plug which has given trouble is handed to almost any garage they will clean and test the plug with special equipment for a nominal charge.

Never fit a sparking plug that is damaged in any way. When a plug is being fitted it should screw into the cylinder head easily; if any resistance is met, remove the plug again and inspect the threaded portion. If the threads are damaged the plug should be replaced with a new one. Alternately if the threads are undamaged, the trouble may be due to dirt between the threads; this can be overcome by brushing the threaded portion of the plug with a small wire brush. If after this the trouble still persists, remove the cylinder head concerned as there may be dirt between the threads in the sparking plug hole. A small brush and paraffin should be used to clean these threads. In the event of the threads being damaged, an Ariel agent should be contacted, who will confirm if the cylinder head can be repaired or if a new cylinder head will be required.

Important: Never interfere with the centre electrode of the sparking plug, as this could lead to numerous troubles. Also, never judge the carburation by the running condition of the sparking plug, as modern two-stroke oils affect the colour of the plug more than the carburetter mixture.

CARBURETTER—LEADER AND ARROW

The carburetter is a metering instrument which mixes the petrol and oil mixture from the petrol tank with air at the correct ratio drawn through the air cleaner, into a form of vapour which will ignite under compression in the engine when fired by the spark plug. Basically the carburetter consists of two chambers, the float chamber which is a reservoir to maintain the supply of petrol/oil to the second chamber which is the mixing chamber, and, as the name implies, the mixing chamber is where the petrol/oil is mixed with air to form a vapour. There is very little that can go wrong with the carburetter, the most common trouble is caused by particles of dirt blocking the jets in the carburetter, or fouling the needle which controls the flow of petrol to the float chamber, and after a very large mileage a certain amount of wear takes place, requiring some parts to be renewed.

In addition to mixing the petrol and oil with air, the carburetter automatically controls the proportion or ratio of petrol/oil to air and any trouble which develops in the carburetter results in an upset of the proportions of the mixture. If the air supply to the carburetter is restricted in any way, such as when the cold start device is in operation, the proportions of the mixture become unbalanced, because while the air supply has been restricted the normal amount of petrol/oil is still being supplied. This results in a rich mixture, and while this is ideal for starting a cold engine, it would be entirely unsuitable for normal running. Alternately the petrol supply could become restricted such as when the petrol tap is only pulled *halfway out* and the flow of petrol/oil from the petrol tank is reduced. Again, the proportions of the mixture become unbalanced as the amount of petrol/oil is reduced, but the normal amount of air is still being supplied. This results in a weak mixture and is extremely harmful to the engine.

Variations in the proportions of the petrol/oil to air mixture do not often occur, but any indication that some variation has taken place should be investigated. If the engine is difficult to start, lacks power, overheats or misfires, the carburetter may be at fault.

An indication of the strength of the petrol/oil to air mixture can be obtained by the engine's performance. If the mixture is too rich the engine will four stroke, i.e. uneven firing, and this could be the result of the air flow to the carburetter being restricted, or an excessive supply of petrol/oil. If, however, the petrol/oil to air mixture is too weak, the motor cycle will be difficult to start and will not accelerate properly, also the engine will become excessively hot. This could be the result of an excessive air supply to the carburetter or a restriction in the petrol/oil supply. Dealing with the air supply first, begin by removing the offside side panel, see page 154. Then examine the air cleaner for contamination, see page 24 for full details, but unless there is something obviously wrong with the air cleaner, it is doubtful if it is at fault.

Next make certain the rubber connector between the rear frame to engine bracket and the carburetter is in good order and *correctly fitted*. If the rubber connector is in order, examine the cold start device and make quite certain that it is functioning correctly. The cold start unit is easily removed for further examination, by pulling off the rubber connector and then slackening the pinch bolt which secures the cold start unit to the carburetter. It can then be rotated anti-clockwise, in order to slip out the control rod (see Fig. 4). The unit can then be pulled rearwards to free it from the machine. The lever on the top of the cold start unit can then be operated, and it can be seen if it is working correctly. There is a spring fitted to retain the lever in either the open or closed position. If this spring has been lost or broken it could result in carburation trouble, and fitting a new spring would be the remedy. If, after checking the foregoing everything mentioned is in order, the air supply to the carburetter is not at fault, the trouble must be in the carburetter itself, or in the petrol supply from the tank. If the petrol/air mixture is too rich, first check the float chamber on the nearside of the carburetter and make certain that the float chamber does not overflow when the petrol tap is pulled on. If petrol does overflow, the float may be punctured or stuck in some way at the bottom of the chamber. Alternatively the nylon needle valve on top of the float may be out of place, or not seating correctly due to dirt on the needle or the seat. It is also possible for dirt or foreign matter to cause the nylon needle to stick on its seat cutting off the petrol/oil supply, and this of course would make it impossible to start the engine, or if the engine was running when the needle became stuck on its seat, the engine would stop when the small quantity of petrol/oil in the float chamber had been used. The remedy for either of these troubles is to remove the carburetter from the motor cycle, and dismantle and clean out the float chamber. See separate instructions for removing and dismantling carburetter, on page 22. Also, if the float or the nylon needle are damaged they should be replaced with new ones. Alternatively if the engine's performance indicates a weak mixture, it may be that the carburetter main jet or needle jet is obstructed, with dirt or foreign matter. Both of these jets are accessible without removing the carburetter from the motor cycle. After removing the offside side panel for the Leader and the electric horn for the Arrow, and making certain the petrol tap is switched off, use the special cranked thin ring spanner which is supplied in the tool kit of each new motor cycle and fit the end of the spanner which has only one ring, to the lowest nut on the bottom of the carburetter mixing chamber, and remove the nut. This will reveal the main jet, which can be removed with the small ring at the other end of the cranked ring spanner. With the main jet removed it can be seen that there is a small hole passing right through the jet; this hole may be blocked with dirt. To clean it out either blow it clear or wash it in petrol or paraffin. *Do not attempt to poke it clear with wire or anything similar as this could damage the jet.* When re-fitting the main jet and the mixing chamber bottom nut they should be tightened firmly but not excessively. To remove the needle jet, first remove the uppermost of the two nuts, using an ordinary spanner. Note that if the bottom nut which covers the main jet has not been removed, it will automatically be removed with the upper nut which will also include the needle jet and the main jet. The needle jet is situated at the end of the threaded portion on the upper nut and it can be removed with the small end of the special thin ring spanner which also fits the main jet. Clean

---

LIST OF PARTS SHOWN IN FIG. 5
CARBURETTER

1. Mixing chamber cap
2. Mixing chamber top
3. Taper needle
4. Throttle valve spring
5. Clip for taper needle
6. Throttle valve
7. Jet block
8. Tickler body
9. Tickler
10. Tickler spring
11. Jet block washer
12. Mixing chamber body
13. Float
14. Float spindle bush
15. Float chamber cover washer
16. Float chamber cover
17. Main jet holder washer
18. Needle jet
19. Main jet holder
20. Main jet
21. Main jet cover nut
22. Banjo bolt
23. Banjo bolt washer
24. Banjo
25. Filter
26. Needle seating
27. Float needle
28. Butterfly spindle spring
29. Butterfly spindle
30. Cold start unit clamp screw
31. Clamp screw nut
32. Cold start unit body
33. Butterfly
34. Air adjusting screw spring
35. Air adjusting screw
36. Jet block locating screw
37. Throttle adjusting screw spring
38. Throttle adjusting screw
39. Carburetter flange rubber seal
40. Pilot jet cover nut washer
41. Pilot jet
42. Pilot jet cover nut.

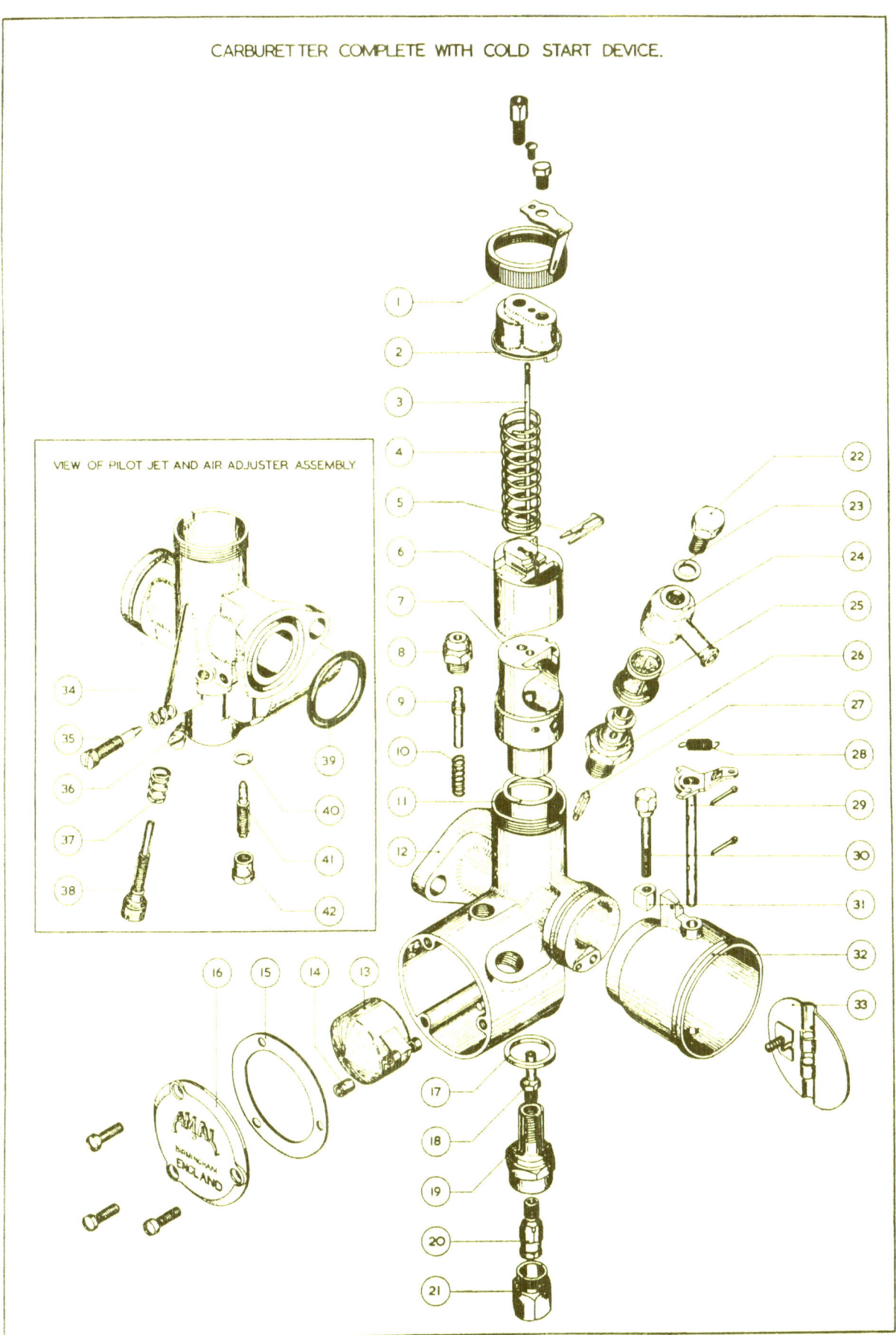

Fig. 5

the needle jet in a similar manner to the main jet, either by blowing it clear or washing in paraffin. When re-fitting the upper nut complete with the needle jet be quite certain that a fibre washer is fitted immediately on top of the hexagon of the upper nut, the fibre washer must be in good condition to prevent a petrol leak. Take extra care when passing the needle jet and upper nut into the bottom of the carburetter, as the needle has to be located into the needle jet before the nut can be screwed into the carburetter.

Removal of Carburetter: To remove the carburetter from the motor cycle, begin by removing both side panels, in the case of the Leader, and the electric horn for the Arrow; then pull off the rubber connector between the cold start unit and the rear engine bracket. Next, slacken the clamp bolt on the offside of the cold start unit, and rotate the unit in an anti-clockwise direction so that the cold start operating rod can be slipped out of the lever on the unit (see Fig. 4). Then remove the petrol pipe from the petrol tap, by undoing the union nut at the top of the petrol pipe. The throttle cable must be released from the carburetter next. This is easily accomplished by unscrewing in an anti-clockwise direction the knurled ring at the top of the mixing chamber but at the same time press the top of the mixing chamber downwards until the knurled ring is free from the carburetter, when the mixing chamber top, throttle cable, slide and needle, etc., can be withdrawn from the carburetter. Unless the throttle cable or any of the other fittings require attention, they can be left dangling but take care not to damage them. If it is required to separate the carburetter fittings from the throttle cable, see instructions on page 127 and 130. Finally, remove the two nuts and washers which secure the carburetter to the engine lug above the crankcase. The carburetter can then be pulled rearwards to free it from the motor cycle.

Dismantling the Carburetter: Important: At no time during the dismantling or assembling of the carburetter must it be clamped in a vice as this could result in irreparable damage, necessitating major replacements of the carburetter parts.

Beginning with the float chamber, on the nearside of the carburetter, remove the three screws from the side of the float chamber. Then the side of the float chamber can be pulled clear, although it may be a little tight and should be prised off carefully. Inside can be seen the large float which pivots up and down controlling the nylon needle valve. At the nearside end of the pivot for the float is a small spacer tube which simply pulls off, the float can be pulled out next. This, will also free the nylon needle and care should be taken not to lose it. If the carburetter has been dismantled because of trouble with either the float or the nylon needle, no further dismantling is necessary as the part required has been removed, but if it is convenient this would be a good opportunity to dismantle and thoroughly clean the complete carburetter. Continue by removing the bolt which secures the petrol pipe union to the top of the float chamber. The petrol pipe, complete with the union can then be pulled off the top of the float chamber. But do not lose the loose nylon gauze filter. If it is required to remove the petrol feed union from the top of the float chamber, fit a spanner to the large hexagon at the base of the union and unscrew. The tickler can also be removed from the top of the float chamber, by fitting a spanner to the nut below the tickler knob and unscrewing it, but note that when the nut is removed the tickler unit can be lifted clear but, as it is in three separate pieces, the knob, the nut and a spring, take care not to lose any of them.

Next remove the lower nut from the bottom of the mixing chamber by turning it with a suitable spanner. This will then reveal the main jet, which is also removed by turning it with the small ring of the special cranked thin ring spanner. The remaining nut on the bottom of the mixing chamber is removed next. The needle jet is at the top end of the threaded portion of the upper nut, which has been removed from the mixing chamber, and the needle jet can be unscrewed with the same spanner used to remove the main jet.

The two screws with springs fitted under their heads, which are fitted to the offside of the mixing chamber, can be removed by screwing them out with a screw-driver. Next remove the small nut from the underside of the mixing chamber, this reveals the pilot jet which has a screw-driver slot in the bottom, and the jet can be removed by unscrewing it in the normal manner. Note, the cold start unit should not be removed unnecessarily as the joint between the cold start unit and the carburetter must be air tight, and for this reason the joint between the two parts is a good fit. If it is required to remove the cold start unit, the clamp bolt should already have been slackened in order to rotate the unit so that the operating rod could be slipped out. It will then have to be pulled carefully but firmly rearward to free it from the carburetter. Finally, the rubber sealing ring which is fitted in a recess in the joint flange of the carburetter should not be disturbed if it is in good condition. If, however, it is damaged or perished, it must be replaced with a new one. The existing sealing ring can easily be prised out with the blade of a small screw-driver, and a new sealing ring can then be pushed into the recess by hand.

This completes the dismantling of the carburetter and all parts should be carefully cleaned and examined. Normally a very large mileage must be covered before any wear takes place, but if any of the carburetter parts are worn or damaged they must be replaced with new ones. The re-assembling can then begin. First fit the spring to the tickler knob, then pass the knob through the nut which secures the tickler to the top of the float chamber, and fit all three items to the top of the float chamber so that the spring is inside, and the tickler knob with a hole passing through it, protrudes above the nut. Next, fit the petrol feed union to the top of the float chamber and securely tighten it. Then insert the nylon needle through the float chamber into the lower end of the petrol feed union, so that only the short round end of the needle is visible. Next pass the float into the float chamber locating it on the hinge, so that the centre of the hinge portion of the float forms a platform to support the nylon needle. The short spacer tube must then be fitted to the end of the float hinge, and then the float chamber cover can be fitted, but the joint washer must be in good condition to ensure a petrol tight joint. Securely tighten the cover with the three screws. Fit the pilot jet next, to the underside of the mixing chamber. Then fit a fibre washer and the nut to the bottom end of the pilot jet, so that the fibre washer is clamped between the nut and the bottom of the mixing chamber. Then fit the two screws with springs to the offside of the mixing chamber, but only tighten the screws until the springs are slightly compressed. Next fit the needle jet and the main jet to the uppermost of the two mixing chamber bottom nuts. Also, there must be a fibre washer fitted directly above the hexagon portion of the nut, and the washer must be in good condition. Then fit and securely tighten the nut to the bottom of the mixing chamber. The mixing chamber bottom nut can then be fitted and tightened firmly, but not excessively.

The nylon filter should then be fitted over the petrol feed union, with the flange of the filter downward, then fit the petrol pipe union over the nylon filter, and locate the petrol pipe union bolt, which must have a fibre washer fitted under its head, through the hole in the petrol pipe union and into the threaded petrol feed union. Tighten the bolt firmly but not excessively.

The carburetter is then ready for fitting to the engine, but first clean the engine lug face where the carburetter securing studs protrude from, then clean and examine the special composition washer which fits over the carburetter studs between the engine lug and the carburetter, if it is in any way damaged it should be replaced with a new one. It is most important that the correct washer is used, as it is made of a special material which insulates the carburetter from the heat of the engine. After fitting the composition washer to the engine lug the carburetter is fitted next, and then to each stud fit a shake-proof washer and a thin nut, but use care while tightening the nuts, and they must each be tightened a little at a time in order to clamp the carburetter evenly to the engine lug. If one nut is tightened more than the other, the carburetter may become distorted, resulting in carburation trouble due to air leakage, etc.

The carburetter parts which are attached to the throttle cable can now be inserted into the top of the mixing chamber, as described on page 127 and 130. Re-fit the cold start unit operating rod as described on page 17 and the air cleaner rubber connector as described on page 17.

Adjustment of Carburetter: On the offside of the carburetter are two screws with springs fitted under their heads. The smaller screw which is fitted horizontally is the pilot air adjusting screw and this screw regulates the strength of the mixture for slow running and tick over. To carry out the adjustment of the pilot air screw, first start the engine and warm up to running temperature, and while it is running slowly screw the adjuster in or out a little at a time until the engine runs slowly and ticks over evenly. This adjustment must be made with the engine at normal working temperature. The second screw which is the larger of the two and is fitted almost vertically to the underside of the mixing chamber, is provided to adjust the position of the throttle slide so that when the twist grip is in the closed position, the engine will continue running. To adjust the screw, first start the engine then close the twist grip control and turn the screw in or out a little at a time until the engine ticks over, as required.

An adjuster for the throttle cable is provided in the top of the mixing chamber, and this adjuster should be screwed in or out until there is just a little slack movement at the beginning of the twist grip operation.

The size of the carburetter jets and throttle slide, and the position of the needle, are of the utmost importance and they should not be varied, except in rare circumstances when the position of the needle may be raised or lowered one notch. If trouble has been experienced with weak or rich mixture, and no other cause can be traced for the variation in mixing strength, raising the needle will enrich the mixture, while lowering it will weaken it.

Carburetter specification: Amal Monobloc Type No. 375/33 with angled spray tube. Choke size, $\frac{7}{8}$ inch. Main jet, 140. Pilot jet, 30. Needle jet, 105. Needle position, centre notch. Throttle Slide, $3\frac{1}{2}$.

Note: Some machines are fitted with a carburetter as specified above, except that the main jet is a 170. This is quite in order as these carburetters do not have an angled spray tube and the larger size jet must be retained. (The 140 jet and angled spray tube is interchangeable, providing both items are replaced.)

Tracing Troubles:

Indication of weak mixture:
  Difficult starting.
  Poor acceleration.
  Engine over heats
  Engine runs better if throttle is not wide open.

To cure weakness:
  Check petrol supply from petrol tank.
  Check and clean main jet and needle jet.

Check and clean the nylon filter in petrol feed union.

Make certain there are no petrol leaks from the carburetter.

Make certain the nylon needle in the float chamber is not sticking.

Make sure the nuts which secure the carburetter to the engine are securely tightened.

Also check the special composition joint washer and rubber sealing ring between the carburetter and the engine lug and make certain they are in good order.

Adjust pilot air screw inwards.

Make certain there are no air leaks at the crankcase end covers, and that the end cover gaskets are in good order, and all nuts and screws are securely tightened. Also ensure that there are no air leaks from the two bolts fitted in the front of the crankcase.

Raise needle one notch (if everything previously suggested fails).

Indication of rich mixture:
Engine four strokes.
Sparking plug sooty.
Excess smoke from exhaust.

To cure richness:
Check the air cleaner and make certain that the element is clean and correctly fitted.

Check the rubber connector between the frame bracket and the cold start unit, and make certain it is correctly fitted and in good order.

Carefully examine the cold start unit and make sure it is operating correctly and is in the open position.

Check the main jet to make certain it has not come unscrewed. Also make sure the pilot jet is fully tight on its seating.

Check the float chamber and make sure the nylon needle is correctly fitted and is seating properly.

Also check the float to make sure it is not punctured.

Adjust pilot air screw outwards.

Lower needle one notch (if everything previously suggested fails).

AIR CLEANER—LEADER AND ARROW

The air cleaner is fitted on the offside of the motor cycle to a short tube on the rear frame to engine bracket. The air cleaner is fitted with a filter element which prevents dust and dirt being drawn in with the air supply for the carburetter.

It is most important that the air cleaner functions correctly as any dirt or dust entering the engine will increase the rate of wear, therefore the engine should never be run with the air cleaner removed. The dirt and dust which the filter prevents from entering the engine, will accumulate on the filter eventually clogging it, and causing a restriction in the air flow. The amount of dirt on the filter must never be allowed to become excessive, as a restriction in the air flow would be detrimental to the engine performance. Under normal conditions the air cleaner filter element should be replaced with a new one every 10,000 miles, but more frequently where extremely dusty conditions prevail. As a temporary measure only the element may be washed in clean petrol.

To remove the air cleaner, first in the case of the Leader remove the offside side panel as described on page 154, then for both models the air cleaner only requires a firm pull outward to free it from the motor cycle. With the air cleaner removed it can be seen that the perforated outer ring is joined at the ends by a stud or clip, and by squeezing the ends of the perforated ring together the stud or clip will simply pull out. Next expand the perforated ring slightly and remove the two side plates and the filter element. Before reassembling the air cleaner, thoroughly clean the side plates and the perforated ring, then fit one of the side plates into the perforated ring followed by the new filter element and the other side plate, squeeze the ends of the perforated ring together so that they overlap, then insert the stud or clip through both ends of the outer ring.

To re-fit the air cleaner to the motor cycle, first fit the spring clip, which clamps the short tube on the air cleaner to the tube on the frame bracket. Then expand the spring clip by squeezing the ends together with a pair of pliers and while the clip is expanded fit the air cleaner over the frame tube and inside the spring clip, then release the clip to secure the air cleaner in position. In the case of the Leader, finally re-fit the offside side panel as described on page 154.

PRIMARY CHAIN CASE—LEADER AND ARROW

The primary chain transmits the engine power to the gear box via the clutch, and it is enclosed in a case on the nearside of the engine unit, which in the case of the Leader is accessible after removing the nearside side panel, as described on page 154. The length of life of the primary chain depends on *correct adjustment and lubrication.*

Primary Chain Lubrication: Use one of the recommended brands of S.A.E. 20 grade oil. See lubrication chart, on page 10. *Important:* On no account must a lubricant or additive containing graphite or Molybdenum Disulphide be used in the primary chaincase, otherwise clutch slip will ensue. The amount of oil required to fill an empty primary chaincase to the oil level plug is approximately three-quarters of a pint. Oil from the primary chaincase is automatically fed to the rear chain, and therefore the oil level in the primary chaincase will slowly reduce, but it must not be allowed to become too low, or rapid wear of the chain will ensue. The oil level in the primary chaincase should be checked and topped up if necessary every 1,000 miles. The oil level plug is marked as shown in Fig. 6, and when the level plug is removed oil should just trickle out. If oil does not trickle out, the level is low and needs topping up. To do this remove the large inspection cap which is situated towards the top edge of the chaincase, and top up through the inspection hole until oil just trickles out of the oil level plug hole, then replace the level plug and the inspection cap. Oil from the primary chaincase is fed to the rear chain by means of a felt wick and a zerk plug, which are set in the rear half of the primary chaincase.

The wick can be replaced with a new one if required, and in the event of the zerk plug becoming blocked with dirt, a piece of wire can be used to clear it.

Primary Chain Adjustment: As the primary chain wears with use it lengthens, therefore it is essential to adjust the chain periodically to keep it tensioned correctly. If the chain tension is allowed to become too slack it will result in rapid wear of the chain sprockets. The chain tension should be checked and if necessary adjusted, at the same time as checking the oil level in the primary chaincase, although it will be found if the chain is kept correctly lubricated, adjustment will only be necessary approximately every 5,000 miles.

To check the chain tension, first remove the large inspection cap from the primary chaincase, then through the inspection hole can be seen the primary chain, and the tension can be checked by moving the chain up and down with one forefinger. The engine must then be rotated slowly by operating the kick starter while at the same time checking the chain tension in a number of places as the chain wear may be uneven, and the position where it is tightest, i.e. with the least amount of up and down movement, is where the tension must be checked for adjustment purposes. If at the tightest spot the total up and down movement exceeds ⅜ inch, the chain must be adjusted until the total up and down movement at the tightest spot is not more than ⅜ inch and not less than ⅛ inch. Note the chain must have a minimum of ⅛ inch up and down movement, otherwise the engine and gear box bearings will be overloaded with consequent damage to the bearings and the chain.

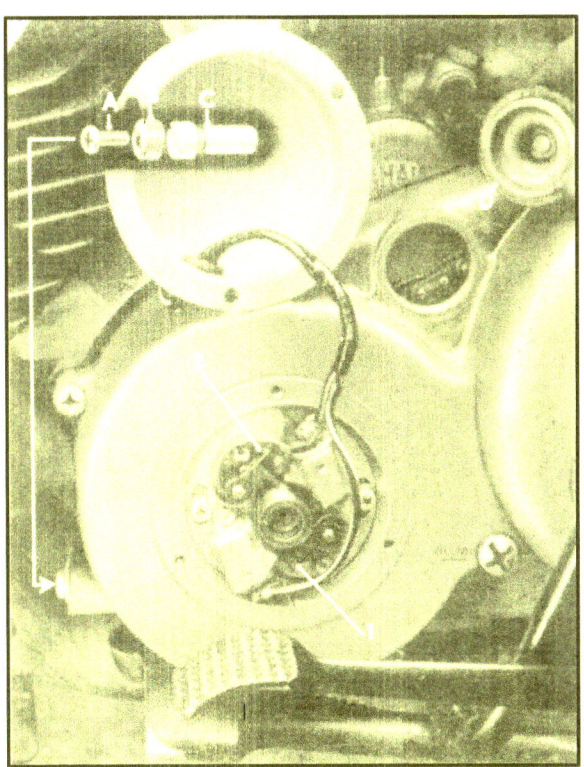

Fig. 7

To adjust the primary chain proceed as follows. Working from the front of the motor cycle, remove the screw and slotted plug from the forward edge of the primary chaincase. (See Fig. 7.) The screw and plug are shown in the insert and marked "A" and "B" respectively. **Important warning** (see Fig. 7) if the screw "A" cannot be removed after unscrewing it four complete turns, tighten plug "B" when it should then be easy to remove the screw. Failure to observe this precaution could result in the chain adjuster inside the chaincase being screwed apart, making it necessary to remove the primary chaincase to re-assemble the chain adjuster.

With the screw and the plug removed, the nylon adjusting sleeve "C" can be reached with an ordinary screwdriver. Turning the adjuster sleeve clockwise will tighten the chain, and anti-clockwise will slacken it. When the chain is adjusted correctly at the tightest spot the plug can be re-fitted in the front of the chaincase, and make sure it is securely tightened. The screw can then be fitted and tightened firmly, but not excessively. Finally re-fit the chaincase inspection cap.

Primary Chaincase: Removal. If it is required to remove the primary chaincase from the engine unit proceed as follows. First, in the case of the Leader, remove the nearside side panel as described on page 154. Then, for both models, remove the rear brake pedal as described on page 108, and the nearside footrest as described on page 182. Next drain the oil from the chaincase by removing the hexagon headed bolt from the bottom edge of the chaincase (see Fig. 6). Then pull apart the snap connectors in the two leads

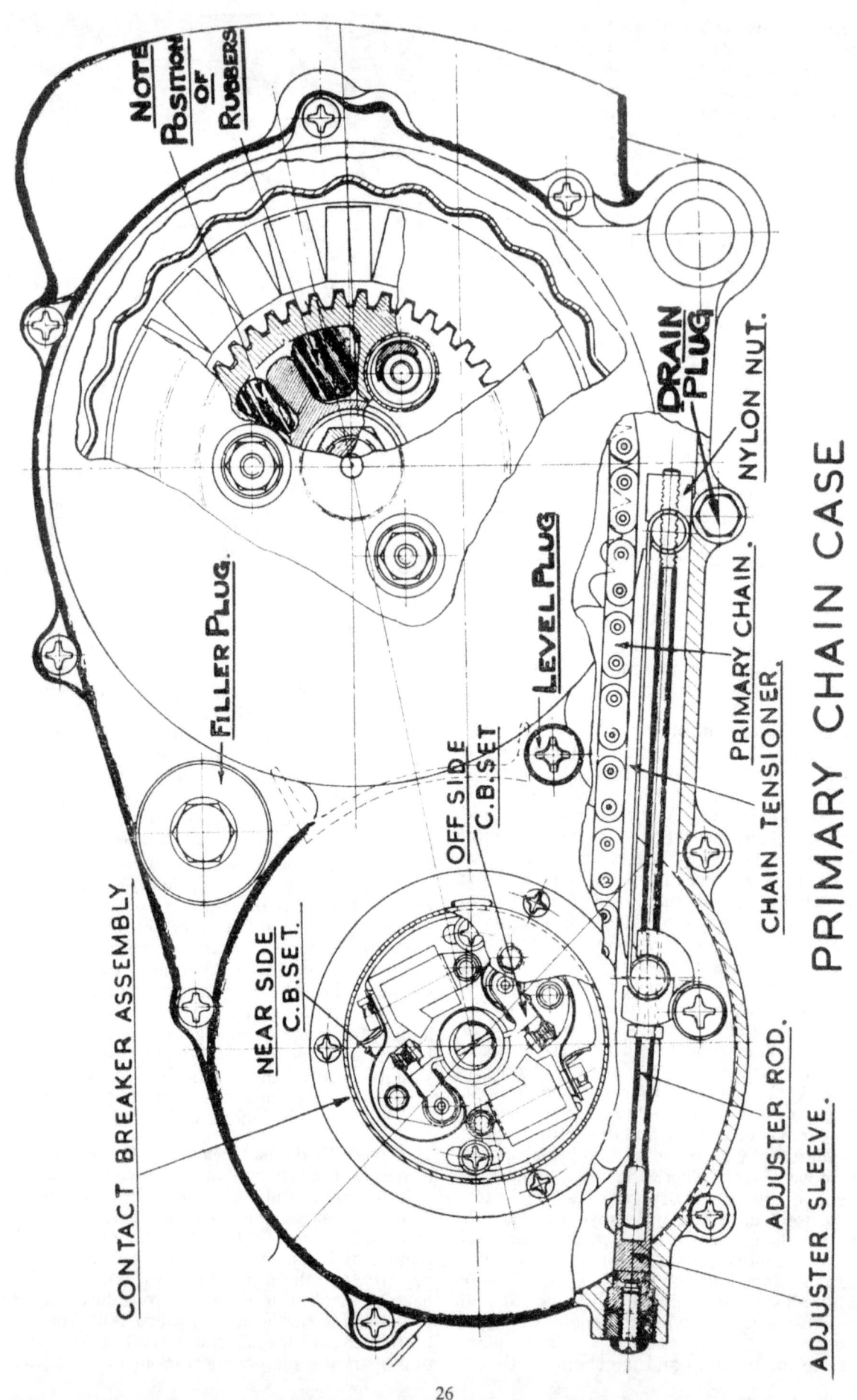

Fig. 6 PRIMARY CHAIN CASE

from the contact breaker, and remove the contact breaker cover by undoing the three screws which secure it to the chaincase. The contact breaker cam must be removed next, as described on page 61, and then the primary chain adjuster must be unscrewed, this is done by first removing the screw and plug from the front of the chaincase, and then if the screw only is loosely re-fitted to the adjuster sleeve, it can be used to extract the adjuster sleeve from the chaincase. Finally remove the eight screws from around the edge of the primary chaincase, when the chaincase can then be lifted clear (see Fig. 8). But note that the centre stand pivot tube passes through the lug on the primary chaincase, from where the brake pedal was removed, and the chaincase may be a little tight on this tube and should be eased off carefully.

Re-fitting Primary Chaincase: Important— When re-fitting the primary chaincase, the greatest care must be taken to avoid damaging or displacing the oil seal which is fitted in the chaincase behind the contact breaker. A service tool, Spares Part No. 43544S, is available, which greatly assists and simplifies fitting. The service tool is in the form of a short sleeve, with a taper at one end and a slot at the other (see Fig. 8). Begin by fitting the service tool over the end of the crankshaft so that the locating peg for the contact breaker cam is located in the slot in the end of the service tool. Then make quite certain that the peg in the crankshaft does not protrude above the service tool, if it does protrude even slightly, remove the service tool and carefully tap the peg further into the crankshaft until it does not protrude above the service tool. Note, if the oil seal is damaged or worn, it must be replaced, see page 34, for instructions on fitting a new one.

Next the old chaincase joint gasket must be removed, and all traces of oil wiped off the joint faces. A new joint washer must be fitted to the engine, and located in position around the nearside crankcase end cover and centre stand pivot tube. Then making sure the service tool is in position on the end of the crankshaft, carefully locate the chaincase in position on the engine unit (see Fig. 9). Note, that the chaincase must be fitted over the centre stand pivot tube, and the service tool on the crankshaft. Also, when locating the chain-

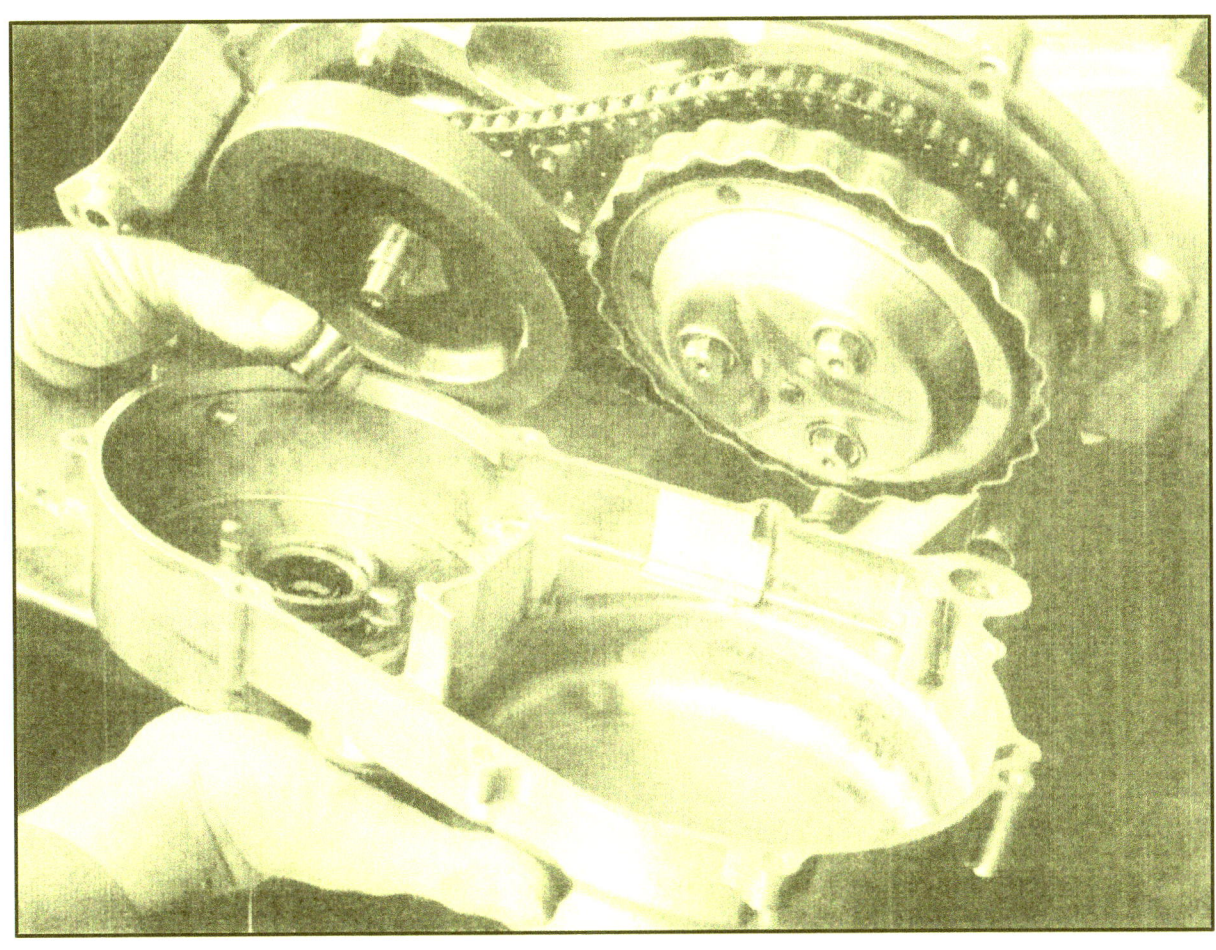

Fig. 8

case in position, the chain adjuster just below the primary chain may need pushing upwards a little, to pass it inside the chaincase. The service tool will then be protruding through the contact breaker and can easily be pulled clear. Next fit the eight screws which secure the chaincase to the engine, and note that there are two long screws and six short ones, one long screw fits above the contact breaker and the other one fits at the rear end of the chaincase. The six short screws fit in the remaining holes around the chaincase, but note the drain screw hole on the bottom edge of the chaincase must have the hexagon headed drain bolt with a fibre washer under its head fitted to it. Make sure all the screws and the bolt are securely tightened evenly, then locate the contact breaker cam on to the end of the crankshaft, making quite certain that the peg in the crankshaft is located in the slot in the cam, and securely tighten the screw in the centre of the cam. Re-fit the contact breaker cover as described on page 60, and connect the contact breaker leads to the leads with corresponding colours on the nearside of the frame. The nylon adjuster sleeve must be fitted next, after passing it into the hole in the front of the chaincase, it may be necessary to rotate the sleeve a little in order to locate it on to the chain adjuster, when the sleeve will then push down inside the hole in the chaincase. At this point adjust the primary chain as described on page 25, and refill the chaincase with fresh oil as described on page 25. Re-fit the brake pedal as described on page 108, and see page 182 for re-fitting the footrest. Finally, in the case of the Leader, re-fit the nearside side panel as described on page 154.

Primary Chain Adjuster: The primary chain adjuster is enclosed in the primary chaincase (see Fig. 6), and full instructions for operating the adjuster are given on page 25. The adjuster consists of a rubber faced tensioner blade, mounted on two trunnions through which the adjuster rod passes, one end of the adjuster rod screws into a nylon saddle nut, while the other end fits into the adjuster sleeve, and the whole assembly is located in a lug on the chaincase (see Fig. 6). The primary chain runs across the top of the tensioner blade, and the sides of the chain will eventually wear two grooves in the rubber surface of the tensioner blade, leaving a strip of rubber in the centre for the chain rollers to run on. Providing the chain is kept lubricated correctly as described on page 25, the tensioner blade will last almost indefinitely. In the rare event of the chain rubbing directly on the metal part of the chain tensioner at any point, or if the rubber is badly torn or damaged, the blade must be replaced with a new one. To remove the primary chain adjuster, first remove the primary chaincase as described on page 25. Then remove the nut, which secures the flywheel to the crankshaft, and withdraw the flywheel slightly towards the end of the crankshaft. See page 29 for description of withdrawing flywheel, but note it is not necessary

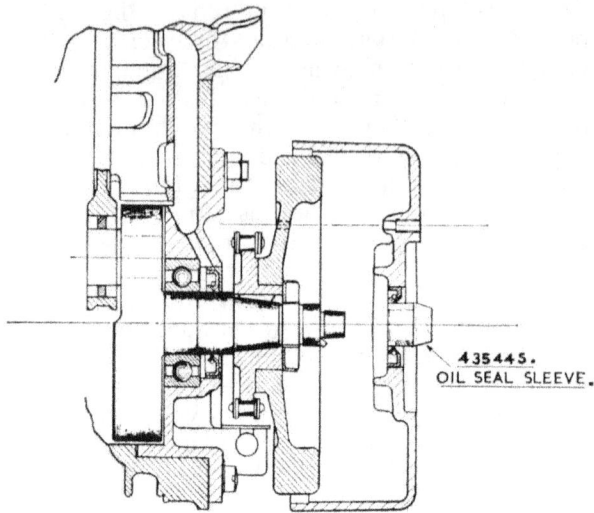

METHOD OF FITTING PRIMARY CHAINCASE TO ENGINE WITH SLEEVE TO PROTECT OIL SEAL

WITH OR WITHOUT CONTACT BREAKER ASSEMBLY

FIG. 9

to remove the clutch as the flywheel need only be withdrawn as far as the primary chain will allow. Then using the nylon adjuster sleeve on the end of the adjuster rod, screw the rod out of the nylon saddle nut. The nylon saddle nut will then be free, and the adjuster rod can be withdrawn from the forward end. This leaves only the tensioner blade and the two trunnions, and these can be carefully eased out of the lug on the engine, by easing the forward end of the tensioner blade outwards while at the same time holding the bottom edge of the flywheel outwards.

To re-fit the chain adjuster, first make certain the two trunnions are fitted in the ends of the tensioner blade, and that the holes through the trunnions are in line with each other. Note if a new tensioner blade is being fitted it can be fitted either way round, but if the original blade is being used again it should be re-fitted the same way as it was originally. Then while holding the bottom edge of the flywheel outward, insert the end of the tensioner blade into the lug on the engine so that the hole through the trunnion lines up with the slot in the lug. Next pass the adjuster rod from the front through both trunnions, and fit the nylon saddle nut to the threaded portion of the adjuster rod where it protrudes through the rear trunnion. The primary chaincase can then be re-fitted as described on page 27, and the chain adjusted as described on page 25. Finally, top up the chaincase with fresh oil, as described on page 25.

Primary Chain: Providing the primary chain is kept correctly lubricated and adjusted it will give long service. Whenever the primary chaincase is removed the chain should be inspected particularly for damaged rollers; if it is damaged or worn badly it must be replaced with a new one, and, in any event, the primary chain should be renewed at approximately 25,000 mile intervals.

To remove the primary chain from the engine, first note that the chain is of the endless type. This means it does not have a detachable connecting link, and the engine and clutch sprockets must be removed together with the chain, and special service tools are available which will greatly facilitate the removal of these parts.

Begin by removing the primary chaincase as described on page 25. Then straighten the turned down edges of the washer which is fitted behind the nut, which secures the flywheel to the engine shaft. The flywheel securing nut must be removed next, and the following service tools will be required:

43552S	Flywheel strap spanner complete.
43545S	Extractor plate.
43547S	Centre screw.
43548S	Bolt (two off).
43544S	Sleeve.
43549S	Box spanner.
43550S	Tommy bar.

Commence by fitting the loop of the flywheel strap spanner (43552S) over the flywheel, then fit box spanner (43549S) over the flywheel securing nut, with the tommy bar (43550S) passing through the box spanner. Hold the handle of the flywheel strap spanner to prevent the flywheel turning, while the flywheel securing nut is removed with the box spanner and tommy bar. (See Fig. 10.)

Next leave the strap spanner in position on the flywheel, and fit the centre screw (43547S) into the threaded hole in the centre of the extractor plate (43545S), but the screw must not yet protrude through the extractor plate. The two bolts (43548S) are then fitted through the two inner holes in the extractor plate, each side of the centre screw. Next fit the sleeve (43544S) over the nearside end of the crankshaft, with the peg in the crankshaft located in the slot in the end of the sleeve. Then fit the extractor plate in position, with the centre screw located on the end of the sleeve on the crankshaft, and the two bolts which are fitted each side of the centre screw, must be

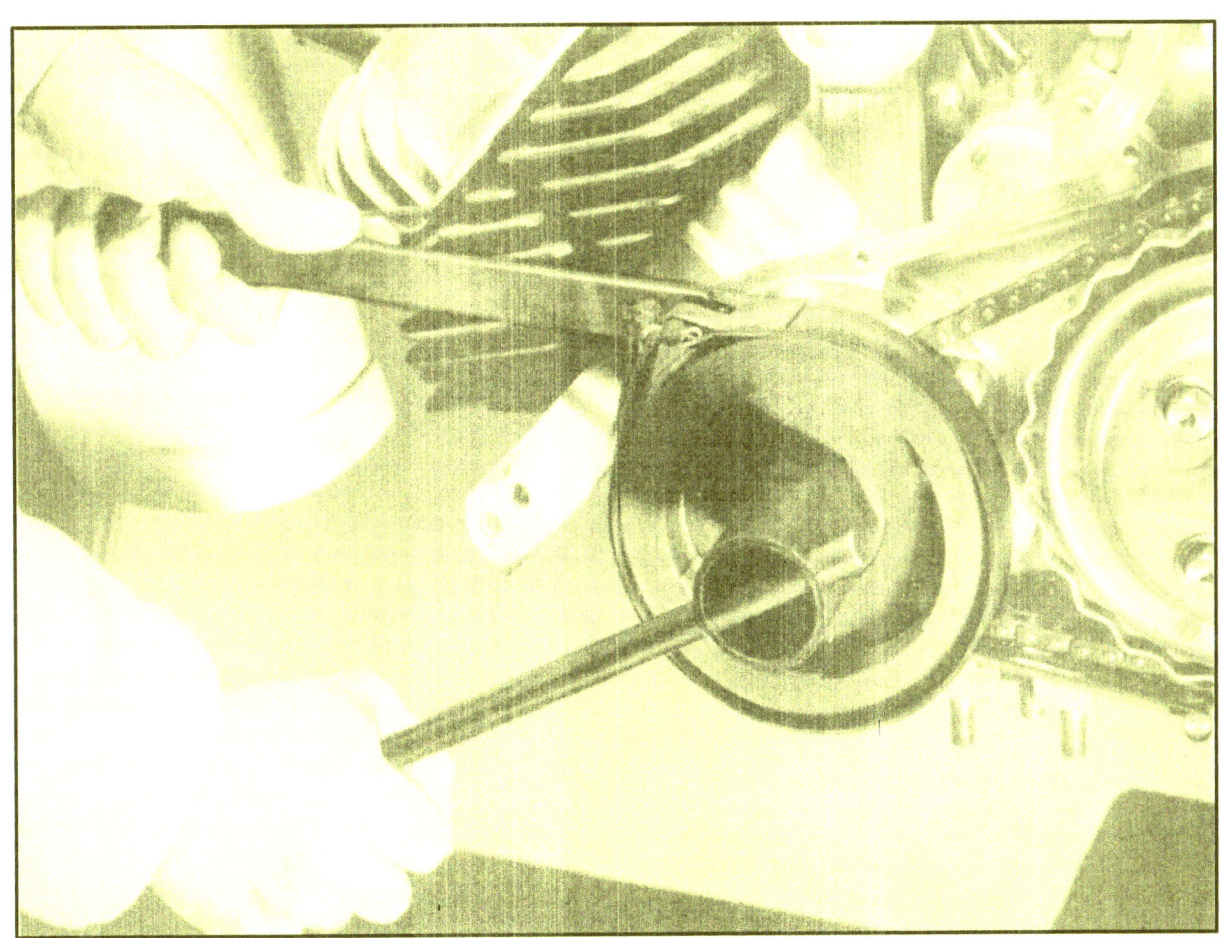

FIG. 10

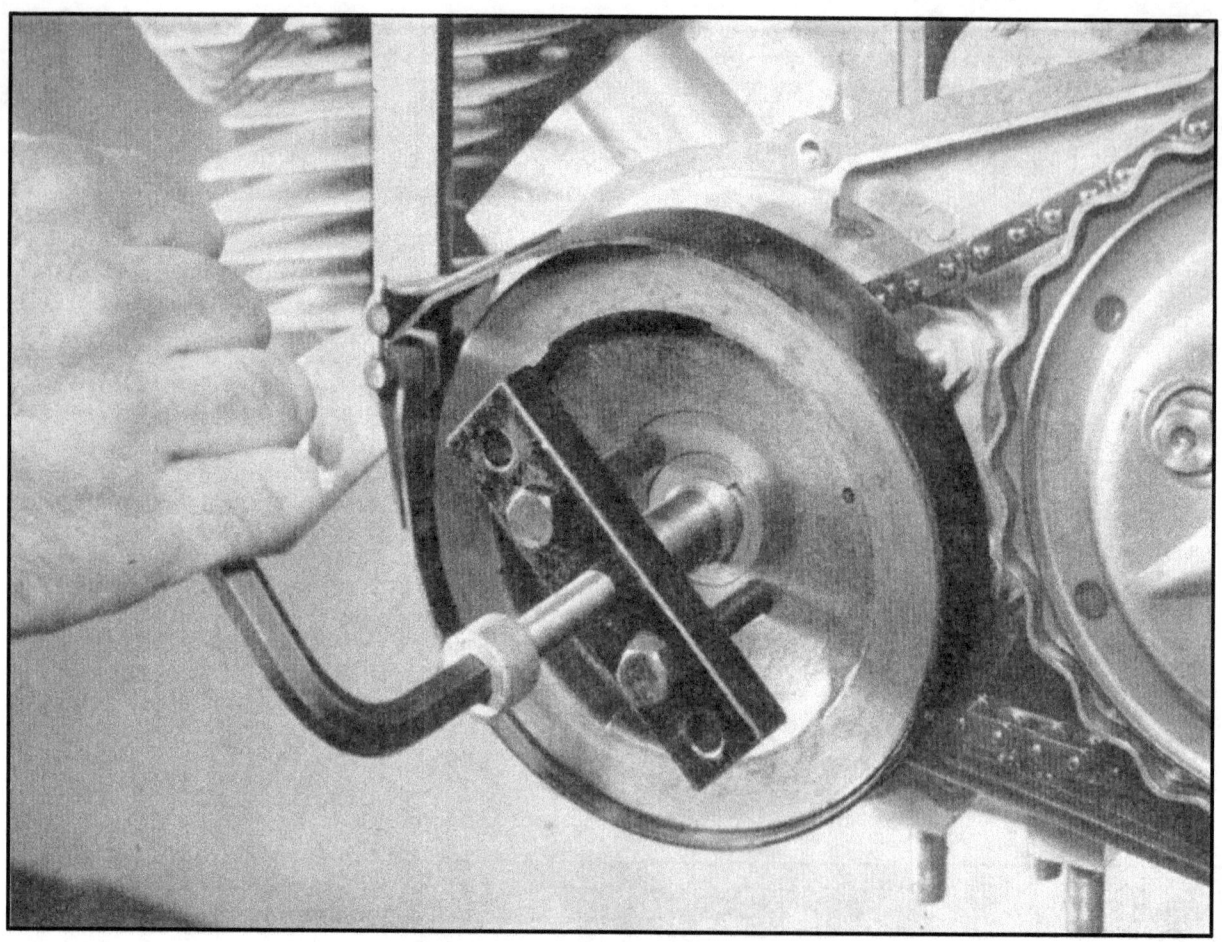

Fig. 11

located through the holes in the flywheel, and screwed finger tight into corresponding threaded holes in the engine sprocket. Then fit the key spanner which is supplied in the tool kit of each new motor cycle for the cylinder head bolts, to the socket head of the centre screw. By turning the centre screw clockwise, while holding the strap spanner to prevent the flywheel turning, the flywheel and engine sprocket will move outward slightly; just sufficient to free them from the taper on the crankshaft (see Fig. 11). The flywheel cannot be completely removed at this stage, but the extractor and strap spanner can be taken away. The clutch must be dismantled next; begin by unscrewing the three sleeve nuts from the outer clutch plate, as these nuts are removed the three clutch springs will also become free. The clutch plates can then be lifted out of the clutch housing, the outer plate will simply pull off, but the remaining plates may have to be levered out. This is easily done by using a piece of strong wire which will hook over the outside of the plates fitted with linings, and inside the unlined plates (see Fig. 12). When all the plates are removed there must be in addition to the outer plate, two plates with linings attached, and two unlined plates.

This now leaves the clutch centre and the clutch case still secured to the gear box mainshaft, and in the middle of the clutch centre can be seen a large nut, and in some cases with a further nut fitted behind it. Before the nuts can be undone the clutch centre must be prevented from turning and the service tool, clutch Banjo 43540S, is specially made for this purpose, the Banjo fits over the teeth of the clutch centre and it has a long handle. With the Banjo in position (see Fig. 13), a tube spanner can be used to remove the clutch centre nuts one at a time. The clutch centre can then be lifted clear taking care not to loosen the clutch rollers, and then the clutch case and the engine flywheel can be withdrawn together, with the primary chain still attached (see Fig. 14), when it will then be a simple matter to lift the chain off the two sprockets.

If the motor cycle has covered a large mileage examine the engine and clutch sprockets, if the teeth are worn or hooked the sprockets should be replaced with new ones. Note that if new sprockets are fitted it is essential to fit a new chain with them. If the engine sprocket requires renewing a hand press will be necessary to remove and re-fit the sprocket to the flywheel. Almost any garage or motor cycle dealer will have a suitable press,

Fig. 12

Fig. 13

Fig. 14

with which the sprocket can be pressed out of the flywheel. Note that the engine sprocket and flywheel are keyed together, and a suitable key must be fitted to the new sprocket before it is pressed into the flywheel.

If the clutch sprocket requires renewing it is supplied complete with a new clutch case ready for assembly to the motor cycle.

The clutch case and sprocket unit is mounted on roller bearings, but it is unlikely that these rollers will need renewing unless there is an appreciable amount of wobble in the clutch case unit when it is fitted.

Re-assembling Primary Chain: If the clutch centre unit has been dismantled, the three large and the three small rubbers which fit around the clutch vane, should be examined, and if any of the rubbers are badly distorted or torn, it would be advisable to take this opportunity and replace all six rubbers. Then to re-assemble the clutch centre unit proceed as follows. Place the clutch centre on a bench with the side into which the rubbers are to be fitted facing uppermost, then place the clutch vane into the clutch centre so that the splined end of the clutch vane is uppermost. Next turn the clutch vane clockwise until the vanes are touching the lobes of the clutch centre, then after smearing all the rubbers with light grease to facilitate fitting, insert the three large rubbers into the three spaces. The clutch vane must then be turned anti-clockwise in order to fit the small rubbers the other side of the vanes, and to make this job easy a screwdriver can be inserted into one of the spaces for a small rubber, and used to lever the clutch vane in an anti-clockwise direction (see Fig. 15). This will increase the size of the spaces for the small rubbers which are then easily fitted, the screwdriver will have to be removed to fit the third small rubber, but with all the other rubbers in place the last one is easily pushed into position.

The clutch centre end plate must be fitted next, but note that one side of the outer edge of the plate is chamfered, and the plate must be fitted with the chamfered edge towards the rubbers, and the three holes in the plate in line with the three holes in the clutch centre. Next fit the three clutch spring bolts through the holes in the end plate and the clutch centre, and place the thrust and locating washer on to the clutch centre end plate, so that the flats on the heads of the clutch spring bolts are located in the slots in the thrust and locating washer.

Fig. 15

Fig. 16

Leave the clutch centre unit assembled on the bench, and next locate the clutch thrust washer on to the back of the clutch sprocket so that the spigot on the thrust washer is located in the hole in the centre of the clutch sprocket. The eighteen clutch rollers must then be assembled into the space between the thrust washer spigot and the edge of the hole in the chain wheel (see Fig. 16). The rollers should be clean and smeared with grease as they are assembled, to help to hold the rollers in position when assembling the clutch sprocket to the gear box mainshaft. The primary chain can then be located over the clutch sprocket and the engine sprocket by holding the two sprocket assemblies side by side (see Fig. 14). Next note the position of the key in the engine shaft, and while holding the sprockets and chain, turn the flywheel and engine sprocket so that the keyway in the engine sprocket corresponds with the position of the key in the engine shaft. Then very carefully locate the two sprocket assemblies on to their respective shafts, making quite certain that the engine sprocket locates correctly over the key in the engine shaft. The clutch centre unit can be fitted next, it must be fitted over the splined gear box mainshaft with the thrust and locating washer next to the clutch rollers, and with the threaded portion of the clutch spring bolts protruding from the nearside of the clutch centre, then pass the service tool—Clutch Banjo 43540S over the clutch centre, and fit the large plain washer and nut to the end of the gear box mainshaft and securely tighten; the thin locknut must then be fitted to the gear box mainshaft and securely tightened (see Fig. 13). If the clutch operating rod has been removed from inside the gear box mainshaft, it should be smeared with clean oil and re-fitted. Next secure the flywheel and engine sprocket to the engine shaft, by first fitting the special tab washer over the end of the engine shaft with the two tabs located into the two holes in the flywheel. Then fit and securely tighten the engine shaft nut, and turn up a portion of the tab washer over the edge of the nut to prevent any possibility of its coming undone. The remainder of the clutch can be assembled next, and proceed in the following order. First fit one of the clutch plates which has linings attached, over the clutch centre, then fit a plain plate followed by a further plate with linings then another plain plate, and finally the special outer plate. The three holes in the outer plate must be in line with the clutch spring bolts which protrude from the clutch centre. Note, on some machines a special washer .080 inches thick is fitted to the clutch spring bolts prior to fitting the spring cups. These washers reduce the load on the clutch and provide a lighter action, and it is desirable that they be fitted to all machines not so fitted if the clutch is in good condition. In the case of machines fitted with an alloy die cast clutch centre, it is only necessary to re-fit the standard .031 inch thick plain washer to provide a large seating surface for the spring sleeve nut.

Then fit a clutch spring cup complete with a spring, followed by a clutch spring washer and a sleeve nut to each of the three clutch spring bolts, and securely tighten. Next re-fit the primary chaincase as described on page 27.

Adjust the primary chain as described on page 25. Top up the chaincase with fresh oil as described on page 25. If the oil seal in the primary chaincase should become worn or damaged it must be replaced. To remove the oil seal, first remove the primary chaincase as described on page 25 and the contact breaker assembly as described on page 60 then the oil seal can be knocked out by locating a drift from the inside of the chaincase, on to the oil seal, and applying a few sharp blows to the drift with a mallet. Before fitting the new oil seal, thoroughly clean the primary chaincase, then begin by using the following service tools:

43593S.   Bolt.
474.   Washer (two off).
43594S.   Nut.
43598S.   Locating collar.
43597S.   Locating collar.

First fit the washer 474 followed by the locating collar 43598S under the head of the bolt 43593S. Then pass the bolt through the primary chaincase from the inside. Next fit the new oil seal on to the locating collar 43597S, and fit the locating collar and oil seal, followed by the second washer 474 and the nut 43594S, to the bolt where it protrudes through the primary chaincase (see Fig. 17). Then tighten the nut and bolt to draw the oil seal into the chaincase. Make sure the oil seal is correctly located, then unscrew and remove the service tools. **Important:** Before fitting the chaincase to the engine, smear the oil seal with oil. Then re-fit the primary chaincase as described on page 27, and re-set the ignition timing as described on page 58.

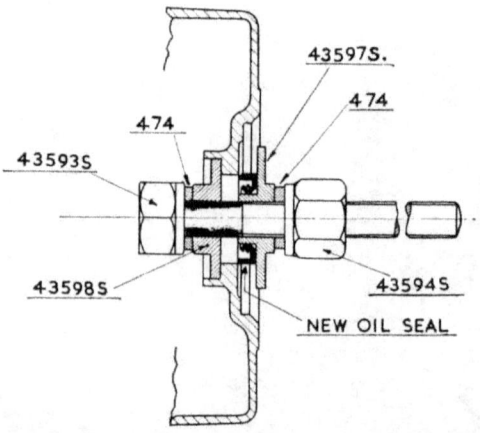

FITTING PRIMARY CHAINCASE OIL SEAL

Fig. 17

Inside the primary chaincase behind the clutch is a second oil seal, fitted in an alloy plate. This seal is to prevent oil leaking out of the primary chaincase, and if it should become worn or damaged, it must be replaced. To remove the plate and oil seal from the engine, first remove the primary chaincase, chain and complete clutch assembly, as described on page 29. Then straighten the tab washers which are folded over the three bolts securing the plate to the engine. The bolts can then be unscrewed and the plate removed. The old oil seal can be removed from the plate, with a drift and mallet. The new oil seal must be fitted so that the spring faces outward, and it should be fitted under a press. Before fitting the plate to the engine, smear the new seal with oil. Also make sure the joint washer behind the plate is in good condition. Then fit the plate to the engine and secure it in position with the three bolts with the tab washers fitted under their heads. When the bolts are tight bend the tabs over the edge of the plate and the flats of the bolt head. Then re-fit the clutch, primary chain and case, as described on page 32.

A breather pipe is fitted behind the primary chaincase, to release any pressure build up. There are no moving parts in the breather and it does not require any attention apart from making sure it is clear and open to atmosphere.

CLUTCH--LEADER AND ARROW

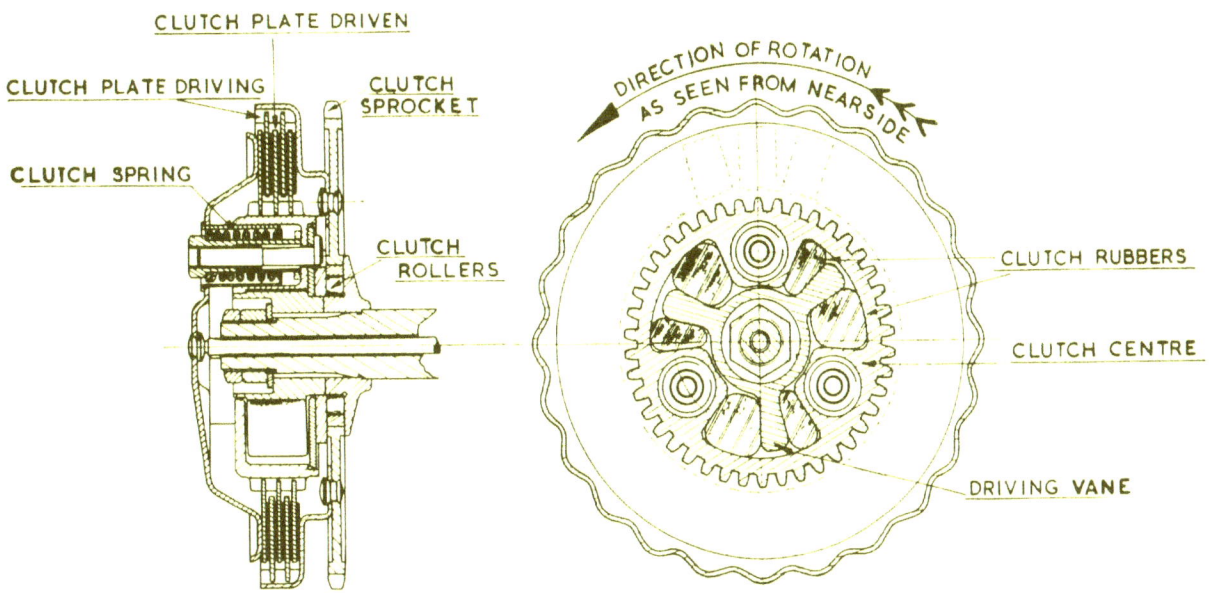

SECTION OF CLUTCH

FIG. 18

A three-plate clutch is fitted to the nearside end of the gear box mainshaft, and is enclosed in the primary chaincase. The clutch will require occasional adjustment, as described on page 126 and 131. Providing the clutch is kept correctly adjusted and not misused, it will give long service, but after a large mileage has been covered, the linings, which are fitted to three of the clutch plates, will begin to wear thin, and this may result in the clutch slipping. When this happens, first check the adjustment and make quite certain that there is 1/16 inch free play in the gear box clutch lever. If the clutch still slips, dismantle the clutch plates as described on page 29. Note, that it is only necessary to remove the primary chaincase in order to dismantle the clutch, do not remove the engine flywheel. Then examine the linings on the three lined clutch plates, and if the linings have a hard and glazed appearance they require renewing. An exchange service is available, whereby plates fitted with worn linings can be exchanged for plates fitted with new linings, ready to assemble to the clutch as described on page 32. Note: If plates with new linings are being fitted, they should be soaked in oil for approximately thirty minutes prior to fitting. The oil should be the same as that used in the primary chaincase.

If the clutch linings and adjustment are in good order, and trouble is experienced with the clutch slipping, it may be that the clutch operating rod which passes through the gear box mainshaft is dry and by removing the clutch rod and smearing it with oil, the trouble will be overcome. Alternatively, if trouble should be experienced with the clutch dragging, that is it will not free properly when the handlebar control lever is pulled in, check the adjustment as there may be too much free play in the handlebar and gear box clutch levers. Also check the clutch operating rod, as it may possibly have broken, which would account for the trouble.

DECARBONISING—LEADER AND ARROW

The burning of the petrol and oil mixture which takes place inside the engine creates a carbon deposit inside the cylinder heads, exhaust ports and silencers; also on the top of the pistons. The amount of carbon that builds up on the parts mentioned must not be allowed to become excessive, and therefore it must be cleaned out periodically. Although the amount of carbon deposited does to some extent depend on the conditions under which the engine has been operating, the time to carry out the work of decarbonising should be based on the mileage covered, and it is strongly recommended that this work is carried out every 5,000 miles.

Before commencing decarbonising, the necessary spares should be obtained, these consist of

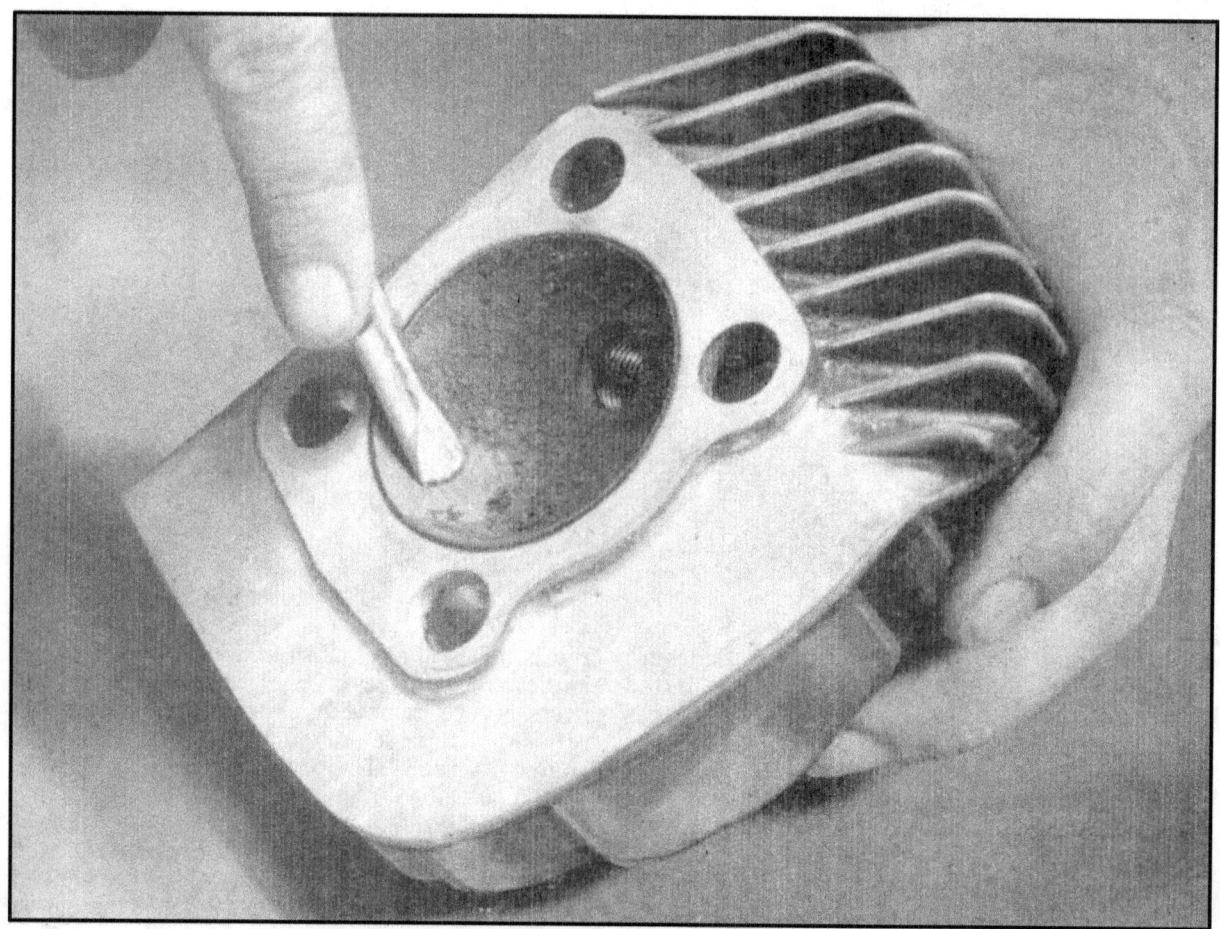

Fig. 19

Fig. 20

the following. Two cylinder head gaskets, two cylinder base washers, two exhaust sealing rings and two silencer end seals. Then in the case of the Leader, begin by removing both side panels as described on page 154, and both legshields as described on page 155. Then remove both exhaust pipes and silencers by first removing the two screws and nuts which secure the rear stop lamp switch to the offside silencer bracket, and leave the loose switch dangling by its leads and spring. Next slacken the acorn nuts at the extreme end of the silencers, just sufficiently to free the silencers from the support stay. Next slacken the nuts on the silencer clamp bolts where they join the exhaust pipe, and pull both silencers rearwards to free them from the motor cycle. In the case of the Arrow, the silencer acorn nuts must be removed completely, then the clamp bolts slackened and the silencers slid forward to free them from the support stays. They can then be pulled outward and rearward to free them from the motor cycle.

Then for both models undo the special nuts which secures each exhaust pipe to the cylinder barrel, with the special spanner supplied in the tool kit of each new motor cycle, which has one end "C" shaped for this purpose and by turning them with this spanner they can be released from the cylinder barrels, and slipped along the exhaust pipes. Then remove the innermost nut which

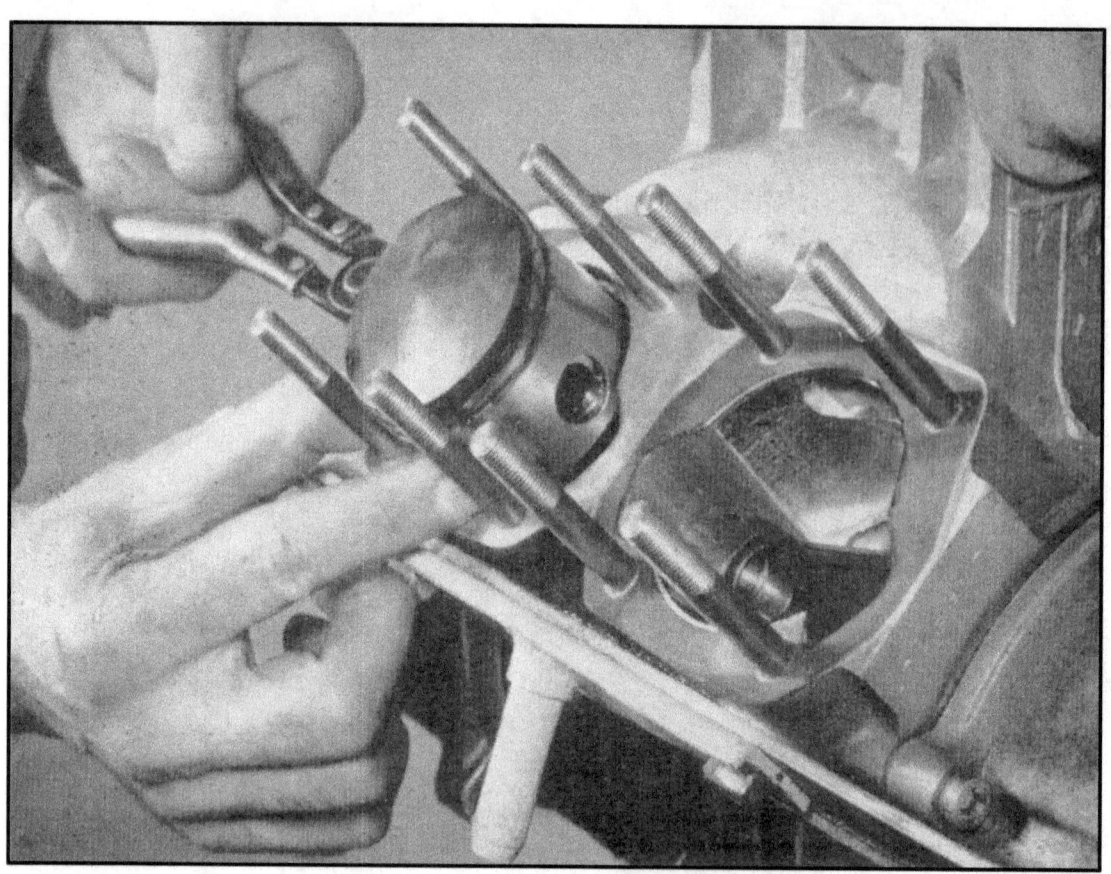

Fig. 21

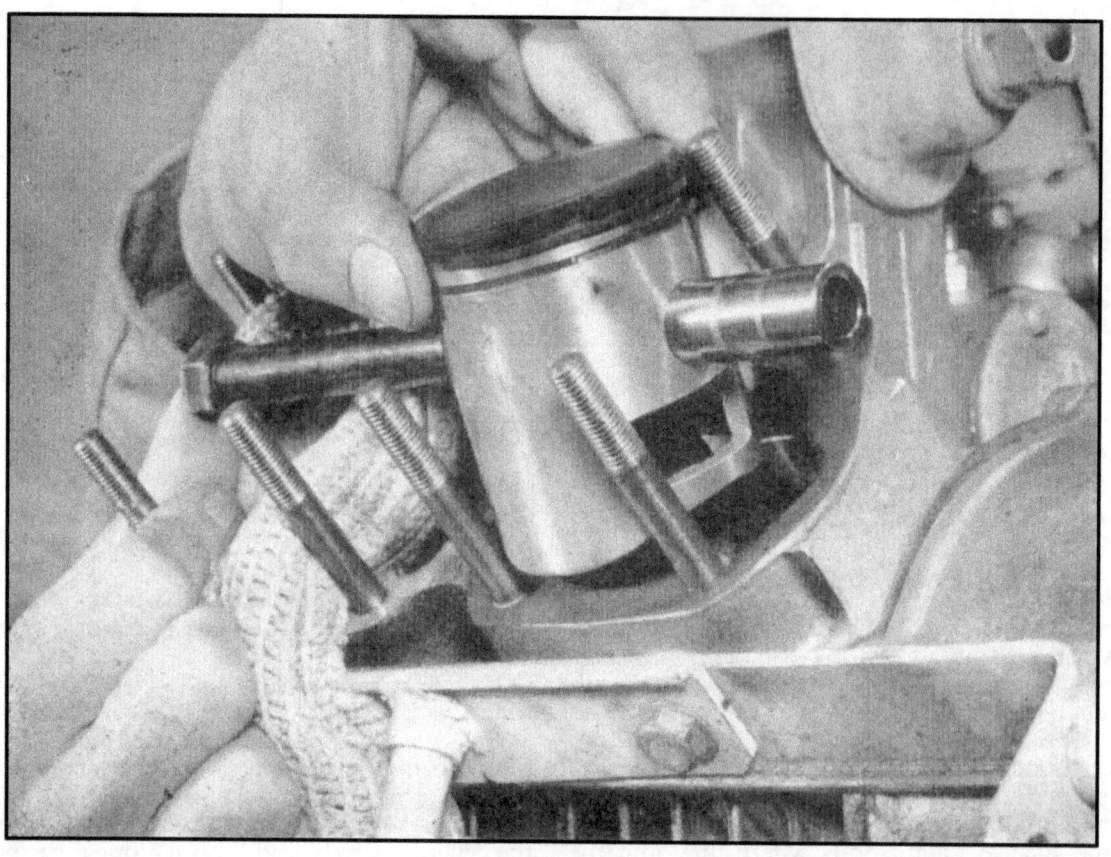

Fig. 22

Fig. 23

secures each footrest and exhaust pipe bracket to the underside of the crankcase. Both exhaust pipes can then be pulled clear of the motor cycle. Next lift off the plastic covers and high tension leads from both sparking plugs, then remove both sparking plugs from the cylinder heads, by unscrewing them with a tube spanner and a tommy bar.

Remove both cylinder heads next, each cylinder head is secured by four sleeve nuts and a special hexagon socket key is supplied in the tool kit of each new motor cycle. Use the socket key to remove each sleeve nut in turn by fitting the short arm of the key into the socket head of the bolt, and then unscrewing them. After removing the four sleeve nuts from each head, the heads themselves can be lifted clear of the motor cycle, but note the special aluminium gasket which is fitted between each cylinder head and cylinder barrel. This gasket must be in perfect condition if it is to be re-fitted when the cylinder heads are re-assembled, otherwise a new gasket must be used.

Note: There are two different design cylinder heads in use, the main difference is in the compression ratio. The high compression heads have a combustion chamber shape like a top hat, whilst the lower compression heads have a hemispherical combustion chamber. Either type of heads may be fitted to an engine but both heads must be of the same shape and compression ratio. It can now be seen that the inside of each cylinder head, the top of both pistons and the exhaust port in each cylinder barrel is coated with a sooty deposit. This deposit will have to be scraped off, but care must be taken not to scratch the metal surface of the pistons or the cylinder heads, and for this reason it is strongly recommended that a stick of soft solder, with a sharp edge, is used to scrape the carbon deposit from the pistons and the cylinder heads.

Beginning with the cylinder heads, carefully scrape all the carbon deposit from the inside of both heads (see Fig. 19). Then finish by polishing with a good quality metal polish. Finally, make quite certain there is no dirt or foreign matter in the threads of the sparking plug hole. The carbon deposit on both pistons must be removed next, and to enable this work to be carried out the pistons must be removed from the engine.

Begin by lifting the cylinder barrels one at a time, in an upward direction. They should lift easily, but if they are a little tight, firm careful pulling in an upward direction will free them. Do not under any circumstances twist the cylinder barrels. As the cylinder barrels are lifted clear it will leave the pistons unsupported, and care should be taken to prevent the pistons falling forward or rearward and becoming damaged (see Fig. 20). The pistons must be removed next, and although they are not rigidly fixed, they are attached to the

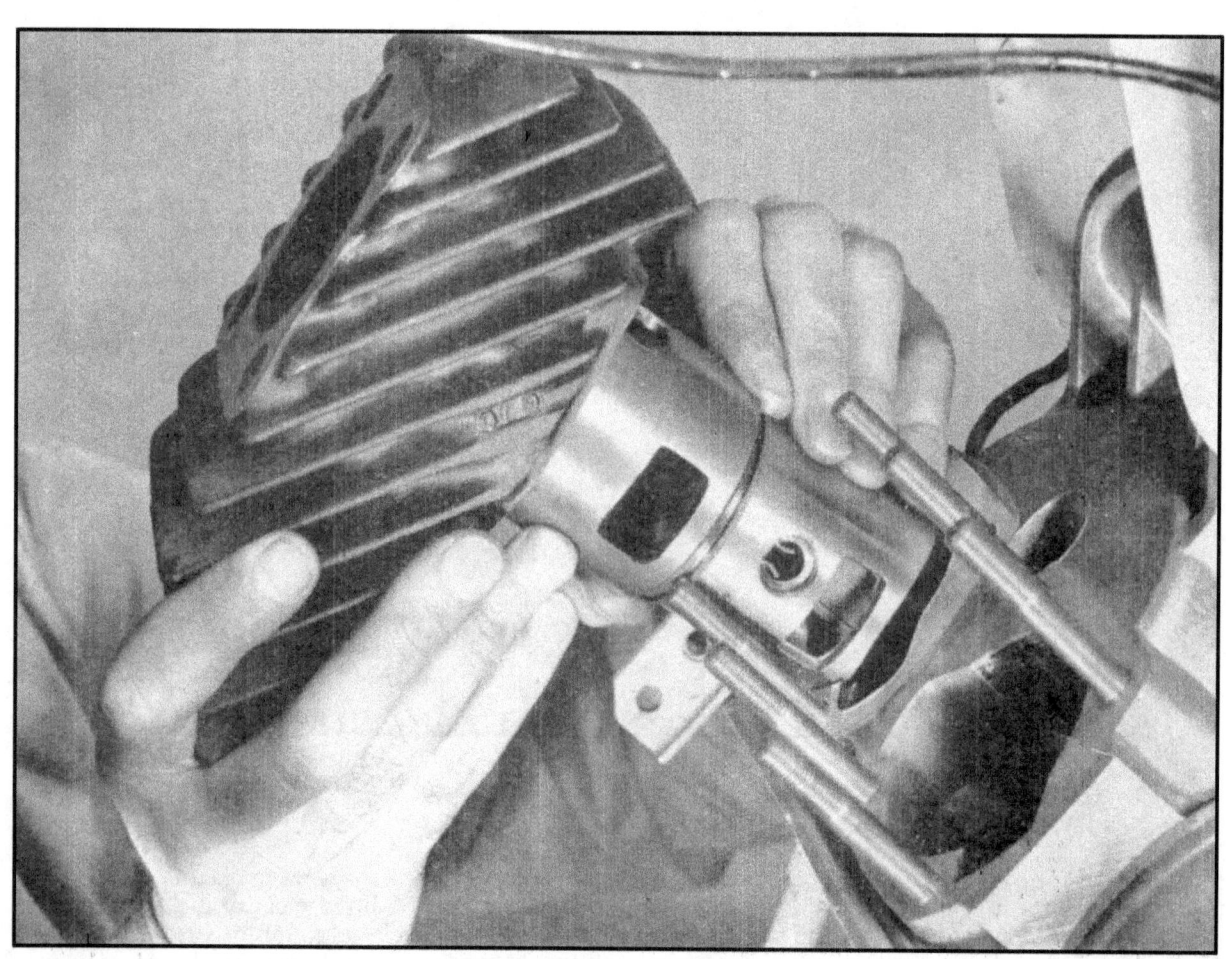

FIG. 24

small end of the connecting rods by the gudgeon pins. At both ends of each gudgeon pin there is a spring wire circlip and these must be removed, but first cover the mouth of the crankcase below the pistons with a large piece of clean cloth, to prevent the possibility of a circlip or anything else falling into the crankcase. Then, using a pair of pointed nose pliers, grip the turned up ends of one of the circlips, and by squeezing the ends together the circlip can easily be withdrawn (see Fig. 21). Remove the circlip from the other end of the gudgeon pin in a similar manner. Then carefully push out the gudgeon pin, this is best done by using a piece of $\frac{1}{2}$ inch diameter wooden dowel approximately 6 inches long. By using a piece of wooden dowel there is no risk of damaging the piston or the small end bush in the connecting rod. While pushing the gudgeon pin through the piston, support the opposite side of the piston with the free hand (see Fig. 22). Do not under any circumstances use force, if the gudgeon pin is a tight fit, removal can be facilitated by wrapping the piston in a cloth which has been dipped in boiling water. The heat from the cloth will expand the piston and free the fit of the gudgeon pin. Take care not to let any water fall into the crankcase.

With the gudgeon pins removed the pistons can be lifted clear, and the next step is to remove the two compression rings from the top of each piston. This job requires extra care as the compression rings could easily be broken if mishandled. The compression rings should be removed one at a time, and note that there is a peg fitted in both the compression ring grooves, these pegs prevent the ring moving around the piston to ensure the ends of the rings do not catch in the ports. Beginning with the ends of the ring each side of the peg, use both thumb nails, one nail on each end of the ring, lever the ends of the ring slightly apart so that the ring is expanded just sufficiently to lift it up clear of the piston (see Fig. 23). Note that this is the top compression ring and when it is re-fitted it must be in its original position at the top of the piston. The lower compression ring must be removed in a similar manner. When working on the piston take the greatest care not to damage or scratch it, and under no circumstances must the piston be clamped in a vice.

Next remove the carbon deposit from the top of the piston, using the same method described for the cylinder heads, by scraping off the carbon with a stick of soft solder and then polishing with metal polish. The piston compression rings and the grooves from where the compression rings were removed must be cleaned; also any stain on the sides of the piston must be cleaned off. The grooves and sides of the piston are best cleaned with metal polish. When the piston and rings have been thoroughly cleaned, they should be washed in petrol, then the rings can be re-fitted to the piston using the same method as described for removing them. The piston can now be re-fitted to its connecting rod. **Important note:** The pistons must always be re-fitted in their respective cylinder barrels and never interchanged. Also note the pistons must always be fitted so that the arrow and the word "Front" which are stamped on the top of the piston, are facing forward. As a further check there is a port each side of the piston, and when the piston is correctly fitted the port is slightly offset forward of the gudgeon pin (see Fig. 20).

To fit the piston to the connecting rod, first locate the piston over the connecting rod and pass the oiled gudgeon pin through one side of the piston then the small end of the connecting rod, and into the other side of the piston. Make sure the groove for the circlip in one side of the piston is visible, then insert one side of the circlip into the groove, then press the other side of the circlip

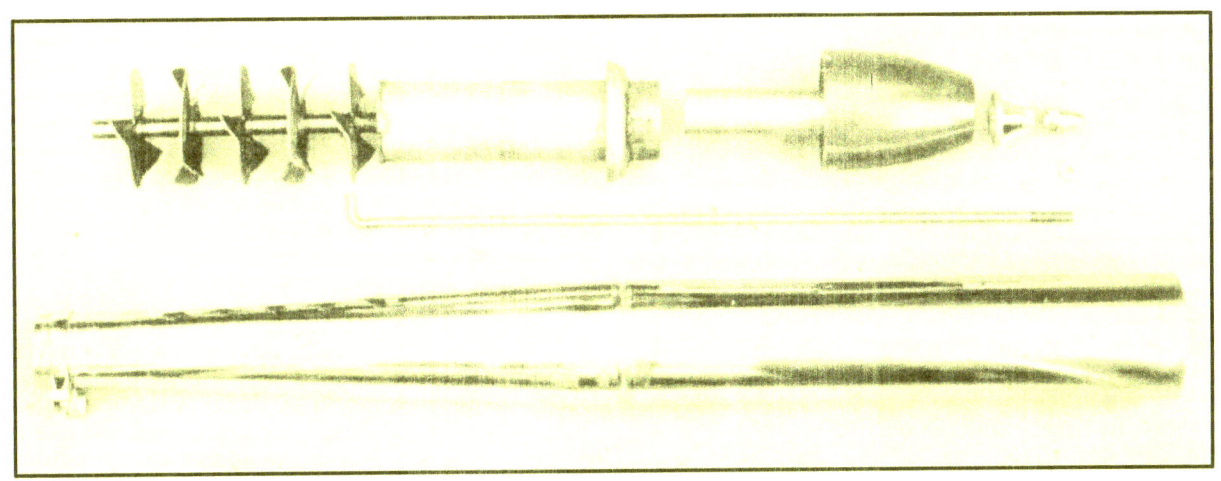

Fig. 25

into the groove by pushing it with a thumb. The circlip for the other end of the gudgeon pin is fitted in a similar manner. But afterwards make quite certain that both circlips are correctly seated in the grooves in the piston.

Next remove the carbon deposit from the exhaust ports of both cylinder barrels. This should be done by working from the end of the ports from where the exhaust pipes were removed, and in addition to scraping with a stick of soft solder, it is permissible to use fine emery cloth wrapped around one finger in order to remove the carbon from inside the curved port, where it cannot be reached with the stick of soft solder. **Important Note:** The exhaust port is the only place where emery cloth may be used, and even then the greatest care must be taken not to touch the inner wall of the cylinder barrel, and under no circumstances may emery cloth be used on the pistons or the cylinder heads.

Then thoroughly clean the cylinder barrel in petrol, removing all traces of loose carbon and any other foreign matter. Next inspect the paper joint washer, which fits between the cylinder base and the crankcase; this washer should only be used again if it is in perfect condition. If in any doubt fit a new washer. The cylinder barrel can then be fitted over the piston and located on to the crankcase, but this job calls for great care and patience. First be quite certain that the cylinder barrel is being fitted to the correct side of the engine. Begin by smearing a little clean oil around the sides of the piston, the same grade of oil as recommended for the gear box would be ideal. Also make quite certain that the pegs in the compression ring grooves are between the ends of the rings.

Then, with one hand, hold the cylinder barrel above the piston with the barrel the correct way round, and lower it slowly on to the piston, but at the same time using the thumb and one finger of the other hand, through the small cut out at the front and rear of the bottom of the cylinder barrel skirt, to squeeze the compression rings into the grooves in the piston, in order to pass the cylinder barrel over the piston and down into the crankcase (see Fig. 24). **Important:** The cylinder barrel must pass easily over the piston and the compression rings, if any resistance or difficulty is met, do not use any force as this would result in damage; instead, re-check the method of assembly and make sure all parts are correctly fitted.

When the first cylinder barrel is correctly located in the crankcase, the second cylinder barrel can be fitted in an identical manner, after making sure the cylinder base joint washer is in good order. **Note:** If a piston compression ring should be broken during the decarbonising work, see page 44 for the important instructions regarding fitting new piston rings.

Next fit new cylinder head gaskets to the top of the cylinder barrels; the old gaskets may be used again only if they are in perfect condition. Then place the cylinder heads in position on top of the barrels, and fit a plain washer under the head of each of the eight socket head cylinder head sleeve nuts. Then locate the sleeve nuts through the holes in the top of the cylinder heads and on to the studs which protrude from the top of the crankcase. Using the hexagon socket key, screw all the sleeve nuts down loosely, then dealing with one cylinder head at a time tighten the front left side sleeve nut a little, then tighten the rear right side sleeve nut a little, then the front right side sleeve nut similarly, and finally the rear left side sleeve nut must be tightened a little. Then commence with the front left side sleeve nut again and follow the same order as before, tightening each sleeve nut a little more.

Continue tightening the sleeve nuts in this manner until they are all equally securely tightened. If this procedure is followed for both cylinder heads, they will be tightened evenly ensuring a good joint between the cylinder head and the cylinder barrel, and eliminating the possibility of distortion of the cylinder head.

Next adjust the gap between the centre electrode and the earthing point on both sparking plugs, as described on page 18. Then smear a little graphite grease on the threaded portion of both sparking plugs, and fit the plugs to the cylinder heads and replace the high tension leads on both plugs. The graphite grease will facilitate the fitting and future removal of the sparking plugs.

This completes the work on the engine; the silencers must be dealt with next (see Fig. 25). Remove the acorn nuts from the end of both silencers, then remove the thin locknut which fits immediately in front of the acorn nut, but note the studs on which these nuts are fitted may tend to revolve with the nuts, this is easily prevented by pulling the studs outward while removing the nuts. The small cone-shaped alloy die casting and the alloy end section can then be pulled free from the silencers. Note the sealing ring fitted between the alloy end section and the main silencer body, this ring fits just inside the end of the main body against the last baffle. Remove the sealing ring from each silencer next, it can easily be prised out with a small screwdriver. Then note the latest baffles as shown in Fig. 25 need not be removed, all that is necessary to clean out the carbon, is to poke clear with a piece of strong wire, the holes around the edge of the end baffle which can be seen. The earlier round type of baffle assembly should be removed to clean, and it would be advantageous to change to the later type when convenient. Next remove as much carbon as possible from both ends of the exhaust pipes.

Re-assembly can then begin. The silencer centre stud must pass through the small diameter tube of the baffle assembly, the stud is fitted into the silencer from the exhaust pipe end, and there is a locating plate in the silencer body through which the stud must pass. Then fit a new sealing ring into the end of both silencer bodies and locate the silencer end section complete with its centre tube into the silencer body. Next fit the cone-shaped alloy die casting over the stud which protrudes from the silencer end section, then fit and carefully tighten the thin locknut on to the silencer centre studs. The acorn nuts can then be loosely fitted.

The exhaust pipes and silencers can now be re-fitted to the motor cycle. Begin with the exhaust pipes, and note new sealing washers must be fitted where the exhaust pipes fit into the cylinder barrel exhaust ports. Two different types of sealing washers have been used, first a copper and asbestos washer and later a soft iron washer. The soft iron washer, which is a dark colour, is the better of the two and should be fitted in place of the copper and asbestos type. First fit the special exhaust pipe nuts on to the exhaust pipes, then fit the new sealing washers over the ends of the exhaust pipes. Locate the pipes into the cylinder barrel exhaust ports, at the same time fitting the exhaust pipe brackets over the inner footrest securing studs. Then making sure the exhaust pipes are as close together as possible under the engine, screw the special exhaust pipe nuts into the cylinder barrel exhaust ports and securely tighten. Fit a plain washer, a shake-proof washer and a nut to the two inner footrest studs and securely tighten. Next fit the silencers over the ends of the exhaust pipes and locate them into the support stay at the rear. Then tighten both silencer clamp bolts and the acorn nuts at the silencer ends. Finally, in the case of the Leader, re-fit both leg shields as described on page 154, and the side panels as described on page 155.

CYLINDER BARRELS AND PISTONS—LEADER AND ARROW

The cylinder barrels are made of hard-wearing, close grain, cast iron, while the pistons are of light alloy, and are fitted with two compression rings. Very careful running in with either a new motor cycle, or new or re-bored cylinder barrels is of the utmost importance, as correct running in beds in the piston rings and creates a hard skin on the surface of the cylinder bore.

PISTON & RING DATA   LEADER & ARROW

PISTON AND BARREL.

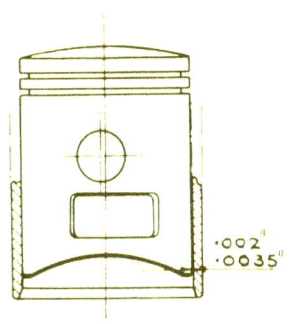

PISTON RING.

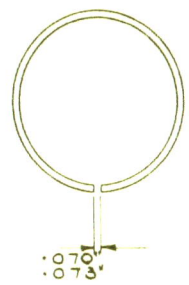

THE PISTON CLEARANCE MUST BE MEASURED AT THE FRONT OR REAR OF THE SKIRT WITH THE PISTON FITTED IN THE LOWER HALF OF THE CYLINDER BARREL. NOTE: WHEN THIS CLEARANCE EXCEEDS .007" THE CYLINDER SHOULD EITHER BE RE-BORED OR EXCHANGED FOR AN OVERSIZE UNIT.

THE PISTON RINGS ARE SUPPLIED WITH THE CORRECT GAP TO CHECK THE GAP THE RING ONLY MUST BE FITTED IN THE CYLINDER BARREL. NOTE: THAT THE GAP ALLOWS FOR THE 1/16 DIA. PEG FITTED IN THE PISTON RING GROOVE.

FIG. 26

Routine Maintenance

If it is required to remove the cylinder barrels and pistons, proceed as described on page 36. The carbon deposit which builds up in the exhaust ports and on the piston crowns must be removed periodically as described on page 36. Under normal conditions the pistons will last until the cylinder barrels require re-boring, but the piston rings should be replaced every ten to fifteen thousand miles. As the decarbonising work is carried out every five thousand miles, a convenient time to change the piston rings would be every second or third time of decarbonising. The piston ring end gap is pre-set, and new piston rings are ready for immediate fitting. *Note:* When fitting new piston rings or pistons to Part worn cylinder bores, the glazed surface must be lightly removed from the cylinder bore. This is easily done by using fine emery cloth and paraffin.

The circlips which secure the gudgeon pins in the pistons should always be removed and re-fitted with special internal circlip pliers, which are obtainable from most good tool dealers. Never under any circumstances re-fit a circlip that has been damaged. Providing the circlips are not damaged, they may be used indefinitely.

After the motor cycle has covered a *very large mileage*, the cylinder bores may become worn, and it will be necessary to re-bore the cylinder barrels and fit oversize pistons. The wear in the bore will be most pronounced at the front and rear of the upper half, and the time to have the cylinders re-bored is when the amount of wear exceeds .0035 inch, the original bore size is 2.125 inch. The rate of wear in the cylinders is very low, and it should not be taken for granted that the cylinders need re-boring when other parts of the engine require overhauling. The wear in the cylinders should be checked with a bore gauge by a competent person. Oversize pistons for use in re-bored cylinders are marked on the top. Two sizes are available and are marked with + 20 and + 40 respectively. An exchange service is available, whereby a worn cylinder barrel can be part exchanged for a re-bored cylinder barrel together with a suitable oversize piston complete with gudgeon pin, rings and circlips, ready for fitting to the engine.

The pistons are marked "front" on the top, to avoid any possibility of fitting them the wrong way round. Also, when the pistons are correctly fitted, the ports in the piston skirt are offset forward of the gudgeon pin. Any time the pistons are removed, they must be re-fitted in their respective cylinders, and never interchanged. A used and worn piston must never be fitted into a new or newly re-bored cylinder, but in the event of a piston being damaged, it is permissible to fit a new piston into a partly worn cylinder. The new piston would of course require carefully running in.

The two compression rings fitted to each piston must be replaced with new ones every ten to fifteen thousand miles as described on page 36. New piston rings are supplied ready for fitting, no gap adjustment being necessary. When new rings have been fitted, the motor cycle must be kept in the lower and medium speed range for approximately 250 miles, to allow the new rings to bed in.

SMALL END BUSH—LEADER AND ARROW

The small ends of both connecting rods are fitted with a bush through which the gudgeon pin for the piston passes. Normally these bushes will last the life of the connecting rod, and when a crankshaft is reconditioned a new connecting rod complete with a new small end bush is included. It is therefore unlikely that these bushes will need attention between general overhauls.

If, however, due to some unusual circumstance a small end bush should become damaged or prematurely worn, it can easily be replaced with the following service tools, after removing the cylinder heads, cylinder barrels and pistons as described on page 36:

- 43593S. Bolt.
- 43594S. Nut.
- 474. Washer (two off).
- 43603S. Guide.
- 43604S. Spacer.

The old small end bush must be removed first (see Fig. 27), commence by fitting the washer 474, followed by the spacer 43604S, under the head of the bolt 43593S. Then pass the bolt through the small end bush, and fit the guide 43603S over the bolt and locate it into the small end bush. Next fit the second washer 474 followed by the nut 43594S to the bolt, and by tightening the nut and bolt the bush will be drawn out of the connecting Rod (see Fig. 28). The service tools can then be unscrewed and removed.

To fit the new bush, first note the oil holes which pass through the bush and the connecting rod; these holes must be in line with one another when the bush is fitted. Then commence by fitting washer 474 under the head of the bolt 43593S, and fit the guide and bush on to the bolt. Then pass the bolt through the small end of the connecting rod. Next fit the spacer 43604S, followed by the washer 474, and the nut 43594S, to the bolt where it protrudes through the connecting rod (see Fig. 27). Then tighten the nut and bolt, making sure the new bush enters the connecting rod true and square. Continue

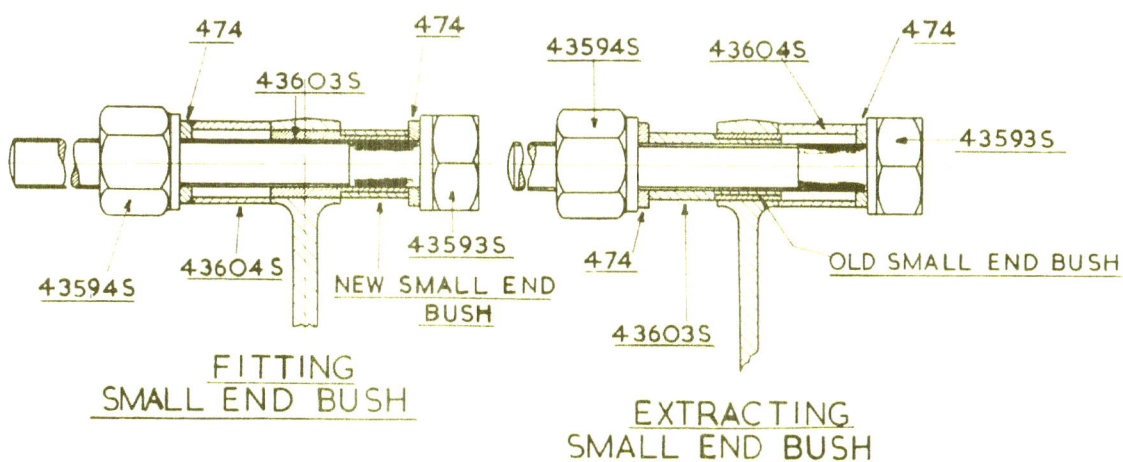

474
474
43603S
43594S
43604S
474
43593S
43593S
43604S
43594S
NEW SMALL END
BUSH
474
OLD SMALL END BUSH
43603S
FITTING
SMALL END BUSH
EXTRACTING
SMALL END BUSH
IMPORTANT:- OIL HOLES IN BUSH AND SMALL END MUST BE LINED UP CORRECTLY BEFORE
FITTING BUSH

FIG. 27

tightening until the bush is correctly located, then unscrew and remove the service tools. *Note*: Normally a new bush does not need reamering, but in the event of a gudgeon pin being tight in the bush, the bush must be carefully reamered to .6003″/.6006″ diameter. The engine can be re-assembled as described on page 41.

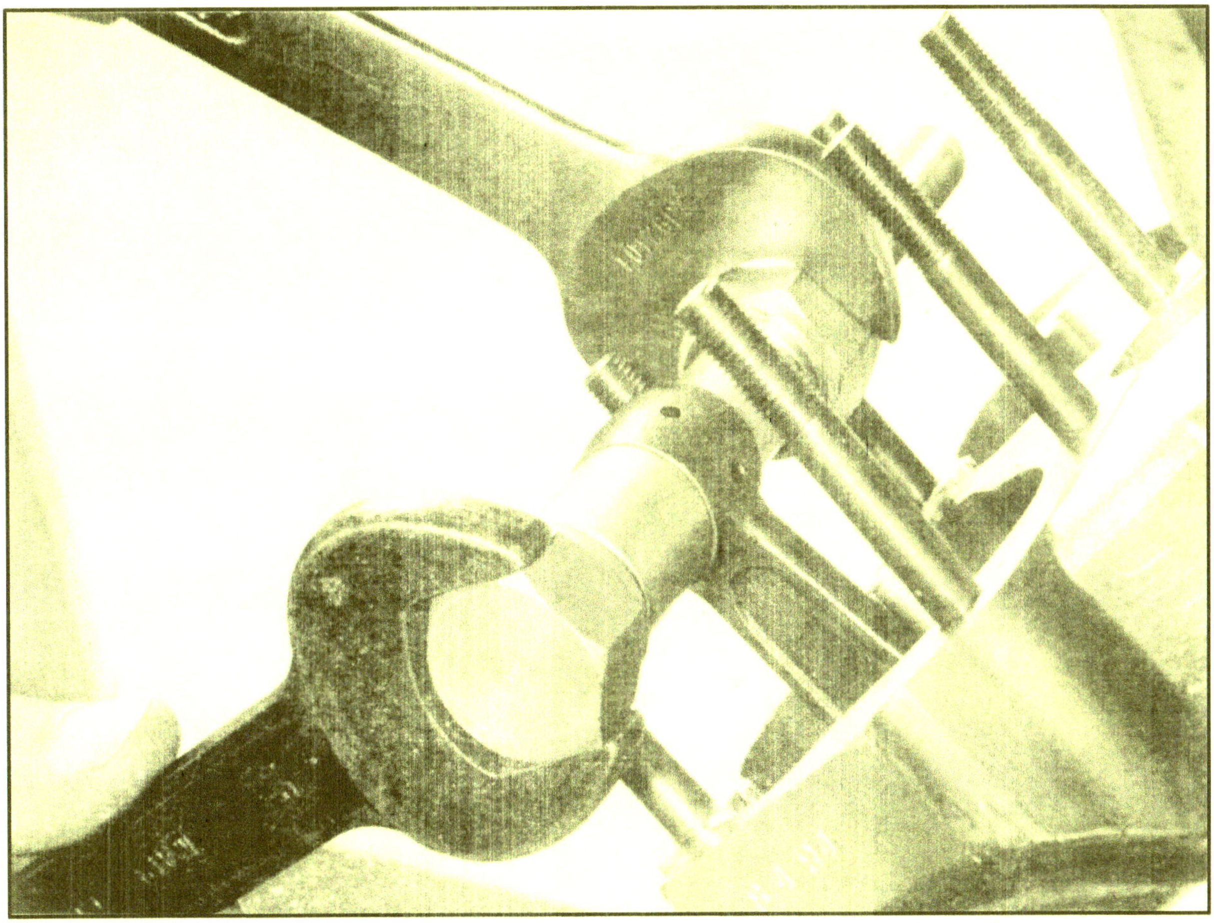

FIG. 28

CRANKSHAFT ASSEMBLY—LEADER AND ARROW

The crankshaft is mounted on three journal ball bearings in the crankcase, and the connecting rods which are fitted to the crankshaft are mounted on roller bearings. The length of the life of these bearings does to some extent depend on the way the machine is driven and serviced, and under normal conditions long life can be expected. When wear in the bearings does become apparent, it will be found that they are all worn a similar amount, and all the bearings and oil seals should be renewed together. Alternatively, it is possible due to some unusual circumstance for one bearing to fail prematurely, and providing the remainder of the bearings are in good condition, it is permissible to change one bearing only.

Excessive bearing wear would be indicated if the engine becomes noisy at low speeds, or if bad vibrations develop, particularly if the motor cycle has covered a large mileage.

The journal bearings which support the crankshaft at each end, can be removed and replaced without disturbing the crankshaft, and if it should be required to replace these bearings only, follow the crankcase dismantling instructions to remove the end covers which contain the bearings.

Crankcase: Dismantling

To dismantle the crankcase, in order to remove the crankshaft, proceed as follows. Remove the exhaust pipes, cylinder heads, barrels and pistons as described on page 36. Then remove the primary chaincase, chain, clutch and engine sprocket as described on page 29. Next remove the alternator as described on page 219. The crankcase end covers can be removed next. Beginning with the nearside, around the cover can be seen four nuts, one screw and one bolt, which secure it to the crankcase. Remove these nuts, bolt and screw, but before removing the nearside crankcase end cover, the woodruff key used to locate the engine sprocket will have to be removed. A few taps with a hammer and drift will usually be sufficient, and then to remove the cover itself,

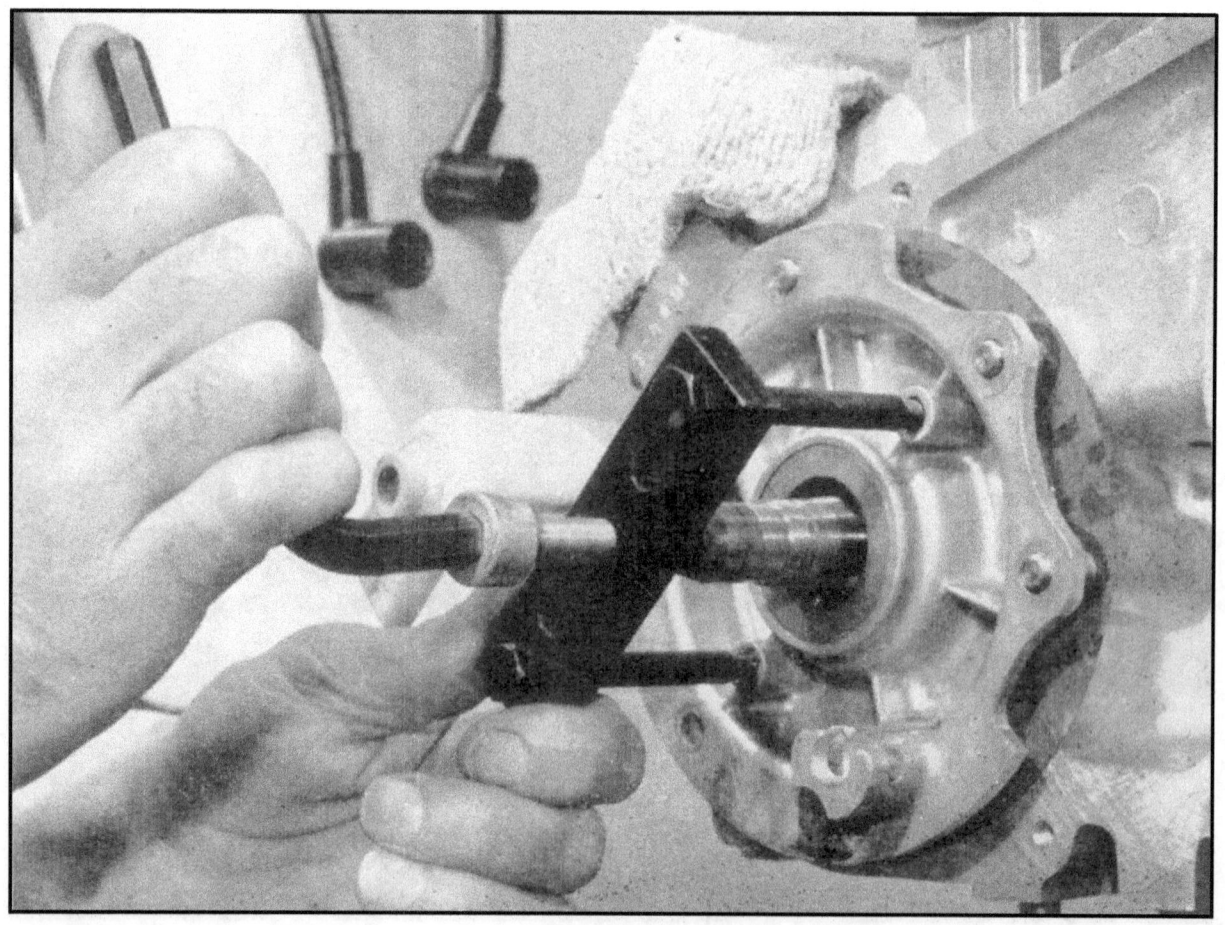

Fig. 29

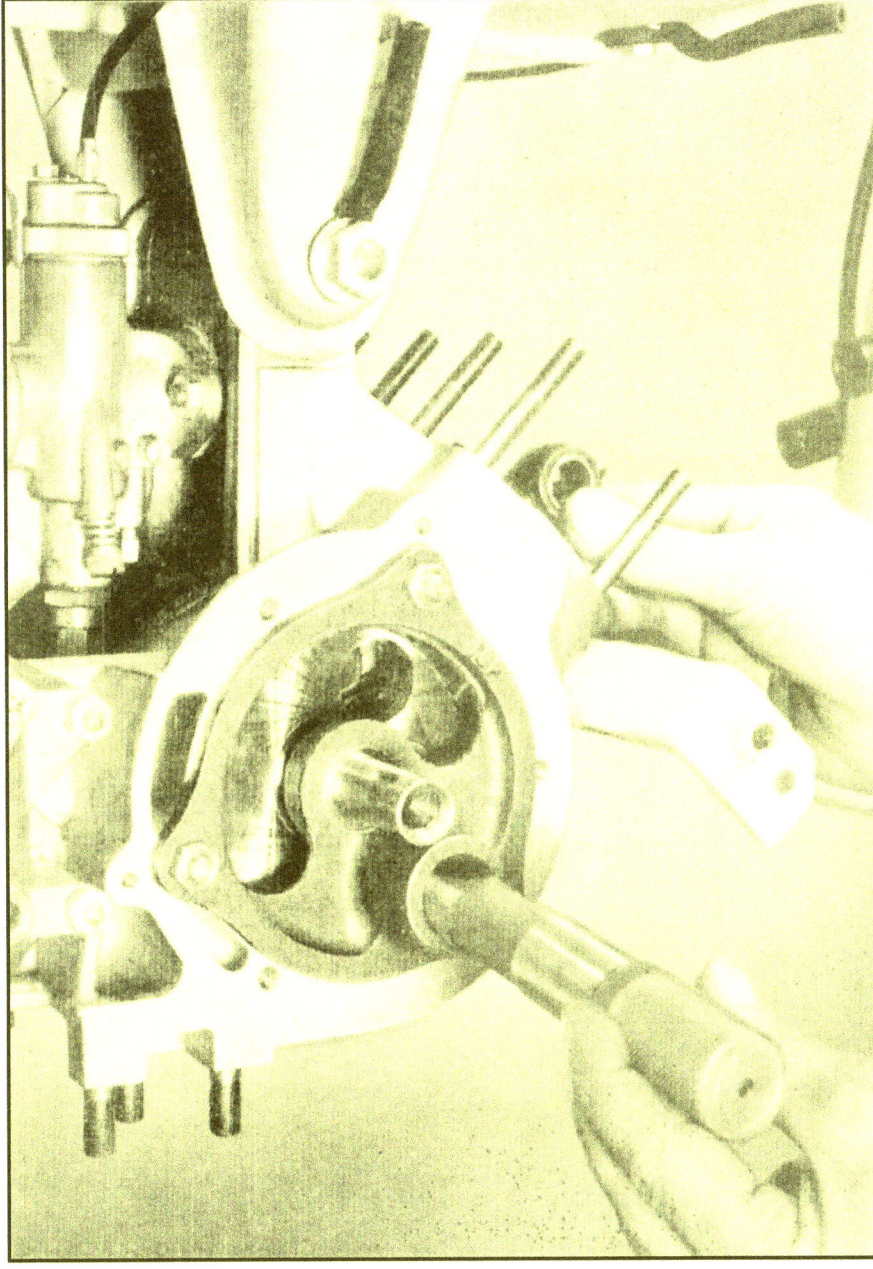

Fig. 30

the following service extractor tools will be required:

    43545S.   Extractor Plate.
    43547S.   Centre screw.
    43546S.   Bolt (two off).
    43544S.   Sleeve.

Commence by fitting the two bolts 43546S through the outermost holes in the extractor plate 43545S. Then fit the sleeve 43544S over the end of the crankshaft, locating the peg into the slot in the sleeve. Next locate the extractor in position with the two bolts screwed into the tapped holes in the end cover. Then fit the centre screw 43547S through the tapped hole in the centre of the extractor plate, so that it locates on the end of the sleeve 43544S. The hexagon socket wrench which is supplied in the tool kit of each new motor cycle, can then be used to turn the extractor centre screw, which will draw the end cover off (see Fig. 29). The extractor tool can then be unscrewed and removed.

To remove the offside end cover begin by first removing the three screws and the three nuts from around the edge of the cover. The key that locates the rotor must be removed before the end cover is withdrawn. A hammer and drift will probably be needed to loosen the key. Then using the service extractor tools, withdraw the offside end cover in the same way as described for the nearside, except instead of fitting the sleeve over the end of the crankshaft, loosely re-fit the rotor bolt for the extractor centre screw to locate on. *Note:* There may be a shim fitted between the outer edge of the offside end cover and the crankcase, or between the end cover bearing and the crankshaft. If a shim is fitted, it is there to position the crankshaft for correct primary chain alignment, and unless a new crankshaft assembly or gear box mainshaft is being fitted, the shim must be re-fitted. If a new crankshaft or gear box mainshaft is being fitted, see page 57 for details of primary chain alignment.

Both ends of the crankshaft are now fully visible, and to remove it from the crankcase the following service tools are required:

43541S. Locating plate.
43542S. Plug.
43551S. Key.

Commence by fitting the locating plate 43541S over the studs which protrude from the offside end of the crankcase, so that the word "top" which is on the locating plate, faces outwards and points to the top of the crankcase mouth (see Fig. 30).

Next fit a nut to each stud and firmly tighten the locating plate in position. The plug 43542S must then be inserted through the boss on the locating plate, and by rotating the crankshaft so that the offside connecting rod is at top dead centre, the plug can be pushed through the offside half of the crankshaft. It may be necessary to turn the plug slightly to allow it to pass the big end and through the crankshaft.

The two halves of the crankshaft are secured together by a bolt, which is accessible through the hollow offside crankshaft. The key 43551S can be fitted into the hollow crankshaft, and located into the socket head of the crankshaft bolt, a tube spanner and tommy bar can then be fitted to the end of the key and the bolt can be undone in the normal way, i.e. in an anti-clockwise direction (see Fig. 31), but note that the bolt acts as an extractor, and after initially loosening it will become tight again. Continue turning the bolt which will at first be extremely tight, until the two halves of the crankshaft become separated. The bolt will remain in position inside the offside crankshaft assembly as it is secured by a circlip. An alternative method of undoing the crankshaft

Fig. 31

FIG. 32

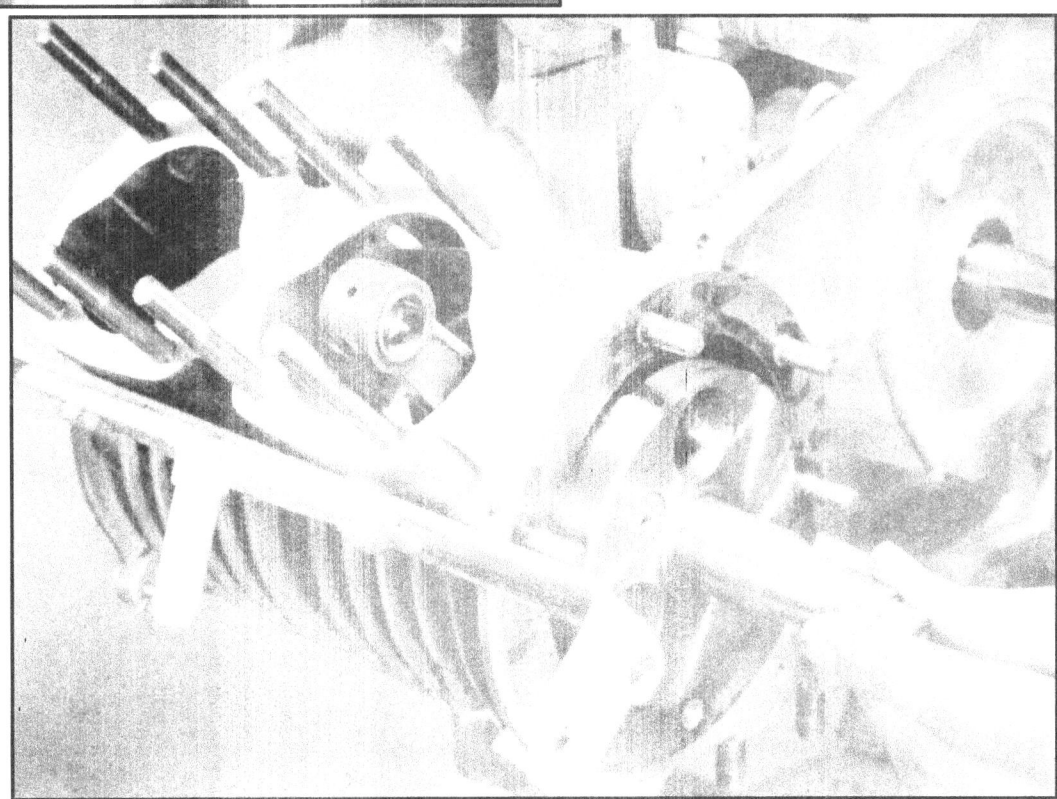

FIG. 33

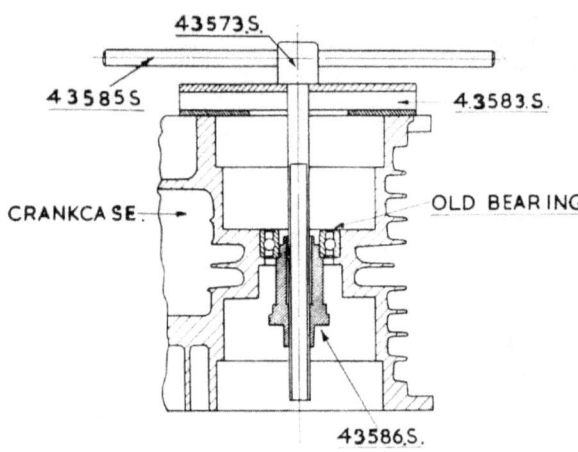

EXTRACTING CRANKCASE BEARING
Fig. 34

bolt, is to fit the key which is used to undo the cylinder head bolts, into the socket head of the crankshaft bolt, then fit a length of steel tube over the right angle portion of the key.

Withdraw the key 43551S and the plug 43542S from the offside crankshaft, and remove the locating plate from the end of the crankcase. The crankshaft halves can then be removed from the crankcase, begin with the offside, by turning it until the connecting rod is at bottom dead centre, then pull the assembly outwards to free it from the centre crankcase oil seal, and tip it at an angle to withdraw it from the crankcase (see Fig. 32). The nearside crankshaft half must be turned until the connecting rod is at top dead centre. Then

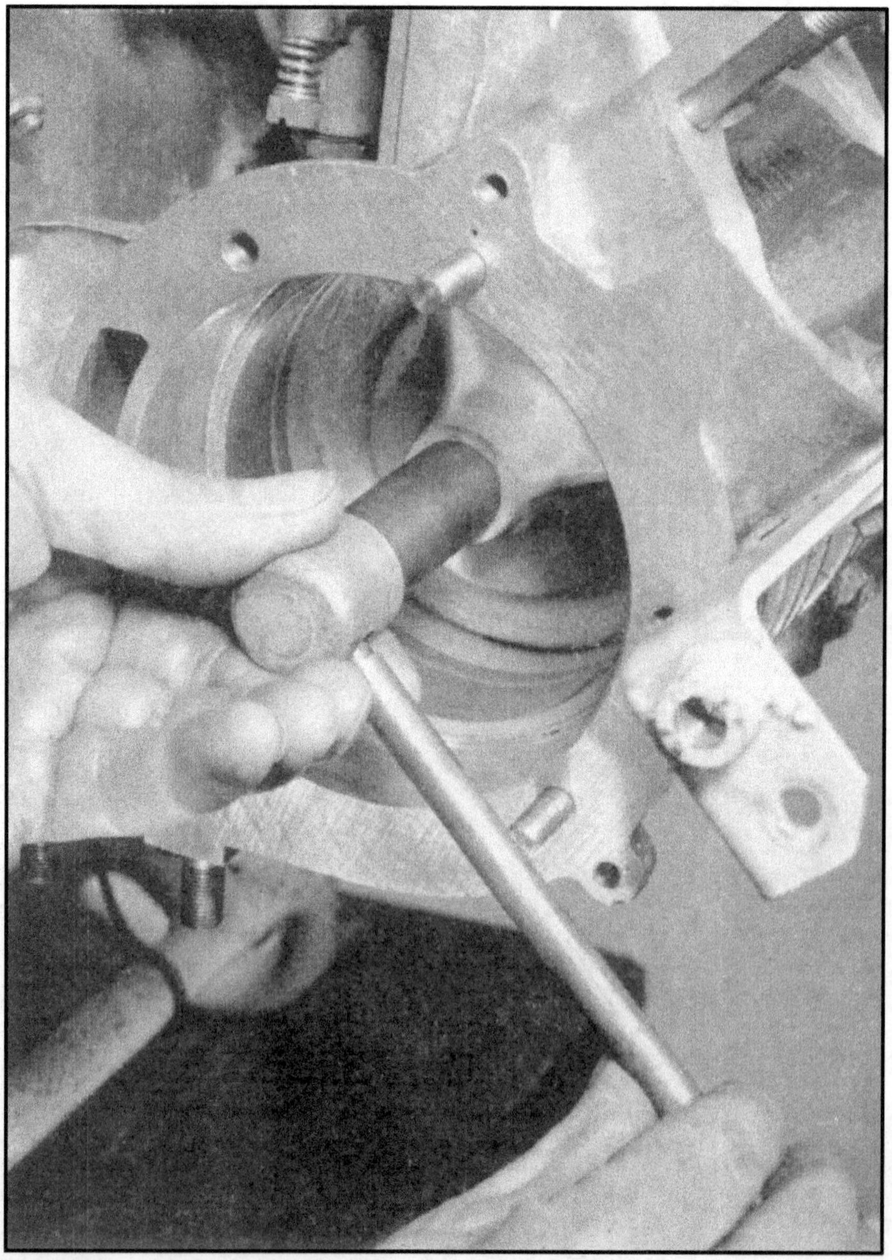

Fig. 35

pull the assembly outward so that the connecting rod is in the crankcase transfer port (see Fig. 33). This will then have freed the assembly from the crankcase centre bearing and the crankshaft can be turned until the connecting rod is at bottom dead centre, when the assembly can be tipped at an angle and withdrawn from the crankcase.

Only the centre main bearing and oil seal now remain in the crankcase, and to remove these the following service tools are required:

43573S.	Spindle assembly.
43585S.	Tommy bar.
43583S.	Extractor channel.
43586S.	Extractor collar.

Commence by passing the spindle assembly 43573S through the extractor channel 43583S. Then pass the spindle through the crankcase centre bearing from the nearside, so that the extractor channel is located against the end of the crankcase. Next fit the extractor collar 43586S to the spindle inside the offside half of the crankcase. Then fit the tommy bar 43585S through the head of the spindle (see Fig. 34), and commence turning the spindle, but make sure that the extractor collar 43586S does not also turn and it can be held by fitting a spanner to the two flats on the collar. Continue turning the spindle until the bearing is removed. The oil seal which is still in the crankcase centre can easily be removed with a drift and mallet. The drift must be passed through the crankcase from the nearside, and located on to the oil seal so that it can be knocked out through the offside half of the crankcase. Some engines are fitted with two single oil seals, while others have one double oil seal. The two types are interchangeable, and when replacing seals, either type can be fitted.

If the connecting rod big end bearings require renewing, this is an extremely specialised job calling for the use of special equipment which means the crankshafts must be returned to the works for servicing, but as this would cause a delay in completing the engine repairs, an exchange service is available whereby worn crankshafts can be part exchanged through an Ariel agent, for crankshafts complete with new big end bearings and connecting rods ready to fit into the crankcase.

Before beginning the engine re-assembly, thoroughly clean out the crankcase. Then commence by fitting the new crankcase centre bearing, using the following service tools. *Note:* New bearings and oil seals should be lightly oiled to facilitate fitting.

43573S.	Spindle assembly.
43585S.	Tommy bar.
43584S.	Spacer.
43582S.	Collar.
43576S.	Bearing locating collar.
43578S.	Locating washer "D".

First fit the spacer 43584S under the head of the spindle assembly 43573S, followed by the collar 43582S. Then pass the spindle assembly through the crankcase from the offside. Next fit locating washer "D" 43578S, followed by the new bearing, on to the bearing locating collar 43576S. The bearing locating collar has an internal thread and it must be fitted complete with the new bearing and washer "D" to the portion of the spindle assembly in the nearside half of the crankcase (see Fig. 36). Next pass the tommy bar 43585S through the head of the spindle assembly, and commence turning (see Fig. 35). Make sure that the bearing enters the crankcase true and square, and continue turning the spindle assembly until the bearing is properly located. Then unscrew and take out the service tools.

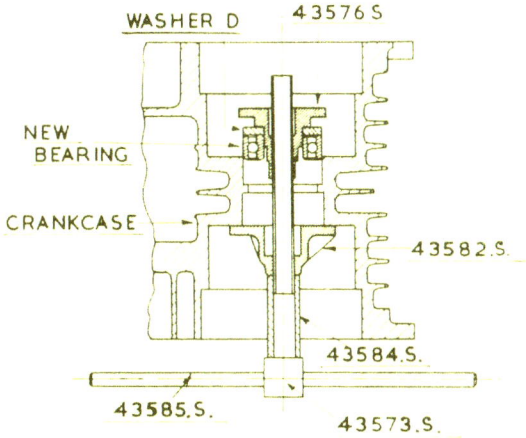

FITTING CRANKCASE BEARING

Fig. 36

The crankcase centre oil seal must be fitted next, and the following service tools will be required:

43593S.	Bolt.
43597S.	Locating collar.
43595S.	Locating collar.
474.	Washer (two off).
43594S.	Nut.
42073.	Distance tube.

Commence by fitting washer 474, followed by locating collar 43597S, under the head of the bolt 43593S, and pass the bolt through the crankcase centre bearing from the nearside, so that the collar 43597S locates in the bearing. Next fit the oil seal on to the locating collar 43595S, but note if the double type oil seal is being used; it can be fitted either way round. If, however, two of the single type are being fitted, they must be assembled back to back. Then fit the locating collar together with the oil seal, on to the portion of the bolt in the offside half of the crankcase. Next fit the spacer 42073 followed by the second washer 474 and the nut 43594S (see Fig. 37).

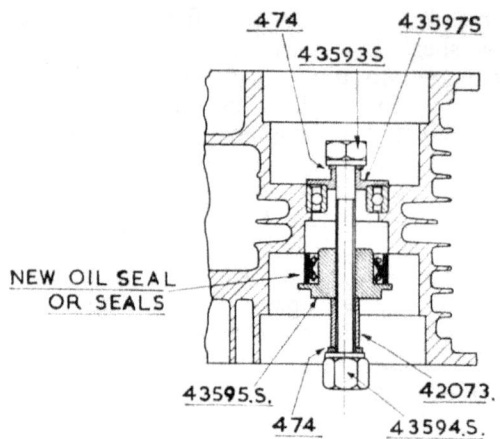

FITTING CENTRE MAIN BEARING OIL SEAL OR SEALS

Fig. 37

Then with a spanner fitted to the head of the bolt to prevent it turning, commence turning the nut until the oil seal is correctly located, then unscrew and take out the service tools.

To remove the old bearings and oil seals and fit new ones in the crankcase end covers, the following service tools are required:

- 43573S. Spindle assembly.
- 43584S. Spacer.
- 43583S. Extractor channel.
- 42586S. Extractor collar.
- 43585S. Tommy bar.
- 43582S. Collar.

Fig. 38

43593S. Bolt.
43594S. Nut.
474. Washer (two off).
43597S. Locating collar.
43598S. Locating collar.

Commence with the offside end cover, by first removing the oil seal with a drift and a mallet. pass the drift through the end cover bearing and locate it on the collar which is fitted between the bearing and the oil seal. Then by applying a few sharp blows to the drift with the mallet, the oil seal and collar can be knocked out (see Fig. 38). Next using a pair of circlip pliers, remove the large circlip which secures the bearing in the end cover. The bearing itself can then be removed. Begin by fitting the spacer 43584S followed by the extractor channel 43583S, under the head of the spindle assembly 43573S. Then pass the spindle assembly through the end cover bearing from the circlip side. Next fit the extractor collar 43586S on to the spindle where it protrudes through the end cover and pass the tommy bar 43585S, through the head of the spindle assembly (see Fig. 39). Commence turning the spindle, making sure that the extractor collar 43586S does not revolve (see Fig. 40), until the bearing is free from the end cover. Then unscrew and remove the service tools.

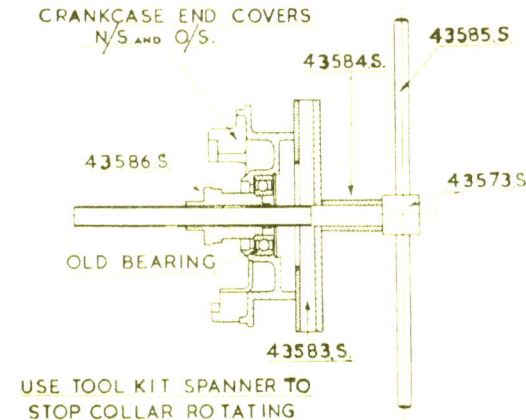

EXTRACTING END COVER BEARING.

Fig. 39

Fig. 40

Before fitting the new bearing and oil seal, thoroughly clean the end cover; then commence by fitting the bearing first, but note it is of the utmost importance to fit the bearing true and square and to ensure accuracy the bearing should be fitted under a press. A private owner should contact his local agent or garage, who will have a suitable press. As an alternative it is permissible to heat the end cover by immersing it in boiling water for several minutes, when the bearing can with care be pushed in by hand, but afterwards make quite certain it is located correctly.

The oil seal can be fitted next, using the service tools. Begin by fitting washer 474, followed by the collar 43582S, under the head of the bolt 43593S. Next locate the new greased oil seal complete with its sleeve, in position on the end cover, and pass the bolt 43593S through the oil seal and end cover bearing. Then fit the locating collar 43597S followed by washer 474 and nut 43594S, to the bolt where it protrudes through the end cover bearing (see Fig. 41). Tighten the nut and bolt to draw the oil seal into the end cover, make sure it is located correctly, then unscrew and remove the service tools. Finally,

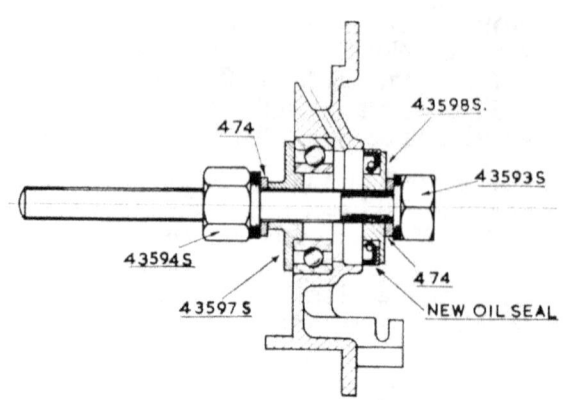

FITTING — OIL SEAL TO NEAR SIDE END COVER.

FIG. 41

fit the large circlip to secure the bearing in position.

The nearside end cover is dealt with in a similar manner, but note there is no circlip fitted to the

FIG. 42

bearing, and the oil seal does not have a sleeve fitted. Commence by removing the old oil seal with a drift and mallet (see Fig. 38), then remove the old bearing (see Figs. 39 and 40), clean the end cover and fit the new bearing in the same way as described for the offside cover. To fit the oil seal into the nearside end cover, use the service tools as follows. First fit washer 474, followed by locating collar 43598S, with the new oil seal mounted on the collar, under the head of the bolt 43593S. Then pass the bolt through the end cover bearing (see Fig. 42), and fit locating collar 43597S, followed by washer 474, and nut 43594S. Next tighten the nut and bolt to draw the oil seal into the end cover (see Fig. 43), and when it is properly located, unscrew and remove the service tools.

With new bearings and oil seals fitted in the crankcase and the end covers, and with the crankshaft re-conditioned, the engine re-assembly can begin. First smear oil on the crankcase and end cover oil seals and bearings. Then, with the connecting rod at bottom dead centre, pass the offside half of the crankshaft into the crankcase (see Fig. 32), and carefully locate it through the

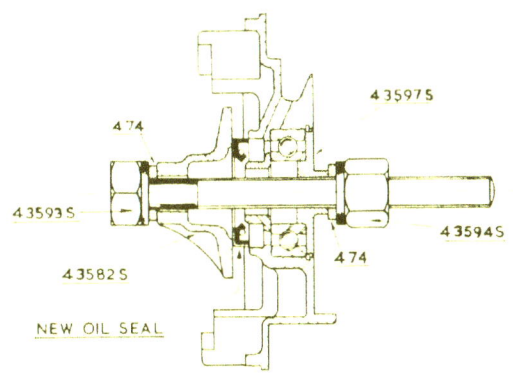

FITTING OIL SEAL TO OFF SIDE END COVER

Fig. 43

oil seal in the centre of the crankcase. The nearside half of the crankshaft must be fitted next, the connecting rod must be at bottom dead centre at first, but as the crankshaft enters the crankcase,

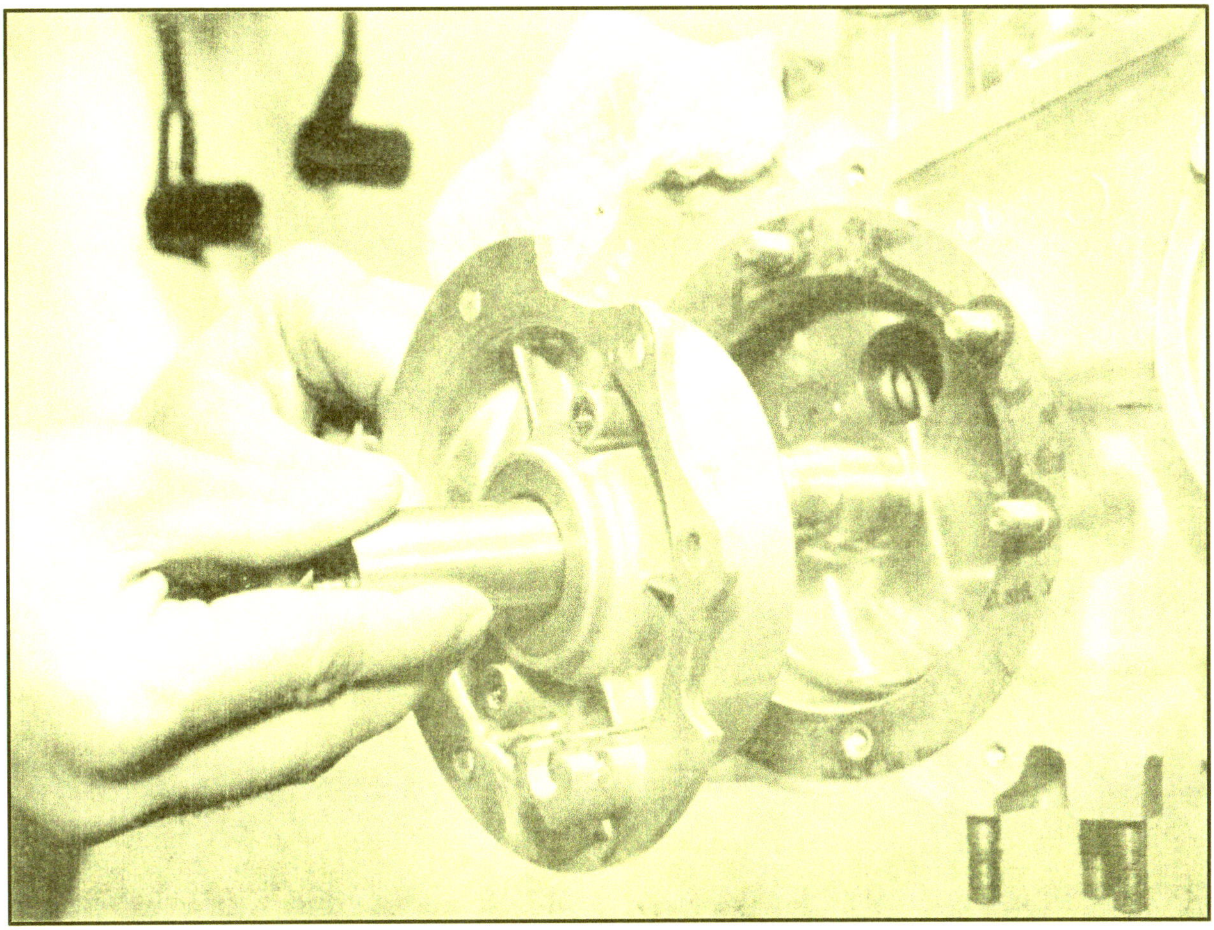

Fig. 45

the connecting rod must be turned to top dead centre and located into the nearside crankcase transfer port (see Fig. 33). The half crankshaft can then be lifted slightly and located through the crankcase centre bearing. Then with one connecting rod at top dead centre and the other at bottom dead centre, fit the key spanner 43551S into the offside crankshaft, which is hollow, and locate it into the socket head of the crankshaft centre bolt. Screw the bolt into the nearside half of the crankshaft until it *only just becomes firm*, then make certain that the two halves of the crankshaft are correctly aligned, they are located together by a key, and if the two halves of the crankshaft are turned slightly in opposite directions to each other, it is quite easy to feel the key locating in the keyway permitting the cranks to move together. When the crankshaft is in line, tighten the centre bolt firmly until a resistance is met, then to enable the bolt to be tightened correctly, fit the nearside end cover with a new joint washer located around its outer edge, using service tool 43543S oil seal fitting sleeve, fitted into the end cover oil seal (see Fig. 44), so that the end cover can be fitted over the crankshaft without any possibility of the oil seal being damaged (see Fig. 45). The end cover will be a firm fit, and it

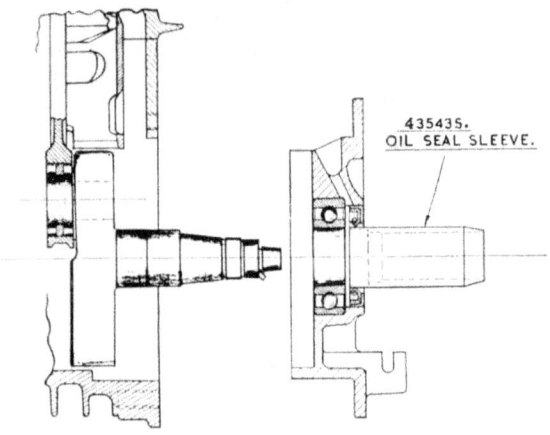

METHOD OF FITTING NEARSIDE CRANKCASE END COVER COMPLETE TO CRANKCASE WITH SLEEVE TO PROTECT OIL SEAL

Fig. 44

Fig. 46

may be lightly tapped with the handle of a mallet to locate it into the crankcase. Then fit a plain washer, a shake-proof washer and a nut to the four studs which protrude from the end cover. Before tightening the nuts, fit a screw (493) with a shake-proof washer under its head into the bottom-most hole in the end cover, and a bolt (46-1412) with a shake-proof washer under its head into the forward bottom hole in the end cover. Then tighten the screw, nuts and bolt a little at a time in turn until they are all securely tightened. Next fit the locating plate 43541S and the plug 43542S to the offside end of the crankcase as described on page 48 (see Fig. 30). A torque spanner must then be used to finally tighten the bolt to a torque of 60 foot/lbs. (see Fig. 46). This is most important, and if a private owner is assembling the engine, he should make some arrangement with an agent or garage who has a suitable torque spanner.

After removing the service tools from the offside end of the crankcase, the crankshaft alignment must be checked with a clock gauge, because although the two separate halves of the crankshaft assembly are true, the joint between the two halves is tapered and this may not have aligned correctly when being assembled. The clock gauge should be attached to one of the crankcase end cover studs, so that the needle rests on the shoulder on the offside end of the crankshaft, then revolve the crankshaft in order to obtain a reading on the clock gauge, the maximum tolerance permitted is .001 inch, if it exceeds this, the alignment must be adjusted. This is done by fitting a suitable piece of tube, which should be a close fit over the shaft and approximately 15 inches long, over the offside end of the crankshaft, and levering it slightly in the required direction. The alignment must then be re-checked with the clock gauge, and the same procedure followed until the alignment is within the .001 inch tolerance. Afterwards a further check must be made with the clock gauge again, but this time the needle must rest on the smaller diameter of the crankshaft towards the end, where it must still be within the .001 inch tolerance.

The offside end cover can then be fitted, first fit a joint washer around the outer edge, then locate the end cover in position on the crankcase, and fit a shake-proof washer and a thin nut (46-55) to the three studs which protrude from the end cover. Before tightening the nuts fit a screw (493) with a spring washer under the head into the three remaining holes in the end cover. Then tighten the nuts and screws a little at a time in turn until they are all securely tightened. Next make sure the key for the rotor is fitted in the keyway in the offside of the crankshaft, then fit the rotor to the crankshaft, locating it over the key and with the *recessed side facing outwards*. Secure it in position with the rotor bolt which must have a plain washer and a shake-proof washer fitted under its head. The rotor bolt fits into the hollow crankshaft, and must be securely tightened.

The woodruff key that locates the engine sprocket must now be fitted to the nearside of the crankshaft. If there is any doubt as to the condition of the key it should be replaced by a new one. It should be lightly tapped into position with a soft drift to avoid damage.

The primary chain alignment must be checked next, and in order to do this the complete clutch and the flywheel and engine sprocket, but without the primary chain, must be fitted in the manner described on page 32. Then using a 12 inch length of ¼ inch diameter silver steel bar, which is obtainable from any good tool dealer, place the bar across the inner faces of the engine and clutch sprockets, the bar should lie flat against both sprockets, but it may be found that when it is held flat on one of the sprockets, there is a small gap between the bar and the other sprocket. Providing this gap does not exceed .010 inch which can be checked with a feeler gauge, this is in order. A final check should then be made, again with a feeler gauge, to ensure that there is a minimum gap of .015 inch between the side of each crank and the inner wall of the crankcase. If the alignment of the chain sprockets varies more than .010 inch, or if the gap between one of the cranks and the crankcase is less than .015 inch, the crankshaft must be repositioned by fitting shims. Two shims are available, one which fits between the bearing in the offside end cover and the crankshaft, is .010 inch thick and will move the crankchaft .010 inch towards the nearside. The other shim fits in place of the joint washer between the outer edge of the offside end cover and the crankcase. This shim is also .010 inch thick and will move the crankshaft .010 inch towards the offside. Therefore if the engine sprocket is nearer the engine than the clutch sprocket by more than .010 inch, the shim for fitting between the offside end cover bearing and the crankshaft should be used. This would then bring the engine sprocket outward and to within the permissible .010 inch alignment with the clutch sprocket. But make sure that moving the crankshaft towards the nearside, does not reduce the gap between the cranks and the crankcase to less than .015 inch. Alternatively, if the engine sprocket is further out from the engine than the clutch sprocket by more than .010 inch, the shim for fitting in place of the offside end cover joint washer should be used. If necessary the end cover joint washer in addition to a shim can be fitted. This would then bring the engine sprocket inward to within the .010 inch alignment with the clutch sprocket. But again make quite certain that there is a gap of at least .015 inch between the cranks and the crankcase. Note if the sprocket alignment is out more than .020 inch, there must be something incorrectly assembled causing the trouble.

To fit these shims it is of course necessary to remove the rotor and the offside end cover, and then re-fit them to check the sprocket alignment and the gap between the cranks and crankcase again. Some engines will not require any shims at all, and in any case it is extremely unlikely that more than one shim will be required. The most important thing is the chain alignment, and if in very rare cases it is necessary to compromise between the chain alignment and the gap between the cranks and the crankcase, it is permissible to reduce the gap slightly below .015 inch in order to bring the chain alignment to within the .010 inch limit.

When the sprocket and crankshaft alignment is satisfactory, make certain the rotor bolt is securely tightened, then fit the remainder of the alternator as described on page 219. The clutch and flywheel with engine sprocket will have to be removed again, in order to fit the primary chain adjuster as described on page 28, and the primary chain as described on page 32. After fitting the primary chaincase, check and if necessary adjust the ignition timing as described on page 58. And the primary chain as described on page 25. Do not forget to re-fill the primary chaincase with oil as described on page 25.

If the motor cycle has covered a very large mileage, the cylinder barrels may need re-boring, see page 44 for instructions on checking wear. In any case the cylinder heads, cylinder barrels, pistons and silencers should be decarbonised and fitted to the engine as described on page 36.

CONTACT BREAKER AND IGNITION TIMING—LEADER AND ARROW

The contact breaker is an automatic switch controlling the flow of electric current to the sparking plugs. In addition to switching the current on and off, the contact breaker must be so adjusted that the current reaches the sparking plugs at the precise moment required.

The contact breaker is secured to the outside of the primary chaincase, over the nearside end of the crankshaft. Mounted on the crankshaft is a cam which revolves with the engine and operates the contact breaker. The cam has a fixed position and cannot be varied, and all adjustments must be made at the contact breaker only.

If an engine has been dismantled, on re-assembling, the ignition timing must be set by adjusting the contact breaker in the way as described for routine maintenance adjustment.

Routine Adjustment

The contact breaker should be checked and if necessary adjusted, after the motor cycle has covered the first 500 miles. Thereafter it should receive attention at 5,000 mile intervals, this could be carried out at the same time as decarbonising.

In the case of Leaders, begin with the near side side panel removed as described on page 154. Then for both models, at the forward end of the primary chaincase can be seen a round metal cover, secured to the chaincase by three screws. Remove these three screws and slip the cover a few inches up the lead which passes through it. On some engines this cover can be removed completely. This will reveal the contact breaker, and, on examination, it will be seen that there are two sets of contact points, one set for each cylinder. In both sets it is the outer point which moves as the engine revolves, making and breaking contact. The inner points normally remain stationary but can be moved for adjustment purposes. Secured to the same mounting plate and connected to the contact points are two condensers, and the mounting plate in turn is secured to the primary chaincase with two screws. In the centre of the mounting plate is a cam which is secured to the engine crankshaft, and as the cam revolves with the engine it pushes the fibre levers outwards, opening and closing the contact points.

There is a lead attached to each condenser, and the lead coloured black with yellow must be attached to the upper condenser, and the lead coloured black with white to the lower condenser.

Commence checking the contact breaker adjustment by rotating the engine slowly, this is easily done by gently pushing the kick starter lever down, then as the contact breaker cam rotates with the engine it will open the upper contact points. When these points reach their *maximum opening*, the gap should be checked with a suitable feeler gauge and it must be between .014 inch and .016 inch. If the gap differs from this it must be adjusted. Adjustment is carried out by slackening the slotted sleeve nut which is situated on the mounting plate within the looped spring. When the sleeve nut is slack the bottom point can be moved to reduce or increase the gap as required. Then when the gap is correct, tighten the sleeve nut making sure the bottom point does not move. After completing the adjustment, check the gap again to make quite certain that it is correct. Next rotate the engine slowly until the lower contact points are at their maximum opening, then check and if necessary adjust the gap between the points in the same way as for the upper contact points. But note the top point of the lower set is the adjustable one.

With both sets of contact points adjusted to produce a gap of between .014 inch and .016 inch, the next stage is to adjust the ignition timing, and this must be carried out in the following manner. In the tool kit of each new motor cycle, there is a

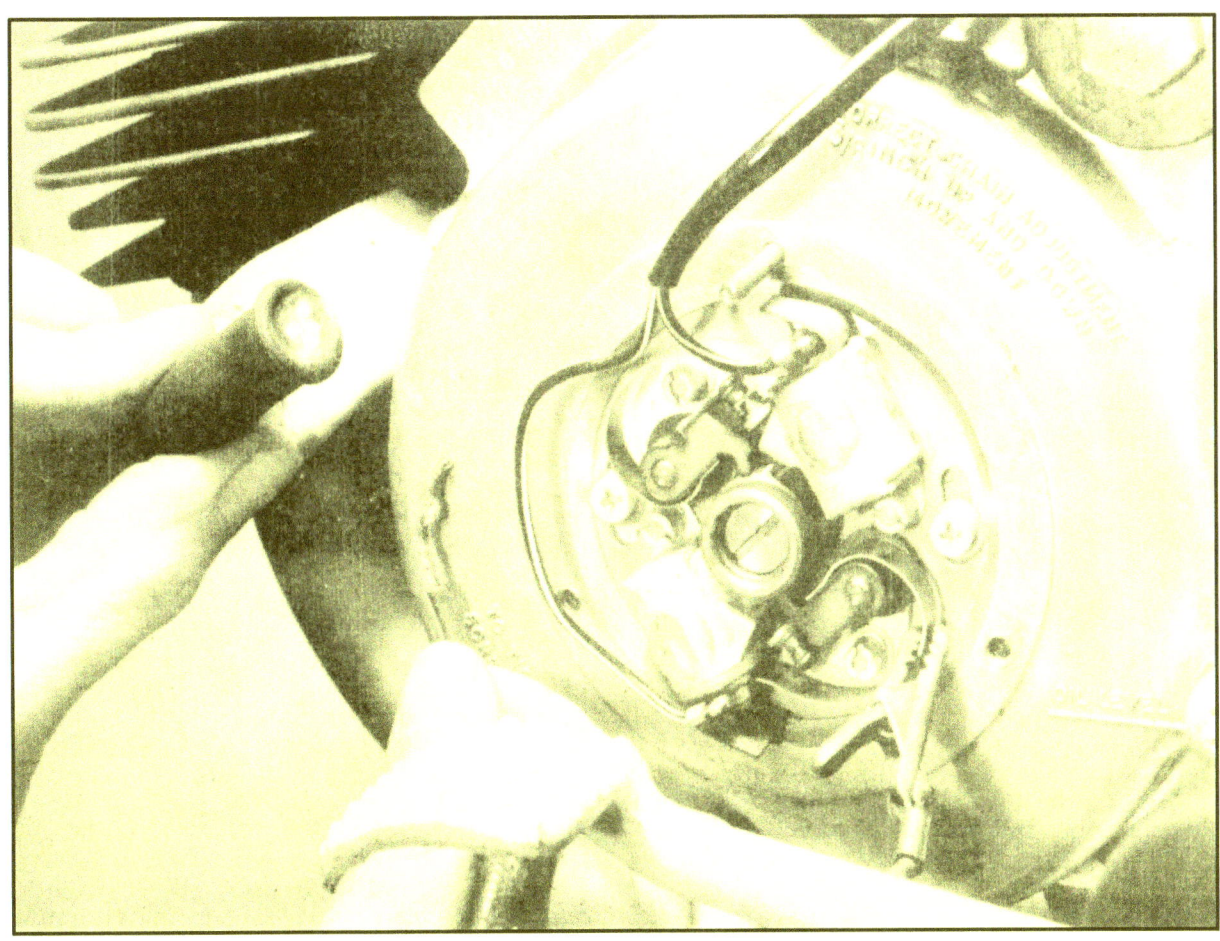

Fig. 47

$\frac{9}{64}$ inch diameter by 3 inch long straight rod, pass this rod through the top contact breaker cover screw hole in the primary chaincase. When the rod is in as far as it will go, gently push down the kick starter lever to rotate the engine very slowly, while at the same time pushing the rod inwards. After the engine has rotated slightly, it will be possible to push the rod further inwards, as there is a locating hole in the flywheel inside the primary chaincase. With the rod located through the chaincase and flywheel, the upper set of contact points should be just beginning to open, but as it is not possible to see this with the naked eye the following method of checking should be adopted. Connect a lead to the metal body of a 6-volt lamp bulb, the lead can be tightly twisted around the body, but the end of the lead must have the covering cut off so that the bare wire makes contact with the body of the bulb. The other end of the lead must also have the covering removed and the bare wire must be attached to a good earthing point on the frame or engine, such as tightly twisting it around one of the smaller cylinder head fins. A second lead must be attached to the loop spring on the upper contact breaker set. The bared end of the lead can be twisted around the spring, but a better way would be to fit a clip to the end of the lead which could be easily clipped on and off the spring. A suitable clip should be obtainable from any electrical dealer. The other end of the second lead must have the covering removed, and the bare wire must be held by hand on to the contact at the base of the bulb. (see Fig. 47). Then with the ignition switched on, the bulb theoretically should just glow therefore if the light is "On" or "Off", rock the rod which is fitted through the chaincase and flywheel, backwards and forwards; if the bulb flickers on and off the adjustment is correct. If, however, the bulb does not flicker, slacken the two screws which secure the contact breaker mounting plate to the primary chaincase, and very carefully turn the plate clockwise or anti-clockwise until the bulb just glows. Then tighten the two screws to secure the contact breaker plate in position, but note while tightening the screws it may be necessary to turn the plate very slightly to keep the bulb glowing.

Next switch off the ignition and detach the lead from the upper loop spring and fit it to the lower loop spring. Partially withdraw the rod from the primary chaincase so that the engine can be rotated by pressing the kick starter down, but while the engine is being rotated, the rod must be pushed inwards as there is a second hole in the flywheel diametrically opposite the first. When the rod is inserted in the second hole, the lower contact point should be just beginning to open. To check this, switch on the ignition and hold the bulb as before, when the bulb should either glow or flicker on and off when the rod in the primary chaincase is rocked back and forth. If, however, the bulb neither glows nor flickers, then the lower contact points must be re-adjusted. Slacken the slotted sleeve nut within the lower loop spring and very carefully move the top point of the lower set until the bulb just glows, then tighten the sleeve nut.

Re-adjusting the lower contact points will, of course, have altered the amount that they open, and if after checking the gap with a suitable feeler gauge, the gap is still between .014 inch and .016 inch, everything is correct, and the contact breaker cover can be re-fitted as described on page 60. However, if upon checking the gap it is found to be larger or smaller than .012 inch to .017 in., it is essential to compromise between the two contact breaker gaps. For example, if the lower contact points gap has had to be reduced to .010 inch, to make the bulb just glow when the rod is located through the primary chaincase and into the flywheel, this is .002 inch smaller than the correct gap. It is already known that the gap between the upper contact points is .015 inch, and the only way to overcome this situation is to re-adjust the upper contact points to .017 inch and follow through the complete procedure again of adjusting the contact breaker plate and the lower contact points, to make the bulb just glow when the rod is located through the primary chaincase and into the flywheel, when it will be found the extra .002 inch added to the upper contact points will give the lower points a gap of .012 inch with the bulb just glowing. Although the upper contact points gap is .001 inch larger than correct, this is permissible in order to obtain the correct ignition timing. Alternately, if after the first adjustment of the contact points, the gap between the lower set was found to be too large, such as .018 inch, then the upper contact points would have to be re-set to a gap of .014 inch which would, after completing the whole adjustment procedure, reduce the gap between the lower contact points to .017 inch, and this would be permissible. The most important thing is that the contact points are just beginning to open when the rod is located through the chaincase and into the respective hole in the flywheel, as this ensures that the ignition timing of 20 degrees before top dead centre is correct. *No advantage can be gained by varying the ignition timing, which is most critical and must be the same for both cylinders*, if it is not, both performance and economy will suffer. When adjusting the contact breaker, make certain that the heads of the two screws which secure the contact breaker unit to the chain cover, do not touch the loop springs. Also ensure that the terminals on the leads at the end of each condenser will not touch the contact breaker cover. Note the felt pad attached to one of the condensers, this pad should have one or two spots of S.A.E. 20 oil put on it after adjusting the contact breaker, to lubricate the cam and fibre levers.

When the contact breaker adjustment and the ignition timing are satisfactory, the contact breaker cover can be re-fitted, but take care to locate the lead coloured black with white from the lower contact set, rearward and around the lower loop spring, to avoid the possibility of this lead being damaged by the moving parts in the contact breaker assembly. Also there must be a joint washer fitted between the cover and the primary chaincase, and the cover must be fitted so that the leads which pass through it are to the rear of the top cover securing screw. Then for the Leader the nearside side panel can then be re-fitted as described on page 154.

Do not dismantle the contact breaker assembly unnecessarily, but if ignition trouble should develop, new condensers and contact points can be fitted. To remove the contact breaker assembly from the motor cycle, first remove the nearside side panel as described on page 154. Then remove the contact breaker cover as described on page 58. Next pull apart the two snap connectors in the leads from the contact breaker, and remove the two screws which secure the contact breaker mounting plate to the primary chaincase, when the assembly can then be lifted clear. To remove one of the condensers and set of contact points, it is only necessary to remove the sleeve nut from within the loop spring and the sleeve nut from the end of the condenser, when the contact points together with the condenser can be lifted off the plate. The one contact point which is attached by the loop spring to the condenser, can be separated from the condenser by removing the small nut from the end.

Trouble with a condenser is rare, but occasionally one does fail, resulting in ignition trouble, which means fitting a new condenser. The contact points may become badly pitted after the motor cycle has covered a large mileage, and it will be necessary to replace them.

When re-assembling the contact breaker parts, begin by fitting the contact point which is attached to a small plate, over the copper stud in the main contact breaker plate with the slot in the small plate located over the short stud in the main plate. Then fit the special fibre washer over the copper stud, followed by the fibre lever which carries the loop spring and the second contact point. The condenser should be fitted to the end of the loop spring, followed by the lead and the nut. At this stage either lead can be attached to either condenser. Next fit a plain washer, a spring washer and a sleeve nut to the short stud within the loop spring. Then locate the condenser over the other short stud in the main plate, and fit a spring washer and a sleeve nut. The contact breaker assembly can then be fitted to the primary chaincase, by passing two screws with plain washers under their heads, through the slots in the main plate and into the primary chaincase, but note the condenser with the lead coloured black with yellow, must be uppermost. Then with the contact breaker cover fitted over the leads, the lead can be coupled by snap connectors to the leads with corresponding colours. The ignition timing and the contact breaker must then be adjusted as described on page 58.

If it should be required to remove the cam which operates the contact breaker, it is only necessary to undo the captive screw in the centre of the cam. The screw will remain in the cam retained by a circlip. Note that there is a small locating peg in the crankshaft and a corresponding slot in the cam, and when re-fitting the cam it must be located over the peg in the crankshaft when tightening the screw.

GEARBOX—LEADER AND ARROW

The four speed gear box in unit with the engine is of proved and robust design, and routine maintenance is reduced to a minimum. The gears are lubricated with oil of S.A.E. 30 grade, using one of the recommended brands as per the lubrication chart on page 10. The capacity of the gear box is approximately one pint of oil, an oil level and an oil drain screw are fitted in the cover on the offside of the gear box and are clearly marked to avoid any confusion. The oil level in the gear box should be checked regularly. This can be done during the periodical general routine maintenance. To check the oil level, first, in the case of the Leader, remove the offside side panel, as described on page 154, and for the Arrow remove the engine cover, described on page 155. Then remove the oil level screw, when oil should just trickle out. If the oil level is low it must be topped up.

Fresh oil can be poured into the gear box after first removing the clutch adjuster cover, which is secured by two screws, top up with oil of the recommended grade until it just trickles out of the oil level screw hole, then re-fit the level screw which must have a fibre washer under its head; re-fit the clutch adjuster cover, which must have a joint washer fitted. *Note:* On no account must the gear box be filled above the oil level screw.

Every 5,000 miles the old oil should be drained and the gear box refilled to the correct level with fresh oil of the recommended grade.

No gear box adjustments are necessary except for the clutch push rod as described on page 126 and 131, and maintenance of the lubricating oil, to the correct level, plus an occasional check that the cover securing nuts are tight.

The position of the kick starter lever and the gear change lever may be varied to suit individual owners, by fitting the levers in the required position on the serrated shafts, but take care in positioning the kick start lever that it does not foul the gear shift lever at the end of its downwards travel.

Kick Starter Case Cover

For the Leader: Remove offside side panel as described on page 154. For the Arrow: Remove the engine cover as described on page 155. Then drain the oil from the gear box into a suitable container; the drain plug is at the bottom edge of the offside end of the gear box. The oil level plug should also be removed as this will facilitate draining. Next remove the two screws which secure the clutch adjuster cover to the gear box, and lift the cover clear. Then slacken the lock nut and adjuster screw, when the clutch cable can easily be slipped out of the operating lever on the top of the gear box.

Next remove the seven nuts and washers from around the gear box end cover, then re-fit the kick starter lever in the normal position on its shaft to prevent the kick starter mechanism springing undone. The end cover can then be withdrawn from the gear box, but be sure to hold the kick starter lever firmly whilst removing the end cover, then afterwards it can be slowly unwound, retaining the mechanism assembled and avoiding bruised knuckles (see Fig. 49). This cover is the kick starter case cover, and it contains parts of the kick starter, clutch and gear change mechanisms. If any of these parts require replacing proceed as follows: The kick starter spindle with the large coil spring simply pulls out of the cover, then the distance piece and the coil spring easily lift off the spindle. If it should be required to separate the spindle and quadrant, locate the long end of the spindle loosely between the jaws of a vice, with the quadrant resting on top of the vice. Then, using a mallet, tap the spindle down through the quadrant. To fit a new spindle or quadrant, place the quadrant on top of the open jaws of the vice, and locate the splines on the spindle into the quadrant and using the mallet again, tap the spindle down into position (see Fig. 50). The quadrant spindle within the large hairpin shaped spring, also simply pulls out of the cover. The oil seal ring, oil seal washer, spring and quadrant, all easily lift off the spindle. Then any new parts which may be necessary can be fitted in the following order. Locate the quadrant

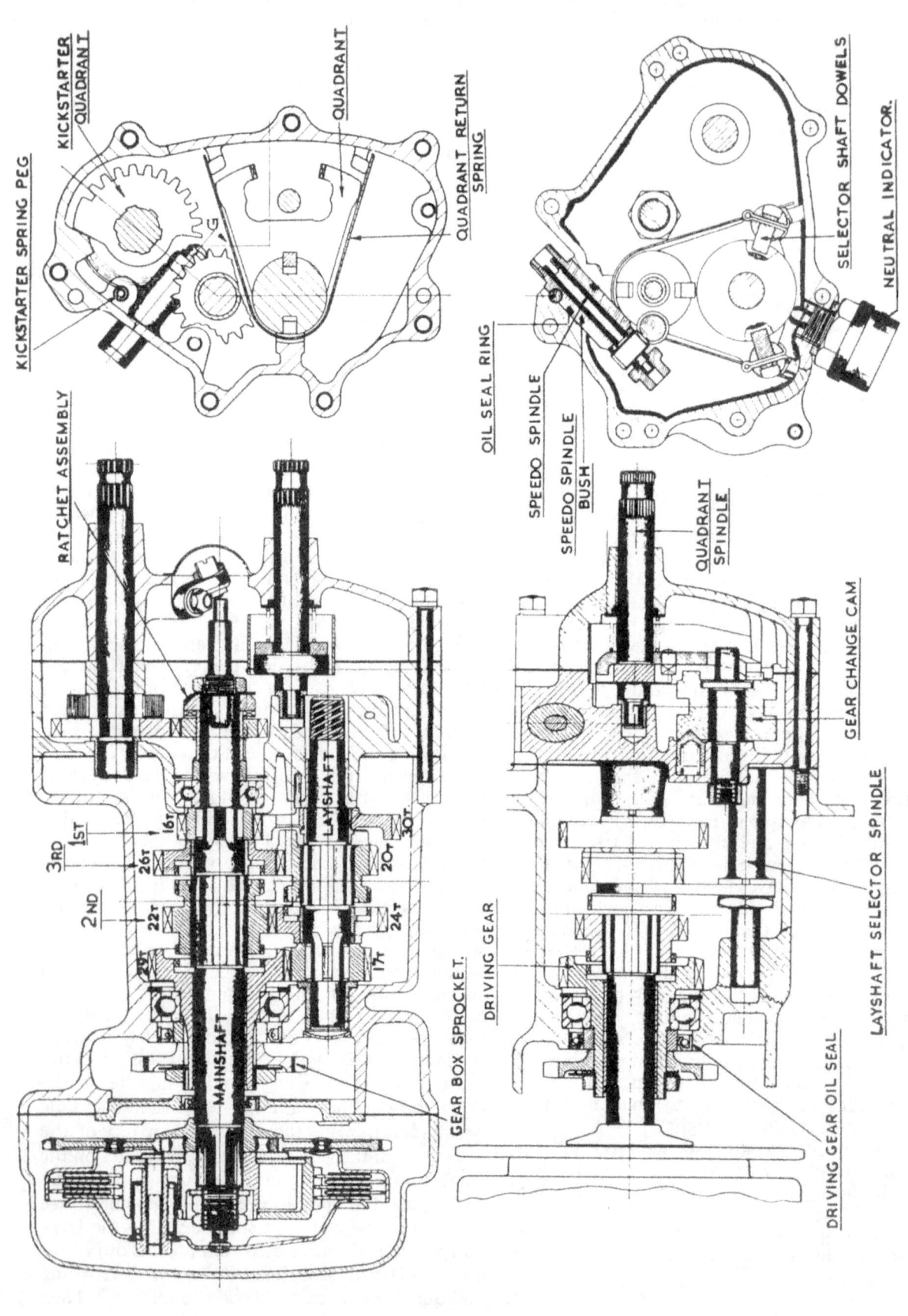

SECTION OF GEAR BOX

Fig. 48

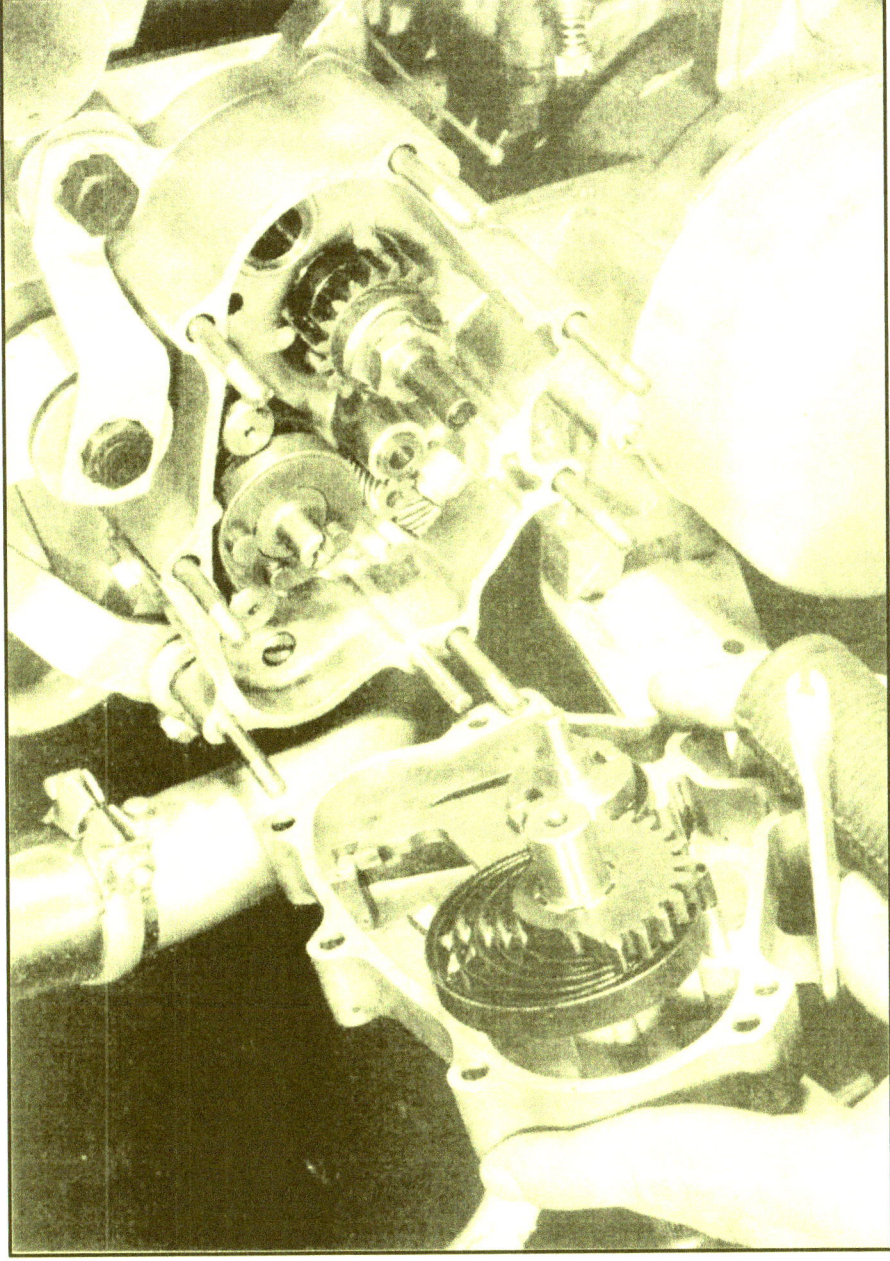

FIG 49

on to the spindle so that the two pegs on the quadrant fit into the slots in the shoulder of the spindle. Then fit the spring followed by the oil seal washer and the oil seal ring. If the large hairpin shaped spring requires replacing, this will only be necessary in the event of it being broken, the original, if still in position, simply pulls out, and the new spring is then fitted by locating the open ends, outside the two lugs on the inner rear edge of the cover. The closed end of the spring locates in a "C" shaped lug the opposite side of the cover.

Important: The open ends of the spring have different shaped cutaways each side, and the side with the larger cutaways must face in towards the gear box when re-fitted. The part of the clutch mechanism which is fitted in the kick starter case cover, can be removed if required by undoing the nut, when the two clutch operating levers can be pulled apart and removed from the cover. When re-assembling the two clutch levers, pass the clutch operating lever and spindle through the hole in the top of the kick starter case cover, then align the lever with the peg for the kick starter spring, and fit the inner clutch lever to the lower end of the spindle, so that the inner clutch lever is at right-angles to the clutch operating lever, with the flat side of the inner clutch lever facing outwards. Then secure both levers in position with the spring

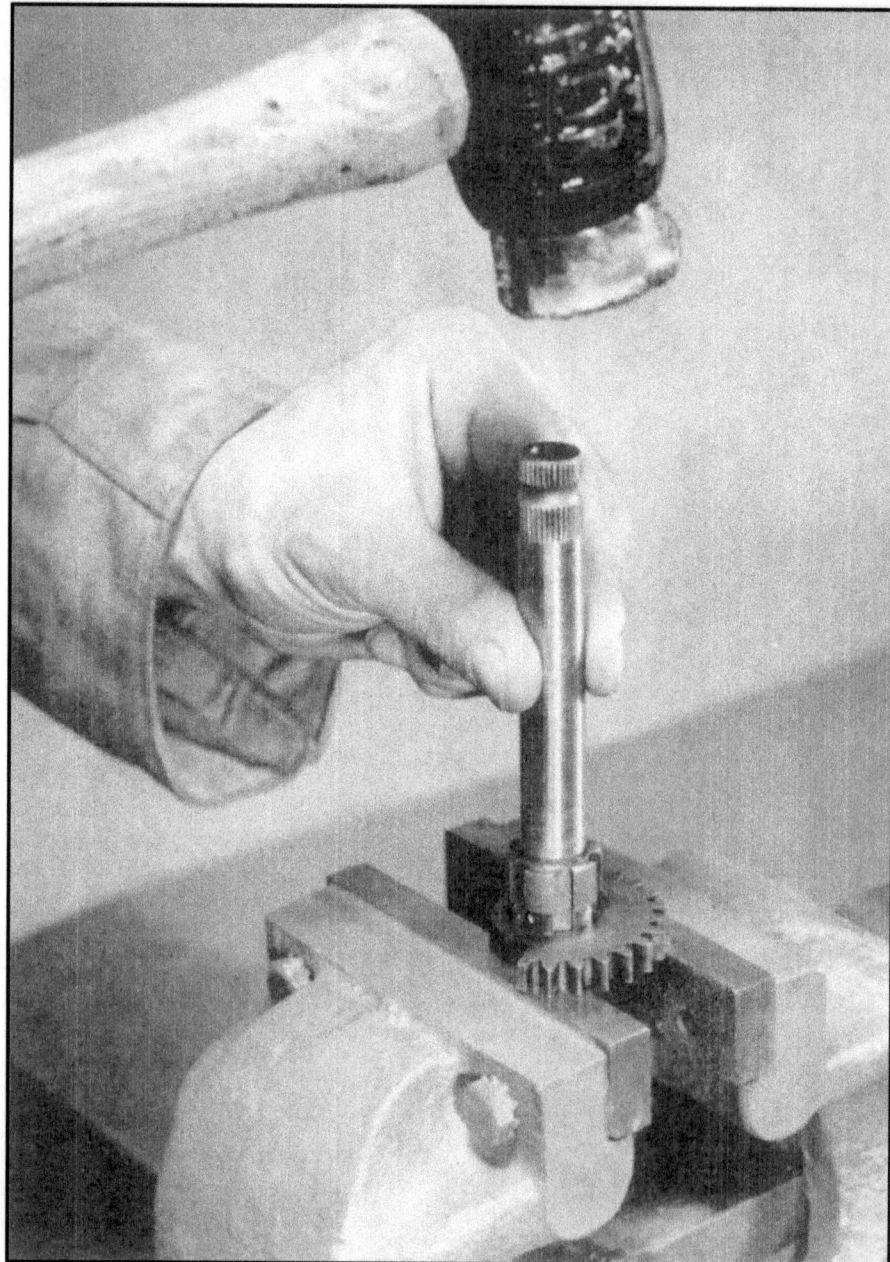

Fig. 50

washer and special nut. The kick starter case and cover should be thoroughly cleaned before re-assembling, and a new joint washer should be fitted. Then locate the quadrant spindle into the kick starter case cover, so that the quadrant is within the large hairpin spring. Next fit the small loop on the outside of the large kick starter coil spring, over the peg which protrudes from the kick starter case cover, so that it is wound in a clockwise direction when viewed from the inside of the kick starter case cover. Fit the distance piece to the kick starter case cover and pass the kick starter spindle through the kick starter spring distance piece and kick starter case cover, and engage the inner end of the kick starter spring in one of the splines of the kick starter spindle.

It can be seen that one of the end teeth on the kick starter quadrant is square, and the kick starter lever must be fitted to the outside end of the kick starter spindle, so that the kick starter lever is in line with the square tooth. Then looking at the outside of the kick starter case cover, turn the kick starter lever anti-clockwise until the spring is fully wound, when still looking at the outside of the cover, with the cover in the upright position, the kick starter lever must be between the three o'clock and one o'clock position. If, however, the kick starter lever is not in the required position when the spring is fully wound, unwind the spring again and locate the inner end in a different spline on the kick starter spindle, and repeat the process until the kick starter lever is in the required position with the spring fully wound. Then note the stop lug inside the top of the kick starter case, as the square tooth on the kick starter quadrant must be located behind this lug when the kick starter case cover is fitted. It maybe necessary to unwind the kick starter lever slightly in order to locate the quadrant. The kick starter case cover can then be secured in position by fitting a spring washer and a nut to the seven studs. The drain plug, with a fibre washer under its head should be fitted next. Then re-fit the clutch cable to the lever on the top of the gear box, and adjust the clutch as described on page 126 and 131. Then, before re-fitting the clutch adjuster cover, refill the gear box with oil as described on page 61. Finally, for the Leader, re-fit the offside side panel as described on page 154, and for the Arrow, re-fit the engine cover as described on page 155.

If at any time it should be necessary to give attention to the speedometer spindle, or the kick-starter ratchet parts on the offside end of the mainshaft, these items are fitted in the gear box inner cover and are accessible after removing the kick starter case cover as described on page 61. Then to remove the speedometer spindle, first disconnect the speedometer cable from the gear box by undoing the union nut at the end of the cable. Next remove the small grub screw from the lug below the top end of the speedometer spindle bush. The speedometer spindle complete with the bush can then be removed, by inserting a screwdriver between the lower end of the speedometer spindle and the small lug on which the spindle rests, and by prising the spindle upward, it will be pushed through the top of the kick starter case.

When re-assembling the speedometer spindle, the thrust washer must first be fitted over the spindle followed by the bush, with the threaded portion of the bush at the opposite end of the spindle to the driving teeth. Also the oil seal ring fitted around the outside of the bush must be in good condition, if in any doubt it should be replaced. The spindle and bush unit can then be inserted through the hole in the top of the kick starter case, making certain that the groove in the bush is in line with the hole for the grub screw. The spindle will drop down and can easily be meshed with the worm on the end of the layshaft. The bush can then be tapped down into position, and the grub screw inserted and tightened.

The kick starter ratchet mechanism is dismantled by first straightening the tab washer, which is fitted behind and folded over one edge of the mainshaft end nut. Then fit a suitable tube spanner and tommy bar over the mainshaft nut, and while holding the spanner in position, strike the tommy bar with a hammer to jar the nut undone, when it can be removed easily. The ratchet parts which consist of the driving ratchet, the ratchet pinion, the pinion spring, the pinion bush and distance piece, can then all be pulled off the mainshaft.

When re-assembling the kick starter ratchet, first fit the distance piece over the mainshaft, followed by the pinion bush with the pinion spring slipped over the bush. Then fit the ratchet pinion with the ratchet teeth facing outward, the driving ratchet is fitted next so that its teeth engage with the ratchet teeth on the ratchet pinion. Then fit the tab washer, with the tab located into the slot in the outside of the driving ratchet. Finally fit and securely tighten the mainshaft nut and bend part of the tab washer over the edge of the nut to prevent any possibility of its coming undone. The kick starter case cover can then be fitted as described on page 63.

DISMANTLING GEAR BOX

If it is required to gain access to the gears themselves, or the remainder of the gear change mechanism which is in the main gear box housing, proceed as follows: First remove the kick starter case cover as described on page 61, then remove the kick starter ratchet parts as described on page 65. Next remove the screw from inside the bottom edge of the kick starter case. *Note:* If the motor cycle is fitted with a neutral indicator, pull the two leads out of the switch which is fitted in the rear edge of the kick starter case. The kick starter case can then be removed, but it may be a little tight and it is permissible to *lightly* tap with a mallet, behind the lug which surrounds the bottom rear fixing stud, while at the same time pulling the top edge of the kick starter case outward. The case will lift clear complete with the layshaft, selector forks and gears, leaving the mainshaft and the driving gear still fixed in the gear box (see Fig. 51). Unless the mainshaft and driving gear need attention, it is not necessary to disturb them. If, however, it is required to remove the mainshaft, commence by removing the primary chaincase as described on page 25. Then remove the primary chain as described on page 29, when the mainshaft can then be withdrawn from the offside end of the gear box. To remove the driving gear, first straighten the tab washers which are fitted under the heads of the three bolts, which secure the oil seal housing to the main engine casting behind the clutch. The three bolts can then be removed, and the oil seal housing lifted

Fig. 51

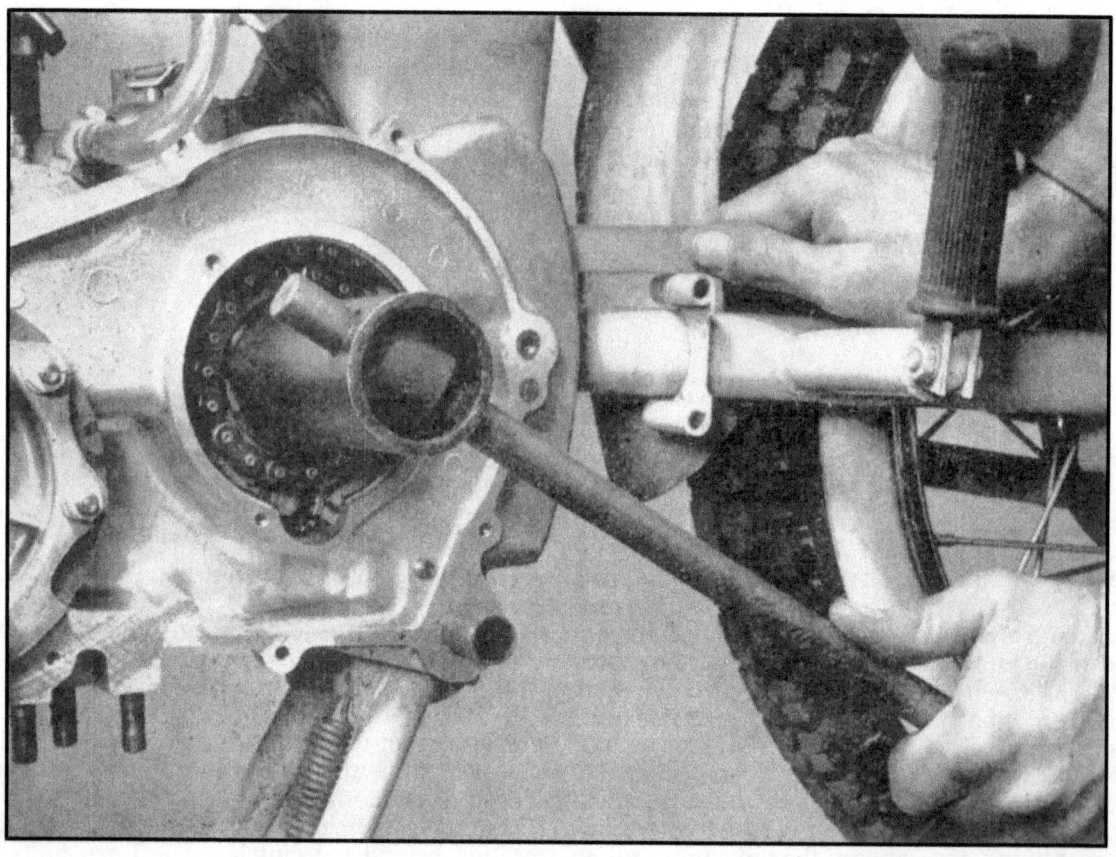

Fig. 52

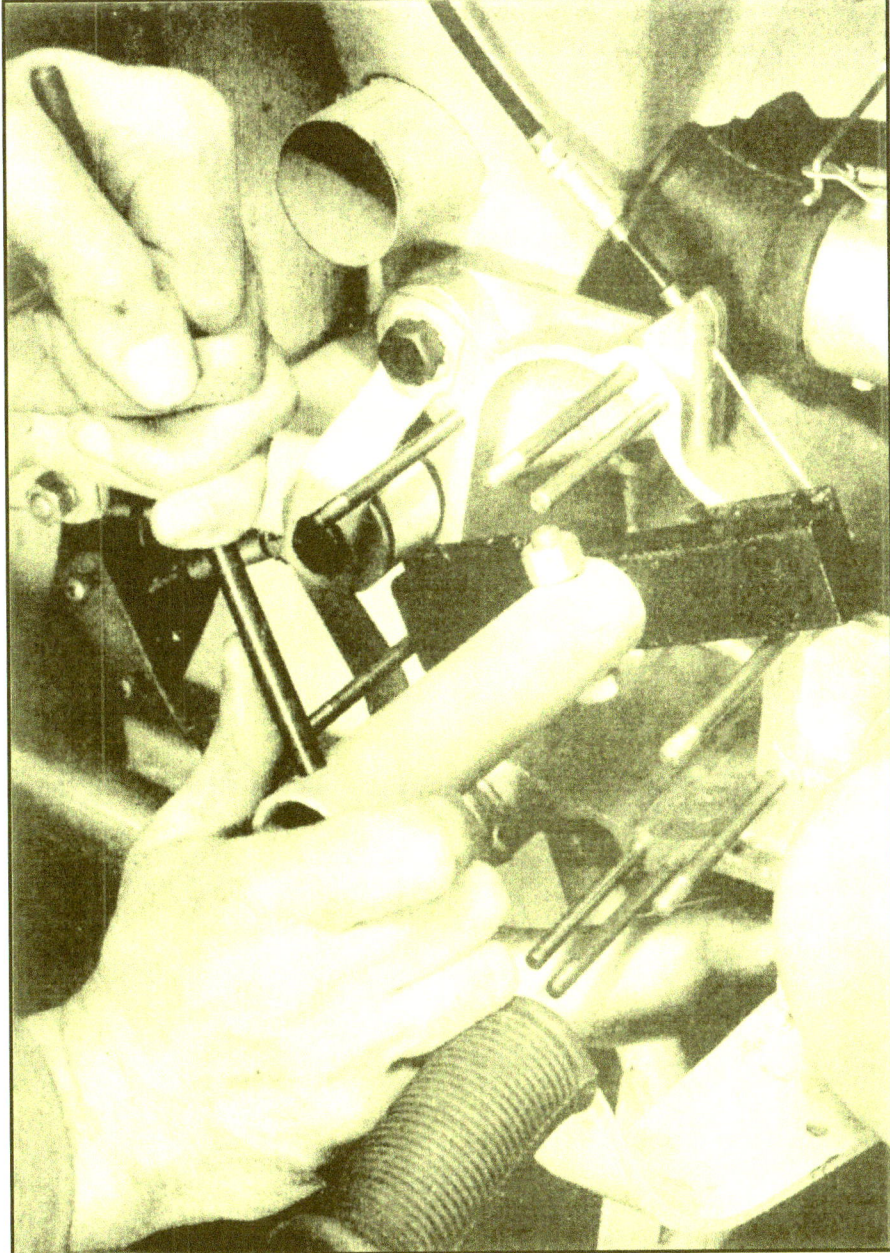

Fig. 54

clear. Next remove the rear chain case as described on page 111, and the rear chain as described on page 120. Then, through the aperture made by removing the oil seal housing, can be seen the gear box driving sprocket which is secured by a large nut. This nut must be removed next, and to facilitate removal a simple tool must be made that will hold the sprocket stationary while the nut is removed. To make the tool, drill a $\frac{1}{4}$ inch diameter hole $\frac{5}{16}$ inch from one end of a length of steel bar, $\frac{3}{4}$ inch wide by $\frac{1}{4}$ inch thick by 12 inches long. Then attach by means of a connecting link, a length of approximately 20 pitches of rear chain ($\frac{1}{2}$ inch by .305 inch) (a piece of old chain would be suitable) to the end of the bar which has been drilled. Then straighten the tab washer which is fitted behind the nut, and pass the loose end of the chain which is attached to the bar, through the top tunnel for the rear chain at the rear of the nearside of the engine unit. Locate the chain over the top of the sprocket and revolve the sprocket until the chain completely surrounds and locks the sprocket. Then fit a 1 inch Whitworth tube spanner over the nut and using a long tommy bar in conjunction with the tube spanner, the nut can be removed (see Fig. 52). The bar and chain can then be withdrawn back out of the top tunnel and the driving sprocket, together with the tab washer and a distance washer, can be pulled clear.

The driving gear can then be withdrawn from inside the gear box, leaving only the ball bearing, oil seal and sprocket spacing collar in the gear box.

If it is required to remove the bearing and oil seal, begin by pushing the sprocket spacing collar out of the oil seal. Next remove the circlip from inside the gear box which secures the bearing. A pair of circlip pliers must be used to do this, then the following service tools are required to remove the bearing:

43573S.	Spindle assembly.
43585S.	Tommy bar.
43583S.	Extractor channel.
43586S.	Extractor collar.

Commence by fitting the extractor channel 43583S under the head of the spindle assembly 43573S. The pass the spindle assembly through the gear box from the offside, and fit the extractor collar 43586S to the spindle where it protrudes through the gear box bearing. Owing to the gear box studs it will be necessary to use the extension tube on the end of the spindle assembly in order to turn the tommy bar (see Fig. 53), see page 150 for details of the extension tube.

Next, pass the tommy bar 43585S through the end of the extension tube (see Fig. 54), and commence turning until the bearing is free from the gear box. The oil seal can then be knocked out with a drift and mallet. Before fitting the new bearing thoroughly clean the gear box. Then the following service tools are required to fit the bearing:

43573S.	Spindle assembly.
43585S.	Tommy bar.
43584S.	Spacer.
43582S.	Collar.
43576S.	Bearing location collar.

Commence by fitting the spacer 43584S, followed by the collar 43582S, under the head of the spindle assembly 43573S. Then pass the spindle assembly through the gear box from the nearside.

Next smear the outer edge of the new bearing with oil, and fit it on to the bearing location collar 43576S. Next fit the location collar and bearing to the spindle which protrudes inside the gear box, then pass the tommy bar 43585S, through the head of the spindle assembly (see Fig. 55) and commence turning.

Make certain the bearing enters the gear box true and square, and continue turning the spindle until the bearing is correctly located, then unscrew and remove the service tools.

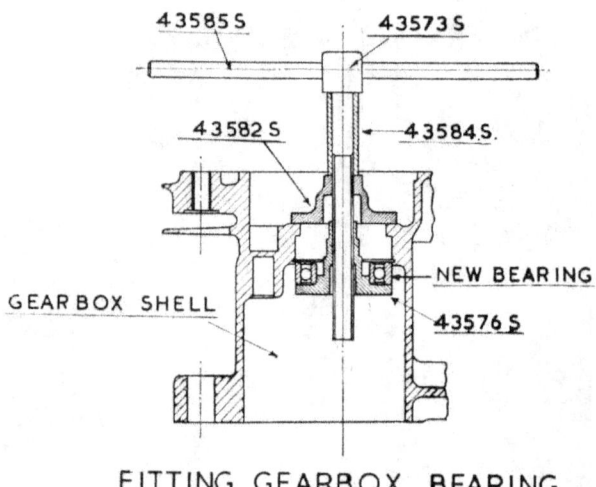

FITTING GEARBOX BEARING

Fig. 55

The new oil seal can be fitted next using the following service tools:

43593S.	Bolt.
43594S.	Nut.
474.	Washer (two off).
42073.	Distance tube.
43595S.	Locating collar.
43596S.	Locating collar.

Commence by fitting washer 474 followed by locating collar 43596S under the head of the bolt 43593S. Then pass the bolt through the gear box bearing from the offside. Next fit the new oil seal on to the locating collar 43595S, and fit the locating collar with the oil seal, followed by the spacer tube 42073, washer 474 and nut 43594S, to the bolt where it protrudes through the gear box bearing (see Fig. 56). Tighten the nut and bolt, making sure the oil seal enters the gear box true and square. Then when the oil seal is correctly located unscrew and take out the service tools. Next smear the oil seal with oil, and push

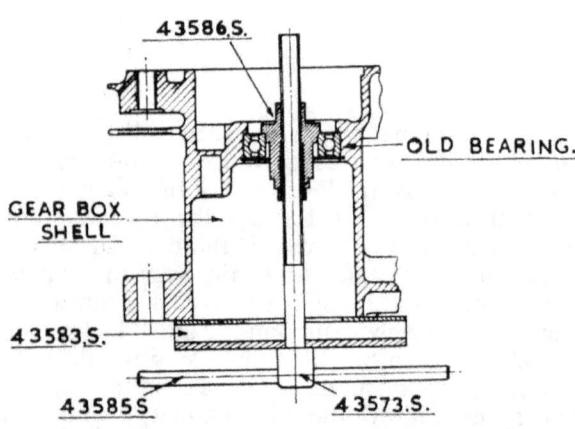

EXTRACTING GEARBOX BEARING

Fig. 53

the sprocket spacing collar into the seal, and re-fit the bearing circlip.

If it should be required to change the layshaft bush which is fitted just below the gear box main-shaft bearing, first remove the core plug which covers the end of the bush. This is easily done by passing a tommy bar into the gear box from the offside, and locating it into the layshaft bush and on to the centre of the core plug. Then a few sharp blows on the tommy bar with a hammer will knock the plug free. Then to remove the bush use the service tool 43587S drift, locate the drift into the nearside end of the bush and apply a few sharp blows with a hammer to the drift, to knock the bush free. To fit the new bush, first locate it into the hole from inside the gear box, and take the utmost care to align the cut-away in the outer edge of the bush with the small peg inside the gear box. Next pass the drift inside the gear box and locate it into the new bush, then very carefully tap the drift with a hammer to push the bush into place, but be quite certain it locates correctly over the peg. *Note:* No reamering is necessary.

A new core plug should now be fitted to cover the nearside end of the bush, and must be fitted as follows. First smear the end of the bush and the edge of the core plug with a good jointing compound, then fit the plug against the end of the bush with the convex side facing outward, then use the drift and hammer to apply one or two

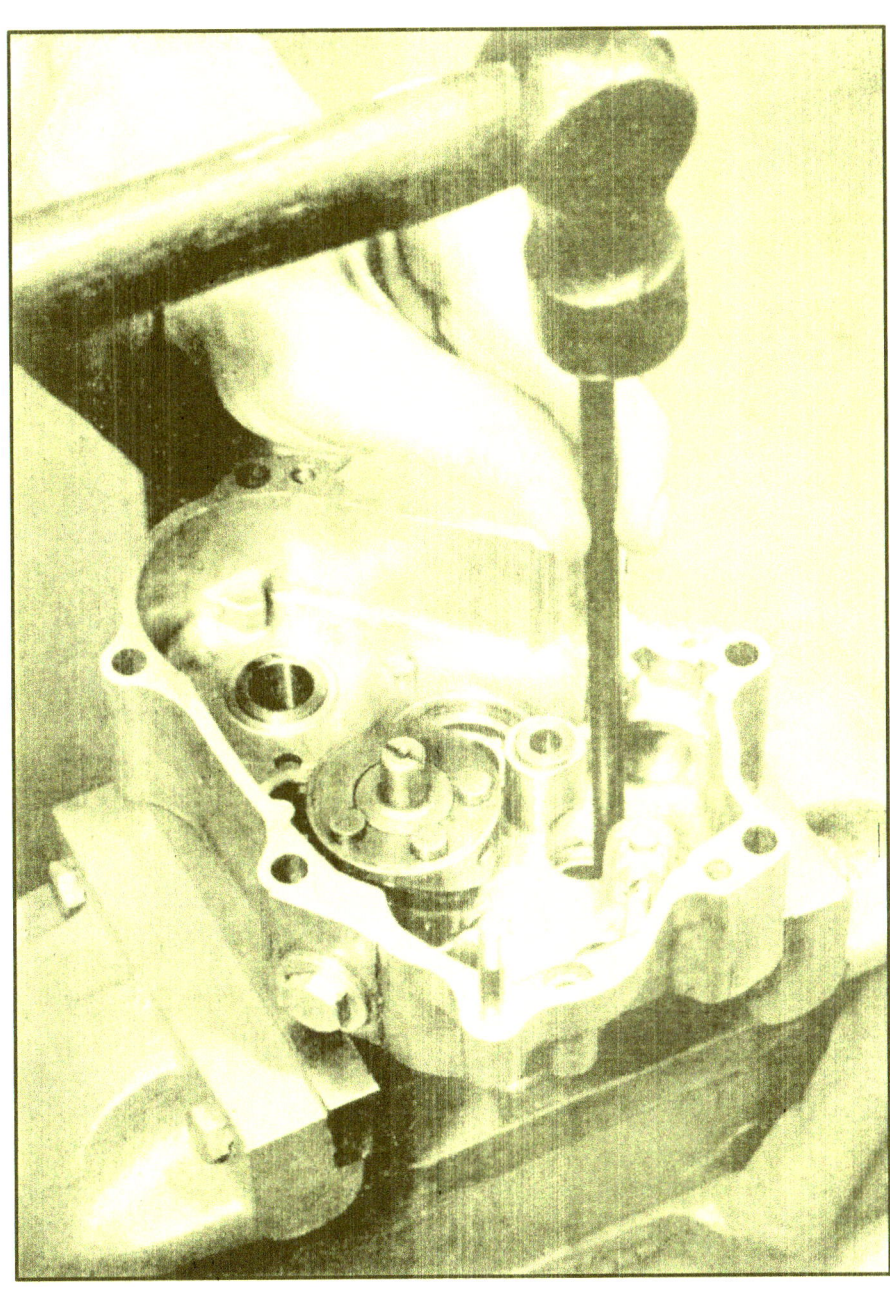

FIG. 57

sharp blows to the convex side of the core plug, which will expand and secure it in position.

Before re-assembling the gear box examine all the gears, and if any are badly worn or have damaged teeth they should be replaced with new ones. All new gears are supplied ready for fitting, including those which incorporate bushes and no reamering is necessary. If, however, the bush in one of the four bushed gears is damaged or prematurely worn, and the gear itself is in good order, a new bush can be fitted. To remove the old bushes and fit new ones, a press is essential, and a private owner who requires a gear re-bushing, should contact a motor cycle agent or garage who will have a suitable press.

The two bushes for the driving gear must be fitted one from each end, and must be pressed into the gear so that they are level with the bottom of the chamfer in each end of the gear. These two bushes do not require reamering, after pressing in. The bushes for the mainshaft third gear and the layshaft second gear, are identical and interchangeable. The bush for the lay shaft first gear is similar in design but smaller. All three bushes are fitted in the same manner, they must first be pressed into the recessed side of the gear, fitting the longer end first, so that the bush fits flush with the back of the gear. After fitting, the bushes must be drilled through the three holes around the edge of the gear, with a $\frac{1}{16}$ inch diameter drill, so

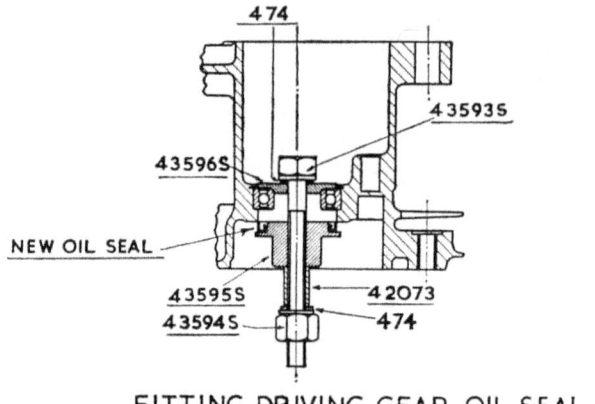

FITTING DRIVING GEAR OIL SEAL

Fig. 56

Fig. 59

that there are three holes through the gear and bush. The bushes must then be reamered as follows:

Mainshaft third gear: } Reamer .861 inch—
Layshaft second gear } .862 inch dia.
Layshaft first gear: Reamer .750 inch—.751 inch dia.

If attention is required to any of the fittings in the kick starter case, first remove it from the gear box as described on page 65. Then slip out the layshaft and any loose gears which may be attached to the selector forks. To remove the selector forks from the kick starter case, straighten and pull out the split pins which secure the selector fork dowels in position. Then by turning the selector forks the dowels can easily be slipped out, and the selector forks can be withdrawn from the kick starter case.

To remove the gear change cam, first straighten the lock washer which is bent against the nut, which secures the gear change cam at the back of the kick starter case. The nut can then be removed and the cam and spindle withdrawn.

Important Note: There may be a shim washer fitted on the cam spindle. Take care not to lose it. Also the cam plunger and spring are now loose and can be lifted out. If it is required to remove the speedometer spindle, proceed as described on page 65. If it should be required to remove the layshaft or kick starter bushes, these can be knocked out with a drift and mallet, providing care is used (see Fig. 57). To remove the quadrant spindle bush, heat the kick starter case by immersing it in boiling water, the bush can then be pulled out with a pair of pliers while the case is hot. To remove the mainshaft ball bearing, first remove the circlip with a pair of circlip pliers. *Note:* There may be a shim washer fitted between the circlip and bearing. Then the following service tools will be required to extract the bearing:

43573S. Spindle assembly.
43585S. Tommy bar.
43583S. Extractor channel.
43586S. Extractor collar.

Then commence by fitting the spindle assembly 43573S through the hole in the extractor channel 43583S, then pass the spindle assembly with the extractor channel under its head, through the mainshaft bearing from the offside of the kick starter case. The extractor collar 43586S must then be fitted to the spindle where it protrudes through the bearing. Next fit the tommy bar 43585S through the head of the spindle assembly (see Fig. 58), and fit a spanner over the flats on the extractor collar to prevent it from turning (see Fig. 59). Then rotate the spindle assembly until the bearing is extracted from the kick starter case. The service tools can then be unscrewed and removed.

Before re-assembling the kick starter case fit-

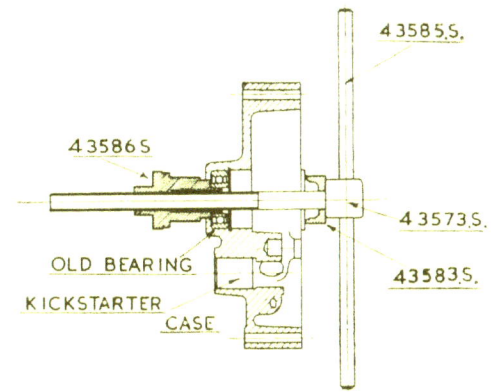

EXTRACTING KICKSTARTER CASE BEARING.

Fig. 58

tings, thoroughly clean the case and all parts which are being fitted. Then commence by fitting new bushes in place of any that have been removed. There must be three bushes in the kickstarter case, the kick starter spindle bush and the quadrant spindle bush, which must be fitted into the offside of the kick starter case, and lastly the layshaft bush which must be fitted from the nearside, also the layshaft bush must be located on the peg which protrudes from the nearside of the kick starter case. These bushes must be fitted by a suitable press, and a private owner should contact his local motor cycle agent or garage, who should have a suitable press. Note that none of these bushes require to be reamed. To fit the mainshaft ball bearing the following service tools are required:

43573S. Spindle assembly.
43585S. Tommy bar.
43584S. Spacer.
43576S. Bearing locating collar.
43577S. Locating washer "A".
43579S. Locating washer "C".

Then commence by fitting the spacer 43584S, followed by locating washer "A" on to the spindle assembly 43573S. Then pass the spindle assembly through the kick starter case from the nearside. Next fit the new bearing followed by locating washer "C", to the spindle where it protrudes from the offside of the kick starter case. The bearing locating collar 43576S must then be screwed on to the spindle and located through washer "C" and the bearing. Then fit the tommy bar 43585S through the head of the spindle assembly (see Fig. 60), and commence turning. Make certain the bearing enters the kick starter case true and square; continue turning the spindle assembly until the bearing is correctly located. Then unscrew and remove the service tools.

Important: If a shim washer was originally fitted next to the old bearing, it must now be re-fitted followed by the large circlip. If a new kick starter case has been fitted it is most unlikely that there will be room for a shim; if this is the case, the shim can be discarded.

Next fit the cam plunger and spring into the kick starter case. Then fit the gear change cam on to the spindle, so that the slotted end of the spindle is the same side as the dogs on the cam. Note if a shim was fitted on the cam spindle when it was dismantled, it must now be re-fitted to the threaded end of the spindle. Then pass the cam spindle, threaded end first, through the offside of the kick starter case, locating the cam plunger into one of the dimples in the cam. Push the cam to compress the plunger spring, and fit the lock washer and nut to the threaded portion of the cam spindle. Securely tighten the nut, and bend one side of the lock washer over the edge of the nut, and the other side over the edge of the kick starter case.

The selector forks can be fitted next, but note that one of the spindles is longer than the other, where it protrudes through the nut, and the fork with the longer spindle is the layshaft selector fork, which fits below the gear change cam. Pass both selector forks through the kick starter case, so that the ends of the spindles with the two holes, are the same side as the cam. Note that the holes for the dowels in the selector fork spindles are counter-bored, and when the dowels are fitted they must protrude from the opposite side to the counter-bore. After locating the dowels in the selector fork spindles, they must be secured in position by passing a $\tfrac{3}{32}$ inch dia. split pin through the small hole in the selector fork spindle and dowel, the split pin must then have its open ends bent over where they protrude through the spindle. Then position the selector forks so that the dowels are located in the gear change cam track.

If the speedometer spindle has been removed it can be re-fitted as described on page 65. To re-assemble the kick starter case to the gear box proceed as described on page 73.

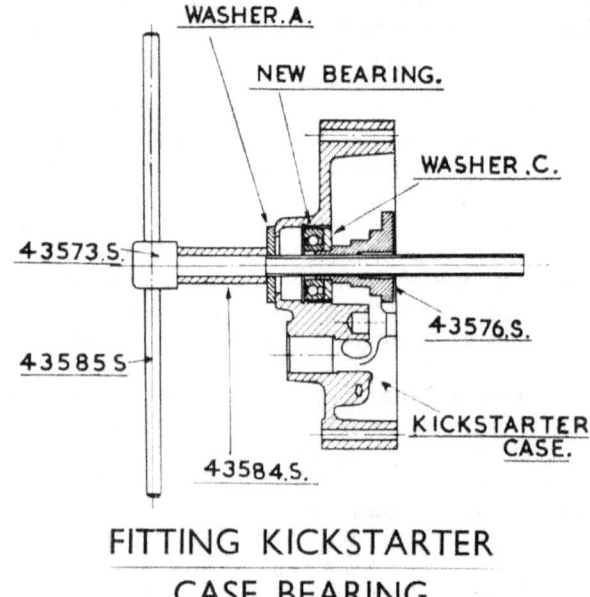

FITTING KICKSTARTER CASE BEARING

Fig. 60

RE-ASSEMBLING GEARBOX

Note that there are two ways of assembling the gear box, one is if the mainshaft and driving gear have not been disturbed, and a second method, if they have. When re-assembling the gear box it is advisable to use new lock washers and joint washers.

Dealing first with assembling a gear box where the mainshaft and driving gear have not been disturbed, first thoroughly clean inside the gear box and all the parts which are being assembled. Then remove the split pins which secure the dowels in the selector fork spindles and slip the dowels out; the selector spindles can then be withdrawn from the kick starter case. Then commence assembling by fitting the 24-tooth layshaft second gear on to the layshaft on the opposite end to the speedometer driving worm, and with the shoulder of the gear facing away from the worm. Then fit the 17-tooth layshaft pinion on to the layshaft, with the shoulder of the pinion facing towards the shoulder of the second gear.

Next fit the layshaft into the bush at the back of the gear box, at the same time meshing the layshaft pinion with the driving gear on the mainshaft. Then fit the mainshaft second gear to the mainshaft selector fork. *Note:* The mainshaft selector fork has a shorter spindle protruding beyond its nut, than the layshaft selector fork. With the second gear fitted to the fork, pass them inside the gear box together, locating the second gear on to the main shaft and the selector fork into the hole at the top of the back of the gear box, meshing the mainshaft and layshaft second gears together. Next fit the layshaft third gear to the layshaft selector fork, so that the five dogs face towards the offside of the machine, then fit the selector fork and third gear into the gear box, locating the third gear on to the layshaft and the selector fork into the hole at the bottom of the back of the gear box. The 26-tooth mainshaft third gear must next be fitted to the mainshaft, with the shoulder facing the offside end of the gear box, and meshed with the layshaft third gear. Then fit the 30-tooth layshaft first gear to the layshaft, with the shoulder facing the offside end of the gear box. The last remaining gear, the 16-tooth mainshaft first gear, can then be fitted to the mainshaft with the shoulder facing the offside end of the gear box, and meshed with the layshaft first gear (see Fig. 61).

The kick starter case is fitted next, but first ensure that the gear change cam is in the neutral position, to determine this, remove the plug, or if fitted, the neutral indicator switch, from the side of the kick starter case, then turn the gear change cam until the dimple in the side of the cam is visible through the plug hole. The plug or neutral indicator switch can then be re-fitted. A new joint washer should be fitted to the end of the gear box. Then with the gear change cam facing outwards, locate the kick starter case over the studs which protrude from the gear box, and over the ends of the selector fork spindles, and the mainshaft and layshaft. It may be necessary to lightly tap the kick starter case with a mallet to locate it against the end of the gear box. Next fit the screw through the hole in the kick starter case at the bottom inner edge and securely tighten it. Then pull outward the upper selector fork spindle, until the hole through the end of the spindle is in line with the channel in the cam. The dowel for the spindle must then be passed through the hole

FIG. 61

in the spindle, so that the end of the dowel with a hole through it is uppermost and the hole in the dowel is in line with the smaller hole through the end of the spindle, and the other end is located in the channel in the gear change cam. A split pin must then be passed through the small hole in the end of the selector fork spindle, and located through the hole through the dowel (see Fig. 62). The open ends of the split pin must pass right through the selector fork spindle, and be bent over.

The dowel for the lower selector fork is fitted in a similar manner, except that the spindle must first be pulled outward as far as possible, so that the dowel can be fitted into the hole in the spindle from the underside, the spindle must then be pushed inwards until the dowel is in line with the channel in the cam, then proceed as described for the upper selector fork.

Next fit the kick starter ratchet mechanism as described on page 65, and the kick starter case cover as described on page 63.

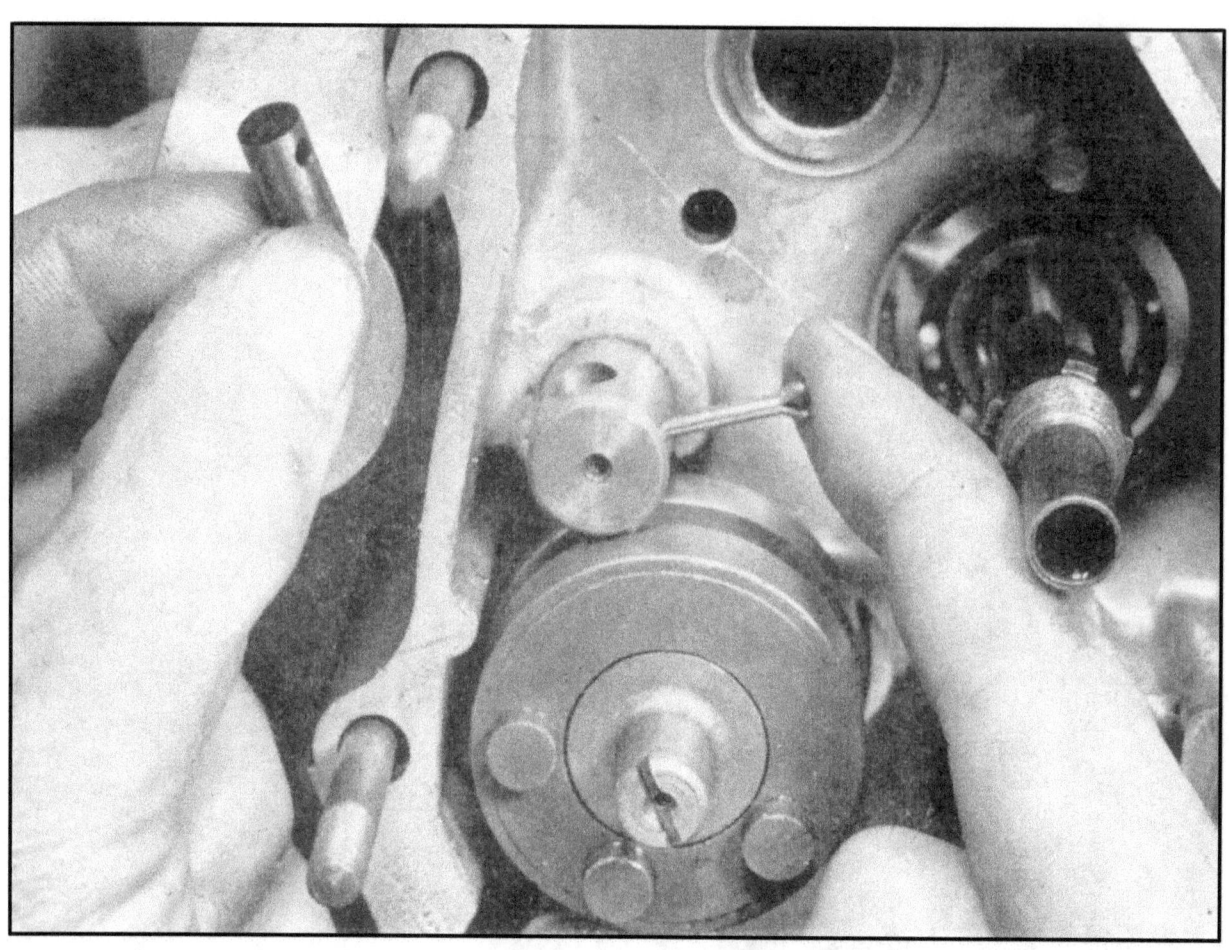

Fig. 62

RE-ASSEMBLING IF THE MAINSHAFT HAS BEEN REMOVED

Commence with the gear box thoroughly clean, and with the main ball bearing, oil seal, circlip and sprocket spacing collar fitted as described on page 68. Then pass the driving gear into the gear box and through the main ball bearing. The driving sprocket can then be located on to the portion of the driving gear which protrudes through the sprocket spacing collar, followed by a large plain washer, the locking washer and the nut. Next fit the special tool comprising of the chain and bar, through the bottom tunnel at the rear nearside of the engine, and locate the chain around the sprocket until the chain is double and the sprocket cannot be turned. Then securely tighten the sprocket nut with a suitable tube spanner and tommy bar (see Fig. 52). One side of the lock washer must then be turned over the edge of the nut.

The gears and shafts are assembled next, but first the kick starter case must be complete with all fittings as described on page 71. Then begin by locating the 16-tooth mainshaft first gear with its shoulder resting on the bearing at the back of the kick starter case. Then place the 26-tooth mainshaft third gear with its shoulder resting on the mainshaft first gear. The mainshaft 22-tooth second gear must then be located into the mainshaft selector fork, and with all three gears in line pass the mainshaft with its smaller threaded end first through the gears and kick starter case. Next assemble the kick starter ratchet parts as described on page 65. Although the nut can only be loosely fitted this will prevent the main shaft from slipping out.

Then assemble the layshaft third gear with the five dogs, into the recessed side of the 30-tooth layshaft first gear which has five corresponding holes. Fit the two gears together so that the layshaft first gear is resting on the kick starter case, and the layshaft third gear is located in the selector fork. Next pass the layshaft with the worm drive end first through the two gears and the kick starter case, making sure it engages correctly with the speedometer spindle. The 24-tooth layshaft second gear must be fitted next; it must be located on the layshaft so that its internal teeth engage with the layshaft third gear. The last remaining gear, the 17-tooth layshaft driving gear, can then be fitted over the layshaft, so that its shoulder rests on the shoulder of the layshaft second gear. Next fit a new joint washer to the gear box. The complete assembly of gears can then be inserted into the gear box (see Fig 63), locating the mainshaft through the driving gear at the back of the gear box, and the kick starter case over the studs in the end of the gear box. It may be necessary to lightly tap with a mallet the kick starter case in order to locate it correctly on to the gear box. Then fit the screw into the hole in the inside bottom edge of the kick starter case and securely tighten. Next securely tighten the kick starter ratchet nut, and bend one side of the

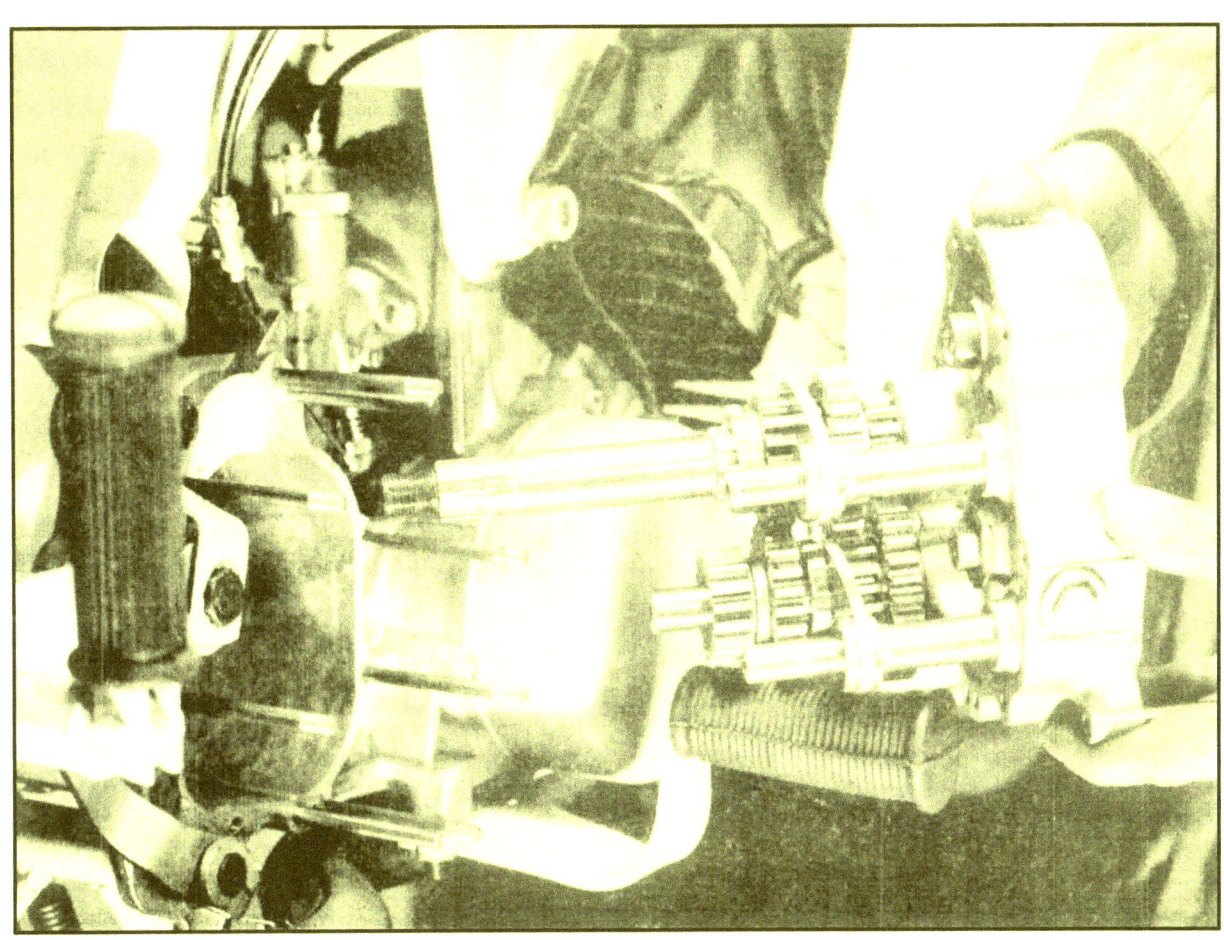

Fig. 63

tab washer over the edge of the nut. The kick starter case cover can then be fitted, as described on page 63. Next fit the rear chain and the rear chaincase as described on page 197.

The oil seal housing plate complete with the oil seal and joint washer, can then be fitted over the nearside end of the gear box mainshaft. The three bolts which secure the plate to the engine must have a lock washer fitted **under their heads**, the bolts can then be fitted and securely tightened, then bend one of the tabs of each lock washer over the edge of the bolt, and one tab over the edge of the oil seal housing plate. Finally fit the clutch, primary chain and primary chaincase as described on page 32.

FRONT WHEEL—LEADER AND ARROW

TO REMOVE

To remove the front wheel from the front fork proceed as follows:—

Put the machine on the centre stand and remove the cover plate from the outer side of each fork leg. Each cover plate has one fixing screw, which must be unscrewed until it floats freely, the screw will remain in the plate as it has a **retaining rubber**; this is done to eliminate the possibility of the screw being lost. The cover plate can then be moved forward and lifted clear (see Fig. 65).

Detach the brake cable from the brake operating arm, by slackening the cable adjuster which is

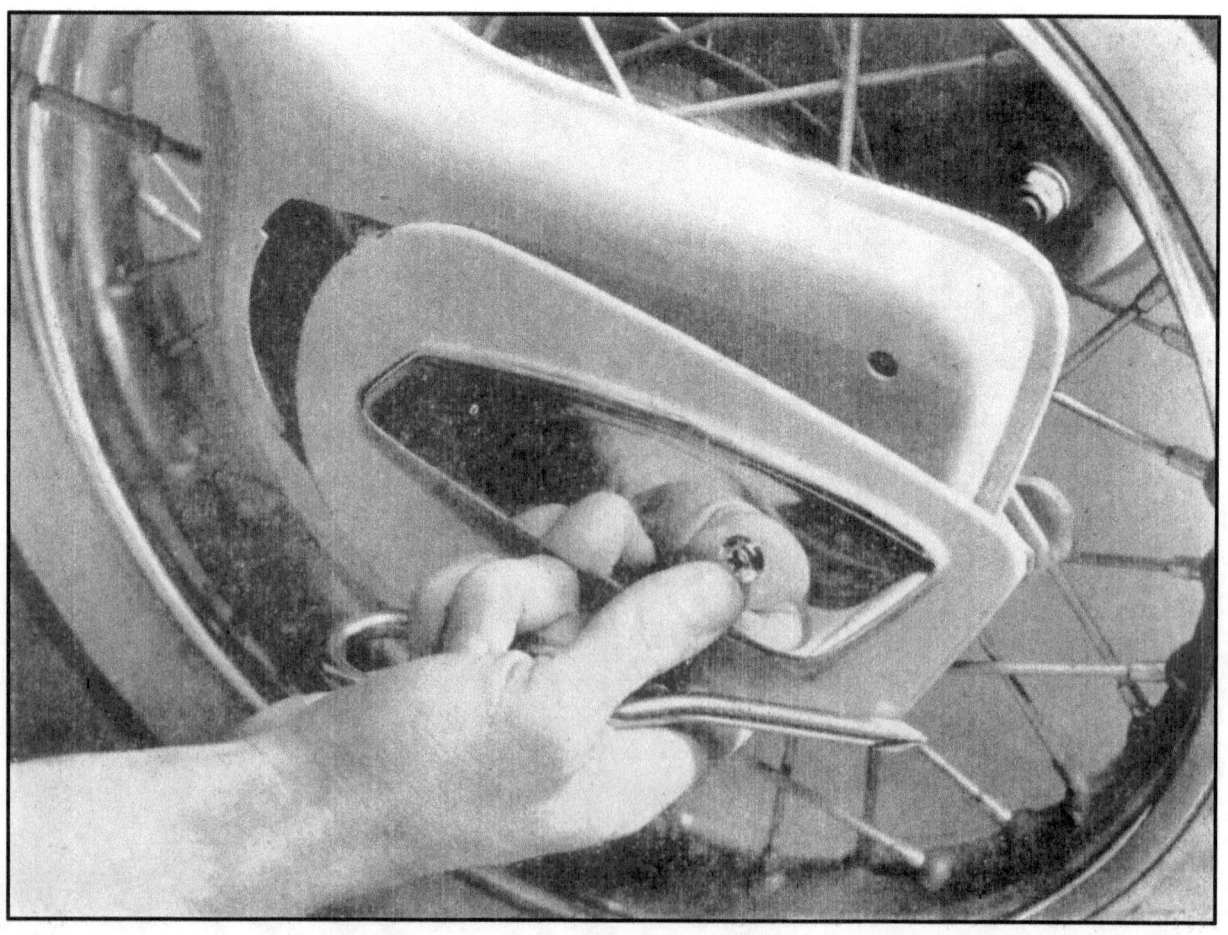

FIG. 65

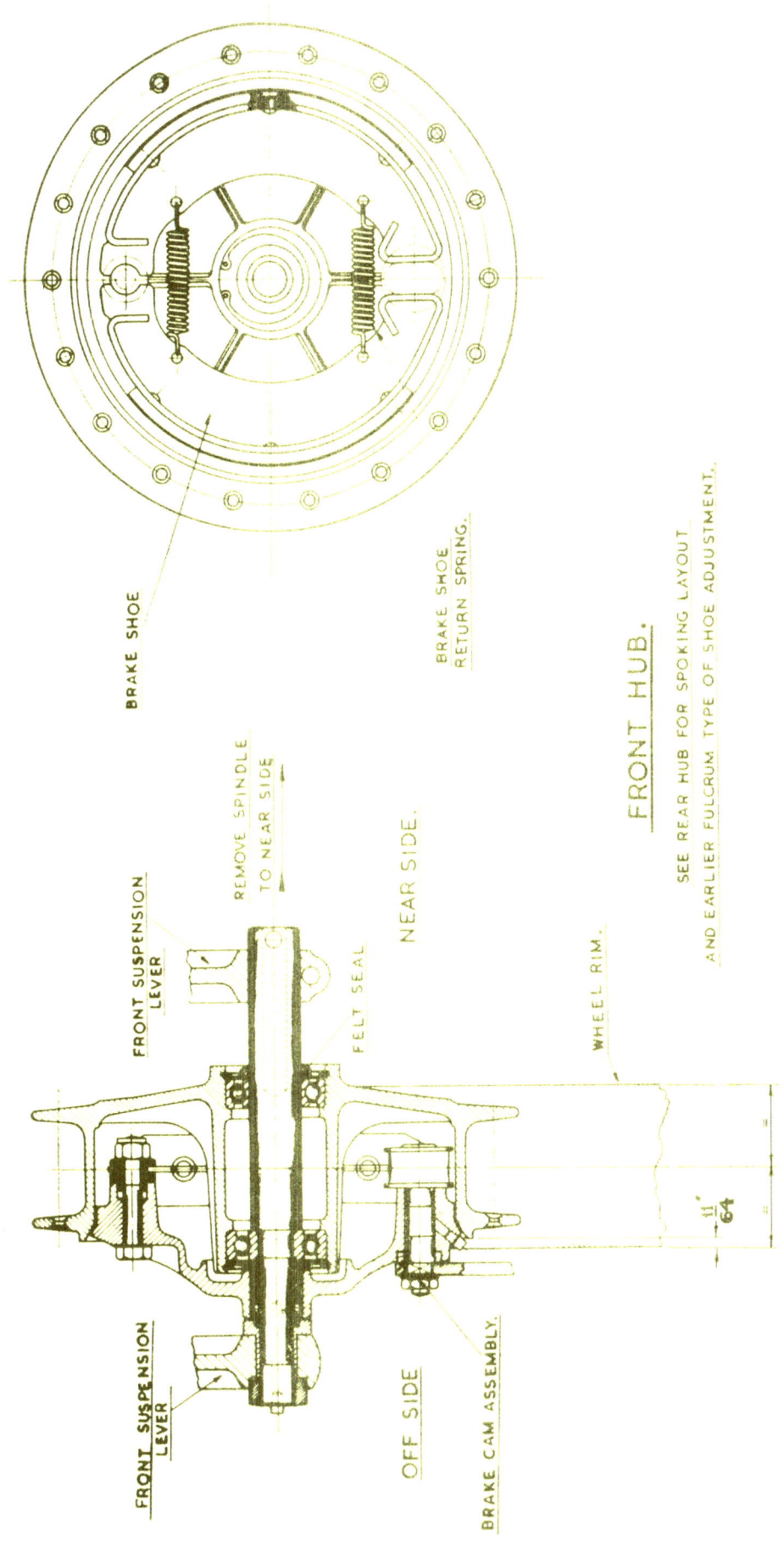

Fig. 64

incorporated in the cable approximately two inches from the operating arm, then pull the cable rearwards and lift the outer cover from the operating arm, the inner cable can then be moved forward to slide the nipple from the slotted stop on the brake anchor plate (see Fig. 66). *Note:* On brakes which have the triangular torque arm bracket on the brake anchor plate (see Fig. 74a), the brake cable outer cover is fitted in the slotted stop and the cable nipple fits in the operating arm, and removal is similar to that described above. If the brake incorporates a fulcrum adjuster (see paragraph on front brake adjustment, page 86), then the adjuster should be screwed out a few turns, i.e. turn in an anti-clockwise direction, when the cable can be easily removed.

Next remove the bolt and special lock nut which secures the brake torque arm to the bottom of the offside fork leg (see Fig. 67), and note the two dust covers, which are fitted to protect the special torque arm pivot bearings. Do not remove the slotted nut which secures the brake torque arm to the brake anchor plate. *Note:* On machines which have the torque arm attached to a triangular bracket on the brake anchor plate, the bolt and nut which secures the torque arm to the bracket should be removed in order to free the wheel. Do not undo the bolt which secures the torque arm to the fork leg, or the bolt and nut which secure the triangular bracket to the brake anchor plate (see Fig. 74a).

Each fork leg has a large aperture which was revealed when the cover plates were removed. Through the offside leg aperture can be seen the bottom end of the hydraulic unit with its two oval-shaped securing brackets. Between these two brackets is the offside, light alloy trailing link, through which the wheel spindle passes, and the spindle is secured by the large nut.

The nearside fork leg has an identical hydraulic unit, but as can be seen, the nearside trailing link incorporates a pinch bolt and nut to the rear of the spindle, and when the pinch bolt is tight it secures the nearside trailing link to the wheel spindle.

The wheel spindle which protrudes through the nearside trailing link is provided with a hole through the end, which is used when withdrawing the spindle.

Before the wheel spindle can be removed,

FIG. 66

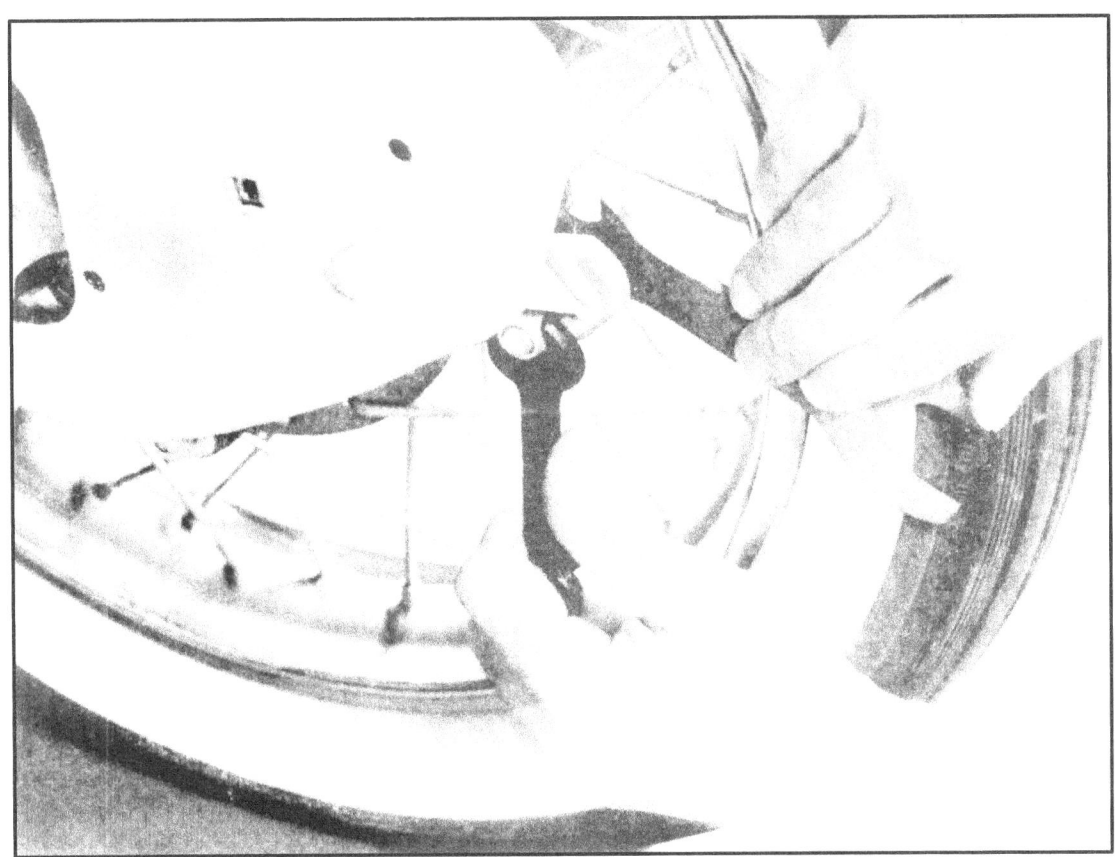

Fig. 67

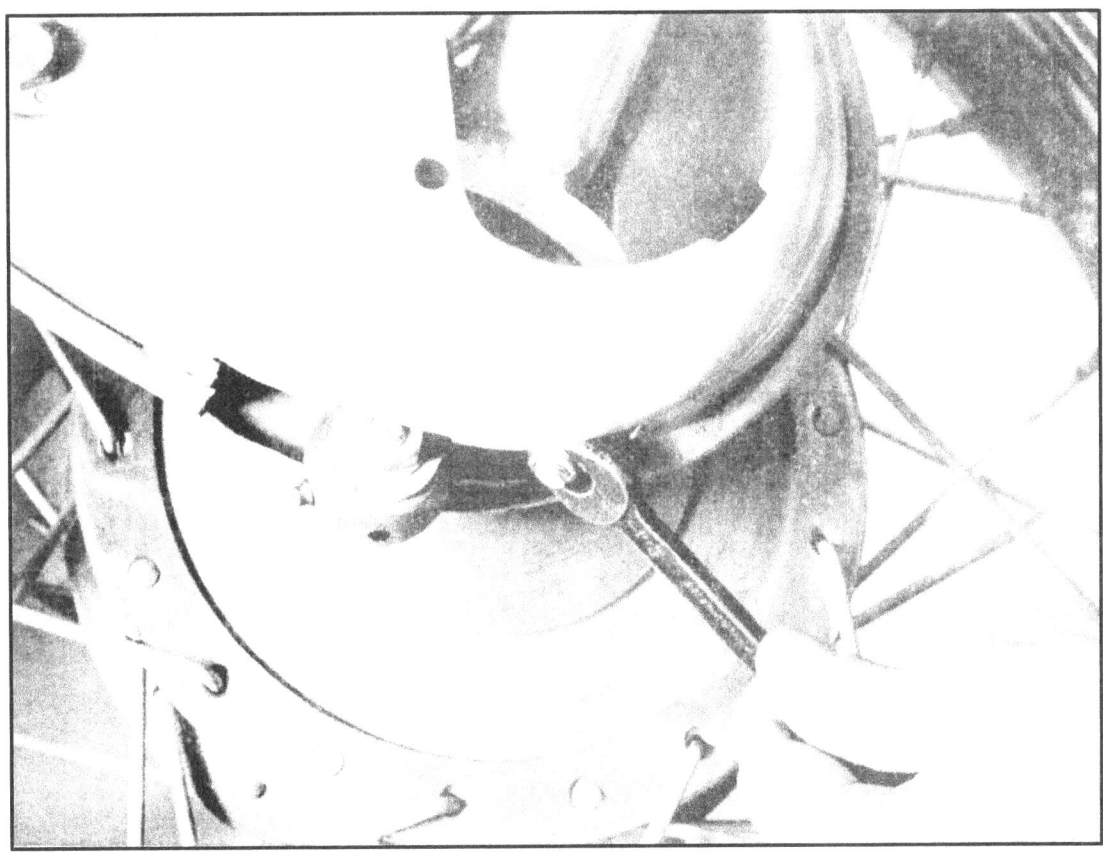

Fig. 68

loosen the pinch bolt nut on the nearside trailing link, two or three turns being quite sufficient (see Fig. 68), then the hydraulic units inside both fork legs must be compressed slightly and retained in that state, to make the hub spindle and nut fully accessible through the fork leg apertures.

No great effort is required to compress the hydraulic units, and this can be accomplished by pushing downwards on the front mudguard, while at the same time inserting in the small hole in front of the fork leg aperture, one at each side, the two ¼ inch diameter rods which are supplied in the tool kit of each new machine, so that passing through the fork legs the rods engage in the holes in the trailing links and the inner faces of each fork leg (see Fig. 69).

An alternative method of compressing the hydraulic units is to insert a steel bar of approximately ⅜ inch diameter by 12 inches long, in the bottom of the fork leg immediately in front of the bottom of the hydraulic unit. The bar can then be used with a levering action to compress the unit while the retaining rods are being inserted (see Fig. 70). If this alternative method is used, care should be taken not to damage the grease nipple in the bottom of each trailing link.

Important: For safety purposes a front stand (listed as optional extra equipment, spares Part No. 42151) should be fitted before withdrawing the wheel spindle (see Fig. 71). If a front stand is not available, a strong box or support 6½ inches

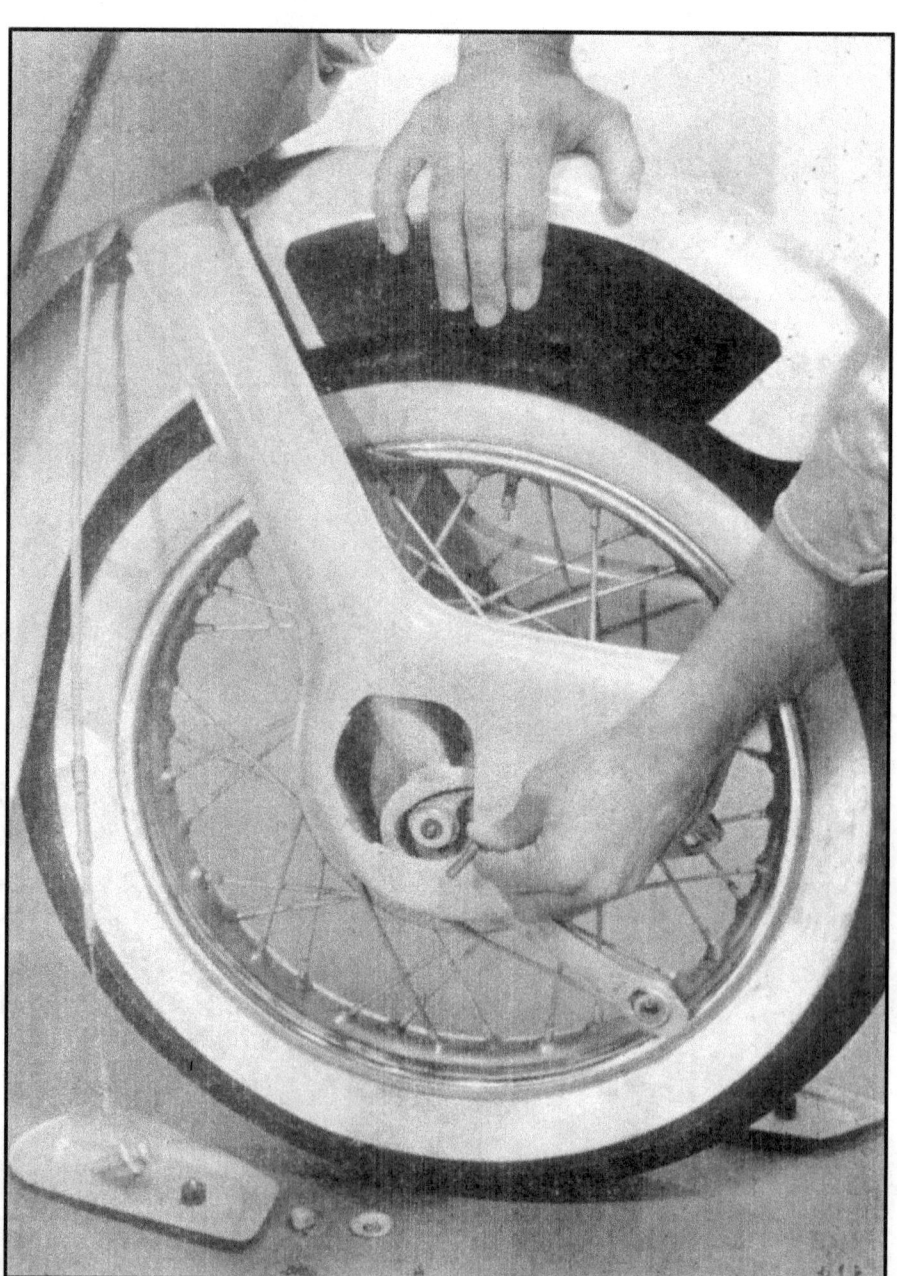

Fig. 69

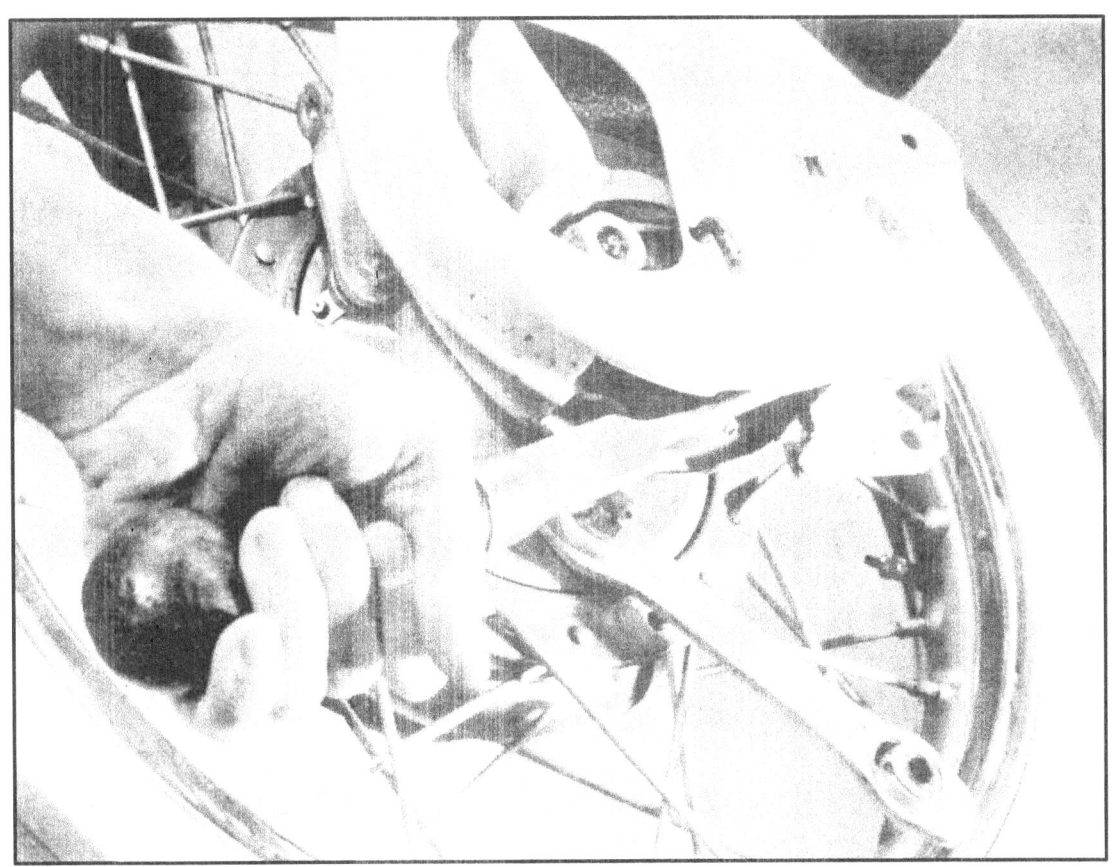

Fig. 70

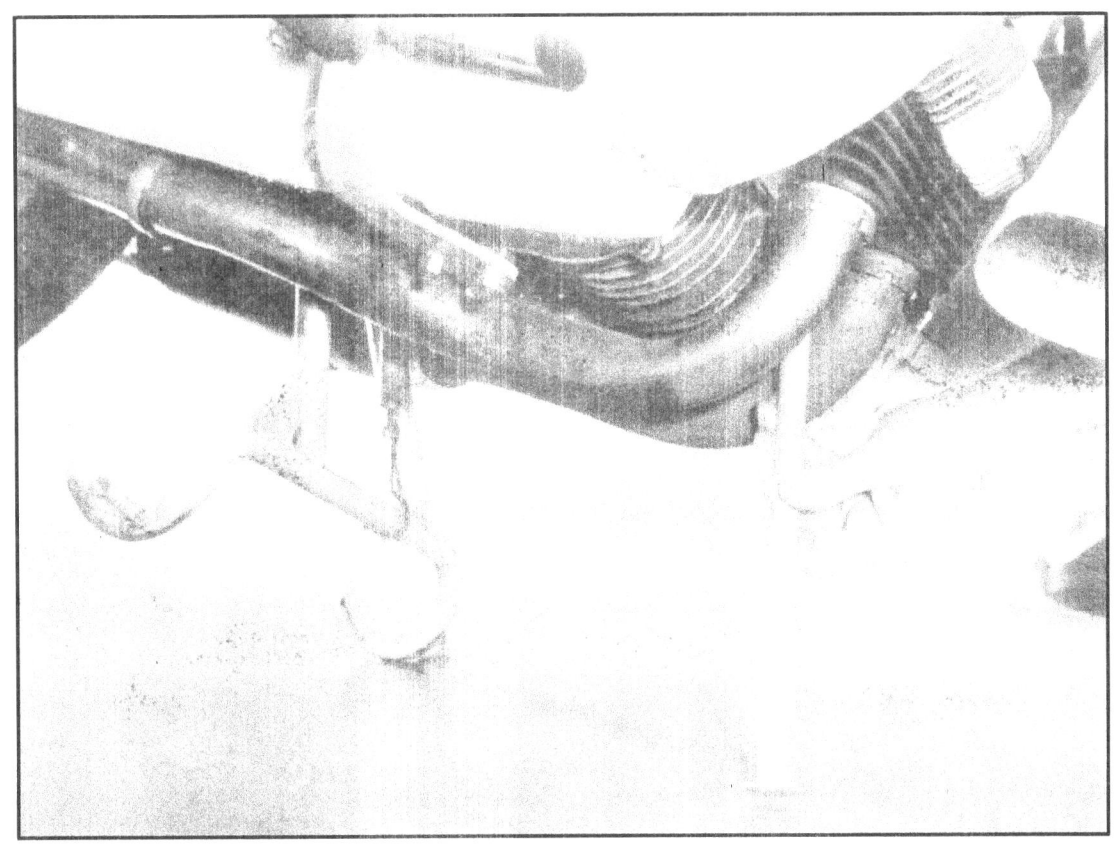

Fig. 71

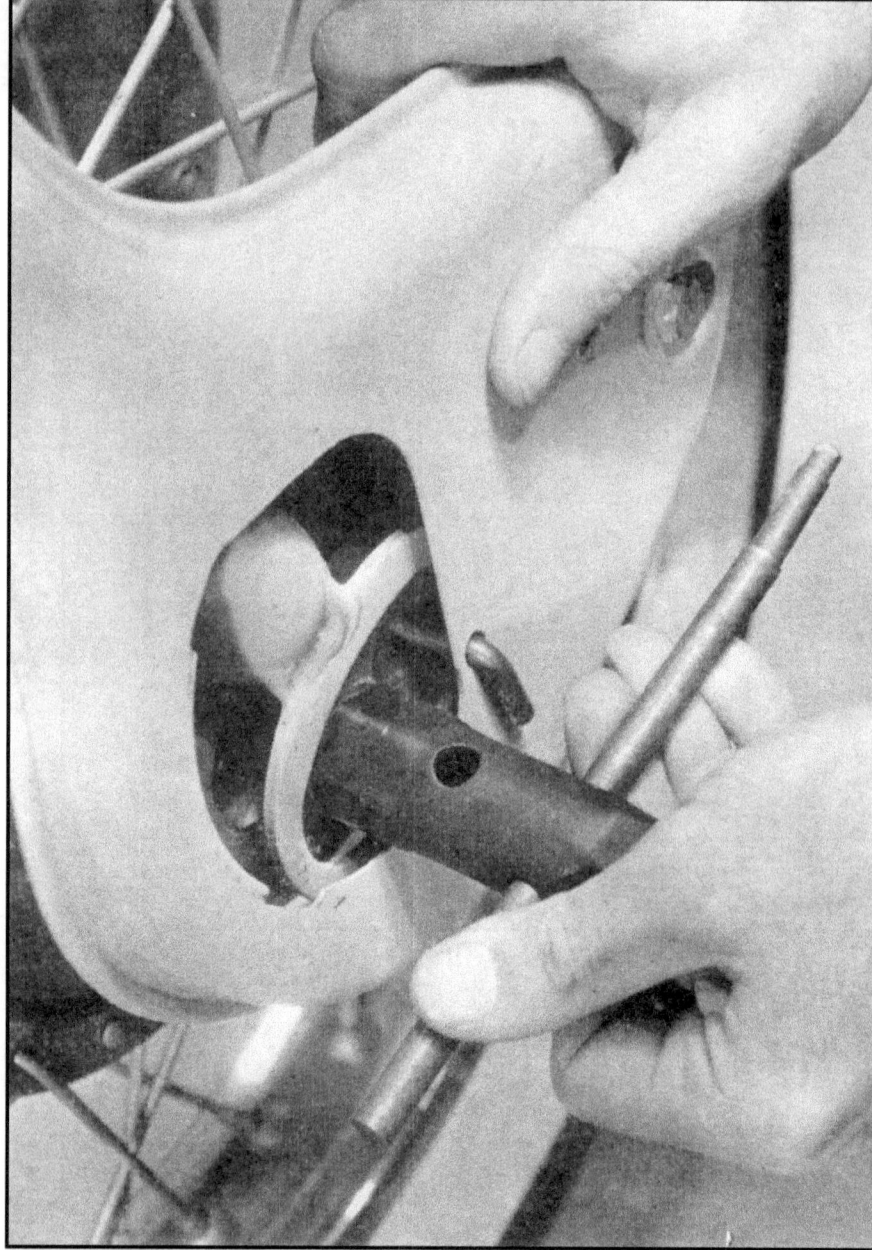

Fig. 72

high should be placed under the forward end of the exhaust pipes. On no account must the fork legs be lowered to ground level, as this would allow the centre stand to spring up and the machine to topple over, with consequent damage.

Next, using a tube spanner ($\frac{1}{2}$ inch, Whitworth) remove from the offside the wheel spindle nut (see Fig. 72). The wheel spindle may then be withdrawn from the nearside, by inserting a $\frac{3}{16}$ inch rod, suitably shaped, through the hole in the spindle end, twisting the rod whilst pulling (see Fig. 73). A spindle withdrawing rod is available as a service tool, or alternatively a tool can be made by bending a length of $\frac{3}{8}$ inch diameter rod to an "L" shape, of a size suitable to fit into the tool box.

Drill a $\frac{7}{32}$ inch diameter hole $2\frac{1}{4}$ inches from the end of the long arm of the "L". Then by passing the rod into the end of the hollow spindle, a $\frac{3}{16}$ inch diameter peg can then be inserted through the hole in the end of the spindle and the hole through the "L" shaped withdrawing tool. The spindle may now be withdrawn by pulling and if necessary, twisting the "L" shaped spindle tool. The wheel can then be pulled free for any maintenance necessary (see Fig. 74), but do not remove the rods which are keeping the hydraulic units compressed. If however the rods have been removed for some reason, they must be re-inserted before the wheel can be re-fitted, and to compress the units in order to insert the rods, the alternative method using a bar as a lever will have to be applied.

Fig. 73

Fig. 74

Fig 74A

Fig. 75

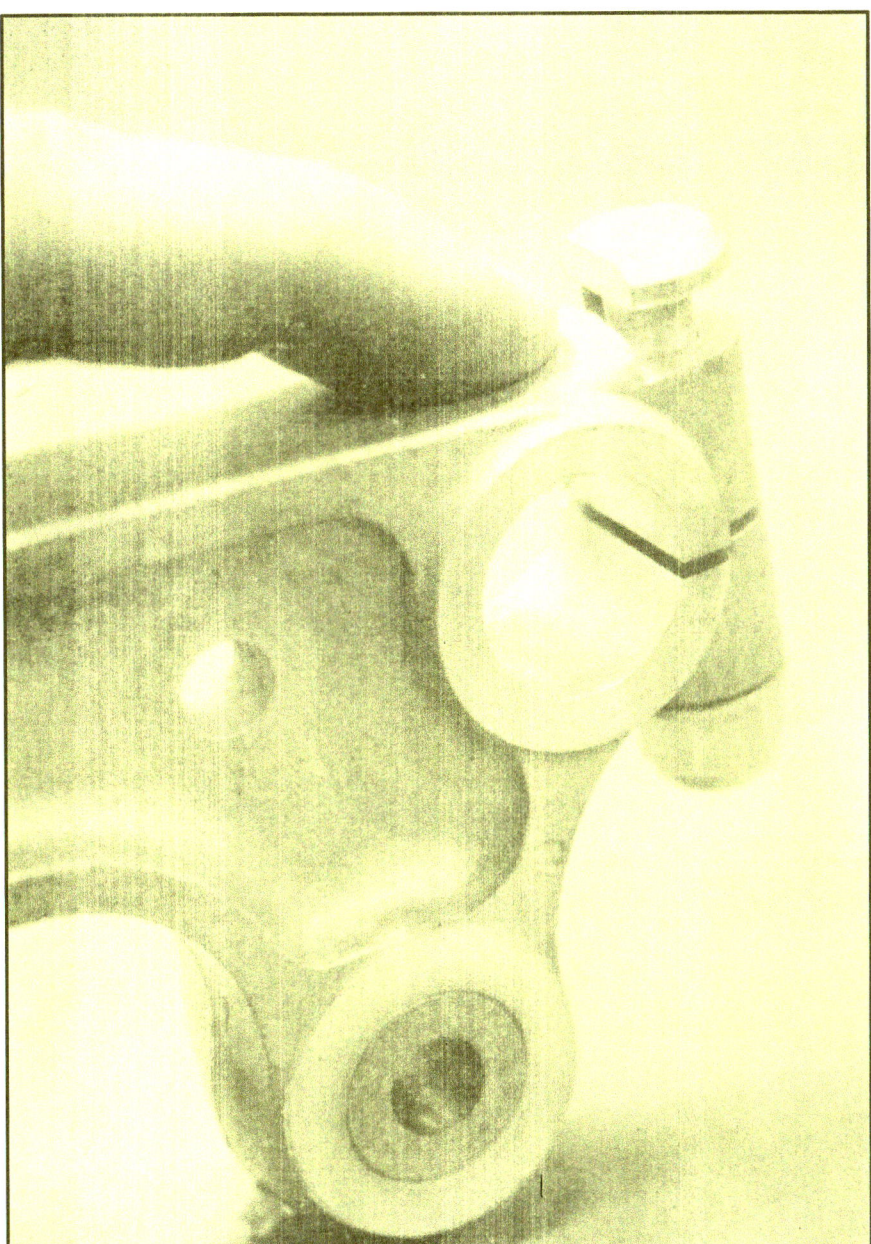

Fig. 76

RE-FITTING FRONT WHEEL

After passing the wheel between the fork legs and lifting same to align the hub, with the links, the spindle can be pushed through the nearside fork link and the hub, this should be done by hand without any undue force. Care must now be taken to align the spindle with the bush in the offside fork link, then the spindle withdrawing rod should be inserted in the spindle again and used to push the spindle through (see Fig. 75). If, however, a strong resistance is met, the alignment of the spindle and the fork link bush should be re-checked. Do not hammer the spindle to force it in, as this may result in internal damage to the hub. When sufficient threaded portion of the spindle protrudes through the offside fork link, the spindle nut can be fitted and will draw the spindle through as it is tightened. After the spindle nut has been tightened, check that the brake anchor plate is free and can be rotated easily. This is most important, as the brake anchor plate could, if tight, interfere with the functioning of the front suspension.

Before tightening the spindle pinch bolt, remove the rods which are keeping the hydraulic units compressed, and make sure that drawing the spindle through has not displaced the nearside fork leg inwards. If this has happened, the fork leg can be eased back by using a piece of wood as a lever between the hub and fork leg. Next move the forks up and down several times, to ensure that alignment is correct, then, making sure that the head of the pinch bolt is seated correctly, i.e. the flat on the bolt head is coincident with the flat on the trailing link (see Fig. 76), tighten the pinch bolt nut. Lightly grease the spherical torque arm bearings, and re-fit the brake torque arm with the dust covers and the correct bolt and self-locking nut. Make doubly sure that this nut is properly tightened. Re-fit the cover plates and finally re-fit and adjust the brake cable.

FRONT BRAKE ADJUSTMENT—LEADER AND ARROW

There are two different types of brakes in use (see Fig. 77), one type is provided with nylon brake shoe fulcrum adjusters screwed into the brake plate, and adjustment is carried out by turning the squared end of the adjuster, clockwise until the brake lining is rubbing the drum, then turn the adjuster anti-clockwise at least five clicks, final adjustment is then made at the brake cable adjuster.

The other type of brake does not incorporate fulcrum adjusters and the method of adjustment is as follows:

Adjust the brake by the cable adjuster, which is situated in the cable near the operating arm, until the wheel cannot be revolved, then re-adjust in the opposite direction, a little at a time and checking until it is just possible to rotate the wheel freely.

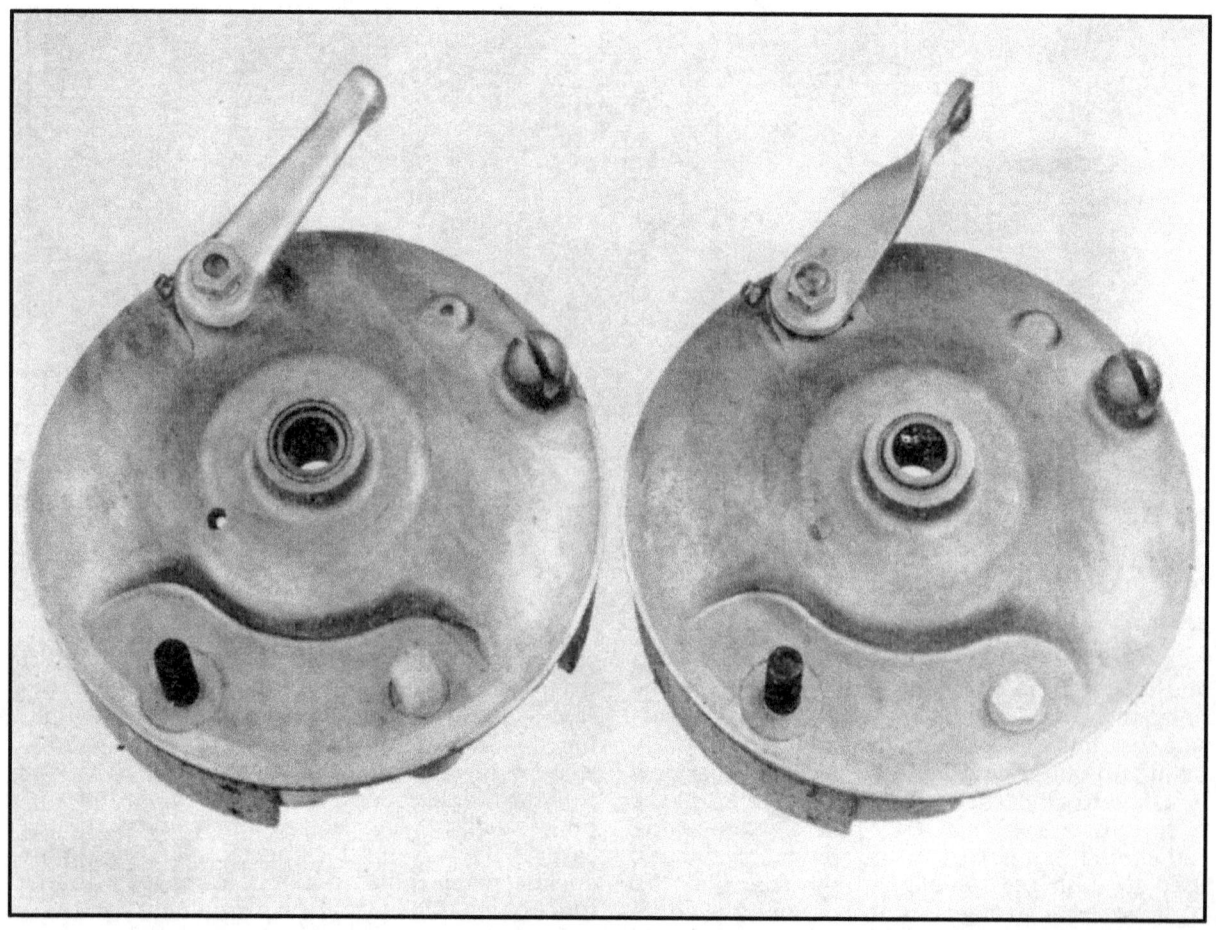

FULCRUM TYPE   Fig. 77   **NON FULCRUM TYPE**

After many thousands of miles it will appear that there is no further adjustment of the cable, even though the brake linings may still be of considerable thickness. To give a new lease of life, it is only necessary to screw the cable adjuster right in until no threads are showing, then remove the nut and spring washer securing the brake operating arm to the brake anchor plate. Withdraw the operating arm from the brake cam spindle, noting the serration of the operating arm relative to the square of the brake cam spindle. Replace the operating arm by moving it radially to the next serration, i.e., thirty degrees in an anti-clockwise direction, when viewing the outside of the brake anchor plate. Replace the spring washer and the nut and securely tighten the operating arm in the new position.

Re-fit the brake cable with the soldered nipple only affixed in the slotted stop on the brake anchor plate, or the operating lever as the case may be, leaving the loose ferrule to float on the inner cable between the slotted stop and the operating arm. Push the operating arm forward and locate the cable outer cover in the cup of the operating arm or slotted stop (see Fig. 78).

Re-adjust the brake by re-setting the cable adjuster in the outer cover.

The two different types of brake can be identified by examining the brake anchor plate at a point directly opposite the operating arm and just above the brake torque arm. The brake incorporating the fulcrum adjuster will have the square ended adjuster protruding from the brake anchor plate, whereas the other type of brake will have a hexagon headed bolt at this point (see Fig. 77).

Note: In the event of any fierceness developing in the brake, this can usually be traced to brake lining dust, collecting in the drum, the remedy is to remove the brake assembly and clear out all dust, etc. In the event of linings being worn down to almost the rivet heads, exchange shoes and linings should be fitted.

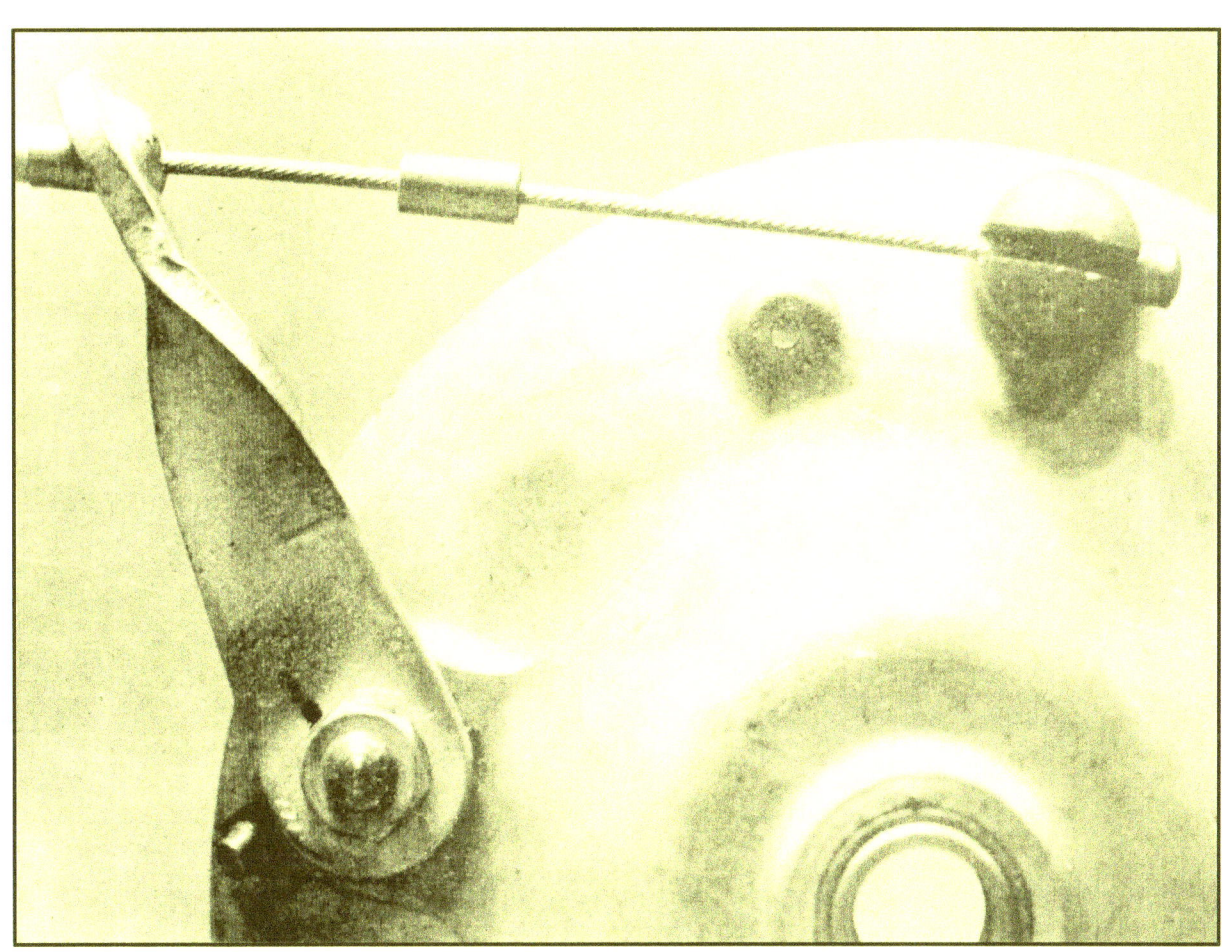

Fig. 78

FRONT WHEEL MAINTENANCE AND LUBRICATION—LEADER AND ARROW

The full width hub is fitted with two journal ball bearings, which are grease packed during assembly, the bearings are not adjustable and when adequately lubricated are trouble free. Every ten thousand miles, as much of the old grease as possible should be removed from the bearings, and fresh grease of the recommended grade inserted. *Note:* There is a grease nipple fitted to the end of the spindle, and this lubricates the floating brake plate bush only, and not the wheel bearings; grease at regular intervals but not excessively. A grease nipple is also fitted to the brake cam spindle bearing. Give only one stroke of the grease gun at one thousand mile intervals, as any excessive supply of grease might reach the brake linings.

The brake plate should be removed and the brake linings inspected for wear whenever the wheel is removed. Do not allow brake lining wear to reach a stage where the securing rivets could score the drum, or irreparable damage could be done (see Fig. 79).

Removal of the brake anchor plate is quite

Fig. 79

Note: A new brake lining is compared with a worn one. When brake linings are worn as shown in the lower half of the photograph they should be replaced.

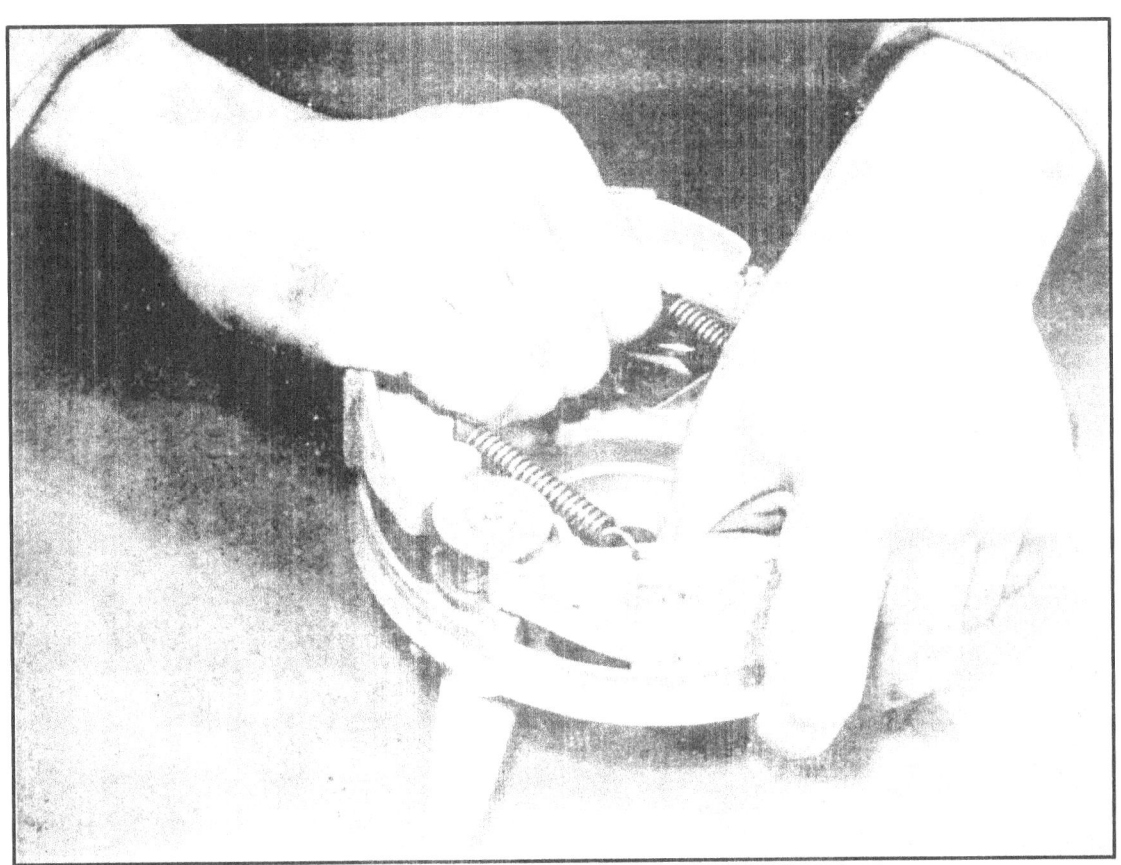

Fig. 80

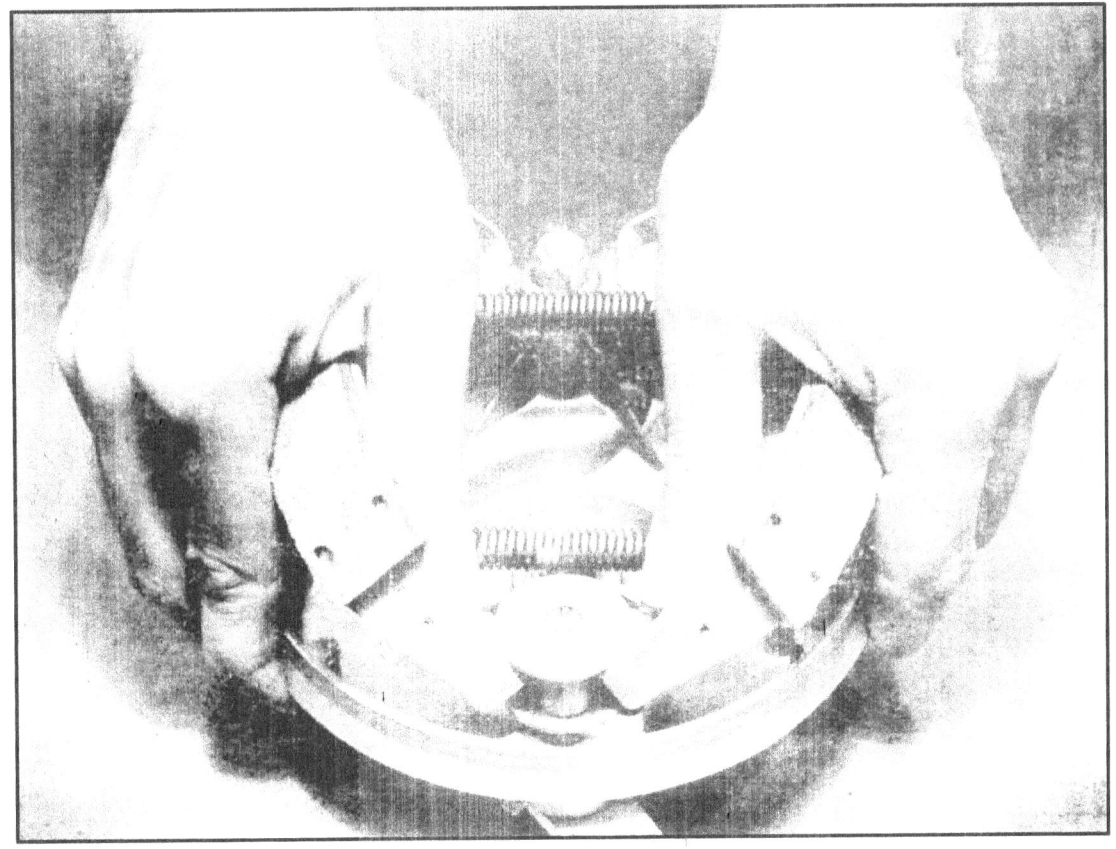

Fig. 81

straightforward, as it is not fixed or attached to the hub in any way, and will easily pull out, although in the case of a brake which incorporates the fulcrum type of adjuster, it may be necessary to screw the adjuster out in order to slacken it, and thereby give greater clearance between the lining and the drum to facilitate removal.

In addition to the two types of brakes already described, minor detail modifications have been introduced from time to time, and the following instructions cover all variations, therefore extra care should be taken to identify the type of brake being dealt with.

When dismantling the brake anchor plate, the main point is removing and refitting the brake shoes, and if the brake shoes are removed for any purpose other than fitting new linings, it is essential that they are replaced on the same side of the brake plate to which they were originally fitted, if this is not done, an inefficient or grabbing brake will ensue. Before removing the shoes a scratch mark may be made on one shoe and on the brake plate for identification purposes, to avoid incorrect re-assembly. *Note:* brakes fitted with fulcrum adjusters should have the adjuster screwed out when this will facilitate brake shoe removal. Also some brakes have special springs fitted from the brake shoe webs to a rib on the brake anchor plate, these springs are to prevent "brake squeal" and it is necessary to disconnect them before the brake shoes can be removed. The best method when removing the shoes, is to leave the shoe springs in place and take a firm grip with one hand on one of the shoes, then with other hand pull the other shoe away from the cam and pivot sufficiently to enable the shoe to be lifted up and clear (see Fig. 80). Both shoes will then be free.

When re-fitting the brake shoes, assemble the two springs to the shoes and hold both shoes as near in position as possible on the brake cam and the brake pivot, then press both shoes down evenly when they will snap into place (see Fig. 81), but afterwards check very carefully to make quite certain that both shoes are correctly located on the cam and pivot by operating the

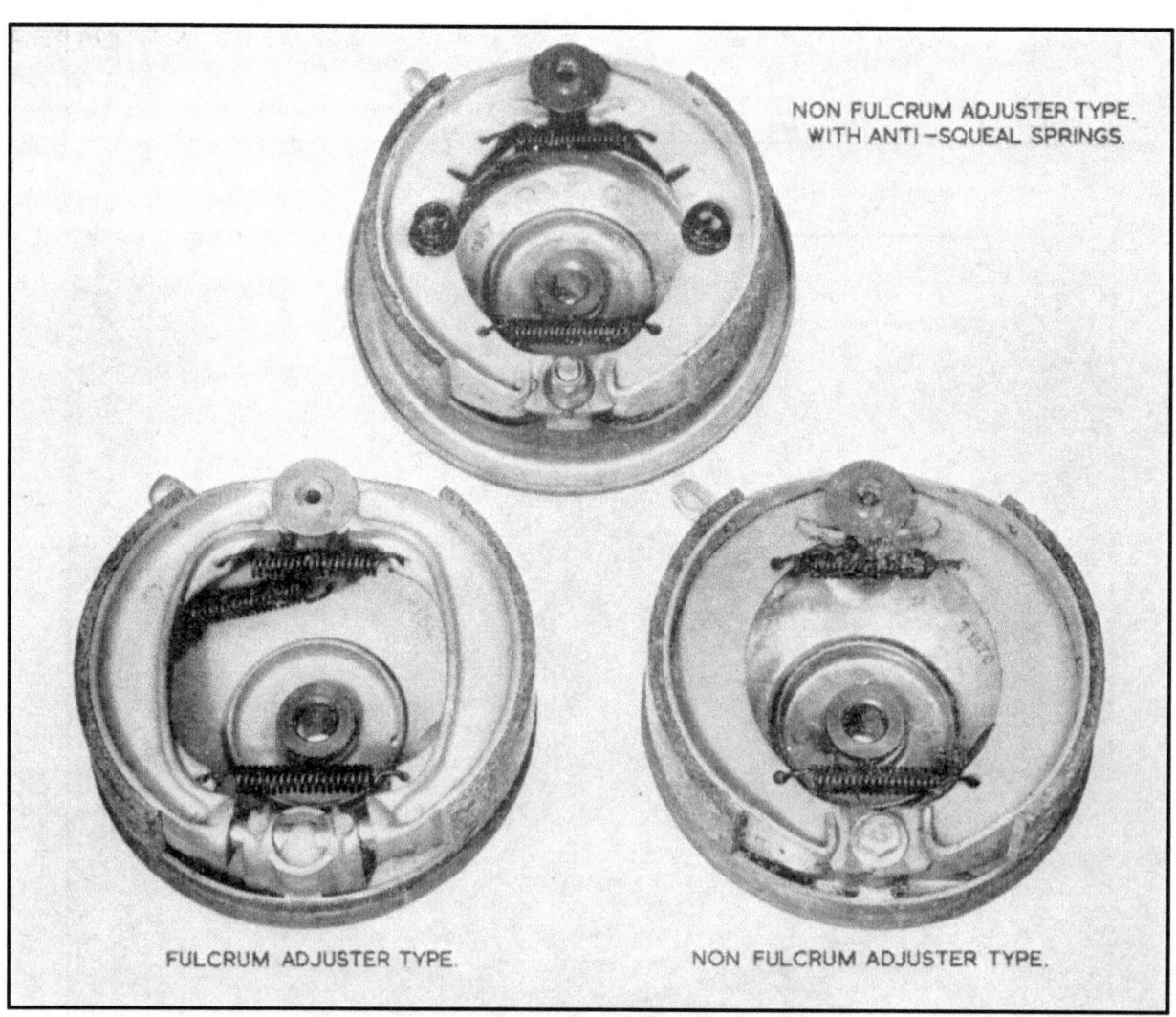

Fig. 82

brake lever. If the brake shoes were fitted with the additional springs to prevent "squeal" these springs should now be re-fitted.

The brake cam is removed by taking off the nut from the brake lever on the outside of the brake anchor plate, when the cam can then be tapped through and removed. Note the felt washer, which is fitted between the operating arm and the brake anchor plate; this must be in good condition and should be semi-stiff, as it is impregnated with tallow. If this washer is damaged or has deteriorated in any way it should be replaced. The pivot fitted to the opposite side of the brake anchor plate to the cam is removed by undoing the self-locking nut and taking out the bolt. As already mentioned in the paragraph on brake adjustment there are two different types of brakes in use, and in place of the pivot already mentioned the other type of brake has the fulcrum adjuster. To take this adjuster apart the two wedges can be pulled out of the casting whilst the square end of the adjuster is merely screwed right in to remove same.

Some brakes are fitted with a cam which incorporates a stop plate and spring to assist return of the cam after the brake has been operated. This plate and spring has since been deleted and the new cam without the plate and spring is interchangeable.

Whenever the brake plate is dismantled, all parts should be thoroughly cleaned and the brake cam and spindle along with the pivot lightly greased before re-assembly. If the brake is fitted with a fulcrum adjuster, then the wedges and thread of the adjuster should also be lightly greased before final assembly.

On machines where the brake torque arm is attached to the brake plate, it should not be removed unnecessarily from the brake anchor plate. If, however, it has to be removed, take out the split pin, which secures the slotted nut, and remove the slotted nut and note that there are also two dust covers protecting the torque arm pivot bearing at the brake plate end. On machines with the triangular bracket on the brake anchor plate, the torque arm is secured to the fork leg by a bolt and special lock nut, which are accessible after pulling the plastic cover off the fork leg bracket. To remove the torque arm pivot bearings, they must be turned sideways and pressed out of the torque arm through the slots provided at each end. When re-fitting the bearings they should be pushed through the slot until they snap into place when they then can be turned sideways into their correct position (see Fig. 83). Any time the torque arm and bearings are removed

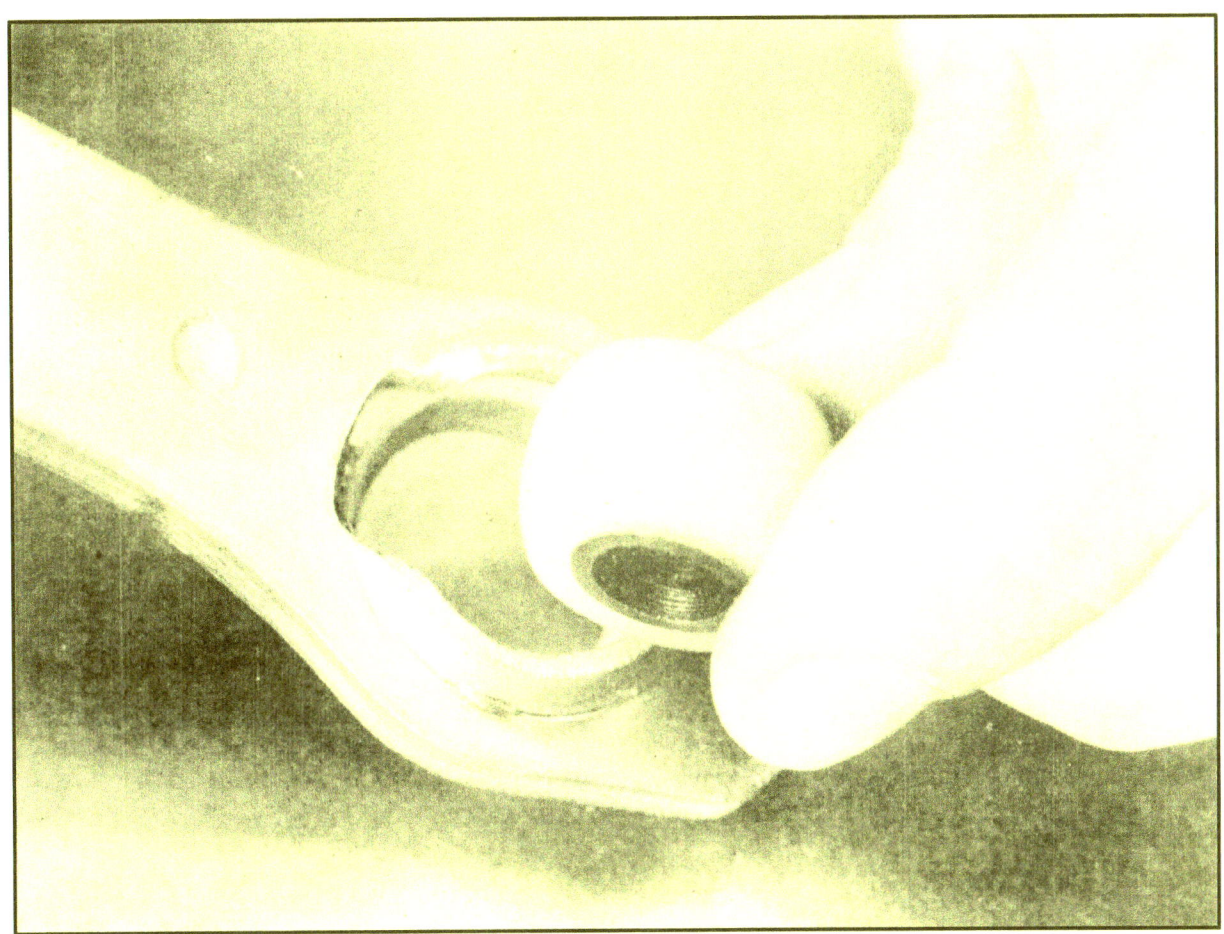

FIG. 83

they should be cleaned and re-greased before assembly.

The greatest care should be taken at all times to avoid getting even the slightest trace of oil or grease on the brake linings. The lining surfaces must be kept free from dirt and grease and they can be cleaned by washing the shoes in clean petrol, **NOT petrol oil mixture,** and after drying, the lining surfaces only may be wiped with carbontetrachloride, which can be purchased from most local chemists.

BRAKE LINING RENEWAL

When the brake linings are worn down nearly to the rivet heads (see Fig. 79), they must be replaced, otherwise the brake drums may become scored. An exchange service is available whereby brake shoes with worn linings can be exchanged for shoes fitted with new linings ready to assemble to the brake anchor plate, and it is strongly recommended that exchange shoes are obtained as re-lining brake shoes by hand is not a satisfactory method. The leading edges of the brake linings must not be chamfered, as dust which develops due to lining wear could find its way on to the lining surfaces if the edges are chamfered, and this would reduce the braking effect.

If new brake linings have been fitted the brake will require re-adjusting. Follow the procedure on page 86 for normal adjustment, but of course, if the brake operating arm and the loose nipple were moved to the alternative position during previous adjustments, they must be replaced in their original positions before commencing any adjustment.

The brake with fulcrum adjusters has light alloy shoes, whereas the brake without the fulcrum adjusters has steel shoes. The steel and the alloy shoes vary considerably in design (see Fig. 84), and are not interchangeable. Therefore when obtaining exchange or replacement brake shoes make certain that the shoes obtained are the same type as those originally fitted.

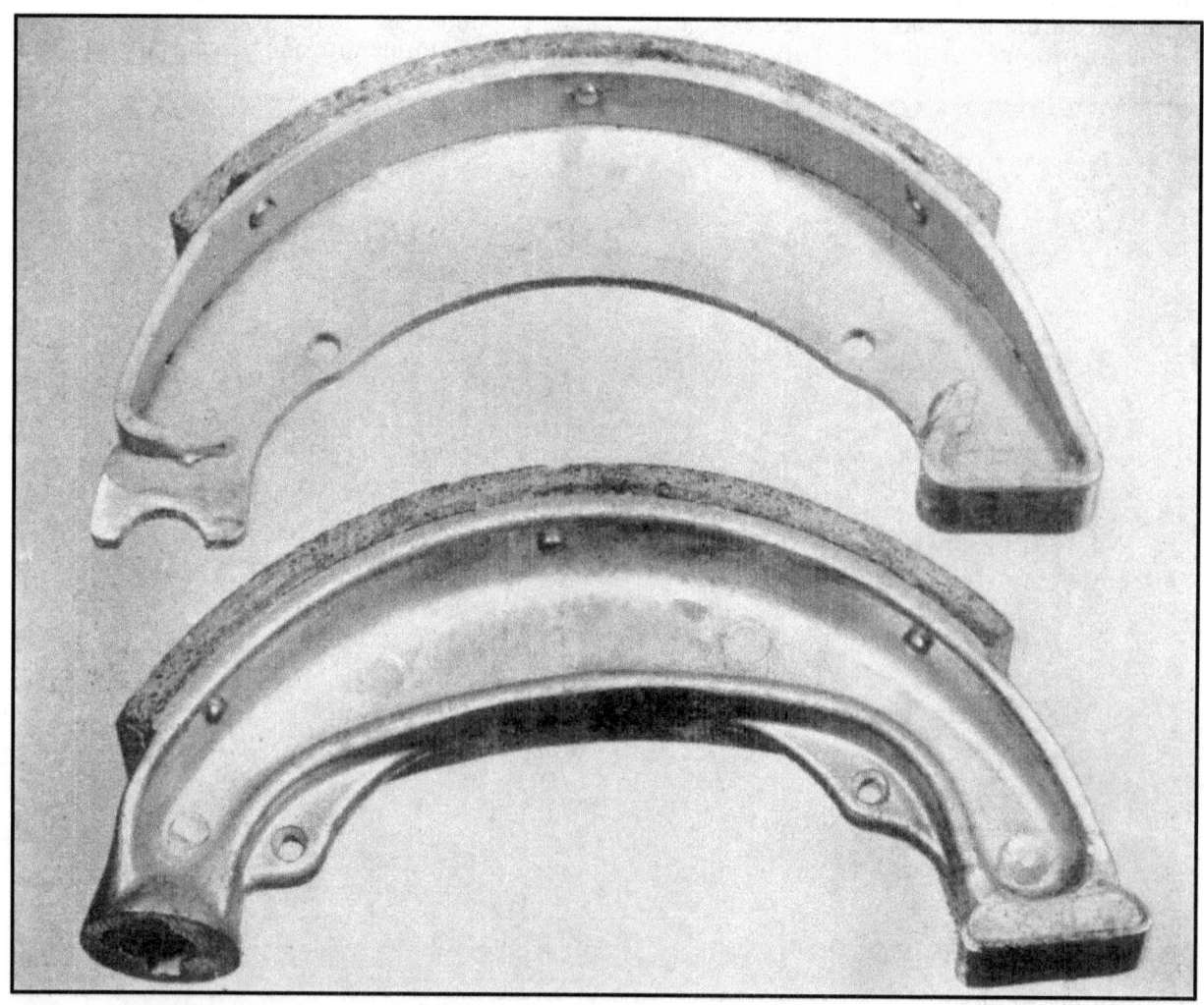

Fig. 84

RENEWING HUB BEARINGS

To carry out the work of removing worn bearings and fitting new ones, in the front hub, the following service tools are required:

43587S. Drift.
43573S. Spindle.
43576S. Bearing locating collar.
43580S. Locating washer "B".
43588S. Collar.
43585S. Tommy bar.
43577S. Locating washer "A".

Commence by removing the large circlips from each side of the hub, to do this easily it is advisable to use a pair of circlip pliers, or round nose pliers of a size suitable to fit the holes in the circlips (see Fig. 85), next take out the grease retaining plates and note there is one plain plate fitted to the offside and two recessed plates with a tallowed felt washer sandwiched between, fitted to the nearside. These plates are easily removed with a suitably pointed rod or the point of the circlip pliers. This leaves only the bearings in the hub, and the offside one must be removed first by passing the drift 43587S through the nearside bearing,

Fig. 85

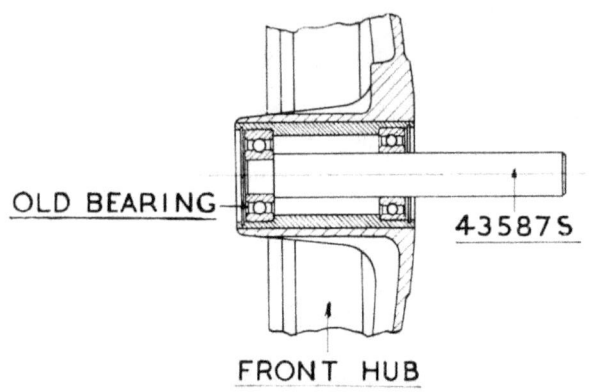

EXTRACTING OFF SIDE
FRONT HUB BEARING

Fig. 86

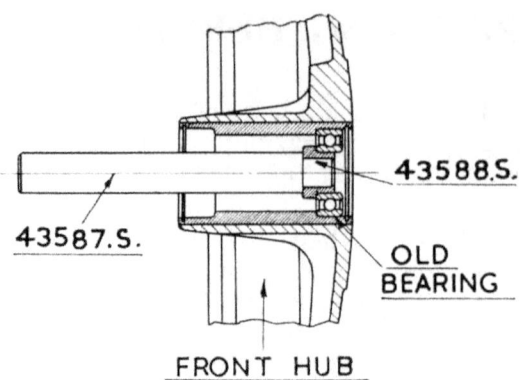

EXTRACTING NEAR SIDE
FRONT HUB BEARING

Fig. 87

Fig. 88

so that the small end of the drift locates in the offside bearing (see Fig. 86), a few sharp blows on the drift with a mallet will then knock the bearing out of the hub. To remove the nearside bearing, the collar 43588S must be placed in the hub from the offside, and located in the nearside bearing the drift 43587S can then be passed through the offside of the hub, and located in the collar (see Fig. 87), then using the mallet as previously, the bearing can be removed (see Fig. 88).

Before fitting new bearings the hub should be thoroughly cleaned out and the inside smeared with clean grease to assist fitting; the new bearings must then be thoroughly packed with grease of the recommended grade. *Note:* The compound

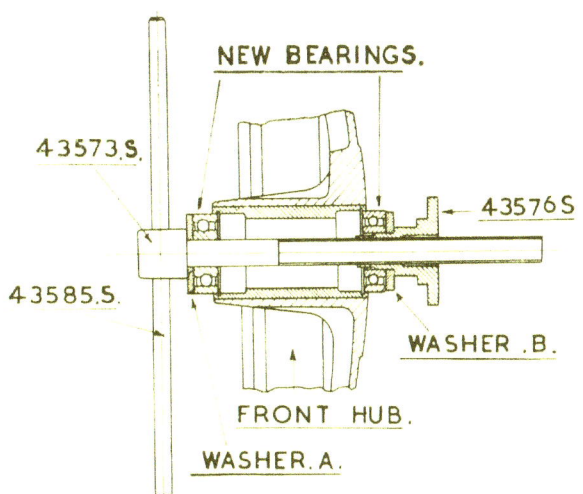

FITTING NEW FRONT HUB BEARINGS

Fig. 90

Fig. 89

Fig. 91

in a new bearing is to prevent corrosion during store life and is *not* a lubricant. Commence by placing locating washer "A" 43577S on the spindle 43573S, next slide the offside bearing on to the spindle then pass the spindle through the hub from the offside (see Fig. 89). Locating washer "B" 43580S is then placed on the bearing locating sleeve 43576S, the nearside hub bearing is also fitted on the locating sleeve, next to the locating washer "B", the sleeve, which has an internal thread is then fitted to the spindle end, which protrudes from the nearside of the hub (see Fig. 90), pass the tommy bar 43585S, through the offside of the spindle and commence turning in a clockwise direction, but at the same time making sure that the locating sleeve with the nearside bearing does not revolve (see Fig. 91). Make certain that the bearings enter the hub true and square and continue turning the spindle until both bearings are properly located in the hub, then unscrew and take out the service tool. Re-fit the grease retaining plates, felt washer and circlips. If either of the grease retaining plates, felt washer or circlips are damaged in any way, they should be replaced.

WHEEL BUILDING

In the event of a wheel being damaged and in need of retruing or the fitting of a new rim or spokes, this work should not be attempted by a novice; wheel building requires expert attention, and an owner who has a damaged wheel should contact his local dealer. The wheel spoking and rim arrangement drawing is given for use by competent wheel builders (see Figs. 64 and 93).

TYRES

Maintaining the correct tyre pressure is of the utmost importance. The front tyre should be kept at a pressure of 18 lb. per square inch; this pressure should be checked weekly and adjusted

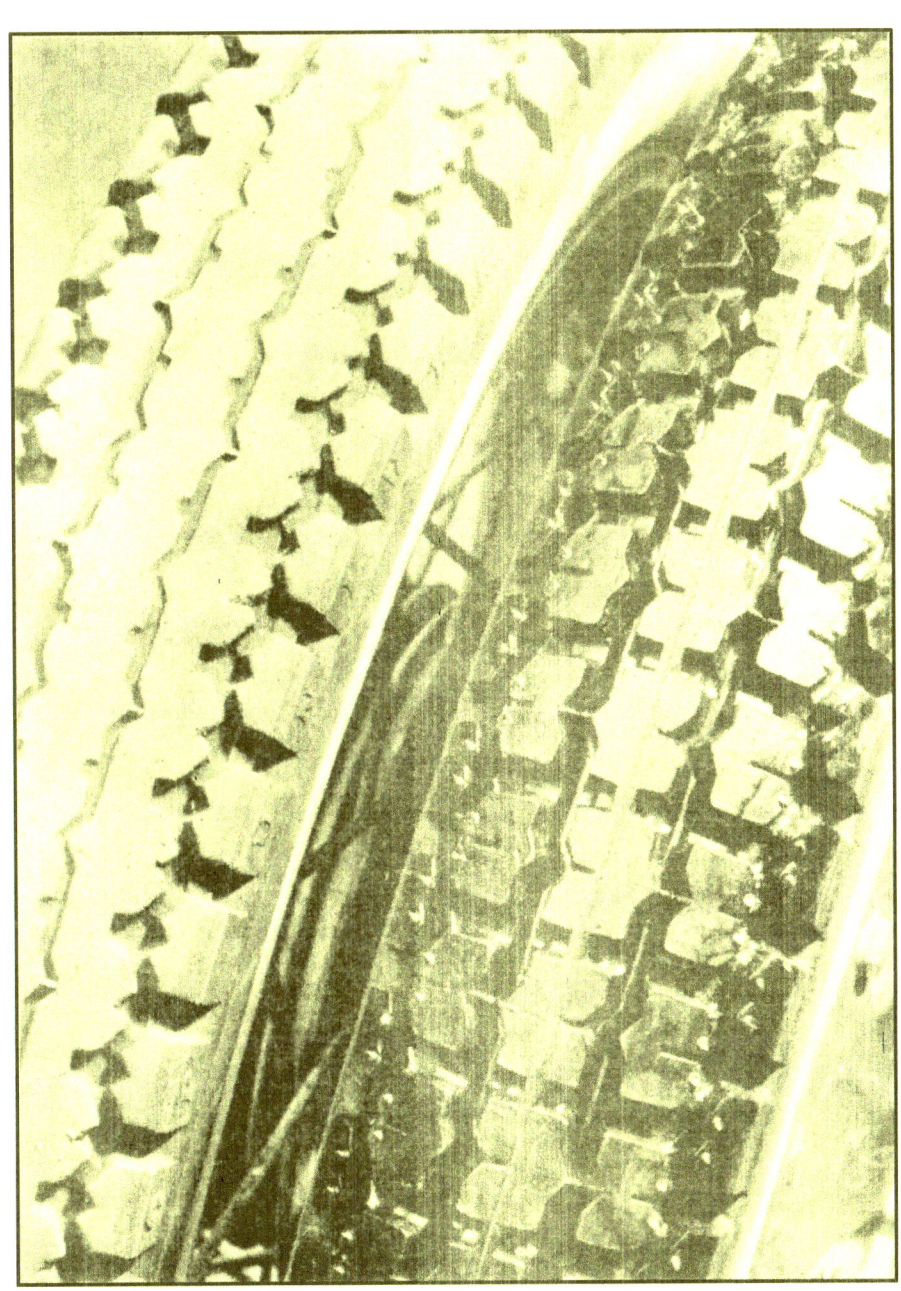

FIG. 92

Note: A new tyre is compared with a worn one, when a tyre becomes worn as shown on the left it should be replaced.

if necessary. *Note:* Always check tyre pressures cold, i.e. before, *not* after, a run. Any serious variation would effect the steering of the motor cycle and cause rapid wear of the tyre and inner tube. When checking the tyres always inspect the outer cover tread and remove any stones, etc., or they will damage the outer cover and puncture the inner tube. Keep the tyre and spokes free from oil and grease; remove any oil or grease with a cloth and a little carbontetrachloride. Never allow a tyre to wear to the extent that the fabric interior is showing through the rubber; this can be extremely dangerous. After many thousands of miles have been covered the tyre will begin to wear smooth (see Fig. 92), and a new outer cover should then be fitted. It is false economy and dangerous to continue using worn tyres.

The tyre pressure is related to the load being carried by the wheel. The recommended inflation pressures are based on a rider's weight of 176 lbs., and allowing for a full tank of fuel. For a rider exceeding 176 lbs., increase the tyre pressure by 1 lb. for every 28 lb. increase in weight above 176 lbs. If additional load is carried in the form of a pillion passenger or luggage, the actual load bearing upon each tyre should be determined and the pressures increased in accordance with the following load and pressure scale:

Inflation pressures = lbs. per square inch:
16   18   20   24   28   32

Load per tyre = lbs.:
190   215   245   295   350   400

The load upon each tyre can be found by placing each wheel in turn on a weighbridge, the weights being taken with the rider seated on the machine. Always check tyre pressures cold, i.e. before, not after, a run.

REAR WHEEL—LEADER AND ARROW

TO REMOVE REAR WHEEL—LEADER

The rear wheel is quickly detachable and can be removed without disturbing the rear chaincase, driving chain or sprocket; the rear portion or tail of the machine hinges upward for easy wheel removal.

With the machine on the centre stand, commence by loosening the acorn nuts at the silencer end bracket (see Fig. 94), these nuts only require unscrewing a few turns sufficient to free the silencers from the bracket. Next loosen the two large chrome plated pivot bolts, which are situated at the forward end of the tail portion (see Fig. 95), there being one each side. Here again these bolts need unscrewing only a few turns, sufficient to allow the sides of the tail portion to open and clear the sides and the body of the machine and the knob of the lifting handle as the tail portion is pivoted up. But before the tail portion can be moved, there are two wing nuts underneath which secure it to the end of the body, and these nuts, which are accessible through the cavity behind the tool tray, must be removed (see Fig. 96). Do not use pliers to remove these nuts, as there is a danger of breaking the wings off; they should be undone by hand. The tail portion can then be pivoted up.

For machines fitted with panniers, in addition to the foregoing, before the tail portion complete with panniers can be pivoted up, there is a bolt securing a bracket behind the forward bottom end of each pannier which must be loosened a few turns, so that the bolt floats freely in the slot in the bracket; then the tail portion and panniers complete can be pivoted up (see Fig. 97), but while pivoting, it will be necessary to ease the lower front end of the tail portion past the pannier brackets. Whether the machine is fitted with panniers or not, use care when moving the tail portion to avoid damaging the enamel.

The rear wheel is now accessible and on the nearside can be seen the rear chaincase, in which are two large rubber grommets, the rearmost grommet which is directly above the wheel spindle nut must be removed leaving a hole in the chaincase through which can be seen as the wheel is revolved the three nuts which secure the rear hub to the driving sprocket; these nuts must be removed next using a tube spanner (⅝ inch across inside flats) through the grommet hole. It will be found, on attempting to undo these nuts, the wheel will tend to revolve and this can be overcome by kneeling or leaning on the brake pedal while undoing the nuts (see Fig. 98). Take extra care when removing these nuts not to let one fall inside the chaincase. The possibility of this happening can be avoided by greasing the inside of the tube spanner and the grease will tend to make the nut stick in the spanner. Next remove the wheel spindle nut (see Fig. 99).

Then moving to the offside of the machine,

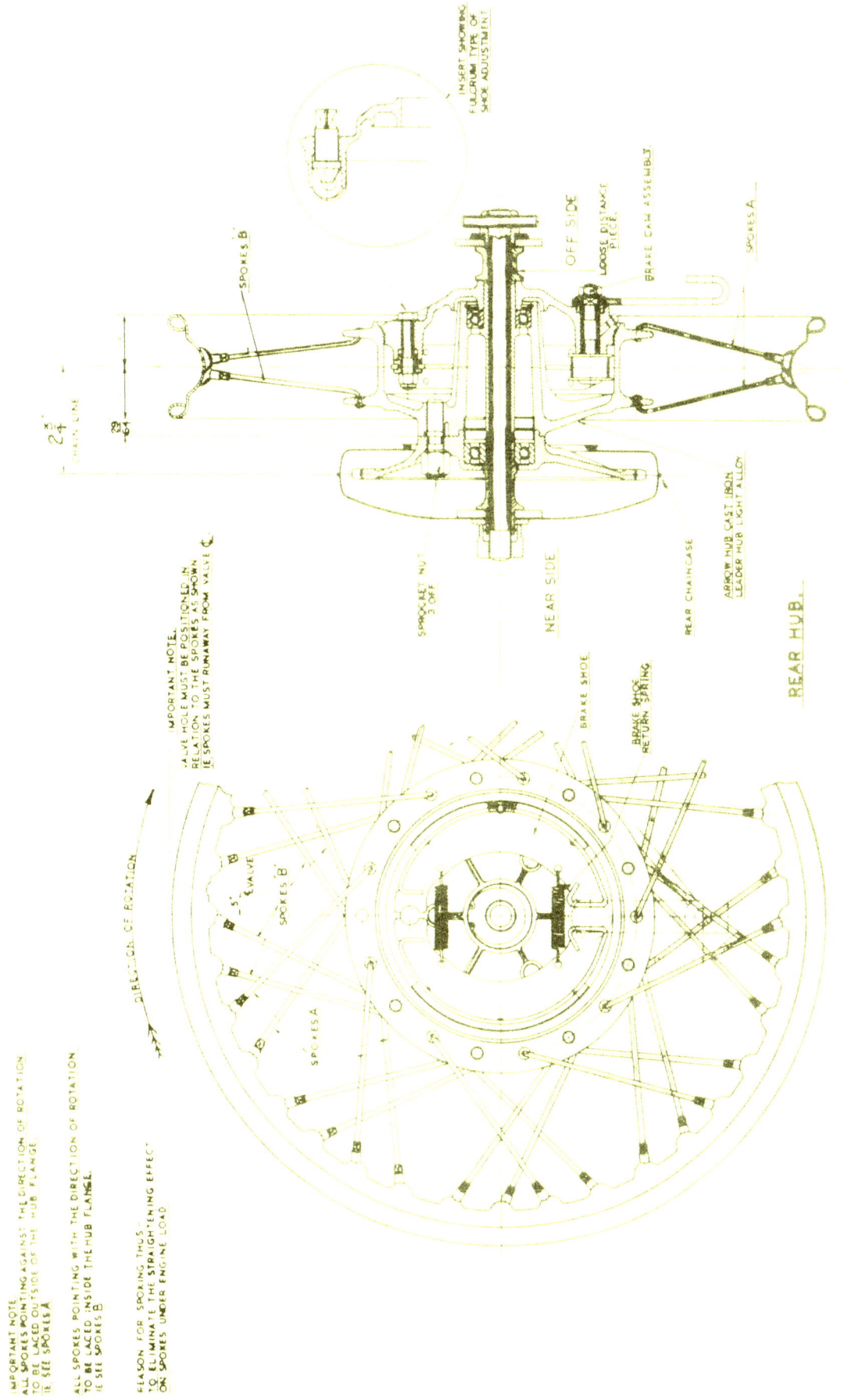

Fig. 93

unscrew the adjuster nut from the brake operating rod (see Fig. 100), and remove the nut which secures the brake torque arm to the brake anchor plate, the torque arm can then be pulled clear of the stud in the brake anchor plate and the brake anchor plate can be revolved clockwise until the brake operating rod is out and clear of the operating arm. The wheel spindle which incorporates the short tommy bar, can now be withdrawn and the spindle distance piece which is fitted between the hub and the offside fork end must be removed (see Fig. 101). The complete wheel can then be moved sideways to the offside disengaging the three hub studs from the driving sprocket. The wheel is then free and can be pulled clear (see Fig. 102).

Fig. 94

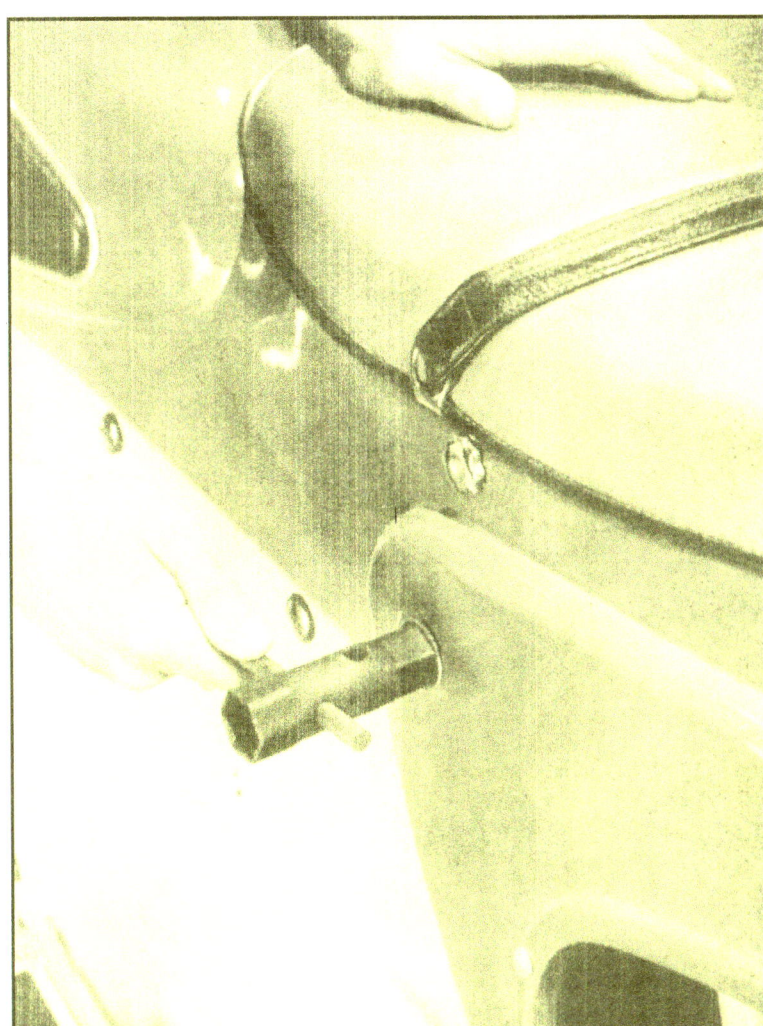

Fig. 95

Fig. 96

101

Fig. 97

Fig. 98

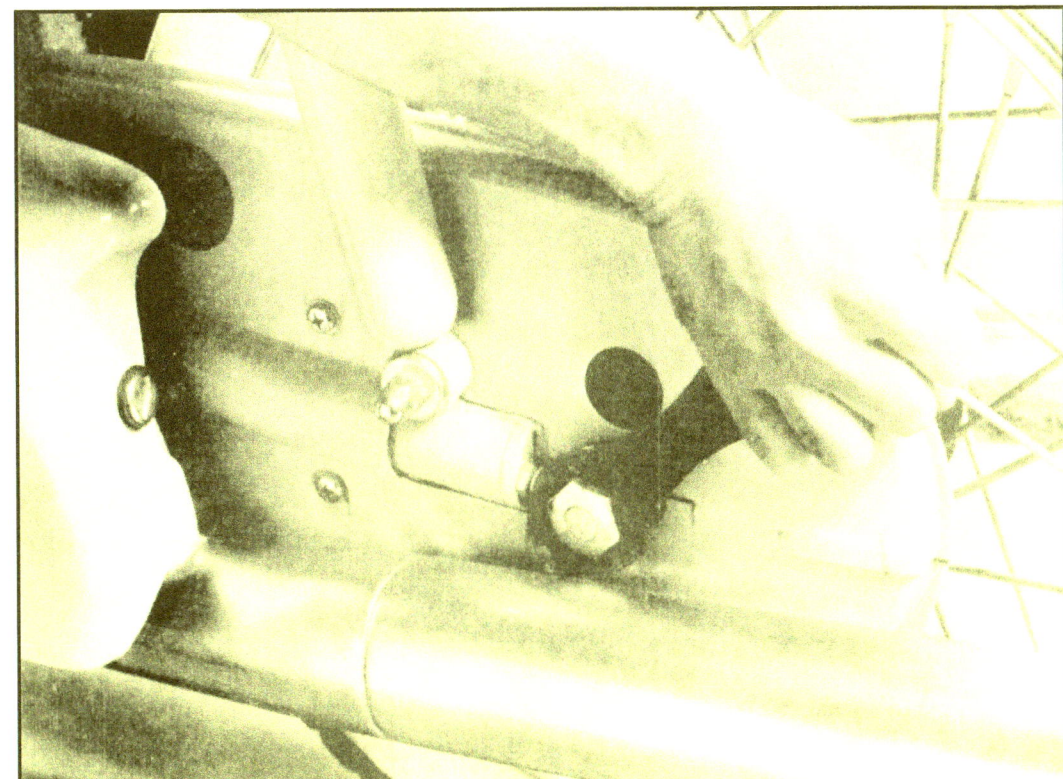

FIG. 99

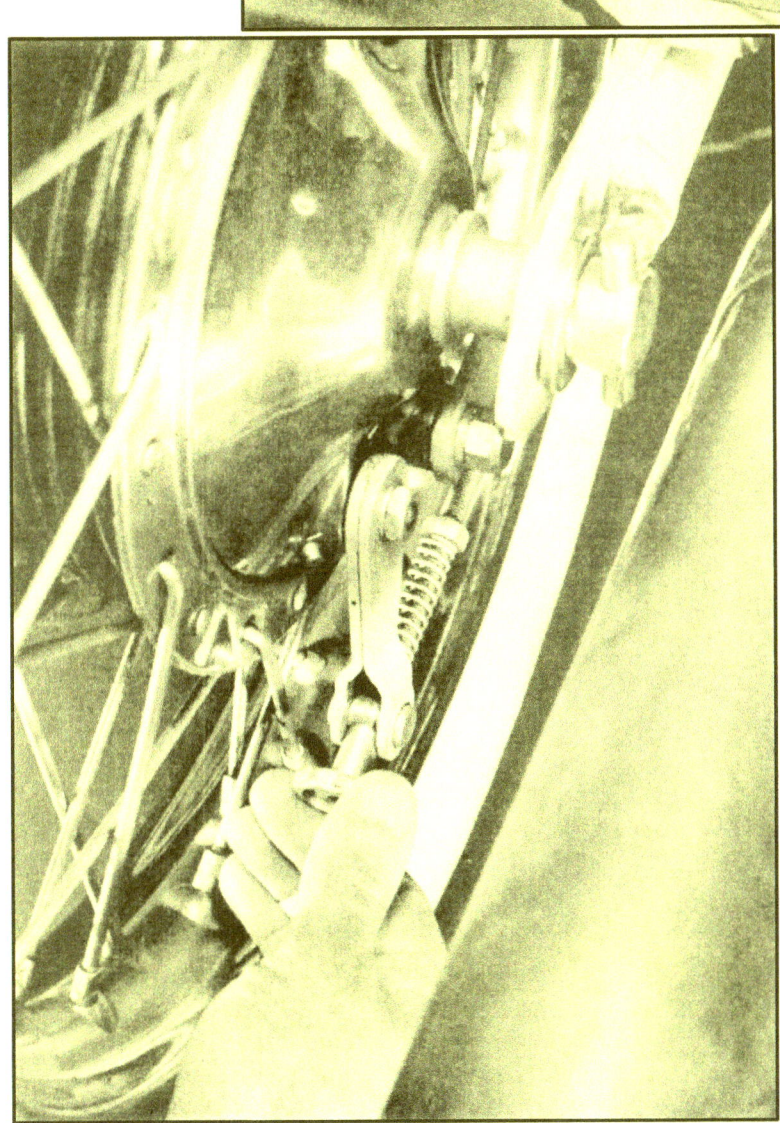

FIG. 100

Fig. 101

Fig. 102

RE-FITTING THE REAR WHEEL—LEADER

Place the wheel between the rear fork ends and carefully locate the three hub studs into the sprocket, then place the wheel spindle distance piece between the hub and the offside fork end, and pass the wheel spindle with a large washer under its head through the offside fork end and the hub (see Fig. 101). Next, through the hole in the rear chaincase, re-fit the three nuts which secure the hub to the driving sprocket and tighten securely (see Fig. 98); replace the rubber grommet in the rear chaincase next, make sure the brake rod spring is in position on the brake rod next to the hexagon nut, then fit the brake rod into the brake operating arm by rotating the brake plate anti-clockwise, and fit the brake adjuster nut to the end of the brake rod (see Fig. 100). Replace the brake torque arm on the stud in the brake anchor plate. The wheel spindle nut is fitted next (see Fig. 99), but first make quite sure that the spindle is correctly located in the offside fork end, when tightening the spindle nut make sure that there is no space between the rear chain adjusters and the spindle to ensure correct wheel alignment, and chain tension. Also, it may be found when tightening the spindle nut, that the spindle will tend to revolve, and this must be prevented as the tommy bar which is incorporated in the offside spindle end may damage the chain adjuster, therefore when tightening the spindle nut, the tommy bar must be held in a vertical position.

Finally adjust the rear brake and fit and securely tighten the washer and special nut, which fixes the torque arm to the brake anchor plate. The tail portion of the machine can then be lowered and the pivot bolts, wing nuts and silencer end nuts re-fitted and tightened. If the machine is fitted with panniers then the two bolts which were loosened behind the panniers must be located in the brackets again and securely tightened.

REMOVAL REAR WHEEL—ARROW

The rear wheel is identical to the Leader, only the instructions for removing and re-fitting varying.

Begin with the motor cycle on the centre stand, then on the nearside is the rear chaincase in which can be seen two large rubber grommets. The rearmost grommet, which is directly above the wheel spindle nut, must be removed leaving a hole in the chaincase through which can be seen, as the wheel is revolved, the three nuts which secure the rear hub to the driving sprocket; these nuts must be removed next using a tube spanner through the hole. It will be found on attempting to undo these nuts that the wheel will tend to revolve; this can be overcome by kneeling or leaning on the brake pedal, whilst undoing the nuts (see Fig. 98). Take extra care when removing these nuts not to let one fall inside the chaincase, the possibility of this happening can be avoided by greasing the inside of the tube spanner, as the grease will tend to make the nut stick inside the spanner. Next remove the wheel spindle nut (see Fig. 99).

Then moving to the offside of the machine, unscrew the adjuster nut from the brake operating rod (see Fig. 100), and remove the nut which secures the brake torque arm to the brake anchor plate, the torque arm can then be pulled clear of the stud in the brake anchor plate, and the anchor plate can be revolved clockwise until the brake operating rod is out and clear of the operating arm. The wheel spindle which incorporates a short tommy bar can now be withdrawn and the spindle distance piece which is fitted between the hub and the offside fork end must be removed (see Fig. 101). The complete wheel can now be moved sideways to the offside, disengaging the three hub studs from the driving sprocket. Then, by leaning the machine over to one side the wheel can be rolled clear between the silencer and tail (see Fig. 103).

RE-FITTING REAR WHEEL—ARROW

Lean the machine over to one side and pass the wheel between the silencer and tail (see Fig. 103), and carefully locate the three hub studs into the sprocket; place the wheel spindle distance piece between the hub and the off-side fork end, and pass the wheel spindle through the off-side fork end (see Fig. 101), the distance piece and the hub. The spindle must have a large

Fig. 103

washer under its head and make sure it locates in the fork end correctly. Next, through the hole in the rear chaincase, fit the three nuts which secure the hub to the driving sprocket and tighten evenly and securely (see Fig. 98), replace the rubber grommet in the rear chaincase. Next make sure the brake rod spring is in position on the brake rod next to the hexagon nut, then fit the brake rod into the operating arm by rotating the brake plate anti-clockwise, and fit the brake adjuster nut to the end of the brake rod (see Fig. 100). Replace the brake torque arm on the stud in the brake anchor plate. The wheel spindle nut is fitted next (see Fig. 99), but first make quite sure that the wheel spindle is located correctly in the offside fork end, then tighten the spindle nut. Note that when the spindle nut is tightened there must be no space between the spindle and the chain adjusters to ensure correct wheel alignment and chain adjustment. Also it may be found when tightening the spindle nut that the spindle will tend to revolve, and this must be prevented as the spindle tommy bar could damage the chain adjuster, therefore when tightening the spindle nut, the tommy bar must be held in a vertical position. Finally, adjust the rear brake and fit and securely tighten the washer and special nut which fixes the brake torque arm to the brake anchor plate. All other details and instructions for the rear wheel are as described for the Leader.

REAR BRAKE ADJUSTMENT—LEADER AND ARROW

As explained when dealing with the front wheel there are two different types of brakes in use, and this also applies to the rear wheel; one type incorporates fulcrum adjusters, whereas the other type does not. For these brakes which incorporate fulcrum adjusters, adjustment of the brake is carried out as follows: Turn the squared end of the adjuster clockwise until the brake lining is just rubbing the drum, then turn the adjuster anti-clockwise at least five clicks. Final brake adjustment is then made by the nut on the extreme end of the brake operating rod. For brakes which do not incorporate fulcrum adjusters, the methods of adjusting the rear brake is to adjust the nut on the extreme end of the brake rod, until the wheel cannot be revolved, then re-adjust in the opposite direction, a little at a time and checking until it is just possible to rotate the wheel freely.

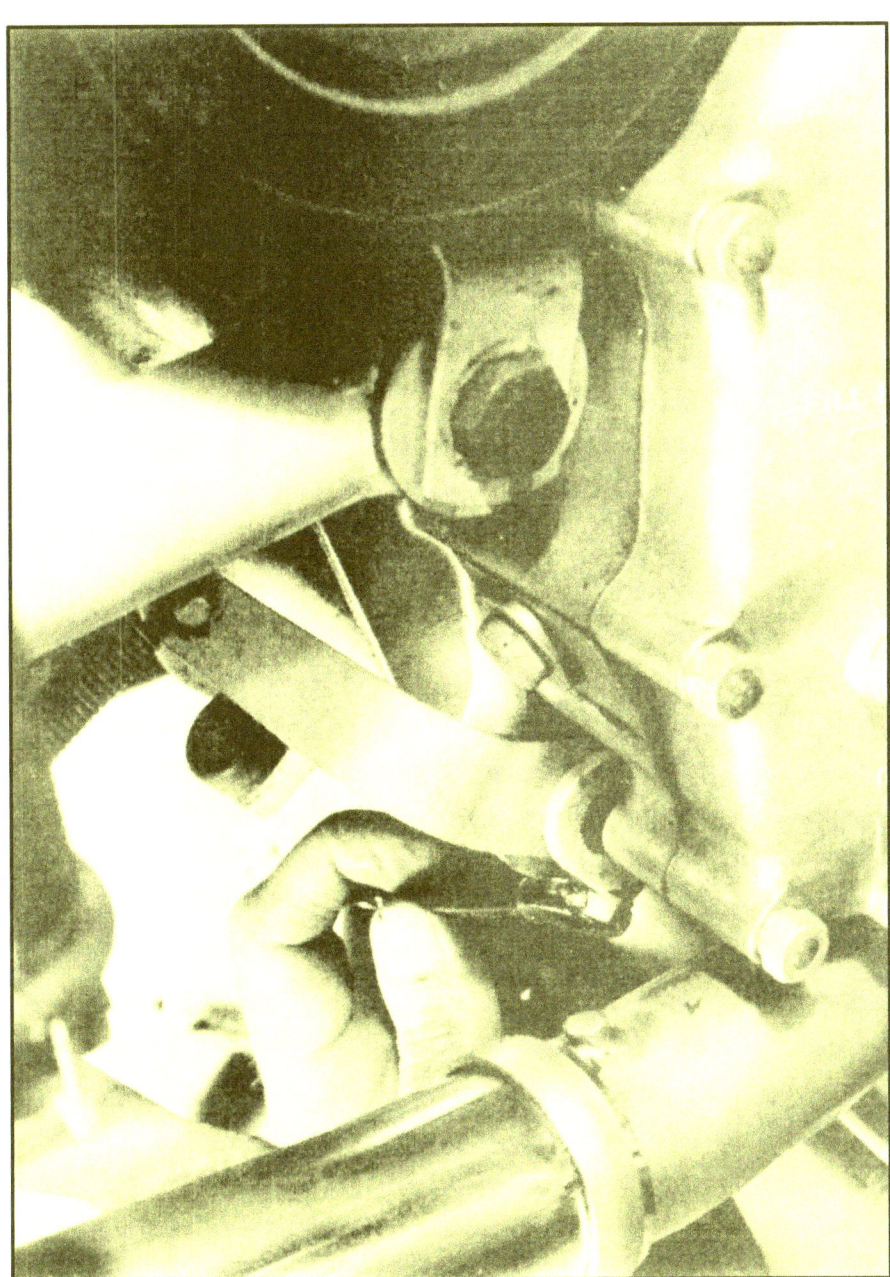

Fig. 104

THE REAR BRAKE PEDAL—LEADER AND ARROW

The brake pedal position is adjustable to suit individual riders. A stop pin is incorporated in the brake pedal and this controls the position of the brake pedal in relation to the footrest. By slackening off the brake adjustment and loosening the pedal stop pin lock nut and screwing the stop pin up or down, the brake pedal can be positioned as required; the lock nut should then be re-tightened. The actual brake adjustment must then be made by the knurled nut on the end of the brake rod.

In unit with the brake pedal is a cross shaft which passes through the engine casting to the opposite side of the machine. The brake rod operating lever is located by serrations to this shaft, with a pinch bolt and nut securing the operating lever to this serrated shaft, and further adjustment of the brake pedal is possible by loosening the pinch bolt and removing the operating lever and re-fitting it in a different position on the serrated shaft. If this operating lever is moved, make quite certain that it does not foul the gear box casting or any part of the machine when the brake pedal is operated. Then tighten the pinch bolt and adjust the brake pedal stop pin and the rear brake.

A grease nipple is fitted to the brake pedal, and this is provided to lubricate the brake cross shaft and central stand pivot and should be greased every 1,000 miles.

To remove the brake pedal loosen the pinch bolt and remove the brake rod operating lever from the splined cross shaft (see Fig. 104). The brake pedal with its integral cross shaft can then be withdrawn from the nearside (see Fig. 105). On re-assembling, clean the cross shaft and re-grease liberally. Also make sure the brake rod operating lever is securely tightened with the pinch bolt and nut.

Note: In the event of any fierceness developing in the brake, this can usually be traced to brake lining dust collecting in the drum, the remedy is to remove the brake assembly, and clean out all dust, etc. In the event of the linings being worn down to almost the rivet heads, exchange shoes and linings should be fitted.

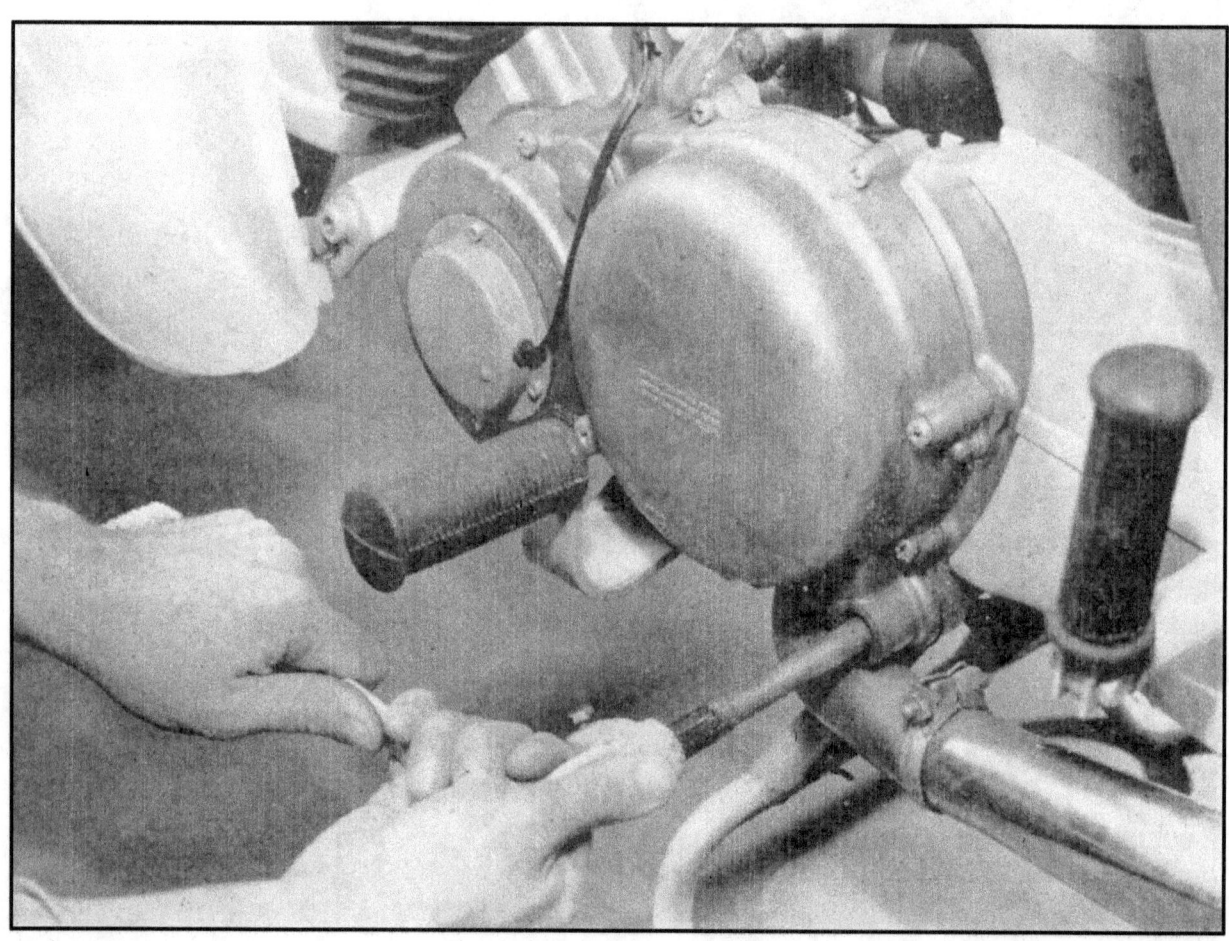

Fig. 105

REAR WHEEL MAINTENANCE AND LUBRICATION—LEADER AND ARROW

The hub and sprocket assembly is mounted on two journal ball bearings which are grease packed during assembly. The bearings are not adjustable, and when adequately lubricated are trouble free. Every ten thousand miles remove as much of the old grease as possible and insert fresh grease of the recommended grade. There is a grease nipple set in the brake anchor plate close to the brake operating arm; this is provided to lubricate the brake cam spindle. Give only one stroke of the grease gun at one thousand mile intervals, as an excessive supply of grease might reach the brake linings.

Whenever the rear wheel is removed, the brake anchor plate should be removed and the brake linings inspected for wear, do not allow brake lining wear to reach a stage where a lining securing rivet could score the drum, or irreparable damage could be done (see Fig. 79).

The brake anchor plate is easily removed as it is not attached to the hub and simply pulls out, although in the case of a brake which incorporates the fulcrum type of adjuster, it may be necessary to screw the adjuster out a little in order to slacken it, and thereby give more clearance between the linings and the drum. If, however, the brake anchor plate will not pull out of the hub easily this is due to it binding on the hub bearing sleeve on which it is mounted, and the best method of removal in this case is to place the wheel on a bench and hold it at an angle of 45 degrees to the bench with the brake anchor plate facing the bench, then gentle tapping around the hub flange surrounding the brake anchor plate with the handle of a mallet will cause the brake anchor plate to fall clear (see Fig. 106).

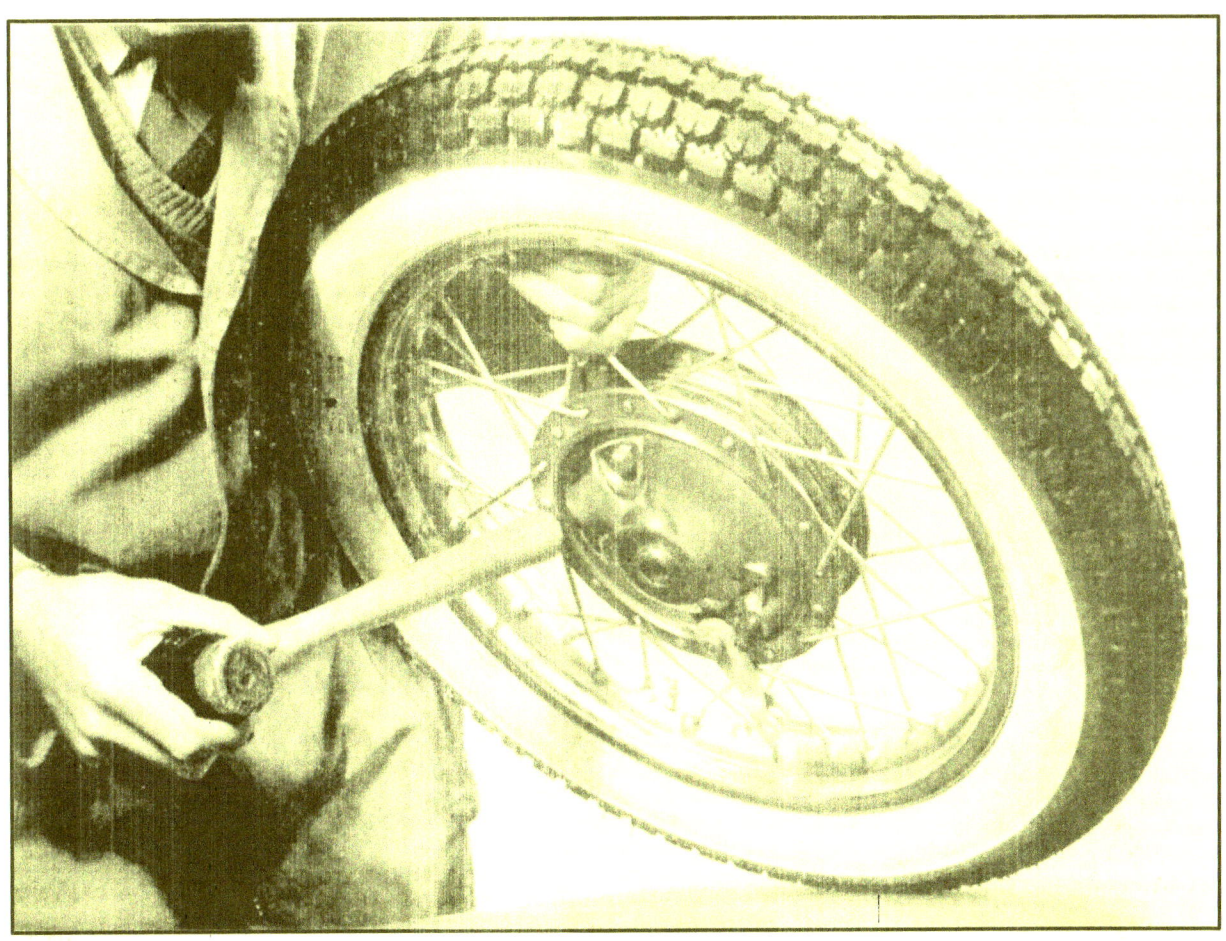

Fig. 106

BRAKE ANCHOR PLATE

The rear brake anchor plate assembly is very similar to the front and the method of dismantling follows closely to that for the front brake.

In addition to the two types of brakes already described, minor detail modifications have been introduced from time to time, and the following instructions cover all variations, therefore extra care should be taken to identify the type of brake being dealt with.

When dismantling the brake anchor plate, the main point is removing and refitting the brake shoes, and if the brake shoes are removed for any purpose other than fitting new linings, it is essential that they are replaced on the same side of the brake plate to which they were originally fitted, if this is not done, an inefficient or grabbing brake will ensue. Before removing the shoes a scratch mark may be made on one shoe and on the brake plate for identification purposes, to avoid incorrect re-assembly. *Note:* brakes fitted with fulcrum adjusters should have the adjuster screwed out when this will facilitate brake shoe removal. Also some brakes have special springs fitted from the brake shoe webs to a rib on the brake anchor plate, these springs are to prevent "brake squeal" and it is necessary to disconnect them before the brake shoes can be removed. The best method when removing the shoes, is to leave the shoe springs in place and take a firm grip with one hand on one of the shoes, then with other hand pull the other shoe away from the cam and pivot sufficiently to enable the shoe to be lifted up and clear (see Fig. 80). Both shoes will then be free.

When re-fitting the brake shoes, assemble the two springs to the shoes and hold both shoes as near in position as possible on the brake cam and the brake pivot, then press both shoes down evenly when they will snap into place (see Fig. 81), but afterwards check very carefully to make quite certain that both shoes are correctly located on the cam and pivot by operating the brake lever. If the brake shoes were fitted with the additional springs to prevent "squeal" these springs should now be re-fitted.

The brake cam is removed by taking off the nut, spring washer and operating arm from the outside of the brake anchor plate; the cam can then be tapped through and removed. Note the felt washer which is fitted between the operating

FULCRUM TYPE FIG. 107 **NON FULCRUM TYPE**

arm and the brake anchor plate; this must be in good condition and should be semi-stiff, as it is impregnated with tallow. If this washer is damaged or has deteriorated in any way, it should be replaced.

The brake shoe pivot is fitted to the brake anchor plate, diametrically opposite to the cam, and is removed by undoing the self-locking nut and taking out the bolt.

As already mentioned in the paragraph on Brake Adjustment, there are two different types of brake in use, and in place of the pivot already mentioned the other type of brake has the fulcrum adjuster (see Figs. 107 and 82), and to take this adjuster apart the two wedges can be pulled out of the casting whilst the square end of the adjuster is merely screwed right in to remove it.

Some brakes are fitted with a cam which incorporates a stop plate and spring to assist return of the cam after the brake has been operated. This plate and spring has since been deleted, and the new cam without the plate and spring is interchangeable.

Whenever the brake anchor plate is dismantled, all parts should be thoroughly cleaned, and the brake cam and spindle along with the pivot lightly greased before re-assembly. If the brake is fitted with a fulcrum adjuster, then the wedges and thread of the adjuster should be lightly greased.

The greatest care should be taken at all times to avoid getting even the slightest trace of oil or grease on the brake linings. The lining surfaces must be kept free from dirt and grease and be cleaned by washing the shoes in clean petrol, not petrol oil mixture, and after drying, the lining surfaces only may be wiped with carbontetrachloride, which can be purchased from most chemists.

When the brake linings are worn down nearly to the rivet heads (see Fig. 79), they must be replaced, and an exchange service is available, whereby brake shoes with worn linings can be exchanged for shoes fitted with new linings ready to assemble to the brake anchor plate. It is strongly recommended that exchange shoes are fitted as relining brake shoes by hand is not always satisfactory.

The leading edges of the brake linings should not be chamfered, as dust which develops from lining wear could find its way to the lining surfaces.

As mentioned previously, there are two types of brake. The brake with fulcrum adjusters has light alloy shoes, whereas the brake without the fulcrum adjusters has steel shoes. The steel and the alloy shoes vary considerably in design and are not interchangeable (see Fig. 84). Therefore when obtaining exchange or replacement brake shoes, make certain that the shoes obtained are the same type as those originally fitted.

REAR WHEEL DRIVING SPROCKET AND CHAINCASE— LEADER AND ARROW

To remove the Sprocket Assembly

The rear wheel driving sprocket is enclosed in the rear chaincase and the rear wheel must first be removed as already described, before the sprocket assembly can be removed.

The rear chaincase must be removed; commence by loosening a few turns the acorn nut which secures the bottom of the nearside rear hydraulic unit, then remove the four Phillips head screws which secure the rear chaincase to the nearside rear fork arm, and note that the screws are secured by nuts and washers behind the chaincase.

The chaincase is formed in two halves and is joined horizontally and can now be parted and removed (see Fig. 108), leaving the sprocket assembly fully exposed, and as can now be seen, the sprocket assembly is mounted on a hollow sleeve and held in the nearside fork end by a circlip fitted to the nearside end of the hollow sleeve. This circlip must be removed and this can be done with the blade of a screwdriver (see Fig. 109). The sleeve complete with the sprocket can then be taken out of the fork arm and detached from the rear chain.

No gasket or joint washer is fitted between the two halves of the rear chaincase, and when fitted together, they overlap. Oil is supplied automatically from the primary chaincase, and additional supplies of oil must not be added to the rear chaincase. If the chain appears to be dry, check the zerk plug and felt wick as described on page 25.

When re-assembling, loop the rear chain over the sprocket before fitting the sprocket in the nearside fork arm. The large washer must be placed on the near side end of the hollow sleeve before the circlip is fitted, and be quite certain that the circlip is in good order before fitting, if in any doubt the circlip should be renewed. The remainder of the re-assembling is straightforward, but do not forget to re-tighten the acorn nut securing the nearside hydraulic unit.

Never continue using a chain sprocket which is badly worn or has hooked teeth (see Fig. 110). If the rear chain is kept adjusted and lubricated correctly, the driving sprocket and chain will give good service, but when a chain or a sprocket is badly worn, it should be replaced. *Note:* Never fit a worn chain on a new sprocket.

Fig. 108

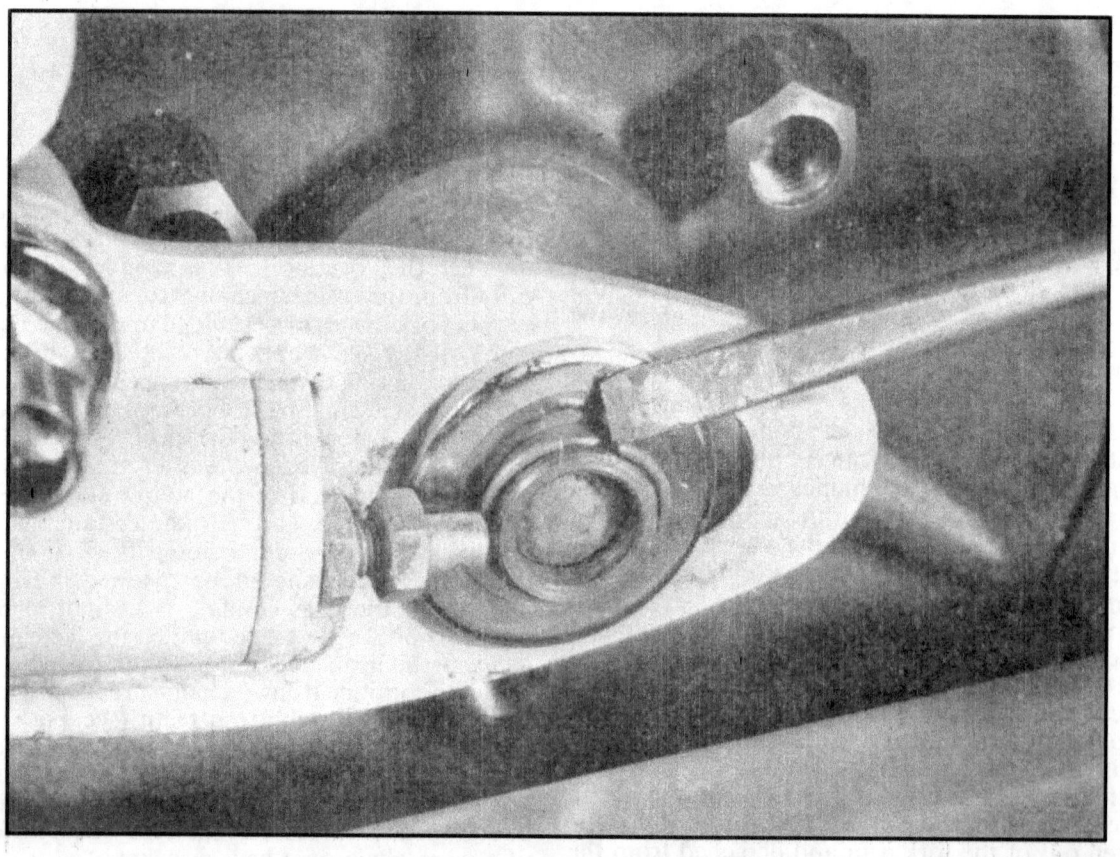

Fig. 109. (*See note on page 117 regarding circlips*)

Fig. 110

A sprocket should never be allowed to become worn or damaged as shown compared with a new one.

RENEWING REAR WHEEL BEARINGS—LEADER AND ARROW

To remove worn bearings and fit new ones in the rear wheel, the following service tools are required:

43587S.	Drift.
43588S.	Collar.
43573S.	Spindle.
43585S.	Tommy bar.
43576S.	Bearing locating sleeve.
43580S.	Locating washer "B".
43577S.	Locating washer "A".
43582S.	Collar.
43584S.	Spacer.

There are two bearings to be removed, one bearing is mounted in the offside of the rear hub, and the other is mounted in the driving sprocket.

Commence with the rear hub by taking out the large circlip from the offside, using a pair of circlip pliers. Next remove the grease retaining plates, and note there is a plain plate in the offside which is easily removed, while in the nearside of the hub is a cupped plate, which must be removed in the following way, using the drift (43587S) carefully locate on the hollow bearing distance piece which protrudes through the bearing, then using a mallet in conjunction with the drift tap the distance piece through the bearing and continue tapping the drift through the bearing until the bearing distance piece and the nearside grease retaining cup are both out of the hub. This will then leave only the bearing in the hub, and to remove the bearing, pass the collar (43588S) through the nearside of the hub and locate it in the bearing, then pass the drift (43587S) through the nearside of the hub and locate it in the collar, next use the mallet in conjunction with the drift as previously and knock the worn bearing out of the hub (see Fig. 111).

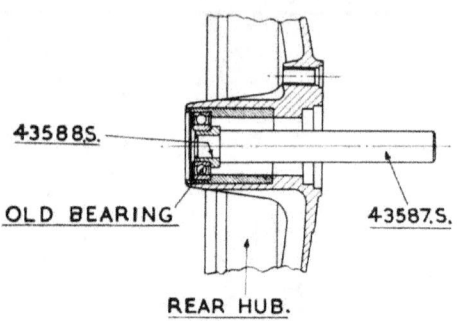

EXTRACTING REAR HUB BEARINGS.

Fig. 111

Before fitting the new bearing thoroughly clean out the hub and smear the inside with clean grease to assist fitting the bearing. The new bearing *must* be packed with grease of the recommended grade. Then commence by fitting collar (43582S) on the spindle (43573S) and pass the spindle through the hub from the nearside. Next fit locating washer "B" (43580S) on to the bearing locating sleeve (43576S) then place the new hub bearing locating sleeve next to locating washer "B". The sleeve which has an internal thread is then fitted on the spindle which protrudes through the offside of the hub (see Fig. 112), next pass the tommy bar (43585S) through the lug of the spindle, and commence turning, but at the same

Fig. 112

time making sure that the locating sleeve with the bearing on it does not revolve. Make certain that the bearing enters the hub, true and square (see Fig. 113), and continue turning the spindle until the bearing is correctly located in the hub, then unscrew and take out the service tool. Re-fit the grease retaining cup, hollow bearing distance piece, plate and the circlip; if either of the grease retainers or the circlip are damaged in any way they should be replaced.

Having completed the work on the hub, the bearing in the driving sprocket can now be dealt with. Commence by removing the grease retaining cup from the sprocket, the cup can easily be prised out (see Fig. 114). It will then be seen that the hollow sleeve which passes through the sprocket bearing is retained by a small circlip on the spindle next to the bearing. Remove the circlip with the aid of a screwdriver (see note on page 117) and tap the sleeve through the bearing with the drift and mallet. This will leave only the bearing in the sprocket and to remove it locate the collar (43588S) in the nearside of the bearing, that is through the small hole in the centre of the sprocket. Then locate the drift (43587S) in the

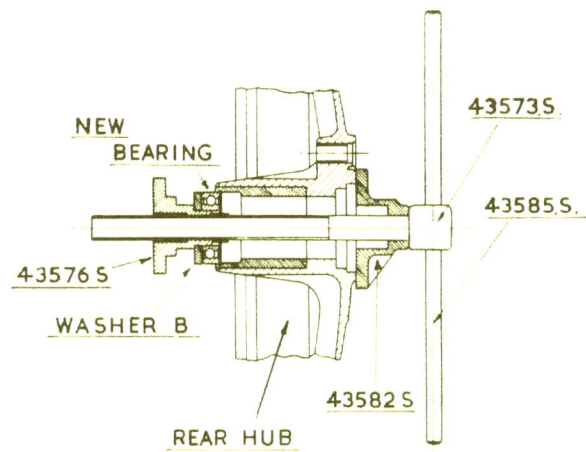

FITTING REAR HUB BEARING

FIG. 113

collar and using a mallet in conjunction with the drift, knock the bearing out (see Figs. 115 and 116).

FIG. 114

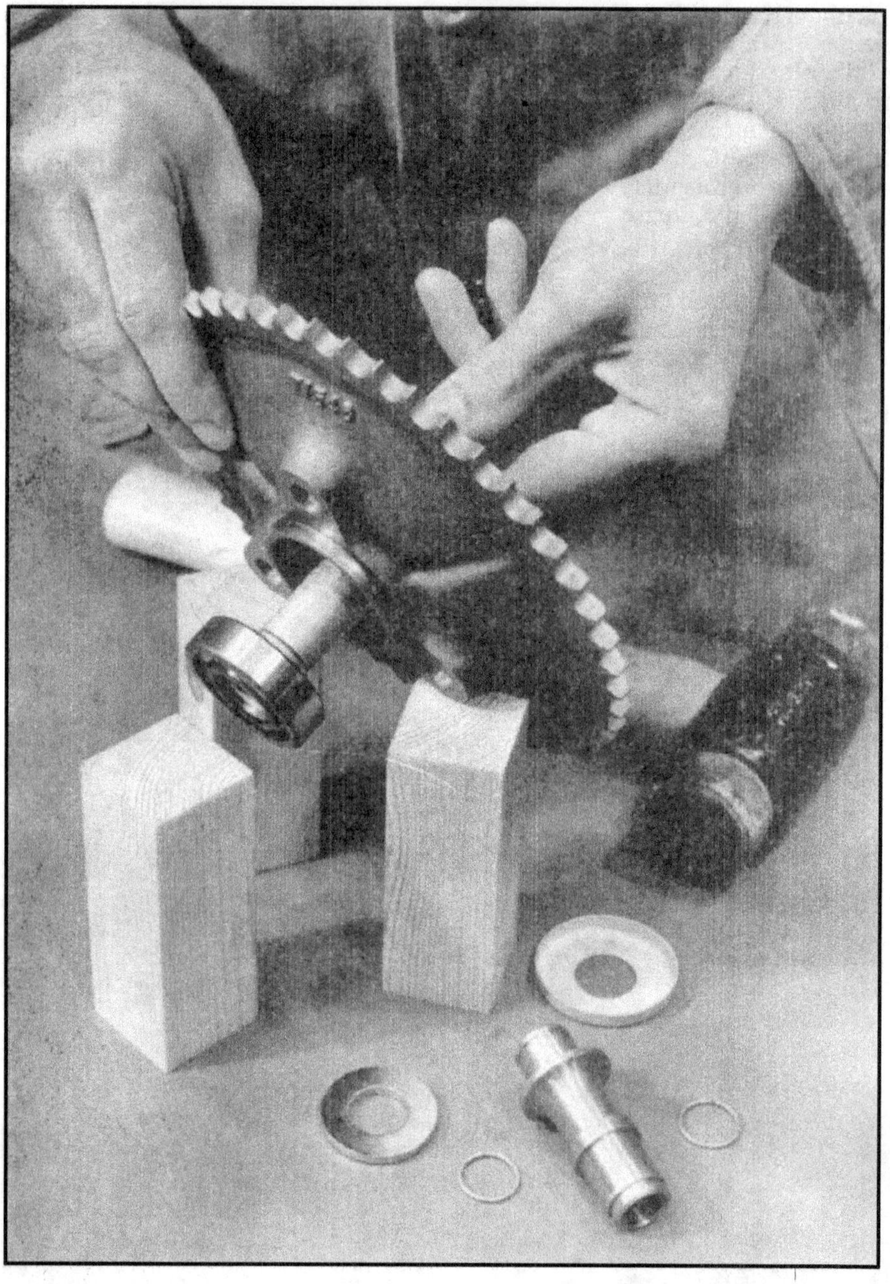

FIG. 151

Before fitting the new bearing, the sprocket should be thoroughly cleaned and checked to make sure the teeth are in good condition (see Fig. 110), if the sprocket is worn this is a good time to replace it, while the assembly is dismantled.

When fitting a bearing in the sprocket commence by smearing the inside of the bearing housing in the sprocket, with clean grease to assist fitting. The new bearing should then be packed with fresh grease of the recommended grade. Next fit the space (43584S) on the spindle (43573S) then fit the locating washer "A" (43577S) on the spindle next to the spacer and pass the spindle through the small hole in the centre of the sprocket from the concave side.

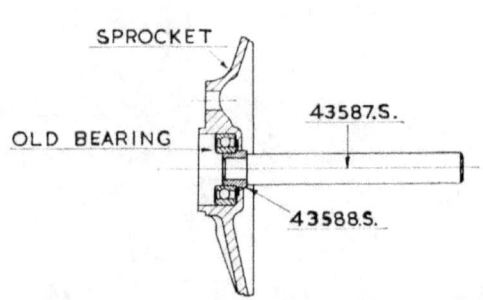

EXTRACTING REAR SPROCKET BEARING

FIG. 116

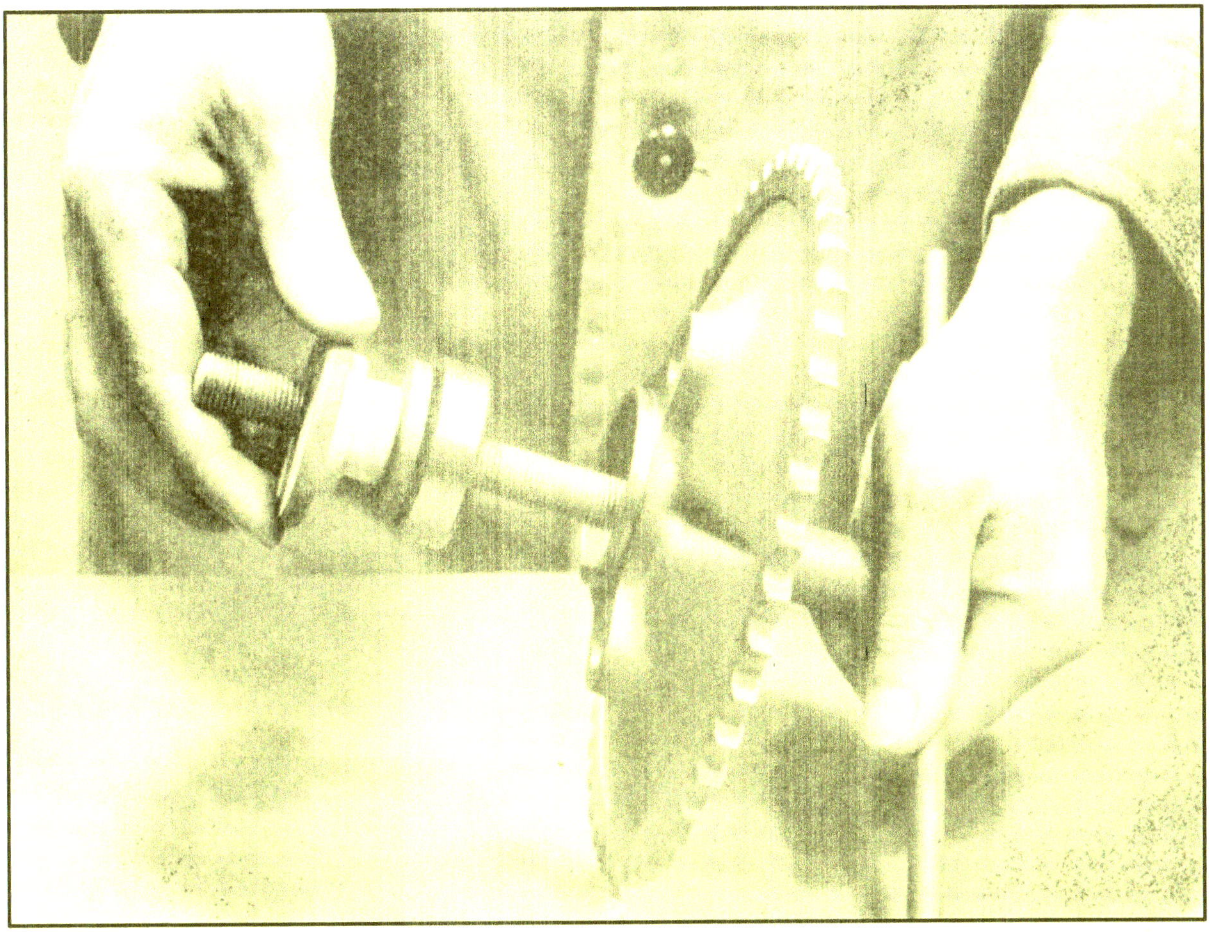

Fig. 117

Next, fit locating washer "B" (43580S) on the bearing locating sleeve (43576S) the new bearing is then placed on the locating sleeve next to the locating washer "B". The sleeve, which has an internal thread is then fitted on the spindle which protrudes through the convex side of the sprocket (see Fig. 117), next pass the tommy bar (43585S) through the spindle and commence turning, but at the same time making sure that the locating sleeve with the bearing does not revolve. Make certain that the bearing enters the sprocket hub true and square and continue turning the spindle until the bearing is correctly located in the sprocket (see Fig. 118), then unscrew and take out the service tool. Re-fit the hollow sleeve, the spindle circlip and the grease retaining cup. If either the circlip or grease retaining plate is damaged in any way, they should be replaced. The two sleeve circlips are identical and therefore interchangeable.

Removal and Re-fitting of Hollow Sleeve Circlips

Use a thin bladed screwdriver and hook it under one end of the circlip. Then prise the circlip end up and over the edge of its groove. It will then peel off easily. When re-fitting the circlip, hold one end securely into the bottom of its groove. Then with a screwdriver or similar tool, feed the rest of the circlip over the end of the hollow spindle. It will then slide down easily and click into position.

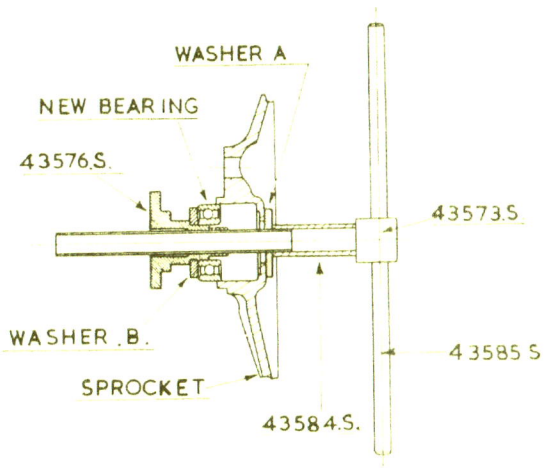

FITTING REAR SPROCKET BEARING

Fig. 118

REAR CHAIN ADJUSTMENT—LEADER AND ARROW

The rear chain is completely enclosed within the rear chaincase and is automatically lubricated, and this enables a large mileage to be covered without constant need for attention.

The chain tension should be checked at approximately every thousand miles although it will be found that most probably adjustment will only be necessary every three to four thousand miles.

When checking the chain, put the machine on the centre stand and remove the forwardmost of the two large rubber grommets in the rear chaincase. The rear chain can then be seen through the grommet hole (see Fig. 119), and the tension can be checked by moving the chain up and down with one forefinger and the total movement must be $1\frac{1}{4}$ inch to $1\frac{1}{2}$ inch. The rear wheel should be revolved and the chain checked in a number of places, as the chain wear may be uneven and the position where the chain is tightest, i.e. with the least amount of up and down movement, is where the tension must be checked and adjusted if necessary.

The correct chain tension is most important, as a tight chain would cause rapid wear of the

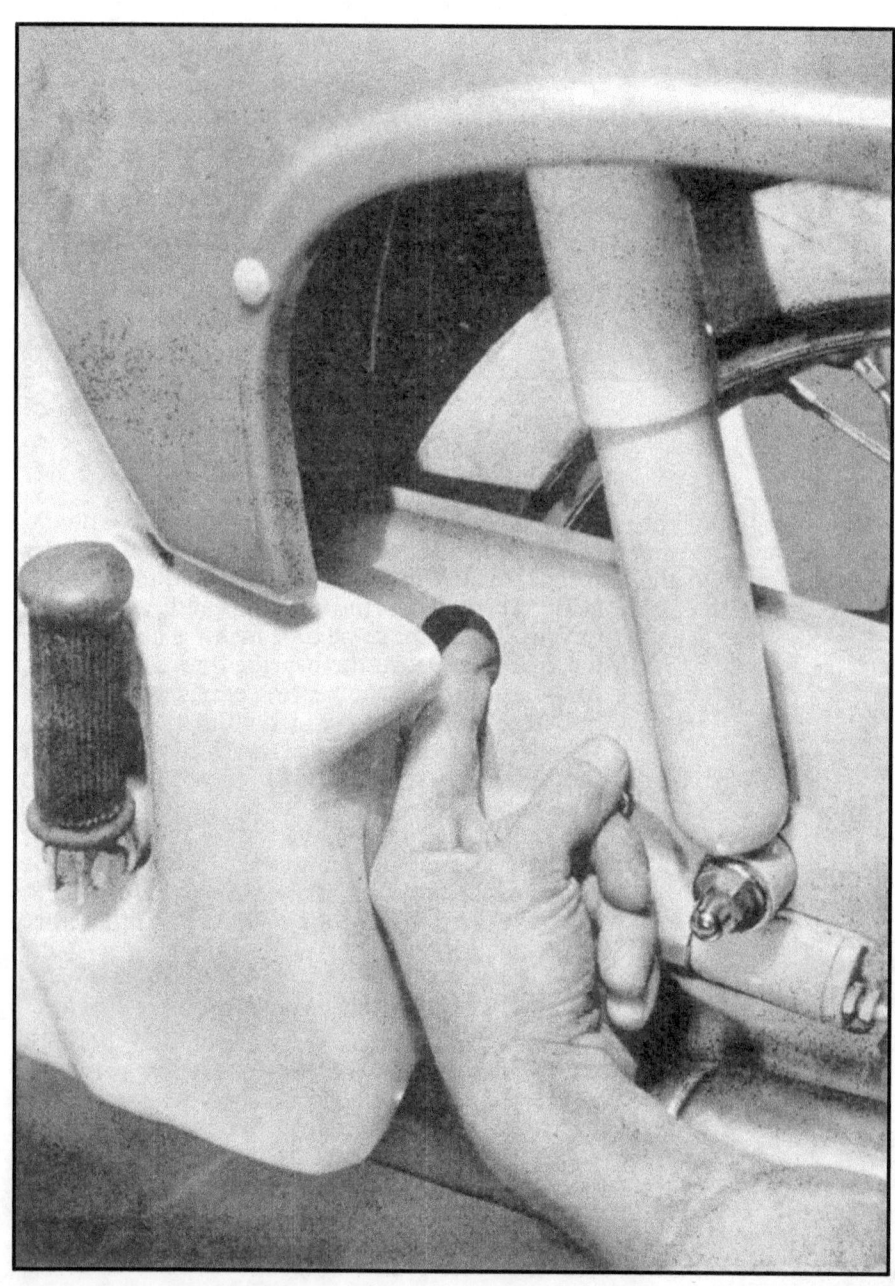

Fig. 119

chain and sprockets, whereas a slack chain would not only damage the chain and sprockets, but could also jump off the sprockets.

To adjust the rear chain, proceed as follows: Loosen the rear wheel spindle nut a few turns; also loosen the special nut which secures the rear brake torque arm to the brake anchor plate. The wheel will then be semi-free within the rear fork, and to take up excessive slack in the chain, the wheel must be moved rearwards until the chain tension is correct at the tightest point. Then the wheel must be secured in the new position.

To move the wheel there are adjusters provided in the rear end of both rear fork arms, these adjusters screw in or out of the fork arms, and at the same time bear against the wheel spindle. Therefore to move the wheel rearwards slacken the locknut which is situated on each adjuster against the fork end. This will free the adjusters which can then be turned so that they screw out, pushing the wheel rearward (see Fig. 120). Both adjusters should be turned the same amount until the chain tension has the correct $1\frac{1}{4}$ inch to $1\frac{1}{2}$ inch up and down movement. At this point the wheel alignment should be checked and corrected if necessary. (See separate paragraph on wheel alignment.) Then tighten the adjuster lock nuts against the end of the fork arm, but make sure the adjuster itself does not move. Next tighten the wheel spindle nut keeping the spindle tommy bar

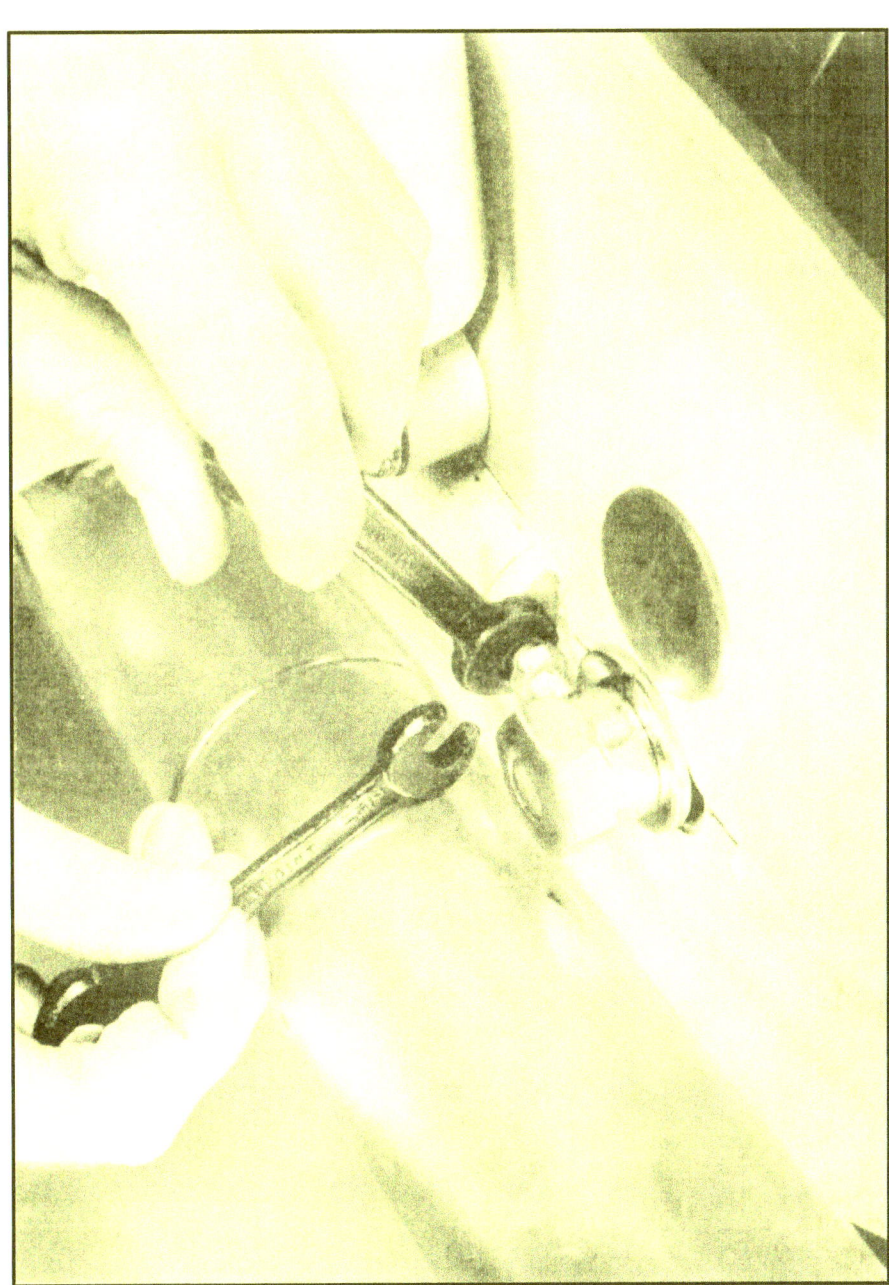

Fig. 120

vertical. Finally securely tighten the special nut which holds the brake torque arm to the brake anchor plate.

It may be that moving the wheel has altered the rear brake adjustment, and this should be checked and re-adjusted if necessary. A chain will not last indefinitely, and when all the adjustment has been utilised, the wheel spindle will be at the extreme end of the slots in the rear fork. Then the rear chain will be badly worn, and should be replaced. If, however, in an emergency only, the chain is suitable for further service, but no more adjustment is available, the chain will have to be shortened by removing one link or removing two links and fitting a cranked link. Any time the rear chain is removed, always, when re-assembling, re-fit the spring clip to the connecting link the correct way. That is, the closed end must face the same direction that the chain moves when driving.

REAR CHAIN

The rear chain transmits the power from the gear box to the rear wheel and is the orthodox roller type of driving chain. A new rear chain has 113 links ½ inch pitch by .305 inch wide.

To remove the rear chain from the motor cycle dismantle the rear chaincase (see paragraph on page 111) and revolve the rear wheel in order to find the split link which joins the chain. The split link is easily recognised as it has a horseshoe-shaped securing clip visible on the side. Remove the clip with a pair of suitable pliers, by pressing with one of the plier jaws on the open end of the

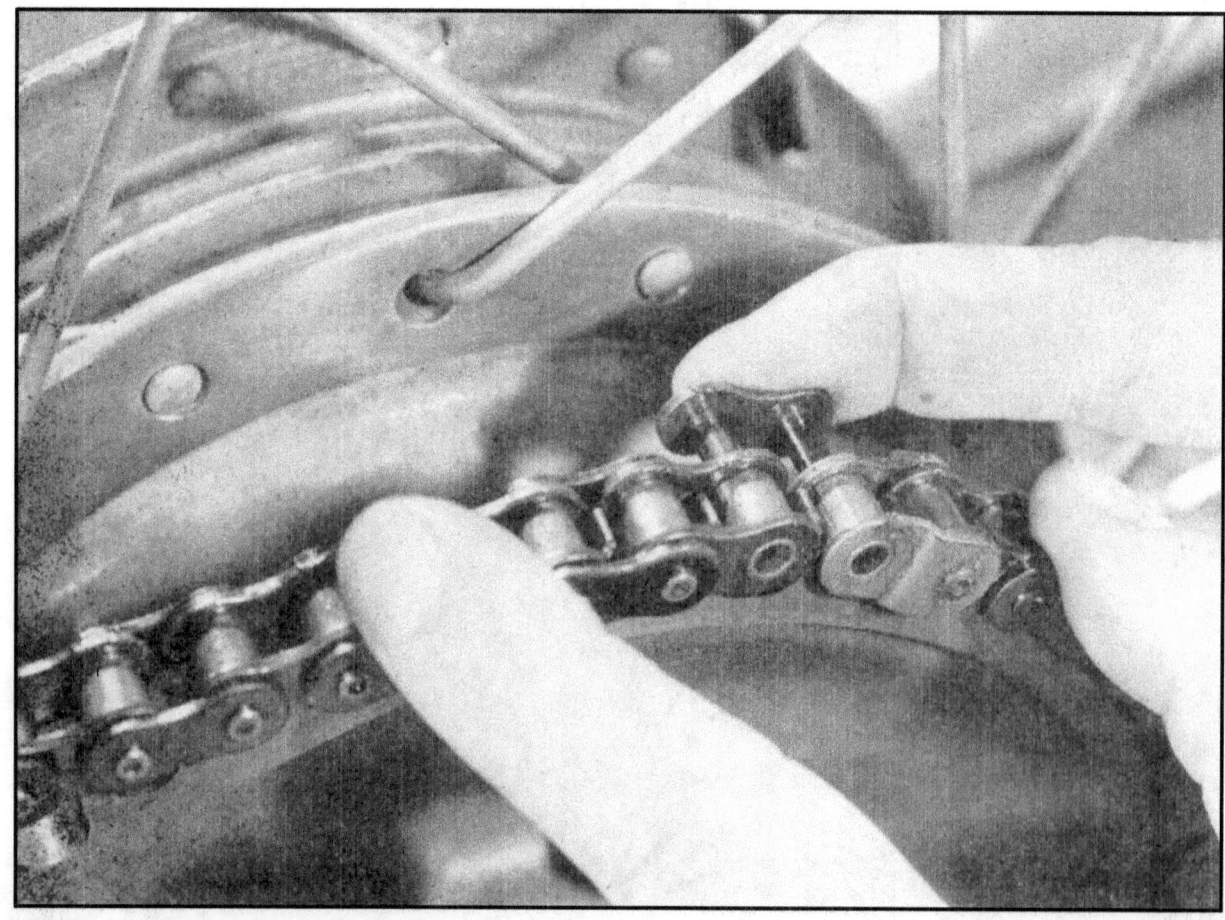

FIG. 121

spring clip with the other jaw engaging the end of the bearing pin; the side plate behind the clip will then pull off and the joint link can be removed (see Fig. 121); this will then have split the chain. When re-fitting the chain, the spring clip must be fitted so that the closed end faces the direction the chain moves when driving, and the clip is re-fitted by pressing one of the plier jaws on the closed end of the spring clip with the other jaw engaging the end of the bearing pin.

A special chain rivet extractor is obtainable from most motor cycle dealers. The chain extractor is used to remove broken or unwanted links in order to repair or shorten a chain. Commence by gripping the chain roller between the jaws of the extractor, then turn the extractor screw clockwise until the tip engages in the end of the bearing pin. Continue turning just sufficiently to force the pin through the plate. Repeat this operation on the bearing pin at the other end of the plate. Detached parts should not be re-fitted.

CHAIN REPAIR AND CLEANING—LEADER AND ARROW

To repair a chain with a broken roller or inner link, remove the parts shown in black in Fig. 122a; replace by two single connecting links and one inner link, parts shown black in Fig 122b.

If the chain has been removed from the motor cycle, and it is convenient, it is worth while cleaning and lubricating it. The chain should be washed thoroughly in several lots of clean paraffin. After allowing the paraffin to drain off, the chain is then immersed in chain lubricant which has been heated in a container until liquid. After about ten minutes immersion during which the chain is moved about with a stick to "work" the joints and ensure penetration of the lubricant, the latter is allowed to cool with the chain still in it. After cooling, the chain is removed and the surplus grease wiped off. The chain can then be re-fitted to the machine after cleaning the sprockets.

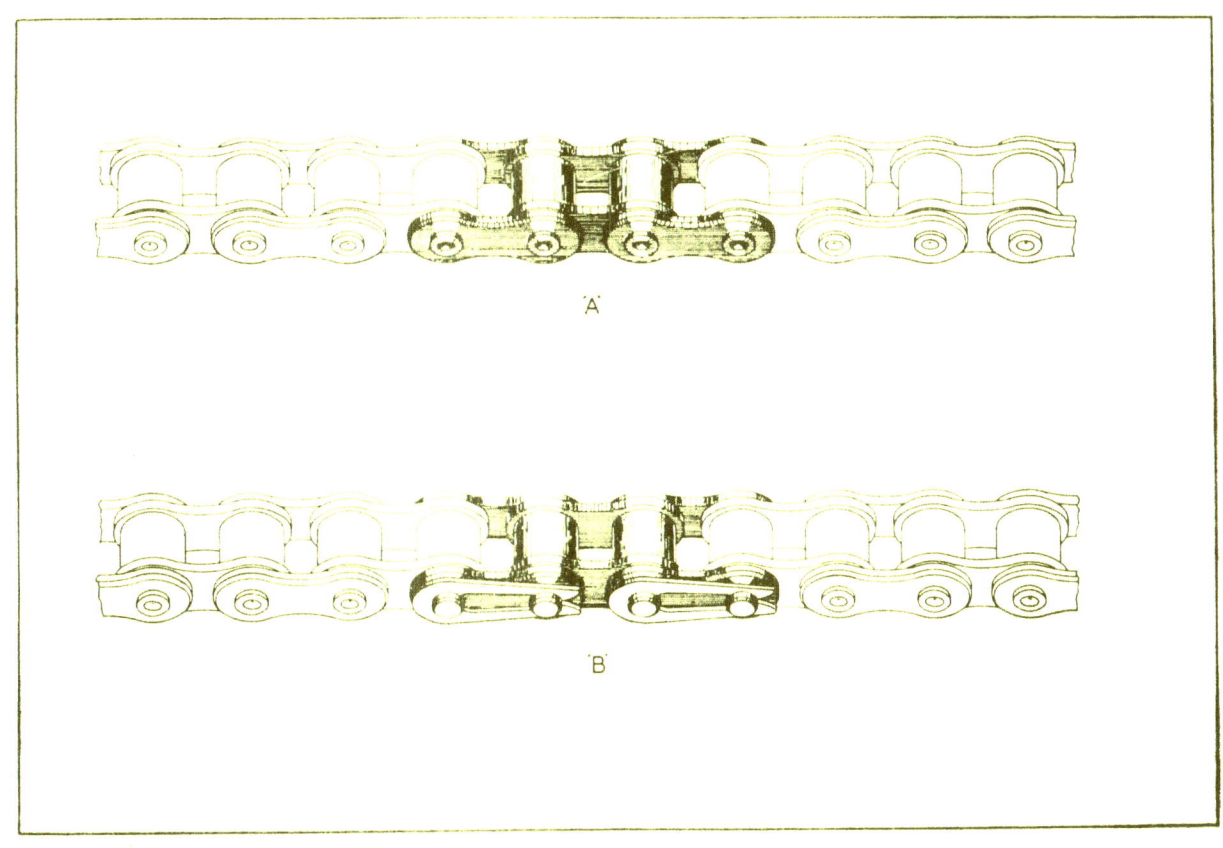

Fig. 122

WHEEL ALIGNMENT—LEADER AND ARROW

The front and rear wheels must be maintained in line with each other to obtain the best steering and the maximum life from the rear tyre and chain. The front wheel is fitted centrally in the front fork and remains in constant alignment, but the rear wheel position is variable for rear chain adjustment and it is possible, especially if the rear chain adjusters have been disturbed, for the rear wheel to be out of alignment.

Therefore at any time the rear wheel has been removed or the rear chain adjusted, the wheel alignment should afterwards be checked.

The best way of checking the wheel alignment is with a long straight edge which will contact both wheels. A six foot length of 3 inch by 1 inch planed wood would make an ideal straight edge, and when placed alongside the machine approximately seven or eight inches from ground level (see Fig. 123) with the front wheel set "straight ahead" the straight edge should contact each wheel at two points. If it is found that when the straight edge is contacting the front wheel correctly it is only touching the rear wheel at one point, then the rear wheel spindle nut and the nut

Fig. 123

securing the brake torque arm to the brake anchor plate must be slackened and the rear chain adjusters must be re-set, either by moving one only, or both until both wheels touch the straight edge correctly, but at the same time, the correct chain tension must be maintained, therefore when the wheels have been correctly aligned, the chain tension should be checked, and if adjustment is necessary, both adjusters should be moved an equal amount of turns until the chain tension is correct.

If a straight edge is not available it is possible to check the wheel alignment with a length of string, by forming a small loop in one end and passing the loop over the rear tyre valve stem, and then taking the string around the back of the rear tyre, which should be positioned with the valve to the rear, so that when the string is taken forward to the front wheel it is clear of all obstructions. Then with the front wheel set straight ahead and the string pulled tight, it should contact each wheel at two points (see Fig. 124). Make this check on each side of the machine and re-set the rear wheel if necessary, as already explained until the alignment is correct.

Fig. 124

WHEEL BUILDING—LEADER AND ARROW

As explained when dealing with the front wheel, if any new spokes or a rim are required or if the wheel needs retruing, the work must not be attempted by a novice and a local dealer should be contacted.

A rear wheel spoking and rim arrangement is given for use by competent wheel builders (see Fig. 93).

TYRES—LEADER AND ARROW

The correct tyre pressure is of the utmost importance. The Arrow rear tyre should be kept at a pressure of 22 lbs. per square inch; and the Leader rear tyre at a pressure of 25 lbs. per square inch. The pressure should be checked weekly and adjusted if necessary. Any serious variation would effect the steering of the motor cycle and cause rapid wear of the tyre and inner tube.

When checking the tyres always inspect the outer cover tread and remove any flints, stones, etc., or they will damage the outer cover and puncture the inner tube. Keep the tyre and spokes free from oil and grease, remove any oil or grease with a cloth and a little carbontetra-chloride.

Never allow a tyre to wear to the extent where the fabric interior is showing through the rubber; this can be extremely dangerous. After many thousands of miles have been covered the tyre will begin to wear smooth (see Fig. 92), and a new outer cover should then be fitted.

The tyre pressure is related to the load being carried by the wheel. The recommended inflation pressures are based on a rider's weight of 176 lbs., and allowing for a full tank of fuel. For a rider exceeding 176 lbs., increase the tyre pressure by 1 lb. for every 14 lbs. increase in weight above 176 lbs. If additional load is carried in the form of a pillion passenger or luggage, the actual load bearing upon each tyre should be determined and the pressures increased in accordance with the following load and pressure scale.

Inflation pressures = lbs. per square inch:
16   18   20   24   28   32

Load per Tyre = lbs.:
190   215   245   295   350   400

The load upon each tyre can be found by placing each wheel in turn on a weighbridge, the weights being taken with the rider seated on the machine.

Always check tyre pressures cold, i.e. *before*, not after, a run.

HANDLEBAR—LEADER AND ARROW

THE HANDLEBAR ASSEMBLY

The only maintenance on the handlebar assembly is lubrication of the control cables and control lever pivots. These should have attention as frequently as is convenient, which should not be less than normal routine maintenance checks. In the case of the Leader, access to the cables is gained by removing he handlebar cover, which is secured in the centrte by a screw which passes through the rear bottom edge of the cover and into a tapped boss. Also one screw at each end of the top of the cover, these screws pass through the handlebar control ever brackets with special lock nuts and washers lto secure them. Remove all three screws, but note that the nuts beneath the two end ones will probably require holding with a spanner to prevent them turning while the screws are being removed. The cover can then be removed by lifting the left hand side first.

Then for the Leader or the Arrow, if the clutch control lever is pulled in towards the handlebar, the inner control cable can be seen between the clutch lever and the bracket on which the lever pivots. A few drops of cycle oil should be applied to this inner cable and the nipple in the handlebar lever. Also the portion of the control lever bracket where the lever pivots should be lightly greased. Apply the grease while holding the lever in towards the handlebar. Repeat this operation for the front brake control cable. The twist grip control cable must be lubricated similarly, and to gain access to the inner control cable, turn the twist grip to the fully open position, then close it slowly, pulling the outer cable out of the twist grip at the same time. This will reveal the inner cable, apply a few drops of oil, but take care not to lose the split bush which fits between the outer control cable and the twist grip. This bush is essential and the twist grip must not be operated unless it is fitted.

In addition to the foregoing, the control cables should be removed from the handlebar levers and the twist grip every two to three months, so that they can be thoroughly lubricated. A good method is to use a toy balloon partly filled with cycle oil. Slip the cable end down the neck of the balloon and tie the neck of the balloon securely around the outer casing of the cable, then holding the balloon uppermost, squeeze it slowly to force the oil down the cable (see Fig. 125). For details of removing the control cables from the handlebar levers and twist grip see pages 126 to 132.

When re-assembling the handlebar cover on the Leader, make sure that the two nylon spacers are in good condition, and fitted in the control lever

FIG. 125

brackets. When the cover has been replaced in position, the end fixing screws with a chrome plated washer under the screw head, pass through the cover and the nylon spacers before the washers and securing nuts are fitted.

HANDLEBAR CONTROL LEVERS—LEADER AND ARROW

The clutch and front brake levers which are fitted to the handlebar, must pivot quite freely, therefore the screws on which they pivot must not be overtightened. In the event of the levers becoming loose, it is in order to tighten the screws and nuts slightly, making quite certain the levers still pivot freely.

If it should be required to remove the levers from the handlebars, first remove the cable, then the nut and pivot screw. The lever can then be lifted clear.

CONTROL CABLES

If the cables are kept well lubricated and correctly adjusted, they will give long trouble-free service, but they will not last indefinitely, and when a control cable begins to fray or breaks it should be replaced with a new one. Repairing a broken cable is rarely satisfactory, and a wise motor cyclist will always carry spares in case of emergency. New cables should have the inner cable lubricated with cycle oil before fitting. In the case of the Leader to remove and re-fit a control cable first detach the handlebar cover as detailed on page 124, and except in the case of a front brake cable, also remove the offside side panel, see page 154, then deal with the cable concerned as follows:

In the case of the Arrow, to remove the clutch cable first remove the engine cover as described on page 155, and to remove the throttle cable first removing the electric horn, as described on page 216.

CLUTCH CABLE—LEADER

The broken cable is easily removed, as irrespective of which end is broken both ends of the cable will have become slack. At the handlebar end a cap is fitted to the outer cover, and this cap fits in the control lever bracket to form a cable stop. The cap may have become wedged in the bracket and need prising out with the blade of a screwdriver. The inner control cable can then be slipped out of the bracket and the control lever, through the slots provided, the cable nipple can then be pushed down and out of the control lever. At the gear box end the inner cable simply pushes down out of the lever, when the outer cover can be pulled up and clear. The complete cable can then be pulled out and clear of the machine, although the cable clip on the offside of the frame may have to be loosened to allow the cable to slide through.

To fit a new cable commence by passing it with the gear box nipple end first through the rubber grommet in the right hand side of the top of the body and guide the cable down until it emerges on the inside of the leg shield. Next fit the nipple, inner cable and the outer cover with the end cap, to the handlebar control lever and bracket. Then pass the cable through the clip on the side of the frame and fit the outer cover into the lug on the gear box. It will now be found that even with the cable midway adjuster completely closed, the nipple on the inner cable will not reach the gear box lever. To overcome this remove the domed cover situated between the kick start and foot change splined shafts. With the cover removed the clutch adjuster can be seen, and this incorporates a threaded stud with a screwdriver slot in the end, and a hexagon lock nut. Slacken the lock nut by turning it anti-clockwise, then turn the stud anti-clockwise a few turns, when this will allow the gear box clutch lever to move nearer to the cable and the nipple can be slipped into the lever easily. The clutch must now be re-adjusted by turning the stud clockwise until there is just free play at the end of the gear box clutch control lever, then secure the stud in this position by preventing it turning by holding it with a screwdriver whilst the lock nut is securely tightened. Final adjustment is then made at the cable adjuster, which is situated in the cable approximately 2 inches from the handlebar lever or the gear box. This adjuster must be set so that there is a minimum of $\frac{1}{8}$ inch free play at the handlebar lever. The correct adjustment is of the utmost importance and for fuller details see page 35.

If an unbroken cable has to be removed, commence by slackening the gear box clutch adjuster so that the cable nipple can be slipped out of the gear box lever. The cable can then be removed from the handlebar without any trouble.

Re-fit the offside side panel and the handlebar cover. See pages 154 and 124.

FRONT BRAKE CABLE—LEADER

Removal: First remove the handlebar cover as described on page 124; then release the old cable from the operating lever on the brake anchor plate. If the cable is broken it will easily pull out, but if the cable is unbroken slacken the adjuster, which is situated in the cable a few inches from the operating lever. Also if the brake incorporates a fulcrum adjuster, this should be screwed out one or two turns. The operating lever on the brake anchor plate can then be pivoted forward and at the same time the cable outer cover can be pulled rearwards enough to free it from the lever. The inner cable can then be pushed forward and sideways to free it from the slotted lug on the brake anchor plate. *Note:* On brakes which have the triangular torque arm bracket on the brake anchor plate, the brake cable outer cover is fitted in the slotted stop lug and the cable nipple fits in the operating arm and removal is similar to that already described. Then tie a four to five foot length of strong thin string to the end of the cable and pull the cable from the handlebar end through the top of the body, making sure the string is also taken through. The cable can then be untied, leaving the string threaded right through the front of the machine. Next detach the cable from the handlebar lever, but note a cap is fitted to this end of the lever, the cap locates into the control lever bracket to form a cable stop. The cap may have become wedged in the bracket, and need prising out with a thin screwdriver blade. The inner cable can then be slipped out of the bracket, and the handlebar lever through the slots provided and the cable nipple can be pushed down and out of the lever. Finally disconnect the stop light switch spring from the cable nipple.

Re-fitting: The new cable can now be fitted. First close the cable adjuster as far as possible, then connect the stop light switch spring to the handlebar end nipple of the cable. Then fit the nipple into the handlebar lever and slip the inner cable through the lever slot and bracket and the outer cover with the cap into the end of the bracket. Next tie the string which protrudes through the top of the body to the end of the cable, which is to be fitted to the brake anchor plate and feed the cable through the grommet in the left hand side of the top of the body, at the same time pulling the string which protrudes just behind the offside fork leg, down to draw the cable through. When the cable is sufficiently through the body remove the string and fit the nipple into the stop lug on the brake anchor plate. Then holding the operating lever forward fit the cable outer cover into the cupped end of the lever.

If a broken cable has been removed from a machine, which has a fulcrum adjuster incorporated in the brake and the old cable was removed without slackening the fulcrum adjuster, it will be necessary now to slacken this adjuster before fitting the new cable.

Finally re-fit the handlebar cover and adjust the brake (see page 86).

Note: In an emergency where a piece of string to draw the cable through is not available, if the headlamp unit is removed from its shell this will give access to where the cable passes and enable a new cable to be fitted without any undue trouble.

THROTTLE CABLE—LEADER

To remove the throttle cable the following procedure applies to broken or unbroken cables.

After removing the handlebar cover and the offside panel (see pages 154 and 124), the split bush which forms a cable stop where the cable enters the twist grip must be removed next, by turning the twist grip to the open position and then closing it slowly, pulling the outer cable out of the twist grip at the same time. The split bush will then be loose on the inner cable and can easily be slipped off. Then remove the two screws from the underside of the twist grip, which will allow the ends of the twist grip to separate. One half can be lifted clear, but the other half will remain attached by the cable (see Fig. 126). The inner cable and nipple can be removed from the twist grip by moving them sideways through the slot provided, when the remaining half of the twist grip can then be removed.

Next push the cable through the grommet in the top of the body, then pass it through the clip on the offside of the frame, so that it is only attached to the carburetter. About an inch below where the cable enters the carburetter is a circular cap which is serrated around its outside edges. This is the mixing chamber cap and it must be removed. Whilst undoing the cap, press down on the mixing chamber top where the cable passes through. This will enable the cap to be removed easily. The throttle cable, mixing chamber top and cap together with the carburetter slide and needle can then be eased out of the carburetter, but take great care not to damage the slide or bend the needle.

To separate the cable from the carburetter parts, first note which notch the needle is positioned, then press out the clip which secures the needle by pushing the open end of the clip, but as a reasonable amount of pressure is required, use the flat of a screwdriver blade under the thumb. Next push the inner cable down and out of the slot to free the throttle slide. The cable will then simply pull out of the mixing chamber top.

If possible, before the new cable is fitted, slide the twist grip off the handlebar and wipe the old grease from inside the grip and off the handlebar, then smear both parts with fresh grease. Also clean and re-grease the groove where the inner cable and nipple are to be fitted. Then replace the twist grip on the handlebar. Then begin by passing the new throttle cable with the carburetter nipple end first through the grommet in the right hand side of the top of the body, so that it emerges at the side of the leg shield. Next feed the cable through the clip on the side of the frame. Then begin assembling the carburetter parts to the new cable, by passing the inner cable end with the smallest nipple through the adjuster in the mixing chamber top with the mixing chamber cap fitted to the top. Next fit the throttle spring over the inner cable which protrudes through the underside of the mixing chamber top. The inner cable must then be passed through the top of the throttle slide and moved sideways to the end of the slot, so that the nipple locates in its seating.

The needle is fitted next, and it must be secured with the clip in the same notch to which it was originally fitted. See instructions on carburetter setting if in doubt. Pass the needle up inside the throttle slide and line the correct notch with the slot for the clip. Then press the clip open end first into its slot, so that the ends pass either side of the needle and the clip will snap into position.

The carburetter parts with the cable attached can now be replaced in the carburetter, but first note that the cut away at the bottom of the throttle slide *must face rearwards when fitted;* also that there is a locating peg on the underside of the mixing chamber top, which must be fitted in the slot in the top edge of the mixing chamber.

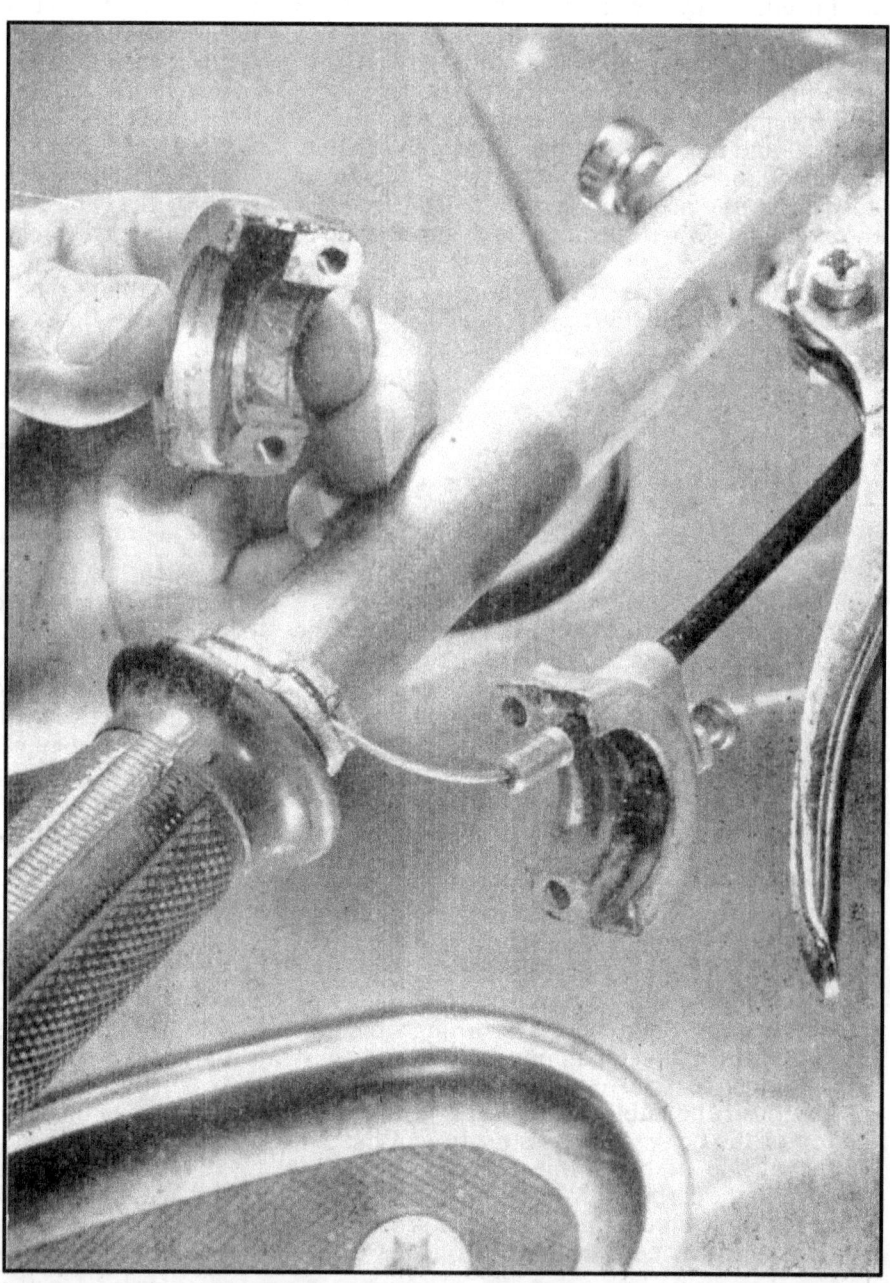

Fig. 126

Commence by very carefully feeding the needle and throttle slide into the mixing chamber, an obstruction may be met inside the mixing chamber *but do not use any force;* the obstruction is the jet block which has a number of holes through it, and the needle must pass through the centre hole, when the throttle slide will then fit into the mixing chamber easily. Use the utmost care when fitting these parts, and remember if any resistance is met, do not force the parts, but re-check the method of assembly. It may be found that although the needle is correctly fitted, the throttle slide will only go into the mixing chamber, level with the top, and it must of course go right down inside. If the slide does stick at the top of the mixing chamber, this is because the cut away is not facing towards the rear correctly; this is easily remedied by revolving the slide until the largest hole in the top of the slide is towards the rear, when it will then move down into the mixing chamber easily.

See that the throttle spring is located on the top of the slide and in the mixing chamber top correctly, then push the top on the mixing chamber making sure that the locating peg is in the slot. Hold the top in this position while the mixing chamber cap is screwed down, but as the thread inside the cap is very fine be sure it is started correctly. If the cap seems tight before it is properly screwed down it may be cross threaded, if this happens, remove the cap carefully and re-start it correctly.

The twist grip can now be re-assembled, and the end cap half with the adjuster screw and hole for the cable must first be slipped on to the cable which protrudes from the top of the body. The cable is then fitted into the twist grip (see Fig. 126), and after making sure that the inner cable is located in its groove, the end cap half which was placed on the cable can now be fitted to the twist grip, but when the cap is in position, the lug which carries the nipple must be visible. The remaining half end cap may now be fitted with the two screws, but before finally tightening the screws, make certain that the twist grip is pushed right on to the handlebar, and the cable faces downwards as it leaves the twist grip, so that there is no obstruction to prevent the front brake lever being operated.

The adjuster screw set in the twist grip end cap controls the closing tension of the twist grip. By screwing the adjuster in or out, the grip can be made to close automatically, or remain open when it is released if it is desired to retain the twist grip in the position in which it is set without being held by hand, such as when giving hand signals. After slackening the lock nut, the adjuster screw should only be screwed in just sufficient to hold the grip open, then the lock nut should be tightened while the screw is held with a screwdriver to prevent it turning, but be quite certain that the twist grip can be closed easily by hand. To make sure the twist grip closes automatically, slacken the lock nut and screw the adjuster out until the twist grip does close automatically, then while holding the adjuster with a screwdriver to prevent it turning, tighten the lock nut.

Re-fit the offside panel and the handlebar cover. (See pages 154 and 124.)

HANDLEBAR AND CONTROLS—ARROW

The handlebar position is easily adjustable, by means of slackening the four clamp bolts at the top of the handlebar stem bracket. The handlebars can then be set in the required position, and the clamp bolts securely tightened.

The only routine maintenance necessary on the handlebar controls is lubrication of the cables and the control lever pivots as described on page 124.

If it is required to remove the handlebars from the motor cycle, there are two alternatives. In both cases it is first necessary to remove the clutch, front brake and throttle cables from the handlebar controls as described on page 130, 131 and 132. Also the dip switch must be removed, if the securing screw is taken out the switch can be left to hang on its lead. Then disconnect the lead from the horn push on the handlebar; there is a snap connector in this lead just inside the front shell, and it is accessible if the bolts securing the headlamp are slackened so that the headlamp can be tilted.

The handlebars can now be removed, either with or without the mounting bracket. If they are being removed with the mounting bracket it is only necessary to remove the pinch bolt and nut which passes through the mounting bracket. The handlebars can then be lifted off the serrated steering column, but note that they may be a little tight and need tapping on the underside with a mallet.

As an alternative to this method the four nuts securing the clamp bolts can be removed and the handlebars can be lifted off leaving the mounting bracket in place on the steering column.

When re-fitting the handlebars, if they were removed with the mounting bracket, take care to fit them on the serrated steering column so that they are at right angles to the front wheel. When fitting the pinch bolt to the mounting bracket, there must be a spring washer under the nut. If the four clamp bolts were removed, note that they have pegs incorporated in their heads, which must be located into the slots in the handlebar clamps on top of the bars.

Then fit a shakeproof washer and a nut to each bolt where it projects from the mounting bracket.

FRONT BRAKE CABLE—ARROW

To remove the front brake cable first slacken the adjuster which is situated in the cable a few inches from the operating arm on the brake anchor plate. Then push the operating arm forward, while at the same time pulling the cable outer cover rearward and out of the cupped operating arm. The inner cable can then be pushed forward to free the nipple from the stop lug on the brake anchor plate. The handlebar control lever will then be slack and the outer cable can be slipped out of the handlebar bracket and the inner cable nipple will easily slip out of the slotted control lever. Finally pull the complete cable upward through the grommet in the top of the front shell. *Note:* On brakes which have the triangular torque arm bracket on the brake anchor plate, the brake cable outer cover is fitted in the slotted stop and the cable nipple fits in the operating arm, and removal is similar to that already described. If the brake incorporates a fulcrum adjuster (see paragraph on Front Brake Adjustment, page 86), then the adjuster should be screwed out a few turns when the cable can be easily removed.

When fitting a front brake cable, first pass the end with the adjuster through the grommet in the nearside of the top of the front shell, and feed it down to the front wheel. Then fit the nipple into the handlebar lever, and locate the inner cable into the slotted bracket and the outer cable into the end of the bracket. Next fit the nipple at the lower end of the cable into the stop lug on the brake anchor plate. Then push the operating arm forward and pull the outer cable rearward and slip it into the cupped end of the operating arm. Finally adjust the front brake as described on page 86.

THROTTLE CABLE—ARROW

To remove the throttle cable the following procedure applies to broken or unbroken cables.

After removing the tool box as described on page 170, and the electric horn as described on page 216, the split bush which forms a cable stop where the cable enters the twist grip must be removed next, by turning the twist grip to the open position and then closing it slowly, pulling the outer cable out of the twist grip at the same time. The split bush will then be loose on the inner cable and can easily be slipped off. Then remove the two screws from the underside of the twist grip, which will allow the ends of the twist grip to separate. One half can be lifted clear, but the other half, which includes the front brake lever, will remain attached by the cable. The inner cable and nipple can be removed from the twist grip by moving them sideways through the slot provided, when the remaining half of the twist grip end can then be removed.

Next push the cable through the grommet in the top of the front shell, then pass it through the gap between the front shell and the offside of the frame, so that it is only attached to the carburetter. About an inch below where the cable enters the carburetter is a circular cap which is serrated around its outside edge; this is the mixing chamber cap and it must be removed. Whilst undoing the cap press down on the mixing chamber top where the cable passes through. This will enable the cap to be removed easily. The throttle cable, mixing chamber top and cap together with the carburetter slide and needle can then be eased out of the carburetter, but take great care not to damage the slide *or bend the needle*.

To separate the cable from the carburetter parts, first note on which notch the needle is positioned, then press out the clip which secures the needle by pushing the open end of the clip, but as a reasonable amount of pressure is required, use the flat of a screwdriver blade under the thumb.

Next push the inner cable down and out of the slot to free the throttle slide. The cable will then simply pull out of the mixing chamber top. If possible, before the new cable is fitted, slide the twist grip off the handlebar and wipe the old grease from inside the grip and off the handlebar, then smear both parts with fresh grease. Also clean and re-grease the groove where the inner cable and nipple are to be fitted. Then replace the twist grip on the handlebar. Then begin by passing the new throttle cable, with the carburetter nipple end first, through the grommet in the right hand side of the top of the front shell, so that it emerges at the side of the frame just above the carburetter. Then begin assembling the carburetter parts to the new cable by passing the inner cable end with the smallest nipple through the adjuster in the mixing chamber top, with the nixing chamber cap fitted to the top. Next fit the throttle spring over the inner cable which protrudes through the underside of the mixing chamber top. The inner cable must then be passed through the top of the throttle slide and moved sideways to the end of the slot so that the nipple locates in its seating. The needle is fitted next, and it must be secured with the clip in the same notch to which it was originally fitted. See instructions on carburetter setting if in doubt. Pass the needle up inside the throttle slide and line the correct notch with the slot for the clip. Then press the clip open end first, into its slot, so that the ends pass either side of the needle and the clip will snap into position.

The carburetter parts with the cable attached can now be replaced in the carburetter, but first note that the cut away at the bottom of the throttle slide must face rearwards when fitted, also that there is a locating peg on the underside of the mixing chamber top, which must be fitted in the slot in the top edge of the mixing chamber. Commence by very carefully feeding the needle and throttle slide into the mixing chamber. An obstruction may be met inside the mixing chamber, but do not use any force; the obstruction is the jet block which has a number of holes through it, and the needle must pass through the centre hole when the throttle slide will then fit into the mixing chamber easily. Use the utmost care when fitting these parts, and remember if any resistance is met do not force the parts but re-check the method of assembly. It may be found that although the needle is correctly fitted, the throttle slide will only go into the mixing chamber level with the top, and it must of course go right down inside. If the slide does stick at the top of the mixing chamber, this is because the cut away is not facing towards the rear correctly. This is easily remedied by revolving the slide until the largest hole in the top of the slide is towards the rear, when it will then move down into the mixing chamber easily.

See that the throttle spring is located on the top of the slide and in the mixing chamber top correctly, then push the top on the mixing chamber making sure that the locating peg is in the slot, hold the top in this position while the mixing chamber cap is screwed down, but as the thread inside the cap is very fine, be sure it is started correctly. If the cap seems tight before it is properly screwed down it may be cross threaded. If this happens, remove the cap carefully and re-start it correctly.

The twist grip can now be re-assembled, and the end cap half with the front brake lever and hole for the cable must first be slipped on to the cable which protrudes from the top of the front shell. The cable is then fitted into the twist grip, and after making sure that the inner cable is located in its groove, the end cap half which was placed on the cable, can now be fitted to the twist grip, but when the cap is in position, the lug which carries the nipple must be visible. The remaining half end cap may now be fitted with the two screws, but before finally tightening the screws, make certain that the twist grip is pushed right on to the handlebar and the cable faces downwards as it leaves the twist grip, so that there is no obstruction to prevent the front brake lever being operated.

The adjuster screw set in the twist grip end cap, controls the closing of the twist grip. By screwing the adjuster in or out, the grip can be made to close automatically, or remain open when it is released if it is desired to retain the twist grip in the position in which it is set, without being held by hand, such as when giving hand signals. After slackening the lock nut, the adjuster screw should only be screwed in just sufficient to hold the grip open, then the lock nut should be tightened while the screw is held with a screwdriver to prevent it turning, but be quite certain that the twist grip can be closed easily by hand. To make sure the twist grip closes automatically, slacken the lock nut and screw the adjuster out until the twist grip does close automatically, then, while holding the adjuster with a screwdriver to prevent it turning, tighten the lock nut.

Re-fit the tool box and the electric horn, see pages 170 and 216.

CLUTCH CABLE ADJUSTMENT—ARROW

It is most important to keep the clutch adjustment correct, in order to obtain satisfactory clutch operation. There are two adjusters provided, one adjusts the clutch directly, while the other adjusts the cable. If the clutch requires adjustment, begin by removing the engine cover as described on page 155. Then check the amount of free play at the end of the clutch operating lever on the top of the gear box. There must be just free play. If the end play is more or less than this, it must be adjust as follows. Unscrew the adapter and screw which secure the domed clutch adjuster cover, which is situated between the kick starter and gear change lever shafts. With the cover removed, the clutch adjuster can be seen, and this incorporates a threaded stud with a screwdriver slot in the end, and a hexagon lock nut. Slacken the lock nut, and turn the stud in the required direction to obtain the correct end play, then hold the stud with a screwdriver to prevent it turning and securely tighten the lock nut.

The domed cover can then be re-fitted, but note there must be a joint washer between the cover and the gear box, and there must be a spring washer under the head of the screw and the adapter. A cable adjuster is incorporated in the cable a few inches from the gear box, and there must be a minimum of $\frac{1}{8}$ inch free play at the handlebar clutch operating lever.

If adjustment is necessary, screw the cable adjuster in or out as required. Finally re-fit the engine cover as described on page 155.

REMOVAL OF CLUTCH CABLE—ARROW

If it is required to remove the clutch cable from the motor cycle, begin by removing the tool box as described on page 170. Then take off the engine cover as described on page 155 and slacken the clutch adjusters sufficiently to allow the inner cable nipple to be slipped out of the gear box clutch operating lever. The cable can then easily be removed from the slotted stop lug on the gear box. It will also now be easy to remove the cable from the slotted handlebar lever. The cable can then be pulled up through the top of the front shell and completely removed.

When fitting a clutch cable begin by passing the gear box end of the cable through the rubber grommet in the offside of the top of the front shell. Guide the cable down the offside of the frame so that it emerges from under the side of the front shell just above the gear box.

Next fit the nipple and cable into the handlebar lever and bracket, then fit the cable into the gear box stop lug, and the nipple into the gear box clutch operating lever. Finally re-adjust the clutch as described on page 131, and fit the tool box and engine cover as described on page 170 and 155.

FRONT FORK—LEADER AND ARROW

The front fork incorporates trailing link suspension which is controlled by coil springs and hydraulic dampers. A light alloy trailing link is fitted in each fork leg and these links have a pivot bolt at the front end, while the wheel spindle and the hydraulic spring units are fitted at the other end. The trailing links pivoting from the front end, move up and down carrying the front wheel with them, to provide the front suspension.

The only routine maintenance necessary on the front fork is lubrication by grease gun of the grease nipples fitted in the trailing links. Each trailing link has one grease nipple situated in the front of the lug to which the lower end of the hydraulic spring unit is secured. These nipples should have two or three strokes of the grease gun every 1,000 miles to prevent ingress of water, etc., due to their exposed position.

The bushes at the forward end of the trailing links, through which the pivot bolts pass, and the steering head bearings on which the fork itself pivots are packed with grease on assembly, and no further attention is necessary until the forks require a general overhaul.

The hydraulic spring units are completely enclosed in the fork legs and are fully protected, and they do not require any attention unless they become damaged or after a very large mileage, are worn when they should be replaced.

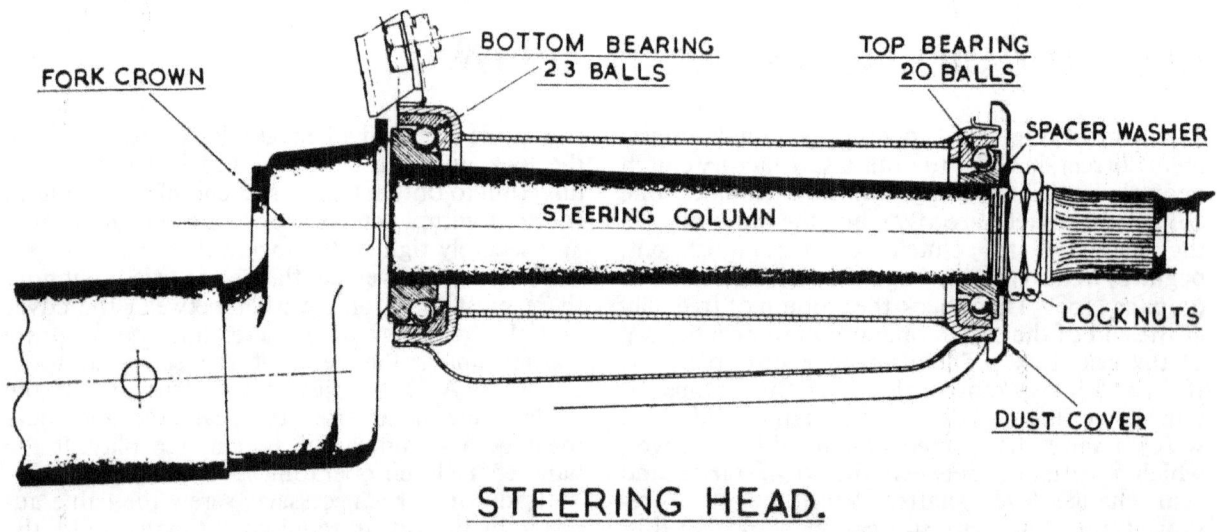

STEERING HEAD.

Fig. 127

Fig. 128

The Steering Head (Leader) is a general term given to that part of the motor cycle where the front fork pivots in the frame in order to steer the machine (see Fig. 127).

To ensure accurate and easy steering there are two bearing assemblies incorporated in the steering head, and the front fork pivots on these bearings. Therefore it is important that these bearings are in good order and correctly adjusted.

A certain amount of bearing wear will of course take place after several thousand miles have been covered, and the steering head is provided with a means of adjustment to compensate for this wear.

When the steering head is correctly adjusted, **the forks must pivot quite freely without any play or rock at the steering head.** The adjustment should be checked periodically, preferably when the front wheel is removed for routine maintenance. For wheel removal see page 76.

With the forks in the "straight ahead" position, using both hands hold the two fork legs and try to move the forks back and forth (see Fig. 128). If any play or rock at the steering head is felt, then adjustment is necessary.

The steering head bearings are of the cup and cone type, and are adjusted by turning a nut which is mounted at the top end of the steering column. The steering column is the shaft which is connected to the top of the fork and passes through the frame for mounting the handlebars. To adjust the steering head bearings it is first necessary to remove certain parts in order to gain access to the adjuster nut.

Commence by taking out the separate centre piece of the glove box lining, this simply pulls out, leaving a hole which gives access to the inside of the frame. The main lining can be left in position.

The anti-thief lock inside the front of the glove box is removed next. The lock is secured to the frame by two bolts which pass through the frame from the inside, with the heads of the bolts welded to a common plate, and with nuts and washers securing the lock to the bolts. Therefore, to remove the lock, take off the two nuts and washers from inside the glove box and at the same time pass one hand inside the frame to prevent the plate dropping, as the lock securing nuts are removed. The lock complete can then be taken out of the glove box.

It is not essential to remove the anti-thief lock, but by doing so, the adjustment of the steering head is made very much easier.

The handlebar unit complete must be taken off next, by first removing the pinch bolt and nut which secures the handlebar unit to the top of the steering column. The complete handlebar assembly, which is located on the steering column by splines, can then be lifted up and clear of the steering column (see Fig. 129), and placed on the instrument panel. As all the control cables, etc., are still attached, the handlebars cannot be completely removed and it would be advisable, after placing them on the instrument panel to tie them with string to the windscreen support stays, to prevent them falling with consequent damage.

Now that the handlebars have been removed from the steering column, a large rubber grommet can be seen, and this must now be removed. Visible through the grommet hole is an alloy die casting below which is a spacer washer and two thin nuts, all mounted on the steering column. The alloy die casting is part of the anti-thief lock, and together with the spacer washer they must be moved up the steering column about half an inch.

Using the two large flat spanners provided, in the tool kit, and working from inside the glove box, the spanners can be located on the two thin nuts on the steering column. Then holding the lower of the two nuts with one spanner to prevent it turning, slacken the top nut with the other span-

Fig. 129

ner by turning it anti-clockwise. Then turn the lower nut clockwise until the forks pivot quite freely, but without any play in the steering head, in other words, take up the play and *no* more. Do not over-tighten the lower nut or the bearings will be damaged. Then holding the lower nut, prevent it turning while tightening the top nut down securely to lock both nuts firmly together.

Re-assembling can now begin, when replacing the handlebars they must be located correctly on the serrated column, to ensure they are straight when the front wheel is in the straight ahead position, re-fit the pinch bolt and nut and securely tighten.

When re-fitting the anti-thief lock, the plate with the two bolts welded to it must be first passed inside the frame and the bolts located through the holes. The remainder of the re-assembling is quite straightforward.

DISMANTLING THE FRONT FORK—LEADER AND ARROW

Removing the front fork from the motor cycle would only be necessary if the fork has been damaged, or if the steering head bearings need replacing. All the working parts inside the fork legs can be removed and replaced without disturbing the actual fork.

Dealing with the working parts of the fork first, if any of these are worn and require replacing, commence by removing the front wheel as described on page 76.

Before withdrawing the pegs which compress the hydraulic units for wheel removal; take out the steel bush through which the wheel spindle passes in the offside trailing link. Then, for the Leader,

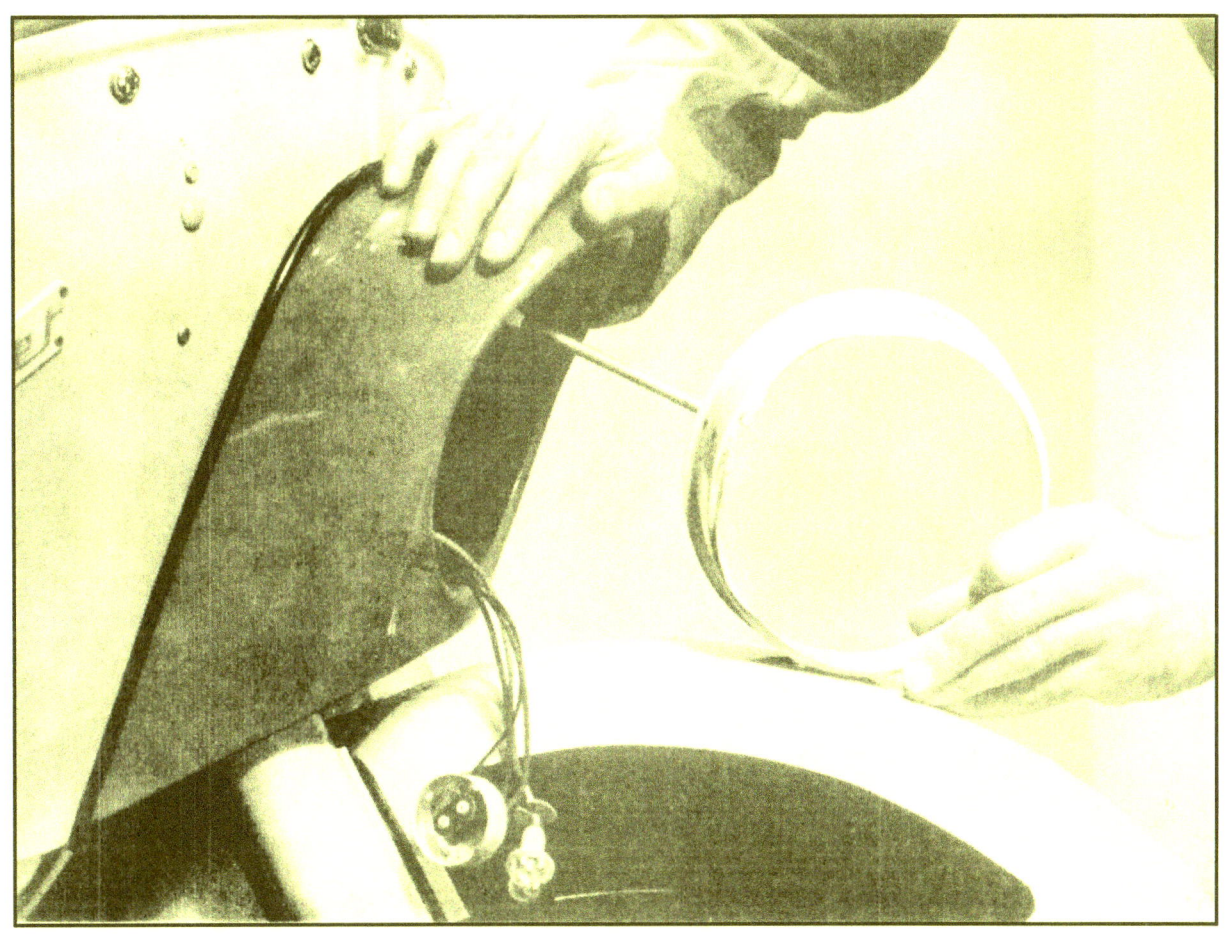

Fig. 130

remove the headlamp unit by turning the handlebars to full lock, and slackening the screw at the base of the lens rim. The rim can then be eased off by pulling forward at the base, which will free the headlamp unit, it will then only be attached by the wiring to the two bulbs, and the simplest way to completely remove the headlamp unit is to take out the bulb holders. The main bulb holder in the centre requires pushing inwards and turning to free it, while the pilot bulb complete with the holder simply pulls straight out. The main bulb will remain in the headlamp unit, but is now loose and should be removed to prevent breakage. Also it would be advisable to remove the pilot bulb from its holder to avoid it being

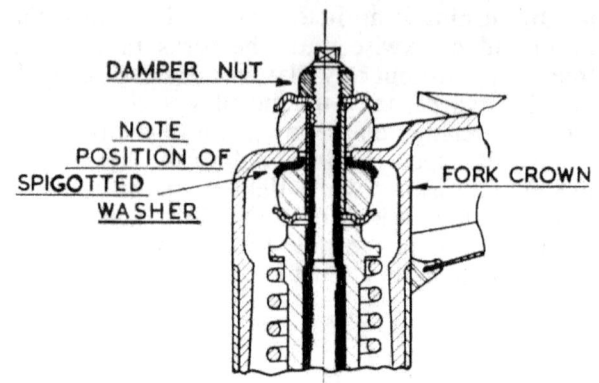

ARRANGEMENT OF TOP MOUNTING FOR FRONT HYDRAULIC SPRING UNIT SHOWING LOCATION OF WASHERS

Fig. 131

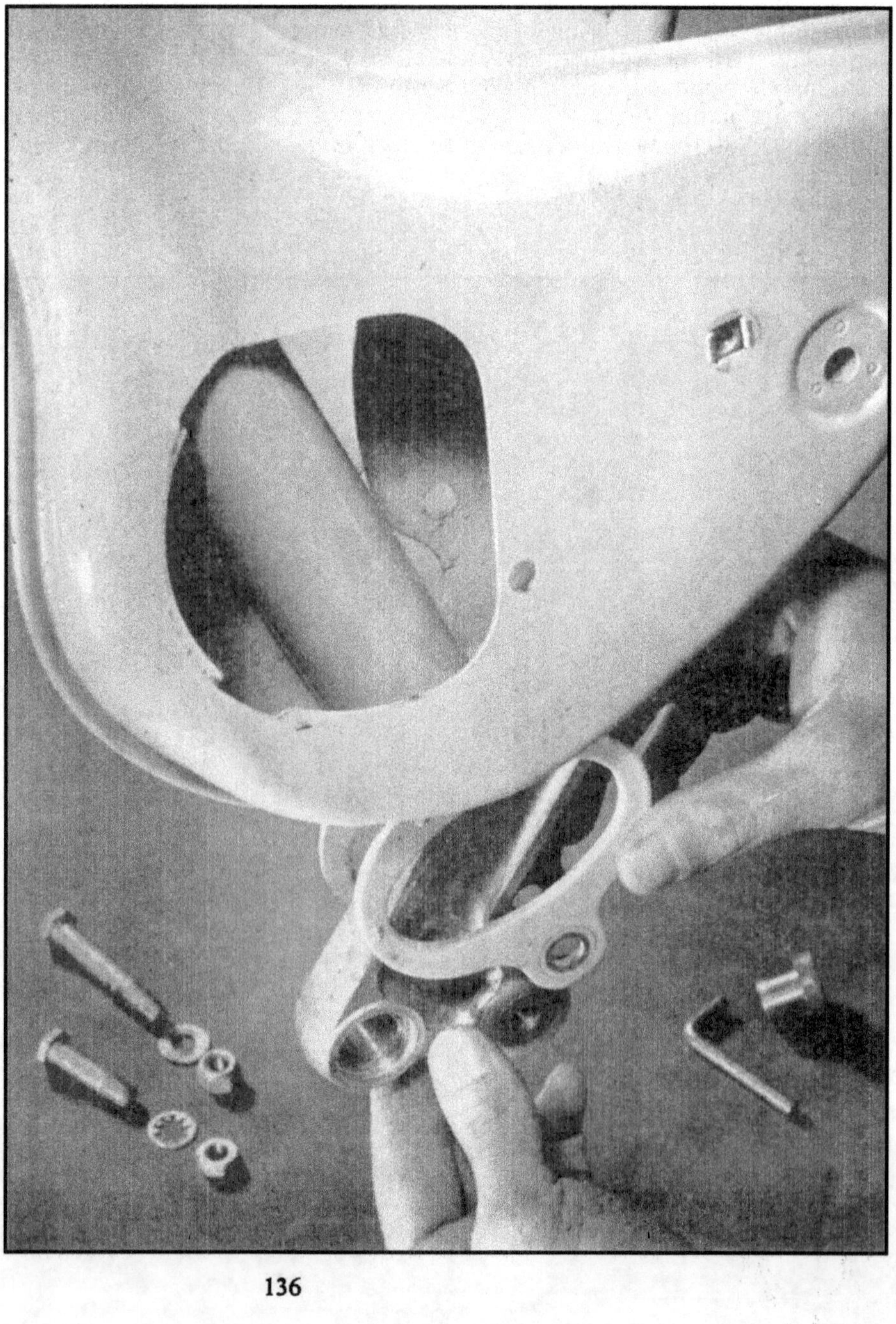

Fig. 132

broken. The headlamp shell should also be removed, from the cowl, to give the maximum accessibility, and the shell can be removed by unscrewing the two large bolts which secure it to the sides of the cowl. If the headlamp shell is then turned sideways it can be eased out complete with trimmer rod (see Fig. 130).

Inside the cowl can be seen the top of both fork legs, through which pass the top fixings for the hydraulic units, secured by special lock nuts with mounting rubbers and washers (see Fig. 131). In the case of the Arrow, it is only necessary to remove the two plastic covers from the top of the fork legs, to gain access to these nuts, etc., these covers can be prised off with a screwdriver. These nuts, rubbers and washers must be removed, but it will be found that the studs on which the nuts are mounted, will tend to revolve while the nuts are being slackened. This, of course, must be prevented, and the stud can be held with the special spanner supplied in the tool kit of each new motor cycle. The special spanner fits the two flats at the top of the stud, while the nut is slackened with a standard $\frac{9}{16}$ inch A.F. spanner. Once the nut has been initially loosened, it can be removed easily without using the special spanner. The special shaped steel washer and mounting rubber fitted below the nut, simply lifts off when the nut is removed.

Then remove the special nut and bolt on which the trailing link pivots. This bolt is the one situated just in front of the nut for the cover plate fixing screws. Next remove the special nut and bolt which secures the oval-shaped brackets at the bottom of the hydraulic unit to the trailing link. Both trailing links can then be eased out of the fork (see Fig. 132), and the hydraulic spring units can then be easily removed, but note that the hydraulic units, if being re-fitted, must be replaced in the same fork leg the same way round in which they were fitted originally. Therefore, they should be marked in some way as they are removed, so that they can be identified with their respective fork leg when the time comes to re-fit them.

If the motor cycle has covered a large mileage, the pivot bearings in the trailing links will almost certainly need renewing. Both links have four nylon bushes, two of these are fitted at the forward end, working on a hardened steel bush, which

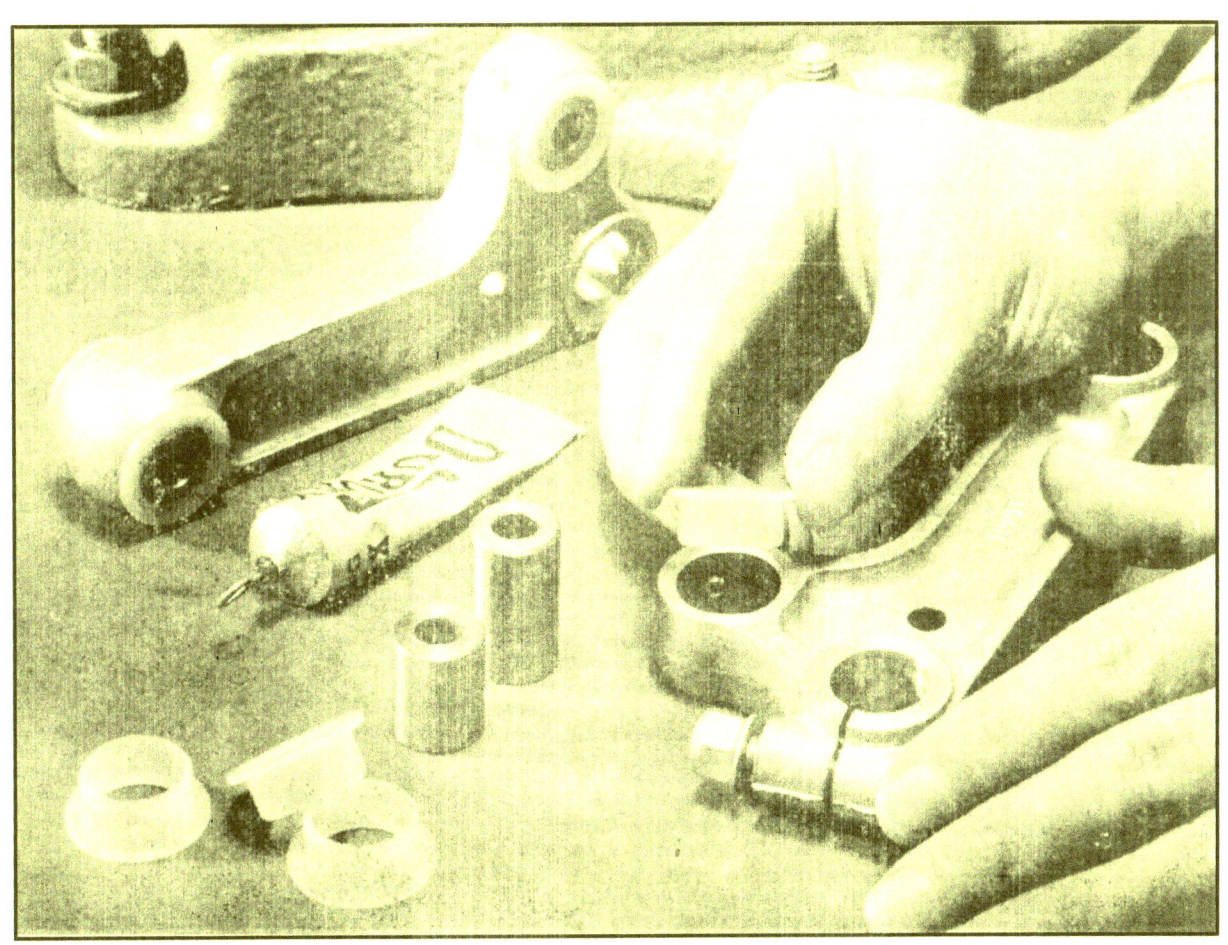

Fig. 133

Fig. 134

remains stationary when the front fork suspension operates; secured by a bolt which passes right through the fork leg; the trailing link pivots with the nylon bushes which are secured in the links with adhesive cement.

The other two nylon bushes are fitted in the lower lug at the rear of the trailing link, working on a stainless iron bush. The iron bush is secured by the hydraulic unit bottom fixing bolt, while the nylon bushes are fixed with adhesive cement in the trailing link. This allows the hydraulic unit bottom fixing point to pivot as the trailing link moves.

All the eight nylon bushes in both trailing links are identical, while the hardened steel bushes fitted at the forward end of the trailing links are easily identified from the stainless iron bushes fitted at the rear, as the latter are ⅜ inch shorter.

To remove the bushes from the trailing links, the steel and iron bushes simply push out, but the nylon bushes may need prising out.

Before fitting new bushes the trailing links should be thoroughly cleaned. Then as each new nylon bush is fitted, it should be pressed into the link just sufficient to hold it, then the outside surface of the bush which will eventually be inside the trailing link, must be coated with adhesive, any well-known brand of plastic adhesive would be suitable. The bush should then be pressed fully home into the trailing link (see Fig. 133). If this procedure is followed with all the nylon bushes, they will be correctly fitted without any adhesive finding its way to the bearing surfaces. With the new nylon bushes fitted in the trailing links, it will be noticed that there is a gap between the bushes in the forward end of the links. This gap should be filled with grease and the inside of the bushes smeared with grease. The bushes fitted to the rear end of the trailing links also have a gap between them, but this is very small, just sufficient to allow grease from the grease nipple to enter the bearing. Grease the inside of the rear bushes, but before re-fitting the steel and iron bushes examine them and if they show signs of serious wear they should be renewed. With all the bushes fitted, work on the trailing links is complete.

The hydraulic spring units are completely self-contained and trouble is rarely experienced. If, however, any trouble does develop or if the units get damaged they should be replaced with new.

Do not attempt to dismantle the hydraulic damper portion of the units. This would only lead to irreparable damage. The springs, however, can be removed if required, by placing the hydraulic unit vertically in a vice, with the alloy cap at the top of the spring, clamped in the jaws of the vice. Then using the special spanner on the two flats at the top of the rod which protrudes through the alloy cap, turn the rod anti-clockwise

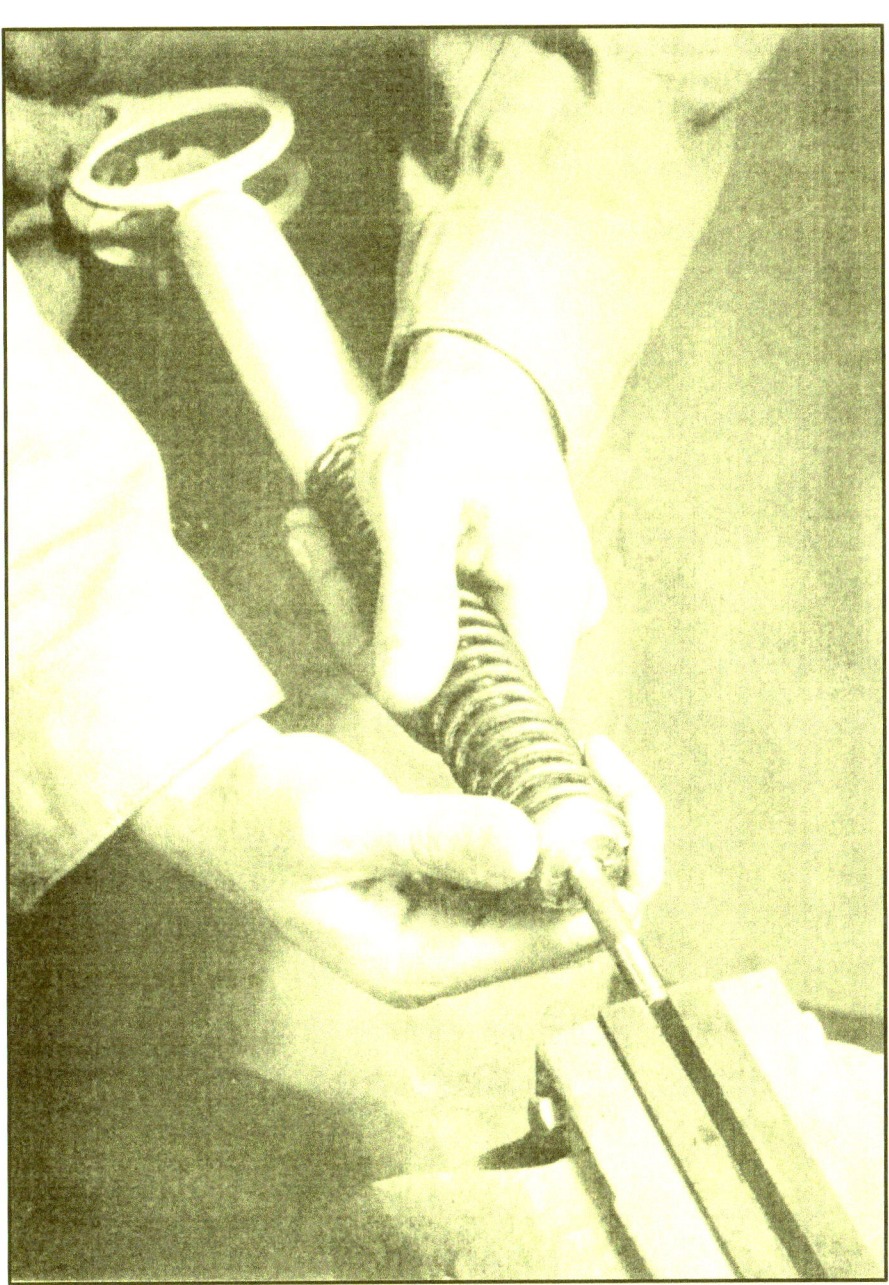

Fig. 135

(see Fig. 134). Note this is a left hand thread. The alloy cap will unscrew from the rod, releasing the spring.

When re-assembling, place the spring and alloy cap on the hydraulic unit, then hold the unit horizontally in a vice by clamping the two flats at the end of the rod, between the jaws of the vice, then using both hands, pull the alloy cap to compress the spring and at the same time turn the cap clockwise to start it on the threaded portion of the rod (see Fig. 135), once it has been started it can be securely tightened easily.

If the hydraulic unit mounting rubbers have deteriorated they should be replaced with new ones.

Before commencing re-assembly, clean out any dirt there may be inside the lower portions of the fork legs, and then begin by making sure the rubbers and washers are correctly assembled on the top of the hydraulic units. One of the two dished washers should be fitted first then the distance tube, with one of the mounting rubbers on it. On top of the rubber, the dished washer with the spigotted centre, should be fitted. The washers when correctly fitted form a retaining cup for the mounting rubber (see Fig. 131).

The hydraulic units can then be fitted inside the fork legs, remembering that if the original units are being re-fitted, each one must be replaced in the same fork leg from which it was removed. They should be located with the top fixing stud only just through the hole in the top of the fork legs. This will leave the oval-shaped bottom fixing brackets projecting, and these must be held at the rear of the aperture in the bottom of each fork leg, whilst the trailing links are inserted between the oval brackets and into the forks (see Fig. 132), but be quite sure that the trailing link with the pinch bolt, is fitted in the nearside fork leg. Ease the links into position, so that the hole through the steel bush in the forward end of the links lines up with the holes in the fork legs for the pivot bolts when only a part of the hole in the steel bush is visible through the hole in the fork legs. A thin pointed tommy bar or steel rod can be inserted to lever the trailing link into position (see Fig. 136). The pivot bolt can then be fitted with a plain washer under the head of the bolt, so that the head of the bolt and the washer face outwards. Note that the two pivot bolts

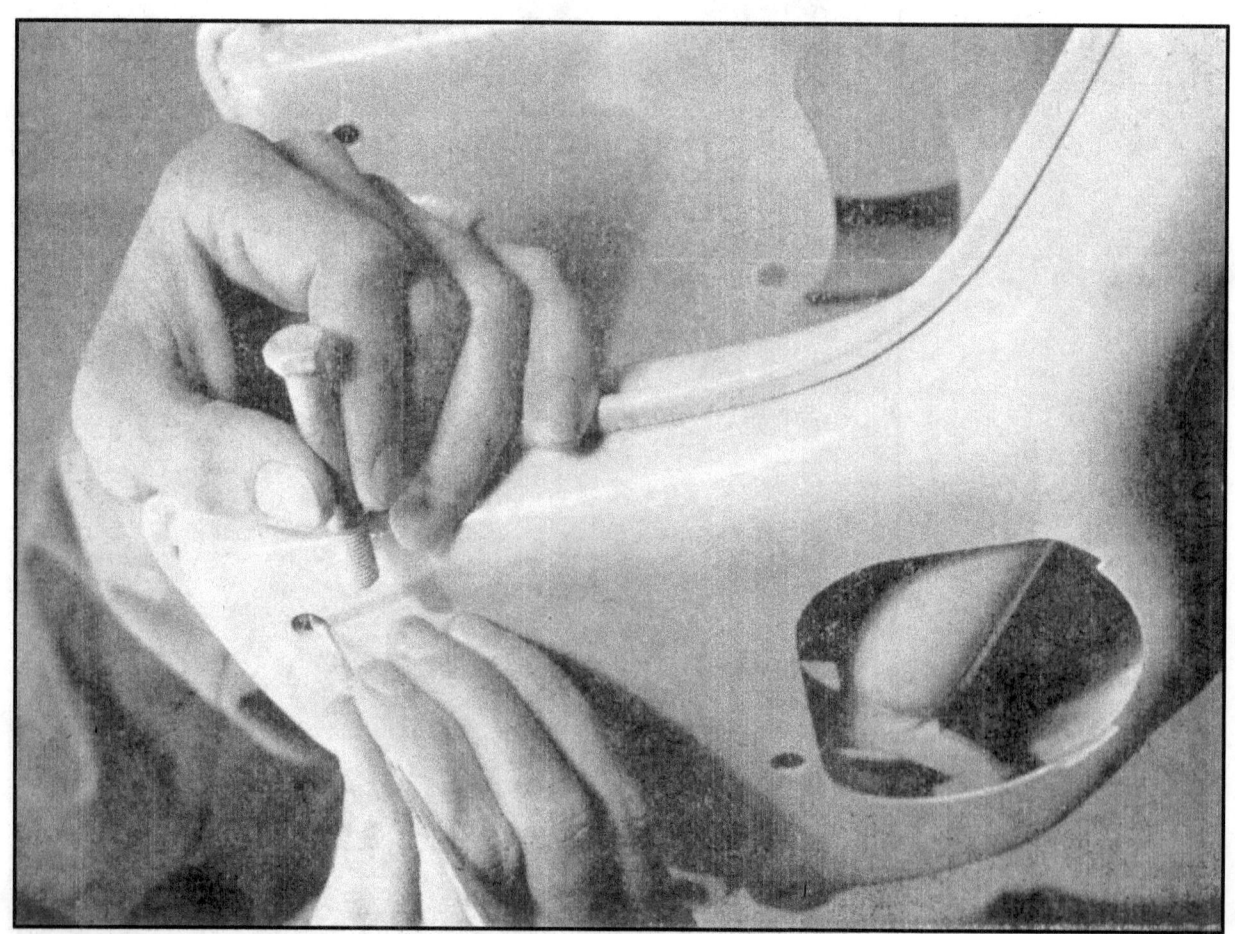

Fig. 136

differ in length, and the longer one must be fitted in the offside fork leg, as it also passes through the lug for the brake torque arm attachment. On machines with the triangular torque arm bracket, the two pivot bolts are the same length, and are interchangeable.

Fit and securely tighten the plain washer and special nut on the pivot bolt. Then line up the hole through the stainless iron bush in the trailing link, with the two holes in the bottom of the oval-shaped brackets at the base of the hydraulic unit, and pass the securing bolt through. Fit the special thin lock nut and shake-proof washer and securely tighten. The hydraulic unit can then be pushed up inside the fork leg, so that the top securing stud and the distance tube for the mounting rubber projects through the top of the fork. The top mounting rubber, dished washer and special self-locking nut can then be fitted (see Fig. 131). Do not tighten the nut excessively, only down to the distance tube when a resistance should be felt. The foregoing procedure applies to both fork legs.

Work on the fork is now complete, but before the front wheel can be re-fitted, the hydraulic units have to be compressed slightly, and this can only be accomplished by the alternative method mentioned in the section dealing with the front wheel, by inserting a 12 inch length of ⅜ inch dia. bar, or a large strong screwdriver in the bottom of the fork leg immediately in front of the bottom of the hydraulic unit. Then use the bar to lever the rear end of the trailing link upward, while the retaining rods are being inserted (see Fig. 70), but take care not to damage the grease nipple in the bottom of each trailing link. Do not forget to re-fit the steel bush in the hole for the wheel spindle, in the offside trailing link. The front wheel can then be re-fitted.

On the Arrow it only remains to push the plastic caps into position on top of the fork legs, but for the Leader proceed as follows: The headlamp shell is fitted in the cowl by inserting it sideways (see Fig. 130), guiding the trimmer rod through the slot at the back of the cowl and up through the grommet in the instrument panel. The shell can then be turned into its correct position and fixed with the special bolts and double coil spring washers. Only the headlamp unit remains to be fitted, and commence by replacing the pilot bulb and holder in the headlamp unit, then the main headlamp bulb, and finally the main bulb holder. On the inside of the chrome plated rim is a metal tag, and this must be located in the slot at the top of the headlamp shell, then holding the screw at the base of the shell up against the shell, push the unit into position on the shell and finally tighten the base screw.

FRONT FORK REMOVAL—LEADER

If the front fork has to be removed from the motor cycle and the machine is being considerably dismantled, it is easiest if the front shielding, and the body together with certain other parts, are removed first, as this will give complete access and simplify the removal of the front fork. For full instructions on dismantling the machine in this manner see page 185. If, however, it is required to remove the front fork only, without dismantling other parts from the motor cycle, proceed as follows: Commence with the motor cycle on the centre stand and with the front wheel removed as described on page 76, take out the centre piece of the glove box lining and remove the anti-thief lock from inside the glove box as described on page 134; next remove the handlebar cover and the handlebars as described on page 134. With the handlebars removed from the steering column, a large rubber grommet can be seen and this must also be removed. Visible through the hole in the body are a spacer washer, an alloy diecasting and two thin nuts, all mounted on the steering column. The alloy diecasting is part of the anti-thief lock and together with the spacer washer they must be moved up the steering column about half an inch. Working from the inside of the glove box and using the two large flat spanners which are supplied in the kit of each new motor cycle, hold the lower of the two nuts with one spanner to prevent it turning and use the other spanner to turn the top nut in an anti-clockwise direction, continue turning until the top nut is free from the threaded steering column, then commence turning the lower nut in a similar anti-clockwise direction until this is also free from the threaded column. The alloy diecasting and nuts which are mounted on the steering column are too large to be removed through the grommet hole in the top of the body, whilst the forks are in place, but this need not present any problem as the steering column can be pushed downwards through the frame (see Fig. 137), although it may need tapping with the handle of a hammer to start it. Having removed the fork, the spacer washer, alloy diecasting and the two nuts, will be left resting on the frame, and can now be removed.

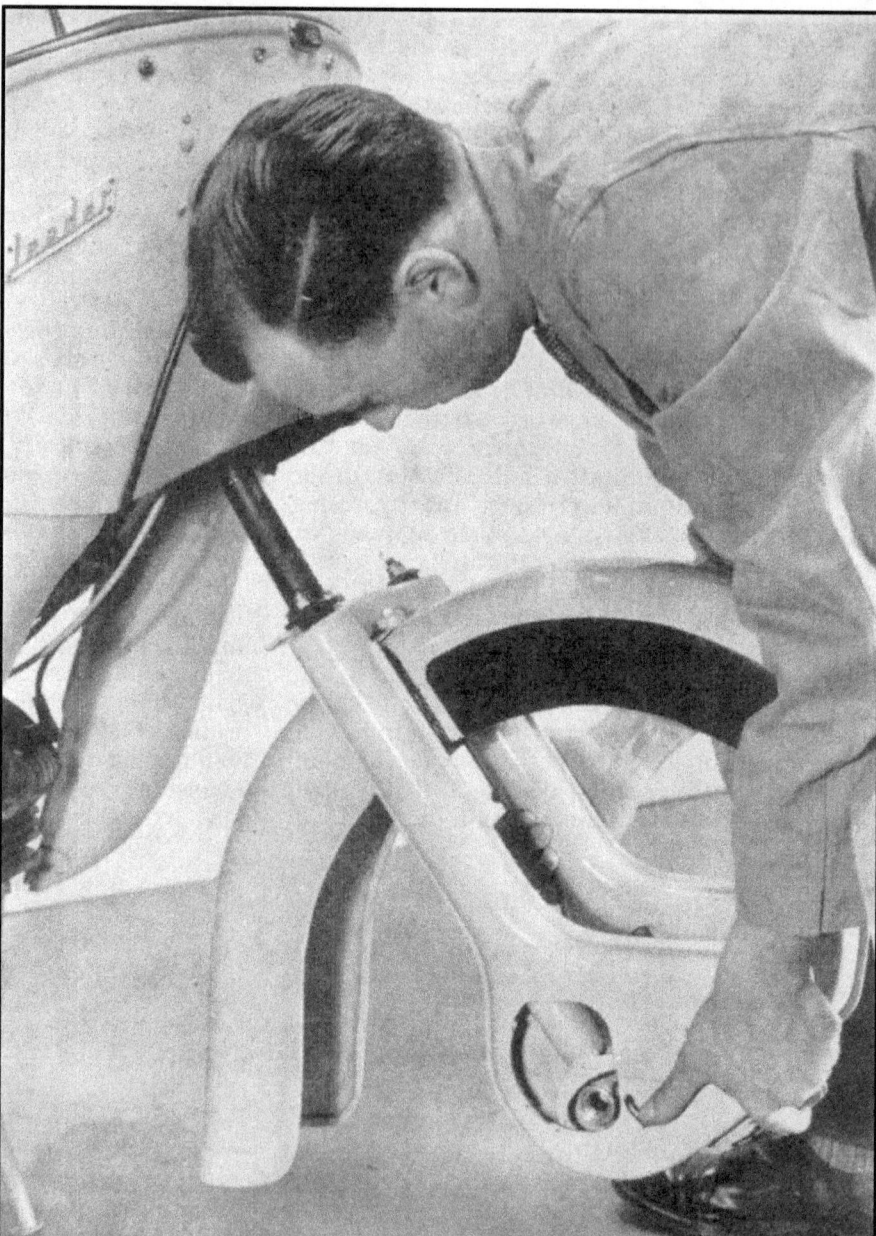

Fig. 137

REFITTING FRONT FORKS—LEADER

If the front fork has been repaired or re-enamelled; before re-fitting it to the motor cycle, examine the steering head bearings and make certain they are in a good order. There are two cupped bearings fitted to the frame, one in the top, and the other in the under side where the steering column passes through, and there are two mating cone-shaped bearings, one fits at the bottom of the steering column immediately on top of the fork crown and the other one is fitted to the top end of the steering column.

If any of these bearings show even the slightest amount of wear or pitting, they should be renewed and in any case when re-assembling the forks even if the old bearings are being used, the steel balls should be replaced with new ones.

For full instructions on renewing the steering head bearings see page 147. In order to simplify the fitting of the front fork to the motor cycle, it is most important that the top steering head cone together with the dust cover and alloy die-casting, which forms part of the anti-thief lock are a push fit on to the steering column. Therefore before fitting the forks, these items should be tried on the column to make certain that they are a push fit. If, however, it is found that any of the items are tight, they should be dealt with in the following manner: The steering head top cone should push down the steering column to a position just below the threaded portion of the column, and if it is found to be tight then it is permissible to use a piece of very fine emery cloth on the steering column in order to ease the fit of the steering head top cone. The emery cloth should be used with great care and should be only applied to that part of the column immediately below the threaded section (see Fig. 138). While using the emery cloth, the fit of the cone should be checked frequently until it is just a push fit. The dust cover, which fits above the steering head top cone, should pass easily over the threaded portion of the steering column, and if any difficulty is experienced with the dust cover due to its being a tight fit on the column, the internal diameter of the cover may be eased slightly with a file so that it will pass easily over the threaded portion of the steering column. The alloy diecasting should next be fitted to the steering column, and if it is found to be a tight fit on the serrations, it should be removed and the serrations inside the alloy diecasting should be carefully filed with a small three-square fine file until the diecasting can be pushed easily down the serrated steering column. Finally, the two thin

Fig. 138

lock nuts should be fitted to the steering column to make sure that they are easily screwed down the threaded portion, and in the event of the nuts being unduly tight it may be that the threads inside the nuts are damaged. If so, the nuts should be replaced, or there may be dirt on the threaded portion of the steering column, causing the trouble, which can be remedied by cleaning with a brush and paraffin. If the threaded portion of the steering column has been damaged in some way, preventing the nuts being fitted, and the damage is not too serious, it may be possible to clean up the threads with a very fine three-square file. If, however, the damage is too serious to be repaired in this manner, then the fork unit should be returned to an Ariel agent for attention.

Having made certain that the fittings for the top of the steering column will assemble easily, the steering column should be thoroughly cleaned. The steering head cone which is fitted to the bottom end of the steering column, should also be thoroughly cleaned and be in good condition. The surface of the cone where the ball bearings run should be liberally coated with grease (see Lubrication Chart); use grease as for hubs, etc. The forks are now ready to be fitted to the motor cycle, but first the frame must be prepared and here again the two steering head cups, which are fitted to the frame, must be thoroughly cleaned and in good condition. The

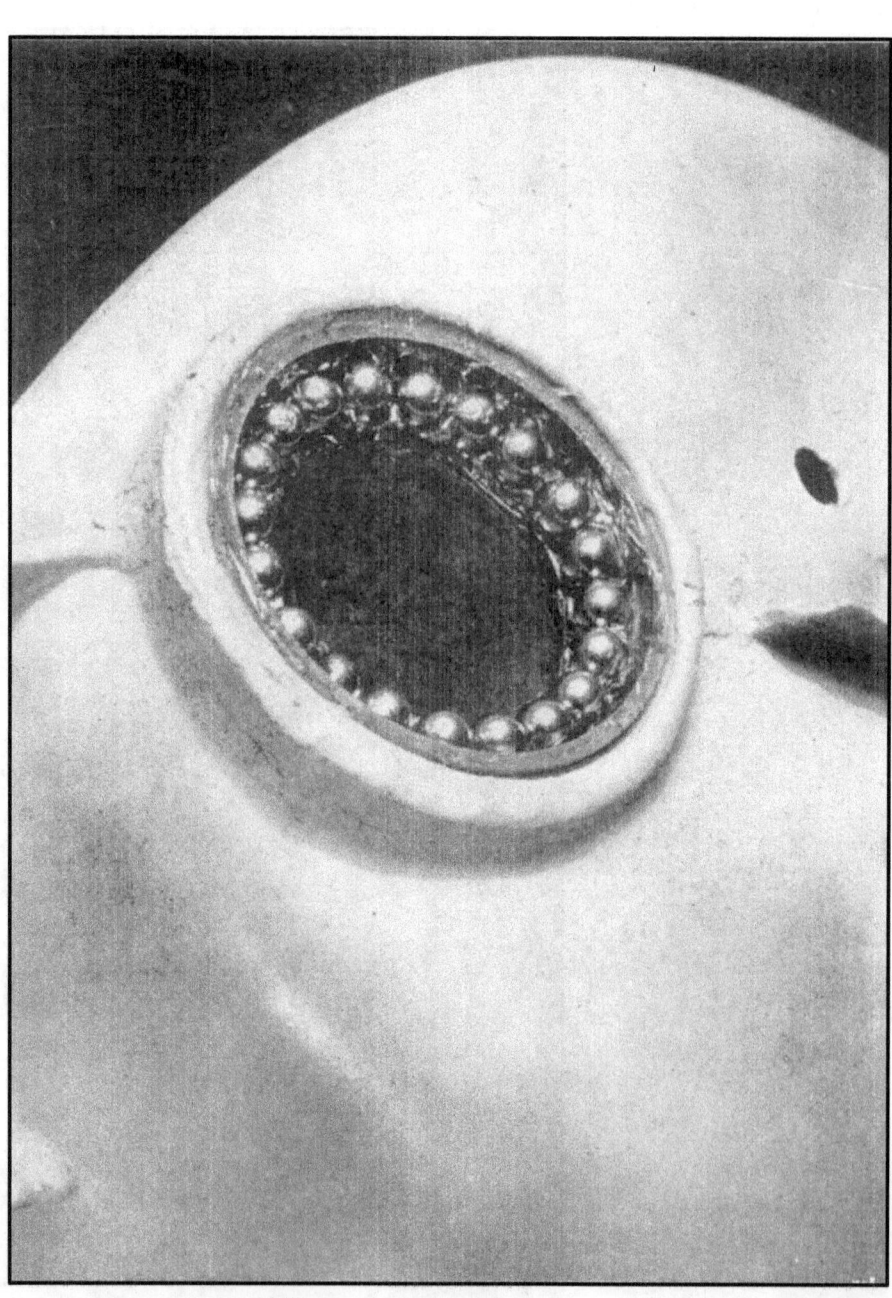

FIG. 139

surface of the cups where the ball bearings will fit must be completely filled with the same grease, which was used for the cone at the bottom of the steering column. Next irrespective or whether new steering head cups and cones have been fitted or not, it is strongly advisable to fit new steel balls, and there must be twenty-three balls fitted to the buttom cup and twenty balls fitted to the top cup. If the balls are carefully placed into the cups, they will remain held by the grease (see Fig. 139), and the greatest care must be taken to make sure that none of the balls fall out during re-assembly. The top steering head cone can now be put into place on top of the balls in the steering head cup in the top of the frame. Next, place the thin washer immediately on top of the cone and then the dust cover is fitted on top of the washer.

The forks can now be fitted to the frame, and this will call for the services of a second person, who must hold the forks and pass the steering column through the steering head cup in the underneath of the frame (see Fig. 137). The other person must hold the top steering head cone while the steering column is passed through, but immediately the top of the steering column is level with the top of the cone, the forks must be held still for a few moments while the two thin nuts and the alloy diecasting are placed on top of the dust cover. At this point it is worth while checking the bottom steering head cup to make quite certain that all the balls are in place. The forks should then be lifted up slowly and centrally, continued passing the steering column through the top cone, the thin nuts, and the alloy diecasting. As the steering column enters the diecasting, it must be positioned so that when the forks are in the straight ahead position, the lug on the alloy diecasting is facing exactly rearwards. This is most important for otherwise the anti-thief lock will not operate. While holding the alloy diecasting nuts and cone, etc., in position, continue to pass the forks and steering column up through the frame until the threaded portion of the column begins to emerge through the top steering head cone.

At this point check again to make quite certain that all the balls are still in place in the bottom steering head cup. There is sufficient room between the top cone and the top of the body of the motor cycle to allow the alloy diecasting and nuts to be raised slightly so that part of the threaded portion of the steering column can be passed through the top cone. The first of the two thin nuts must then be started on the threaded portion of the steering column by turning it in a clockwise direction. Continue turning the nut until all the play has been taken out of the steering head and it is correctly adjusted (see the instructions on page 133). When the steering head is correctly adjusted the lower nut must be held with a spanner to prevent its turning whilst the top nut is then started on the threaded portion of the column by turning it also in a clockwise direction, and screwed down on to the lower nut, then while still holding the lower nut, tighten the top nut securely to lock them together. Re-check the steering head adjustment to be quite certain that it is correct. The thick spacer washer is then fitted on to the steering column immediately on top of the alloy diecasting. The handlebars are fitted next, but make certain that they are squarely in position in relation to the front wheel. Then the handlebar securing pinch bolt and nut can be fitted and securely tightened. Any cables, etc., which have been disconnected can be re-fitted and finally the handlebar cover can be re-fitted. For separate details on the fitting of the handlebar, control cables and handlebar cover, see page 124.

FRONT FORK—ARROW

The front fork is the same as fitted to the Leader, but due to the different handlebar design the method for adjusting the steering head bearings, and removing and re-fitting the fork, vary slightly.

The steering head is a general term given to that part of the motor cycle where the front fork pivots in the frame in order to steer the machine (see Fig. 127).

To ensure accurate and easy steering there are two bearing assemblies incorporated in the steering head, and the front fork pivots on these bearings. Therefore, it is important that these bearings are in good order, and that no excessive wear develops.

A certain amount of bearing wear will of course take place after several thousand miles have been covered, and the steering head is provided with a means of adjustment to compensate for this wear.

When the steering head is correctly adjusted, the forks must pivot quite freely without any play or rock at the steering head. The adjustment should be checked periodically, preferably when the front wheel is removed for routine maintenance. For wheel removal see page 76.

With the forks in the "straight ahead" position, using both hands hold the two fork legs and try to move the forks back and forth (see Fig. 128). If any play or rock at the steering head is felt, then adjustment is necessary.

The steering head bearings are of the cup and cone type, and they are adjusted by turning a nut which is mounted at the top end of the steering column. The steering column is the shaft which is connected to the top of the fork and passes through the frame for mounting the handlebars. To adjust the steering head bearings it is first necessary to remove certain parts in order to gain access to the adjuster nut.

Commence by removing the bolt from each side of the headlamp, taking care not to let it drop; let the headlamp hang by its wiring harness. Next remove the pinch bolt and nut from the handlebar stem bracket, the handlebars complete can then be lifted up off the serrated steering column, and laid on the front shell with a suitable piece of cloth to prevent the front shell being scratched. The tool box must be removed next as described on page 170. Then working through the hole in the top of the front shell, remove the two nuts and bolts which pass through the brackets securing the forward end of the front shell to the top of the frame. Next slacken the four screws which secure the bottom edge of the front shell, two each side of the machine. Slip the plastic cover off the steering column, and lift the front shell sufficiently to insert on to the two thin steering head nuts the two special flat spanners supplied in the tool kit of each new machine. Then holding the lower of the two nuts with one spanner to prevent it turning, slacken the top nut with the other spanner. Then turn the lower nut until the forks pivot quite freely, but without any play in the steering head, in other words, take up the play and *no* more. Do not over tighten the lower nut or the bearings will be damaged. Then holding the lower nut, prevent it turning while tightening the top nut down securely to lock both nuts firmly together.

Re-assembling can then begin. First slip the plastic cover over the steering column, then fit the handlebars, but take care to locate the handlebars correctly on to the serrated steering column, so that the handlebars are at right angles to the front wheel. The pinch bolt must then be fitted to the handlebar stem bracket, and a spring washer and nut is then fitted to the pinch bolt and securely tightened. Next tighten the four screws at the bottom of the front shell; two each side of the machine. Then fit the two bolts and nuts through the brackets inside the forward end of the front shell, but note there should be a plain washer under the heads of the bolts, and a plain washer and a shake-proof washer under the nuts.

The tool box can then be fitted as described on page 170. Then only the headlamp remains to be fitted, the two headlamp securing bolts must have a plain washer fitted under their heads, and there must be a distance piece between each side of the headlamp and the front shell. Also the licence holder should be fitted between the nearside distance piece and the headlamp. Note there may be an additional plain washer fitted together with one of the distance pieces, in order to centralise the headlamp.

FRONT FORK REMOVAL—ARROW

If it should be required to remove the front fork from the motor cycle, commence by removing the front wheel as described on page 76. Then proceed exactly as described for adjusting the steering head bearings, but instead of turning the two thin nuts to adjust the bearings, remove both nuts completely from the steering column. The forks can then be withdrawn from the frame, although it may be necessary to give the top of the steering column a tap with a mallet to initially free the fork.

RE-FITTING FRONT FORK—ARROW

If the front fork has been repaired or re-enamelled, before re-fitting it to the motor cycle, first examine the steering head bearings and make certain they are in a good order. There are two cupped bearings fitted to the frame, one in the top, and the other in the underside where the steering column passes through, and there are two mating cone-shaped bearings, one fits at the bottom of the steering column immediately on top of the fork crown, and the other one is fitted to the top end of the steering column.

If any of these bearings show even the slightest amount of wear or pitting, they should be renewed and in any case when re-assembling the forks, even if the old bearings are being used, the steel balls should be replaced with new ones. For full instructions on fitting new steering head bearings see page 147.

The front forks should then be thoroughly cleaned and all grease, etc., must be removed from the steering head bearings. Then the steering head cups in the top and bottom of the frame must be packed with fresh grease of the same grade as recommended for the hubs. Then place new steel balls in the grease-packed steering head cups (see Fig. 139). There must be twenty-three steel balls in the bottom cup and twenty in the top cup. Next lift the fork assembly and pass the steering column up through the steering head tube in the frame (see Fig. 137), and locate the steering head bottom cone, which is situated at the bottom of the steering cloumn, into the steering head cup in the bottom of the frame, but take the utmost care not to let any of the steel balls fall out of either of the steering head cups. Then, holding the fork in position, pass the top steering head cone down the steering column and locate it into the top steering head cup, and again make certain that none of the steel balls have fallen out of the steering head cups. Then still holding the forks in position, pass the thin washer, followed by the dust cover, down the steering column, next fit one of the thin nuts to the steering column; it should be possible to screw this nut down finger tight with one hand while holding the forks up with the other. The thin nut should then be tightened with one of the special flat spanners which is supplied in the tool kit of each new motor cycle, until all the free play in the steering head bearings has been taken up. See page 145 for full instructions on steering head bearing adjustment. Then fit the scond thin nut to the steering column, and while holding the lower thin nut with one of the special flat spanners to prevent it turning, tighten the second thin nut securely to lock both nuts together. Afterwards check the adjustment of the steering head bearings again, to make quite certain it is in order. Next the front wheel can then be fitted as described on page 85.

Then re-fit the plastic cover and handlebars to the steering column, secure the front shell and re-fit the tool box and the headlamp as described on page 146.

If it should be required to remove the plastic covers from the top of the front fork crown, they can easily be prised off with a screwdriver. When re-fitting they merely require pushing on.

All other details for the front fork are as described for the Leader.

RENEWING STEERING HEAD BEARINGS—LEADER AND ARROW

It is of the utmost importance to keep the steering head bearings in good order. If they are allowed to become excessively worn it will seriously affect the steering and stability of the motor cycle. The bearings are packed with grease on assembly and require no further lubrication, but they will have to be adjusted from time to time, and if they are kept correctly adjusted they will give long trouble free service. If the machine has covered a large mileage and a roughness can be felt in the steering head bearings, that is to say when the forks are turned from side to side, they no longer pivot smoothly although the bearings appear to be adjusted correctly, the front fork should be removed and the bearings examined and if the frame cups or the fork cones show the slightest trace of wear or pitting they should be replaced. In the top of the frame through which the steering column passes is a cupped ball bearing race which holds twenty steel ball bearings, and mounted on the steering column is a cone-shaped ball bearing race; when the parts are assembled they form the top steering head race. Similarly in the bottom of the frame is a cupped ball bearing race which contains twenty-three balls, and a cone-shaped ball bearing race is fitted to the bottom of the steering column, these parts form the bottom steering head race. Apart from waiting until roughness can be felt in the head bearings when they are then obviously worn, if the front forks are removed for any reason the bearings should be examined, and if they show any signs of wear they should be replaced with new ones. To give access to replace the steering head bearings, it is only necessary to remove the front fork, but, if the machine is being considerably dismantled, it is a little easier to fit the new bearings to the bare frame. The following instructions for removing the old bearings and fitting new ones apply to a motor cycle that has been completely dismantled, or to a machine where the front forks only have been removed.

The following service tools are required for renewing the steering head bearings.

43585S. Tommy bar.
43573S. Spindle assembly.
43581S. Locating washer for head lug tube.
43576S. Bearing locating collar.
43589S. Locating washer for head lug tube bottom race marked "E".
One Off. Plain washer with $\frac{9}{16}$ inch inside dia.

When the front fork is removed from the motor cycle the bottom steering head cone will remain on the steering column portion of the fork assembly, and the bottom steering head cup will remain in the frame, while the top steering head cup and cone will remain assembled together at the top of the frame. The top cone can be lifted clear of the steering head and the steel balls can then be removed; also any steel balls which remain in the bottom steering head cup can also be removed. The old steering head cups in the frame are removed with a drift and a hammer, but before commencing to knock the old cups out of the steering head if the motor cycle is on the centre stand, make certain that it is well supported underneath and that knocking out the steering head bearing cups will not unbalance the machine. To remove the bottom steering head cup pass a drift through the top of the frame and locate it on the inner edge of the bottom steering head cup.

Note: A drift for this purpose is not supplied with the service tools as it need only be a length of steel bar approximately twelve to fifteen inches long and ⅜ inch in diameter. With the drift in position on the bottom steering head cup, give the top end of the drift one or two sharp blows with a hammer (see Fig. 140), then move the drift to a point diametrically opposite on the inner edge of the cup and again apply a few sharp blows with the hammer to the drift. Continue using the hammer and drift in this manner and moving from side to side of the steering head cup until it is knocked out of the frame. It will be found that it is much easier if a large and heavy hammer is used in preference to a light one.

The top steering head cup is removed in a similar manner to the bottom one except that the drift must be passed through from the underside of the frame to locate it on the inner edge of the

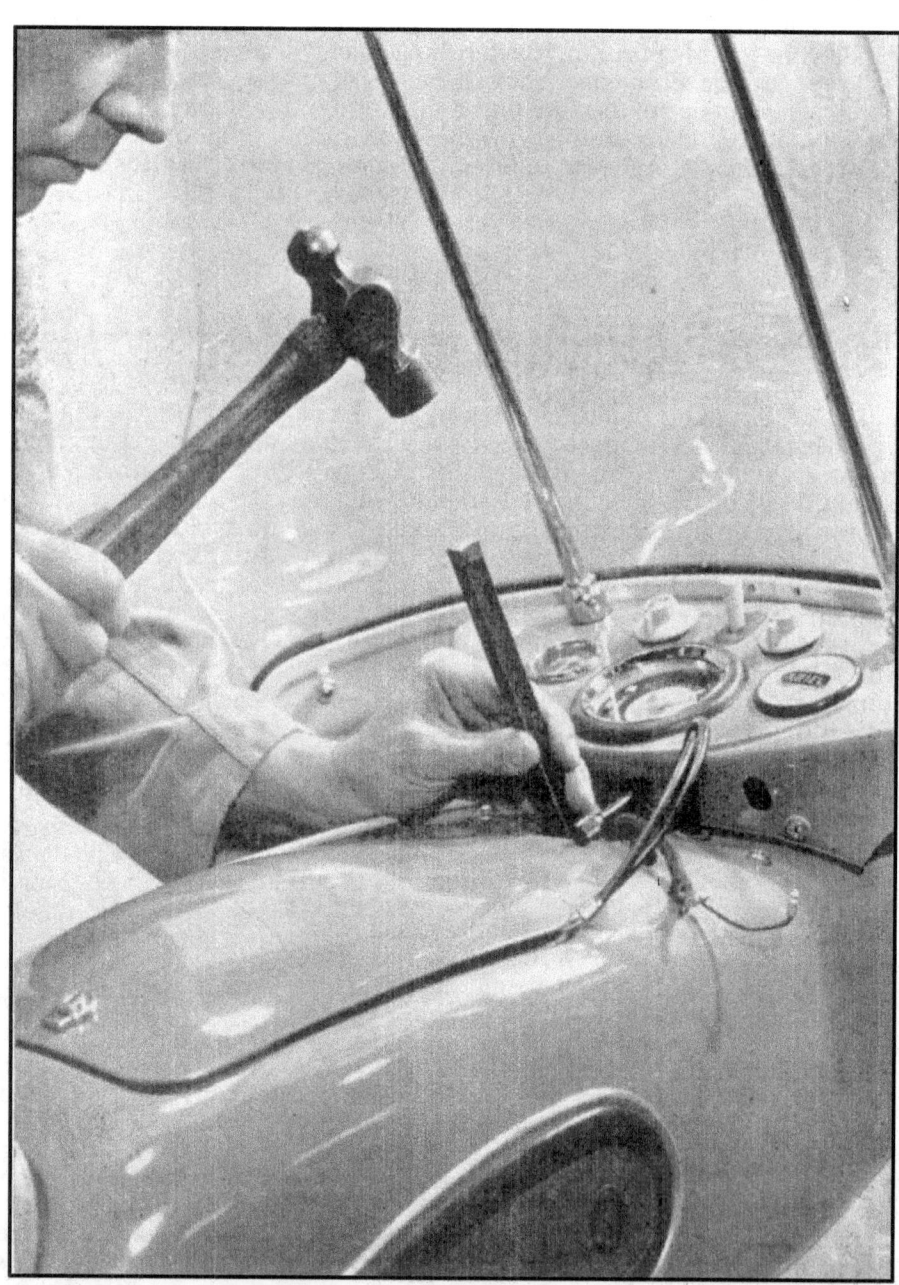

Fig. 140

top steering head cup (see Fig. 141); and here the greatest care must be taken as there is a *lip inside the frame immediately below the top steering head cup*, and on no account must the drift be knocked against this lip. If a finger is passed through the top steering head cup it is possible to feel where the lip finishes leaving approximately $\frac{1}{16}$ inch of the underside of the top steering head cup exposed, and the drift must be located on this $\frac{1}{16}$ inch wide inner edge of the top steering cup. Then using the drift and hammer and moving from side to side of the top steering head cup, the cup can be knocked out.

With the steering head cups removed from the frame the steering head lug tube should be thoroughly cleaned, removing all traces of dirt and old grease. Then the recesses in the steering head lug tube where the new steering head cups are to be fitted to the top and bottom of the frame should be smeared lightly with fresh clean grease to assist fitting the new bearings. The fitting of the new steering head cups can now begin. Commence by placing the $\frac{9}{16}$ inch inside dia. plain washer on the spindle assembly 43573S. Next fit the head lug tube locating washer 43581S to the spindle assembly. Then place the new top steering head cup part No. 4-1203 over the spindle assembly and locate the outer edge of the steering head cup on the outer edge of the head lug tube locating washer 43581S, and then pass

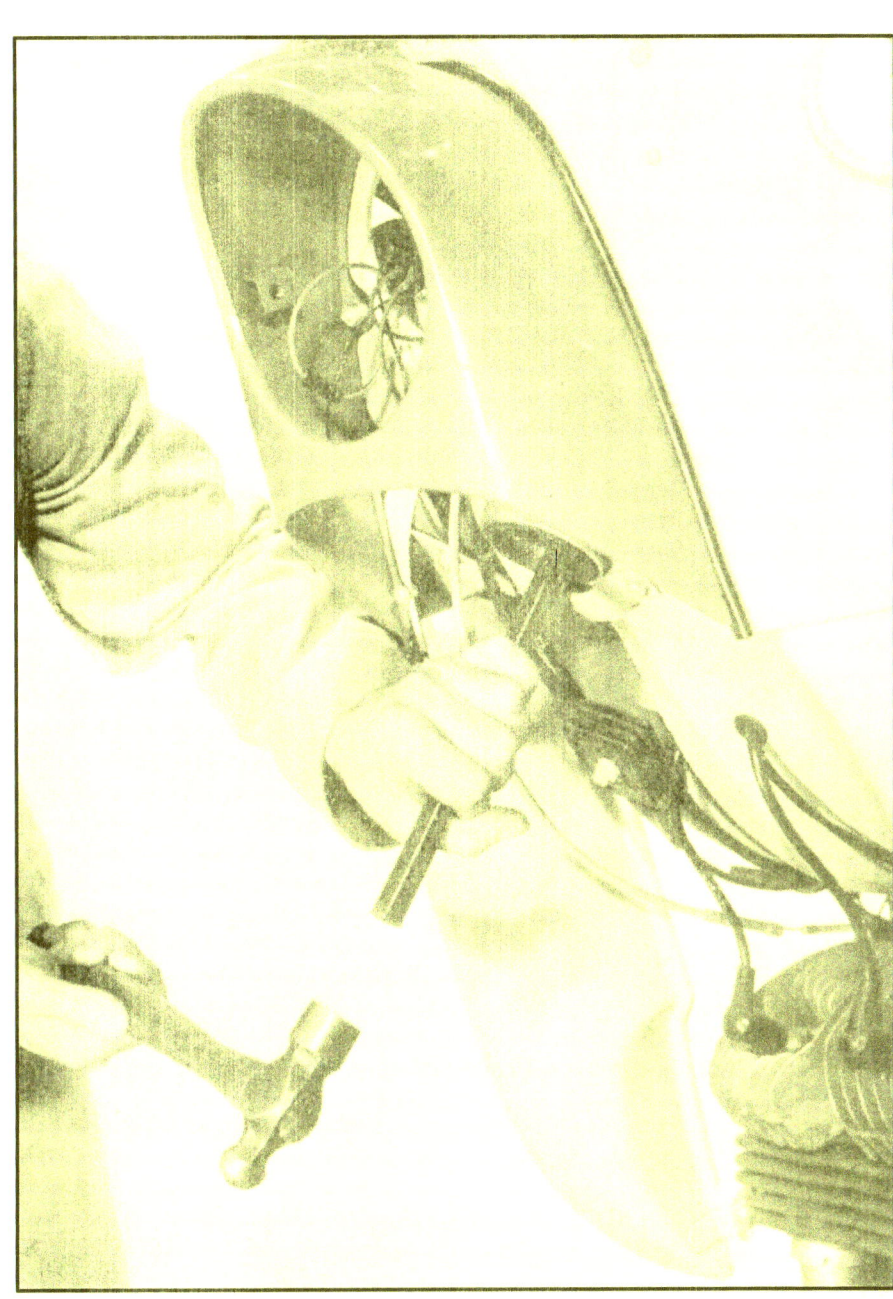

Fig. 141

the spindle assembly through the top of the frame and down through the steering head lug tube so that the new steering head cup 4—1203 is in position on top of the recess in the head lug tube. Next fit the bottom head lug tube locating washer 43589S to the bearing locating collar 43576S, then place the new bottom steering head cup Part No. 41043 over the bearing locating collar 43576S, so that the outer edge of the new steering head cup locates on the outer edge of the bottom head lug tube locating washer 43589S, then fit the bearing locating collar 43576S, which has an internal thread, to that portion of the spindle assembly which projects through the bottom of the steering head lug tube in the frame, so that the new steering head cup 41043 is in position against the recess in the bottom of the steering head lug tube (see Fig. 142).

Note if the machine has been dismantled and the new steering head cups are being fitted to the bare frame, the tommy bar 43585S can be passed through the lug at the top of the spindle assembly 43573S. If, however, in the case of the Leader, the forks only have been removed from the machine, an extension tube for the spindle assembly will be required, and this can be made from a 6 inch length of $1\frac{1}{16}$ inch inside dia. tube with a $\frac{3}{8}$ inch clearance hole drilled through $\frac{1}{2}$ inch from each end. The extension tube can be fitted to the lug at the top end of the spindle assembly 43573S and secured in position with a nut and bolt passing through the $\frac{3}{8}$ inch clearance hole, and the spindle assembly lug. Then the tommy bar can be passed through the other end of the extension tube when this will allow the tommy bar to be turned without it meeting any obstruction (see Fig. 143).

Using the tommy bar, commence turning the spindle assembly in a clockwise direction at the same time making sure that the bearing locating collar 43576S does not rotate with the spindle assembly. Proceed with care making quite certain that the new steering head cups enter the recesses in the steering head lug tube true and square, and continue turning the spindle assembly until both steering head cups are correctly located in the recesses in the steering head lug tube. Then unscrew and take out the service tool. This completes the work on the frame.

The steering head bottom cone which is fitted to the bottom of the steering column of the fork

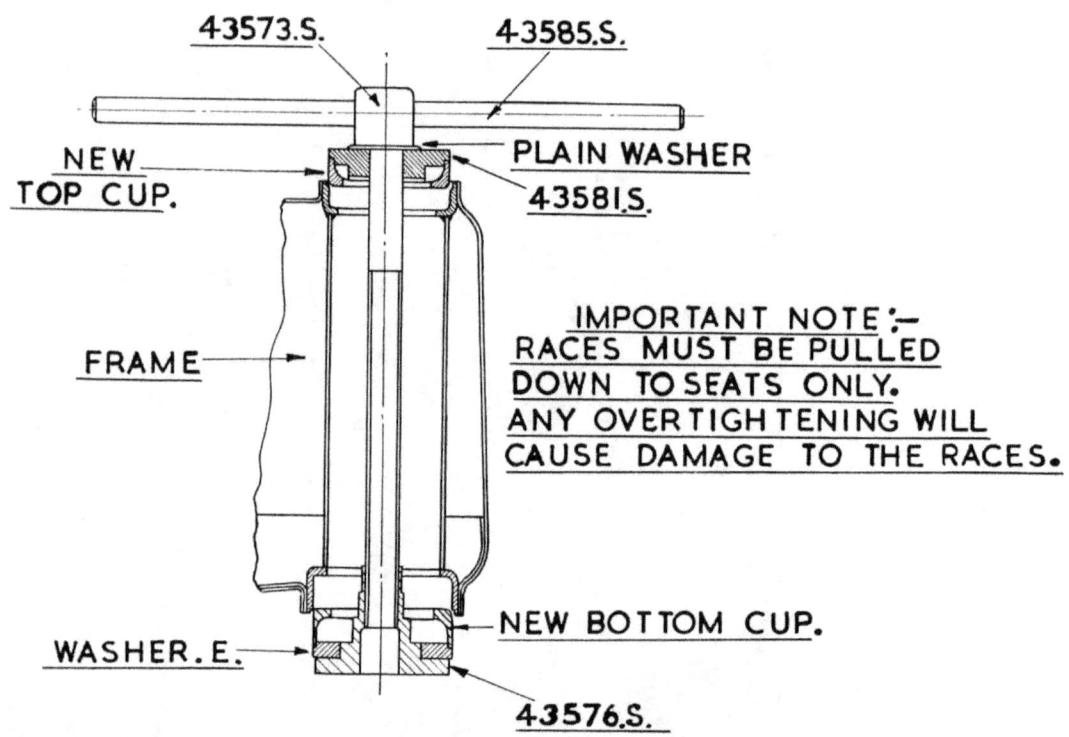

FITTING STEERING HEAD RACES.

Fig. 142

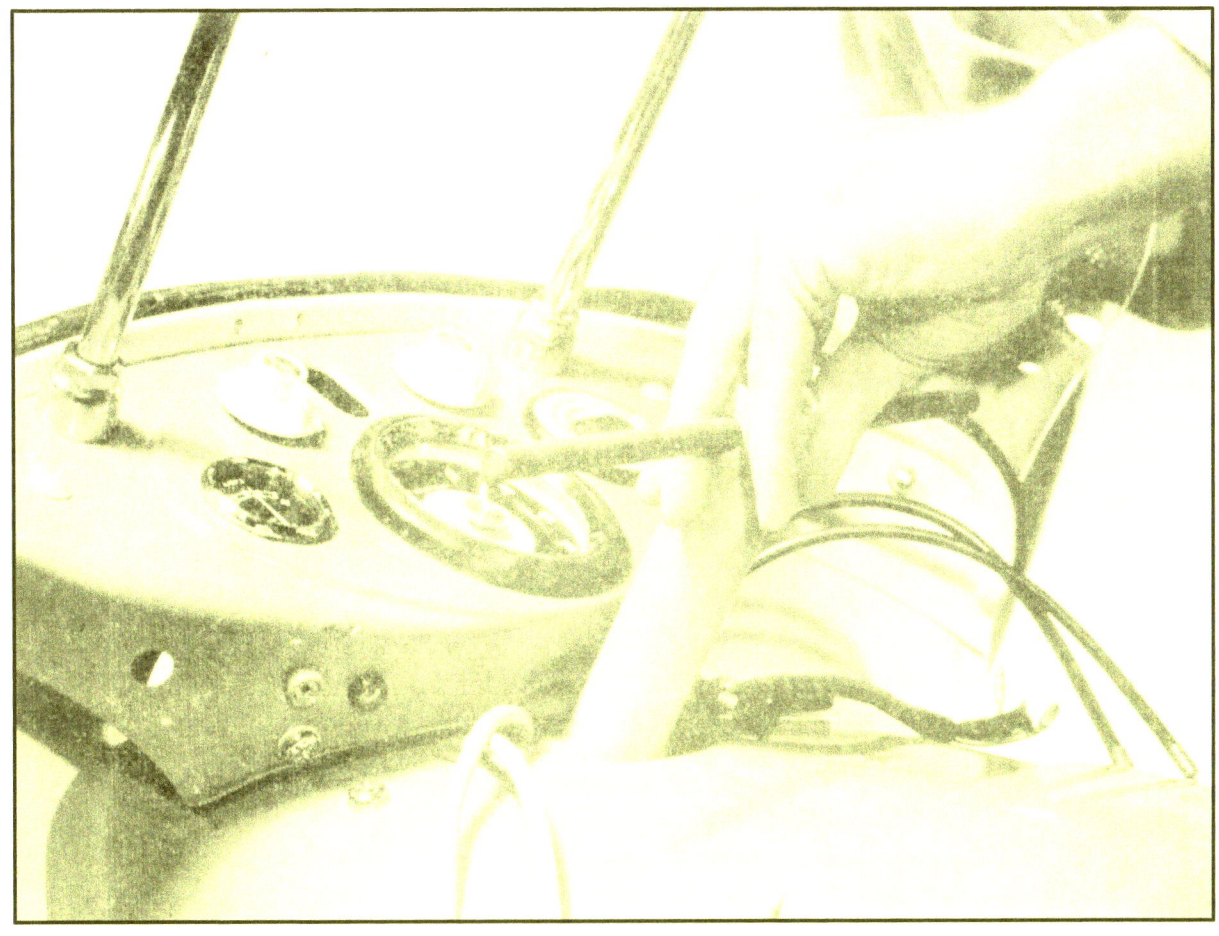

Fig. 143

assembly is dealt with next, but first the front mudguard must be removed from the front fork (see page 153 for instructions on removing front mudguard. The best method of removing the old steering head cone from the steering column is to clamp the steering column vertically in a vice so that the fork assembly is upside down with the rear of the fork legs facing outwards. It can then be seen that a portion of the underside of the bottom steering head cone is exposed at the rear of the fork crown. Then using a drift located at one end of the underside of the exposed portion of the bottom steering head cone apply one or two sharp blows to the drift with a hammer then move the drift to the other end of the exposed portion of the underside of the cone and again apply one or two sharp blows with the hammer (see Fig. 144). Continue in this manner working from end to end using the drift in conjunction with the hammer until the cone is knocked free from the bottom of the steering column. Before fitting the new bottom steering head cone remove any dirt or old grease from the bottom of the steering column, then place the new bottom steering head cone on the steering column and to prevent damage to the new cone fit the old cone, which was removed from the steering column, immediately on the top of the new cone only upside down, so that the inner rims of each cone are touching each other.

A piece of tube will now be required, which will fit over the steering column, and when located on top of the old fork steering head cone, will project above the steering column (see Fig. 145). The tube should be made of steel, 12 inches long and with an inside diameter of $1\frac{5}{16}$ inch, then with the tubing in place on the steering column and resting on top of the old cone, apply a few sharp blows to the top of the tube with a mallet until the new steering head bottom cone is properly located at the bottom of the steering column. Make quite certain that the new bottom cone is correctly seated at the base of the steering column true and square, then remove the piece of tubing and the old cone from the steering column. The forks are now ready to be re-fitted to the motor cycle. For instructions on re-fitting the forks see pages 196 and 205 for a motor cycle which has been dismantled and the forks are being fitted to the bare frame, and pages 142 and 146 for a motor cycle where the fork only has been removed. When assembling the forks it is essential that new steel balls are fitted in the steering head races, and there must be twenty steel balls in the top race and

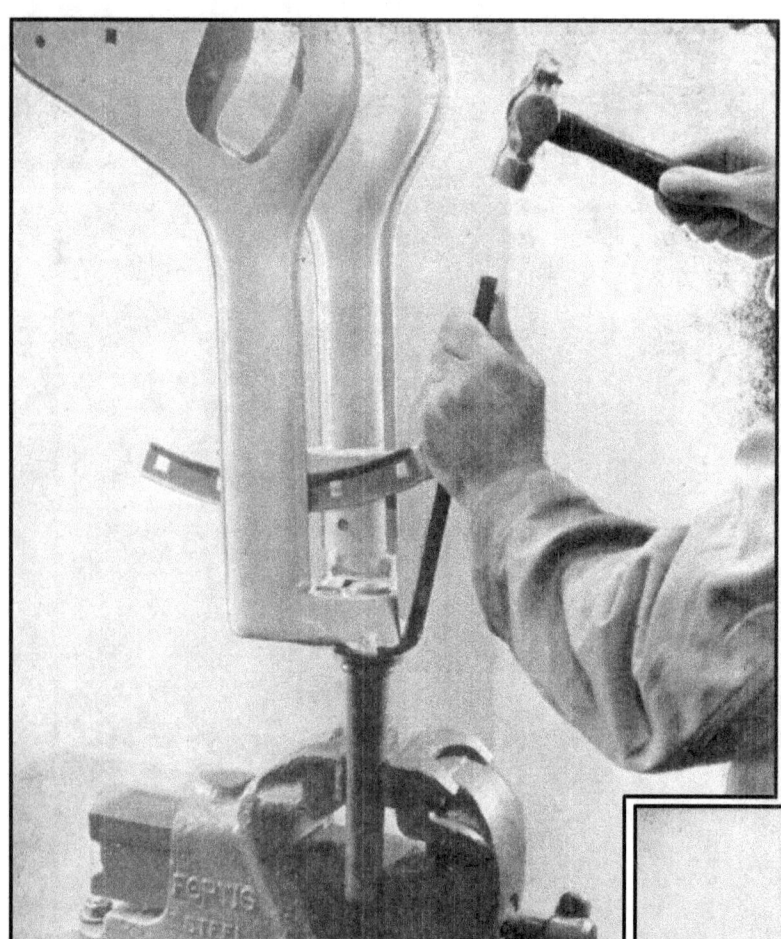

Fig. 144

Fig. 145

twenty-three in the bottom race, and both races must be packed with grease (see Lubrication Chart; use grease as for hubs, etc.). A new top steering head cone should be assembled to the top of the steering head when the forks are being re-fitted.

FRONT MUDGUARD: REMOVAL—LEADER AND ARROW

To remove the front mudguard the motor cycle must be on the centre stand with a front stand also fitted, or a support under the forward end of the exhaust pipes with the front wheel removed (see page 76). Then inside the mudguard at each side can be seen four bolts which screw into brackets welded to the fork legs; there are also two bolts in the centre of the mudguard which secure it to the fork crown. The mudguard is in two separate halves and the front half should be removed first by removing the bolt and nut, which pass through the centre to secure the guard to the front of the fork crown casting, and then the two forward most bolts from each side, when the front section of the guard can then be pulled clear (see Fig, 146). The rear section is removed similarly by taking out the bolt which secures the centre of the guard to the rear of the fork crown and, then removing the two rearmost bolts from each side of the mudguard, when it can be pulled clear. Take care not to lose or damage the two rubber mouldings which fit between the mudguard halves and fork legs.

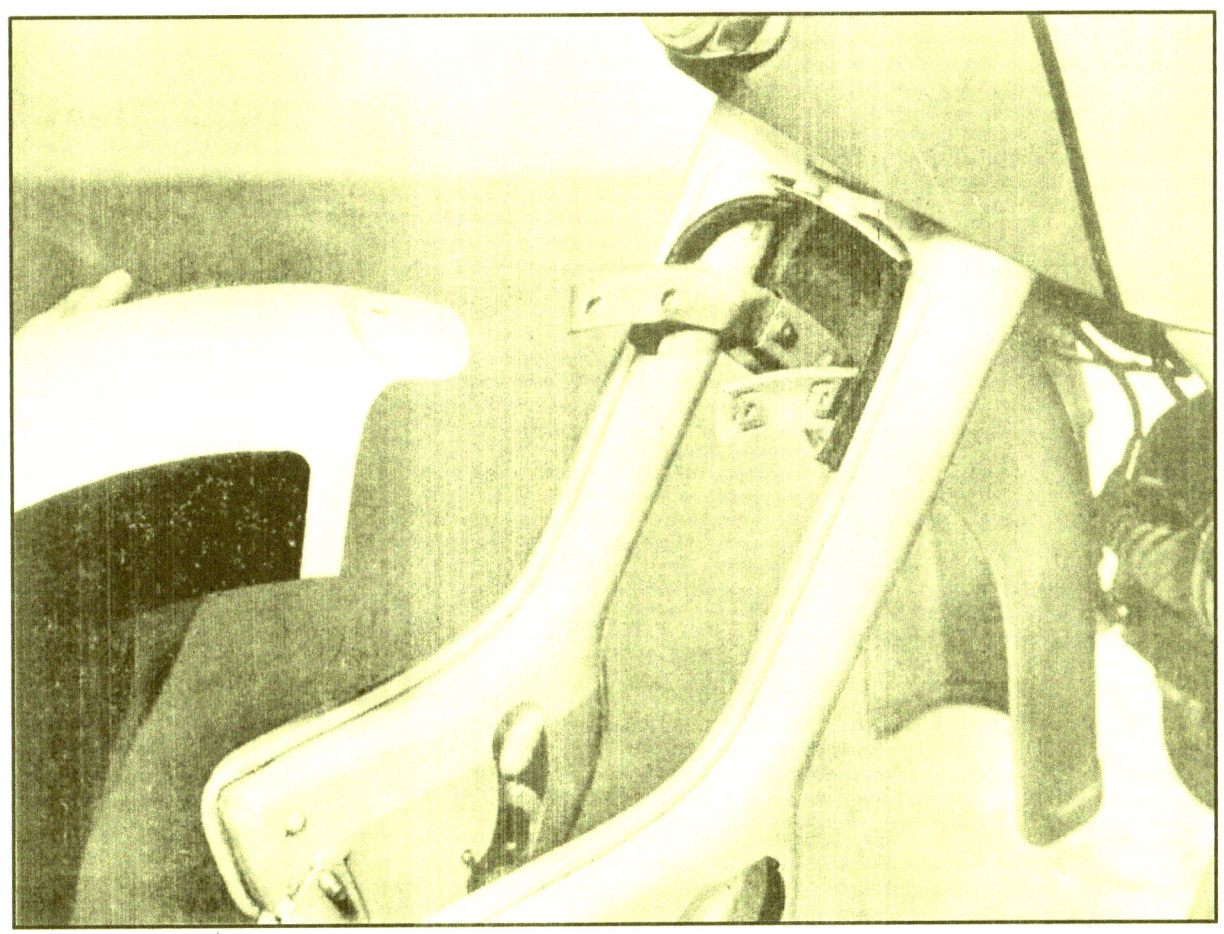

Fig. 146

RE-FITTING FRONT MUDGUARD

Commence with the two rubber mouldings which seal the joint between the front mudguard and the fork legs. To facilitate assembly these mouldings should be liberally moistened with liquid soap in the channel in the moulding into which the mudguards are to be fitted. Fit the rubber mouldings to each side of the rear section of the mudguard, and place the rear section in position on the front forks. Loosely assemble the centre bolt with a shake-proof washer under the head, then see that the two rubber mouldings pass on the inside of each fork leg, making sure that the moulding is correctly located on the rear section of the mudguard. Loosely assemble the two bolts on each side of the rear section of the mudguard with a plain and a shake-proof washer under the head of each bolt, then place the front section of the mudguard in position on the front fork at the same time carefully locating it into the rubber moulding; a thin bladed screwdriver will assist fitting the rubber moulding on to the mudguard. Next loosely assemble the centre nut and bolt which secures the front section of the guard to the fork crown, so that the nut is inside the mudguard together with a shake-proof washer, then loosely assemble the four bolts to the sides of the front section of the mudguard with a plain, and a shake-proof washer under the head of each bolt. Carefully check the two rubber mouldings which seal the joints between the mudguard sections and the fork legs, and if they are fitted satisfactorily, securely tighten the two centre bolts which secure the mudguard sections to the fork crown, then finally tighten the four bolts at each side.

SIDE PANELS—LEADER

Removal of the nearside side panel gives access to almost all engine and primary drive adjustments.

The side panel is secured by five screws, four of which are visible from the side of the machine, and these only require slackening until they float freely, as they will remain attached to the panel by circlips to prevent loss. The remaining screw is at the rear end of the side panel just above the silencer, and this screw must be completely removed. Under each screw head a rubber washer is fitted, and besides preventing damage to the enamel finish, acts as a self-locking device. With the five fixing screws undone, the panel should be carefully removed, easing it over the petrol tap knob, the cold start lever knob and the pillion footrest.

To remove the offside side panel, which is secured in a similar manner, it is necessary to first detach the kick starter and gear change levers. Both are fitted to serrated shafts and secured by pinch bolts and nuts, which should be completely removed before easing the levers off their respective shafts. When removing the gear lever, first ease it half way from its serrated shaft until it is "free", then rotate it to the vertical position and completely remove. This makes it quite unnecessary to disturb the footrest. The five fixing screws are then undone and the side panel eased over the pillion footrest and lifted clear.

Re-fitting—Leader

When re-fitting the nearside side panel, first pull out the cold start control to the start position, and the petrol tap to the on position. Then pass the side panel over the pillion footrest and behind the drivers' footrest, and locate it in position so that the cold start control and petrol tap project through the holes provided and re-fit the five securing screws. Finally push in the petrol tap and cold start control if required. The offside side panel is fitted by passing it over the pillion footrest and behind the drivers' footrest. Then locate it in position so that the kick starter and gear change lever shafts project through the holes provided, and re-fit the five securing screws. Partially re-fit the footchange lever by locating it on its shaft in a vertical position, then rotate it to the position required and press it correctly on to the shaft. Refit the kick start lever in the position required making sure it does not foul the gear change lever at the end of its stroke. Then finally re-fit and securely tighten the pinch bolts in both levers.

If the machine is fitted with panniers, extra care should be taken to avoid damaging the enamel finish when removing and re-fitting the side panels.

LEG SHIELDS—LEADER

As can be seen with the side panels removed, each leg shield is secured at two points, and to remove them unscrew the bolt which passes through the leg shield top bracket and into the frame, and the nut and bolt which secures the bottom of the leg shield to the side panel bracket which passes across the front of the engine. The leg shield can then be pulled down and free. Both leg shields are dealt with similarly.

A rubber bead is fitted to the top of each leg shield where it fits into the front shield, and if these rubbers do not come out with the leg shields as they are removed, they should be taken out of the front shield to prevent loss; also as they must be fitted to the leg shields when re-assembling.

Re-assembling the leg shields is straightforward, first fit the rubber bead to the top edge of the leg shield, towards the outer edge and insert them into the bottom of the front shield. If, however any trouble is experienced through the rubber bead and leg shield being too tight for the front shield, smear the outside of the rubber bead with soft soap, when this will then assist fitting.

Once the leg shield is in position, the top securing bolt and washer can be fitted. The bottom securing brackets are then easily lined up, and the bolt, nut and washer can be fitted and tightened.

ENGINE COVER—ARROW

The engine cover encloses the offside of the crankcase and gear box. Removal of the cover gives access to the gear box oil filler and drain plugs and the clutch adjusters.

To remove the cover, begin by taking off the kick starter and gear change levers. They are both fitted to serrated shafts, and secured with pinch bolts. Both pinch bolts must be completely removed, the kick starter lever can then be eased off its shaft, but when removing the gear change lever, first ease it halfway along its serrated shaft until it is "free", then rotate it to the vertical position and completely remove. This makes it quite unnecessary to disturb the footrests. Next remove the bolt which passes through the forward end of the cover and into the crankcase, then remove the screw from the middle of the cover, and the cover can be lifted clear.

When re-fitting the engine cover, first make sure there is one felt washer fitted to the kick starter shaft, and two on the gear change shaft. Then locate the cover in position, making sure no cables are trapped or pinched, and fit the bolt with a plain washer under its head, through the bracket on the cover and into the front of the crankcase. Next fit the screw with a plain washer under its head, through the middle of the cover and into the adapter on the gear box.

Note: A large rubber grommet is fitted in the side of the engine cover, and removal of this grommet provides access to the gear box oil level plug, if the oil level needs topping up this can be done by using an oil can of the pump type, through the level plug hole. Greasing the end of the screwdriver will facilitate replacing the level plug.

WINDSCREEN—LEADER

REMOVAL—LEADER

Undo the two nylon screws which secure the windscreen to the top of the support stays, and slide the nylon eye bolts and sockets out of the screen and off the support stays. Then unscrew the two sleeve nuts at the base of the support stays to remove them. Next slacken the six screws which secure the windscreen in the front shield. The screen can now be removed, but it may be found that it is a tight fit in the front shield, therefore the procedure suggested below should be followed.

If the screen is damaged and is going to be renewed, do not hesitate to break it completely and carefully remove the pieces remaining in the front shield with a pair of pliers, for whilst the screen is perspex it can still be very sharp.

Note: If the front shield and windscreen are both undamaged, but the motor cycle is being dismantled, the front shield can be removed complete with the windscreen (see page 185).

If, however, an undamaged screen has to be removed from the front shield, the greatest care must be taken to avoid breakage. After undoing the fixings, the only method to be adopted with safety is to strike the screen with the palm of the hand in an upward direction, along the front underside of the bulge (see Fig. 147).

FITTING WINDSCREEN—LEADER

Commence with the rubber sealing strip and corner pieces, together with the six screws with spacer tubes and washers, assembled into the top of the front shield. The screws must not be

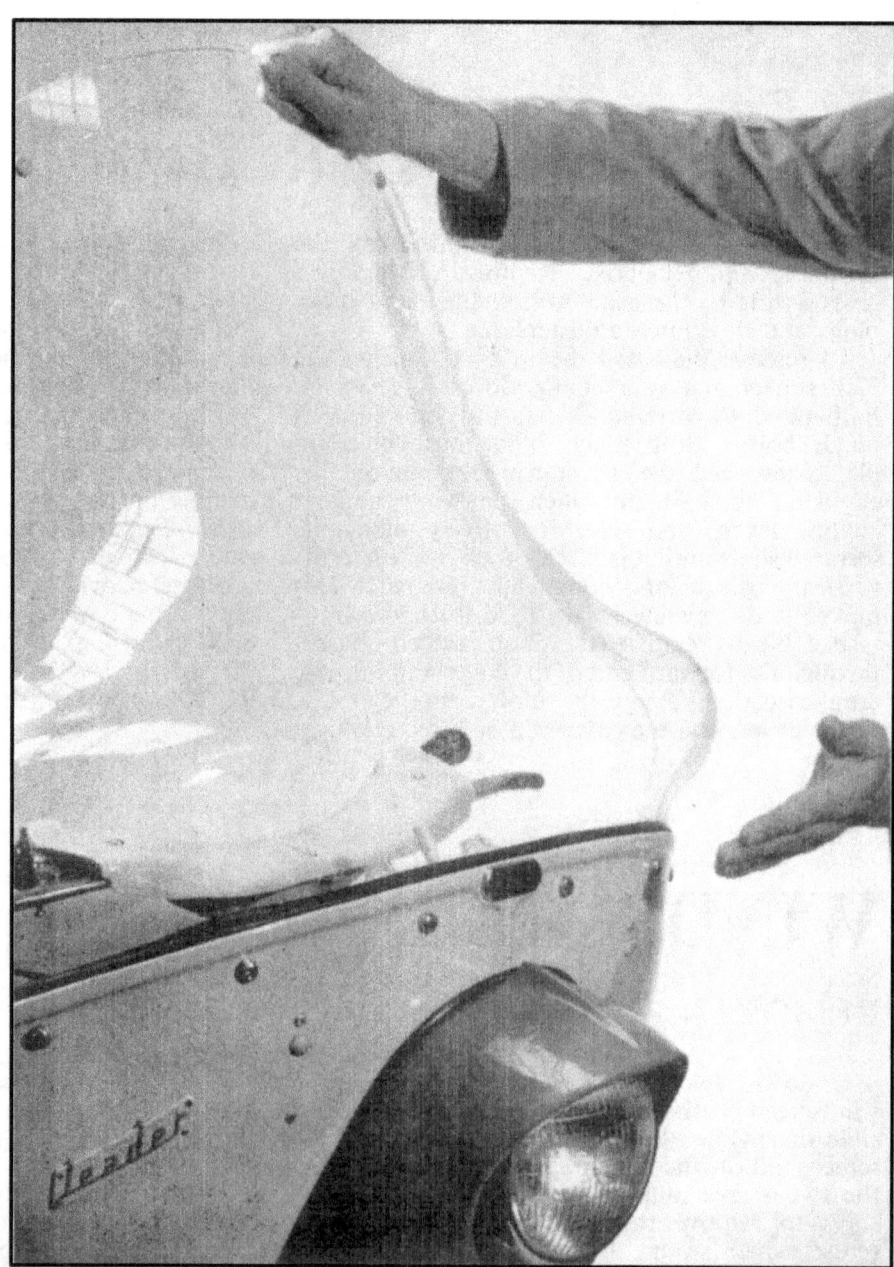

Fig 147

tightened and should only be screwed loosely into the nuts. Then liberally wet the inside of the rubber sealing strip and the bottom of the windscreen with liquid soap. Carefully insert the windscreen into the rubber sealing strip, starting at one end, and gently easing it into position until the screen is in the rubber sealing strip along its entire length. At this stage check that the slots in the bottom of the screen are in line with the fixing screws, then carefully press the windscreen into its correct position on the fixing screws, but do not tighten the screws.

Assemble the windscreen support stays with the sleeve nuts to the sockets in the instrument panel, but leave loose. Fit the nylon eye bolts and sockets together and slide them on to the support stays and into the screen. The nylon screws should then be loosely fitted. Next ease the screen forward to its correct position, and tighten the sleeve nuts at the bottom of the support stays. Position the rubber corner pieces to make a neat joint with the main rubber sealing strip, then tighten all the screws along the top of the front shield. Finally tighten the nylon screws at the top of the support stays, but take care not to over tighten them as this would damage the screws and make subsequent removal very difficult.

EXTENSION FOR WINDSCREEN—LEADER

An adjustable extension for the windscreen is available as an optional extra, and is intended for use by the taller rider who finds the height of the standard windscreen inadequate.

The extension is supplied complete with nylon screws and nuts, and can be fitted or removed in a matter of minutes. To fit an extension, first remove the two plug grommets from the upper half of the windscreen, then locate the extension *on the front of the windscreen*, so that the slots in the extension are in line with the two holes in the windscreen. The two nylon screws must then be fitted through the slots in the extension and holes in the windscreen, then fit the nylon nuts to the screws where they project through the back of the windscreen, but before the screws are fully tightened, the extension should be set at the required height. To make further adjustments of the position of the windscreen extension, first slacken the nylon screws and nuts.

INSTRUMENT PANEL—LEADER

If for any reason it is desired to remove the instrument panel from the motor cycle, follow the instructions on page 166.

However, in the event of any trouble being experienced with any of the instruments or fittings, they can be removed and replaced without disturbing the actual instrument panel, and to deal with any particular item proceed as follows:—

SPEEDOMETER—LEADER

Two types of speedometers are in use, and they vary considerably. They are easily identified as the "Chronometric" type reads up to 80 m.p.h., while the "Magnetic" type reads up to 120 m.p.h. They are interchangeable as a complete unit with cable and grommet. But if a "Magnetic" type is substituted for the "Chronometric" type, then the instrument panel will require slight modification, i.e. a hole must be drilled in the rear of the panel to allow for the different position trip control. A half inch diameter hole $\frac{9}{16}$ inch from the panel top edge and $1\frac{13}{16}$ inch centres to left of the original hole, would be suitable.

If trouble develops in the speedometer it should be returned to the makers for their expert attention. This only applies to the speedometer head, and not to the drive cable and driving gears in the gear box, for which there are separate instructions on page 65 and page 158.

To remove the speedometer from the instrument panel first remove the headlamp unit as described on page 136 in order to gain access, through the hole in the front shield, to the underside of the instrument panel. Also, remove the handlebar cover, as described on page 124, and for the "Magnetic" speedo pull the "trip" control out. Then working through the headlamp cowl with one hand, the underside of the speedometer head can be reached, when it will be found that there are two knurled rings on the underside of the speedometer. The knurled ring which is situated towards the left, when standing in front of the motor cycle, secures the speedometer driving cable from the gear box to the speedometer head. *Note:* With the "Magnetic' speedometer there is only one knurled ring, and this is on the driving cable. In place of the second knurled ring there is a "pull-out" bulb holder. Detach the driving cable by unscrewing the knurled ring by hand. Then push the forward bottom edge of the speedometer head upward to free it from its rubber moulding. *Note:* If the speedometer head is the "Chronometric" type and is fitted with a trip control, it must be tilted so that the front edge is removed first, allowing the trip control rod which is flexible, to be pulled through the back of the instrument panel as the speedometer head is lifted clear. With the speedometer head lifted out of the instrument panel, the only remaining attachment is the lead to the bulb, and this can be detached by unscrewing the second knurled ring or pulling out the bulb holder. The speedometer head is then free.

RE-FITTING SPEEDOMETER HEAD—LEADER

First make certain that the rubber moulding which secures the speedometer head to the instrument panel is in good condition; if in any doubt it should be renewed. Then with the rubber moulding fitted to the instrument panel, liberally wet the inner channel in the moulding and the outer edge of the chrome rim of the speedometer head, with liquid soap. Next fit the bulb with its knurled securing ring or push-in holder to the underside of the speedometer head, then push the speedometer head into the rubber moulding, but note for the "Chronometric" type if a trip control is fitted the control rod must first be passed through the rubber moulding and located through the hole in the back of the instrument panel. The outer edge of the chrome rim can then be fitted into the channel in the rubber moulding, and this is best accomplished with the aid of a thin bladed blunt screwdriver, which if inserted between the speedometer head and the rubber moulding can be used to lever the top edge of the moulding over the outer rim of the speedometer head whilst at the same time pushing the speedometer head down into the channel in the rubber moulding. Continue working in this manner around the speedometer head until it is correctly fitted in the rubber moulding.

Re-fit the speedometer driving cable with its knurled securing ring, to the underside of the speedometer head and with the "Magnetic" type push into position the trip control.

Re-fit the headlamp unit as described on page 141 and finally re-fit the handlebar cover as described on page 124.

To illuminate the speedometer head during darkness, a bulb is fitted which automatically lights up when the motor cycle lights are switched on. In the event of this bulb requiring to be renewed, it will be necessary to remove the headlamp, see page 136; and then to remove the horn so that it hangs by its lead. See page 214 for details on the horn. Undoing the speedometer drive cable, will then enable the bulb holder to be easily removed. The bulb then becomes exposed and it is a simple matter to change on the "Chronometric" type, by pushing it down into its holder and turning sideways. The new bulb must be a 6-volt, 0.3 amp single contact with bayonet fitting and is fitted by locating the pegs at the base of the bulb in the slotted holder and pushing down and turning. In the case of the "Magnetic" speedometer the bulb unscrews from its pull-out holder. The new bulb must be a 6-volt 3-watt screw fitting, and replacements must be the same type. The driving cable, horn and headlamp can then be re-fitted.

The speedometer head is operated by a cable drive from the gear box, and if the speedometer does not function correctly or stops altogether, it may be that the driving cable has broken. To investigate this possibility the complete cable must be removed from the motor cycle. Commence by removing the headlamp unit, and detaching the knurled ring which secures the driving cable to the underside of the speedometer head as already described in the paragraph dealing with removal of the speedometer head. Next remove the offside side panel as described on page 154. This will expose the speedometer driving cable, which is the large cable leading to the front of the gear box, where it is secured by a nut. Undo the nut by turning it with a suitable spanner. Then remove the bolt from the side of the frame, which secures the cable clip to the frame. The speedometer driving cable complete can then be removed from the motor cycle. The large cable is an outer casing to cover and protect the inner driving cable which is very flexible, except for a short portion at each end which is square shaped to provide a coupling for the drive. At the gear box end of the cable there is a further loose coupling into which the square ended inner cable fits. Remove the inner cable, and if it, or one of the square ends are broken, a new inner cable must be fitted. At the same time examine the outer casing as this must be in good condition. If it is damaged this may have been the cause of the inner cable breaking. Therefore, in a case like this the outer casing also should be renewed.

Before fitting a new inner cable it should be smeared with a medium grease, except for the square ends which should be kept clean. Then insert the inner cable into the outer casing and fit the loose coupling to the gear box end of the cable making certain that the square end of the inner cable is fitted into the socket in the loose coupling. The cable can then be fitted to the gear box, but make sure the flat peg on the loose coupling locates correctly into the lug on the gear box. If the peg will not go in, rotate the rear wheel slowly while pushing the cable into the lug on the gear box, when the peg will then locate itself. The nut on the cable outer casing can then be fitted to the lug on the gear box and tightened firmly, but not excessively. Next re-fit the cables and cable clip to the side of the frame, then pass the speedometer cable behind the offside leg shield and up behind the front shield. Then working through the headlamp cowl fit the speedometer cable with its knurled ring to the underside of the speedometer head. Finally re-fit the headlamp unit, as described on page 141, and the offside side panel as described on page 154.

Note: If trouble has been experienced with the speedometer and the speedometer head and cable is in good order, the parts inside the gear box which drive the cable should be examined and rectified or renewed if required. See page 65 for details on the gear box.

AMMETER—LEADER

The ammeter is an instrument which indicates the amount of charge to, or discharge from, the battery. With the engine and all electrical equipment switched off, the needle on the ammeter dial should indicate zero, i.e. in the centre position. The needle may not point exactly to the zero mark, but this is quite in order providing the needle always returns to the same position when everything is switched off. With a new motor cycle or ammeter the zero position of the needle should be noted and if it is slightly out of centre this should be kept in mind when checking the amount of charge or discharge.

With the engine running and the motor cycle travelling at over 20 m.p.h. in top gear, the ammeter should always show a charge, i.e. the needle should be between the centre position and the plus sign. The only times when the ammeter should show a discharge, i.e. when the needle is between the centre position and the minus sign are when the engine is running very slowly, or when the engine is stopped but with the ignition or the lights switched on. If a discharge is shown at any other times than these, this indicates a fault in the electrical equipment which must be rectified immediately. The cause could be either a short in the wiring circuit, i.e. the cover of a lead may have worn through allowing two bare leads to touch, or a bare lead to touch a part of the motor cycle; or a defect may have developed in the rectifier or the A.C. generator. See separate instruction for electrical equipment on page 212.

Occasionally after considerable use the ammeter indicator needle may become loose and stick in one position, and although the ammeter is still functioning it will not give a true reading, and it should therefore be renewed.

If trouble develops in the ammeter itself, the engine cannot be started and the lights will not operate. A method of checking the ammeter, or starting the engine and making the lights usable, as a temporary measure in an emergency, is to detach one of the leads from the underside of the ammeter and fit it to the same terminal as the other ammeter lead. This in effect joins the two leads together by-passing the ammeter, and if the engine can then be started and the lights switched on this will prove the ammeter to be at fault, and it must be renewed as soon as possible.

To remove the ammeter from the instrument panel, first to avoid the possibility of a short, disconnect the battery as described on page 213, then, if the motor cycle is fitted with a parking lamp, the switch which is fitted to the left hand side of the instrument panel must be removed. The thin nut which can be seen on the switch, secures it to the panel, remove the nut by turning it in an anti-clockwise direction, when the switch can then be pushed through to the inside of the instrument panel. Take care not to lose the on-off indicator plate which will become detached as the switch is pushed through the instrument panel. Leave the switch inside the instrument panel, where it will remain attached by its lead.

Insert one hand under the nearside of the instrument panel, so that the fingers can be used to push the ammeter upward, then with the other hand pressing on the top of the instrument panel, push the ammeter up and out of the panel, but note a strong push will be required.

With the ammeter free from the instrument panel the two leads to the underside can be detached by simply removing the nuts and washers; note the colour of the leads and to which side of the ammeter they are fitted, as they must be fitted in the same order to the new ammeter.

To fit a new ammeter, first connect the leads to their respective terminal screws on the underside of the ammeter. Then note that the ammeter chrome rim has four tags; place the ammeter in the hole in the instrument panel with the four tags located through the four slots around the edge of the hole in the instrument panel, and with the rubber sealing ring between the instrument panel and the ammeter chrome rim. Then working from under the nearside end of the instrument panel with a small screwdriver, use the blade of the screwdriver to bend the two nearside tags outward. The front offside tag can be reached and bent outward with a long thin screwdriver, by working through the headlamp cowl after removing the headlamp unit as described on page 136. The fourth tag cannot be reached, but if three have been bent outwards properly this will be sufficient to secure the ammeter.

Finally, if the motor cycle is fitted with a parking lamp, the switch must be passed back into the hole in the instrument panel, so that the threaded portion and the knob are outside the panel. The on-off indicator plate is then re-fitted, but note there is a tag on the indicator plate which must be located in the groove in the threaded portion of the switch, then re-fit and tighten the thin nut.

WARNING LIGHTS—LEADER

For machines fitted with flashing indicators or a neutral gear indicator; warning lights are provided in the instrument panel. The warning light for the flashing indicators is fitted in the nearside of the top of the instrument panel, and shows an amber light when the flashing indicators are operating. The warning light for the neutral gear indicator is fitted in the offside of the top of the instrument panel, and shows a white light whenever the gear box is in the neutral position with the ignition switched on.

The two warning lights are almost identical, the only variations being the colour of the lead to the bulb holder and the colour of the lens on the instrument panel. Therefore the following instructions apply to both warning lights.

To change a bulb in one of the warning lights, it is only necessary to insert one hand under the end of the instrument panel and pull the lower portion of the warning light which is the bulb holder, sideways. This will free the holder and expose the bulb, the bulb simply screws out and it is a 6-volt 3-watt screw-in type, and replacements must be of the same type. The new bulb must be pushed into the holder at the same time as it is turned clockwise to screw it in. The bulb and holder can then be pushed back into the warning light body.

To remove a warning light from the instrument panel first insert one hand under the end of the instrument panel and pull apart the snap connector in the lead to the warning light, the snap connector will be found approximately four to five inches from the warning light, and the lead simply pulls out. Still working from under the end of the instrument panel, hold the portion of the warning light which is immediately under the instrument panel and turn it clockwise, when it will come free, but do not lose the shake-proof washer which is fitted between the warning light body and the instrument panel. The lens in the instrument panel can be removed by simply lifting it out.

When assembling the warning light to the instrument panel, the bulb holder and the body with the lead all assembled together should be placed under the instrument panel with the shake-proof washer on top of the body. Then line up the hole in the centre of the body with the hole in the instrument panel, and place the lens in the top of the panel so that the threaded portion of the lens locates in the hole in the body, then push the lens and body down so that the lens is fitted in the panel correctly and turn the body to screw it on to the threaded portion of the lens until the warning light is properly secured. Finally fit the warning light lead into the snap connector under the instrument panel, which is already fitted with a lead with a corresponding colour.

LIGHTING AND IGNITION SWITCHES—LEADER AND ARROW

There are two different types of lighting and ignition switches in use, they are easily identified as one type has the ignition switch operated by a key, whereas the other type does not have a key and is a normal switch. Dealing first with the type without a key, the two switches are almost identical in appearance, and the instructions for removing and re-fitting are similar, only varying in the number and assembly of leads, but this variation together with the difference in switch operation, makes the switches non-interchangeable. It is therefore essential to obtain the correct type, when fitting a new switch.

To replace a damaged or lost switch knob is quite simple. If the old knob has to be removed, unscrew the small screw in the top of the knob, when the knob and screw can be lifted clear, but take care not to lose the chromium plated washer from below the screw. The new knob is then located on the square portion of the switch which projects above the Leader instrument panel, or the Arrow headlamp, and secured in position with the screw and washer which were removed when the old knob was taken off.

If trouble should develop in one of the switches, a satisfactory repair is not practical and a new switch should be fitted. In order to fit a new switch the existing one must first be removed from the cable harness. Begin by removing the screw from the top of the switch knob and lifting the knob clear, this will expose a flat square nut which secures the switch to the Leader instrument panel, or the Arrow headlamp, remove the nut, taking care not to lose the small split ring from below the nut, and push the top of the switch down through the instrument panel or headlamp as the case may be. Then, for the Leader, continue by inserting one hand under the end of the instrument panel, the switch and cable harness can be pulled out a few inches from the end of the instrument panel.

Note: If a lighting switch is being removed it will pull from under the nearside end of the instrument panel easily and sufficiently to enable the necessary work to be carried out. If, however, an ignition switch is being removed, in order to gain full accessibility pull the main harness as well as the switch towards the offside end of the instrument panel, when the switch will then extend from the end of the panel sufficiently to carry out the necessary work. In the case of the Arrow, remove the headlamp unit. *Note:* The battery should be disconnected to prevent the possibility of a short.

Then with the switch and harness assembly protruding from the end of the instrument panel, or the inside of the headlamp shell in the case of the Arrow, roll back the rubber shroud and remove the switch by cutting through all the leads, as close as possible to the switch, using a pair of pliers or wire cutters.

A new switch is supplied with short leads and snap connectors already fitted, together with spare connectors for soldering to the leads which were cut from the old switch. To fit the spare connectors to the leads which were cut from the switch, first cut away approximately ¼ inch of the insulating cover from the end of each lead. Then dealing with the leads one at a time, pass a connector over the lead so that the bare wire just projects through the hole in the end of the connector, and then solder the connector in this position taking care to keep the outside of the connector free from solder. When connectors have been fitted to all the leads pass them through the rubber shroud, and then they can be pushed into the snap connectors which are fitted to the short leads from the new switch. *Note:* There may be a slight variation in the colour marking of the leads on the new switch, but if the leads are coupled as detailed in the following chart no mistake can be made. The terminal numbers are marked on the underside of the switch.

Lighting Switch No. 54033004

Terminal Number	New Switch Lead Colour	Harness Lead Colour
1	Red with black	Red with black
2	Brown with white	Brown with white
3	Blue	Blue
4	No lead fitted	No lead fitted
5	Black	Black
6	No lead fitted	No lead fitted
7	Green with black	Green with black or green
8	Brown with green	Brown with green
9	No terminal	No terminal
10	No lead fitted	No lead fitted
11	Brown with green	Brown with green

Note: The two brown and green leads in the harness can be fitted to either of the brown and green leads from the switch.

Ignition Switch No. 54033003

Terminal Number	New Switch Lead Colour	Harness Lead Colour
12	Brown with white	Brown with white
13	Purple	Brown with purple
14	White	White
15	Black with white	Black with white
16	Green with yellow	Green with yellow
17	No lead fitted	No lead fitted
18	Black	Black
19	No lead fitted	No lead fitted

When all the leads have been coupled with the snap connectors, in accordance with the relative chart, the switch is passed back under the instrument panel, or into the headlamp in the case of the Arrow, and the threaded portion at the top of the switch must be located through the "D" shaped hole in the instrument panel, or headlamp; the split ring and the flat square nut are then fitted to the threaded portion of the switch. Finally, re-fit the knob to the switch and secure it in position with the screw which passes through the top of the knob, not forgetting the chromium plated washer.

For machines which are fitted with a key operated ignition switch, the following instructions apply. To replace a lost or damaged lighting switch knob is quite simple. If the old knob has to be removed, unscrew the small screw in the top of the knob, when the knob and screw can be lifted clear, but take care not to lose the chromium plated washer from below the screw. The new knob is then located on the square portion of the switch which projects above the Leader instrument panel, or the Arrow headlamp, and secured in position with the screw and washer which were removed when the old knob was taken off. The ignition switch has a rubber cover in place of a knob, and this cover simply pulls off or pushes on as required.

If trouble should develop in one of the switches, a satisfactory repair is not practical and a new switch should be fitted. Begin by removing the knob or rubber cover as already described, this will expose a thin nut which secures the switch to the Leader instrument panel or the Arrow headlamp, remove the nut, if a lighting switch is being dealt with take care not to lose the small split ring from below the nut, then push the top of the switch down through the top of the instrument panel or headlamp as the case may be. For the Leader continue by inserting one hand under the end of the instrument panel, the switch and cable harness can be pulled out a few inches from the end of the instrument panel. In the case of the Arrow remove the headlamp unit. *Note:* the battery should be disconnected to prevent the possibility of a short.

The switch is comprised of a plug and socket, the socket is connected to the main wiring harness and the switch can easily be pulled free from the socket, and a new switch inserted. Due to the lay out of the pins on the switch, it is not possible to fit a switch incorrectly. The new switch can then be passed back under the instrument panel, or into the headlamp in the case of the Arrow. The threaded portion at the top of the switch must be located through the "D" shaped hole in the instrument panel or headlamp. The thin nut, and for a lighting switch the split ring, are then fitted to the threaded portion of the switch. Finally refit the switch knob or rubber cover.

INSPECTION LAMP—LEADER

The inspection lamp is an optional extra and if it is desired to add an inspection lamp to the equipment of the motor cycle, no special fitting is involved. Every motor cycle is provided with inspection lamp plug sockets fitted to the instrument panel, as part of the standard equipment. The inspection lamp is supplied complete ready to plug into the sockets, when it will immediately light up.

Note: The inspection lamp should only be plugged in when it is being used. When not in use, the plugs must be withdrawn from the sockets, and it is advisable to keep the inspection lamp in the glove compartment or the tool tray, for use in an emergency. If the inspection lamp has red and black leads, these should be pushed into their corresponding sockets only, i.e. red lead into red socket. This is to avoid any possibility of a short occurring should the bulb holder come into contact with the motor cycle.

To renew the bulb in the inspection lamp first remove the two screws from the sides of the lamp, when the lamp lens and clip can then be lifted clear. The bulb can then be unscrewed in an anti-clockwise direction. The new bulb must be a 6-volt, 3-watt screw fitting type, and it is fitted by screwing it in, in a clockwise direction. The lamp lens and clip can then be re-fitted and secured in position with the two screws.

PLASTIC LAMP

In the case of the all plastic inspection lamp the question of a possible short circuit does not arise, therefore, either wire can be plugged into either plug.

To replace a bulb grasp the lamp body in the left hand and with the right forefingers and thumb around the plastic lens it can be easily snapped out of its retaining groove; in cold weather it may be necessary to warm the lens in the hand for a few moments to facilitate removal. The bulb is a 6-volt 6-watt bayonet fitting and to remove press in slightly and rotate anti-clockwise to withdraw.

The two inspection lamp sockets fitted to the instrument panel do not require any attention unless one should become broken, or it is required to remove the lead from the one socket. In this event, both sockets are removed in a similar manner. The sockets are provided with screwdriver slots and they must be turned in an anti-clockwise direction. It will be necessary while unscrewing the sockets to pass one hand under the end of the instrument panel, and hold the round nuts at the back of the sockets and prevent them turning.

As the sockets become free from the round nut, take care not to lose any of the washers, etc., and note only the black socket has a lead attached to it. The red one being the earth return.

When fitting a new socket or re-assembling the originals, commence by passing the socket pin, with its coloured plastic insulator in position, through the instrument panel, so that the coloured insulator remains outside the instrument panel. Then if it is the red socket that is being fitted, working from under the end of the instrument panel, assemble a plain washer and a shake-proof washer to the socket pin, then fit the round nut, and hold it to prevent it turning, while the socket is tightened by turning it with a screwdriver.

If it is the black socket that is being fitted, when the socket pin and insulator are in position in the instrument panel, working from under the end of the panel, assemble the two fibre washers and the rectangular fibre insulator card to the socket pin, then fit the lead, followed by a shake-proof washer and the round nut. Hold the nut to prevent it from turning, also hold the rectangular fibre insulator card so that it is positioned between the two socket pins, then tighten the socket by turning it with a screwdriver.

Note: In the event of the lamp not operating, a quick check can be made by touching the lamp plugs to the battery terminals; if the lamp operates in this manner but does not when plugged in correctly, the trouble will probably be a bad earth at the red plug this must be checked and any paint or corrosion scratched away at the back of the panel.

AMMETER—ARROW

The ammeter is an instrument which indicates the amount of charge to or discharge from the battery. With the engine and all electrical equipment switched off, the needle on the ammeter dial should indicate zero, i.e., in the centre position. The needle may not point exactly to the zero mark, but this is quite in order providing the needle always returns to the same position when everything is switched off. With a new motor cycle or ammeter the zero position of the needle should be noted and if it is slightly out of centre this should be kept in mind when checking the amount of charge or discharge.

With the engine running and the motor cycle travelling at over 20 m.p.h. in top gear, the ammeter should always show a charge, i.e., the needle should be between the centre position and the plus sign.

The only times when the ammeter should show a discharge, i.e., when the needle is between the centre position and the minus sign are when the engine is running very slowly, or when the engine is stopped but with the ignition or the lights switched on. If a discharge is shown at any other times than these, this indicates a fault in the electrical equipment which must be rectified immediately. The cause could be either a short in the wiring circuit, i.e., the cover of a lead may have worn through allowing two bare leads to touch, or a bare lead to touch a part of the motor cycle; or, a defect may have developed in the rectifier or the A.C. generator. See separate instructions for electrical equipment on page 212.

Occasionally after considerable use the ammeter indicator needle may become loose and stick in one position, and although the ammeter is still functioning it will not give a true reading, and it should therefore be renewed.

If trouble develops in the ammeter itself, the engine cannot be started and the lights will not come on. A method of checking the ammeter, or starting the engine and making the lights usable, as a temporary measure in an emergency, is to detach one of the leads from the underside of the ammeter and fit to the same terminal as the other ammeter lead.

This in effect joins the two leads together, by-passing the ammeter, and if the engine can then be started and the lights can be switched on this will prove the ammeter to be at fault, and it must be renewed as soon as possible.

To remove the ammeter from the top of the headlamp, first remove the headlamp unit as described on page 214, then detach the leads from the two terminals on the underside of the ammeter, by removing the two nuts. Next bend down the four tags which secure the ammeter into the headlamp, the ammeter can then be pushed up and out of the headlamp.

When re-fitting the ammeter, there must be a rubber sealing ring between the ammeter rim and the top of the headlamp. Then when the ammeter is in position, the four tags must be bent up against the inside of the headlamp. Next connect the leads to the terminals at the bottom of the ammeter, the lead coloured brown with blue must be connected to the offside terminal, while the leads coloured brown with white must be connected to the nearside terminal. Finally, re-fit the headlamp unit as described on page 214.

SPEEDOMETER—ARROW

If any trouble should develop in the speedometer, it should be returned to the makers for their expert attention. This only applies to the speedometer head, and not to the driving cable and driving gears in the gear box, for which there are separate instructions on page 65.

To remove the speedometer from the headlamp, first remove the headlamp unit as described on page 214. Then inside the headlamp can be seen the body of the speedometer, and the driving cable which is attached to the bottom of the speedometer by a knurled ring, unscrew the knurled ring to free the cable, then on the same boss as the knurled ring is a hexagon nut; remove this nut and the bracket above, when the speedometer head can be pushed up out of the headlamp.

When refitting the speedometer the rubber grommet must be in place under the rim. The speedometer can then be passed through the hole in the top of the headlamp, and the bracket and hexagon nut fitted to the bottom of the speedometer. Next locate the inner cable into the boss on the bottom of the speedometer, and secure the cable in position with the knurled ring. Then re-fit the headlamp unit as described on page 214. The speedometer head is operated by a cable drive from the gear box, and if the speedometer does not function correctly or stops altogether, it may be that the driving cable has broken. To investigate this possibility commence by removing the headlamp unit, and detaching the knurled ring which secures the driving cable to the underside of the speedometer head as already described in the paragraph dealing with removal of the speedometer head. Next remove the engine cover as described on page 155. This will expose the speedometer driving cable, which is the large cable leading to the front of the gear box, where it is secured by a nut. Undo the nut by turning it with a suitable spanner, then pull the inner cable out of the main speedometer cable in the headlamp, if only a portion of the inner cable is pulled out due to it being broken, the remainder must be withdrawn from the gear box end. The large cable is an outer casing to cover and protect the inner driving cable which is very flexible, except for a short portion at each end which is square shaped to provide a coupling for the drive.

At the gear box end of the cable there is a further loose coupling into which the square ended inner cable fits. If the inner cable or one of the square ends are broken, a new inner cable must be fitted. At the same time examine the outer casing as this must be in good condition. If it is damaged this may have been the cause of the inner cable breaking.

Therefore, in a case like this the outer casing also should be renewed. Before fitting a new inner cable it should be smeared with a medium grease, except for the square ends which should be kept clean.

Then insert the inner cable into the outer casing and fit the loose coupling to the gear box end of the cable, making certain that the square end of the inner cable is fitted into the socket in the loose coupling. The cable can then be fitted to the gear box, but make sure the flat peg on the loose coupling locates correctly into the lug on the gear box. If the peg will not go in, rotate the rear wheel slowly while pushing the cable into the lug on the gear box, when the peg will then locate itself. The nut on the cable outer casing can then be fitted to the lug on the gear box and tightened firmly, but not excessively.

Then working inside the headlamp fit the speedometer cable with its knurled ring to the underside of the speedometer head. Finally re-fit the headlamp unit, as described on page 214 and the front shell as described on page 171.

Note: If trouble has been experienced with the speedometer, and the speedometer head and cable are in good order, the parts inside the gear box which drive the cable should be examined and rectified or renewed if required. See page 62 for details on the gear box. If it should be required to remove the speedometer outer cable from the motor cycle, begin by detaching both ends as already described. Then remove the front shell as described on page 170 and disconnect and withdraw the electric horn leads from the plastic sheath. The speedometer outer cable can then be carefully withdrawn down through the plastic sheath. When fitting the outer cable, pass it up through the sheath and reconnect the two electric horn leads as described on page 216.

Next re-fit the front shell as described on page 171, then fit the speedometer inner cable as already described.

EIGHT-DAY CLOCK—LEADER

The eight-day clock is not a standard fitting, but an optional extra, and is therefore not fitted to all motor cycles, but for motor cycles fitted with an eight-day clock, or for machines to which it is desired to fit a clock, the following instructions apply.

First, to fit an eight-day clock to a machine which has not previously had one fitted. The new clock must be of the correct type, which is obtainable from all Ariel agents. Then commence by removing the Ariel badge from the offside of the top of the instrument panel, by inserting one hand under the end of the panel and pushing the badge upward. This will free the badge when it is an easy matter to remove from the panel the grommet which secured the badge. The clock can then be fitted into the badge hole, as described below.

Fitting the Eight-Day Clock

After removing the two knurled nuts, washers and the "U" shaped bracket from the underside of the clock, pass the clock with the winder knob first, through the hole in the top of the instrument panel, and locate the winder knob through the oval-shaped hole in the rear of the instrument panel. It may be found that the winder knob appears to be too tight in the oval-shaped hole to pass through. This can be overcome by inserting one hand under the end of the instrument panel and pushing the knob firmly. When the clock is in position in the instrument panel, the rubber sealing ring must be seated in the loose metal ring between the clock chrome rim and the instrument panel. Then working from under the end of the instrument panel, fit the "U" shaped bracket to the clock so that the bracket is located on the two studs in the bottom of the clock, and against the underside of the instrument panel. Then fit the spring washers and knurled nuts to the studs in the bottom of the clock. The clock can then be wound up and started, by turning the winder knob. To adjust the fingers of the clock pull the winder knob outwards and turn it in the required direction.

Removing Eight-Day Clock

To remove the clock from the instrument panel insert one hand under the offside end of the instrument panel, when it will be found that there are two knurled nuts at the bottom of the clock. Remove the knurled nuts, do not lose the spring washer which is fitted under each nut. Mounted on the studs from which the knurled nuts were removed is a "U" shaped bracket, which will now simply pull off. The clock can then be lifted or pushed out of the instrument panel, but it will have to be eased and tilted in order to draw the winder knob through the panel.

Note: In the event of any trouble developing

in the mechanism of the clock, it should be returned to the makers for their expert attention. However, if the clock gains or loses slightly it can be adjusted, and to do this remove the clock from the instrument panel as already described. Then if the clock is examined it will be seen that there is a small slot in the side of the clock just below the "three" on the dial. The slot has a cover which slides open by pulling the small knob on the cover with a thumb or finger nail. Through the slot with the cover open, can be seen a lever, and the slot is marked at each end. One end is marked "F" and the other "S". If the clock has been gaining move the lever very slightly towards the "S", or if the clock has been losing move the lever very slightly towards the "F".

Then before re-fitting the clock it should be checked several times against a reliable time check, such as a radio time signal, and adjusted further if necessary. When the clock is operating satisfactorily it can be re-fitted to the motor cycle as already described.

If it should be desired to re-fit the badge in the instrument panel clock hole, first fit the grommet into the hole, but note the grommet must be fitted so that the recess for the badge is uppermost, then place the badge on the grommet, with as much of the badge as possible inserted into the recess in the grommet. Then using the blade of a small screwdriver, prise the edge of the grommet over that portion of the badge which is still outside the recess.

PARKING LAMP—LEADER

The parking lamp is an optional extra, fitted to new motor cycles by special order only, but a parking lamp can be obtained from an Ariel agent and easily fitted to a machine that has not previously had one fitted.

Dealing first with fitting a parking lamp to a motor cycle to which one has not previously been fitted.

Note: If flashing indicators are not fitted to the motor cycle, the lead from the parking lamp must have one of the small washer type of terminals soldered to the loose end, in place of the existing snap connector.

Commence by fitting the parking lamp centrally to the top rear edge of the front shield. There are two tapped holes at this point, and screws which fit into the tapped holes are supplied with the parking lamp. When the parking lamp has been secured in position, by passing the screws through the parking lamp and into the tapped holes, the lead from the parking lamp must be passed through the slot in the grommet, through which the headlamp trimmer rod also passes.

Then, for a machine not fitted with flashing indicators, remove the thin nut and the on-off indicator plate from the parking lamp switch, and working from under the nearside end of the instrument panel, attach the lead from the parking lamp to either of the switch terminals. Next, remove the lead which is coloured red with black, from the sub-harness supplied with the lamp. The remaining leads coloured brown with blue are not required and can be discarded. Then attach the lead, coloured red with black, to the other terminal on the parking lamp switch.

Next remove the headlamp unit as described on page 136, the electric horn can then be seen through the back of the headlamp cowl. The lead, which is attached to the electric horn, incorporates a double snap connector which has only three leads connected to it. Push into the spare socket on the double snap connector, the lead coloured red with black, which is already attached at the other end to the parking lamp switch. Then re-fit the headlamp unit as described on page 141. It now only remains to fit the parking lamp switch to the instrument panel. The threaded portion of the switch should have one thin nut fitted, and then be passed through the hole in the instrument panel, to the left of the inspection lamp sockets, so that the threaded portion and the knob are outside the panel. The on-off indicator plate is then fitted. But note there is a tag on the indicator plate which must be located in the groove in the threaded portion of the switch, then fit the second thin nut. The thin nut inside the instrument panel can be adjusted on the threaded portion of the switch, so that when the second thin nut is tightened to secure the switch in position, the switch will fit flush and neatly in the instrument panel.

If the motor cycle is fitted with flashing indicators, when the parking lamp has been fitted to the front shield, and its lead passed inside the instrument panel as already described, connect the sub-harness supplied with the parking lamp to the switch. The lead coloured red with black must be connected to the left side terminal of the switch while the lead coloured brown with blue is connected to the right side. Then working from under the nearside end of the instrument panel, the large terminal on the second lead coloured brown with blue, must be connected to the black inspection lamp socket. For details of inspection, lamp sockets (see page 162). Next the lead from the parking lamp must be pushed into the snap connector fitted to the lead coloured red with black and the remaining brown with blue lead must be connected to the ammeter terminal nearest to the speedometer. Finally, fit the switch to the instrument panel as already described.

To remove the parking lamp from the motor cycle, it is only necessary to remove the two screws which secure the lamp to the front shield, and then detach its lead. If the motor cycle is not fitted with flashing indicators, the parking lamp lead is attached to one of the parking lamp switch terminals, and this is from where it must be removed. If, however, the motor cycle is fitted with flashing indicators, the parking lamp lead is attached by a snap connector to the lead coloured red with black, and it is detached by separating the snap connector.

The parking lamp switch is removed by simply removing the nut and the on-off indicator plate from the outside of the instrument panel. The switch can then be pushed inside the instrument panel and pulled down below the nearside end, when the leads which are attached to the two switch terminals can be removed to free the switch by removing the screw from each terminal.

To renew the bulb in the parking lamp it is not necessary to remove the parking lamp from the motor cycle. Commence by removing the two small screws, which are situated each side of the lamp just below the lens. The lens and clip can then be lifted clear, and the bulb can be unscrewed in an anti-clockwise direction. The new bulb must be a 6-volt, 3-watt screw fitting type, and is fitted by screwing it in. The lamp lens and clip can then be re-fitted and secured in position with the two small screws.

Rubber Grommet for the Headlamp Trimmer Control: Leader

This is the oval-shaped grommet fitted in the instrument panel, through which the knob for setting the angle of the headlamp passes.

If the grommet has been removed, or if a new grommet is being fitted, it is an easy matter to fit the grommet into the instrument panel with the assistance of the blade of a small screwdriver. The grommet should first be wetted with liquid soap, and it must be fitted with the smooth side uppermost, then after placing it in position, the screwdriver blade can be used through the hole in the grommet to locate the grommet properly with the edge of the hole in the instrument panel fitting into the channel in the rubber grommet.

INSTRUMENT PANEL—LEADER

If it should be required to remove the instrument panel only; first remove the windscreen support stays as described on page 155. Then disconnect the driving cable and the lead to the bulb from the speedometer head as described on page 157. Next disconnect the leads from the ammeter as described on page 159. Also detach the lighting and ignition switches from the instrument panel, and the lead from the black inspection lamp socket. Then if the motor cycle is fitted with a parking lamp, the switch must be detached from the instrument panel, and the snap connector in the lead from the parking lamp must be separated as described above. Also, if the motor cycle is fitted with flashing indicators or a neutral indicator, the warning lights in the instrument panel must be disconnected as described on page 160.

Next remove the handlebar cover as described on page 124. Then the four centremost screws along the top edge of the instrument panel must be removed next. The nuts for these screws are special captive nuts and they will remain attached to the instrument panel, but do not loose the spacer tubes through which the screws pass in the front shield. The screw fitted each side of the rear edge of the instrument panel must be removed next, the nuts for these screws are inside the instrument panel and can be reached from under the ends of the panel. The instrument panel can then be lifted clear.

For details on the fittings in the instrument panel, see the pages already referred to when removing the panel. When re-fitting the instrument panel, begin by fitting a plain washer under the heads of the two screws for the rear of the instrument panel. Then pass the screws through the holes in the rear of the panel and the corresponding holes in the brackets on the top of the body. Next fit a plain washer, a shake-proof washer and a nut to each screw where it protrudes inside the instrument panel. Fit a plain washer under the heads of the four screws for the top edge of the front shield, then making sure the spacer tubes are in position in the four holes, pass the screws through the front shield and the spacer tubes and locate them into the special captive nuts in the front edge of the instrument panel, and securely tighten.

Note: If one of the captive nuts should be dislodged, it is permissible to fit a plain washer, a shake-proof washer and a nut to the end of the screw inside the instrument panel, by passing the washers and nut under one end. The instruments and fittings can then be re-connected as described on the pages referred to when dealing with the removal of the instrument panel. Re-assemble the windscreen stays as described on page 157, and finally re-fit the handlebar cover as described on page 124.

HEADLAMP COWL AND SHELL
—LEADER

For details of removing the headlamp shell, see page 136, and for the headlamp cowl, see page 185.

The headlamp cowl is a single unit incorporating a threaded boss each side for the headlamp shell pivot bolts, if either of these bosses should become damaged the headlamp cowl must be replaced. The headlamp shell incorporates a control rod for adjusting the headlamp beam. The control rod is secured to the headlamp shell by two nuts, so that there is one nut each side of the bracket on the top of the headlamp shell. Note that there is a shake-proof washer fitted between the top nut and the bracket, and a plain washer between the lower nut and the bracket. To separate the control rod from the headlamp shell, it is only necessary to remove the lower nut.

The headlamp shell is secured inside the headlamp cowl by two pivot bolts, which pass through the sides of the headlamp shell into the threaded bosses each side of the headlamp cowl. There must be a double coil spring washer fitted under the head of each pivot bolt, to retain the lamp in any desired position, and the bolts must be securely tightened when fitted.

FRONT SHIELD—LEADER

The front shield is the vertical panel fitted between the windscreen and the leg shields. To remove the front shield from the motor cycle, follow the instructions from page 185 until the front shield is removed.

Fitted to the front shield are two badges, one at the centre of the top edge and the other on the offside. To remove either of these badges proceed as follows:—Dealing first with the Ariel badge at the centre of the front shield top edge, first remove the windscreen from the front shield as described on page 155. Also remove the rubber sealing strip from the channel in the top edge of the front shield. The Ariel badge is secured to the front shield by its stainless steel surround, which has two tags passing through the front shield into the channel where they are turned over. By straightening the two tags, the badge can be pulled free. A new badge is fitted by first fitting the badge and its surround on the front shield with the two tags on the surround located through the slots in the front shield. The tags must then be bent over to secure the badge in position. The rubber sealing strip and the windscreen can then be fitted as described on page 156.

The Leader badge which is fitted to the offside of the front shield is removed by tapping out the rivets which secure the badge to the front shield. The rivets are easily tapped out by locating a one-inch nail in the end of each rivet in turn. At one end the rivets are split slightly where they were punched over when originally fitted, and this is the end to locate the nail. With all the rivets removed, the badge becomes free. To fit a new badge, first pass a new rivet through one of the holes in the front of the badge, then locate the badge with the rivet through the corresponding hole in the front shield, and while a small drift or something similar is pressed hard against the head of the rivet, carefully punch over, with a small punch and hammer, the other end of the rivet which projects through the front shield. Fit the remaining rivets in an identical manner.

There are two brackets welded to the top rear edge of the front shield, and these brackets carry the sockets for the windscreen support stays. The sockets are easily removed after removing the front shield from the motor cycle. Each socket is secured to the top of its bracket by a nut, which is fitted to a threaded portion of the socket, which passes down inside the bracket.

Note that there is a plain washer fitted between the nut and the underside of the bracket. These sockets must be fitted to the brackets before fitting the front shield to the motor cycle.

The licence holder is fitted to the nearside of the front shield, and if required it can be removed by undoing the nearside end screw in the top edge of the front shield. To change a licence, it is only necessary to peel back the edge of the licence holder to free the glass.

If the motor cycle is fitted with flashing indicators, on the front shield, see page 220. Also, for details of rear view mirrors, see page 211.

BODY AND FITTINGS—LEADER

The body of the motor cycle is the main section which covers the top half of the frame. If it should be required to remove the body from the frame for any reason, follow the instructions for general dismantling. See page 185 until the body is removed.

Inside the front end of the body there is a bracket fitted to each side. Each bracket has six threaded holes, and there are two $\frac{1}{4}$ inch dia. by $\frac{5}{8}$ inch underhead bolts with a shake-proof washer fitted under their heads, screwed through the longer arm of each bracket from the inside. Then through the holes in the section between the arms of each bracket are screwed from the inside two $\frac{1}{4}$ inch dia. by $\frac{3}{4}$ inch underhead bolts with a shake-proof washer fitted under their heads. Then the brackets are fitted into the body with the bolts projecting through corresponding holes in the body; two $\frac{1}{4}$ inch. dia. by $\frac{1}{2}$ inch underhead bolts with a shake-proof washer and a plain washer fitted under the heads are then passed through the holes in the longer arm of the bracket which secures the rear of the instrument panel to the top of the body. The black headlamp earth lead is fitted under the head of the offside bolt, unless flashers are fitted in which case it should be fitted to the corresponding bolt on the nearside. The bolts are then located through the forward hole each side of the top of the body, and screwed into the holes in the threaded bracket. In the remaining hole each side of the top of the body, fit a $\frac{1}{4}$ inch dia. by $\frac{1}{2}$ inch underhead chromium plated screw with a chromium plated washer under the head. Note that the brackets with the threaded holes differ slightly and will only fit their respective side of the body. This also applies to the brackets fitted to the top of the body for the instrument panel, and when these brackets are fitted the short arm must project upward and be at an angle to suit the rear of the instrument panel. If the motor cycle is fitted with flashing indicators, the flasher unit should be secured inside the body, by fitting its bracket under the head of the offside front bolt in the top of the body, after removing the shake-proof washer from this bolt.

The glove compartment lid is secured to the link hinges by special screws and nuts. The lid is easily detached from the body by simply removing the screws. The lock which is fitted to the lid is also easily removed, by undoing the small screw at the base of the lock.

Towards the rear end of the body at each side are fitted the tail cover pivot bosses. They consist of a plate with three studs attached, fitted to the outside of the body with the studs projecting inside. A plain plate is then fitted over the studs inside the body, and a shake-proof washer and a nut is fitted to each stud and securely tightened. The knee grip rubber pads each side of the glove compartment are held in place by plugs incorporated in the back of the rubber pads. These plugs pass through holes in the motifs which surround the rubber pads and through corresponding holes in the body. The knee grip rubber pads and motifs are easly removed by prising them outward by hand. When re-fitting, use a little soft soap on the plugs to facilitate assembly.

A right-angle shaped stop plate to prevent the dualseat grab handle screw damaging the body is fitted to the offside top edge of the body immediately above the tail cover pivot boss, and the stop plate is secured by a $\frac{3}{16}$ inch diameter screw and special locking nut.

The lifting handle which is fitted into the nearside of the body, is retained in the tube across the body by a large hairpin spring. The ends of this spring can be seen projecting through two holes in the offside end of the body tube. To withdraw the lifting handle it is only necessary to turn the serrated knob at the nearside end, when the handle will spring out. To return the handle, push it in to the body tube, locating the peg under the handle knob through one of the slots in the body, then turn the knob slightly to trap the peg inside the body, to retain the lifting handle. To remove the lifting handle from the motor cycle, first withdraw it in the normal way, then push the two ends of the hairpin spring into the body tube. The lifting handle can then be pulled completely out. To fit the lifting handle to the body, first pass the coil spring over the closed end of the hairpin spring, then fit the closed end of the hairpin spring into the end of the lifting handle. Next pass the short peg through the hole through the lifting handle end, in order to retain the hairpin spring in the lifting handle. Then squeeze the open ends of the hairpin spring together and pass the assembly inside the body tube, and locate the open ends of the hairpin spring through the two holes in the offside end of the body tube. On some machines the hairpin spring has formed eyes, instead of turned out ends. When the lifting handle is fitted a split pin locates the hairpin spring in position by passing through the body cross tube, and the two spring eyes. The ends of the split pin should be opened out to retain the lifting handle.

There must be a rubber grommet fitted in the hole at each side of the steering column for the control cables to pass through. A similar grommet must be fitted at the rear of the glove compartment, where the dualseat catch operating rod passes through. A further rubber grommet must be fitted in the hole in the offside rear end of the body for the tail lamp harness to pass through. There must be six small rubber buffer grommets fitted in the holes around the top of the body where the dualseat rests. A rubber sealing band for the glove compartment lid must be fitted in the channel in the top of the glove compartment, with a suitable adhesive.

DUALSEAT—LEADER

Two hinged brackets secure the dualseat to the body. Each hinged bracket is fastened to the body by two screws passing through holes in the offside top edge of the body, and corresponding holes in the portion of the hinged bracket which is fitted inside the top edge of the body. Special locking nuts are then fitted to the screws. By removing the four screws and nuts which secure the hinged brackets to the body, the complete dualseat can be removed. Note that the portion of the hinged bracket which fits inside the top edge of the body is offset slightly to match the curved shape of the top of the body, and although the two brackets assemblies are similar, they are not interchangeable.

If the dualseat has to be removed for any reason, it is not necessary to remove the hinged brackets; the easiest method is to remove the two screws which secure each hinged bracket to the underside of the dualseat.

Fitted to the underside of the dualseat are two spring clips which locate on the body tube when the dualseat is down. Also, a portion of the dualseat catch for locking the seat down, and the ends of the grab handle. All these items are secured to the underside of the dualseat by screws. On some machines the screws are fitted into special nuts inside the seat and the screws can be removed leaving the nuts in place. On other machines the screws are self tapping wood screws, and are fitted directly into the marine plywood seat base. If with one of the latter screws the hole in the dualseat wood base should become a loose fit around the screw, the next larger size of self-tapping screw can be fitted.

DUALSEAT WATERPROOF COVER—LEADER AND ARROW

A waterproof cover for the dualseat is available as an optional extra. No fitting instructions are necessary as the cover simply stretches over the dualseat, and can be removed and re-fitted as required.

Note: When fitting a cover insert the nose end of the dualseat first then it is an easy matter to stretch the cover over the back of the seat.

DUALSEAT—ARROW

The dualseat is fitted to the top of the frame, and hinges upward from the nearside to give access to the petrol filler cap and the battery.

If it should be required to remove the dualseat from the motor cycle, it is only necessary to prise off with a screwdriver the two special lock washers which are situated at the end of the hinges on the underside of the dualseat. The dualseat can then be moved rearwards and lifted clear. Note when re-fitting the dualseat it is advisable to use two new locking washers.

Fitted to the base of the dualseat is a sponge rubber pad which locates on the top of the battery to prevent it moving, and four large rubber buffers which locate into the four cups on the top of the frame. The rubber pad and buffers are glued to the dualseat base, and should not be removed unnecessarily. Also, fitted to the dualseat base are the two hinge brackets and two spring clips. These are secured in position by self-tapping wood screws which have plain washers under their heads. In the event of one of the screw holes becoming worn, the next larger size of self-tapping wood screw can be fitted.

The dualseat fittings which are secured to the top of the frame are all removable except the front hinge bracket and the front spring clip bracket, these two items are part of the frame. The four cups for the rubber buffers can be removed after undoing the bolt and nut which secures each one. The bolt which secures the nearside rear cup also secures the strap which prevents the dualseat being opened too far. The rear hinge bracket is similarly secured with a bolt and nut, while the rear spring clip bracket has two screws and nuts. When fitting these items the two front cups must have a $\frac{1}{4}$ inch dia. by $\frac{1}{2}$ inch underhead bolt passed through them, then a spacer must be fitted under the cups, and the battery earth lead must be fitted to the nearside bolt and then a shake-proof washer. The offside bolt must have a cable clip as well as the spacer fitted to it before the bolts are passed through the frame and the bulkhead. Then fit a plain washer with a shake-proof washer and a nut to each bolt where it projects inside the frame. The two rear cups are secured similarly, except that the bolt must be a $\frac{1}{4}$ inch dia. by $1\frac{1}{8}$ inch underhead, and on the nearside a large diameter, plain washer and the dualseat strap is fitted instead of a spacer. The dualseat rear hinge bracket is secured by a $\frac{1}{4}$ inch dia. by $\frac{1}{2}$ inch underhead bolt with a cable clip fitted under its head. Pass the bolt through the frame and fit a plain washer, a shake-proof washer and a nut to the bolt where it projects inside the frame. The rear spring clip bracket is secured by two screws with plain washers under their heads, and with plain washers and locking nuts fitted inside the frame.

GRAB HANDLE: DUALSEAT—ARROW

If required a grab strap can be fitted to the dualseat, a strap and fittings are available as an optional extra. To fit a grab handle first remove the dualseat from the motor cycle as described on page 169.

Then at a point $3\frac{7}{8}$ inches in front of the rear pair of dualseat base rubbers there is a hole through the base at each side. These holes cannot be seen as they are covered by the dualseat skirt, but if the tacks securing the skirt at this point are removed the two holes will become accessible. Next locate the brackets at each end of the grab handle, over the holes in the dualseat base, so that the strap crosses the top of the dualseat. Then secure the brackets in position with the special self-tapping screws, and finally re-tack the dualseat skirt in position.

FRONT SHELL—ARROW

The front shell covers the front half of the frame and incorporates a deep tool box. The lid of the tool box is on the top of the front shell, and can be opened by using a coin or screwdriver to slacken the screw when the lid will lift off. If it is required to gain access to the inside of the front shell, the tool box can be removed by slightly straining upwards and rotating the lid retaining strap anti-clockwise.

The strap and the tool box can then be lifted clear. When re-fitting the tool box it can be placed in the front shell either way round. There must be a rubber bead fitted around the outer edge of the tool box, then the lid retaining strap can be inserted into the wider portion of the slots in the sides of the tool box and rotated clockwise into position. Note when the strap is fitted, the convex side must be uppermost, the tool box lid can then be re-fitted.

To remove the front shell from the motor cycle, first remove the handlebars and control cables as described on page 129, then separate the snap connector in the horn push lead just under the forward end of the front shell. In order to withdraw the dip switch leads from the front shell, slacken the screw at the top of the headlamp rim and pull the rim and light unit free. The three leads from the dip switch can then be seen, they are coloured blue, blue with red and blue with white, and they have snap connectors which can be pulled apart, when the leads can then be withdrawn through the front shell. Next remove the dualseat as described on page 169 and remove the headlamp from the front shell as described on page 146. The tool box must be removed next as described on page 170.

Then inside the forward end of the front shell are two bolts and nuts which secure the front shell to two brackets on the frame, remove these bolts and nuts next, then remove the two screws from each side of the under edge of the front shell. The front shell can then be lifted up, by pulling the bottom edge each side outward a little and lifting the nearside first to clear the rectifier, which is fitted to the side of the frame. The front shell can then be lifted clear. The badge which is fitted each side of the front shell is retained by a grommet, and if required they are easily pushed out. The same applies to the knee grip rubbers, except that they are retained by projections on their backs, which pass through holes in the front shell, but to remove them they only require pushing out. When re-fitting these items, the grommet for the badge is easily located into the hole in the front shell, then if the inner edges of the grommet are smeared with soapy water, the badge can be fitted with the aid of a small screwdriver. The projections on the back of the knee grip rubbers should also be wetted with soapy water, when the rubber can easily be pushed into place. *The two front shell support brackets which are fitted each side of the frame, must on no account be removed unless the petrol tank is also being removed*, as the nuts and washers inside the frame are only accessible after removing the petrol tank. If the frame and fittings are being dismantled and it is required to remove the support brackets, it is only necessary to undo the bolt securing each bracket, when the bracket will be free.

When re-fitting the support brackets to the sides of the frame, first locate the tags on the back of the support bracket through the hole in the side of the frame, then fit the special washer which has two slots and a hole, inside the frame and locate the slots over the tags on the back of the support bracket.

Next locate a square nut between the tags on the support bracket, then fit a shake-proof washer and a large outside diameter plain washer under the head of a ¼ inch dia. by ½ inch underhead bolt, and pass the bolt through the square hole in the support bracket and the frame, and into the square nut inside the frame and securely tighten. The two top support brackets which are secured to the top of the frame, should not be removed unnecessarily. If it is required to remove them it is only necessary to remove the nut securing each bracket when they can then be lifted clear. Note that the two bolts from which the nuts and brackets were removed are welded to a plate inside the frame, and this plate with the bolts can only be removed after removing the ignition coils as described on page 216. When re-fitting the top support brackets, the plate and bolt assembly must first be in position in the frame, then locate the support brackets over the bolts where they project above the frame, so that they face outward.

Then secure them in position by fitting a plain washer, a shake-proof washer and a nut to both bolts, but do not tighten until the front shell is fitted.

RE-FITTING FRONT SHELL

The two knee grip rubbers and badges should be fitted, before fitting the front shell to the frame. Also fit the two short pieces of rubber beading to the rear edge of the front shell, where it rests on the frame. Then commence by lowering the front shell on to the offside of the frame first, then pull the nearside edge of the front shell outward and ease it past the rectifier, but make certain the wiring harness is located through the cut away in the rear edge of the front shell with beading above the harness.

Next fit a shake-proof washer and a plain washer under the heads of the four screws for the bottom edge of the front shell. Pass the screws through the brackets on the frame and tighten them into the threaded bosses in the front shell. Then fit a plain washer under the head of two ¼ inch dia. by ½ inch underhead bolts, and pass the bolts through the brackets inside the forward end of the front shell. Next fit a plain washer, a shake-proof washer and a nut to both bolts, and securely tighten followed by tightening the two nuts previously left loose if the forward support brackets have been disturbed. Re-fit the handlebars and control cables as described on page 129 and connect the horn push lead to the snap connector under the front end of the shell. Re-fit the headlamp as described on page 146. Then pass the dip switch leads through the grommet in the nearside of the top of the front shell, and into the headlamp. The snap connectors must be coupled to the headlamp unit and the main harness so that the leads with corresponding colours are fitted together. Re-fit the headlamp rim and light unit by locating the projection inside the headlamp rim into the slot at the bottom of the headlamp shell, then push the rim into place and firmly tighten the screw on the top of the headlamp. Re-fit the dualseat as described on page 169 and the tool box as described on page 170.

TAIL SECTION—LEADER

The rear portion of the motor cycle is known as the tail section, and in order to gain access to the rear wheel the tail section pivots upwards as described on page 98.

The tail section incorporates the rear number plate, stop/tail lamp, and the silencer support stay. Also, if the motor cycle is fitted with panniers, rear luggage carrier or fender, these too are fitted to the tail section.

If it should be required to remove the tail section from the motor cycle, first slacken the acorn nuts at the silencer ends, just sufficiently to free the silencers from the support stay. Then remove the wing nuts from the underside of the top of the tail section, there are two wing nuts and they secure the tail section to the end of the body and are accessible through the cavity under the dualseat. If the motor cycle is fitted with panniers, slacken the bolt behind the forward bottom edge of each pannier, so that it is free in the slotted bracket. Next disconnect the leads under the dual seat for the stop and tail lamp, and for the rear flashing indicators if fitted. Finally remove the two pivot bolts, when the tail section can be slightly sprung open and lifted clear.

Note: There is a distance tube and a plain washer fitted between the tail section and the body, where the pivot bolt passes through, on some machines the distance tube is loose, while on others it is welded to the tail section. If it is the loose type be certain to re-fit it when assembling the tail section to the motor cycle.

When re-fitting the tail section, begin by locating it in position, then pass the tail lamp lead through the rubber grommet in the side of the body. Make sure the two studs in the under side of the tail section are located through the holes in the end of the body, and if panniers are fitted, the bolt at the back of each pannier must be fitted into the slotted bracket. Then fit the pivot bolt to each side of the tail section, not forgetting the distance tube and plain washer, before finally tightening the pivot bolts, secure the silencers to the support stay by tightening the acorn nuts at the silencer ends, then securely tighten the pivot bolts. Next tighten the bolt at the back of each pannier to secure it to the slotted bracket. Then fit a plain washer, a spring washer and a wing nut to the two studs in the under side of the tail section. Finally re-fit the stop and tail lamp leads; also the flasher leads, if fitted, to the corresponding snap connectors in the main wiring harness under the dual seat.

Tail Lamp—Leader

If it should be required to gain access to the tail lamp bulb, this is done by removing the two screws which pass through the tail lamp lens, when the lens can then be removed. Then to remove the bulb push it inwards and turn it slightly anti-clockwise, when it will become free. A new bulb must a a 6-volt, 18/3 watt double filament, bayonet fitting. Note that the pegs on the base of the bulb are offset, and when fitting a bulb it will only go into the holder one way; it must be pushed in and turned clockwise. If a resistance is met when attempting to turn the bulb, take it out again and re-fit it reversing the position of the pegs. The tail lamp lens can then be fitted and note the lens is in two pieces, the clear section at the bottom fits in two slots in the red portion. A rubber joint washer must be fitted between the lens and the tail lamp. The two screws which secure the lens should be tightened firmly but not excessively.

If it should be required to remove the tail lamp from the motor cycle, pivot the tail section upward as described on page 98. Then separate the two leads just behind the tail lamp by pulling apart the snap connectors. Then inside the tail section at the back of the tail lamp are two nuts, remove these nuts and the tail lamp will be free.

When re-fitting the tail lamp there must be a plain washer, a shake-proof washer and a nut fitted to each stud inside the tail section. When fitting the leads into the snap connectors, make certain the colours correspond.

The Silencer Support Stay

If it should be required to remove this stay, slacken the acorn nuts at the silencer ends to free the silencers from the stay. Then if a rear fender is fitted, it must be removed as described on page 211. Finally, remove the two screws from the bottom edge of the number plate, when the support stay can be pulled clear. When re-fitting the support stay, the two screws which pass through the number plate must have a plain washer under their heads, then after passing through the brackets on the support stay behind the number plate, fit a plain washer, a shake-proof washer and a nut. Note if a fender is fitted see instructions on page 211. Finally, secure the silencers to the stay by tightening the acorn nuts.

For instructions on removing and fitting the Leader badge on the rear number plate, see page 167, and proceed as described for the badge on the front shield.

For details of panniers, see page 208.

For details of rear luggage carrier, see page 210.

For details of fender, see page 211.

TAIL SECTION—ARROW

The tail section blends from the rear end of the frame to form a broad mudguard. The rear wheel, number plate and tail lamp are fully accessible without disturbing the tail section. If, however, it is required to remove the tail section, proceed as follows:—First remove the dualseat as described on page 169. Then remove the rear hydraulic units as described on page 180. Next pull apart the snap connectors which join the tail lamp leads. These connectors are under the dualseat, and the leads are coloured brown and brown with green, and brown with blue, after separating them pull the leads which are inside the tail section, down through the grommet in the top of the tail section so that they no longer protrude. Next remove the small screw and nut from each side of the under edge of the tail section where it joins the frame. Then remove the three screws and nuts from each side of the tail section, where it joins the frame. Next remove the dome nut from the end of each silencer, and the four bolts and nuts from across the forward top edge of the tail section, where it joins the frame. *Note:* It will be advantageous to remove the dual seat, rear hinge, by prising off with a screwdriver, the special locking washer which secures the dualseat hinge to the frame. The tail section can then be pulled rearward to free it from the motor cycle.

When re-fitting the tail section, first make certain the suspension bracket inside the end of the frame and the alloy spacers between the suspension bracket and the frame are in line with the holes for the securing bolts. Then begin by locating the tail section on to the frame and fit the two strips of rubber beading between the underside of the tail section and the top of the frame. Then commence fitting the four bolts across the top of the tail section, where it joins the frame. Beginning with the nearside bolt, it must have a cup, a large plain washer and the webbing strap fitted under its head.

The next bolt must have a plain washer only fitted under its head. The third bolt must have a cable clip and the seat hinge bracket under its head. While the offside bolt must have a cup and a spacer fitted under its head. Pass the bolts through the tail section and frame and locate them through the alloy spacers and the suspension bracket. The two centre bolts must also pass through the rear mudguard bracket. Then fit a plain washer, a shake-proof washer and a nut to each bolt, but do not tighten these bolts yet. Next fit a plain washer under the heads of the six screws which fit, three each side of the tail section. Note that the two longer of these screws must pass through the forward end of the lifting handles, the others must pass through the holes above and forward of the lifting handles. Then fit a shake-proof washer and a nut to each screw, but do not tighten them yet. Next fit a plain washer under the heads of the two screws which fit each side of the machine, through the underedge of the tail section and frame. Locate the screws into position and fit a plain washer and a special locking nut to both screws, and securely tighten. Then tighten the three screws and nuts each side of the tail section, and the four bolts and nuts across the top. Next fit and securely tighten the acorn nut for each silencer end. Then pass the stop switch and tail lamp leads through the grommet in the top of the tail section and connect the leads with corresponding colours. Then re-fit the rear hydraulic units as described on page 181. The dualseat rear hinge should be fitted next, to the bracket on the frame. Note that a new locking washer may be required. Then fit the dualseat as described on page 169.

The rear number plate is secured to the tail section by two bolts which pass from inside the tail section into two nuts which are located in brackets inside the number plate. To remove the rear number plate, first remove the two bolts from inside the tail section, the number plate will then be free, but the tail lamp leads are still attached by the two snap connectors inside the number plate and must be pulled apart. When re-fitting the number plate, first couple the corresponding coloured leads with the snap connectors. Then locate the number plate on to the tail section with the rubber beading between the number plate and tail section, and fit the two bolts from inside the tail section into the nuts inside the number plate.

Tail Lamp—Arrow

To change a tail lamp bulb first remove the two screws from the tail lamp lens, the lens will then be free and the old bulb can then be taken out by pushing it inward and turning it slightly. A new bulb must be a 6 volt, 18/3 watt, double filament, bayonet fixing. Note that the pegs at the base of the bulb are offset, and the bulb will only fit one way round. There are two grooves in the bulb holder for the pegs on the bulb to locate into, after pushing the bulb in, turn it to secure it in the holder. Then re-fit the tail lamp lens with the two screws, but note there must be a rubber joint washer between the lens and the tail lamp. Also the lens is in two pieces, the clear portion at the bottom slides into slots in the red portion.

If it should be required to remove the tail lamp from the motor cycle, first remove the rear number plate as described above. Then inside the number plate are two nuts and shake-proof washers, which, when removed will free the tail lamp.

The lifting handles which are fitted each side of the machine, are secured by a screw and a nut at each end. The screw at the forward end has a plain washer under the head, and a shake-proof washer and a nut inside the tail section. While the screw at the rear has a plain washer under the head, and a plain washer, a shake-proof washer and a nut inside the tail section.

The silencer support stays are secured to the tail section by two screws each.

The screws have a plain washer under their heads, then after passing them through the tail section, the support stays, a plain washer, a shake-proof washer and a nut is fitted to each screw; sufficient clearance has been provided in the fixing holes to allow both brackets to be accurately aligned with each other. To remove the support stays, the two screws which secure them to the tail section and the acorn nut at the silencer end must be removed.

PETROL TANK—LEADER

The petrol tank is fitted inside the frame, and the standard petrol tank has a capacity of approximately $2\frac{1}{4}$ gallons, a larger petrol tank with a capacity of 3 gallons is available, and is standard on 1961 machines. Both types of petrol tanks are fitted and removed in the same way. Also, the fittings for both petrol tanks are similar.

The petrol filler cap which is accessible under the dualseat, is fitted with two special sealing rings. If these sealing rings become worn, damaged or loose, they should be replaced with new ones.

The petrol tap is operated by pulling the knob outward and a reserve supply of petrol for an emergency is obtainable by turning the knob in a clockwise direction and pulling it further outwards.

A fibre washer is fitted between the petrol tap and the bottom of the petrol tank, to prevent any possibility of the petrol leaking. If a leak should develop, examine the fibre washer and if it is worn or damaged in any way, it should be replaced with a new one. *Note:* Some machines have two fibre washers fitted to the petrol tap, one washer being thicker than the other. This is in order to position the petrol tap so that the knob is in line with the hole in the side panel.

To remove the petrol tap, first remove the nearside side panel, then disconnect the petrol pipe from the petrol tap, by undoing the nut at the top of the petrol pipe. Then if there is any petrol in the tank, it must now be drained into a suitable container. Remove tap knob by unscrewing its retaining nut. At the top of the petrol tap there are two flats to which an open ended spanner can be fitted, then by unscrewing the tap it can easily be removed. The upper portion of the petrol tap is fitted with a gauze filter, and the filter should be thoroughly cleaned by washing in clean petrol before the tap is re-fitted, also make certain the fibre washer for the tap is in good condition.

If for any reason it is required to remove the petrol tank from the motor cycle, proceed as follows. First disconnect and remove the battery as described on page 213. Then remove both side panels and the petrol pipe; also if there is any petrol in the tank it should be drained, as already described, then remove the petrol tap. Next remove the tail section from the motor cycle as described on page 172. Also remove the rear wheel as described on page 98. Then remove the rear chaincase and the rear hydraulic units as described on page 180. The rear mudguard must be removed next. The bolt which secures the mudguard to the underside of the end of the body should be unscrewed first, then remove the two bolts and nuts which secure the mudguard to a bracket, at the bottom rear edge of the frame. Also remove the four bolts and nuts from inside the rear of the tool tray. The rear stop switch leads must then be disconnected, the switch is fitted on the offside silencer and the leads simply pull out. Also, if the motor cycle is fitted with a neutral indicator the two leads coloured white with blue and white, which are included in the stop switch harness, must be pulled out of the sockets in the neutral gear indicator switch at the rear of the gear box. These leads are clipped to the rear mudguard by spring clips. Remove clips complete with the leads from the mudguard.

The rear mudguard can then be lifted clear.

Next remove the two screws and nuts from each side of the motor cycle, which pass through the body and frame just above the point where the rear hydraulic units pass inside the frame. The rear suspension bracket inside the rear of the frame can then be withdrawn. Note the two alloy die cast double spacers which fit between the rear suspension bracket and the frame. These spacers will come free with the suspension bracket.

Then remove the bolts and nuts which secure the battery carrier to the top of the frame, this will also free part of the dualseat catch which is mounted on the frame. The battery carrier can then be lifted up and out of the frame.

Finally, remove the bulkhead and petrol tank from the frame, as described on page 193.

When work on the petrol tank has been completed and it is ready for re-assembling, proceed as follows. Fit the petrol tank, the bulkhead and battery carrier as described on page 194. Next locate the four $\frac{1}{4}$ inch dia. by $1\frac{1}{8}$ inch underhead bolts with a plain washer under their heads, through the holes in the right angle brackets, the bottom of the tool tray and the frame. Then locate the two die cast double ended spacers on the bolts where they project through the frame, and then fit the rear suspension bracket to the bolts, and secure it in position by fitting a plain washer, a shake-proof washer and a nut to the two outer bolts only. Also fit the two screws with plain washers under their heads through each side of the body and suspension bracket. Then fit a plain washer, a shake-proof washer and a nut to each screw, and securely tighten. Next fit the rear mudguard and the rear hydraulic units as described on page 196, and the rear chaincase as described on page 197. The leads to the rear stop switch on the offside silencer should be fitted next; these leads are coloured brown with blue and brown, and can be fitted in the sockets in the switch either way round. Also if the motor cycle is fitted with a neutral indicator, the leads coloured white with blue and white must be fitted to the sockets in the neutral gear indicator switch at the rear of the gear box, the leads can be fitted either way round. The sub-harness from the stop switch can then be clipped to the rear mudguard with the two cable clips. Next fit the rear wheel as described on page 105, and the tail section as described on page 172. Then fit the petrol tap to the petrol tank as described on page 196 and screw the petrol pipe union nut on to the petrol tap. Finally, re-fit the side panels as described on page 154 and the battery as described on page 213.

PETROL TANK—ARROW

The petrol tank is fitted inside the frame, and the standard petrol tank has a capacity of approximately $2\frac{1}{4}$ gallons, a larger petrol tank with a capacity of 3 gallons is available and is standard on 1961 machines. Both types of petrol tank are fitted and removed in the same way. Also, the fittings for both petrol tanks are similar.

The petrol filler cap, which is accessible under the dualseat, is fitted with two special sealing rings, if these sealing rings become worn, damaged or loose, they should be replaced with new ones.

A fibre washer is fitted between the petrol tap and the petrol tank boss, to prevent any possibility of the petrol leaking. If a petrol leak should develop, examine the fibre washer, and if it is worn or damaged in any way, it should be replaced with a new one. *Note:* Some machines have two fibre washers fitted to the petrol tap, one washer being thicker than the other. This is in order to position the petrol tap so that the knob is in an accessible position.

To remove the petrol tap first disconnect the petrol pipe from the petrol tap, by undoing the nut at the top of the petrol pipe. Then if there is any petrol in the tank, it must now be drained into a suitable container. At the top of the petrol tap there are two flats to which an open spanner can be fitted, then by unscrewing the tap it can easily be removed.

The upper portion of the petrol tap is fitted with a gauze filter, and the filter should be thoroughly cleaned by washing in clean petrol before the tap is re-fitted, also make certain the fibre washer for the petrol tap is in good condition.

If for any reason it is required to remove the petrol tank from the motor cycle, proceed as follows. First disconnect and remove the battery as described on page 213; also if there is any petrol in the tank it should be drained as already described, then remove the petrol tap. Next remove the tail section from the motor cycle as described on page 173. Also remove the rear wheel as described on page 105. The rear mudguard must be removed next by removing the two bolts and nuts which secure the mudguard to a bracket at the bottom rear edge of the frame. The rear stop switch leads must then be disconnected, the switch is fitted on the offside silencer and the leads simply pull out. The rear mudguard can then be lifted clear. The rear suspension bracket inside the rear of the frame can then be withdrawn. Note the two alloy die cast double spacers which fit between the rear suspension bracket and the frame. These spacers will come free with the suspension bracket. Then remove the bolts and nuts which secure the battery carrier to the top of the frame, the battery carrier can then be lifted up and out of the frame. Finally, remove the bulkhead and petrol tank from the frame, as described on page 203.

When work on the petrol tank has been completed and it is ready for re-assembling, proceed as follows. Fit the petrol tank, the bulkhead and battery carrier as described on page 204.

Next locate the four $\frac{1}{4}$ inch dia. by $1\frac{1}{8}$ inch underhead bolts with a plain washer under their heads, through the holes in the top of the rear end of the frame. Then locate the two die cast double ended spacers on the bolts where they project through the frame, and then fit the rear suspension bracket to the bolts and secure it in position by fitting a plain washer, shake-proof washer and nut to the two outer bolts only, but do not tighten the nuts. Next fit the rear mudguard by locating the bracket on the mudguard, on to the two middle bolts which project from the suspension bracket. Then fit a plain washer under the heads of two ¼ inch dia. by ½ inch underhead bolts, and pass the bolts through the holes in the rear mudguard, and the bracket on the bottom rear end of the frame, then fit a plain washer, a shake-proof washer and a nut to both bolts, and securely tighten. Next carefully remove the four bolts which pass through the top of the frame and the suspension bracket, and fit the tail section as described on page 173 and the rear hydraulic units as described on page 181; also re-fit the rear chain-case as described on page 206. The leads to the rear stop switch on the offside silencer should be fitted next; these leads are coloured brown with blue and brown, and can be fitted in the sockets in the switch either way round. Next fit the rear wheel as described on page 105. Then fit the petrol tap to the petrol tank as described on page 175 and screw the petrol pipe union nut on to the petrol tap. Finally, re-fit the battery as described on page 213.

REAR FORK—LEADER

Note: Before the pivot bolt can be unscrewed, the rearmost primary chain case screw must be removed.

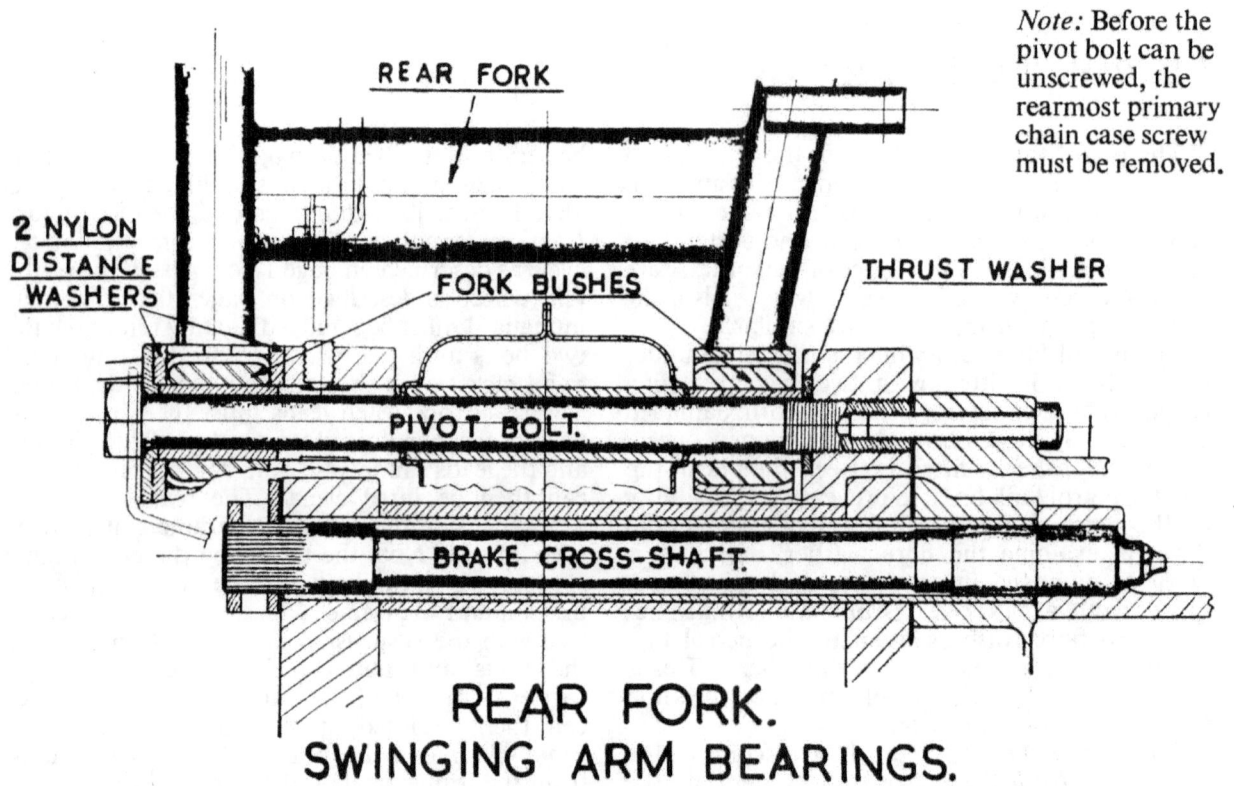

REAR FORK.
SWINGING ARM BEARINGS.

Fig. 148

The rear fork moves up and down from a pivot at the rear of the gear box, carrying the rear wheel to provide the rear suspension. The movement of the fork is controlled by the rear hydraulic units, for the details of these units see page 180.

The rear fork does not require any routine maintenance. The two bushes which are fitted in the lugs at the forward end of the fork are of special steel and bonded rubber construction and do not require any lubrication. After the motor cycle has covered a large mileage and is being generally overhauled the bushes may require replacing with new ones.

To remove the rear fork, if the motor cycle is being generally dismantled as described on page 185, the rear fork will be removed during the process, if however, it is required to remove the rear fork only, procced as follows: Remove the rear wheel as described on page 98. Then remove the rear chaincase and chain as described on page 111. The rear mudguard must be removed next, the bolt which secures the mudguard to the underside of the end of the body should be unscrewed first, then remove the two bolts and nuts which secure the mudguard to a bracket at the bottom rear edge of the frame. Also remove the two middle bolts and nuts from inside the rear of the tool tray. The rear stop switch leads must then be disconnected, but first disconnect the battery as described on page 213 to prevent the possibility of an electrical short. The stop switch is fitted on the offside silencer and the leads simply pull out. Also if the motor cycle is fitted with a neutral gear indicator, the leads coloured white, and white with blue, which are included in the stop switch harness, must be pulled out of the sockets in the neutral gear indicator switch at the rear of the gear box. These leads are clipped to the rear mudguard by spring clips. Remove the clips complete with the leads from the mudguard.

The rear mudguard can then be lifted clear. Next remove the rear hydraulic units as described on page 180. Then remove the air cleaner, the top rear engine mounting bolt, the pivot bolt and the rear fork as described on page 191. If it is required to remove the chain sprocket from the rear fork see page 111.

To replace the old bushes with new ones in the

REAR FORK.
EXTRACTING SWINGING ARM BUSHES.
474.
43602S.
474.
43593S.
43594S.
42073.
43601S.
IMPORTANT:-THE HEAD OF THE BOLT MUST ALWAYS BE ON OUTSIDE FACE.

FIG. 149

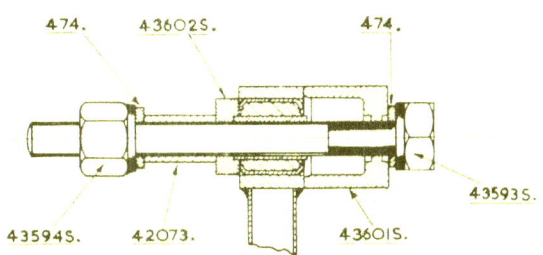

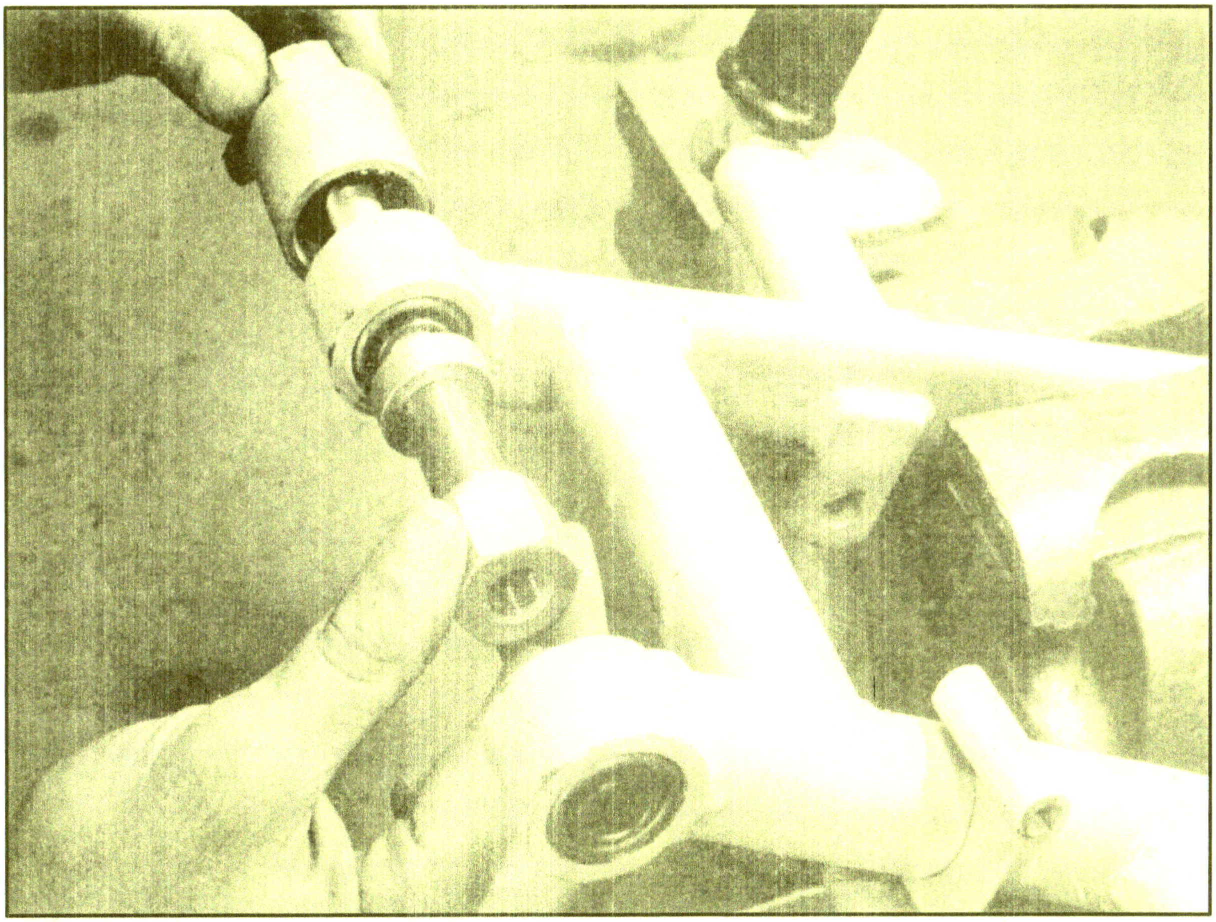

FIG. 150

rear fork, the following instructions apply to the Leader and the Arrow and the following service tools are required:—

43593S. Bolt.
43594S. Nut.
474. Washer (two off).
42073. Distance tube.
43602S. Washer.
43601S. Spacer.

To remove the old bushes, they must be dealt with one at a time, begin by fitting one washer 474 under the head of the bolt 43593S. Then fit spacer 43601S under the head of the bolt so that the closed end of the spacer is next to the washer.

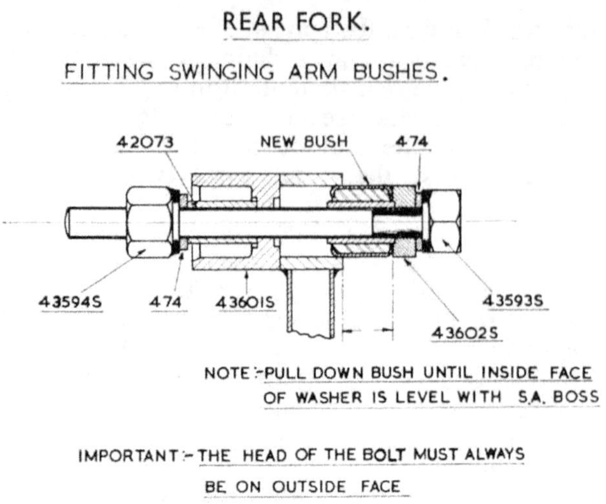

REAR FORK.
FITTING SWINGING ARM BUSHES.
42073
NEW BUSH
474
43594S
474
43601S
43593S
43602S
NOTE:-PULL DOWN BUSH UNTIL INSIDE FACE OF WASHER IS LEVEL WITH S.A. BOSS
IMPORTANT:-THE HEAD OF THE BOLT MUST ALWAYS BE ON OUTSIDE FACE

Fig. 151

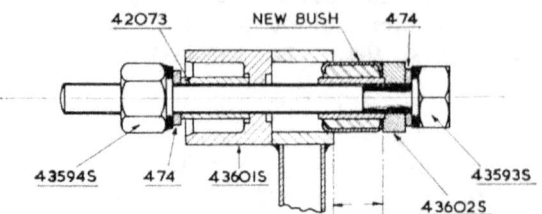

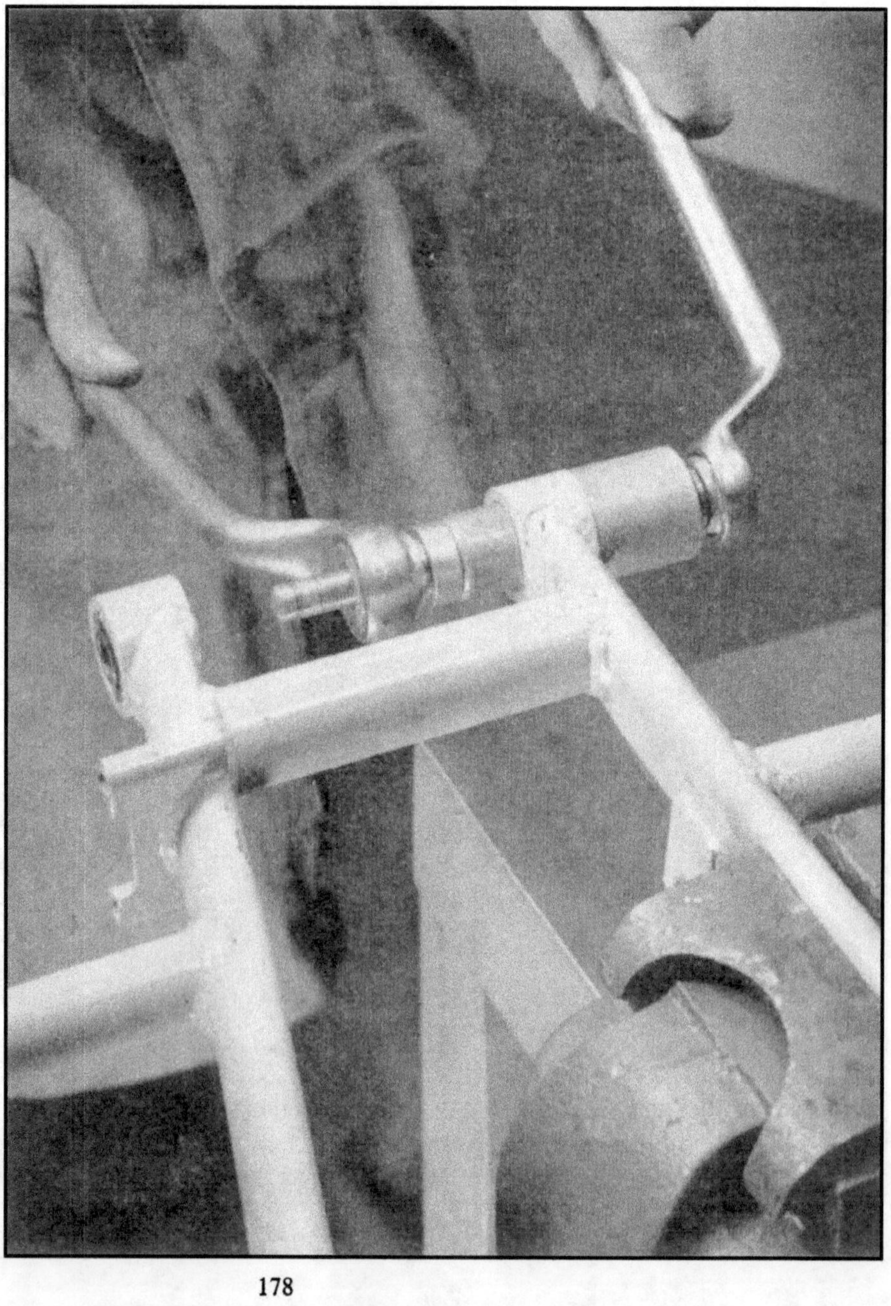

Fig. 152

Pass the bolt through the old bush from the outside, then fit washer 43602S to the bolt where it projects through the bush, with the recess in the washer next to the bush. The distance tube 42073 is then fitted, followed by the second washer 474 and finally the nut 43594S. (See Figs. 149 and 150). Then fit a spanner on the head of the bolt to prevent it turning, while a second spanner is used to tighten the nut. Continue tightening the nut until the old bush has been drawn out of the fork and into the spacer 43601. The service tools can then be unscrewed and removed with the old bush. The bush in the other side of the fork must be removed in an identical manner.

The two bushes are identical and interchangeable and can be fitted either way round. To fit new bushes in the rear fork, proceed as follows. First smear a little thin grease on the outside diameter of both bushes, to avoid any possibility of their picking up, then, dealing with one side of the fork at a time, begin by fitting one washer 474 under the head of the bolt 43593S, then fit washer 43602S, with its plain side next to the washer 474. Followed by the new bush 41074 on to the bolt. Next pass the bolt through one of the fork pivot lugs from the outside of the fork, i.e. the head of the bolt must not be between the two fork pivot lugs. Fit spacer 43601 with the closed end first, on to the portion of the bolt which projects between the two pivot lugs. Next fit the distance tube 42073, followed by washer 474, and finally the nut 43594S, to the end of the bolt (See Fig. 151). Then with the end of the new bush located in the fork pivot lug, commence turning the nut 43594S at the same time making sure the head of the bolt does not turn and that the new bush enters the fork pivot lug true and square (see Fig. 152). Continue turning the nut until the new bush is correctly located in the fork pivot lug, i.e. when the edge of the washer 43602S is level with the face of the fork pivot lug. Then unscrew and remove the service tools.

The new bush for the other side of the fork must be fitted in an identical manner. The fork can then be re-fitted to the motor cycle in the manner described on page 195.

Next re-fit the rear mudguard as described on page 196. Then re-fit the rear hydraulic units as described on page 180 and the rear chain and chaincase as described on page 197. The air cleaner can be fitted next as instructed on page 24. The rear stop switch leads should be fitted next together with the neutral gear indicator leads if an indicator is fitted, see page 225 for full details. The side panels can then be re-fitted as described on page 154, and finally, the rear wheel as described on page 105.

REAR FORK—ARROW

The rear fork moves up and down from a pivot at the rear of the gear box, carrying the rear wheel to provide the rear suspension. The movement of the fork is controlled by the rear hydraulic units, for the details of these units see page 180.

The rear fork does not require any routine maintenance. The two bushes which are fitted in the lugs at the forward end of the fork are of special steel and bonded rubber construction and do not require any lubrication. After the motor cycle has covered a large mileage and is being generally overhauled the bushes may require replacing with new ones as described for the Leader on page 177.

To remove the rear fork, if the motor cycle is being generally dismantled as described on page 201, the rear fork will be removed during the process, if however, it is required to remove the rear fork only proceed as follows: Remove the rear wheel as described on page 105, and the dualseat as described on page 169. Then remove the rear chaincase and chain as described on page 111. The rear mudguard must be removed next; remove the two bolts and nuts which secure the mudguard to a bracket at the bottom rear edge of the frame. Also remove the two middle bolts and nuts from under the dualseat where the tail section joins the frame. The rear stop switch leads must then be disconnected, but first disconnect the battery as described on page 213 to prevent the possibility of an electrical short. The stop switch is fitted to a bracket just above the offside silencer and the leads simply pull out. The leads are clipped to the rear mudguard by spring clips. Separate the snap connectors in these leads where they pass under the dualseat.

The rear mudguard can then be lifted clear. Next remove the rear hydraulic units as described on page 180. Then remove the air cleaner, the top rear engine mounting bolt, the pivot bolt and the rear fork as described on page 202. If it is required to remove the chain sprocket from the rear fork see page 111.

When re-fitting the rear fork, assemble it to the motor cycle as described on page 205. Next re-fit the rear mudguard by locating it in position at the end of the frame, the bracket on the mudguard must be under the edge of the suspension bracket, then pass the two middle bolts through the frame, etc., and the holes in the mudguard bracket. Note that the nearside one of these two bolts must have a plain washer under its head, while the offside one must have a cable clip and the seat hinge bracket under its head. Then fit a plain washer, a shake-proof washer and a nut to both bolts where they protrude through the mudguard bracket. Next locate the mudguard on to the bracket at the bottom rear edge of the frame, and pass two ¼ inch dia. by ½ inch underhead bolts, with plain washers under their heads, through the holes in the mudguard and the corresponding holes in the bracket on the frame, and fit a plain washer, a shake-proof washer and a nut to both bolts and securely tighten.

Next re-fit the rear hydraulic units as described on page 206 and the rear chain and chaincase as described on page 206; the air cleaner can be fitted next as instructed on page 24. The rear stop switch leads should then be fitted, the leads can be pushed either way round into the sockets in the switch, but they must be connected under the dualseat to the leads with corresponding colours. Next re-fit the rear wheel as described on page 105, and finally the dualseat as described on page 169.

REAR HYDRAULIC UNITS—LEADER AND ARROW

The two hydraulic units which are fitted with coil springs are fitted between the rear fork and the top of the frame, and control the movement of the rear fork which pivots from the rear of the gear box, and together these parts provide the rear suspension. The springs which are fitted in the hydraulic units are suitable for average conditions, but if required, special auxiliary springs are available which fitted together with the existing springs, stiffen the action of the rear suspension, permitting extra weight to be carried.

The hydraulic units are sealed, and do not require any attention, after a very large mileage has been covered new units may be required.

If it is required to remove the rear hydraulic units from the motor cycle begin with the motor cycle on the centre stand, then remove the rear chaincase as described on page 111. Also remove the acorn nut and washers from the bottom end of both hydraulic units. Next, with the dualseat open, the top of the rear hydraulic units can be seen where they project through top of the frame. Remove the special nut from the top of both units, but note the studs on which the nuts are fitted must be prevented from turning whilst the nuts are being removed. A special spanner is supplied in the tool kit of each new motor cycle which will fit the two flats at the top of the studs whilst the nuts are being removed. Next, remove the steel washers and the mounting rubbers from the top of both hydraulic units.

The rear wheel of the motor cycle must next be lifted a few inches off the ground, this is most easily done by placing a suitable block of wood under the centre stand. As an alternative, the rear wheel can be removed, but obviously, if the motor cycle is lifted at the rear, it will save a considerable amount of work. Then with either, the rear end of the motor cycle raised or the rear wheel removed, the rear fork and hydraulic units can be pulled downwards sufficiently to free the top of the units from the frame, when they can then be pulled sideways to free them from the rear fork and the motor cycle.

To gain access to the springs inside the rear hydraulic units, place the unit horizontally with the two flats at the top of the stud clamped between the jaws of a vice. Then unscrew the top cover up the stud, but note this has a *left-hand thread*. When the cover is free from the threaded portion of the stud, the hydraulic unit can be taken out of the vice and the top cover and coil spring lifted off. Do not attempt to dismantle the sealed hydraulic damper portion of the units, as this could lend to irreparable damage. Trouble with the hydraulic units is rare, but if trouble should be experienced, the units should be replaced with new ones. To re-fit the coil springs and top covers to the hydraulic units, first place the springs and covers in position, and clamp the flats at the top of the stud between the jaws of a vice, so that the hydraulic unit is horizontal. Then pull the top cover firmly to compress the spring, sufficiently to start screwing the cover on to the threaded portion of the stud. Once the cover has been started on the thread, it is an easy matter to screw it down securely. Do

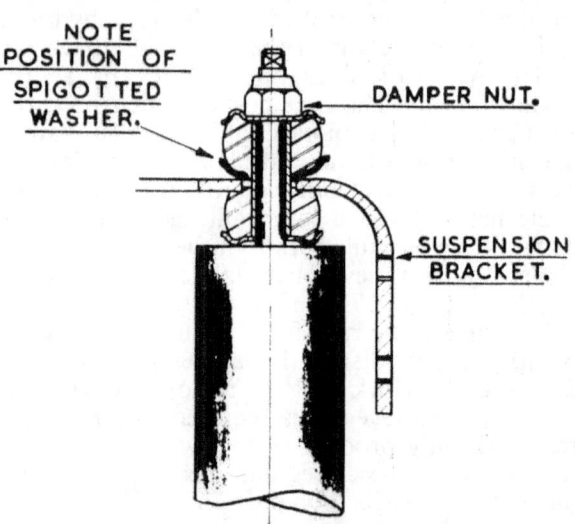

ARRANGEMENT OF TOP MOUNTING FOR REAR HYDRAULIC SPRING UNIT SHOWING LOCATION OF WASHERS.

Fig. 153

not forget that the top cover *has a left-hand thread*.

Before fitting the rear hydraulic units to the motor cycle first assemble to the stud which projects from the top cover of the unit, one of the cupped washers (not the one with a spigoted-centre), one of the mounting rubbers and the distance tube (see Fig. 153). *Note:* The rubbers must be in good condition, if in any doubt they should be replaced with new ones. Next fit both hydraulic units to the studs each side of the rear fork, then lift the rear fork whilst at the same time guiding the studs at the top of the hydraulic units, through the holes in the rear suspension bracket and the top of the frame. Then to the portion of the studs which now project through the frame, fit the spigoted washer with the spigot located into the hole in the frame, next fit a mounting rubber and a cupped washer, so that the rubbers are in a cup formed by the washers. Then fit the special locking nut to the top of each stud and tighten firmly but not excessively.

If the rear wheel was removed, it should now be re-fitted as described on page 105, for the leader and page 105 for the Arrow, or if a wood block was placed under the centre stand, it should now be removed. The rear chain case must be fitted next as described on page 197. Finally, fit a plain washer, a cupped chromium plated washer and an acorn nut to the studs which secure the bottom end of the hydraulic units.

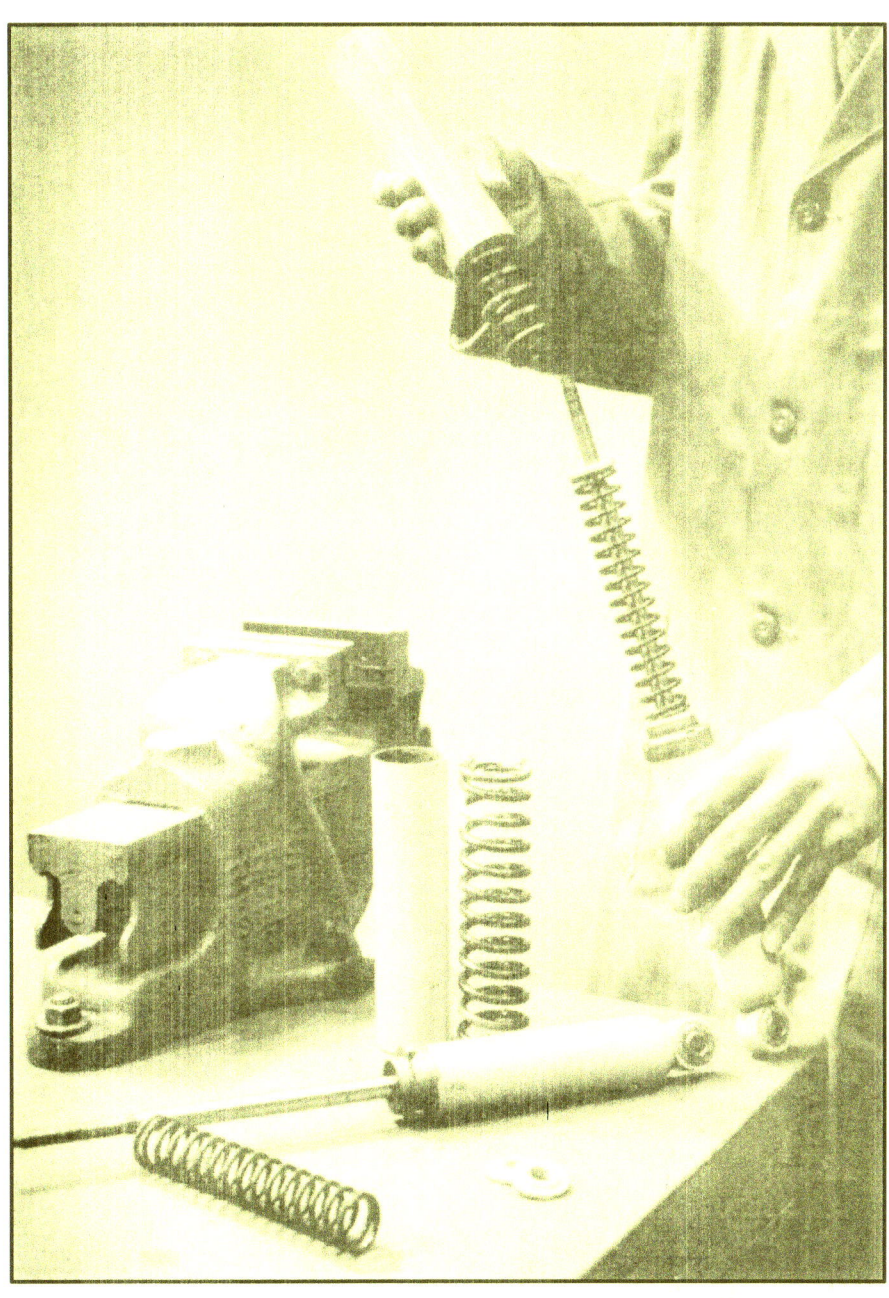

Fig. 154

SUPPLEMENTARY SPRINGS—LEADER AND ARROW

These springs are available as an optional extra, to be fitted in addition to the standard springs, if it is found that the standard springs are not strong enough for the weight being carried by the motor cycle. These springs are supplied with special locating washers, and to fit them, first remove both hydraulic units and remove the top covers and springs from the units as already described, then place one of the locating washers over the hydraulic unit top stud, so that the larger diameter spigot of the locating washer fits in the tube at the bottom of the stud. Next fit the supplementary spring on top of the locating washer, and fit a second locating washer on top of the spring with the smaller diameter spigot located in the top of the supplementary spring. Then fit the standard spring and the top cover and re-assemble the hydraulic units to the motor cycle, as described on page 180. (See Fig. 154.)

FOOTRESTS—LEADER AND ARROW

The footrests are secured to lugs on the underside of the crankcase. There are three studs screwed into each crankcase lug and the footrests are secured in position with nuts and washers. One footrest stud each side also secures the exhaust pipes to the underside of the crankcase.

If it is required to remove the footrests, the exhaust pipes and silencers must be removed first as described on page 37. This will then leave two nuts only securing each footrest, remove these nuts and the footrests will be free.

Note that the footrests are not interchangeable and must be fitted to their respective sides of the motor cycle. When the footrests are in the correct position, the portion which supports the rider's foot must be rearward of the portion, which is fitted to the studs under the engine. When fitting the footrests, first locate them on the studs under the engine, and to the two studs each side which do not take the exhaust pipes fit a plain washer, a shake-proof washer and a nut, but before tightening, pull the offside footrest outward as far as possible, and push the nearside footrest inward and securely tighten the two nuts each side. This is most important to ensure that the gear change lever and the rear brake pedal do not foul the footrests.

Finally, re-fit the exhaust pipes and silencers as described on page 43.

If it should be required to change a footrest rubber, the easiest method of removing the old rubber is to cut it off with a sharp knife. The new rubber is simply fitted by wetting and tapping it on to the footrest, with a mallet.

PILLION FOOTRESTS—LEADER AND ARROW

To remove the pillion footrests it is only necessary to remove the nut and bolt which secures the footrest to the lug on the rear fork, when the pillion footrests will be free. The pillion footrests are interchangeable and can be fitted either side. When fitting the pillion footrests, first locate the pivot lug at the end of the footrest into the lug on the rear fork, then in the small gap between the two lugs where they fit together, fit the special spring shim washer. Only one shim washer is fitted to each footrest and it can be fitted either side of the pivot lug on the footrest. Next pass the bolt through the holes in both lugs and the shim washer, and fit a shake-proof washer and a nut to the bolt and tighten sufficiently to retain footrest in up position.

If it should be required to change a pillion footrest rubber, proceed in the same way as described for the rider's footrest rubber.

CENTRE STAND—LEADER AND ARROW

The centre stand which pivots from the rear of the gear box, is a standard fitting and is always ready for immediate use. A spring is fitted between the centre stand and the underside of the engine, and this spring is fitted in such a way that it holds the centre stand up when it is not in use, it also holds the stand down in position when it is in use.

At one end of the spring a hook is fitted, and the hook in turn is fitted to the cross tube of the centre stand. The other end of the spring is fitted to a "C" shaped link and the link in turn is fitted to the underside of the engine.

To prevent the centre stand striking any part of the motor cycle when not in use, a rubber buffer is fitted to a lug on the stand. If this buffer becomes worn or damaged it should be replaced.

Any time work is being carried out on the centre stand or its fittings, the motor cycle must not be supported by the stand as there is the possibility it may fold up, allowing the motor cycle to topple with consequent damage.

To remove the centre stand spring use a strong screwdriver to lever the hook off the stand cross tube. The spring can then be slipped off the "C" shaped link. The spring and the hook are easily separated. The "C" shaped hook pivots between two spacers on a special screw fitted in the underside of the engine casting. To remove the "C" shaped link it is first necessary to remove the special screw on which the link pivots. The head of the screw is located inside the primary chaincase, therefore remove the chaincase as described on page 25. Then fitted in the engine portion of the primary chaincase can be seen a slotted screw just above the lug where the brake pedal is fitted. By removing this screw the "C" shaped link and the two spacers will be free. When re-fitting the link, first smear the threads of the screw with jointing compound, then pass the screw partially into position and fit one spacer on the screw where it projects under the engine, then fit the link with its ends facing forward, and place the second spacer on the screw so that there is a spacer each side of the link, then securely tighten the screw. Re-fit the primary chaincase and brake pedal as described on page 27. The centre stand, spring and hook can then be fitted to the "C" link, and the hook can be pulled over the cross tube of the stand.

To remove the centre stand first disconnect the springs as already described. Then remove the rear brake pedal as described on page 108. Through the rear engine lugs from where the brake pedal cross shaft was removed, a tube is fitted which forms a pivot for the brake pedal and the centre stand. The tube is a firm push fit in the engine lugs, and may need light tapping with a suitable drift and a mallet to remove; it must be pushed through from the offside to the nearside. With the tube removed the centre stand is free from the motor cycle.

When re-fitting the centre stand begin by pushing the pivot tube partially through the lug at the rear of the engine on the primary chaincase side. Then locate the centre stand in position with the curved feet of the stand facing rearwards, and push or lightly tap the pivot tube through the top cross tube of the stand, and the lug on the offside of the engine until the tube is just below the surface of the primary chaincase. Then re-fit the brake pedal as described on page 108 and finally re-fit the centre stand spring as described above.

FRONT STAND—LEADER AND ARROW

The front stand is not part of the standard equipment, but is available as an optional extra. The stand consists of three parts: a bracket which is a permanent fixture on the crankcase, a loose tube which fits over a peg on the bracket, and the front stand leg which fits into the tube. The tube and the leg are normally carried in the glove compartment or tool tray and only fitted to the bracket on the crankcase when required to support the front of the machine. The tube and front stand leg are easily fitted to the bracket on the crankcase, by leaning the motor cycle to one side and fitting the tube and leg over the peg which projects from the bracket between the exhaust pipes. Then, when the motor cycle is in the upright position the front stand will contact the ground, lifting and supporting the front end of the machine. See Fig. 71.

If the motor cycle was originally supplied with a front stand, the bracket for the stand will already be fitted to the front of the crankcase. If, however, the front stand is purchased separately the bracket will have to be fitted to the crankcase, and this is easily done by first removing the two bolts which secure the large bracket across the front of the crankcase. Then pass the bolts through the holes in the front stand bracket, and locate it in position on the large bracket across the crankcase, with the peg on the front stand bracket between the exhaust pipes and pointing downwards. Locate the two bolts through both brackets and into the tapped holes in the crankcase and securely tighten.

PROP STAND—LEADER

The prop stand is not part of the standard equipment but is available as an optional extra. It is supplied complete with the securing bolts and washers. Fitting the prop stand is a simple matter. On the underside of the crankcase, just forward of the nearside footrest, are two threaded bosses, and any dirt which may have collected inside these bosses must be removed without damaging the threads. Then locate the prop stand bracket on to the underside of the crankcase so that the holes in the prop stand bracket line up with the threaded bosses in the crankcase. Next fit a shake-proof washer under the heads of the two bolts supplied, and locate the bolts through the holes in the prop stand bracket, and into the threaded bosses in the bottom of the crankcase, and securely tighten both bolts. The prop stand should fold along the nearside of the engine when not in use.

Note: Some motor cycles have a tapped hole incorporated in the nearside footrest, and this is provided so that a stop pin for the prop stand can be fitted, to prevent the prop stand fouling the brake pedal. The stop pin is a bolt $\frac{5}{16}$ inch dia. by $\frac{5}{8}$ inch under head, and must first have a thin lock nut fitted to it, it can then be screwed into the underside of the tapped hole in the footrest, and when it has been screwed in sufficiently to form a satisfactory stop for the prop stand, the locknut should be tightened against the underside of the footrest, making sure the bolt does not move. In the case of the footrest hole being plain (not tapped) use a $\frac{1}{4}$ inch dia bolt and two lock nuts, one each side of the footrest to provide the necessary adjustments.

PROP STAND—ARROW

The prop stand is not part of the standard equipment and is available as an optional extra. It is supplied complete with bracket securing bolts and washers. Fitting the prop stand is a simple matter. Commence by securing the large cranked bracket, supplied with the prop stand, to the lug at the top of the prop stand leg. Locate the bracket on to the lug so that the two middle holes in the bracket are in line with the two holes in the lug, and with the two end holes in the bracket on the nearside, and the curved edge of the bracket facing forward. Then pass a bolt through each of the two holes in the bracket and lug, and fit a shake-proof washer and a nut to both bolts and securely tighten. Then with the bracket fitted to the prop stand, it is ready for fitting to the motor cycle, as follows:

On the underside of the crankcase, just forward of the nearside footrest, are two threaded bosses, and any dirt which may have collected inside these bosses must be removed without damaging the threads. Also the innermost nut and washers securing the offside footrest must be removed. Then locate the prop stand bracket which is at the top of the prop stand leg, on to the underside of the crankcase, so that the holes in the prop stand bracket line up with the threaded bosses in the crankcase, while the other end of the bracket fits over the innermost offside footrest stud. Next fit a shake-proof washer under the heads of two of the bolts supplied with the prop stand, and locate the bolts through the holes in the prop stand bracket and into the threaded bosses in the bottom of the crankcase, and securely tighten both bolts. Then re-fit the plain washer, shake-proof washer and nut to the inner offside footrest stud. The prop stand should fold along the nearside of the engine when not in use.

Note: Some motor cycles have a tapped hole incorporated in the near side footrest, and this is provided so that a stop pin for the prop stand can be fitted to prevent the prop stand fouling the brake pedal. The stop pin is a bolt $\frac{5}{16}$ inch dia. by $\frac{5}{8}$ inch under head, and must first have a thin lock nut fitted to it, it can then be screwed into the underside of the tapped hole in the footrest, and when it has been screwed in sufficiently to form a satisfactory stop for the prop stand, the lock nut should be tightened against the underside of the footrest, making sure the bolt does not move.

GENERAL DISMANTLING—LEADER

The following instructions cover the procedure for generally dismantling the motor cycle in order to remove the frame, but if it is required to remove the forks or certain other parts only, follow the instructions until the parts concerned are removed.

Proceed in the following order. *First disconnect and remove the battery to prevent the possibility of an electrical short.* The two leads to the battery are easily detached by removing the screw and nut which secures each lead to the battery terminals. The battery will then simply lift up and out of the motor cycle. Remove the front wheel as described on page 76; next take off the handlebar cover, see page 124, and detach the clutch, brake and throttle control cables—remove them completely from the motor cycle, see page 126. Undo the screw which secures the dip switch and remove the switch from the handlebar leaving it attached by its lead. Disconnect the snap connector on the electric horn button lead. This is the lead which emerges from the underside of the handlebar, just to the right of the centre, and the snap connector which is a joint in the lead, simply pulls apart, although it is only necessary to pull out one end to separate the lead from the main hardness.

Disconnect the two leads from the stop lamp switch on the handlebar; these simply pull out, one from each side. If the motor cycle is fitted with flashing indicators, the switch complete should be removed by undoing the nut which secures it to the bracket on the handlebar, leaving it attached to its lead.

The handlebar can then be removed by taking out the pinch bolt and nut and lifting the bars up clear of the serrations on the steering column (see Fig. 129).

The side panels and leg shields must be removed next, see page 154; then take the headlamp unit and shell out of the headlamp cowl, see page 136. Also pull out the black lead from the socket on the headlamp bulb holder.

Before removing the headlamp cowl, see page 155 regarding the windscreen, and take off the two screen support stays from the instrument panel. Then if it is desired to remove the windscreen from the front shield, proceed as instructed on page 155. Otherwise if the screen and shield are being removed together, only the four centre screws along the top edge of the front shield need be removed. Then inside the headlamp cowl at the back can be seen, one bolt at the top and two nuts at each side; these must be removed. There are also two screws with special nuts securing the bottom edges of the cowl to the front shield; these must also be removed. The screws are readily accessible from the front by turning the forks to full lock and the special nut securing each screw is easily reached behind the bottom of the front shield.

With the screws, nuts and bolt removed, the headlamp cowl can be eased forward and pulled clear.

Next remove the two nuts from each side of the motor cycle which secure the front shield to the underside of the body. If the motor cycle is fitted with flashing indicators, the lead from each lamp on the front shield must be separated from the main harness. These leads are joined by a double snap connector, which is reached through the large aperture in the front shield. The leads are easily identified as one is coloured light green and white, and the other light green and red, and they simply pull out of the snap connector. Also if a parking light is fitted it will have to be removed from the front shield. Undo the two screws which secure the lamp and rest it on the instrument panel. The front shield can then be removed; it must be eased forward to free it from the bolts in the front of the body, then downards, as the sockets for the windscreen support stays which project through the instrument panel are attached to the back of the front shield (see Fig. 155).

The instrument panel is the next main item to be removed, but first the speedometer cable and the wiring harness must be disconnected from the instruments and fittings in the panel. On the underside of the speedometer head are two knurled nuts, unscrew these to free the speedometer cable and light bulb, and then remove the speedometer cable from the motor cycle as instructed on page 158. Next pull apart the snap connector which joins the lead from the inspection lamp socket, then undo the two nuts from the underside of the ammeter and detach the leads. If the motor cycle is fitted with a parking light, the snap connector in the inspection socket lead need not be parted, as the parking light, switch and inspection socket becomes separated from the main wiring harness when the two ammeter leads are detached. Also if flashing indicators or a neutral gear indicator are fitted, the snap connector in the lead from each warning light must be pulled apart. Next remove the screw from the top of the lighting and ignition switches, and detach both switch knobs, but do not lose the chromium plated washer from the top of each knob. It can then be seen that the switches are secured to the instrument panel by a square flat nut; unscrew both nuts, taking care not to lose the small split ring which is fitted below each, the switches can then be pushed out of the instrument panel.

The instrument panel can now be removed by removing the two screws and nuts from the bottom rear edge of the panel (see Fig. 156).

Note: If the motor cycle is fitted with flashing indicators, the sub wiring harness from the flasher unit must be disconnected next. The flasher unit is mounted in the offside of the front of the body, and there are two leads still to be disconnected by separating the snap connectors at the end of the sub harness. Disconnect the green with brown lead and the brown with blue lead.

Before the body of the machine can be removed, the tail section must first be taken off. Begin by loosening the acorn nuts at the extreme end of the silencers; they only require undoing a few turns.

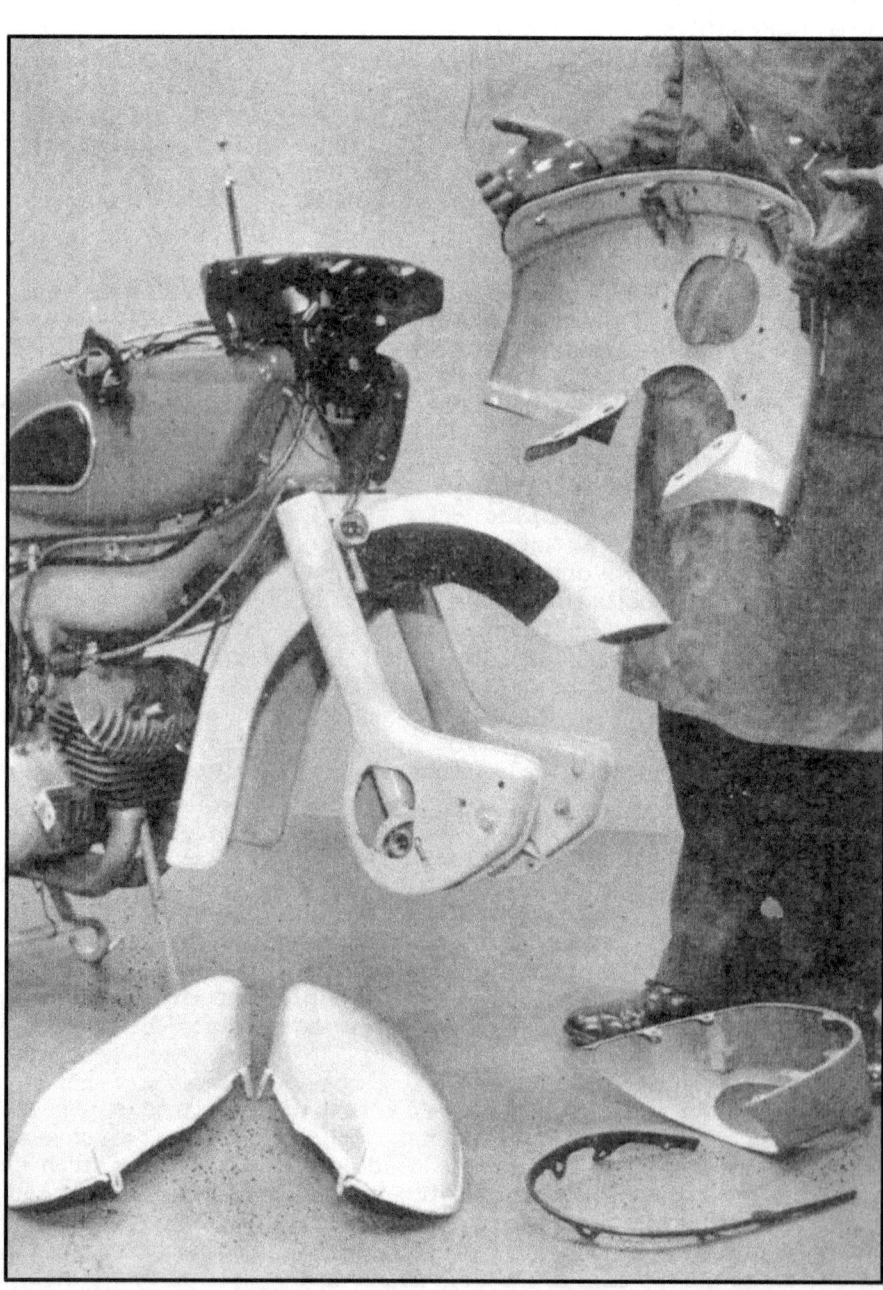

Fig. 155

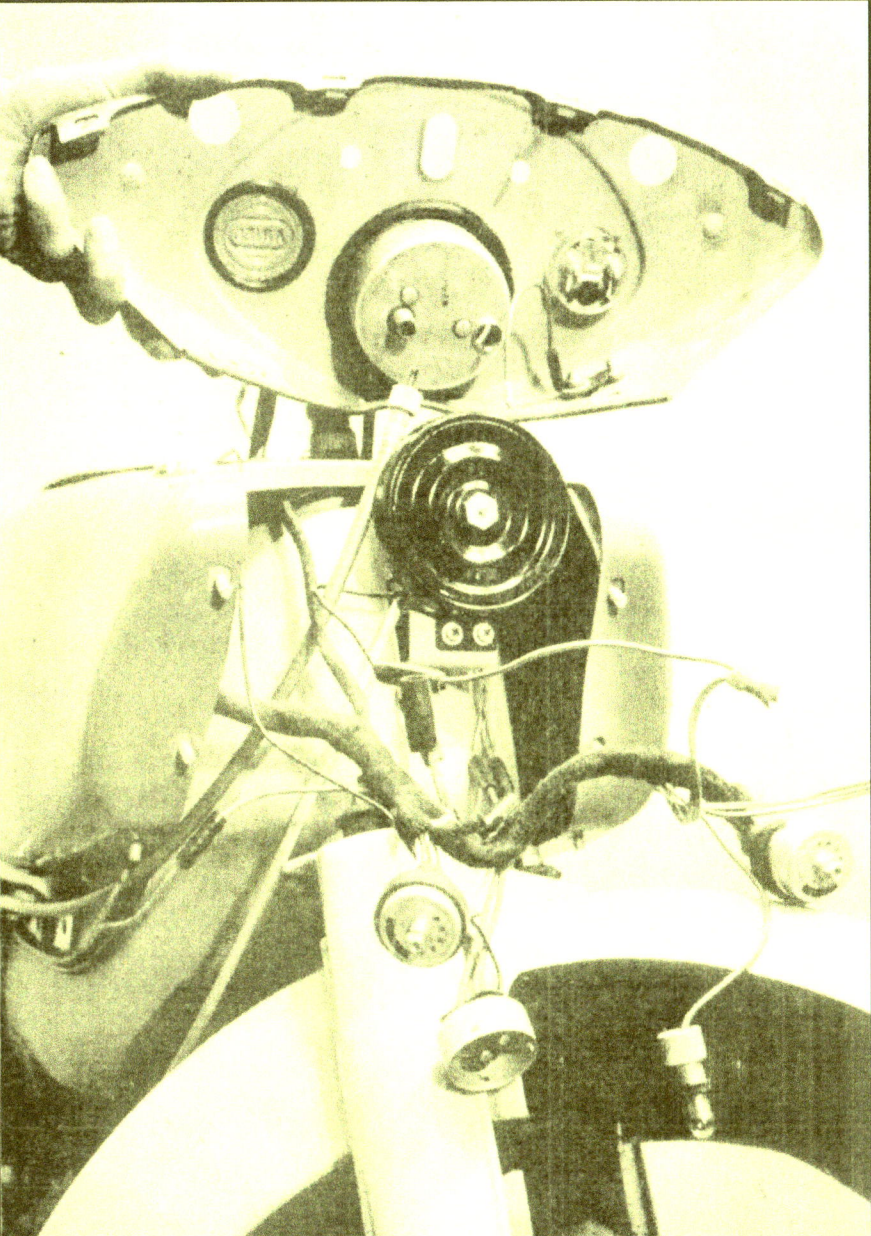

Fig. 156

just sufficient to free the silencers from the tail section stay. Next remove the two wing nuts which secure the tail section to the end of the body, these nuts are accessible through the cavity behind the tool tray; do not use pliers to remove them as there is a danger of breaking off the wings; they should be undone by hand. Then remove the two large chrome plated pivot bolts, which are situated at the forward end of the tail section, there being one bolt each side. *Note:* When the pivot bolts are removed, a loose distance tube and washer which fits on the bolts between the tail section and the body, will become free and may fall to the ground. Take care not to lose these parts. But note also that on some machines the distance tubes are not loose, but welded to the tail section.

If the motor cycle is fitted with panniers; in addition to the foregoing, loosen a few turns the bolt which secures a bracket behind the forward bottom end of each pannier, so that the bolt floats freely in the slot in the bracket.

The leads to the stop and tail lamp, also the leads to the rear flashing indicators if fitted, must be disconnected. The snap connectors for these leads are located under the dualseat. The stop and tail lamp leads are coloured brown for the stop lamp and brown with green for the tail lamp. If flashing indicators are fitted, the leads are coloured light green with white for the offside indicator lamp and light green with red for the nearside indicator lamp. Disconnect the leads by pulling them out of the snap connectors.

The tail section complete can then be removed by pulling the front ends outwards as it is lifted up and clear (see Fig. 157).

The silencers should be removed next, by first pulling out the snap connectors from each side of the stop switch, and then slackening the nut which secures the pinch bolt fitted to the clamp at the forward end of each silencer where it joins the exhaust pipe. With the clamps loosened the silencers can be pulled rearwards to withdraw them from the exhaust pipes, when they will be free from the motor cycle.

The rear mudguard which then projects from the end of the body is secured to the end of the body with one bolt and a large washer, which passes from the underside of the mudguard into a boss on the body. Remove this bolt and washer next.

If the tyre inflator or any tools are still in the tool tray, they should be removed. Next slacken the bolt which secures the dualseat locking catch to the frame, so that the catch can be turned sideways when the rod which operates it can then be slipped out.

Next remove the bolt and nut which secures a bracket to the inside of the body at each side of the tool tray; remove the two screws and nuts from

Fig. 157

each side of the body at the point where the rear hydraulic units pass inside the frame.

At each side of the motor cycle where the body joins the frame, there are three bolts which secure the body to the frame. Remove these bolts next, noting that the rearmost bolt each side is secured by a nut, while the remainder screw into tapped bosses in the frame. Next remove the lining from the glove compartment. *Note:* If the motor cycle is fitted with panniers, then the brackets on each side of the rear end of the body and frame, which secure the bottom front end of each pannier, must now be removed. Each bracket is secured the three bolts and nuts, two passing through the side of the body and the frame and one through the under edge of the frame. Remove these bolts and nuts and free the brackets, then the body complete with the dualseat can be lifted upwards and clear of the machine. (See Fig. 158.)

The front forks can be removed next. Begin by taking the alloy die casting and spacer washer from off the steering column; they are not secured in any way and simply slide up the serrated steering column. This will leave two thin nuts mounted on the column, and these are removed next by using the two large flat spanners which are supplied in the kit of each new motor cycle. Hold the lower of the two nuts with one of the flat spanners to prevent it turning and use the other spanner to turn the top nut in an anti-clockwise direction. (See Fig. 159.) Continue turning until the top nut is free from the steering column. Then commence turning the lower nut in a similar direction, until it is also free from the steering column. The forks can then be pulled down and out of the frame, although it may be necessary to apply a sharp blow with a mallet to the top of the steering column to loosen the forks initially.

At this point of the dismantling, the front forks are free from the motor cycle and any work necessary to the forks or the steering head can now be carried out, see pages 135 and 147.

If, however, the frame of the motor cycle has to be removed continue dismantling as follows:—

First disconnect the wiring harness by separating the snap connectors in the three leads from the generator on the offside of the engine. Then detach the high tension leads from both sparking plugs. Then remove the spring clips which secure

Fig. 158

Fig. 159

the stop lamp switch harness to the side of the mudguard. These clips simply pull off. Next, moving to the nearside of the engine, separate the two snap connectors in the leads from the contact breaker. Finally, if the motor cycle is fitted with a neutral indicator there are two leads attached to the indicator switch, which is fitted in the rear of the gear box, just above where the rear brake pedal cross shaft emerges, and these leads must be removed. They will simply pull out as they are fitted with snap connectors.

Remove the rear chaincase as instructed on page 111. Remove the rear chain as instructed on page 120. Next remove the rear brake pedal as instructed on page 108. Then remove the rear wheel as instructed on page 98. The rear mudguard is removed next. It is secured to the frame by four bolts and nuts. The two lower bolts pass through the mudguard and a bracket which is welded to the frame, and they are easily visible and accessible. The other two bolts pass through the top of the frame and a bracket which is welded to the mudguard. These two bolts are accessible in the rear of the tool tray. After the tool tray lining has been pulled out, remove the two centre bolts and nuts from the rear of the tool tray, and the two bolts and nuts which secure the mudguard to the bottom of the frame. The mudguard can then be lifted clear.

Next, remove the rear hydraulic spring units by

first removing the acorn nut chromium plated and spacer washer from the side of the bottom end of each unit. Then remove the nut from the top of each unit, where it projects above the frame. But note that the stud on which the nut is mounted may also turn when undoing the nut and this must be prevented. A special spanner is supplied in the tool kit, and this can be used to hold the stud whilst undoing the nut. The rear fork complete with the hydraulic units can then be pulled downwards to free the hydraulic units from the top of the frame. It is then an easy matter to pull them off the rear fork to free them from the motor cycle (see Fig. 160). Take care not to lose any of the top mounting rubbers and washers for the hydraulic units.

Then disconnect the petrol pipe by undoing the union nut between the tap and the petrol pipe, leaving the pipe attached to the carburetter. Then drain the petrol from the tank into a suitable container. Next the cold start control must be disconnected, and this is easily done by first pulling off the rubber connector tube between the carburetter and the frame, and then slackening the clamp bolt on the offside of the cold start unit, so that the unit can be rotated in an anti-clockwise direction when at the same time the operating rod can be slipped out and removed from the machine.

The air cleaner is removed next, and this

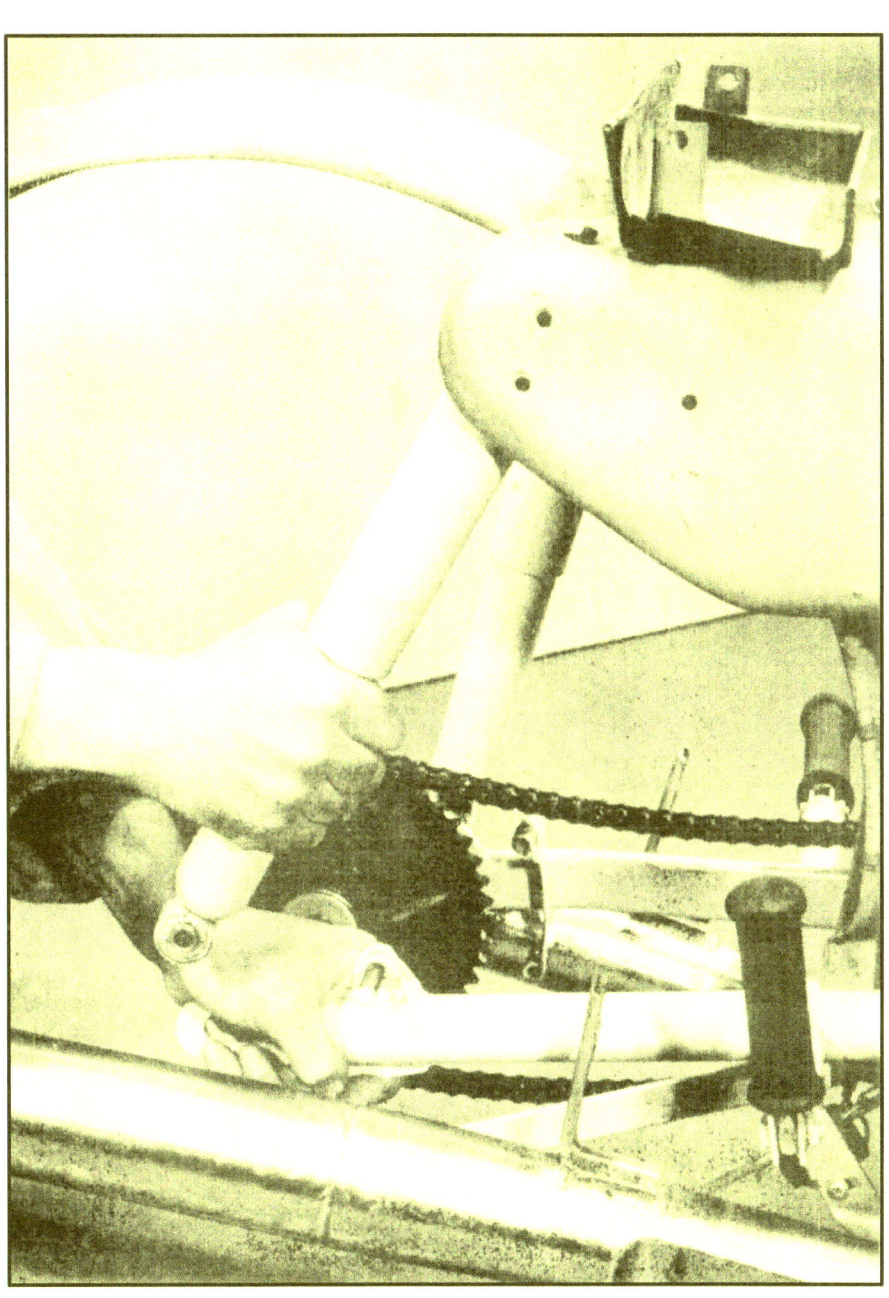

Fig. 160

simply pulls off. Then directly under the tube from where the air cleaner was removed, can be seen the hexagon head of the top rear, engine mounting bolt. Remove this bolt which has a shake-proof washer under its head. As the bolt is removed take care not to lose the special large washer, which fits on the bolt between the nearside of the frame bracket and the engine casting. Also the cranked locking plate which is fitted under the head of the bolt, must be removed. If it does not come away with the bolt, it must be pulled off the head of the lower bolt, on which it is only located and will pull off easily before the lower bolt is removed.

The lower bolt, which is the pivot bolt for the rear fork, is removed next, but it will first be necessary to remove the rearmost screw from the primary chaincase on the opposite side of the engine. This screw is at the rear of the large dome on the primary chaincase, and in line with the pillion footrest when the rear fork is horizontal. It is essential to remove this screw, as it is screwed into the end of the pivot bolt. The pivot bolt can then be removed by turning it with a tube spanner in an anti-clockwise direction.

The rear fork can then be pulled rearwards to free it from the engine although it will be necessary to ease the rear fork sideways and downwards while pulling it rearward. At the offside of the rear fork there are one steel and two nylon thrust plates fitted, through which the pivot bolt passes. The steel plate and one of the nylon plates may have come free when the pivot bolt was removed, and the remaining nylon plate which is on the other side of the rear fork lug will be removed at the same time as the rear fork. The important thing is not to lose these thrust plates.

The engine is now only secured to the frame by the stud which passes through the two forward frame brackets and the large engine lug at the rear of the cylinders. Remove the nut from either end of the stud and then withdraw the stud from the machine. The frame can then be lifted clear of the engine.

The last remaining items can now be removed from the frame. Begin by removing the two bolts and nuts which still secure the tool tray to the top of the frame. This will then free the tool tray and the two brackets which secured the frame to the edge of the body, also it will free the rear suspen-

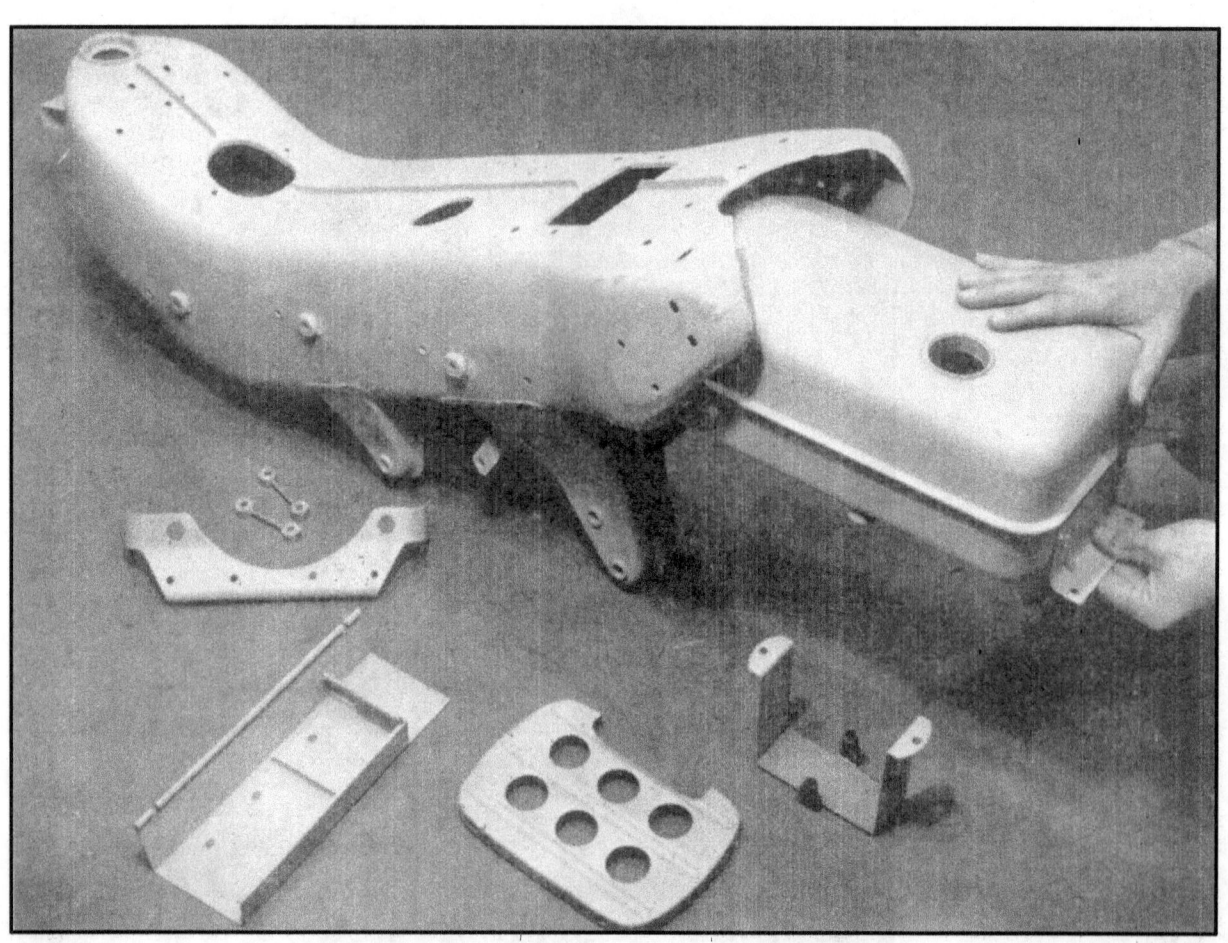

Fig. 161

sion bracket from inside the frame. Note the two alloy diecast double spacers which are fitted between the rear suspension bracket and the top of the inside of the frame. These spacers will become loose when the rear suspension bracket is removed. Next remove the nuts and bolts which secure the battery carrier to the top of the frame, this will also free the part of the dualseat catch which is mounted on the frame. The battery carrier can then be lifted up and out of the frame.

The bulkhead which is fitted in the frame immediately in front of the battery carrier is removed next by first removing the two bolts and nuts which secure the bulkhead to the top of the frame, and the two bolts and nuts which secure it to the bottom of the frame. The bulkhead can then be withdrawn. The battery earth lead will automatically be detached when the nearside top bulkhead securing bolt is removed.

Next remove the petrol tap by fitting an open-ended spanner to the portion of the tap above the knob. Also remove the petrol tank filler cap. Then remove the petrol tank by first undoing the bolt which is in the bottom of the frame, a few inches in front of the forward engine bracket, and just to the offside of the frame centre rib. Then remove the two bolts and special locking nuts which secure the bracket at the rear of the tank to the bottom of the frame. There are two rubber washers fitted to each bolt, one outside, and one inside the frame. The petrol tank can then be withdrawn through the rear of the frame. There is no need to remove the bracket from the tank (see Fig. 161).

Then unscrew the plastic spark plug caps from the end of both high tension leads. Disconnect the snap connectors in the white lead from each ignition coil and the snap connector in the one black with white lead from the offside coil. The ignition coils and the snap connectors are inside the forward end of the frame. The remaining black with white lead to this coil and the black with yellow lead from the nearside coil became disconnected when the snap connectors in the contact breaker leads were parted. The ignition coils can then be removed, but on some machines the coils are fitted inside the frame at the bottom and secured with two bolts and nuts each, while on other machines the coils are fitted at the top and secured with screws and special clip nuts. In either case it is only necessary to remove the four bolts and nuts, or the four screws, whichever is applicable to free the coils. It is then an easy matter to withdraw both coils from the frame, taking care to pass the leads which are still attached to the coils, through the frame as the coils are withdrawn.

The rectifier can be taken off next and this is secured by a nut inside the frame. Remove the nut and pull the rectifier clear, but note if the ignition coils were fitted to the bottom of the frame, there is an earthing lead from the rectifier to one of the coil securing bolts. Whilst machines which have the ignition coils fitted in the top of the frame, some have an earth lead incorporated in the wiring harness, while others do not have an earth lead and are self-earthing. The three leads from the rectifier can be separated from the main harness by parting the snap connector in each lead.

Next remove the anti-thief lock from the top of the frame after undoing the nut from each side of the lock. The lock can be removed, but note the bolts from which the two nuts were removed are welded to a plate inside the frame, and the two bolts together with the plate are removed as one unit. The electric horn can then be removed First separate the snap connector in the lead from the electric horn to the main harness then remove the two screws immediately below the horn, which secure it to the frame. Note the screws are secured by a tapped plate which becomes free when the screws are removed. If required the steering stop bracket can be removed from the bottom of the frame, by undoing the two bolts and nuts which secure it. Finally, detach the main wiring harness, and remove all the rubber grommets from the frame when the frame will then be completely bare and ready for any repair or re-enamelling work, although before re-enamelling the steering head cups should be removed, see page 147.

RE-ASSEMBLING—LEADER

If the motor cycle is being generally overhauled, or even if lesser work is being carried out, while the machine is in a dismantled state the following parts should be checked and attended to if necessary.

Front and rear wheel bearings, brake linings, brake cams, etc., and tyres.
Front fork bushes and hydraulic units.
Steering head bearings.
Rear fork bushes and hydraulic units.
Rear chain and chain wheel.

Also, if the engine unit requires any attention this would be a good opportunity to carry out the necessary work, although the whole of the engine unit is equally accessible when it is fitted to the motor cycle.

When all work on the parts concerned has been completed, before beginning the re-assembly of the motor cycle every component should be thoroughly cleaned. Also all nuts and bolts should be washed in a mixture of paraffin and oil to remove any dirt from the threads, and they should be examined to ensure they are not damaged. If in any doubt they should be replaced with new ones. The six rubber washers for mounting the petrol tank and the fibre washer, or in some cases, two washers, for the petrol tap, should also be replaced with new ones, as these items do tend to perish over a period of time.

Commence re-assembling by first fitting the two rubber grommets for the high tension leads into the underside of the frame. The holes for these grommets are the two largest towards the front end of the frame.

The anti-thief lock can now be fitted to the frame. Begin by passing the plate with the two bolts welded to it inside the frame and locate the bolts through the two forwardmost holes in the top of the frame. Then place the anti-thief lock over the bolts and fit a plain washer, a shake-proof washer and a nut to both bolts and tighten firmly but not excessively.

The rectifier is fitted next, but first note if a rectifier earth lead is incorporated in the wiring harness, or if a separate lead is used, it must be placed over the centre fixing stud, together with a shake-proof washer. Then pass the rectifier into position with the centre stud through the hole in the bottom of the frame. This is the forwardmost hole towards the offside. Then with the rectifier leads facing rearward, fit a shake-proof washer and a $\frac{5}{16}$ inch B.S.F. nut to the rectifier centre stud which is inside the frame, and securely tighten. If the rectifier does not have an earthing lead, assemble it to the frame with the nut and a *shake-proof washer each side of the frame*, as described above.

Then fit the two ignition coils, they should be passed inside the frame with the leads already assembled, as follows: The high tension leads should be pushed firmly into the centre terminal of each coil, the clip on the end of the high tension lead acting as a snap connector. Also the rubber covers must be fitted where the high tension leads enter the coils. The short white leads must be fitted, one to each coil and attached to the negative terminal. Then the coil which is fitted to the offside of the frame must have the two black with white leads attached to its positive terminal, while the coil fitted to the nearside of the frame must have the black with yellow lead attached to its positive terminal. Also, if the coils are secured to the top of the inside of the frame, the clip nuts must be fitted to the coils before they are passed inside the frame. The coils can then be secured to the frame, if they are fitted to the top of the frame they should be secured with four screws with plain washers under the heads. *Note:* These screws have a special thread to suit the clip nuts already fitted to the coils. If the coils are fitted to the bottom of the frame, they should be secured with four $\frac{1}{4}$ inch dia. by $\frac{1}{2}$ inch under head bolts with plain washers under the heads. Then, after passing the bolts through the coil brackets and the frame, fit a plain washer, a shake-proof washer and a nut to three of the bolts and securely tighten. To the fourth bolt fit a shake-proof washer, the loose end of the rectifier earth lead, a further shake-proof washer and a nut, and securely tighten. If it is not certain whether the coils are to be fitted to the top or the bottom of the inside of the frame, this is easily determined as there are four $\frac{1}{4}$ inch clearance holes in a line across the forward end of the frame, either in the top or bottom of the frame, and the coils are fitted to these holes. Next pass the high tension leads through the grommets which have already been fitted in the underside of the frame, also pass through the nearside grommet the small harness which combines a black and white lead and a black with yellow lead.

If the steering stop bracket was removed from the frame, it should now be re-fitted. Place the stop bracket in position on the underside of the frame, and pass two $\frac{1}{4}$ inch dia. by $\frac{1}{2}$ inch under head bolts fitted with plain washers through the holes in the stop bracket and through the two forwardmost holes in the underside of the frame. Then fit a plain washer, a shake-proof washer and a nut to both bolts where they project inside the frame, and securely tighten.

Fit the electric horn next to the bracket which is welded to the nearside of the front of the frame. A small plate with two tapped holes fits inside the horn bracket, and then pass two $\frac{3}{16}$ inch dia. by $\frac{7}{16}$ inch under head screws with shake-proof washers through the holes at the bottom of the electric horn and through the holes in the horn bracket. The screws are then located in the tapped holes in the plate inside the horn bracket and securely tightened.

Next place a plain washer and a petrol tank mounting rubber on each of the three special petrol tank securing bolts. Then pass one of the securing bolts through the hole in the frame, which is just to the offside of the centre and a few inches forward of the front engine bracket. Place a further petrol tank mounting rubber over the portion of the bolt which is now inside the frame. Then pass the petrol tank into the frame (see Fig. 161) and locate the tank front bracket over the front securing bolt. The tank front bracket incorporates a tapped boss and the bolt should be screwed in finger tight. Next pass the other two petrol tank securing bolts through the holes in the frame which are in line with the holes in the tank rear bracket, and fit a further tank mounting rubber to each bolt, so that there is now a mounting rubber under the head of each bolt and a second rubber between the inside of the frame and the petrol tank brackets. Then pass the two bolts at the rear of the tank through the tank rear bracket and fit a special lock nut to each bolt. Then firmly tighten all three petrol tank securing bolts.

The bulkhead can then be fitted into the frame.

The cutaway in the flange of the bulkhead must be at the bottom and the flange must face rearwards. The bulkhead can then be secured in position, but only fit the two bolts at the top and the two at the bottom. Do not fit the side bolts. The bolts for securing the bulkhead must be $\frac{1}{4}$ inch dia. by $\frac{1}{2}$ inch under head, and have a plain washer fitted under the head, except the top nearside bolt which must have a plain washer and the battery red earth lead terminal under the head. Then pass the four bolts through the holes in the frame and the holes in the bulkhead and fit a plain washer, a shake-proof washer and a nut to each bolt where it projects inside the frame, and securely tighten.

After making sure the rubber mat for the bottom of the battery carrier, and the two rubber sleeves for the short side brackets are in position, pass the battery carrier into the frame. Then secure it in position with two $\frac{1}{4}$ inch dia. bolts by $\frac{1}{2}$ inch under head, the offside securing bolt must have a plain washer fitted under the head before it is passed through the hole in the battery carrier and the frame, and then a plain washer, a shake-proof washer and a nut must be fitted to the bolt where it protrudes inside the frame. The nearside securing bolt is assembled the same, except after fitting the plain washer under the head of the bolt, the dualseat catch is also fitted. The bolt is then passed through the hole in the battery carrier and the frame, and a plain washer, together with a shake-proof washer and a nut is fitted to the portion of the bolt which is inside the frame. *Note:* The offside bolt and nut can be securely tightened, but the nearside bolt and nut with the dualseat catch must be left slack.

Next, place the tool tray in position on top of the frame together with the two right-angle brackets which are used to secure the body to the frame. Both these brackets have two bolt holes in one arm, and there are corresponding holes in the bottom of the tool tray and the frame. Then fit a plain washer under the heads of four $\frac{1}{4}$ inch dia. by $1\frac{1}{4}$ inch under head bolts, and pass the bolts through the holes in the right-angle brackets, the bottom of the tool tray and the frame. Next, locate the two die cast alloy double ended spacers on the bolts where they project through the frame, and then fit the rear suspension bracket to the bolts, and secure it in position by fitting a plain washer, a shake-proof washer and a nut to the two outer bolts only.

The frame is then ready to be fitted to the engine unit. Commence with the engine on the centre stand, and with a support under the forward end of the exhaust pipes, or use front stand if available. Then slacken the two socket head set screws which are situated in the two engine lugs at the top and rear of the gear box on the offside. A special key spanner will be required to slacken these screws and this can be obtained from most tool dealers. The key required is Unbrako W5 $\frac{5}{32}$ inch across flats. When the screws have been slackened, the distance tube which is fitted in each lug will become loose but they must not be removed from the lugs. Then locate the brackets on the underside of the frame on to the lugs on top of the engine and gear box. The front engine securing stud must be fitted first, it can be passed through the frame brackets and the engine lug from either side, and there must be a cable clip, a plain washer, a shake-proof washer and a nut on each side. The cable clip is shaped like a large washer with a long tag attached, and with a rubber sleeve covering the tag. Do not fully tighten the nuts on the front engine stud at this stage. Next, locate the frame correctly on the lugs at the top and rear of the gear box and pass the top securing bolt partially through the engine lug and the frame bracket. This bolt should only be pushed in loosely in order to hold the frame in position whilst fitting the rear fork. Next check to make certain there is a washer fitted to the lug on the nearside of the gear box where the rear fork pivot bolt screws in. This washer is not loose, but fixed in a recess in the lug and is secured in position by punching over the metal surrounding the washer in a number of places. Then fit the distance washer on to the rear fork pivot bolt. This washer is $1\frac{1}{2}$ inches in diameter and has a spigot in the centre, and when fitted to the pivot bolt the spigot must face away from the head of the bolt. Next, place one of the nylon thrust washers on the pivot bolt, and locate it on the spigot in the centre of the distance washer. The pivot bolt is then ready for securing the rear fork in position, and it should be placed somewhere convenient whilst the rear fork is located in position at the rear of the gear box. The rear fork must be placed with the pivot lugs in line with the two engine lugs at the rear of the gear box, and the offside fork pivot lug must be outside the offside engine lug. Also, at the same time as the fork is being placed in position, the second nylon thrust washer must be placed between the offside fork pivot lug and the offside engine lug, so that the rear fork and the nylon thrust washer are located into position together. It will be found that the fork will not push straight into position, and it will be necessary to push the fork at a slight angle with a twisting action to locate it correctly. Then pass the pivot bolt through the fork and engine lugs from the offside of the machine. Carefully locate the threaded portion of the pivot bolt into the nearside engine lug and securely tighten. But make sure the rear fork hydraulic unit securing studs are approximately $12\frac{1}{4}$ inches from the underside of the suspension bracket in the frame when tightening the pivot bolt otherwise the life of the suspension rubber bushes will be shortened. Note the cranked locking plate which couples the pivot bolt to the top engine bolt, must be fitted over the hexagon head of the pivot bolt in a position whereby the hole in the other end of the locking plate is in line with the hole in the engine lug where the top engine bolt is fitted. At this point the top engine bolt which had previously been loosely fitted, should be removed in order to line up the cranked locking plate with the top bolt hole. Also, a shake-proof washer must be fitted under the head of the bolt, when it can then be passed through the hole in the cranked locking plate and the engine lug and frame bracket (see Fig. 3) but before the threaded portion of the bolt is located in to the nearside engine lug, the special spacer washer must be fitted between the frame bracket and the nearside engine lug and located on the bolt, as it is passed into the nearside engine lug. The top engine bolt can then be securely tightened. The two socket headed set screws in the two offside engine lugs must also be securely tightened. Then fit the long screw into the hole at the rear edge of the primary chaincase. This screw locates into the end of the pivot bolt. Tighten the two nuts on the front engine stud.

The petrol tap can be fitted next, and it would be advisable to fit new fibre washers on the petrol tap to ensure a good joint between the tap and the tank. Also the knob of the petrol tap must face outward when fitted, so that it will be in line with the hole in the nearside side panel. Normally one fibre washer is fitted, but if the knob of the tap is in the wrong position when the tap is tightened, a further special thin washer is available, which together with the normal washer will permit the tap to be tightened to the correct position.

Fit the cold start operating rod into the bracket on the frame, and slip the cranked end of the rod through the small hole in the end of the lever on the cold start device (see Fig. 4). When the operating rod was removed, the cold start device was rotated in an anti-clockwise direction in order to position the lever vertically on the nearside of the machine, to facilitate removal of the operating rod, and the cold start device must be in this same position to re-fit the rod. It can then be rotated clockwise until the lever is uppermost and horizontal, then the clamp bolt on the offside of the cold start device should be securely tightened. Then fit the rubber connector between the cold start device and the rear frame to engine bracket. But first liberally wet the rubber connector with petrol or petrol-oil mixture. This will greatly facilitate fitting the connector, and in this particular instance the petrol will not harm the rubber as it is special petrol and oil proof material. The oval-shaped end of the connector has a channel moulded around the outer edge, and this end of the connector fits into the oval-shaped hole in the frame bracket, but note that the end of the connector is also shaped to suit the angle of the frame bracket and the connector can only be fitted one way up, also the seam along the top of the connector must be central and the edge of the hole in the frame bracket must be located in the moulded channel. It is then an easy matter to slip the other end of the connector over the end of the cold start unit, but afterwards check to make certain that the connector is correctly located at both ends.

The air cleaner is fitted next to the tube incorporated in the offside of the rear frame to engine bracket. Begin by clamping the ends of the air cleaner spring clip together with a pair of pliers in order to increase the internal diameter of the clip. Then pass the clip only over the tube on the frame bracket, and keep it clamped between the pliers while the air cleaner is fitted over the frame bracket tube and inside the clip, then release the clip from the pliers when it will secure the air cleaner in position.

Next fit the petrol pipe from the carburetter to the petrol tap by locating the pipe on the tap and tightening the union nut. Tighten the nut firmly but not excessively. The front fork and mudguard assembly are fitted next. The steering head cups in the top and bottom of the frame must be packed with fresh grease of the same grade as recommended for the hubs. Then place new steel balls in the grease-packed steering head cups, there must be twenty-three steel balls in the bottom cup and twenty in the top cup (see Fig. 139). Next lift the fork assembly and pass the steering column up through the steering head tube in the frame and locate the steering head bottom cone which is situated at the bottom of the steering column, into the steering head cup in the bottom of the frame, but take the utmost care not to let any of the steel balls fall out of either of the steering head cups. Then, holding the fork in position, pass the top steering head cone down the steering column and locate it into the top steering head cup, and again make certain that none of the steel balls have fallen out of the steering head cups. Then still holding the forks in position, pass the thin washer, followed by the dust cover, down the steering column, next fit one of the thin nuts to the steering column. It should be possible to screw this nut down finger tight with one hand while holding the forks up with the other. The thin nut should then be tightened with one of the special flat spanners which is supplied in the tool kit of each new motor cycle, until all the free play in the steering head bearings has been taken up. See page 133 for full instructions on steering head bearing adjustment. Then fit the second thin nut to the steering column, and whole holding the lower thin nut with one of the special flat spanners to prevent it turning, tighten the second thin nut securely to lock both nuts together (see Fig. 159). Afterwards check the adjustment of the steering head bearings again, to make quite certain it is in order. Next fit the alloy diecasting which froms part of the anti-thief lock to the steering column, but take care to position it correctly with the lug facing rearward when the forks are in the straight ahead position. Then pass the thick spacer down the steering column, and rest it on top of the alloy die casting. The front wheel can then be fitted as described on page 85.

The rear mudguard should be fitted next, the bracket which is welded to the mudguard has two holes, and the two centre bolts which pass through the tool tray and the frame are not yet fitted with nuts, and the mudguard bracket must be located on to these bolts, then a plain washer, a shakeproof washer and a nut must be fitted to each bolt, but do not tighten the nuts yet, as the mudguard must also be secured to the bracket which is welded to the underside of the rear edge of the frame. The bracket is provided with two holes and there are corresponding holes in the mudguard. Fit a plain washer under the head of two $\frac{1}{4}$ inch dia. by $\frac{1}{2}$ inch under head bolts, and pass the bolts through the holes in the bracket which is welded to the frame, and through the holes in the mudguard. Then fit a plain washer, a shakeproof washer and a nut to both bolts, and securely tighten. Also tighten the bolts and nuts which secure the mudguard to the top edge of the frame.

Next fit the hydraulic units to the frame and rear fork. Take care to assemble the steel washers and mounting rubbers in the right order on the top of the hydraulic units (see Fig. 153). Also the mounting rubbers must be in good condition and if in any doubt fit new ones. First fit one of the larger washers with the cupped side uppermost to both hydraulic units, then fit the spacer tube and one mounting rubber directly above the cupped steel washer. Next locate the stud and the spacer tube at the top of the hydraulic units, through the holes in the rear suspension bracket and the top of the frame, at the same time locate the bottom end of the hydraulic units on to the studs which project from each side of the rear fork (see Fig. 160). Then fit the two smaller steel washers to the hydraulic unit studs which project above the frame, again with the cupped side of the washer uppermost and the spigot in the centre of the washer located through the hole in the frame. Next fit the second mounting rubber to both hydraulic unit top studs, followed by the second of the larger washers, and this time the cupped side of the washers must face downwards. Finally fit the special locking nut to the top of both hydraulic unit studs and tighten firmly but not excessively. Next fit a plain washer, a chromium plated cup washer and an acorn nut to the bottom securing studs for both hydraulic units. Securely tighten the offside acorn nut, but leave the nearside one loose until the rear chaincase has been fitted.

The rear chain sprocket should be in good condition and fitted to the rear fork. If in any doubt, or for instructions on removing and fitting the rear chain sprocket to the rear fork, see page 111. The rear chain can then be fitted, but it must be in good condition and be thoroughly cleaned, before being treated with fresh lubricant, see page 120 for full details on rear chain. To fit the rear chain to the gear box sprocket, first move the gear change lever on the gear box up or down to engage a gear, then pass the end of the rear chain into the top of the housing for the gear box sprocket, and at the same time operate the kick starter slowly but continuously. The kick starter can be operated with one hand while feeding the chain on to the sprocket with the other, but it will be necessary to use a tommy bar, or something similar to guide the chain on to the sprocket, also the kick starter will be easier to operate if both sparking plugs are removed. Operating the kick starter in gear will cause the gear box sprocket to rotate, and if the rear chain is fed on to the top of the sprocket it will be carried round, and can then be pulled out of the bottom of the housing which surrounds the gear box sprocket. With the chain around the sprocket, locate the two ends round the rear chain sprocket with the two end links only separated by one tooth of the sprocket, then from the offside, pass the chain connecting link through the two end links and assemble the loose side plate to the nearside of the connecting link. Finally, fit the spring clip with the closed end facing towards the direction of chain travel. The spring clip is fitted by first locating it as near as is possible in position on the connecting link rivets, then by using a pair of pliers with one jaw behind the closed end of the spring clip, and the other jaw behind the rivet inside the clip, pressure on the pliers will cause the clip to snap into position. Afterwards, check very carefully to make quite certain the spring clip is correctly fitted.

The rear chaincase is fitted next, and this is simply located in position on the rear fork, with the half with the rubber grommets in fitted at the top, there is no gasket or joint involved but the top half must overlap the lower half. Then fit a plain washer under the heads of the four screws which are used to secure the chaincase to the rear fork, and note that the two shorter screws fit at the front end of the chaincase. After passing the four screws through the chaincase and the brackets on the rear fork, fit a plain washer and a nut to each screw and securely tighten. Then tighten the acorn nut at the bottom end of the nearside rear hydraulic unit. The rear wheel can then be fitted as described on page 105. Also fit the rear brake pedal as described on page 108.

The main wiring harness with the lighting and ignition switches can now be assembled to the motor cycle. Place the harness on the frame with the switches at the forward end. The branch in the harness which includes the plain white, and the white with black leads; also the green with black, green with yellow and brown with blue leads, must be passed through the hole in the offside of the frame, which is situated above the two forwardmost threaded bosses on the offside of the frame. Note that as there is no grommet fitted in this hole, to prevent the harness becoming chaffed and damaged, the joint where the branch harness leaves the main harness should be protected by binding it with insulation tape. Next connect the leads inside the frame. There are two white leads and a white with black lead already attached to the coils, and these must be coupled by the snap connectors to the leads with corresponding colours in the branch harness. The remainder of the branch harness must then be passed through the hole in the underside of the frame, through which the offside high tension lead also passes. Then couple the leads from the end of the branch harness as follows. The green with black lead must be coupled with a double snap connector to the green with black lead from the alternator and the green with black lead from the rectifier. The green with yellow lead from the branch harness must be connected to the green with yellow lead from the alternator. The brown with purple lead from the branch harness must be coupled to the brown with purple lead from the rectifier. Then the green with white lead from the alternator must be connected to the green with white lead from the rectifier. The branch harness should then be looped around the cable clip which is attached to the offside end of the engine securing stud. Also some machines have a cable clip attached to the bolt which secures the front of the petrol tank to the frame, and for these machines the branch harness should also be fitted under this clip. Next connect the black with white and the black with yellow leads, which protrude from the hole in the underside of the frame through which the nearside high tension lead also passes, to the black with white and the black with yellow leads from the contact breaker. Then re-fit the plastic covers to the high tension leads by screwing them on tightly and snap the covers over the sparking plug terminals.

The separate sub harness for the rear stop switch should be fitted next, by clipping it to the offside of the rear mudguard. Then connect the brown and the brown with blue leads in the sub harness to the leads with corresponding colours, at the end of the main harness. If a neutral indicator is fitted, the white with blue and white leads should be fitted to their respective snap connectors.

The assembling of the motor cycle can now continue, and the silencers should be fitted next, but note the flat on the forward ends of the silencer bodies must face outwards to clear the stand, and when the silencers are in position the brackets must be vertical. After fitting the clamp to the forward end of each silencer, continue by locating them over the ends of the exhaust pipes and against the stop pegs which are incorporated on the exhaust pipes. The clamps should be securely tightened by tightening the nut on the clamp bolts. If the stop lamp switch was removed from the front bracket on the offside silencer, it should be re-fitted with its operating arm facing forward. The stop switch should be secured to the back of the front silencer bracket, with two screws which have plain washers fitted under the heads, and special locking nuts fitted to the screws. The stop switch spring can then be fitted to the switch operating arm, then fit the other end of the spring over the front end of the brake rod between the brake rod operating lever and the plain washer. Next fit the stop switch leads into the stop switch. The leads have snap connectors fitted, and they simply push into the sockets each end of the switch. It is not important to fit the different coloured leads in any particular order to the switch. If a neutral indicator is fitted, push the white with blue and white leads into the sockets on the switch at the rear of the gear box.

The body of the motor cycle can now be fitted and it should be fitted complete with the dualseat, the glove compartment lid and sealing rubber, the two knee grip rubbers and the two brackets with five bolts and one screw fitted to each bracket. Also the headlamp earthing lead and the flasher unit if the motor cycle is fitted with flashing indicators. If any of these items are not fitted, then do so before fitting the body to the motor cycle. For details of fitting dualseat, see page 169. For other items see details on body, page 168. When fitting the body, locate the main wiring harness in the space between the body and the frame on the offside of the machine.

Locate the body in position on the frame, see Fig. 158), then fit a shake-proof washer and a plain washer which has a large outside diameter, to a $\frac{1}{4}$ inch diameter by $\frac{1}{2}$ inch under head bolt, and pass the bolt up through the hole towards the end of the rear mudguard, and locate it in the threaded boss at end of the body, but do not tighten the bolt until the other body securing bolts have been located in position. Next fit a plain washer under the heads of four $\frac{1}{4}$ inch diameter by $\frac{1}{2}$ inch under head screws, and fit two screws to each side of the body through the holes just above the point where the rear hydraulic units pass inside the frame. There are corresponding holes through the frame and rear suspension bracket, and the screws must pass right through, when a shake-proof washer and a nut can be fitted to each screw where it protrudes through the rear suspension bracket, but do not tighten the screws yet. Then fit a shake-proof washer and a plain washer under the heads of two $\frac{1}{4}$ inch diameter by $\frac{1}{2}$ inch under head bolts, and pass the bolts through the holes each side of the body and frame, which are in line with a corresponding hole through the flange of the bulkhead inside the frame. Then fit a plain washer and a shake-proof washer and a nut to the bolts where they project through the bulkhead. Next fit a shake-proof washer and a plain washer under the heads of four $\frac{1}{4}$ inch diameter by $\frac{3}{8}$ inch under head bolts, and fit two bolts to each side of the body, through the holes which are in line but forward of the last bolts fitted. Note, the bolt which is fitted forwardmost of these two on the offside of the motor cycle, must also have a cable clip fitted under its head. The forwardmost bolt of all which secures the body to the frame and which is in line with those already fitted, also secures the leg shields and should be left out or loose for the time being. There are threaded bosses in the frame for the bolts to screw in to, but they should only be screwed in loosely. Then fit a shake-proof washer under the heads of two $\frac{1}{4}$ inch diameter by $\frac{3}{8}$ inch under head bolts, and fit the bolts inside the top channel edge of the body, each side of the tool tray, and pass the threaded portion of the bolts through the holes in the inner face of the channeling, and through the holes in the top end of the right-angle brackets which are situated each side of the tool tray. Then fit a shake-proof washer and a nut to both bolts, but before tightening them check that the body is correctly fitted and located on the frame. Then securely tighten the bolt which fastens the rear mudguard to the end of the body, and the two screws each side of the body in line with the top end of the hydraulic units; also the three bolts each side which secure the body to the frame, and finally the two bolts which fasten the body to the right angle brackets in the tool tray. *Note:* If the motor cycle is fitted with panniers, the brackets which secure the panniers to the frame must now be fitted. Each bracket is secured to the frame by three ¼ inch diameter by ⅜ inch under head bolts with a plain washer fitted under the head of each bolt. Two bolts pass through the holes in the top end of the brackets and the holes in the sides of the body and frame which are situated a few inches forward of the hydraulic units. The third bolt passes through the holes in the right-angle brackets and the hole in the under edge of the frame. All bolts are then fitted with a plain washer, a shake-proof washer and a nut, and securely tighten. For full details on fitting panniers, see page 208.

The tail cover is fitted next, locate it in position on the rear end of the body (see Fig. 157), and note that there must be a distance tube fitted between the pivot bolts holes in the tail cover and the body. On some machines the distance tube is loose, while on others it is welded to the tail cover. If the distance tube is of the loose type, there must be a large plain washer fitted between the end of the distance tube and the tail section. If the distance tubes are the loose type be quite certain to fit them. Then fit a large chromium plated washer under the heads of both pivot bolts, and pass the bolts through the tail cover, the second large washer, the distance tubes and screw into the threaded bosses in the body, and securely tighten both bolts. Next fit a plain and a spring washer and a wing nut to the two studs which protrude from the underside of the tail cover and through the holes in the end of the body, and tighten the wing nuts firmly by hand. The silencer support stay at the rear of the tail cover should be located on to the ends of the silencers, the acorn nuts can then be securely tightened to fasten the silencers to the support stay. If the machine is fitted with panniers, there is a bolt behind the forward bottom end of each pannier which must be located in the slotted bracket which secures the pannier to the frame, then the bolts must be securely tightened.

The sub wiring harness from the tail lamp, which is clipped along the offside inner face of the tail cover, must be passed through the rubber grommet in the offside rear end of the body. The sub harness can then be connected to the main wiring harness. The lead coloured brown must be connected to the double snap connector which is already fitted with two brown leads. The lead which is coloured brown with green must be coupled to the triple snap connector which is already fitted with a brown with green lead. If the motor cycle is fitted with flashing indicators, the two leads from the rear indicators are also included in the tail lamp sub harness, and they must be connected to the triple snap connector to which the brown with green tail lamp lead has been fitted. The rear flashing indicator leads are coloured as follows: one is green with white and the other is green with red, and they must be connected to the leads with corresponding colours in the triple snap connector.

Next fit the operating rod for the dualseat catch through the grommet in the rear of the glove compartment, and locate it into the hole in the hook of the dualseat catch, then with the hook facing rearwards, securely tighten the bolt which fastens the catch to the frame.

The instrument panel is the next main item to be fitted, and this should be complete with the ammeter, speedometer, clock or badge, inspection lamp sockets, trimmer rod grommet and if the motor cycle is fitted with extras, the parking lamp switch and flasher and neutral great indicator lights. Also the four special captive nuts must be fitted inside the front edge of the instrument panel. For separate details on any of these items, see page 157. The instrument panel must have a rubber beading fitted along the bottom rear edge. It can then be located on the frame so that the holes in the rear edge of the instrument panel correspond with the holes in the two brackets which are fitted on each side of the top of the body. Then fit a plain washer under the heads of two ¼ inch diameter by ½ inch under head chromium screws, and pass the screws through the holes in rear edge of the instrument panel and the brackets on the body, then fit a shake-proof washer and a nut to each screw and securely tighten. The instruments and fittings can now be connected. Begin by fitting the speedometer cable, first to the gear box and then to the speedometer head in the instrument panel, as described on page 158. Then fit the speedometer bulb and holder to the underside of the speedometer. The bulb and holder are attached to the main harness, and simply screw into the bottom of the speedometer.

The leads to the ammeter are attached next. They extend from the main harness and have washer-type terminals attached to the ends. One lead consists of three brown with blue leads and these must be attached to the stud on the underside of the ammeter, nearest the speedometer. The other lead consists of two brown with white leads which must be attached to the stud on the nearside of the bottom of the ammeter.

Next assemble the lighting and ignition switches into the "D" shaped holes in the instrument panel, with the ignition switch in the offside hole and the lighting switch in the nearside. The main portion of the switch fits under the instrument panel with its securing stud projecting above the panel. Fit a split ring and flat square nut to both switch studs, to secure the switches to the instrument panel. Then locate the switch knobs on top of the switches, and secure them in position by fitting a chromium plated washer and screw through the centre of both knobs.

The leads which are to be connected to the fittings on the handlebars, should be passed through the steering column grommet hole in the top of the body. Begin with the electric horn push lead which is coloured black. Next pass the two front stop switch leads through the grommet hole, these leads are coloured brown and brown with blue and are enclosed in a common cover. The dipper switch leads are next, but as the switch is too large to pass through the grommet hole, the leads must be disconnected from the headlamp bulb holder and the main harness, so that the switch can be placed on top of the body and its lead passed down through the rubber grommet and the grommet hole in the body and re-connected to the headlamp bulb holder and the main harness. The lead from the dipper switch to the main harness is coloured blue, and is joined by a snap connector to a lead with a corresponding colour. The two leads from the dipper switch to the headlamp bulb holder are coloured blue with white and blue with red, and they have snap connectors close to the bulb holder. Separate, and rejoin the leads at these snap connectors, but in addition to passing the leads through the grommet hole in the top of the body, first pass the leads through one of the smaller holes in the rubber grommet which will be fitted in the grommet hole.

If the motor cycle is fitted with flashing indicators, the indicator switch must be dealt with in a similar manner to the dipper switch. The indicator switch has three leads, one is coloured green with brown, one is green with white and the other is green with red. Separate the snap connectors in these leads, and after passing the leads attached to the switch down through the same hole in the rubber grommet as the dip switch leads, and then through the grommet hole in the body, rejoin them with the snap connectors.

Next thread the horn push lead and the front stop switch leads through the other small hole in the steering column rubber grommet, then fit the grommet into the hole in the top of the body. The handlebars can now be fitted. Locate them on the splined steering column, making quite certain that the handlebars are fitted squarely in relation to the front wheel. Then fit the handlebar pinch bolt through the lug just below the centre of the handlebars. This bolt is $\frac{5}{16}$ inch diameter by $1\frac{1}{2}$ inches under head and is made from a special high tensile steel, and it is therefore essential to use the correct bolt. A spring washer and a thin lock nut are then fitted to the pinch bolt, and securely tightened.

The control cables and fittings can now be assembled to the handlebars. Begin by fitting the dipper switch to the underside of the handlebar, and next to the dummy grip rubber, so that the switch knob faces the nearside end of the handlebar. Next fit the two leads coloured brown and brown with blue, to the front stop switch on the offside of the handlebar. There are snap connectors on the ends of the leads and sockets incorporated in the switch, and it is not important to fit the different coloured leads in any particular order. The lead from the horn push should be joined next, by coupling the black lead which extends from the offside of the steering column grommet, to the snap connector on the horn push lead. If the motor cycle is fitted with flashing indicators, the indicator switch can now be fitted to the bracket on the nearside of the handlebar. The hole in the bracket and threaded portion at the end of the switch are both "D" shaped to ensure the switch is fitted correctly. Pass the switch through the bracket from the offside locating the threaded portion through the bracket, then fit the switch securing nut over the knob and on to the threaded portion of the switch which protrudes through the nearside of the handlebar bracket, and tighten the nut firmly but not excessively.

Next fit the throttle cable, clutch cable and the front brake cable, and adjust them as described on pages 126 to 129. Then fit the handlebar cover as described on page 124.

The front shield complete with the windscreen can be fitted next (see Fig. 155), but note if the windscreen and the front shield are separate, the front shield only should be fitted at this stage, and the windscreen should be assembled to the front shield afterwards as described on page 156. In either event it is essential that the two sockets for the windscreen support stays are securely fitted to the two brackets at the upper rear edge of the front shield, *before fitting the front shield to the motor cycle*. Then commence by locating the front shield on to the four bolts which project from the underside of the body, two each side of the motor cycle. Then carefully ease the front shield into position on to the four bolts which project from the front of the body, and at the same time locating the sockets for the windscreen stays through the holes in the instrument panel. Then fit a plain washer, a shake-proof washer and a nut to the four bolts which protrude from the underside of the body and through the bottom of the front shield, but leave the nuts loose. Next fit the beading which seals the joint between the headlamp cowl and the front shield over the four bolts which project from the front of the front shield. Then fit the headlamp cowl over the same four bolts, and fit a plain washer, a shake-proof washer and a nut to each bolt, but leave the nuts loose. Next fit a shakeproof washer and a plain washer under the head of a $\frac{1}{4}$ inch diameter by $\frac{1}{2}$ inch under head bolt, and pass the bolt through the hole towards the top edge at the back of the headlamp cowl, and into the threaded boss in the front shield, but do not tighten the bolt yet. Each side of the headlamp cowl at the inner bottom edge there is a hole with a corresponding hole in the front shield. Through each of these holes fit a screw $\frac{3}{16}$ inch diameter by $\frac{3}{8}$ inch under head and with a plain washer under the head, the screws should be first passed through the holes in the headlamp cowl and rubber beading, then where they protrude through the back of the front shield, fit a special locking nut and securely tighten. The nuts which are loosely fitted to the four bolts in the underside of the body, and the four bolts at the back of the headlamp cowl together with the bolt at the top of the back of the headlamp cowl, must now be securely tightened. The screws for the top of the front shield should be assembled next. There must be six $\frac{1}{4}$ inch diameter by $\frac{3}{4}$ inch under head screws, each with a chromium plated washer under its head. There must also be a spacer tube fitted in all six holes along the top of the front shield, and the screw which is to be fitted to the nearside end must have the licence holder assembled to it. Pass four of the screws through the four centremost holes in the top of the front shield, locating them through the spacer tubes and into the special captive nuts in the front edge of the instrument panel, but do not tighten the screws yet. *Note:* If when assembling these four screws, one of the captive nuts should be pushed out of the instrument panel, it is permissible to avoid dismantling the front shield again, to fit a plain washer, a shake-proof washer and a nut, in place of the captive nut, and this can be done by passing the nut and washers under the end of the instrument panel. Next pass the two end screws through the front shield and spacer tubes, then fit a chromium plated plain washer and an acorn nut to each screw where it protrudes at the back of the front shield, but leave the screws loose.

If the windscreen is not already fitted, assemble it next. Then assemble the windscreen support stays and tighten the screws along the top of the front shield. See page 156 for full details on fitting windscreen and **stays.**

The leg shields can then be fitted, as described on page 155. Next fit the headlamp shell into the headlamp cowl, and fit the headlamp complete with bulbs, into the headlamp shell, as fully described on page 141.

If the motor cycle is fitted with flashing indicators, couple the leads from the flasher lamps on the front shield to the snap connectors under the instrument panel which are fitted with leads of a corresponding colour, i.e. the nearside leads are coloured green with red and the offside are green with white. Also if the motor cycle is fitted with a parking lamp, assemble the lamp to the back of the front shield and connect the lead as fully described on page 165. Then fit the three sections of lining into the glove compartment.

Next, check and if necessary adjust the rear chain, as described on page 118. Then check the wheel alignment and if required, re-set it as described on page 122. Check and if necessary adjust the tyre pressures, see pages 98 and 124. Adjust the rear brake, see page 107. Check the adjustment of the front brake, clutch and throttle cables, and if necessary re-adjust them. If required top up the primary chaincase and gear box with oil as recommended on page 25 and 61. Replenish the petrol tank with a quantity of the correct mixture of petrol and oil, see page 10.

When fitting the petrol filler cap note the two sealing rings which are fitted to the sleeve portion of the cap. These sealing rings must be in good condition. If in any doubt replace them with new ones and smear with grease. Next check the motor cycle over generally and make certain that all nuts and bolts are securely tightened. The side panels can then be fitted, as described on page 154.

The battery can be fitted next, but first check the state of the charge with a hydrometer, and if the charge is low, the battery should be re-charged before fitting it to the motor cycle. *Note:* If a hydrometer and battery charger are not available a local agent or garage will carry out this work for a nominal charge. Then check the level of the acid in the battery and if necessary top up with distilled water to the correct level. Clean the battery terminals, and then coat them with clean vaseline. The battery can then be fitted into the carrier in the top of the frame, but note the positive terminal which is marked with a plus sign, must be on the near side of the motor cycle when the battery is fitted. Then connect the battery earth lead which is coloured red and already fitted to the frame just forward of the battery carrier, to the battery positive terminal + and securely tighten. Next fit the leads which are coloured brown with blue to the negative battery terminal — and securely tighten. See page 212 for full details on the battery.

Finally fit the tyre inflator between the brackets on the nearside of the top of the frame, and place the tool kit in the tool tray. The motor cycle is then ready for use.

GENERAL DISMANTLING—ARROW

The following instructions cover the procedure for generally dismantling the motor cycle in order to remove the frame.

Commence by disconnecting and removing the battery, to prevent the possibility of an electrical short while dismantling the motor cycle. The leads to the battery are easily detached by removing the screw and nut which secures each lead to the battery terminals. The battery will then simply lift up and clear off the motor cycle. Next completely remove the handlebars and control cables as described on page 129, also remove the speedometer cable as described on page 163. The headlamp must be removed next by pulling apart the four snap connectors in the leads inside the headlamp; also pull the black earth lead from the socket in the headlamp shell. Next detach the leads from the ammeter, then remove both switches from the top of the headlamp by removing the screw in the top of the switch knobs and lifting the knobs off, then remove the nuts from below the switch knobs, take care not to loose the spring ring washer from below each nut. The switches can then be pushed through into the headlamp. Next remove the bolt from each side of the headlamp and remove the headlamp from the motor cycle.

The front shell should be removed next as described on page 170, then remove the front wheel and the front fork as described on pages 76 and 146; also remove the tail section and the rear wheel as described on pages 105 and 173. The silencers should be removed next by slackening the nut which secures the pinch bolt fitted to the clamp at the forward end of each silencer where it joins the exhaust pipe. With the clamps loosened the silencers can be pulled rearwards to withdraw them from the exhaust pipes.

Then disconnect the wiring harness by separating the snap connectors in the three leads from the generator on the offside of the engine. Then detach the high tension leads from both sparking plugs. Also pull out the snap connectors from each side of the rear stop lamp switch, which is mounted on a bracket above the offside silencer. Then remove the stop lamp switch harness from the clips which secure it inside the mudguard. Next, moving to the nearside of the engine, separate the two snap connectors in the leads from the contact breaker, and remove the three leads from the rectifier, by undoing the screw which secures each lead.

Remove the rear chain case as instructed on page 111 and the rear chain as instructed on page 120. Next remove the rear brake pedal as instructed on page 108. The rear mudguard is removed next. It is secured to the frame by two bolts and nuts. The bolts pass through the mudguard and a bracket which is welded to the frame, and they are easily visible and accessible, after removing them the mudguard can be lifted clear. Next remove the rear hydraulic spring units by first removing the acorn nut and chromium plated washer, from the side of the bottom end of each unit. Then remove the nut from the top of each unit, where it projects above the frame. But note that the stud on which the nut is mounted may also turn when undoing the nut, and this must be prevented. A special spanner is supplied in the tool kit, and this can be used to hold the stud while undoing the nut. The rear fork complete with the hydraulic units can then be pulled downwards to free the hydraulic units from the top of the frame; it is then an easy matter to pull them off the rear fork to free them from the motor cycle (see Fig. 160). Take care not to lose any of the top mounting rubbers and washers for the hydraulic units.

Then disconnect the petrol pipe by undoing the union nut between the tap and the petrol pipe, leaving the pipe attached to the carburetter. Then drain the petrol from the tank into a suitable container. Next the cold start control must be disconnected, and this is most easily done by first pulling off the rubber connector tube between the carburetter and the frame, and then slackening the clamp bolt on the offside of the cold start unit, so that the unit can be rotated in an anti-clockwise direction, when at the same time the operating rod can be slipped out and removed from the machine. The air cleaner is removed next, and this simply pulls off. Then directly under the tube from where the air cleaner was removed, can be seen the hexagon head of the top rear engine mounting bolt.

Remove this bolt which has a shakeproof washer under the head by turning it with a tube spanner. As the bolt is removed take care not to lose the special larger washer, which fits on the bolt between the nearside of the frame bracket and the engine casting. Also the cranked locking plate which is fitted under the head of the bolt, must be removed. If it does not come away with the bolt, it must be pulled off the head of the lower bolt, on which it is only located, and will pull off easily, before the lower bolt is removed.

The lower bolt which is the pivot bolt for the rear fork is removed next, but it will first be necessary to remove the rearmost screw from the primary chaincase on the opposite side of the engine. This screw is at the rear of the large dome on the primary chaincase, and in line with the pillion footrest when the rear fork is horizontal.

It is essential to remove this screw, as it is screwed into the end of the pivot bolt. The pivot bolt can then be removed by undoing it with a tube spanner.

The rear fork can then be pulled rearwards to free it from the engine, although it will be necessary to ease the rear fork sideways and downwards while pulling it rearwards. At the offside of the rear fork there are one steel and two nylon thrust plates fitted through which the pivot bolt passes. The steel plate and one of the nylon plates may have come free when the pivot bolt was removed, and the remaining nylon plate which is on the other side of the rear fork lug will be removed at the same time as the rear fork.

The important thing is not to lose these thrust plates. The engine is now only secured to the frame by the stud which passes through the two forward frame brackets and the large engine lug at the rear of the cylinders.

Remove the nut from either end of the stud and then withdraw the stud from the machine. The frame can then be lifted clear of the engine.

The last remaining items can now be removed from the frame. Begin by removing the nuts and bolts which secure the battery carrier to the top of the frame, the battery carrier can then be lifted up and out of the frame. The bulkhead which is fitted in the frame immediately in front of the battery carrier is removed next, by first removing the two bolts which secure the bulkhead to the top of the frame, and the two bolts and nuts which secure it to the bottom of the frame, and finally the one screw from each side, the bulkhead can then be withdrawn.

The battery earth lead will automatically be detached when the nearside top bulkhead securing bolt is removed. Next remove the petrol tap, by fitting an open-ended spanner to the portion of the tap above the knob. Also remove the petrol tank filler cap.

Then remove the petrol tank by first undoing the bolt which is in the bottom of the frame, in front of the forward frame to engine bracket, and just to the offside of the frame centre rib. Then remove the two bolts and special locking nuts, which secure the bracket at the rear of the tank to the bottom of the frame. There are two rubber washers fitted to each bolt, one outside, and one inside the frame. The petrol tank can then be withdrawn through the rear of the frame (see Fig. 161). Then unscrew the plastic sparking plug caps from the end of both high tension leads.

Next disconnect the snap connectors in the white lead from each ignition coil and the snap connector in the one black with white lead from the offside coil. The remaining black with white lead to this coil, and the black with yellow lead from the nearside coil became disconnected when the snap connectors in the contact breaker leads were parted. The ignition coils and the snap connectors are inside the forward end of the frame, at the top and secured with screws and special clip nuts, it is only necessary to remove the four screws to free the coils. It is then an easy matter to withdraw both coils from the frame, taking care to pass the leads which are still attached to the coils through the frame as the coils are withdrawn.

The rectifier can be taken off next and this is secured by a nut inside the frame. Remove the nut and pull the rectifier clear. If required the steering stop bracket can be removed from the bottom of the frame by undoing the two bolts and nuts which secure it. Also the front shell support brackets can be removed as described on page 171. *Note:* Under no circumstances must these brackets be removed unless the fuel tank is out. Finally detach the main wiring harness and remove all the rubber grommets from the frame when the frame will then be completely bare and ready for any repair or re-enamelling work, although before re-enamelling, the steering head cups should be removed, see page 147

RE-ASSEMBLING—ARROW

If the motor cycle is being generally overhauled, or even if lesser work is being carried out, while the machine is in a dismantled state the following parts should be checked and attended to if necessary:

Front and rear wheel bearings, brake linings, brake cams, etc., and tyres.
Front fork bushes and hydraulic units.
Steering head bearings.
Rear fork bushes and hydraulic units.
Rear chain and chain wheel.

Also if the engine unit requires any attention this would be a good opportunity to carry out the necessary work, although the whole of the engine unit is equally accessible when it is fitted to the motor cycle.

When all work on the parts concerned has been completed, before beginning the re-assembly of the motor cycle every component should be thoroughly cleaned. Also all nuts and bolts should be washed in a mixture of paraffin and oil to remove any dirt from the threads, and they should be examined to ensure they are not damaged. If in any doubt they should be replaced with new ones. The six rubber washers for mounting the petrol tank and the fibre washer, or in some cases, two washers for the petrol tap, should also be replaced with new ones, as these items do tend to perish over a period of time. Commence re-assembling by first fitting the front shell support brackets to the top and sides of the frame, see page 171, and then fitting the two rubber grommets for the high tension leads, into the underside of the frame. The holes for these grommets are the two largest towards the front end of the frame. Then fit the two ignition coils, they should be passed inside the frame with the leads already assembled, as follows: The high tension leads should be pushed firmly into the centre terminal of each coil followed by the rubber cover, the clip on the end of the high tension lead acting as a snap connector. The short white leads must be fitted, one to each coil and attached to the negative terminal. Then the coil which is fitted to the offside of the frame must have the two black with white leads attached to its positive terminal, while the coil fitted to the nearside of the frame must have the black with yellow lead attached to its positive terminal.

Also, the clip nuts must be fitted to the coils before they are passed inside the frame. The coils can then be secured to the frame with four screws with plain washers under the heads. *Note:* These screws have a special thread to suit the clip nuts already fitted to the coils. Next pass the high tension leads through the grommets which have already been fitted in the underside of the frame, also pass through the grommet in the offside of the frame, just forward of the rear front shell bracket, the small harness which combines a black and white lead and a black with yellow lead. If the steering stop bracket was removed from the frame, it should now be re-fitted. Place the stop bracket in position on the underside of the frame and pass two $\frac{1}{4}$ inch diameter by $\frac{1}{2}$ inch under head bolts fitted with plain washers through the holes in the stop bracket and through the two forwardmost holes in the underside of the frame. Then fit a plain washer, a shake-proof washer and nut to both bolts where they project insider the frame and securely tighten.

Next place a plain washer and a petrol tank mounting rubber on each of the three special petrol tank securing bolts. Then pass one of the securing bolts through the hole in the frame, which is just to the offside of the centre, and a few inches forward of the front frame to engine bracket. Place a further petrol tank mounting rubber over the portion of the bolt which is now inside the frame. Then pass the petrol tank into the frame and locate the tank front bracket over the front securing bolt (see Fig. 161). The tank front bracket incorporates a tapped boss and the bolt should be screwed in finger tight. Next pass the other two petrol tank securing bolts through the holes in the frame which are in line with the holes in the tank rear bracket, and fit a further tank mounting rubber to each bolt, so that there is now a mounting rubber under the head of each bolt and a second rubber between the inside of the frame and the petrol tank brackets.

Then pass the two bolts at the rear of the tank through the tank rear bracket and fit a special lock nut to each bolt. Then firmly tighten all three petrol tank securing bolts. The bulkhead can then be fitted into the frame. The cutaway in the flange of the bulkhead must be at the bottom and the flange must face rearwards. The bulkhead can then be secured in position. The bolts for securing the bulkhead to the bottom of the frame must be $\frac{1}{4}$ inch diameter by $\frac{1}{2}$ inch under head, and have a plain washer fitted under the head while the top nearside bolt must have a cup for the dualseat rubber, then a spacer washer, a shake-proof washer and the battery red earth lead terminal under the head. The top offside bolt must have a cup, a spacer washer and a cable clip fitted under its head. Then pass the four bolts through the holes in the frame and the holes in the bulkhead and fit a plain washer, a shake-proof washer and a nut to each bolt where it projects inside the frame and securely tighten. The screws which pass through the sides of the frame and the bulkhead, must be a $\frac{1}{4}$ inch diameter by $\frac{1}{2}$ inch under head, and they have a plain washer under their heads. Then after passing the screws through the frame and bulkhead, fit a plain washer, a shake-proof washer and a nut to both screws. Next after making sure the rubber mat for the bottom of the battery carrier, and the two rubber tubes for the short side brackets are in position, pass the battery carrier into the frame. Then secure it in position with two $\frac{1}{4}$ inch diameter bolts by $\frac{1}{2}$ inch under head, the securing bolts must have a plain washer fitted under their heads and the offside bolt must also have a fibre insulating plate under its head, before they are passed through the hole in the battery carrier and the frame, and then a plain washer, a shakeproof washer and a nut must be fitted to the bolts where they protrude inside the frame. Then fit a plain washer under the heads of four $\frac{1}{4}$ inch diameter by $1\frac{1}{4}$ inch under head bolts, and pass the bolts through the holes in the top of the rear end of the frame. Next locate the two die cast alloy double-ended spacers on the bolts where they project through the frame, and then fit the rear suspension bracket to the bolts, and secure it in position by fitting a plain washer, a shake-proof washer and a nut to the two outer bolts only, but do not tighten the nuts.

The frame is then ready to be fitted to the engine unit. Commence with the engine on the centre stand, and with a support under the forward end of the exhaust pipes, or use front stand if available. Then slacken the two socket head set screws which are situated in the two engine lugs at the top and rear of the gear box on the offside of the machine. A special key spanner will be required to slacken these screws and this can be obtained from most tool dealers. The key required is Unbrako W5 $\frac{5}{32}$ inches across flats.

When the screws have been slackened, the distance tubes which are fitted in each lug will become loose but must not be removed from the lugs. Then locate the brackets on the underside of the frame on to the lugs on top of the engine and gear box. The front engine securing stud must be fitted first, it can be passed through the frame brackets and the engine lug from either side, fit a plain washer, shake-proof washer and a nut on the nearside, and the electric horn bracket, a plain washer, a shake-proof washer and a nut on the offside end. Do not fully tighten the nuts on the front engine stud at this stage.

Next, locate the frame correctly on the lugs at the top and rear of the gear box, and pass the top securing bolt partially through the engine lug and the frame bracket. This bolt should only be pushed in loosely in order to hold the frame in position whilst fitting the rear fork. Next check to make certain there is a washer fitted to the lug on the nearside of the gear box where the rear fork pivot bolt screws in.

This washer is fixed in a recess in the lug and is

secured in position by punching over the metal surrounding the washer in a number of places. Then fit the distance washer on to the rear fork pivot bolt. This washer is 1½ inches in diameter and has a spigot in the centre, and when fitted to the pivot bolt the spigot must face away from the head of the bolt.

Next place one of the nylon thrust washers on the pivot bolt, and locate it on the spigot in the centre of the distance washer. The pivot bolt is then ready for securing the rear fork in position, and it should be placed somewhere convenient while the rear fork is located in position at the rear of the gear box. The rear fork must be placed with the pivot lugs in line with the two engine lugs at the rear of the gear box, and the offside fork pivot lug must be outside the offside engine lug. Also, at the same time as the fork is being placed in position, the second nylon thrust washer must be placed between the offside fork pivot lug and the offside engine lug, so that the rear fork and the nylon thrust washer are located into position together. It will be found that the fork will not push straight into position, and it will be necessary to push the fork at a slight angle with a twisting action to locate it correctly (see Fig. 2). Then pass the pivot bolt through the fork and engine lugs from the offside of the machine. Carefully locate the threaded portion of the pivot bolt into the nearside engine lug and securely tighten after making sure the rear fork hydraulic unit securing studs are approximately 12¼ inches from the underside of the suspension bracket in the frame when tightening the pivot bolt. Note the cranked locking plate which couples the pivot bolt to the top engine bolt, must be fitted over the hexagon head of the pivot bolt in a position whereby the hole in the other end of the locking plate is in line with the hole in the engine lug where the top engine bolt is fitted. At this point the top engine bolt which had previously been loosely fitted, should be removed in order to line up the cranked locking plate with the top bolt hole. Also, a shake-proof washer must be fitted under the head of the bolt, when it can then be passed through the hole in the cranked locking plate and the engine lug and frame bracket (see Fig. 3), but before the threaded portion of the bolt is located into the nearside engine lug, the special thrust washer must be fitted between the frame bracket and the nearside engine lug and located on the bolt, as it is passed on to the nearside engine lug.

The top engine bolt can then be securely tightened. The two socket headed set screws in the two offside engine lugs must also be securely tightened. Then fit the long screw into the rear edge of the primary chaincase, and then tighten the two nuts in the front engine stud. The petrol tap can be fitted next, and it would be advisable to fit new fibre washers on the petrol tap to ensure a good joint between the tap and the tank. Fit the cold start operating rod into the grommet in the bracket on the frame, and slip the cranked end of the rod through the small hole in the end of the lever on the cold start device (see Fig. 4). When the operating rod was removed, the cold start device was rotated in an anti-clockwise direction in order to position the lever on the nearside of the machine, to facilitate removal of the operating rod, and the cold start device must be in this same position to re-fit the rod. It can then be rotated clockwise until the lever is uppermost and horizontal, then the clamp bolt on the offside of the cold start device should be securely tightened. Then fit the rubber connector between the cold start device and the rear frame to engine bracket. But first, liberally wet the rubber connector with petrol or petroil mixture. This will greatly facilitate fitting the connector, and in this particular instance the petrol will not harm the rubber as it is special petrol and oil proof material. Then insert the oval shaped end of the connector which has a channel moulded around the outer edge into the hole in the frame bracket, but note that the end of the connector is also shaped to suit the angle of the frame bracket and the connector can only be fitted one way up, also the seam along the top of the connector must be central and the edge of the hole in the frame bracket must be located in the moulded channel. It is then an easy matter to slip the other end of the connector over the end of the cold start unit, but afterwards check to make certain that the connector is correctly located at both ends. The air cleaner is fitted next, to the tube incorporated in the offside of the rear frame to engine bracket.

Begin by clamping the ends of the air cleaner spring clip together with a pair of pliers in order to increase the internal diameter of the clip. Then pass the clip only over the tube on the frame bracket, and keep it clamped between the pliers while the air cleaner is fitted over the frame bracket tube and inside the clip, then release the clip from the pliers when it will secure the air cleaner in position.

Next fit the petrol pipe from the carburetter to the petrol tap by locating the pipe on the tap and tightening the union nut firmly but not excessively. The front fork and mudguard assembly are fitted next. The steering head cups in the top and bottom of the frame must be packed with fresh grease of the same grade as recommended for the hubs. Then place new steel balls in the grease-packed steering head cups, there must be twenty-three steel balls in the bottom cup and twenty in the top cup.

Next lift the fork assembly and pass the steering column up through the steering head tube in the frame and locate the steering head bottom cone, which is situated at the bottom of the steering column, into the steering head cup in the bottom of the frame, but take the utmost care not to let any of the steel balls fall out of either of the steering head cups. Then, holding the fork in position, pass the top steering head cone down the steering column and locate it into the top steering head cup, and again make certain that none of the steel balls have fallen out of the steering head cups. Then still holding the forks in position, pass the thin washer, followed by the dust cover, down the steering column, next fit one of the thin nuts to the steering column. It should be possible to screw this nut down finger tight with one hand while holding the forks up with the other. The thin nut should then be tightened with one of the special flat spanners which is supplied in the tool kit of each new motor cycle, until all the free play in the steering head bearings has been taken up. See page 145 for full instructions on steering head bearing adjustment. Then fit the second thin nut to the steering column, and while holding the lower thin nut with one of the special flat spanners to prevent it turning, tighten the second thin nut securely to lock both nuts together (see Fig. 159). Afterwards check the adjustment of the steering head bearings again, to make quite certain it is in order.

The rear mudguard should be fitted next, the bracket which is welded to the mudguard has two holes, and the two centre bolts which pass through the frame and the suspension bracket are not yet fitted with nuts, and the mudguard bracket must be located on to these bolts.

The mudguard must also be secured to the bracket which is welded to the underside of the rear edge of the frame. The bracket is provided with two holes and there are corresponding holes in the mudguard.

Fit a plain washer under the head of two $\frac{1}{4}$ inch diameter by $\frac{1}{2}$ inch under head bolts, and pass the bolts through the holes in the bracket which is welded to the frame and through the holes in the mudguard. Then fit a plain washer, a shake-proof washer and a nut to both bolts, and securely tighten. Next fit the silencers to the exhaust pipes, and securely tighten the silencer clamps. Note that the flats on the silencers must face outward to provide clearance for the centre stand when retracted. The four bolts which pass through the frame and the rear suspension bracket must then be carefully removed, and the tail section fitted as described on page 173. Next fit the hydraulic units to the frame and rear fork. Take care to assemble the steel washers and mounting rubbers in the right order on the top of the hydraulic units (see Fig. 153). Also the mounting rubbers must be in good condition and if in any doubt fit new ones. First fit one of the larger washers with the cupped side uppermost to both hydraulic units, then fit the spacer tube and one mounting rubber directly above the cupped steel washer.

Next locate the stud and the spacer tube at the top of the hydraulic units, through the holes in the rear suspension bracket and the top of the frame, at the same time locate the bottom end of the hydraulic units on to the studs which project from each side of the rear fork.

Then fit the two smaller steel washers to the hydraulic unit studs which protrude above the frame, again with the cupped side of the washer uppermost and the spigot in the centre of the washer located through the hole in the frame. Next fit the second mounting rubber to both hydraulic unit top studs, followed by the second of the larger washers, and this time the cupped side of the washers must face downwards. Finally fit the special locking nut to the top of both hydraulic unit studs and tighten firmly until resistance is felt, but not excessively.

Next fit a plain washer, a chromium plated cup washer and an acorn nut to the bottom securing studs for both hydraulic units.

Securely tighten the offside acorn nut, but leave the nearside one loose until the rear chaincase has been fitted. The rear chain sprocket should be in good condition and fitted to the rear fork. If in doubt, or for instructions for removing and fitting the rear chain sprocket to the rear fork, see page 111. The rear chain can then be fitted, but it must be in good condition and be thoroughly cleaned, before being treated with fresh lubricant, see page 120 for full details on rear chain.

To fit the rear chain to the gear box sprocket, first move the gear change lever on the gear box up or down to engage a gear, then pass the end of the rear chain into the top of the housing for the gear box sprocket, and at the same time operate the kick starter slowly but continuously.

The kick starter can be operated with one hand while feeding the chain on to the sprocket with the other, but it will be necessary to use a tommy bar, or something similar to guide the chain on to the sprocket, also the kick starter will be easier to operate if both sparking plugs are removed. Operating the kick starter whilst in gear will cause the gear box sprocket to rotate, and if the rear chain is fed on to the top of the sprocket it will be carried round, and can then be pulled out of the bottom of the housing which surrounds the gear box sprocket. When the centre of the chain is around the gear box sprocket, locate the two ends around the rear chain sprocket with the two end links only separated by one tooth of the sprocket, then from the offside pass the chain connecting link through the two end links and assemble the loose side plate to the nearside of the connecting link. Finally, fit the spring clip with the closed end facing towards the direction of chain travel. The spring clip is fitted, by first locating it as near as is possible in position on the connecting link rivets, then by using a pair of pliers with one jaw behind the closed end of the spring clip, and the other jaw behind the rivet inside the clip, pressure on the pliers will cause the clip to snap into position. Afterwards, check very carefully to make quite certain the spring clip is correctly fitted. The rear chaincase is next to be fitted, and this is simply located in position on the rear fork, the half with the rubber grommets in, fitted at the top, there is no gasket or joint involved but the top half must overlap the lower half.

Then fit a plain washer under the heads of the four screws which are used to secure the chaincase to the rear fork, and note that the two shorter screws fit at the front end of the chaincase. After passing the four screws through the chaincase and the brackets on the rear fork, fit a plain washer and a nut to each screw where it protrudes from the back of the chaincase and securely tighten. Then tighten the acorn nut at the bottom end of the nearside rear hydraulic unit. The rear wheel can then be fitted as described on page 105. Also fit the rear brake pedal as described on page 108. The main wiring harness with the lighting and ignition switches can now be assembled to the motor cycle.

Place the harness on the frame with the switches at the forward end.

The branch in the harness which includes the plain white, and the white with black leads, must be passed through the hole in the side of the frame, which is situated just forward of the front shell rear support bracket on the offside of the frame. Note that as there is no grommet fitted in this hole, to prevent the harness becoming chaffed and damaged, the joint where the branch harness leaves the main harness should be protected by binding it with insulation tape. Next connect the leads inside the frame. There are two white leads and a white with black lead already attached to the coils, and these must be coupled by the snap connectors to the leads with corresponding colours in the branch harness.

Two remaining leads which are attached to the coils are coloured black with white and black with yellow, and are combined in a small sub harness which must then be passed through the hole in the side of the frame, through which the coil branch harness passes, so that it then protrudes outside the frame. Next fit the speedometer driving cable to the gear box, as described on page 164. Then slip the plastic tube, which protects the cables and leads between the frame and the engine, over the speedometer cable.

The sub harness from the alternator must then be passed up inside the plastic tube, and when it emerges at the top, couple the three leads to the three leads with corresponding colours in the main harness. Next pass the small sub harness from the coils, which contains the black with white and the black with yellow leads, down through the plastic tube and through the gap between the engine and the gear box. Then secure it in the cable clip under the nearside footrest, and couple the leads in the sub harness to the leads with corresponding colours from the contact breaker. Next connect the leads from the main harness, which are coloured brown with blue and brown with black, to the electric horn leads as described on page 216. The rectifier is fitted next, begin by placing the rectifier red earth lead which is incorporated in the branch harness from the main wiring harness, over the rectifier centre fixing stud, together with a shake-proof washer. Then pass the rectifier into position with the centre stud through the hole in the side of the frame. This is the forward most upper hole in the nearside. Then with the rectifier terminals facing upward, fit a shake-proof washer and a $\frac{5}{16}$ inch B.S.F. nut to the rectifier centre stud which is inside the frame, and securely tighten. Then connect the remaining leads in the branch harness to the rectifier terminals. The lead coloured green with white must be connected to the forward terminal, the lead coloured brown with purple must be connected to the middle terminal, and the double lead coloured green with black must be connected to the rear terminal. These leads are secured by passing a screw through the terminal on the end of each lead, then fit the screws and leads to their respective rectifier terminal and fit a plain washer and a nut to each screw and securely tighten. The leads from the rear stop switch and the tail lamp can be connected next to the leads with corresponding colours at the end of the main harness. The stop switch lead which is coloured brown must be connected to the lead coloured brown from the stop lamp. The two stop switch leads must be fitted to the sockets each side of the switch. It is not important to fit the different coloured leads in any particular order to the switch.

The front shell can be fitted next as described on page 171, followed by the dualseat as described on page 169, and the handlebars and control cables, etc., as described on page 129.

Then fit the headlamp to the front shell as described on page 146, but before fitting the headlamp rim, fit the speedometer, driving cable to the boss on the underside of the speedometer, then fit the lighting and ignition switches to the headlamp shell, the lighting switch should be fitted to the nearside. Note that the holes for fitting the switches are "D" shaped, and the switches will only fit one way. After locating them in position fit a spring wire washer and a square nut to the portion of each switch, where it projects out of the headlamp, then fit the respective knob to each switch, and secure them in position with a chromium plated washer and screw. Next connect the ammeter leads to the terminals on the underside of the ammeter, and note the lead coloured brown with blue must be connected to the offside of the ammeter, and the brown with white leads to the nearside. Then the lead coloured red with black from the main harness must be connected to the lead with corresponding colours from the pilot bulb. The blue lead from the main harness and the two leads from the main headlamp bulb must be connected to the leads with corresponding colours from the dip switch. The black earth lead from the main headlamp bulb holder, must be fitted to the socket inside the headlamp shell. The headlamp rim can then be fitted as described on page 214. Next check the following, and if necessary adjust accordingly. The rear chain as described on page 118.

The wheel alignment as described on page 122. The tyre pressures as described on pages 98 and 124. The rear brake as described on page 107.

The front brake as described on page 86.

The clutch cable as described on page 131.

The throttle cable as described on page 130. If necessary top up the primary chaincase with oil, as described on page 25, and the gear box as described on page 61. Replenish the petrol tank with a quantity of the correct mixture of petrol and oil see page 10. *Note*, when fitting the petrol filler cap, the two sealing rings which are fitted to the sleeve portion of the cap. These sealing rings must be in good condition.

If in any doubt replace them with new ones. Next check the motor cycle over generally and make certain that all nuts and bolts are securely tightened.

The engine cover can now be fitted as described on page 155. The battery can be fitted next, but first check the state of the charge with a hydrometer, and if the charge is low the battery should be re-charged before fitting it to the motor cycle.

Note: If a hydrometer and battery charger are not available a local agent or garage will carry out this work for a nominal charge. Then check the level of the acid in the battery and if necessary top up with distilled water. Clean the battery terminals, and then coat them with clean vaseline. The battery can then be fitted into the carrier in the top of the frame, but note the positive terminal which is marked with a plus sign must be on the nearside of the motor cycle when the battery is fitted. Then connect the battery earth lead which is coloured red and already fitted to the frame just forward of the battery carrier, to the battery positive terminal + and securely tighten. Next fit the leads which are coloured brown with blue to the negative battery terminal —, and securely tighten. See page 212 for full details on the battery. The motor cycle is then ready for use.

PANNIERS—LEADER

Panniers for carrying luggage which fit each side of the tail section are available as optional extras. The panniers are complete with detachable lids, and locks are fitted as an anti-thief precaution. There are also available specially shaped holdalls, so that luggage can be pre-packed and then very conveniently slipped in and out of the panniers. Once panniers are fitted to a motor cycle, they become a permanent fixture, and rear wheel removal and accessibility are unaffected.

Dealing first with fitting panniers to a motor cycle to which they have not previously been fitted. Begin by removing the existing bolt which is fitted each side of the tail cover, through the lower ends of a bracket and into tapped bosses which are welded to the inside of each side of the tail section. At point "A" in Fig. 162. The tail section is provided with two further holes each side. These holes are fitted with rubber plugs which must be removed from points "E" and "C" as shown in Fig. 162. *Note:* If these further two holes are not already in each side of the tail section, they must be drilled through. Begin by fitting a large plain washer under the head of a $\frac{1}{4}$ inch diameter by 1 inch under head bolt, then pass the bolt through the uppermost hole in the back of the pannier, with the head of the bolt inside the pannier. Next fit the spacer 4-2280 to the bolt where it projects through the back of the pannier and locate the pannier in position on the tail section, screwing the bolt into the tapped boss which is welded inside the tail section. Make sure that the tail section bracket is fitted properly to the bolt where it protrudes inside the tail cover and then fit a shakeproof washer and a nut, and securely tighten. Then, very carefully, align the pannier with the forward top edge of the tail section, so that the pannier lid is $\frac{1}{8}$ inch lower than the top edge of the tail section. Again using extra care mark the tail section through the holes in the back of the pannier at points "E" and "C". Then remove the pannier from the tail section and drill through the positions marked on the tail cover with a $\frac{9}{32}$ inch diameter drill. **Important Note:** If flashing indicators are being fitted, a further hole must be drilled through the tail cover. Irrespective of whether the tail section has had to be drilled for fixing the pannier or not. There is already a suitable hole provided in the rear end of the back of the pannier, and it is a simple matter to mark the tail section through the hole in the pannier, and after removing the pannier from the tail section a $\frac{9}{32}$ inch diameter hole must be drilled through where the tail section has been marked as shown in Fig. 166.

Next fit the smaller rubber bead to the rear edge of the pannier as shown in Fig. "F", and then fit the pannier to the tail section as shown in Figs. "A", "C" and "E". The tail section complete with the panniers must then be removed from the motor cycle by first disconnecting the stop and tail lamp leads under the dualseat, and slackening the silencer acorn nuts, then removing the wing nuts from the underside of the tail cover and finally removing the pivot bolts from the forward end of the tail cover. With the tail section removed from the motor cycle, the brackets for securing the bottom of the panniers to the frame must be fitted to the frame as shown

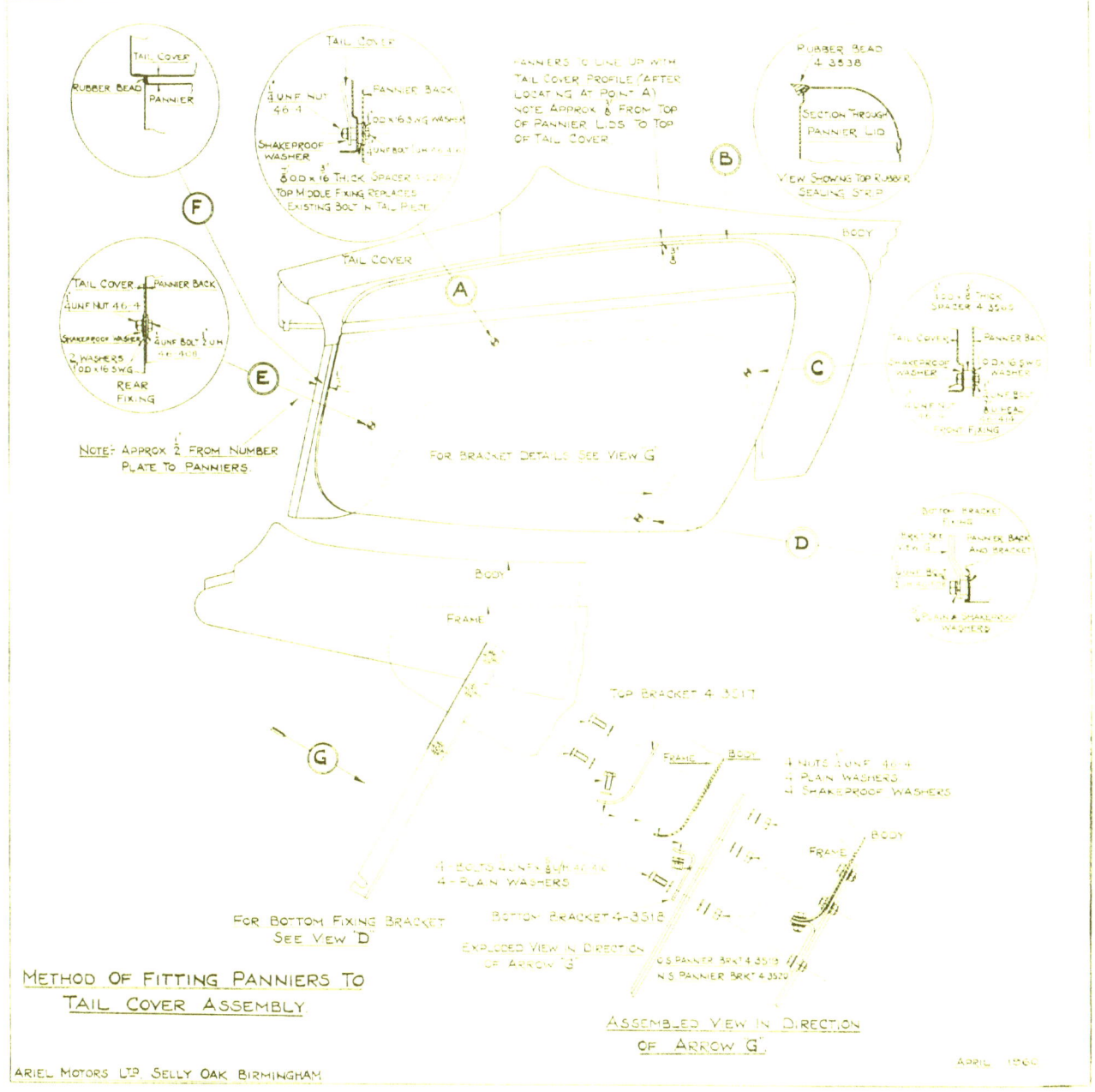

FIG. 162

in Fig. "G". Before the bolts, which secure the brackets are fully tightened, the tail section, complete with the panniers must be re-fitted to the motor cycle, so that the brackets can be aligned with the threaded boss on the forward bottom edge of the back of each pannier, by loosely assembling the bolts and washers through the slot at the bottom of the brackets as shown in Fig. "D". Then, without disturbing the brackets, remove the tail section and panniers from the motor cycle again and fully tighten the bolts and nuts which secure the pannier brackets to the frame as shown in fig. "G". Next re-fit the tail section and panniers to the motor cycle, and secure the brackets to the back of the panniers as shown in Fig. "D".

Next fit the large rubber bead to the back edge of the pannier lids as shown in Fig. "B". The lids can then be fitted to the panniers. At the rear end the lids have a tongue which locates in a slot in the top rear edge of the pannier, a lock complete with keys is provided at the front end of the panniers. If flashing indicators are being fitted proceed as described on page 220. Otherwise the holes provided for flashing indicators must be plugged with grommets to prevent the ingress of water.

For instructions on rear wheel removal when panniers are fitted see page 98. If it should be required at any time to remove the panniers from the tail section, it is only necessary to remove the bolts shown in Figs. "A", "C", "D" and "E". If flashing indicators are fitted, disconnect the leads from the rear indicators by separating the snap connectors in the leads. The panniers can then be lifted clear.

If the keys for the pannier locks should be lost or damaged, replacement keys are obtainable. Also if it should be required, new locks can be fitted to the panniers. The main portion of the lock is secured by tags on the back of the lock, which pass through holes and are turned over inside the pannier. By straightening the tags the lock can be removed from the pannier. The portion of the lock which is fitted to the pannier lid is secured by two "Pop" rivets, and to remove it, the rivets must be drilled out. The rivets for fitting the new lock are of a special design and must be fitted with a special "Pop" rivet gun. Most car body repair agents have a suitable rivet gun, and would carry out the riveting for a nominal charge.

REAR LUGGAGE CARRIER—LEADER

A luggage carrier complete with adjustable rubber straps to fit on the top of the tail section at the rear of the dualseat is available as an optional extra. The tail section is already provided with four holes for fixing the luggage carrier, and the holes are temporarily filled with rubber plugs which can easily be pulled out. *Note:* A few machines may not have these holes in the tail section and if it is desired to fit a luggage carrier, the holes must be drilled first. This is easily accomplished by locating the luggage carrier squarely on top of the tail section, with the rear edge of the luggage carrier $\frac{7}{16}$ inch forward of the rear edge of the tail section. Then mark the tail section through the four holes in the luggage carrier, remove the carrier and drill through the tail section where it has been marked, using a $\frac{5}{16}$ inch diameter drill. *Note:* Remove the tail lamp lens while drilling rear two holes.

The tail section will have to be pivoted upwards as described on page 98, in order to gain access to the underside, to facilitate fitting the carrier. Then pass the four screws supplied with the carrier through the holes in the carrier and locate it on the tail section with the screws protruding through to the inside of the tail section, and fit a plain washer, a shake-proof washer and a nut to each screw and securely tighten. The tail section can then be returned to its normal position as described on page 105.

The rubber straps are supplied with hooks which can be moved along the straps to adjust their length. At the front and rear edges of the carrier there are two recesses for the luggage strap hooks to fit into.

REAR LUGGAGE CARRIER—ARROW

A luggage carrier complete with adjustable rubber straps, to fit on top of the tail section at the rear of the dualseat is available as an optional extra.

The tail section is already provided with four holes for fixing the luggage carrier. The two forward holes in the top of the tail section are already fitted with suitable screws, nuts and washers, which must be removed in order to fit the carrier. Also remove the rubber plug grommet from each side of the tail section, to uncover the holes for the carrier rear fixing.

The rear support stays should already be assembled to the carrier, the stays must be fitted to the lug each side of the carrier, and secured by a screw with a plain washer under its head with a plain washer, a shake-proof washer and a nut fitted to secure the screw. The stays must also be fitted so that they are set inward at their lower ends. Then locate the carrier in position on the tail section, and fit a plain washer under the heads of the four fixing screws. Pass the screws through the two front lugs on the carrier, and the lower ends of the support stays, then where the screws protrude inside the tail section, fit a plain washer, a shake-proof washer and a nut, and securely tighten.

The rubber straps are supplied with hooks which can be moved along the straps to adjust their length.

REAR VIEW MIRRORS—LEADER

These are not part of the standard equipment but are available as optional extras. A mirror can be fitted either to the nearside or the offside of the motor cycle, or if required to both sides. The mirror only is interchangeable and can be fitted to either side of the motor cycle, but the brackets which are supplied with the mirrors are specially shaped and handed, one for the offside and one for the nearside. To avoid confusion, the brackets are marked "L" for the left-hand side and "R" for the right-hand side. The brackets have a set in them, making a long and a short arm. The mirror must be fitted to the long arm of the bracket, by locating the stud in the back of the mirror through the slot in the bracket, and securing it in position by fitting the plain washer, shake-proof washer and acorn nut which are supplied with the mirror. Then to fit the mirror to the motor cycle, first remove the end screw which secures the windscreen to the front shield, from the side to which the mirror is to be fitted. Next locate the mirror with its bracket on the front of the front shield, and fit the front shield screw with a plain washer under the head, or if it is the nearside, the licence holder, through the hole in the short arm of the mirror bracket, and the hole and the spacer tube in the front shield. Then fit a plain washer, a shake-proof washer and an acorn nut to the screw where it protrudes through the back of the front shield.

To adjust the angle of the mirror, slacken the acorn nut at the back of the mirror, set the mirror to the required angle and firmly but not excessively tighten the acorn nut.

REAR FENDER—LEADER

The rear fender is not part of the standard equipment, but is available as an optional extra. *It is designed for use in conjunction with panniers.* The fender is chromium plated and incorporates twin reflectors and a Leader badge, and when fitted it adds to the eye appeal of the rear of the motor cycle and to the rider's safety at night.

To fit a rear fender to a motor cycle proceed as follows: First, if the fender is new, begin by removing the two screws which secure the brackets inside. Next remove the two screws from the bottom edge of the motor cycle rear number plate, then with a plain washer fitted under the head of each screw, pass the screws through the plain holes in the fender brackets, and re-fit the screws to the rear number plate so that the fender brackets hang downward. Behind the rear number plate, the screws must pass through the brackets on the silencer support stay, then a shake-proof washer and a nut must be fitted and securely tightened. Next locate the fender on to the two brackets, and fit the two screws with plain washers under their heads, through the holes in the fender and into the captive nuts on the brackets.

Any time it is required to remove the fender from the motor cycle it is only necessary to remove the two screws from the fender to free it. The reflectors at each end of the fender are easily removed, by first removing the fender from the motor cycle, then inside can be seen a hair-pin spring clip. By pulling the top ends of the clip outwards, the clip together with the reflector and backing washer can be removed. When re-assembling, fit the reflector first, followed by the backing washer, then insert the closed end of the spring clip through the slot in the bottom of the fender and locate the open ends behind the bracket at the top of the fender. *Note:* It is important to fit the reflector backing washers, otherwise mud, etc., will get behind the reflector rendering it inoperative.

For full instructions on removing and fitting the Leader badge see page 167.

WINDSCREEN—ARROW

A windscreen is available as an optional extra, it is supplied complete, and fitting it to the machine is simple. The main bracket is secured to the handlebars by the two clamps, while the lower bracket locates through the adjustable lugs on the main bracket, but note that the two large washers must be fitted to the adjustable lugs, so that the washer is between the rods of the two brackets, then tightening the bolts in the adjustable lugs will secure the screen in the required position.

ELECTRICAL EQUIPMENT
—LEADER AND ARROW

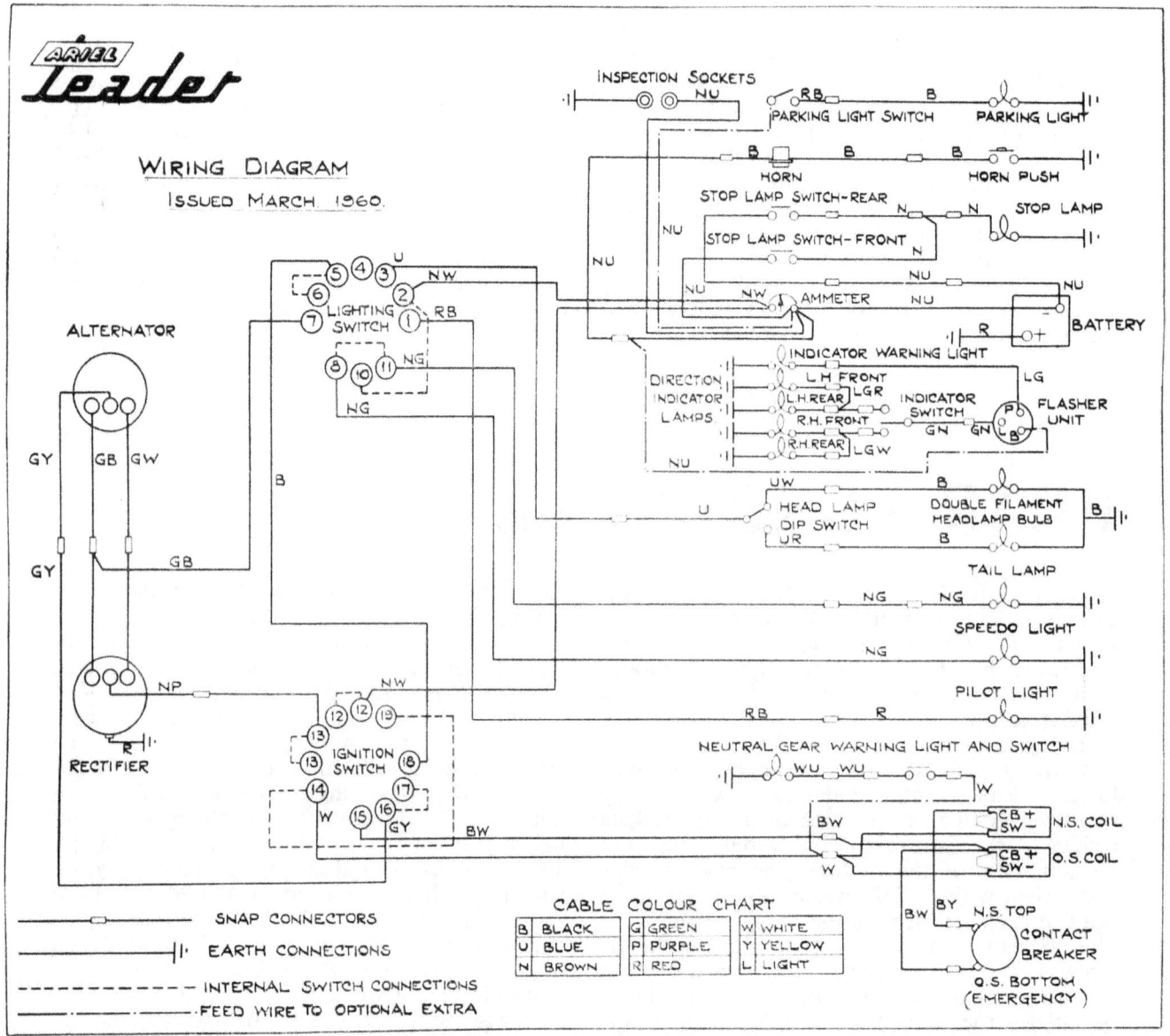

1958-1961 inclusive (see page 240)

Fig. 163

BATTERY—LEADER AND ARROW

The 6-volt 13-amp. hour battery is a Lucas type MLZ. 9E. The battery is fitted into a rubber-lined carrier under the dualseat, and a sponge rubber pad on the dualseat base holds the battery lid in position and protects it from road vibrations. Gas which is generated as the battery is being charged, is released through vent holes in the filler plugs and escapes into the atmosphere via an elbow-shaped breather.

The terminals at each end of the battery are clearly marked, the positive terminal by a plus sign +, and the negative terminal by a minus sign —. *It is of the utmost importance that the battery earth lead is attached to the positive terminal*, if the battery is wrongly connected it could result in damage to the rectifier and generator.

The battery outer case is moulded in a semi-transparent plastic material through which the acid level can be seen. On the outside of the case is a coloured line marked "maximum acid level", and the level of the acid inside the battery must be maintained to this mark. A weekly inspection should be made by lifting the battery from its carrier sufficiently to see the acid level, if it is below the line it must be topped up with *distilled water*, which is obtainable from most garages and chemists; under no circumstances must the battery be topped up above the line. In order to top up the battery, remove the three filler plugs from the top. The battery is divided into three sections, and each section must be topped up individually as required. Before re-fitting the filler plugs, make certain that the breather holes through the plugs are clear and that the rubber sealing rings are in good order. Make sure both terminal connections are clean and tight and lightly coated with Vaseline to prevent corrosion.

If it is required to remove the battery from the motor cycle, first remove the bolt and nut which secures the lead to the positive + terminal, then the bolt and nut which secures the lead to the negative — terminal. The battery can then be lifted clear.

When re-fitting the battery be quite certain to fit the earth lead to the positive terminal. When fitting the lead to the battery terminal, fit the shake-proof washer to the bolt, followed by the lead. Then pass the bolt, washer and lead through the battery terminal, fit the nut and tighten it fully. The main harness lead should be fitted to the negative terminal in a similar manner. Make sure both connections are tight and that the connections are not touching any part of the motor cycle.

If the battery is given regular attention it will give long, trouble-free life. If the battery should become fully discharged the engine can be started on the emergency system and then switched to normal. If the engine will not run after switching to the normal position, the battery should be tested. Each cell can be checked with a hydrometer and a private owner who possesses a trickle charger can re-charge the battery and re-check it with a hydrometer. *Note:* In order to use a hydrometer the battery must be removed from the motor cycle and tilted to allow the electrolyte to rise above the separator guards. Alternatively, the battery should be returned to an Ariel or Lucas agent for test and attention. If one of the battery cells will not hold a charge, a new battery must be fitted.

TECHNICAL DATA

Nominal voltage: 6.

Amp-hour capacity: 12 at 10 hr. rate.
13 at 20 hr. rate.

Re-charge current: 1.5 amperes.

Specific gravity of electrolyte:
Battery fully charged: 1.285.
Battery half charged: 1.230.
Battery fully discharged: 1.142.

Note: If it should be necessary to replace the battery with a new one, there are two models available, the MLZ. 9E. and the ML. 9E., and either one is equally suitable. The difference between these two batteries lies in the method of initial charging. The MLZ. 9E. is a dry charged battery and only requires filling with the correct electrolyte to the mark on the side of the battery and leaving to stand for at least one hour when it is then ready for use. The ML. 9E. battery requires filling with suitable electrolyte and charging in the normal way at 1.0 ampere.

HEADLAMP UNIT—LEADER

The headlamp has a 6 inch diameter lens, and is fitted with a pre-focus double filament bulb and a separate pilot light bulb.

To fit a headlamp or pilot bulb, first remove the headlamp unit and the bulb holders as described on page 136. The headlamp bulb will remain in the headlamp unit, but it is only necessary to turn the unit on to its back when the headlamp bulb will drop out. The pilot light bulb merely requires pushing into its holder slightly and turning to free it. The new bulbs can then be fitted. The pilot bulb has two pegs at the base which must be in line with the grooves in the holder as the bulb is pushed in, the bulb is turned to lock it in position. The headlamp bulb only requires

placing into the back of the headlamp unit, but note the small cutaway in the collar on the bulb, as this must be in line with the ridge in the back of the light unit. The headlamp unit can then be re-fitted as described on page 141.

A new headlamp bulb must be a 6-volt, 30/24-watt double filament, pre-focus type. A new pilot light bulb must be a 6-volt, 3-watt single contact bayonet fitting.

In the event of the headlamp glass requiring renewing, a light unit consisting of the glass and reflector must be fitted. If a new chromium plated rim is required, it is fitted in the same way as a new light unit. First remove the headlamp unit from the motor cycle, then prise the ends of the five wire clips out of the inner edge of the headlamp rim. This will free the light unit from the headlamp rim. When fitting a rim and light unit together, note the projection on the outer edge of the back of the reflector. This projection must be located between the arms of the small bracket inside the headlamp rim. The five wire clips can then be fitted; insert one end of a clip under the edge of the rim, so that only the centre portion of the clip touches the light unit, then spring the other end of the clip under the edge of the headlamp rim. The five clips are all fitted in the same way and should be spaced equally round the rim.

HEADLAMP UNIT—ARROW

The headlamp has a 6 inch diameter lens and is fitted with a pre-focus double filament bulb and a separate pilot light bulb.

To fit a headlamp or pilot bulb first remove the headlamp unit by slackening the small screw at the top of the headlamp, the rim can then be pulled off from the top together with the light unit; it will then only be attached by the leads to the two bulbs.

The main bulb holder in the centre requires pushing inwards and turning to free it, while the pilot bulb holder simply pulls out of the reflector.

The headlamp bulb will remain in the headlamp unit, but it is only necessary to turn the unit on to its back when the headlamp bulb will drop out. The pilot light bulb merely requires pushing into its holder slightly and turning to free it. The new bulb can then be fitted. The pilot bulb has two pegs at the base which must be in line with the grooves in the holder as the bulb is pushed in, the bulb is turned to lock it in position. The headlamp bulb only requires placing into the back of the headlamp unit, but note the small cutaway in the collar on the bulb, as this must be in line with the ridge in the back of the light unit. The headlamp unit can then be re-fitted.

Commence by locating the tag inside the bottom of the headlamp rim into the slot in the headlamp shell. Then push the rim into place and tighten the screw at the top of the headlamp. A new headlamp bulb must be a 6-volt, 30/24-watt, double filament, pre-focus type. A new pilot light bulb must be a 6-volt, 3-watt single contact bayonet fitting.

In the event of the headlamp glass requiring renewing, a light unit consisting of the glass and reflector must be fitted. If a new chromium plated rim is required, it is fitted in the same way as a new light unit. First remove the headlamp unit from the motor cycle, then prise the ends of the five wire clips out of the inner edge of the headlamp rim. This will free the light unit from the headlamp rim. When fitting a rim and light unit together, note the projection on the outer edge of the back of the reflector. This projection must be located between the arms of the small bracket inside the headlamp rim. The five wire clips can then be fitted, insert one end of a clip under the edge of the rim, so that only the centre portion of the clip touches the light unit, then spring the other end of the clip under the edge of the headlamp rim. The five clips are all fitted in the same way and should be spaced equally round the rim.

ELECTRIC HORN—LEADER

There are two types of horn in use, Lucas model HF.1849 and Lucas model 8H. Either type may be fitted as they are fully interchangeable. To identify the two types, the model 8H has the model number clearly stamped on the rim, whereas the model HF.1849 has the model number stamped on the back. The horn is secured to a bracket on the front of the frame and is operated by the push button on the handlebar. Access to the horn is gained by removing the headlamp unit as described on page 136. If it is required to remove either type of horn from the motor cycle, begin by removing the two screws which secure the horn to the bracket on the frame, but note that the horn securing screws fit into a single lose tapped plate, the plate will remain inside the bracket on the frame, but if the motor cycle has to be moved before the horn is refitted, the tapped plate should be removed to prevent loss. The two horn leads must be disconnected next, and with the model 8H the leads have flat connectors directly on the horn, the connectors simply pull off and the horn is free. With the model HF.1849 one lead must be separated from the snap connector in the main wiring harness, while the other lead has a snap connector under the handlebar just to the offside of the steering column, after separating this lead tie a length of string to the end which will be pulled through the grommet in the top of the body when the horn is removed, this string should protrude through the grommet after the horn has been removed, so that when refitting, the string can be used to draw the lead back up through the grommet in the top of the body.

When refitting the horn, begin by connecting the leads. With the model 8H this is a simple

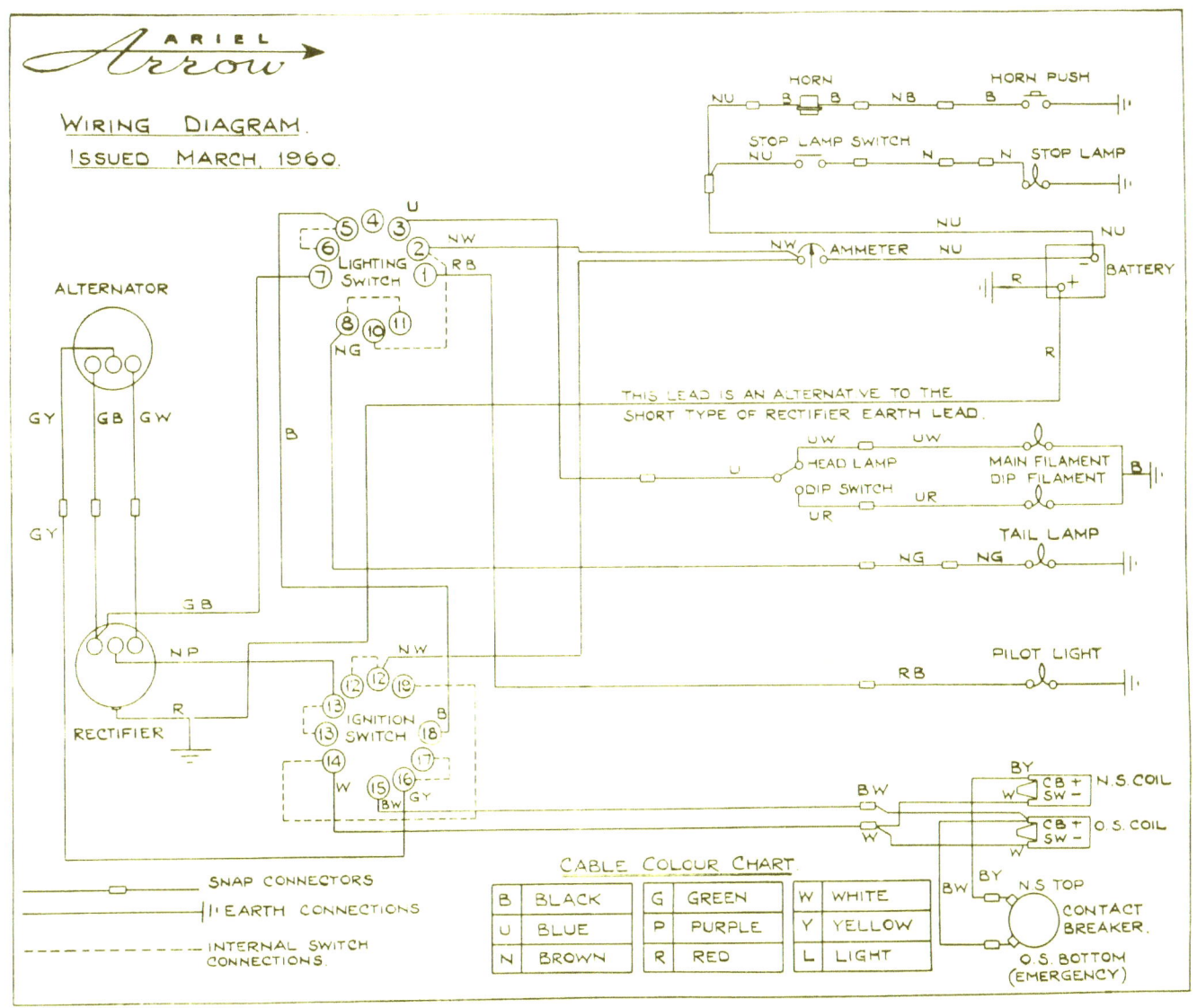

1958-1961 inclusive (see page 240)

FIG. 164

matter as the flat connectors only require pushing onto the terminals on the horn, and either lead may be fitted to either terminal. With the model HF.1849, connect the lead from the horn to the snap connector in the main wiring harness. Then draw the other lead through the grommet in the top of the body by gently pulling the string which is tied to the lead. The lead can then be connected by fitting it to the snap connector from under the offside of the handlebar, and the string can be removed. Next secure the horn to the bracket on the frame, insert one finger into the offside end of the bracket on the frame and lift the tapped plate into position. Then while holding the tapped plate, locate the horn in position and fit a screw with a shakeproof washer under the head, through the hole in the horn and frame bracket and into the tapped plate. The second screw is fitted similarly, then make sure they are both securely tightened. Finally refit the headlamp unit.

The horn should not require any attention, its tone is adjusted during manufacture. If the tone should deteriorate, examine the horn leads and renew any which are badly worn or chafed, ensure that all connections are clean and tight, and that the snap connector nipples are firmly soldered to the cables. Check that the screws securing the horn to the frame are tight. If after this the horn is still unsatisfactory, remove the horn from the motor cycle as described on page 214, and return it to an Ariel or Lucas agent for repair. Do not dismantle or interfere with the horn.

ELECTRIC HORN—ARROW

There are two types of horn in use, Lucas model 8H and Lucas model HF.1849. Either type may be fitted as they are fully interchangeable. To identify the two types, the model 8H has the model number clearly stamped on the rim, whereas the model HF.1849 has the model number stamped on the back. The horn is secured to a bracket which in turn is secured to the front engine mounting stud. If it is required to remove the horn from the motor cycle, begin by removing the engine cover as described on page 155. Then remove the two screws which secure the horn to the frame bracket. *Note:* the screws are located into a tapped plate which will become free when the screws are removed. The horn leads must be disconnected next, with the model 8H the leads have flat connectors directly on the horn, and these simply pull off, and the horn is free. With the model HF.1849 the leads must be separated from the snap connectors which are enclosed within the plastic sleeve which covers the leads from the engine to the frame. If the two horn leads are pulled downward where they enter the sleeve, they can be parted from the snap connectors, and the horn will be free.

When refitting the horn, begin by connecting the leads. With the model 8H it is a simple matter as the flat connectors only require pushing onto the terminals on the horn, and either lead may be fitted to either terminal. With the model HF.1849, slide the plastic sleeve down so that the two horn leads from the harness can be pulled out of the top. *Note:* the two snap connectors must be attached to these leads and not to the two from the horn. Then pass a length of strong wire down inside the sleeve, and when it emerges at the bottom fix it to one of the horn leads, then pull the wire together with the horn lead up and out of the top of the sleeve. Fit the lead to one of the snap connectors, then repeat the process for the other lead. The horn can be located onto its bracket, and secured in position with the two screws which must have, shakeproof washers under their heads, the screws pass through the horn and frame bracket and locate into the tapped plate. Finally refit the engine cover as described on page 155.

The horn should not require any attention, its tone is adjusted during manufacture. If the tone should deteriorate, examine the horn leads and renew any which are badly worn or chafed, ensure that all connections are clean and tight, and that the snap connector nipples are firmly soldered to the cables. Check that the screws securing the horn to the frame bracket are tight. If after this the horn is still unsatisfactory, remove the horn from the motor cycle as described above, and return it to an Ariel or Lucas agent for repair. Do not dismantle or interfere with the horn.

IGNITION COILS—LEADER AND ARROW

There are two ignition coils, one for each cylinder. They are secured inside the frame and are accessible through the hole in the bottom of the glove compartment. Periodically inspect that the high tension leads are in good condition and fitted securely into the coils. Also that the rubber covers are in place where the high tension leads enter the coils.

Ignition coil failure is very rare, but the coils could become damaged if the ignition was left switched on for any length of time without the engine running. In the event of ignition trouble it is most unlikely that a coil has failed, and the other components should be checked first. Begin with the sparking plugs, then check the battery and the contact breaker. Also check all leads and connections. If all the foregoing are in order and the trouble persists, pull apart the two snap connectors in the leads from the contact breaker, then with the ignition switched on scrape the connectors on the ends of the upper leads against the cylinder head. This should cause a spark which would prove the coils and circuit to be in order. If, however, one of the leads does not spark, the coil concerned should be removed and returned to an Ariel or Lucas agent for test.

REMOVAL OF COILS

If it is required to remove the coils begin by pulling the high tension leads out of the ends of the coils, then pull apart the snap connector which joins the two white leads and the snap connector which joins the one black with white lead.

There is a further black with white lead attached to the offside coil and a black with yellow lead attached to the nearside coil. These two leads pass through the frame and down to the contact breaker, and there are snap connectors incorporated in the leads between the frame and the contact breaker. These snap connectors must be pulled apart.

On some machines the coils are fitted inside the frame at the bottom and secured with two bolts and nuts each; while on other machines the coils are still fitted inside the frame, but at the top and secured with screws and special clip nuts. In either case it is only necessary to remove the four bolts and nuts, or the four screws, whichever is applicable, to free the coils. It is then an easy matter to withdraw both coils from the frame, taking care to pass the leads which are still attached to the coils, through the frame as the coils are removed.

When re-fitting the coils they should be passed inside the frame with the leads already assembled, as follows: The high tension leads should be pushed into the centre terminal of each coil, the clip on the end of the high tension lead acting as a snap connector. The short white leads must be fitted, one to each coil and attached to the negative terminal. Then the coil, which is fitted to the offside of the frame must have the two black with white leads attached to its positive terminal; while the coil fitted to the nearside of the frame must have the black with yellow lead attached to its positive terminal. Also, if the coils are secured to the top of the inside of the frame, the clip nuts must be fitted to the coils before they are passed inside the frame. The coils can then be secured to the frame, if they are fitted to the top of the frame they should be secured with four screws with plain washers under the heads. *Note:* These screws have a special thread to suit the clip nuts already fitted to the coils. If the coils are fitted to the bottom of the frame, they should be secured with four $\frac{1}{4}$ inch diameter by $\frac{1}{2}$ inch under head bolts with plain washers under the heads. Then, after passing the bolts through the coil brackets and the frame, fit a plain washer, a shake-proof washer and a nut to three of the bolts and securely tighten. To the fourth bolt fit a shake-proof washer, the loose end of the rectifier earth lead, a further shake-proof washer and a nut, and securely tighten. If it is not certain whether the coils are to be fitted to the top or the bottom of the inside of the frame, this is easily determined as there are four $\frac{1}{4}$ inch clearance holes in a line across the forward end of the frame, either in the top or bottom of the frame, and the coils are fitted to these holes. Next pass through the nearside high tension lead grommet which is fitted in the underside of the frame, the small harness which combines a black with white lead and a black with yellow lead. The two leads in this harness must then be connected to the leads with corresponding colours from the contact breaker. Finally connect the two white leads and the one black with white lead from the coils, to their respective snap connectors in the main wiring harness inside the frame.

RECTIFIER—LEADER AND ARROW

The rectifier converts alternating current from the generator into direct current for the battery. There is little to go wrong with the rectifier and trouble is very rare. It must be kept dry and clean; the rectifier nut and cable connections must always be tight, and the rubber cable sheath in position for protection against road grit and moisture. When cleaning the rectifier do not wash it with water, but dust it lightly or use a small brush to remove any foreign matter from the plates. No adjustments can be made to the rectifier, cleaning is the only maintenance required.

If the rectifier should become damaged or defective, the generator would cease to charge the battery. But as long as there was a charge in the battery the electrical equipment would continue working, but this would not last more than a few hours. The remedy would be to fit a new rectifier, if this fails to overcome the trouble the generator should be checked and tested as described on page 218.

The rectifier is secured by a nut inside the frame and to remove the rectifier it is only necessary to disconnect the three leads and remove the nut from inside the frame when the rectifier can be pulled clear. Note that if the ignition coils are fitted in the bottom of the frame, there is an earthing lead from the rectifier to one of the coil securing bolts; while for machines which have the coils fitted in the top of the frame, some have an earth lead incorporated in the wiring harness; while others do not have an earth lead and are self earthing, which makes it important to keep the rectifier fixing tight.

When fitting a rectifier to the frame, if a rectifier earth lead is incorporated in the wiring harness, or if a separate lead is used, it must be placed over the centre fixing stud, together with a shake-proof washer. Then pass the rectifier into position with the centre stud through the hole in the frame. Then fit a shake-proof washer and a $\frac{5}{16}$ inch B.S.F. nut to the rectifier centre stud which is inside the frame and securely tighten.

If the rectifier does not have an earthing lead, assemble it to the frame with the nut, and a shake-proof washer each side of the frame as described above. Finally re-connect the three leads as follows, the leads coloured green with white and green with black, to the two outer rectifier terminals, and the remaining brown with purple lead to the middle one.

Note: Three different types of rectifier are in use, Type FSX.1501, Type FSX.1589 and type 2DS.506. They are all interchangeable and either type may be fitted, but note that the 2DS.506 rectifier has a $\frac{1}{4}''$ diameter fixing stud and nut, and the method of connecting the leads varies slightly. If a type 2DS.506 is used to replace one of the other types, suitable 'Lucas' connectors must be soldered to the wiring harness.

Important. Never disturb the tension of the nuts which hold the element together on the through bolt.

ALTERNATOR—LEADER AND ARROW

The alternator is mounted on the offside of the engine and, as the engine revolves, the alternator generates A.C. current which is rectified to D.C. before charging the battery, which serves all the electrical equipment on the motor cycle.

No routine maintenance is required, and trouble

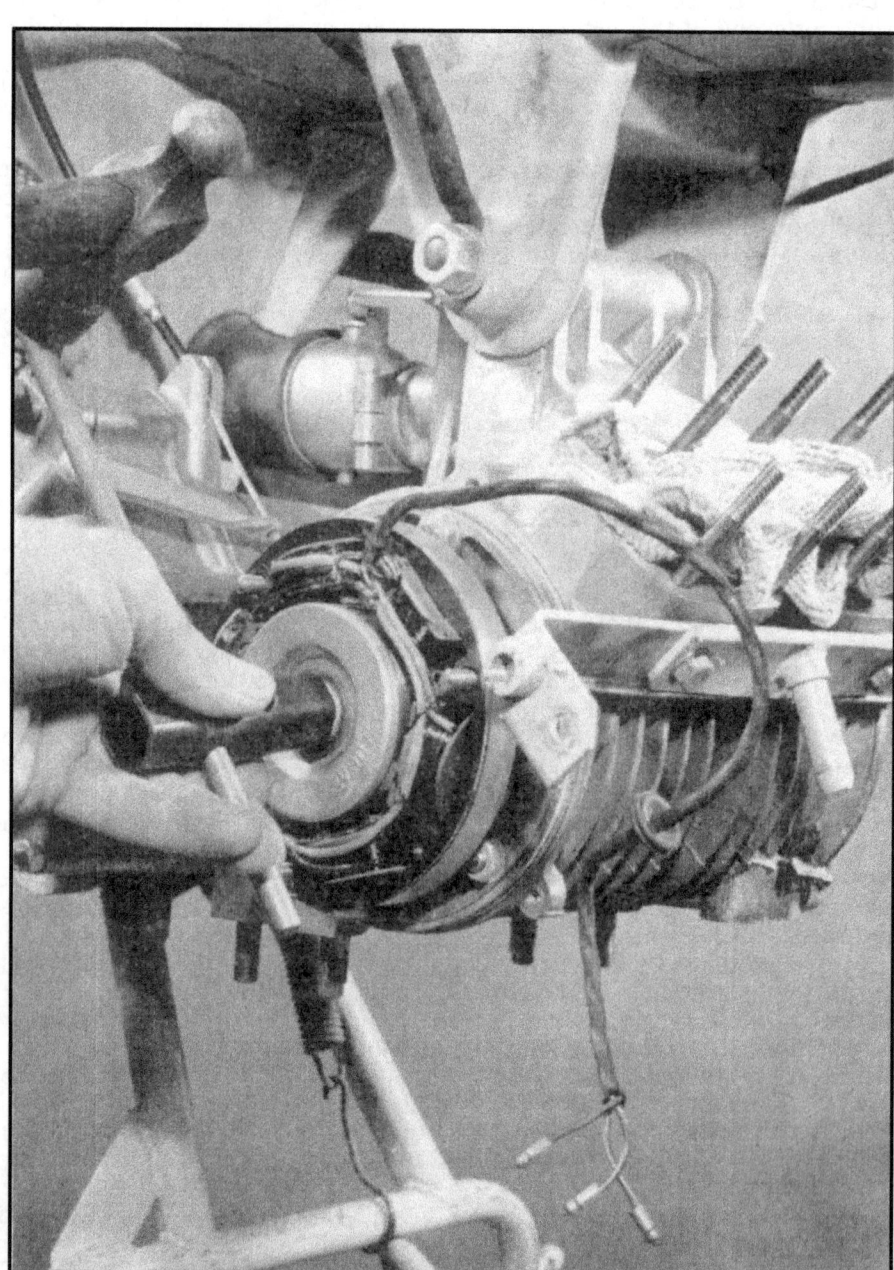

Fig. 165

with an alternator is very rare, but if trouble should develop it will stop generating, leaving only the charge in the battery to operate the electrical equipment, and this would not last more than an hour or two. The ammeter which is fitted in the instrument panel indicates when the alternator is generating, whenever the machine is running above 20 m.p.h. the needle on the ammeter dial should be towards the plus sign. If the needle points to the zero position in the middle of the dial, it may be that the alternator has developed some fault, but first check that the ammeter itself is not at fault as described on pages 162 and 159. Then check that all the electrical leads are intact and connected correctly. If the ammeter and all the leads are in good order the alternator must be removed from the motor cycle and returned to an Ariel or Lucas agent for test and repair. Private owners are strongly advised not to interfere with the alternator apart from removing and re-fitting it.

To remove the alternator from the engine proceed as follows: First remove the offside side panel, as described on page 154, or the engine cover for the Arrow as described on page 155, then disconnect the three leads which protrude from the alternator cover, by separating the snap connectors. The alternator cover can then be removed by unscrewing the three small screws from around the outer edge. Note the rubber joint ring which fits between the alternator cover and the engine. The alternator can then be seen, and it is composed of two units, the rotor, which incorporates magnets and is secured to the engine shaft by a bolt, and the stator, which incorporates the coils and is secured to the engine by the special locking nuts and washers. Begin by removing the three nuts and washers which secure the stator, and then, very carefully, ease the stator off the engine; it will be a little tight but careful pulling will free it. The rotor bolt must be removed next, and this is done by fitting a suitable tube spanner and tommy bar to the bolt, then while holding the spanner and tommy bar in position, strike the tommy bar with a hammer to jar the bolt undone, when it can then be removed easily (see Fig. 165). The rotor will then simply pull off the engine shaft.

Note: There are two types of Alternator in use, Lucas RM.15 and Lucas RM.18. The RM.18 type is narrower and has a compensating spacer fitted on the engine shaft behind the Rotor, there may also be a thick spring washer fitted under the head of the Rotor securing bolt. In the event of a replacement Alternator being required, it is permissible to fit the RM.18 type in place of the RM.15 type, providing the correct spacer is also fitted behind the rotor. Also as the RM.18 Stator is narrower, the three studs which secure the Stator to the engine would require thicker or additional washers to ensure that the securing nuts tighten correctly.

When re-assembling the alternator, begin by fitting the Rotor to the engine shaft, making quite certain that the key for locating the Rotor is fitted in the engine shaft, and that it is in line with the key way in the Rotor. Also if a spacer was fitted on the engine shaft behind the Rotor, make sure that it is in place upon re-assembly. Then fit a shakeproof washer and a plain washer (also if originally fitted, a thick spring washer), under the head of the Rotor bolt, and fit the bolt into the offside end of the engine shaft and securely tighten.

Next locate the stator on to the three studs which protrude from the offside of the engine, and note that the leads which are attached to the stator must be at the top and facing outward. Then fit a plain washer and a special locking nut to the three studs, and securely tighten. Make sure the rubber joint ring is in position on the engine where the alternator cover is to be fitted. Then pass the leads from the stator through the rubber grommet in the alternator cover and carefully locate the cover on to the engine, so that the stator leads protrude from the top of the cover, and the three securing tags line up with the three threaded holes in the engine casting. Then fit a screw through the hole in each of the securing tags and if each screw is tightened a little at time in turn, the cover will be secured evenly in position. The leads which protrude from the alternator cover must then be fitted to the snap connectors on the leads with corresponding colours. Finally, fit the offside side panel as described on page 154, or the engine cover as described on page 155.

STOP LAMP SWITCH—LEADER AND ARROW

The stop lamp switch automatically operates the stop lamp when the rear brake is applied, and in the case of the Leader; also when the front brake is applied. The Leader has one stop switch fitted to the handlebar which is coupled to the front brake lever. While both the Leader and the Arrow have a stop switch fitted just above the offside silencer, which is coupled to the rear brake. The switches are coupled to the brake levers by a spring, so that as the lever is operated the switch is pulled on; a second spring inside the switch pulls it off as the brake lever is released. If trouble is experienced with the stop lamp not illuminating when the brakes are applied, this is most likely due to bulb failure, and fitting a new stop and tail lamp bulb will effect a cure. If this does not overcome the trouble, check that the leads are all connected correctly and are in good condition.

Also check that the spring which couples the

switch to the brake lever is in order and make sure the switch operates freely; any dirt or corrosion should be cleaned off and the operating lever which protrudes from the switch should be lightly greased. To check the stop switch, pull the two leads from the sockets each side of the switch, and place the terminals at the ends of the leads together, when the stop lamp should illuminate. If it does illuminate this proves all the leads to be in order, and the stop switch to be at fault, and the switch should be replaced with a new one. If trouble should be encountered with the stop lamp being constantly illuminated, it may be that the switch position requires re-adjustment, or it could be due to a short in the switch or the leads to the switch. If removing the leads from the switch causes the stop lamp to go off this eliminates the leads, and the switch must be the cause of the trouble. The switch must be clean and operate freely as already described, and if this does not effect a cure, a new switch should be fitted.

DIP SWITCH—LEADER AND ARROW

The headlamp dip switch is fitted to the nearside of the handlebar, and when the headlamp is switched on the dip switch is used to control the double filament headlamp bulb, to obtain either the main light beam or a short dipped beam. If trouble should develop and only one beam position is obtainable, it is most likely that the bulb is at fault and fitting a new bulb will overcome the trouble. If this does not effect a cure, check that all the leads are correctly fitted and in good condition. Also remove the switch from the handlebar by undoing the screw which secures the dip switch bracket, then make sure the connections inside the switch are secure and that none of the leads are damaged. The switch incorporates a spring loaded lever, which moves from side to side as the knob is operated, making contact with the terminals each side. Make quite certain that this mechanism is operating correctly, and that it is not corroded with dirt, etc. The mechanism should be thoroughly cleaned and lightly coated with Vaseline, particularly where the knob pivots. Note that if a new dip switch is being fitted, replacement switches differ slightly to the original type. The difference is in the method of attaching the leads, instead of being soldered in position, the leads are passed up into the hollow terminals and secured by pointed screws.

FLASHING INDICATORS—LEADER

Flashing direction indicators are available as optional extras for use on machines which are with or without panniers.

If it should be required to fit flashing indicators to a machine which has not previously had them fitted, proceed as follows for a machine fitted with panniers; if the machine is not fitted with panniers, see page 223: Supplied with the flasher set is a new sub-wiring harness, which in addition to containing the flasher leads, also includes new stop and tail lamp leads, and the new sub-harness must be fitted in place of the existing tail lamp harness. Begin by removing the tail section as described on page 172. Then disconnect the tail lamp sub-harness, by separating the two leads which are coloured brown and brown with green, inside the tail section behind the number plate. Unclip the sub-harness from along the side of the tail section; it can then be pulled clear. Next fit the new sub-harness supplied with the flashers. At the end where the leads are of an even length, fit the leads coloured brown and brown with green to the snap connectors from where the original sub-harness was removed from under the dualseat. The additional leads which are coloured green with white and green with red, must be fitted to the snap connectors in the main harness which are already fitted with leads with corresponding colours. Next pass the new sub-harness through the rubber grommet in the side of the body. Next the tail section must have a $\frac{9}{32}$ inch diameter hole drilled through each side for the flasher leads to pass through. There is already a suitable hole in the back of the pannier which is plugged with a rubber grommet. Remove the grommet and mark the tail section through the hole. Then remove the panniers as described on page 209 and drill through the tail section where it has been marked. Next fit one of the rubber grommets supplied with the flashers into the hole in the back of each pannier, and the hole which has been drilled each side of the tail section. The panniers can then be re-fitted to the tail section as described on page 208, and the tail section complete must next be re-fitted to the motor cycle, but first only fit the two pivot bolts with the tail section in the lifted up position, so that the new sub-harness can be fitted, clip it along the inside of the tail section, then fit the leads coloured brown and brown with green to the leads with corresponding colours from the back of the tail lamp. Then pass the lead coloured green with white through the grommets in the offside of the tail section and the pannier back, and the lead coloured green with red through the grommets in the nearside of the tail section and the pannier

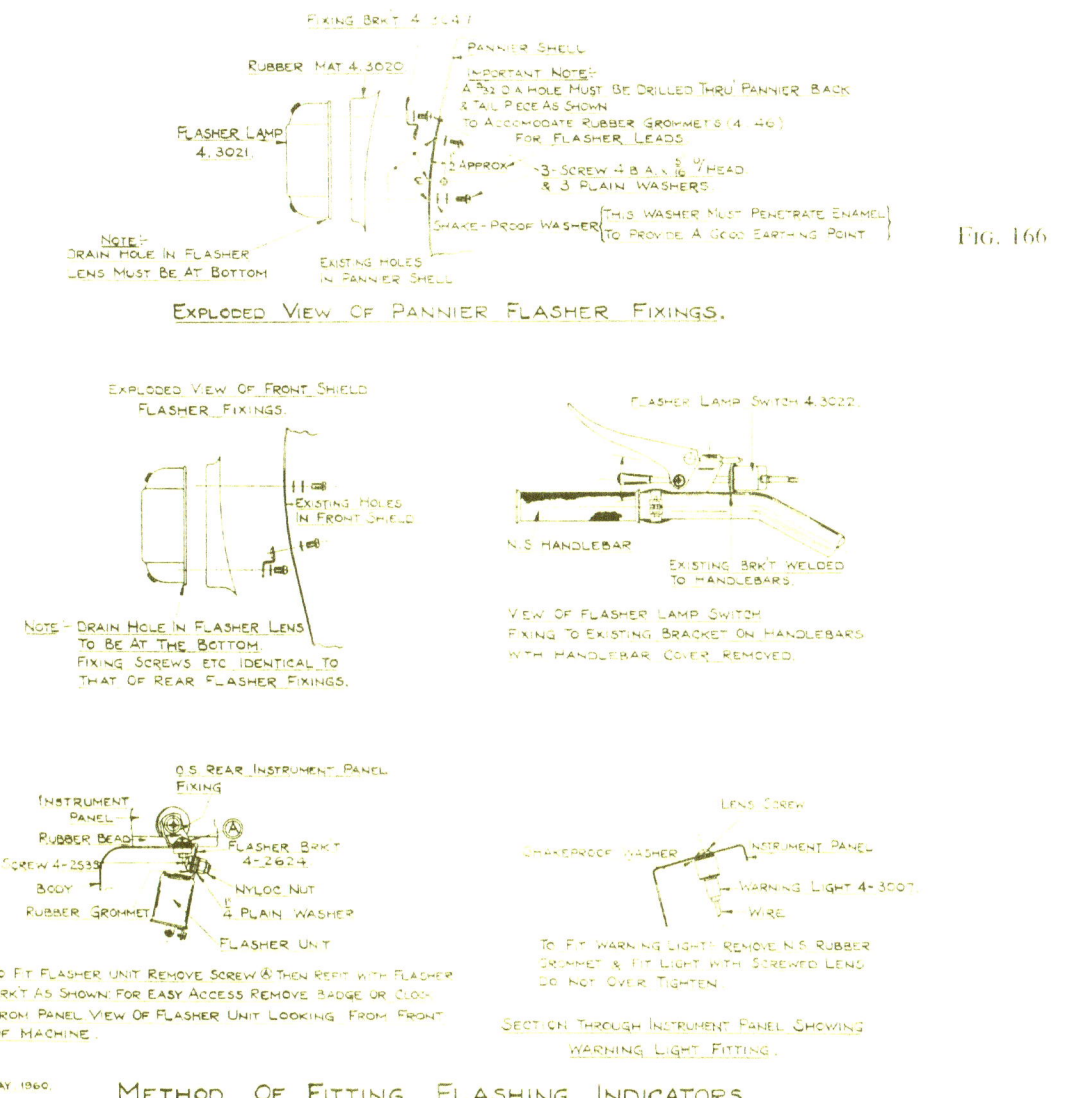

METHOD OF FITTING FLASHING INDICATORS

back. The tail section can then be secured in position as described on page 172.

Next remove the two screws which secure the lens of the flasher lamps, and pull off the lens of each lamp. Then fit the small cranked brackets to the back of the flasher lamps. Two of the lamps must have the brackets fitted at the opposite end to the bulb holder. The other two must have the brackets fitted the same end as the bulb holder, by first fitting a plain washer under the head of a screw, then pass the screw through the plain hole in the cranked bracket, and locate the bracket on to the back of the flasher lamp so that the portion of the bracket with the threaded hole in it, protrudes from the back of, and faces towards, the centre of the flasher lamp, then securely tighten the screw into the threaded hole in the back of the flasher lamp. Next fit one of the large rubber mouldings to the back of each flasher lamp; there is a square hole in the moulding so that it can be fitted over the cranked bracket. Next remove the three plug grommets from the rear end of both panniers, and fit one of the grommets supplied with the flasher set into the middle of the three holes, then pass the lead which is inside each pannier, through the grommet in the rear end. Next remove from the flasher lamps the small connector which is pushed into the terminal at the side of the lamp glass, then pass the lead which protrudes from the back of each pannier through the grommet in the back of a flasher lamp just above the bulb. Note the flasher lamps for fitting to the panniers must have the cranked brackets fitted at the bulb holder end. Locate a lamp in position on each pannier so that the wider portion of the large rubber moulding is uppermost, then secure the lamps in position by fitting a plain washer under the head of a screw; the screw is then passed from inside the pannier through the top hole and into the threaded hole in the cranked bracket on the back of the lamp. Next fit a plain washer and a shake-proof washer under the head of a screw, and fit the screw through the lower hole in the pannier and into the threaded hole in the back of the lamp. The loose connector which was removed from the lamp must now be fitted over the lead which protrudes through the back of the lamp. Approximately half an inch of the end of the lead must be bare, and the wires spread and turned back outside the connector. Then re-fit the connector with the lead to the terminal at the side of the bulb glass. The flasher lamp lens can then be re-fitted with the two screws, but note that the small cutaway in the joint face of the lens must be at the bottom.

The front two flasher lamps are fitted in a similar manner. Begin by removing the head-lamp unit as described on page 136. Then fit the two short separate leads which are coloured green with red and green with white to the front flasher lamps. Pass one lead through the back of each lamp and fit it to the connector at the side of the bulb glass. Next remove the three plug grommets from each side of the front shield, and in the middle hole each side fit one of the grommets supplied with the flasher set. The lamp with the green with white lead must be fitted to the offside of the front shield; pass the lead through the grommet in the front shield, and locate the lamp in position with the wide portion of the large grommet at the bottom. Then secure the lamp in place by fitting a screw with a plain washer under its head through the front shield and into the threaded hole in the cranked bracket at the back of the lamp, and a second screw with a plain washer and a shake-proof washer under its head, passing through the front shield and into the threaded hole in the back of the lamp. The flasher lamp lens can then be fitted, making sure the cutaway is at the bottom. Fit the flasher lamp for the nearside of the front shield in the same manner as the one for the offside. Next pass the lead from the two front flasher lamps under the instrument panel and loop them through the brackets from the windscreen support stays, then working through headlamp cowl, fit the lead from each of the front flasher lamps into the snap connectors in the main wiring harness, which are already fitted with leads with corresponding colours.

The flasher unit should be fitted next, but first fit one of the rubber grommets supplied with the flasher set into the hole in the bracket at the end of the flasher unit. Next fit the small loose right-angle bracket under the head of the ¼ inch diameter screw, and pass the screw through the grommet in the flasher unit bracket, so that the right-angle bracket is on the inside of the flasher bracket. Then fit a plain washer and a special locking nut to the screw and tighten the nut so that the right-angle bracket is away from the end of the flasher unit. But note the nut must not be over-tightened as it is most important that the flasher unit is flexible on the right-angle bracket. Next attach the flasher unit sub-harness; this harness consists of three leads which have open-ended terminals at one end. The end of the flasher unit has three screws which are marked "B", "L" and "P", and the open-ended terminals must be fitted under the heads of these screws, the lead coloured brown with blue must be fitted to screw "B", the lead coloured green with brown must be fitted to screw "L", and the lead coloured green to screw "P". Then fit the flasher unit to the motor cycle, begin by removing the badge or clock from the instrument panel as described on page 164. It can then be seen that a bolt passes through a bracket inside the instrument panel, and through the top of the body; unscrew and remove this bolt. In addition to securing the instrument panel, the headlamp earth lead is also attached to this bolt. The bolt must now have a shake-proof washer and the headlamp earth lead fitted under its head, and then be passed through the right-angle bracket at the end of the flasher unit. Next re-fit the bolt through the instrument panel bracket and into the threaded hole in the top of the body, so that the flasher unit is secured inside the body.

The flasher control switch must be fitted next, and the lead from the switch must be passed through the same hole in the grommet in the top of the body as the dip switch lead. The easiest method of doing this is to tie a length of string to a piece of strong wire then thread the wire and string through the hole in the grommet, leaving some string on the top of the body. Next tie the leads from the flasher switch to the string, then smear the leads with liquid soap and draw them through the grommet by pulling the string. Then untie and remove the string and wire. This will leave the switch on top of the body and the leads can be connected through the headlamp cowl. The lead coloured green with brown must be connected to the lead with a corresponding colour from the flasher unit. The other two leads which are coloured green with white and green with red, must be connected to the same snap connectors as the leads from the flasher lamps which have corresponding colours. The lead coloured brown with blue from the flasher unit must be fitted to the double snap connector in the main harness which is already fitted with leads of corresponding colour. The flasher switch can then be fitted to the handlebar, but the handlebar cover must first be removed as described on page 124. Then remove the large thin nut from the bottom of the switch control rod, and pass the control rod through the bracket on the nearside half of the handlebar. Then re-fit the nut to the switch to secure it to the handlebar bracket.

Next fit the flasher warning light to the instrument panel. Begin by removing the rubber grommet from the offside of the instrument panel. Then unscrew the lens from the top of the warning light, and place a shake-proof washer on the top of the warning light and locate it in position under the instrument panel. Then fit the lens through the hole in the instrument panel, and locate it through the shake-proof washer and into the top of the warning light. The warning light can then be screwed firmly on to the lens. The lead from the warning light which is coloured green must be connected to the lead from the flasher unit which has a corresponding colour.

It now only remains to re-fit the handlebar cover as described on page 124. The clock or badge in the instrument panel as described on page 164 and the headlamp unit as described on page 141. Finally, make certain the panniers and the tail section are secured correctly.

If it should be required to fit a new bulb to one of the flasher lamps, first remove the lens by undoing the two small screws. The bulb is then accessible and can be removed by pressing it down slightly and turning in either direction, when the bulb will become free. A new bulb must be a 6-volt, 18-watt, single contact, bayonet fitting, and it is fitted by simply pushing it into its holder, with the pegs located each side of the holder, then turn the bulb either direction so that the pegs lock under the holder. Then re-fit the flasher lamp lens.

For full details of the warning light and bulb, see page 160.

If any trouble should be experienced with the flashing indicators if only one lamp fails to work, it may be that the bulb requires renewing. If the fitting of a new bulb does not overcome the trouble, check that all wiring connections are fitted correctly, and that all the leads are in good condition. Also that all screws, etc., securing the flasher lamps, switch and unit are in order. If two lamps on one side should fail, it may be the switch on the handlebar causing the trouble. The rubber cover over the end of the switch can be rolled back and the lead connections can be checked; also the switch can be cleaned. In the event of all four lamps failing, check all items already mentioned, and if no fault is located the flasher unit may be the cause of the trouble. In this case the fitting of a new unit would be the remedy.

FITTING FLASHING INDICATORS TO A MOTOR CYCLE WHICH IS NOT FITTED WITH PANNIERS—LEADER

The flashing indicator set is supplied complete, and if it is specified for a machine without panniers, two special P.V.C. mouldings are included for mounting the rear flasher lamps. Supplied with the flasher set is a new sub-wiring harness, which in addition to containing the flasher leads, also includes new stop and tail lamp leads and the new sub-harness must be fitted in place of the existing tail lamp harness. Begin by removing the tail section, as described on page 172. Then disconnect the tail lamp sub-harness, by separating the two leads which are coloured brown and brown with green, inside the tail section behind the number plate. Unclip the sub-harness from along the side of the tail section; it can then be pulled clear.

The tail section must then have four holes drilled through each side for the fixing screws and flasher lamp leads. To ensure these holes are drilled accurately, a template is supplied with the flasher set. The template should be located in position on the nearside of the tail section, and the hole positions marked with a centre punch. The template can then be located on the offside, and the hole positions again marked with a centre punch. Next using a $\frac{3}{16}$ inch diameter drill, drill the three fixing screw holes through each side of the tail section. The remaining hole to be drilled each side must be $\frac{9}{32}$ inch diameter, and one of the grommets supplied with the flasher set must be fitted to each of the $\frac{9}{32}$ inch diameter holes, for the flasher lamp leads to pass through. Next remove the two screws which secure the flasher lamp lens, and pull off the lenses from all four lamps. Then dealing with the two lamps which are to be fitted to the tail section, begin by fixing them to the P.V.C. mountings.

The lamps must be positioned so that the bulb holder will be at the top when the lamps are fitted to the machine. The lamps are secured to their mountings by fitting a plain washer under the head of the fixing screws; the screws must then be passed through the holes in the support plate, and the holes in the P.V.C. mounting from the inside and then located into the corresponding holes in the back of the flasher lamp and securely tightened.

Next the new sub-wiring harness, which was supplied with the flasher set and which incorporates the stop and tail lamp leads as well as the rear flasher lamp leads, must be fitted to the tail section. The end of the sub-harness where the leads are of an uneven length must be connected to the tail lamp by fitting the leads coloured brown and brown and green to the leads with corresponding colours from the tail lamp.

The lead coloured green with white must be passed through the grommet which has been fitted into the offside of the tail section; while the lead coloured green with red must be passed

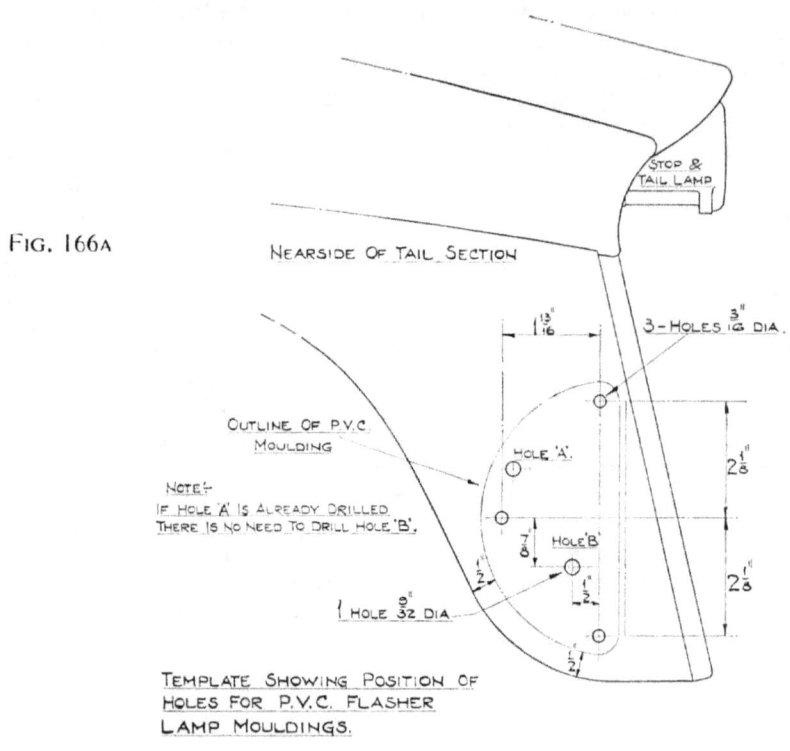

Fig. 166A

TEMPLATE SHOWING POSITION OF HOLES FOR P.V.C. FLASHER LAMP MOULDINGS.

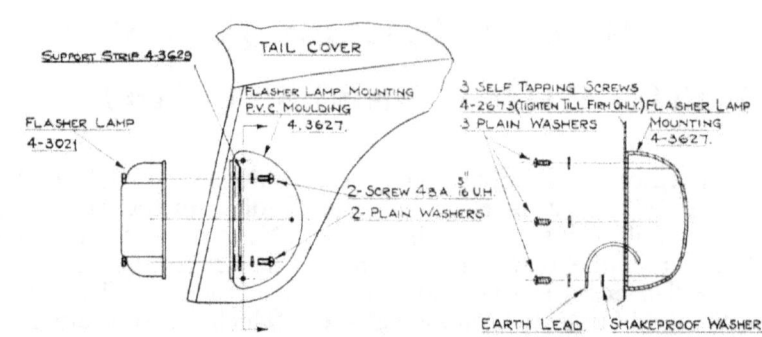

FITTING FLASHERS WITHOUT PANNIERS.

Ariel Motors Ltd. May, 1960.

through the grommet which has been fitted into the nearside of the tail section. The sub-harness should then be clipped along the offside inner edge of the tail section. Then pass the earth lead for each of the rear flasher lamps through the grommet each side of the tail section so that the washer type terminal on each earth lead is inside the tail section. Next pass the two leads which protrude from each side of the tail section through the open side of the P.V.C. moulding and the grommet in the back of the flasher lamp. Then locate the P.V.C. mouldings in position on the tail section, remembering that the bulb holders must be at the top. To secure the mouldings and lamps in position, fit a plain washer under the heads of the six self-tapping screws and fit two screws through two of the holes in each side of the tail section, and into the corresponding holes in the P.V.C. mouldings. The remaining screw for each side must be passed through the washer type terminal on the end of each earth lead, and then have a shake-proof washer fitted next to the terminal. The screws can then be fitted through the remaining hole each side of the tail section, and into the P.V.C. moulding. All six screws should then be firmly tightened. The leads which protrude through the back of the flasher lamps must be connected to the terminals. Begin by removing the two loose connectors from each flasher lamp and fit them over the leads. Approximately half an inch of the end of each lead must be bare and the wire spread and turned back over the connectors. Then re-fit the connectors so that the earth leads are at the side of the bulb holder, while the lead coloured green with white or green with red as the case may be, must be in the terminal at the side of the lamp glass. The flasher lamp lens can then be re-fitted making sure the drain hole is at the bottom. Then re-fit the tail section to the motor cycle as described on page 172.

Before the front flasher lamps can be fitted to the front shield there must be a small cranked bracket and a large rubber moulding fitted to the back of each lamp. The cranked brackets must be fitted at the opposite end to the bulb holder, by first fitting a plain washer under the head of a screw, then pass the screw through the plain hole in the cranked bracket and locate the bracket on to the back of the flasher lamp so that the portion of the bracket with the threaded hole in it protrudes from the back of, and faces towards, the centre of the flasher lamp.

Then securely tighten the screw into the threaded hole in the back of the flasher lamp. Then fit one of the large rubber mouldings to the back of each flasher lamp; there is a square hole in the moulding so that it can be fitted over the cranked bracket. The front two flasher lamps, the flasher unit and the control switch can then be fitted as described on page 222.

NEUTRAL INDICATORS—LEADER

The neutral indicator incorporates a warning lamp in the offside of the instrument panel, which illuminates whenever the gear lever is in the neutral position, while the ignition is switched on.

The neutral indicator is not part of the standard equipment but is available as an optional extra. To fit a neutral indicator to a motor cycle that has not previously been fitted with one, begin by removing the large plug from the offside end of the rear of the gear box, but note this plug is below the oil level in the gear box, and if any oil is spilled, it must afterwards be replaced with fresh oil. Spilling the oil can be avoided by leaning the motor cycle to the nearside while changing the plug. The plunger switch for the neutral indicator fits in place of the plug that has been removed, and there must be a fibre washer fitted on the threaded portion of the switch, to make an oil-tight joint between the switch and the gear box. If the fibre washer which was removed with the plug is in good condition, it can be fitted to the switch, otherwise a new fibre washer must be fitted.

The sub-wiring harness supplied with the neutral indicator incorporates new rear stop switch leads, and before it can be fitted the existing rear stop switch leads must be removed. These leads are coloured brown and brown with blue, and will simply pull out of the sockets in the stop switch, the other ends of the leads are joined by snap connectors to the main harness under the dualseat. The leads can then be unclipped from the rear mudguard and pulled free. Next fit the new sub-wiring harness by connecting the leads which are coloured brown and brown with blue to the snap connectors in the main wiring harness which are already fitted with leads with corresponding colours. The other ends of the brown and brown with blue leads in the sub-wiring harness, must be pushed into the sockets in the rear stop switch; they can be fitted either way round. There are two more leads in the new sub-harness, and these are coloured white and white and blue. The upper ends of these leads must be fitted into the snap connectors in the main wiring harness, which are already fitted with leads with corresponding colours. The lower ends of the leads can then be fitted either way round, into the sockets in the neutral gear indicator switch in the rear of the gear box.

The warning light for the instrument panel is all that remains to be fitted, and full instructions for fitting this light are included on page 160.

CLEANING AND POLISHING
—LEADER AND ARROW

Regular cleaning and polishing of the motor cycle will protect and maintain the finish in the best possible condition. The enamelled exterior parts of the machine must never be dry cleaned, as this will inevitably lead to a scratched and dull surface. The enamelled parts should first be washed with warm water to remove any dirt, etc. Do not use detergents. Any tar spots which may be on the machine can be removed with a cloth moistened with turpentine. After washing and drying the enamelled parts with a chamois leather, they can be polished with one of the well-known brands of car polish. The windscreen should only be cleaned with genuine Perspex cleaner, obtainable from any good accessory dealer. All chromium plated parts should be washed and dried as described for the enamelled parts and then polished with a soft duster. Stains, etc., can be removed with a well-known brand of chromium cleaner. Do not use metal polish under any circumstances, as this will ruin the plating.

The dualseat cover should always be cleaned with warm soapy water; never use detergents or chemical cleaners which would be harmful to the material. To clean the engine unit and the hubs and spokes use one of the well-known oil and grease solvents, which can be purchased from any good motor cycle dealer. Use care when applying and washing off the solvent, to avoid the possibility of water entering the carburetter or any of the electrical equipment.

RE-TOUCHING ENAMEL

Tins of synthetic enamel in all Leader and Arrow colours are available for re-touching scratched or damaged enamel surfaces. A good quality child's paint brush is ideal for applying the enamel, but the brush must be shaped to a point to ensure a neat job.

The enamel will take approximately one hour to dry and should therefore be applied indoors in a dust free atmosphere. The parts being re-touched must first be thoroughly cleaned and then wiped over with a cloth damped with cellulose thinners.

If the enamel is too thick for the job in hand, a small quantity should be poured into a suitable container and mixed with a little cellulose thinners. The enamel should then be carefully applied to the parts concerned, and left to dry for at least one hour. Afterwards if required, cutting down paste, which is obtainable from paint shops and garages, can be used to blend in the re-touched parts.

FAULT FINDING CHART
—LEADER AND ARROW

FAULT	CAUSE	REMEDY
Engine will not start	Lack of fuel	Turn on petrol tap to main and reserve positions. Make certain there is fuel in the tank. Check that the cold start device is working, and that fuel is reaching the carburetter; make sure the breather hole in the petrol filler cap is clear by removing the cap and blowing through from the outside. Also make quite certain that the carburetter securing nuts and float chamber screws are tight.
	No spark at plugs	Check battery by switching lights on and off, if lights operate the battery is in order, if the lights do not operate move ignition switch to emergency position, to start the engine. If necessary dry the sparking plugs, and check and re-set the gap to .030 inch—.035 inch. Alternatively fit two clean plugs. Check all coil connections and high tension leads to the sparking plugs. Make certain the connections are clean and tight, and the leads are in good condition. Check the contact breaker gap and re-set if necessary. Make sure that electrical current is reaching the contact breaker and leaving the coils, check battery connections and earth wire. Make certain that the heads of the two screws which secure the contact breaker unit to the chaincase, are not touching the loop springs. Also ensure that the contact breaker cover does not touch the terminals on the leads at the end of each condenser.
	Too much fuel	If the engine is "flooded" it will be difficult to start. Switch off petrol, remove sparking plugs and kick the engine over several times; fit clean and dry sparking plugs, and start engine in the normal way. If "flooding" persists, check that the float in the carburetter is not punctured; also make sure the float needle is in position and good order.
Engine runs erratically	Electrical	Check and if necessary clean and re-set the sparking plugs and the contact breaker. If in doubt fit new sparking plugs. Check the high tension leads and coil connections, make sure the leads are not damaged. Make certain the battery connections are clean and tight, and that there is a good charge in the battery.
	Carburation	Check petrol supply from tank; make certain the breather hole in the petrol filler cap is clear by removing the cap and blowing through from the outside. Also

Fault	Cause	Remedy
		check that the float chamber needle is not stuck on its seat. Clean the float chamber and all jets. Make sure the cold start device is operating correctly. Check that the carburetter securing nuts and the float chamber screws are tight. Make sure the two bolts in the front of the crankcase are securely tightened. See carburetter fault-finding chart on page 23.
Engine lacks power	Electrical	Check and if necessary re-set ignition timing; also check sparking plugs.
	Carburation	Check for weak or rich mixture, as described on page 23.
	Mechanical	Engine and silencers require decarbonising, air cleaner element requires renewing. If the engine has covered a large mileage, the crankcase oil seals and bearings may be worn resulting in loss of pressure. Cylinder barrels may need reboring. Check that brakes are not over adjusted and rubbing drums. Also that the chains are not adjusted too tight.
Engine will not run slowly	Ignition timing	Check and re-set if necessary.
	Carburation	Check for weak mixture as described on page 23.
	Mechanical	Make certain the two bolts in the front of the crankcase are securely tightened. Check for air leak at cylinder head or base joints; also at crankcase end covers, and tighten any nuts and bolts as required. Renew any joint washers or gaskets which are damaged. Also check crankcase oil seals and make sure they are in good order.
Excessive fuel consumption	Electrical	Check that the sparking plugs are in good condition, and of the correct type and make; the plug gap must be between .030 inch and .035 inch. Check ignition timing and contact breaker gaps, and re-set if necessary.
	Carburation	Check for rich or weak mixture as described on page 23.
	Mechanical	Check for petrol leaks from carburetter, petrol pipe, tap and tank. Make certain that the brakes and driving chains are not over adjusted and causing a drag on the engine power. If the engine has covered a large mileage, it may be in need of decarbonising or a general overhaul.
Engine noisy	Pinking	Check that the sparking plugs are the correct make and type, and that they are in good condition with the correct gap. Check for weak mixture as described on page 23. Engine and silencers may need decarbonising. Check ignition timing and re-set if necessary.

Fault	Cause	Remedy
	Mechanical	Check the primary chain or the clutch are not damaged. If the engine has covered a large mileage, the bearings may require renewing, or a rebore may be necessary.
Clutch slips	Adjustment or wear	Re-adjust the clutch, but if the trouble persists exchange clutch plates should be fitted.
Clutch drags	Adjustment or lubrication	Re-adjust the clutch, if the trouble persists dismantle the clutch and clean all the plates; check the clutch operating rod and the adjuster in the gear box, if they are worn or damaged they should be replaced. Liberally smear the clutch rod with oil before fitting it. After re-assembling the clutch and the primary chaincase; top up with one of the recommended brands of S.A.E. 20 grade oil.
Kick starter lever does not return or operate Gear change lever does not return or operate	Broken springs or worn parts	Remove kick starter case cover and check for broken spring, or damaged or worn parts.
Difficulty in selecting gears Slips out of gear	Worn or damaged parts inside gear box	Dismantle the gear box as described on page 61 and replace parts as necessary.
Motor cycle does not steer correctly	Tyre pressures incorrect	Check and adjust the tyre pressure as described on page 98 and page 124.
	Wheel alignment incorrect	Check and adjust as described on page 122. Also make certain wheel spindle nuts, rear hub sprocket nuts and the nearside trailing link clamp bolt are all securely tight.
	Steering head bearings	Check adjustment, if the bearings are too slack or tight they must be re-adjusted. If the steering head bearings are worn or damaged they must be replaced.
	Wheel bearings	If the wheel bearings are worn, they must be replaced.
	Wheel rims and spokes	If there are loose spokes, or if the wheel rims are out of true, the wheel must be repaired by a competent wheel builder.
Inefficient brakes	Incorrect adjustment	Re-adjust the brakes as described on page 86 and page 107.
	Dirt or grease on linings	Clean all brake parts and the drum, wipe the linings with a cloth and a little carbon tetrachloride or replace brake linings.
	Worn linings	Fit exchange brake shoes with new linings.
	Worn brake cam	Check all brake parts and renew any which are worn or damaged.
Fierce or grabbing brakes	Excessive dust deposits	Remove brake anchor plate and thoroughly clean all parts.
	Rust in brake drum	Remove all rust deposits with fine emery cloth. Also clean all brake parts.

Fault	Cause	Remedy
	Chamfered brake linings	The leading edges of the linings must not be chamfered. If the linings have been chamfered it must be either removed or exchange shoes with new linings fitted.
	Excessive wear of front torque arm pivot bearings	Check the bearings and replace if necessary.
	Excessive wear of front brake plate centre bush	Check bush for wear and replace if necessary.
Poor suspension	Weak springs	Remove hydraulic spring units and fit new springs or new units complete.
	Worn hydraulic units	Fit new units complete.
	Soft rear suspension	Fit supplementary springs, see page 182.
	Hard suspension	Check hydraulic units and make certain they operate satisfactorily. If the units are not working replace them with new ones. Check that the front trailing links pivot freely; also the rear fork. If the machine was purchased secondhand, it may be fitted with supplementary springs, removing these springs will effect a cure.
Squeak from suspension	Dry springs	Remove hydraulic units. Dismantle and grease springs.
Rough or noisy transmission	Chain adjustment	Check front and rear chain adjustment and correct if necessary.
	Chain alignment	Check wheel alignment and correct if necessary. If the engine or gear box has been dismantled check sprocket alignment as described on page 57.
	Worn chains and sprockets	Check chains and sprockets and replace any part necessary.
Electrical fault		Refer to the section dealing with the component concerned for full details. If a light fails fit a new bulb. Check the wiring and connections as per the wiring diagrams on pages 212 and 215.
	Alternator	Page 218
	Rectifier	,, 217
	Battery	,, 212
	Headlamp	,, 213 and 214
	Tail lamp	,, 172 and 173
	Electric horn	,, 214 and 216
	Ignition coils	,, 216
	Stop switches	,, 219
	Lighting and ignition switches	,, 160
	Flashing indicators	,, 220
	Neutral indicator	,, 225
	Warning lamps	,, 160
	Parking lamp	,, 165
	Inspection lamp	,, 162

SERVICE TOOLS—LEADER AND ARROW

The following list is the complete range of special service tools, which can be purchased either individually or collectively:

43569 ENGINE SET

Part No.	Description	No. Off.
43540S	Clutch Banjo	1
43552S	Flywheel Strap Spanner	1
43545S	Extractor Plate	1
43547S	Centre Screw—Extractor	1
43546S	Bolt—End Cover Extractor	2
43548S	Bolt—Flywheel Extractor	2
43544S	Sleeve	1
43541S	Locating Plate	1
43542S	Plug—Locating Plate	1
43551S	Key—Crankshaft Bolt	1
43549S	Box Spanner—Flywheel Nut	1
43550S	Tommy Bar	1
43543S	Sleeve	1
43570S	Service Ignition Timing Peg	1
43500	Combination Spanner	1
43523	D.E. Tube Spanner	1
43524	D.E. Tube Spanner	1
43525	D.E. Tube Spanner	1
43501	Wrench—Cylinder Head Bolt	1

43572S BEARING REMOVAL AND REPLACEMENT KIT

Part No.	Description	No. Off.
43573S	Spindle Assembly	1
43576S	Bearing Location Collar	1
43577S	Locating Washer	1
43578S	Locating Washer—Crankcase	1
43579S	Locating Washer—Gear Box	1
43580S	Locating Washer—Hubs	1
43581S	Locating Washer—Head Lug	1

43572S—continued

Part No.	Description	No. Off.
43582S	Collar	1
43583S	Extractor Channel Complete	1
43584S	Spacer	1
43585S	Tommy Bar	1
43586S	Extractor Collar	1
43587S	Drift	1
43588S	Collar—Drift	1
43589S	Locating Washer—Head Lug	1

43592S OIL SEAL AND BUSH FITTING AND EXTRACTING KIT

Part No.	Description	No. Off.
43593S	Bolt	1
43594S	Nut	1
42073	Distance Tube	1
43595S	Locating Collar	1
43596S	Locating Collar	1
43597S	Locating Collar	1
43598S	Locating Collar	1
43601S	Spacer—P.R.F. Bush	1
43602S	Washer—P.R.F. Bush	1
43603S	Guide—S.E. Bush	1
43604S	Spacer—S.E. Bush	1
474	Washer	2

FOR FRONT WHEEL SPINDLE

Part No.	Description	No. Off.
43624/1S	Spindle Withdrawing Rod complete	1
43624S	Spindle Withdrawing Rod (front)	1
43625S	Peg—Spindle Withdrawing Rod	1

OPTIONAL EXTRA EQUIPMENT
—AVAILABLE FOR LEADER AND ARROW

Any of the following items can be supplied with a new machine, or be fitted to a machine already in service.

LEADER

	Page
Prop Stand	184
Front Stand	183
Windscreen Extension	157
Rear View Mirrors	211
Dualseat Waterproof Cover	169
Pannier Cases	208
Pannier Bags	208
Rear Carrier and Straps	210
Rear Fender	211
Flashing Indicators	220
Neutral Gear Indicator	225
Parking Lamp	165
Inspection Lamp	162
Eight-Day Clock	164
Tins of Enamel for Retouching	226

ARROW

	Page
Rear Carrier with Straps	210
Prop Stand	184
Front Stand	183
Dualseat Waterproof Cover	169
Dualseat Strap	170
Petrol Tap with Reserve	—
White Wall Tyres	—
Tins of Enamel for Retouching	226
Windscreen	211

PROPRIETARY EQUIPMENT AND ACCESSORIES

Although every effort is made to obtain the most suitable and highest quality fittings of a proprietary nature for incorporating into our motor cycles, our guarantee does not cover such parts.

If premature trouble is experienced with proprietary fittings and it is intended to make a claim under the guarantee, the part or parts should be returned to and claims made direct on the actual manufacturers who will deal with them on the terms of their respective guarantees. Date of purchase and mileage covered should always be clearly stated when submitting a claim.

CHAINS
Renold Chains Ltd., Wythenshawe, Manchester.

Perry Engineering Co. Ltd., Stockfield Road, Tyseley, Birmingham 27.

CARBURETTER
Amal Ltd., Holdford Road, Witton, Birmingham 6.

ELECTRICAL EQUIPMENT
Joseph Lucas Ltd., Service Dept., Great Hampton Street, Birmingham 18.

SPARK PLUGS
Lodge Plugs Ltd., Rugby.

SPEEDOMETER
S. Smith (M.A.) Ltd., Cricklewood, London.

TYRES
The Dunlop Rubber Co. Ltd., Fort Dunlop, Erdington, Birmingham 24.

The Avon India Rubber Co. Ltd., Melksham, Wilts.

EIGHT DAY CLOCK
S. Smith (M.A.) Ltd., Cricklewood, London.

CONDITIONS OF GUARANTEE

NOTICE

We do not appoint agents for the sale on our behalf of our motor cycles or other goods, but we assign to motor cycle Dealers areas in which we supply to such Dealers exclusively for re-sale in such areas. No such Dealer is authorised to transact any business, give any warranty, make any such representation or incur any liability on our behalf.

GUARANTEE

We give the following guarantee with our motor cycles, motor cycle combinations and sidecars including all accessories and component parts other than tyres, saddles, chains and lighting and electrical equipment, and other than accessories and component parts supplied to the order of the Purchaser and differing from those comprised in the standard specifications supplied with our motor cycles, motor cycle combinations and sidecars, but including accessories and parts supplied by way of exchange as hereinafter provided. This guarantee is given in place of any implied conditions or warranties or any liabilities whatsoever statutory or otherwise; no guarantee except that hereinafter contained and no condition or warranty whatsoever statutory or otherwise is given or is to be implied nor are we to be under any liability whatsoever except under the guarantee hereinafter contained. Any statement, description, condition or representation contained in any catalogue, advertisement, leaflet or other publication shall not be construed as enlarging, varying or overriding anything herein contained. In the case of machines (a) which have been used for "hiring out" purposes or (b) any motor cycle and/or sidecar used for any dirt tracks, cinder track or grass track racing or competitions (or any competition of any kind within an enclosure for which a charge is made for admission to take part in or view the competition) or (c) machines from which the trade mark name or manufacturing number has been altered or removed or (d) any machine in which parts have been used not supplied by or approved by the motor cycle manufacturer, or (e) any machine from which the silencing system as fitted by the manufacturer has been partially or wholly removed or interfered with, no guarantee, condition or warranty of any kind statutory or otherwise is given or is to be implied nor are we to be under any liability whatsoever in respect of any such machine.

We guarantee, subject to the conditions mentioned below, that all precautions which are usual and reasonable have been taken by us to secure excellence of materials and workmanship, but this guarantee is to extend and be in force for six months only from date of purchase, or date of exchange in case of any accessory or part supplied by way of exchange as hereinafter provided, and damages for which we make ourselves responsible under this guarantee are limited to the free repair of or supply of a new part or accessory in exchange for the part of the motor cycle, motor cycle combination or sidecar or accessory which may have proved defective. We undertake, subject to the conditions mentioned below, to make good in manner aforesaid any part or accessory covered by this guarantee which has proved defective within the said period of six months. We do not undertake to replace or refix, or bear the cost of replacing or refixing any such new part or accessory in the motor cycle, motor cycle combination or sidecar. As motor cycles, motor cycle combinations and sidecars are easily liable to derangement by neglect or misuse, this guarantee does not apply to the defects caused by wear and tear, misuse or neglect.

The term "misuse" shall include amongst others the following acts:

1. The attaching of a sidecar to a motor cycle in such a manner as to cause damage or calculated to render the latter unsafe when ridden.

2. The use of the motor cycle or of a motor cycle and sidecar combined when carrying more persons or a greater weight than that for which the machine was designed by the manufacturers.

3. The attaching of a sidecar to a motor cycle by any form of attachment not provided, supplied or approved by the manufacturers, or to a motor cycle which is not designed for such use.

We do not guarantee tyres, saddles, chains or lighting and electrical equipment or any accessories or component parts supplied to the order of the Purchaser differing from those comprised in the standard specifications supplied with our motor cycles, motor cycle combinations or sidecars. As regards all such tyres, saddles, chains, lighting and electrical equipment, accessories and component parts, no guarantee, condition or warranty of any kind statutory or otherwise is given or is to be implied, and we are to be under no liability whatsoever in respect thereof.

CONDITIONS OF GUARANTEE

If a defective part or accessory should be found in our motor cycles, motor cycle combinations or sidecars or in any part or accessory supplied by way of exchange as before provided, it must be sent to us **Carriage Paid,** and accompanied by an intimation from the owner that he desires to have it repaired or exchanged free of charge under our guarantee and he must also furnish us at the same time with the number of the machine, the date of the purchase or the date when the alleged defective part or accessory was exchanged as the case may be.
Failing compliance with the above, such articles will lie here at **the risk of the owner,** and this guarantee and any implied guarantee, warranty or condition shall not be enforceable.

REPAIRS

Any motor cycle, motor cycle combination or sidecar sent to us to be plated, enamelled or repaired will be repaired upon the following conditions, i.e. we guarantee that all precautions which are usual and reasonable have been taken by us to secure excellence of materials and workmanship, such guarantee to extend and be in force for three months only from the time such work shall have been executed, and this guarantee is in lieu and in exclusion of all conditions and warranties statutory or otherwise and all liabilities whatsoever and the damages recoverable are limited to the cost of any further work which may be necessary to amend and make good the work found to be defective.

**ARIEL
MOTORS LIMITED
SELLY OAK
BIRMINGHAM 29**

INDEX

	LEADER page	ARROW page
AIR CLEANER	24	24
Element	24	24
Rubber connector	17	17
ALTERNATOR	218	218
Removal	219	219
Re-fitting	219	219
Rotor	219	219
Stator	219	219
AMMETER	159	163
Removal	159	163
Re-fitting	159	163
ANCHOR BAR		
Front	91	91
Rear	100	105
BATTERY	212	212
Removal	213	213
Re-fitting	213	213
Carrier	193, 195	203, 204
BODY	168	—
Removal	185	—
Re-fitting	198	—
BRAKE		
Front	77	77
Adjustment	86	86
Cable	126	130
Cam	90	90
Linings	88, 92	88, 92
Plate	88	88
Pivot	90	90
Shoe	92	92
Rear	99	99
Adjustment	107	107
Cam	110	110
Lining	88, 111	88, 111
Plate	110	110
Pivot	110	110
Shoe	110	110
Pedal	108	108
Rod	103, 108	103, 108
BULKHEAD		
Removal	193	203
Re-fitting	194	204
CABLES	126	126
Lubrication	124	124
Brake	126	130
Clutch	126	131
Throttle	127	130
CARBURETTER	19	19
Removal	22	22
Re-fitting	23	23
Cleaning	20	20
Dismantling	22	22
Re-assembling	22	22
Tracing troubles	23	23
CARRIER (REAR)	210	210
CENTRE STAND	183	183
Removal	183	183
Re-fitting	183	183
CLOCK: EIGHT-DAY	164	—
Removal	164	—
Re-fitting	164	—
Adjustment	165	—
CLUTCH	35	35
Adjustment	126	131
Dismantling	28	28
Re-assembling	32	32
COILS	216	216
Removal	216	216
Re-fitting	217	217
CONTACT BREAKER	58	58
Adjustment	58	58
Removal	60	60
Re-fitting	60	60
Points	60	60
Capacitors	60	60
COLD START UNIT	17, 22	17, 22
CRANKCASE	46	46
Centre Bearing	51	51
Centre Oil Seal	51	51
CRANKCASE END COVER N/S	46	46
Ball bearing	52	52
Oil seal	52	52
Joint washer	56	56
CRANKCASE END COVER O/S	47	47
Ball bearing	53	53
Oil seal	53	53
Oil seal collar	53	53
Circlip	53	53
CRANKSHAFT	46	46
Removal	46	46
Re-fitting	55	55
Sprocket alignment	57	57
CYLINDER BARREL	43	43
Removal	37	37
Re-fitting	42	42
CYLINDER HEAD	36	36
Removal	39	39
Re-fitting	42	42
DECARBONISING	36	36
DIP SWITCH	220	220
DUALSEAT	169	169
Removal	169	169
Re-fitting	169	169
Grab handle	169	170
Strap	—	170
Waterproof cover	169	169
ENGINE	14	14
Removal	15	15
Re-fitting	15	15
Sprocket	30	30
Cover	—	155

	LEADER page	ARROW page		LEADER page	ARROW page
EXHAUST PIPES	41	41	INSTRUMENT PANEL	166	—
Removal	37	37	Removal	166	—
Re-fitting	43	43	Re-fitting	166	—
Decarbonising	42	42	INSTRUMENTS	157	—
FILLER CAP (PETROL TANK)	174	175	Removal	157	—
Sealing rings	174	175	Re-fitting	157	—
FLASHING INDICATORS	220	—	LEG SHIELD	155	—
Fitting	220	—	Removal	155	—
Switch	222	—	Re-fitting	155	—
Warning light	160	—	LICENCE HOLDER	167	146
Unit (flasher)	222	—	LIFTING HANDLE	168	173
FLYWHEEL	29	29	LUBRICATION CHART	10	10
FOOTREST	182	182	MIRROR (REAR VIEW)		
Removal	182	182	Fitting	211	—
Re-fitting	182	182	MUDGUARD		
FORK LEG ASSEMBLIES	135	135	Front	153	153
Dismantling	135	135	Removal	153	153
Re-assembling	140	140	Re-fitting	154	154
FRAME			Rear		
Removal	185	201	Removal	190	202
Re-fitting	193	203	Re-fitting	196	206
Fittings	192	203	NEUTRAL INDICATOR	225	—
FRONT FORK	132	132	Fitting	225	—
Removal	141	146	PANNIERS	208	—
Re-fitting	142	146	Fitting	208	—
FRONT SHIELD	167	—	Removal	209	—
Removal	185	—	Lock and keys	210	—
Re-fitting	200	—	PARKING LIGHT	165	—
FRONT STAND	183	183	Fitting	165	—
GEAR BOX	61	61	Removal	166	—
Kick starter case cover	61	61	PETROL TANK	174	175
Kick starter case	71	71	Removal	174	175
Dismantling	65	65	Re-fitting	175	175
Re-assembling	72	72	Special three gallon	174	175
Sprocket	67	67	PETROL TAP	174	175
GLOVE BOX	168	—	PILLION FOOTREST	182	182
Lid	168	—	PISTON	43	43
Lock	168	—	Removal	37	37
Lining	168	—	Re-fitting	41	41
HANDLEBAR	124	124, 129	PISTON RINGS	41, 43	41, 43
Control levers	125	125	PRIMARY CHAIN	24	24
Cover	124	—	Adjustment	25	25
Removing	185	129	Alignment	57	57
Re-fitting	200	129	Case	25	25
HEADLAMP	213	214	Removal	29	29
Cowl	167	—	Re-fitting	32	32
Shell	167	214	Oil seals	34	34
Trimmer rod	167	—	PROP STAND	184	184
Unit	213	214	Fitting	184	184
Removal	136	214	REAR CARRIER	210	210
Re-fitting	141	214	REAR CHAIN	120	120
HORN	214	216	Adjustment	118	118
Removal	214	216	Removal	120	120
Re-fitting	215	216	Re-fitting	197	206
HYDRAULIC UNITS					
Front	139	139			
Rear	180	180			
Supplementary springs	182	182			

	LEADER page	ARROW page		LEADER page	ARROW page
REAR CHAIN CASE	111	111	SPEEDOMETER—*continued*		
Removal	111	111	Cable	158	163
Re-fitting	197	206	Spindle (gear box)	65	65
REAR FENDER	211	—	STEERING HEAD	133	145
			Adjustment	133	145
REAR FORK	176	179	Bearings	147	147
Removal	176	179	STOP LIGHT		
Re-fitting	179	179	Switches	219	219
Pivot bushes	177	177			
			TAIL SECTION	172	173
REAR MUDGUARD			Removal	172	173
Removal	190	202	Re-fitting	172	173
Re-fitting	196	206	TOOL BOX	—	170
REAR NUMBER PLATE	172	173	TYRES	97, 124	97, 124
RECTIFIER	217	217	WHEEL ALIGNMENT	122	122
SIDE PANELS	154	—	WHEEL FRONT	76	76
Removal	154	—	Removal	76	76
Re-fitting	154	—	Re-fitting	85	85
SILENCER	41	41	Bearings	93	93
Removal	37	37	WHEEL REAR	98	98
Re-fitting	43	43	Removal	98	105
Decarbonising	42	42	Re-fitting	105	105
SMALL END BUSH	44	44	Bearings	113	113
Removal	44	44	Sprocket	111	111
Re-fitting	44	44	WHEEL BUILDING	97, 123	97, 123
SPARKING PLUGS	18	18	WINDSCREEN	155	211
SPEEDOMETER	157	163	Removal	155	—
Removal	157	163	Re-fitting	156	211
Re-fitting	158	163	Extension	157	—

SUPPLEMENTARY INSTRUCTIONS FOR SPORTS ARROW

The Workshop Manual covers the Sports Arrow apart from the following additional information:—

Technical Data

Specially tuned engine.

Compression ratio	10 : 1 (as standard 1961 Arrow).
B.H.P.	20 at 6,500 r.p.m.
Carburetter	Amal Monobloc Type 376/277.
Choke size	$1\frac{1}{16}$ in.
Main Jet	230.
Pilot Jet	30.
Needle Jet	105.
Needle Position	No. 3.
Throttle Valve	$3\frac{1}{2}$.

Important Note

All details in the Manual are applicable apart from the carburation, the adjustments are as stated, but as this is a relatively high performance engine, the adjustment is more critical, and whilst the needle position is stated as No. 3, this may not be entirely satisfactory for every engine, and in the event of apparent weak mixture, after normal adjustment has been carried out, it may be desirable to raise the needle one notch, and in the event of rich mixture to lower the needle one notch, followed by resetting the external adjuster as required.

IT IS ESSENTIAL TO USE PREMIUM GRADE FUEL IN THIS ENGINE AT ALL TIMES WITH OIL AS RECOMMENDED ON PAGE 10

SUPPLEMENTARY INSTRUCTIONS FOR THE 200 c.c. ENGINE MODEL 1964

The normal Workshop Manual covers the 200 Model apart from the following additional information:—

Technical Data: Ariel Twin Two-Stroke Engine.

Capacity	199.4 c.c.
Bore	48.5 m.m. (1.909 in.)
Stroke	54 m.m. (2.125 in.)
Compression ratio	9.5 to 1
Maximum power	14 B.H.P. at 6,250 r.p.m.
Maximum speed	Approx. 65 m.p.h.
Fuel consumption	90 to 100 m.p.g. at 40 m.p.h.
M.P.H. per 1,000 r.p.m. in top gear	10.7
Sprocket sizes	Engine ... 22 T
	Clutch ... 50 T
	Gearbox ... 18 T
	Rear wheel ... 49 T
Rear chain	$\frac{1}{2}$ in. pitch 114 links
Overall gear ratios	Top ... 6.2 to 1
	3rd ... 8.15 to 1
	2nd ... 11.5 to 1
	1st ... 19.8 to 1
Carburetter	Amal Monobloc $\frac{13}{16}$ in. bore Type 375/57
	Main Jet ... 130
	Pilot Jet ... 30
	Needle Jet ... 104 (with angled spray tube)
	Slide 375 ... $3\frac{1}{2}$
	Needle B
	No. 3 Notch
Petrol/Oil ratio	32 to 1

For all other details refer to the respective sections of the Workshop Manual. Maintenance should be regularly carried out as recommended, particular attention being paid to tyres, brakes and chains.

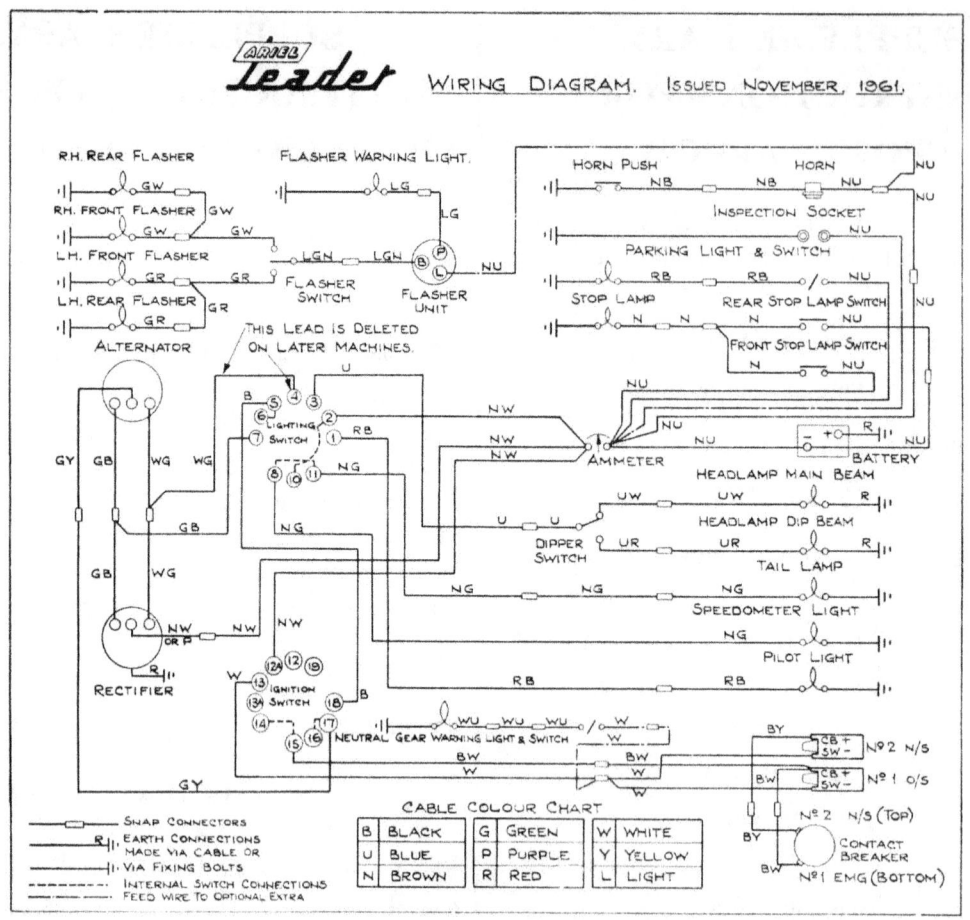

1962 onward (with key type ignition switch).

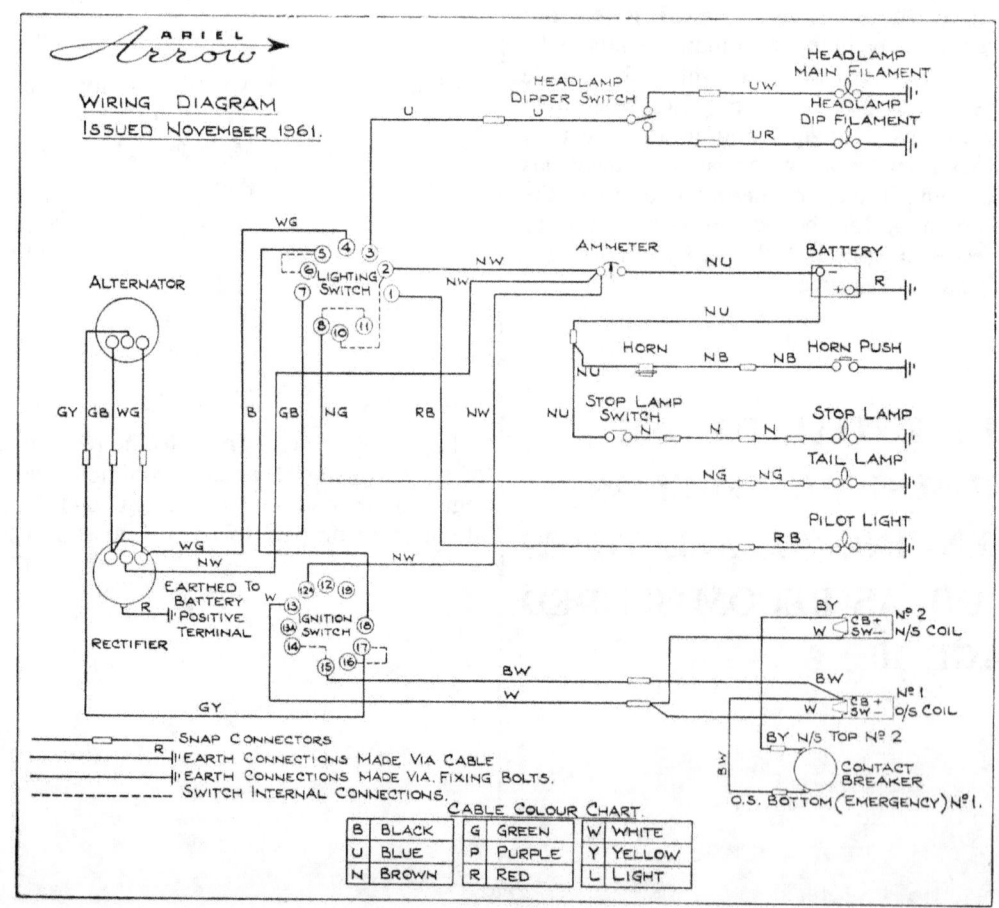

SPARE PARTS LIST
FOR
ARIEL
THE MODERN MOTOR CYCLE

AND

250 c.c. TWIN CYLINDER
TWO STROKE

ARIEL MOTORS LTD.
BIRMINGHAM

PLATE NO. 1 Ref. Nos.	PART NO.	DESCRIPTION OF PART	NO. PER SET
		CYLINDERS, CRANKCASE AND FITTINGS	
1	A7-1057	Carburetter flange joint washer (inter 12019-54)	1
	T137	Carburetter flange washer ... Sports Arrow only	1
2	T136	Cylinder head L/S	1
3	T55	Cylinder base joint washer	2
4	T43	Cylinder head gasket	2
5	T70	Washer for cylinder head sleeve nut	8
6	T37	Sleeve nut for cylinder head	8
7	T90	Stud (crankcase—cylinder)	8
8	T2051	Sealing washer for exhaust pipe nut	2
9	T2050	Nut securing exhaust pipe	2
10	T135	Cylinder head R/S	1
11	T88	Stud, for footrest	6
12	TSW-7	⅜" Shakeproof washer for T88	6
13	UN1/6F	Nut, for footrest stud	6
	UN2/5F	Nut, for R/S end cover stud	3
	UN2/5F	Nut, carburetter fixing stud	2
14	T94	Stud, crankcase end covers	7
	T94	Stud, carburetter fixing	2
15	TSW-5	5/16" Shakeproof washer	7
16	UN1/5F	Nut, for L/S end cover stud	4
17	T91	Stud for alternator	3
18	TW-17	1" Plain washer	3
19	SN-39	Nut for alternator stud	3
20	T83	Screw for alternator cover	3
21	T41	Cylinder barrel, R/S	1
22	T93	Screw for crankcase end covers	4
23	S5-3	Washer for T93 screw	3
24	T109	Rubber grommet, for alternator cover	1
25	T120	Shim, crankcase cover R/S	as req
	T122	Paper washer, R/S end cover (not used if T120 fitted)	as req
26	T131	Crankcase end cover R/S	1
27	T21	Alternator cover	1
28	T53	Joint ring for alternator cover	1
	T10	Crankcase c/w fixed fittings ... Sports Arrow only	1
29	T10/1	Crankcase c/w fixed fittings	1
	UN5/8C	Crankcase plug bolt ... Arrow only	2
30	T82	Joint washer—oil seal housing	1
31	T40	Cylinder barrel, L/S	1
32	TW-20	7/16" Plain washer for L/S end cover stud	4
33	UN5/12C	Bolt for L/S end cover	1
34	UN4/10C	Bolt for oil seal housing	3
35	T72	Tab washer for oil seal housing bolt	3
36	T12	Crankcase end cover L/S	1
37	T11	Oil seal housing (G box—chaincase)	1
	T753	Oil seal	1
	5775-56	Rubber grommet for T2198/1 cowl ... Arrow	1
	T121	Paper washer for L/S end cover	1
	T2198/1	Cowl for gearbox and crankcase ... Arrow	1
	T2198/2	Cowl for gearbox and crankcase Sports Arrow only	1
	T2202	Felt washer for kickstarter and foot change spindles Arrow only	3
	T71	Anchor pin (connecting link to centre stand)	1
	T2200	Hexagon adaptor, clutch adjuster to T2198/1 cover Arrow	1
	T2110	Spacer for connecting link	2
	T124	Breather pipe assembly	1

PLATE 1 CYLINDERS, CRANKCASE AND FITTINGS

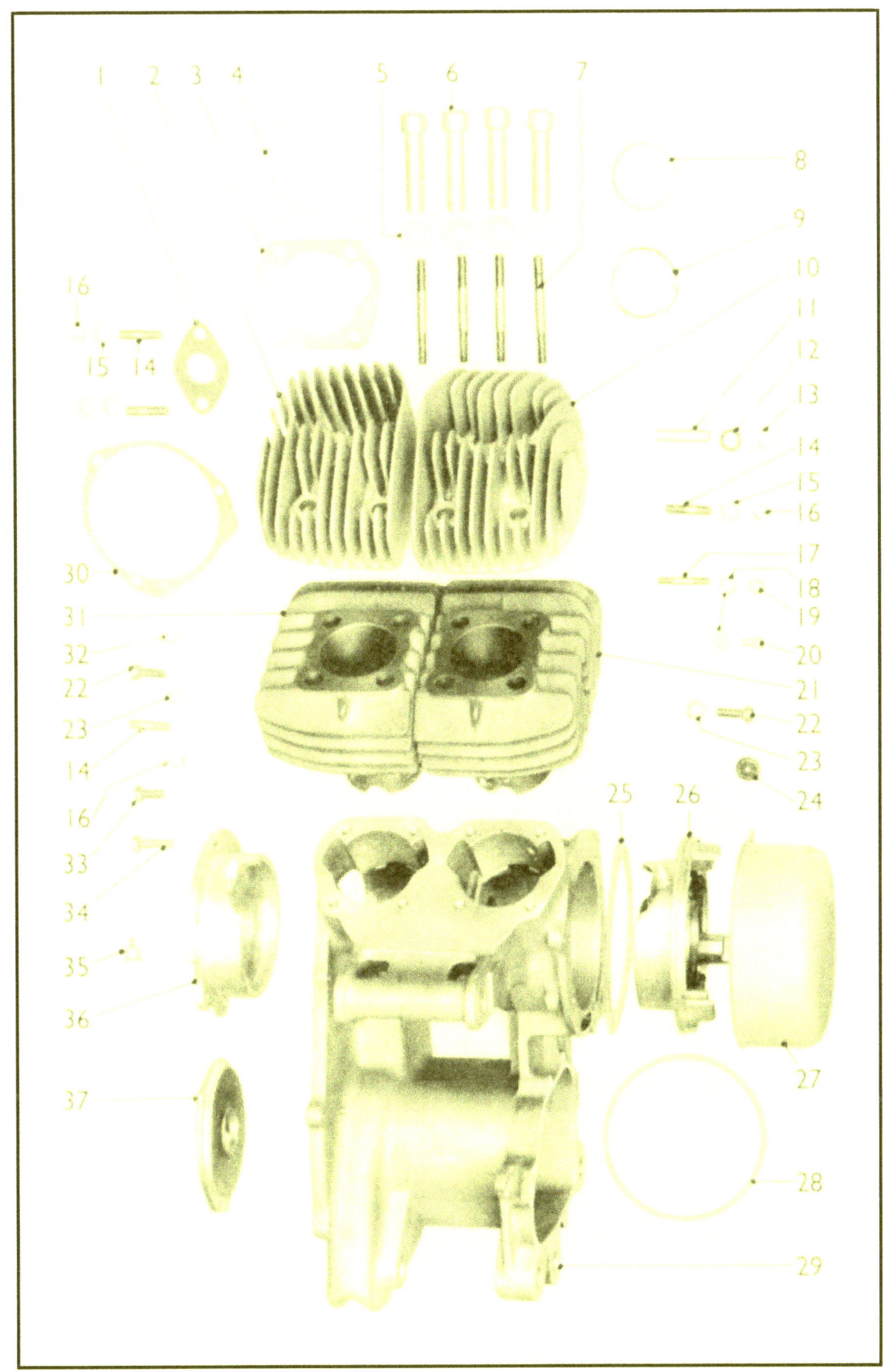

243

PLATE NO. 2 Ref. Nos.	PART NO.	DESCRIPTION OF PART	NO. PER SET
		PISTONS, CON-ROD AND CRANKSHAFT ASSEMBLY	
1	T18	Piston complete (standard)	2
2	T18/2	Piston ring (standard)	4
	T18/3	Piston complete (·020" o size)	2
	T18/5	Piston ring (·020" o size)	4
	T18/6	Piston complete (·040" o size)	2
	T18/8	Piston ring (·040" o size)	4
3	T18/10	Circlip for gudgeon pin	4
4	T18/9	Gudgeon pin	2
5	T31	Small end bush	2
6	T30/1	Connecting rod c/w crankpin, bearings and S.E. bush	2
7	T19/1	Flywheel and sprocket	1
7	T19	Flywheel only	1
9	T80	Key (flywheel—engine sprocket)	1
12	T33	Thrust washer for crankpin	2
13	T79	Key for engine sprocket	1
14	T22	Engine sprocket (22T)	1
15	T50	Oil seal for end covers	2
16	T34	Ball bearing for crankcase (LJ.25) (SKF 6205)	1
16	T34	Ball bearing for end covers (LJ.25) (SKF 6205)	2
17	T26	Outer shaft (L/S crankshaft)	1
18	T25	Inner shaft (L/S crankshaft)	1
	T103	Crankshaft assembly (R/S) c/w inner and outer shafts, con-rod and big end complete	1
	T104	Crankshaft assembly (L/S) c/w inner and outer shafts, con-rod and big end complete	1
19	T49	Oil seal for crankcase	2
20	T45	Key, for locking bolt T29	1
21	T24	Inner shaft (R/S crankshaft)	1
22	T23	Outer shaft (R/S crankshaft)	1
23	T98	Key, mainshaft—rotor	1
24	T101	Circlip for R/S cover bearing	1
25	T58	Collar for R/S crankshaft	1
26	T3011	Alternator complete	1
27	T3012	Cam assembly (contact breaker)	1
28	T51	Oil seal for contact breaker	1
29	T76	Nut for engine sprocket	1
30	T75	Engine sprocket tab washer	1
31	T44	Washer for crankshaft locking bolt	1
32	T29	Locking bolt for inner L/S and R/S crankshaft	1
33	T105	Circlip for T29 locking bolt	1
34	TW-33	Plain washer for rotor bolt	1
35	TSW-9	Shakeproof washer for rotor bolt	1
36	T89	Bolt (rotor—R/S crankshaft)	1
	T128	Shim, R/S end cover bearing (·010")	as req

PLATE 2 PISTON, CON-ROD & CRANKSHAFT ASSEMBLY

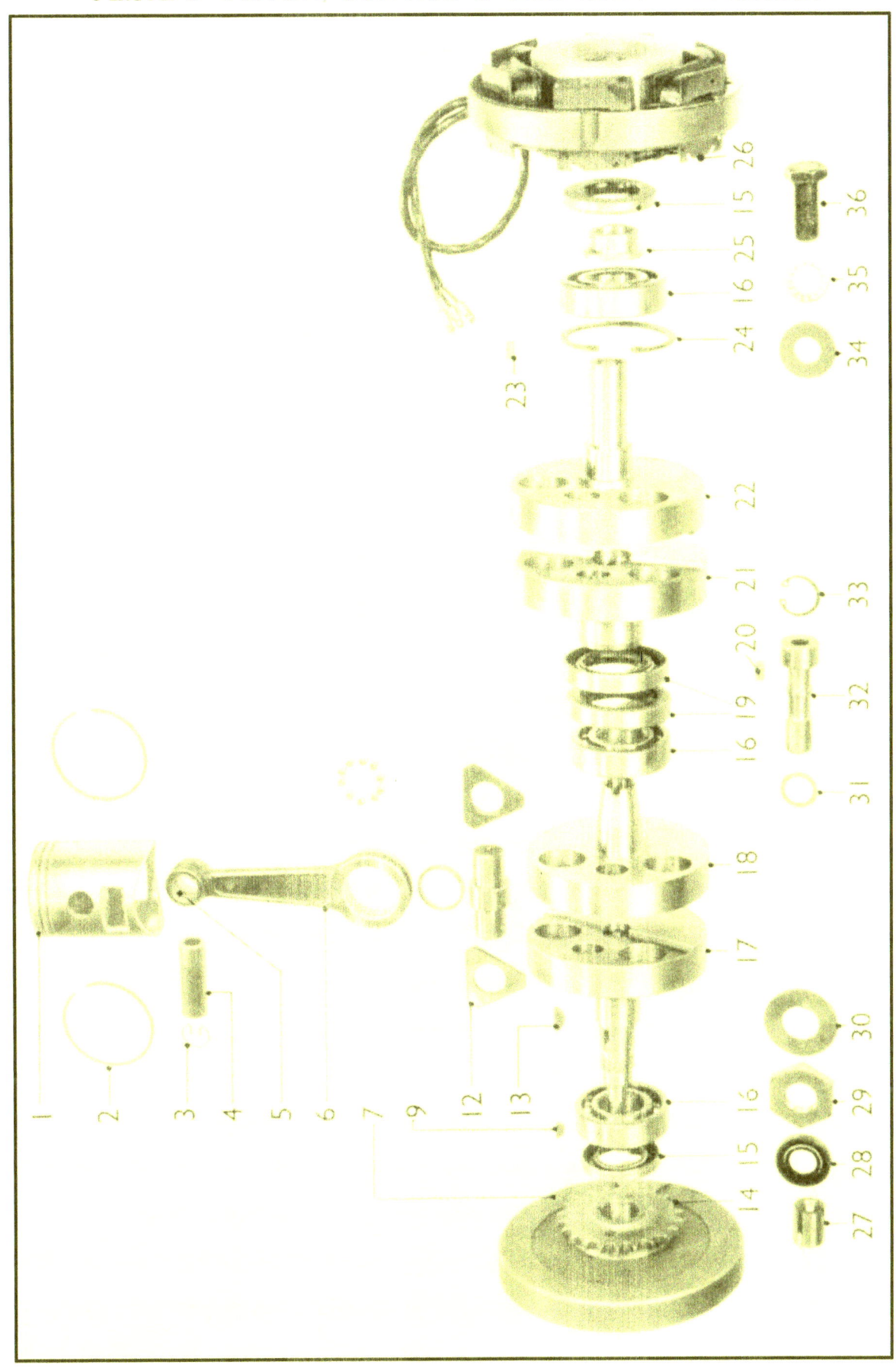

245

PLATE NO. 3 Ref. Nos.	PART NO.	DESCRIPTION OF PART	NO. PER SET
		CONTACT BREAKER, CHAINCASE, CLUTCH AND FITTINGS	
1	ET-428A	Inspection cap for outer chain cover (inter 1596-33, 3342-31)...	1
	ET-428A/1	Inspection cap for outer chain cover Sports Arrow	1
2	T46	Rubber grommet for contact breaker cover	1
3	K359	Washer for inspection cap (inter 10219-54)	1
4	T65	Primary chain adjusting rod	1
5	T3015	Contact breaker complete	1
6	T42	Cover for contact breaker Leader	1
6	T42/F	Cover for contact breaker ...Arrow	1
	T42/1	Cover for contact breaker Sports Arrow	1
	T127	Joint washer for contact breaker cover	1
7	T116	Oil level plug for outer chain-cover	1
8	A6-769	Washer for oil level plug (inter 2101-30)	1
9	UN4/28C	Drain bolt for outer chain-cover	1
	T77	Washer for drain bolt	1
10	T86	Screw (long) for chain-cover	2
11	T87	Screw (short) for chain-cover	6
12	T85	Screw securing contact breaker cover	3
12	T85	Screw securing contact breaker	2
13	T111	Plain washer for contact breaker screw	2
14	T69	Adjuster sleeve for chain tensioner adjusting rod	1
15	T106	Oil seal "O" ring for T69 sleeve	1
16	T64	Tensioner blade for primary chain	1
17	T2570	Screw for adjuster locking plug	1
18	T60	Locking plug for tensioner	1
19	T61	Trunnion for tensioner blade	2
20	T57	Felt plug in crankcase for rear chain lubrication	1
21	T529	Clutch push rod	1
22	T52	Joint washer for chain cover	1
23	T112	Primary chain ($\frac{3}{8}$" pitch × ·225 × 70 pitches)	1
24	T17	Chain cover, outer	1
	T17.1	Chain cover, outer Sports Arrow only	1
25	T97	Saddle nut (nylon) for chain adjuster	1
26	T526	Clutch spring plate c w liners	1
27	T518	Clutch locknut	1
28	T504	Clutch driving plate	2
29	T522	Clutch plate and liners	2
30	T517	Clutch lockwasher... (cancelled)	
31	T532	Clutch mainshaft nut	1
32	T509	Clutch centre	1
	T531	Seating washer	3
33	T515	Washer for T516 clutch nut	1
34	T508	Vane for clutch centre	1
35	T524	Cush drive rubber (large)	3
36	T511	Clutch centre end plate	1
37	T523	Cush drive rubber (small)	3
38	T512	Thrust and locating washer	1
39	T528	Clutch spring nut	3
40	T501	Clutch chainwheel complete	1
41	T521	Clutch spring	3
	T530	Washer for clutch spring	3
42	T507	Clutch spring cup	3
43	T525	Clutch thrust washer	1
44	T519	Clutch spring bolt	3
45	T527	Roller bearing (HOFF B2274A) for clutch chainwheel	18

PLATE 3 CONTACT BREAKER, CHAINCASE, CLUTCH AND FITTINGS

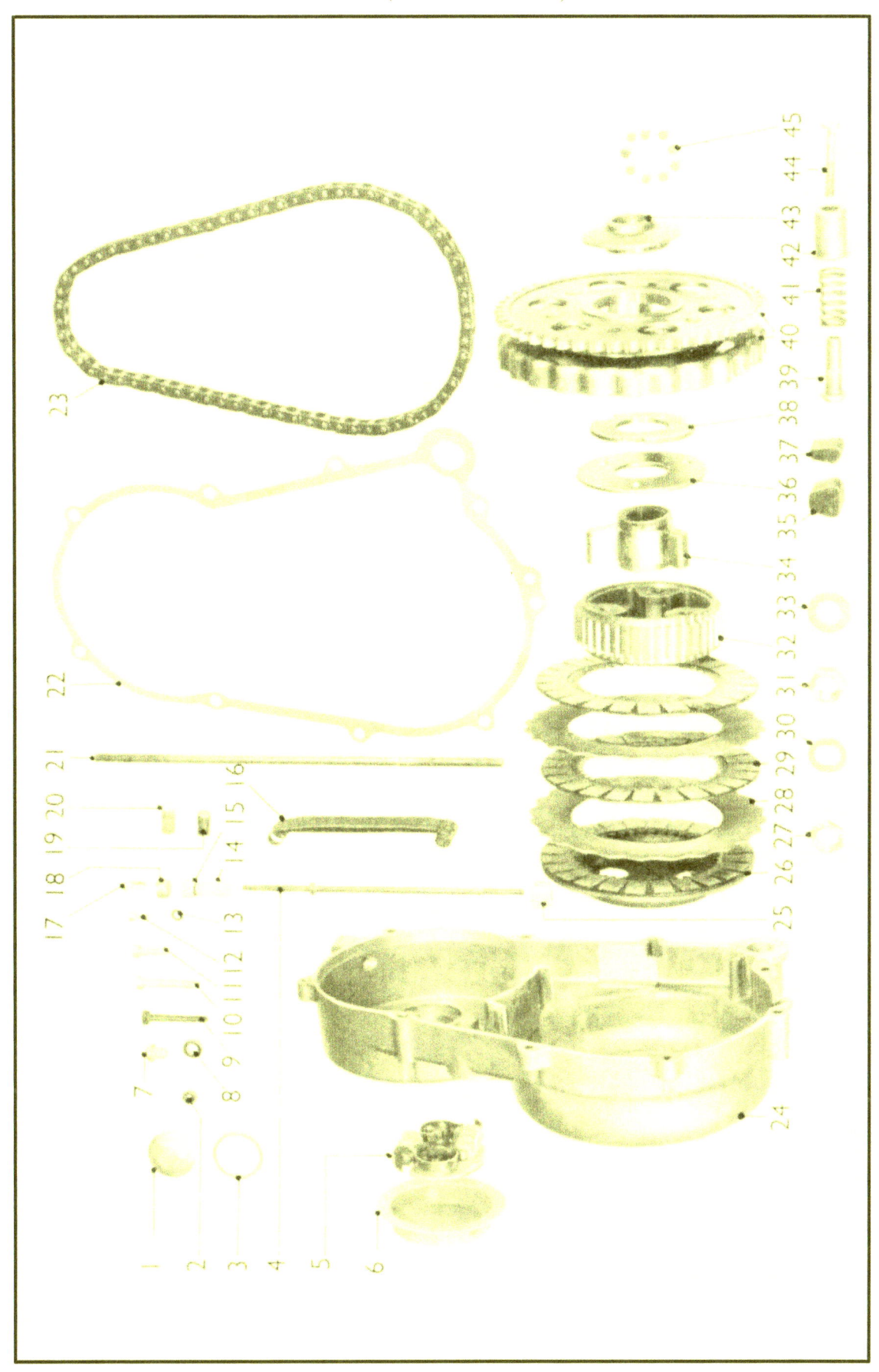

PLATE NO. 4 Ref. Nos.	PART NO.	DESCRIPTION OF PART		NO. PER SET
		KICKSTARTER CASE AND FOOT GEAR CONTROL		
1	T806	Nut, securing inner clutch operating lever		1
2	T770	Spring washer (inter 3752-52 or S5-2)		1
3	T805	Locknut for adjusting screw		1
4	T802	Adjusting screw and ball		1
5	T801	Inner clutch operating lever		1
6	T767	Kickstarter case cover		1
7	T798	Clutch operating lever and spindle		1
	T864	Kickstarter lever (folding type) complete	Sports Arrow	1
8	T760	Kickstarter lever		1
	T865	Kickstarter lever (folding type)	Sports Arrow	1
9	T764	Kickstarter lever pedal (inter 12503-54)		1
	T866	Kickstarter lever pedal (folding type)	Sports Arrow	1
	T853/1	Kickstarter pedal rubber		1
10	T857	Distance collar for kickstarter spindle		1
11	T785	Kickstarter spring pin		1
12	T784	Kickstarter spring (inter 3335-48)		1
13	T792	Cam spindle		1
14	T751	Joint washer, between kickstarter case and gearbox		1
15	T768	Joint washer for kickstarter case cover		1
16	T783	Kickstarter quadrant		1
17	UN1/4F	Nut for gearbox-cover studs		7
	S5-2	Spring washer (¼" I dia.)		7
18	T777	Screw, kickstarter case cover—kickstarter case to gearbox		1
19	T756	Stud, kickstarter case to kickstarter case cover		1
20	T779	Washer for drain plug and oil level plug		2
21	T778	Oil level plug and oil drain plug		2
22	T757	Dowel, gearbox—kickstarter case covers		2
23	T755	Stud, gearbox—kickstarter case cover		6
24	T782	Kickstarter spindle		1
25	T773	Kickstarter spindle bush		1
26	T771	Kickstarter case c/w bushes		1
27	T759/1	Foot change lever		1
	T863	Chromed cover for foot change lever		1
	T761	Foot change lever rubber		1
28	T807	Clutch adjuster cover		1
29	T790	Oil seal ring (inter 12493-54)		1
30	T766	Oil seal washer		1
31	T808	Joint washer for T807 cover		1
32	T789	Spring for quadrant spindle (inter 3746-52)		1
33	UN5/22F	Bolt for foot change lever		1
	T872	Washer for T870 bolt	Sports Arrow	1
	T871	Nut for T870 bolt	Sports Arrow	1
	T867	Nut for folding kickstarter pedal	Sports Arrow	1
	UN2/5F	Nut for UN5/22F bolt		1
33	T765	Bolt for kickstarter lever (inter 12502-54)		1
	T870	Bolt for kickstarter lever	Sports Arrow	1
34	T809	Screw for T807 adjuster cover		2
	T869	Spring washer for kickstarter pedal	Sports Arrow	1
	T868	Washer for kickstarter pedal (inter 3701-55)	Sports Arrow	1
35	T791	Quadrant return spring		1
36	T787	Quadrant and peg		1
37	T793	Gear change cam		1
38	T786	Quadrant spindle		1
39	T812	Speedometer spindle thrust button (inter 3160-31)		1
40	T774	Quadrant spindle bush (inner) (inter 3720-52)		1
41	T810	Speedometer spindle		1
42	T795	Washer for cam spindle		1

Continued

PLATE 4 KICKSTARTER CASE AND FOOT GEAR CONTROL

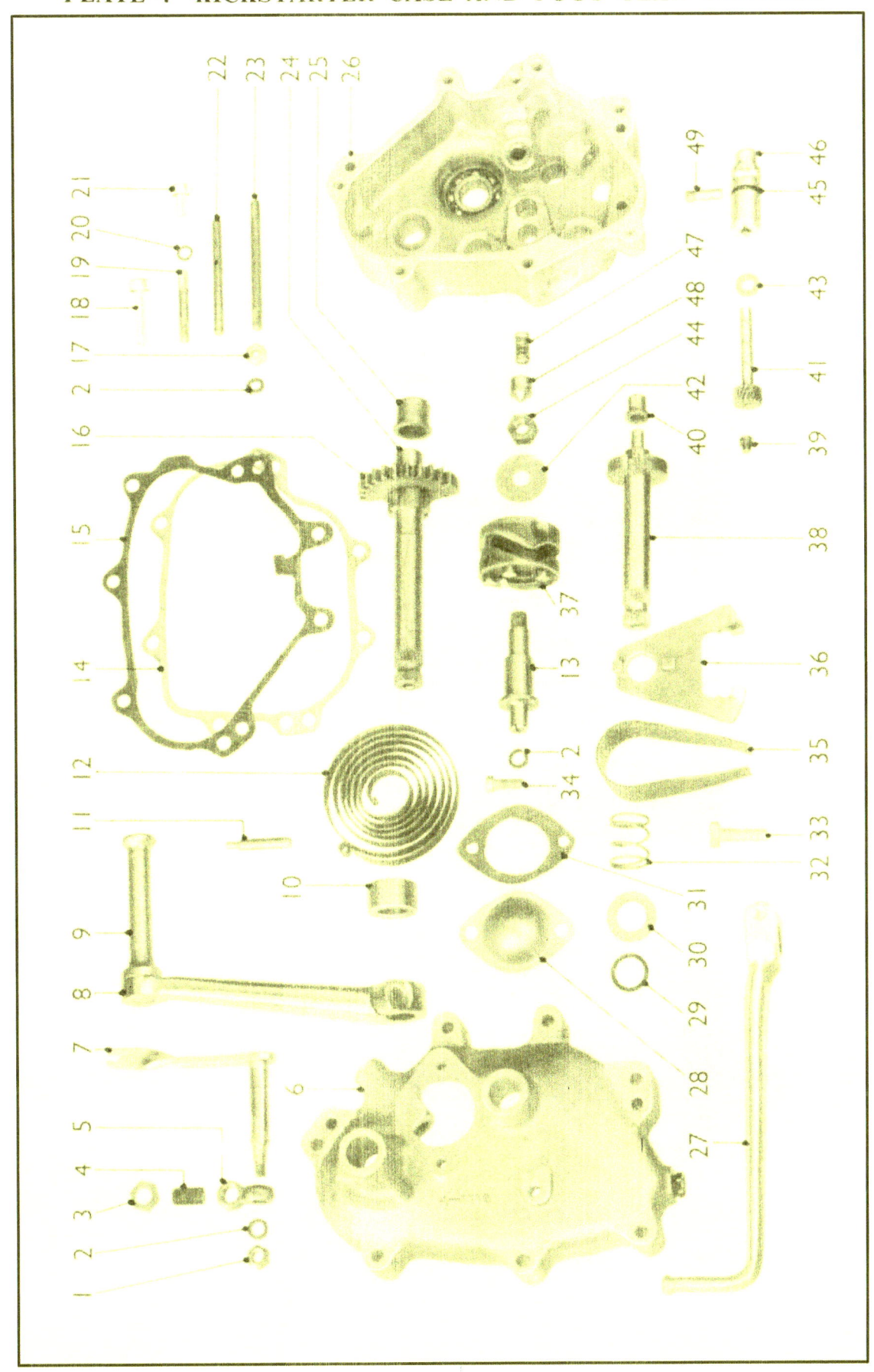

PLATE NO. 4 Ref. Nos.	PART NO.	DESCRIPTION OF PART	NO. PER SET

KICKSTARTER CASE AND FOOT GEAR CONTROL

Ref.	Part No.	Description	No.
43	T811	Speedometer spindle thrust washer (inter 3665–52)	1
44	T794	Nut for cam spindle	1
45	T781	Oil seal for speedometer spindle bush (inter 3666–52)	1
46	T775	Speedometer spindle bush	1
47	T797	Cam plunger spring (inter 3709–52)	1
48	T796	Cam plunger (inter 3707–55)	1
49	T780	Cotter pin, securing speedometer spindle bush (inter 3164–31)	1
	T854	Plug for kickstarter case	1
	T859	Washer (fibre) for T854 plug	1
	S5–3	Spring washer for T765	1

PLATE NO. 5 Ref. Nos.	PART NO.	DESCRIPTION OF PART	NO. PER SET

GEARBOX FITTINGS

Ref.	Part No.	Description	No.
1	T828	Split pin for dowel (inter 3741–52)	1
2	T827	Dowel for selector spindle (inter 3739–52)	2
3	T849	Selector fork complete (mainshaft)	1
4	T851	Selector fork (mainshaft)	1
5	T826	Washer	1
6	T825	Selector spindle nut (mainshaft)	1
7	T830	Mainshaft nut (kickstarter end) (inter 3626–52)	1
8	T831	Mainshaft nut lockwasher (inter 3684–55)	1
9	T832	Driving ratchet (inter 3680–52)	1
10	T833	Ratchet pinion	1
11	T835	Ratchet pinion spring (inter 3196–33)	1
12	T834	Ratchet pinion bush (inter 3683–52)	1
	T858	Distance piece for T834 bush	1
13	T837	Bearing retaining ring, kickstarter end (inter 3628–52)	1
14	T836	Ball race, kickstarter end (3176–33)	1
15	T838	First gear, mainshaft	1
16	T820	Bush for third gear, mainshaft	1
17	T840	Third gear and bush (mainshaft)	1
18	T839	Second gear, mainshaft	1
19	T842	Driving gear and bush	1
20	T844	Driving gear bush	2
21	T752	Circlip (driving gear ball race)	1
22	T750	Ball bearing (62 mm × 35mm × 14mm)	1
23	T754	Driving gear oil seal	1
24	T845	Sprocket spacing collar	1
25	T846	Driving sprocket	1
26	T856	Driving gear nut distance washer	1
27	T848	Driving gear nut lockwasher (inter 3091–33)	1
28	T847	Driving gear nut (inter 3089–33)	1
29	T829	Mainshaft	1
30	T813	Layshaft	1
31	T815	Layshaft first gear and bush	1
32	T762	Layshaft bush	2
33	T817	First gear bush (layshaft)	1
34	T821	Third gear (layshaft)	1
35	T822	Selector fork complete (layshaft)	1
36	T824	Selector fork (layshaft)	1
37	T818	Second gear and bush (layshaft)	1
	T820	Bush for second gear (layshaft)	1
38	T814	Layshaft pinion	1
39	T763	Washer (crankcase—layshaft)	1
40	T758	Dowel for layshaft bushes (inter 12443–55)	2

PLATE 5 GEARBOX FITTINGS

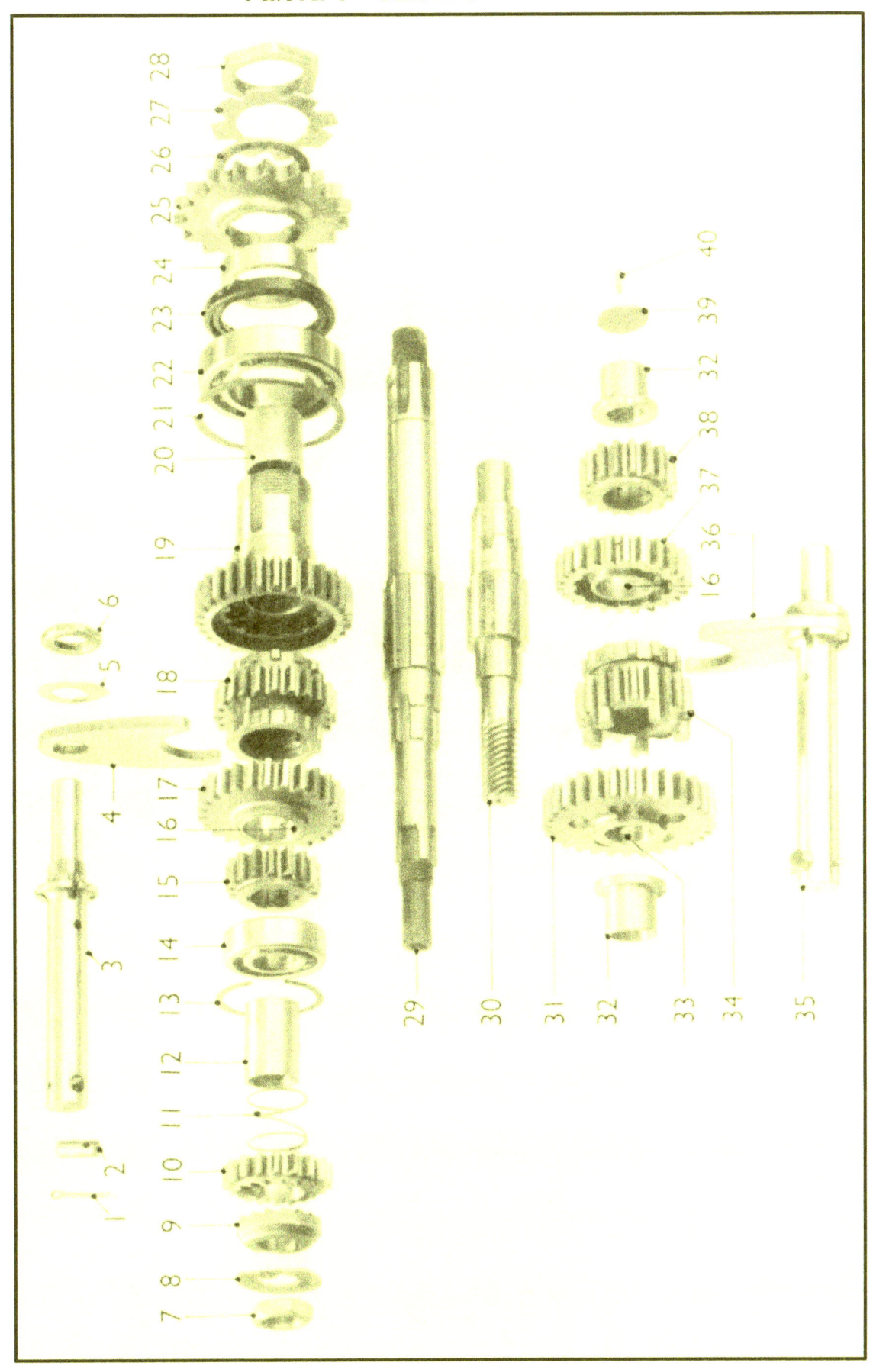

PLATE NO. 6 Ref. Nos.	PART NO.	DESCRIPTION OF PART	NO. PER SET
		FRONT FORKS, MUDGUARD AND FITTINGS	
	T1157	Front forks complete	1
1	SN-34	Nut for anchor bar bolt	1
2	T1564	Dust cover for anchor bar	4
3	T1056	Ball and bush for anchor bar	2
4	T1526	Slotted nut for anchor bar bolt	1
5	T1558	Split pin for slotted nut	1
6	T1585	Anchor bar c/w ball and bush	1
7	T1159	Bolt securing anchor bar, front	1
	SN-34	Bolt for T1159 bolt	1
8	SN-37	Nut for cover plate screw	2
9	T1055	Screw for T1034 and T1035 cover plate	2
	T1116	Rubber for T1055 screw	2
10	T1054	Pinch bolt for L S suspension lever	1
11	TW-20	Plain washer	1
12	SN-42	Nut for T1054 pinch bolt	1
13	T1049	Suspension lever pivot bolt	2
	SN-34	Nut for T1049 pivot bolt	2
14	T1001	Suspension lever L S	1
15	T1053	Bush for suspension lever	8
16	T1061	Damper unit complete	2
	T1033	Spring for damper unit	2
17	T1061/2	Centre cap, damper top	2
18	T1061/1	Damper nut, top fixing	2
19	UN1 5F	Nut for mudguard bolt UN5 14F	1
	TSW-5	Shakeproof washer for UN1 5F nut	1
20	UN5 14F	Bolt, mudguard, front section to crown	1
21	TW-20	Plain washer for UN5/14F bolt	1
22	UN5 10F	Bolt, for mudguard, rear section	1
	TSW-5	Shakeproof washer for UN5 10F bolt	1
23	T1061/3	Outer cap for damper top	4
24	T1061/4	Rubber for damper top	4
	T1125	Front damper cover ... Arrow	2
25	TW-17	¼" Plain washer	8
26	UN4 8F	Bolt, mudguard to fork bracket	8
	TW-17	Plain washer for UN4 8F bolt	8
	TSW-4	Shakeproof washer for UN4 8F bolt	8
	SN-37	Nut for UN4 8F bolt	8
27	T1061/5	Distance tube for damper top	2
28	T1051	Bearing distance piece (long)	2
29	T1059	Pivot bolt for R/S suspension lever	1
	SN-34	Nut for T1059 pivot bolt	1
30	T1040	Distance piece for R S suspension lever	1
31	T1000	Front suspension lever R S	1
32	UN2 6F	Nut for fork end bolt	2
	TSW-7	Shakeproof washer for fork end bolt	2
33	T1058	Tab washer for fork end bolt (cancelled)	
34	T1052	Bearing distance piece (short)	2
35	T1050	Bolt for fork end	2
36	T1039	Handlebar lock ... Leader	1
37	D8-21	Nut for steering column (inter 4835-36)	2
38	T1017	Dust cover for steering head race	1
39	D10-2	Cone for steering head ball race (top) (inter 4818-31)	1
40	D10-137	Ball race for frame head lug (top) (inter 4820-36)	1
41	T1044	Bottom steering head cone	1
42	T1043	Ball race for frame head lug (bottom)	1
	S9-2	Steel ball for head races (23 for bottom race, 20 for top race)	43
	T1126	Handlebar bracket ... Arrow	1
	T1111	Pinch bolt for T1126 bracket ... Arrow	1
	T1128	Handlebar clamp ... Arrow	2
	T1129	Bolt for T1128 clamp ... Arrow	4
	TSW-5	Shakeproof washer for T1129 bolt ... Arrow	4
	UN1 5F	Nut for T1129 bolt ... Arrow	4
	T1130	Cover for handlebar stem ... Arrow	1

Continued

PLATE 6 FRONT FORKS, MUDGUARD AND FITTINGS

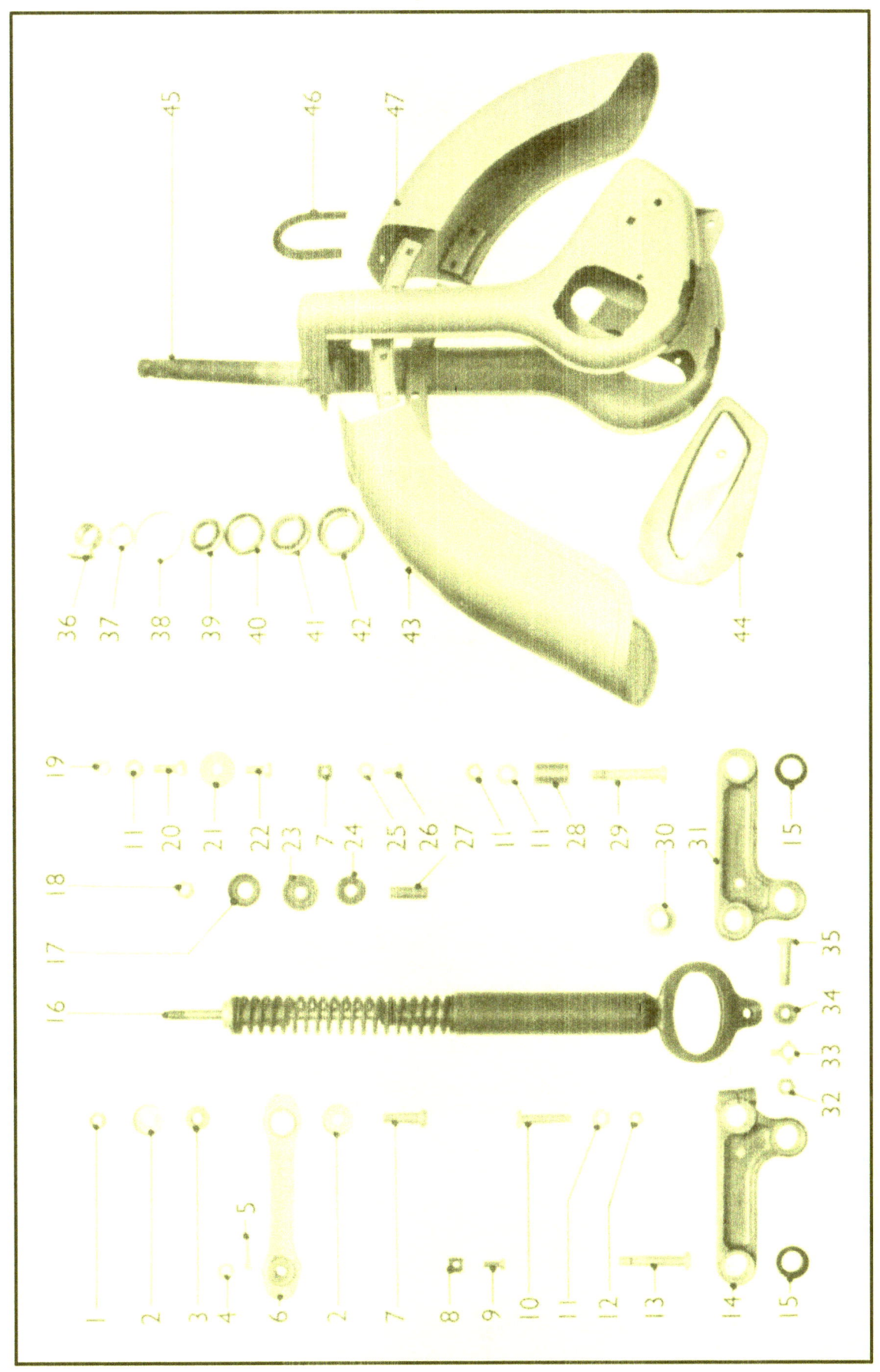

PLATE NO. 6 Ref. Nos.	PART NO.	DESCRIPTION OF PART	NO. PER SET

FRONT FORKS, MUDGUARD AND FITTINGS

PLATE NO. 6 Ref. Nos.	PART NO.	DESCRIPTION OF PART	NO. PER SET
43	T1021 1	Front mudguard, rear section	1
	T1034 1	Front fork cover plate L/S ... Sports Arrow	1
44	T1034	Front fork cover plate L/S ... ... Leader	1
	T1034 F	Front fork cover plate L/S ... ...Arrow	1
44	T1035	Front fork cover plate R/S ... ... Leader	1
	T1035 F	Front fork cover plate R/S ... ...Arrow	1
	T1035 1	Front fork cover plate ... ... Sports Arrow	1
45	T1161	Steering column and fork leg assembly	1
46	T1046	Rubber moulding	2
47	T1020 1	Mudguard, front section	1
	T1019	Front mudguard complete (front and rear section) ...	1
	T2610	Rubber grommet for fork leg	2
	T1156	Cover for anchor bar bracket	1
	UN2/5F	Nut for T1111 bolt	1

PLATE NO. 7 Ref. Nos.	PART NO.	DESCRIPTION OF PART	NO. PER SET

FRONT WHEEL AND FITTINGS

PLATE NO. 7 Ref. Nos.	PART NO.	DESCRIPTION OF PART	NO. PER SET
	T1578 1	Front wheel complete (less tyre and tube)	1
	T1579	Front hub, rim and spokes only, built up	1
1	T1573	Front hub only	1
2	T1509	Circlips for bearings	2
3	T1556	Grease retaining cup, L/S	1
4	T1513	Felt washer, L/S	1
5	T1557	Felt washer retaining cup, L/S	1
6	T1511	Hub bearing, L/S	1
7	T1510	Hub bearing, R/S	1
8	T1515	Grease retaining plate, R/S	1
9	T1516	Hub spindle	1
10	T1518	Nut for hub spindle	1
	T1562	Grease plug for hub spindle	1
11	UN6 18F	Bolt securing anchor bar	1
12	SN-34	Nut for anchor bar bolt	1
13	T1056	Ball and bush for anchor bar	2
14	T1585	Anchor bar c/w ball and bush	1
	T1154	Anchor bar bracket	1
15	T1564	Dust cover for anchor bar	4
16	T1569 1	Brake shoe c/w lining	2
17	T1508	Brake lining c/w rivets	2
	T1588	Spring (brake shoe to brake plate)	2
18	C13-5	Brake shoe return spring (inter 4110-26) ...	2
19	T1568	Pivot for brake shoe	1
20	T1528	Front brake cam lever	1
21	T1523 1	Brake cam	1
	UN2 5F	Nut for brake lever	1
	T1575	Spring washer	1
22	T1529	Felt washer for cam spindle	1
23	C13-66	Washer for cam spindle (inter 4118-29) ...	1
24	T1517	Bush (hub spindle to brake plate)	1
25	T1522	Bush for brake plate	1
26	T1587	Front brake plate	1
	T1587 1	Front brake plate c/w brake shoes, etc. ...	1
	T1154	Anchor bar bracket	1
27	UN5 36F	Bolt for pivot	1
28	TW-20	Washer for pivot bolt	1
29	SN-42	Nut for pivot bolt	1
	T1520	Spoke	36
	T1520 1	Nipple for spoke	36
	T1519	Rim (WM2-16)	1
	T1562	Grease nipple for brake plate	1
	SN-34	Nut for anchor bolt	1

PLATE 7   FRONT & REAR HUB, BRAKES AND FITTINGS

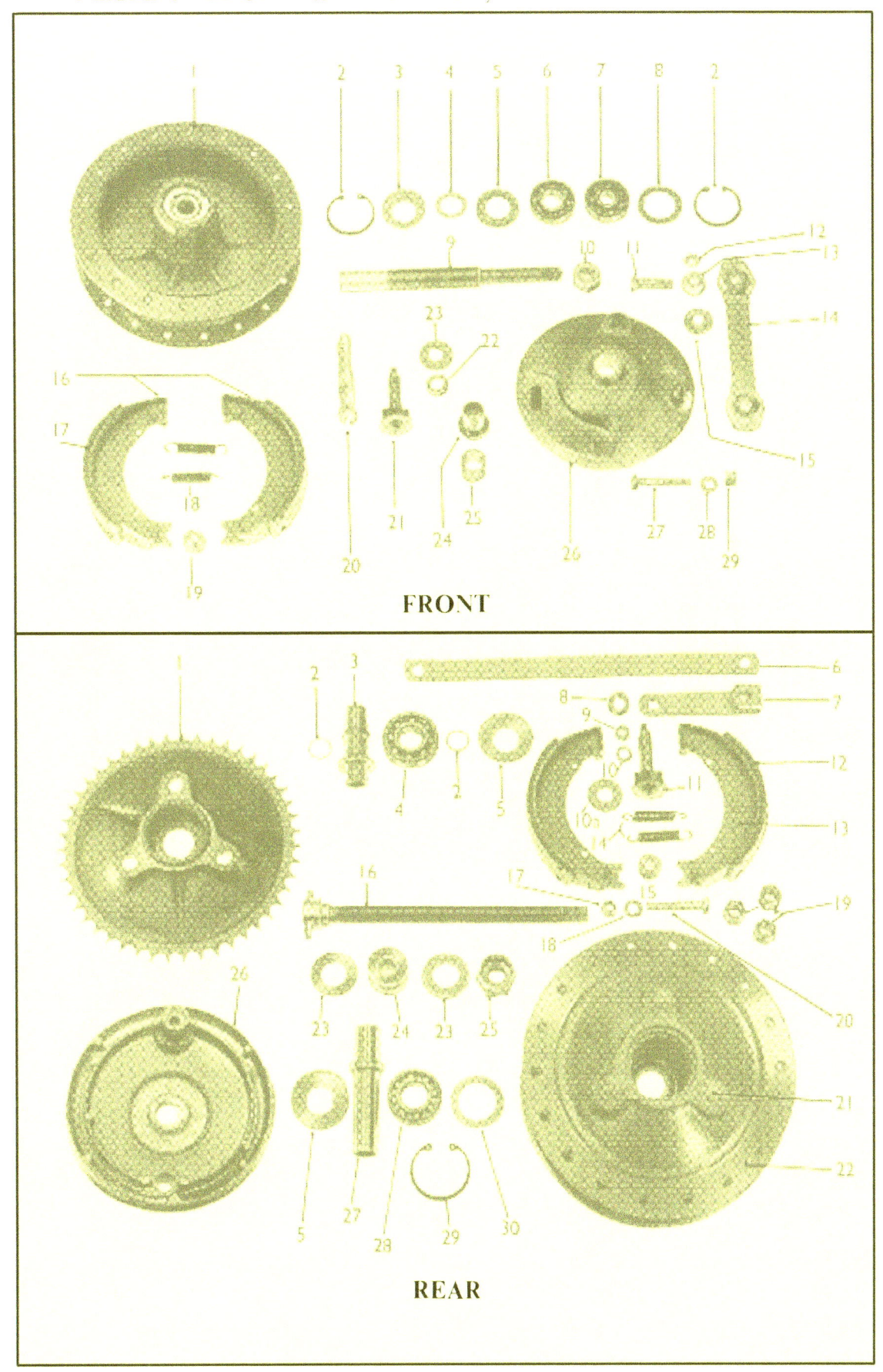

FRONT

REAR

PLATE NO. 7 Ref. Nos.	PART NO.	DESCRIPTION OF PART	NO. PER SET
	T1581/1	Rear wheel complete (less tyre and tube)	1
	T1582	Hub, rim and spokes only, built up	1
1	T1546/1	Rear chain sprocket	1
2	T1537	Circlip for fixed spindle	2
3	T1536	Fixed spindle	1
4	T1534	Bearing for sprocket	1
5	T1535	Grease retaining cup	2
6	T1552	Anchor bar	1
7	T1576	Brake cam lever	1
	T1577	Washer for brake lever	1
8	T1529	Felt washer for brake cam spindle	1
9	UN2 5F	Nut for brake lever	1
10	T1575	Spring washer	1
10A	4118-29	Plain washer for cam spindle	1
11	T1523/1	Brake cam assembly	1
12	T1508	Brake lining c/w rivets	2
13	T1569/1	Brake shoe c/w lining	2
14	C13/5	Brake shoe return spring (inter 4110-26)	2
15	T1568	Pivot for brake shoe	1
16	T1538	Rear hub spindle	1
17	SN-42	Nut for pivot bolt	1
18	TW-20	Plain washer for pivot bolt	1
19	T1547	Spherical nut securing chain sprocket	3
20	UN5 28F	Bolt for pivot	1
21	C30/19	Brake drum drive stud	3
	4218-56	Peg securing C30/19 stud	3
22	T1584	Rear hub c/w studs only	1
23	T1545	Outside washer for hub spindle	2
24	T1543	Slip collar	1
25	T1542	Hub spindle nut	1
26	T1586	Rear brake plate	1
	T1586/1	Rear brake plate c/w shoes, etc.	1
	T1588	Spring, brakeshoe to brake plate	2
27	T1544	Ball race distance piece	1
28	T1511	Bearing for hub	1
29	T1509	Circlip for hub tube	1
30	T1515	Grease retaining plate	1
	T1519	Rim (WM2-16)	1
	T1520	Spoke	36
	T1520/1	Nipple for spoke	36
	T1562	Grease plug	1
	T1087	Bolt for anchor bar	1
	TW-25	Plain washer for anchor bolt	1
	SN-34	Nut (¼" UNF NT D126) for anchor bar bolt	1
	SN-34	Nut for anchor bolt	1

PLATE 7 FRONT & REAR HUB, BRAKES AND FITTINGS

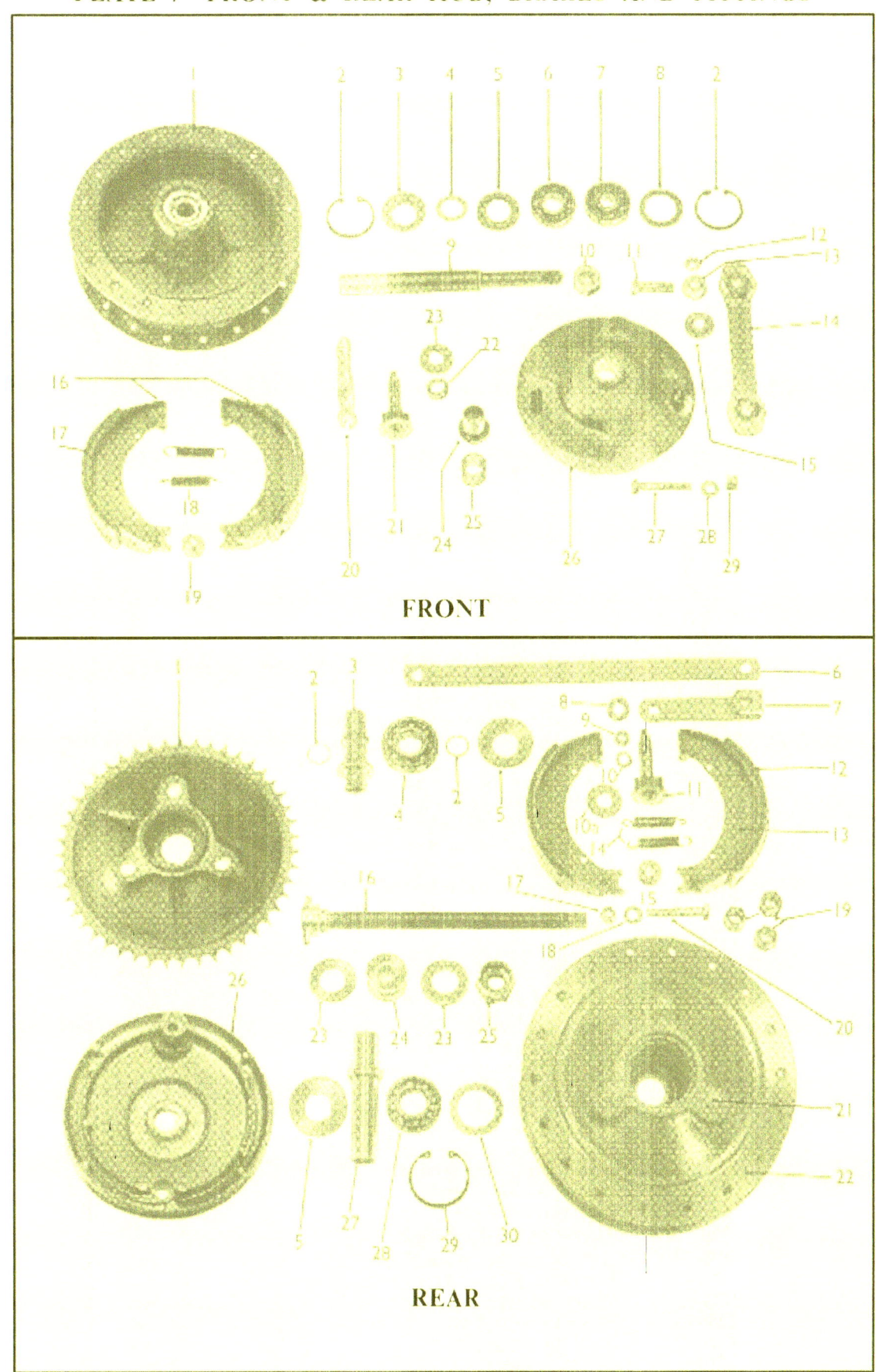

FRONT

REAR

PLATE NO. 8 Ref. Nos.	PART NO.	DESCRIPTION OF PART		NO. PER SET
		REAR SUSPENSION AND REAR CHAINCASE		
1	T2118	Rear chain (⅜" × ·305" × 113 pitches)		1
2	T2102	Rubber pad for pillion footrest		2
3	T1062/1	Locknut for rear damper unit (top)		2
4	T1061 1	Locknut for damper unit (top)		2
5	T1061 3	Outer cap for damper unit (top)		4
6	T1061 5	Distance tube for damper unit (top)		2
7	T1061 4	Rubber for damper unit (top)		4
8	T1061 2	Centre cap for damper unit (top)		2
	T1078	Spring for rear damper unit		2
	T1123	Supplementary spring for rear damper unit		2
	T1124	Seating washer for T1123 spring		4
9	T1062	Rear damper unit		2
10	T1112	Pillion footrest only		2
	T2129	Pillion footrest and rubber pad		2
11	T1552	Rear brake plate anchor bar		1
12	SN-34	Nut for anchor bar bolt		1
13	TW-25	Plain washer		1
14	T1066	Nut for damper unit fixing bolt (bottom)		2
15	T1564	Dished washer for T1066 nut		2
16	T1087	Bolt for anchor bar		1
17	TW-25	Plain washer for T1087 bolt		2
18	T1073	Pivoted rear fork assembly c w flexible bushes		1
19	T2111	Screw, chaincase front fixing		2
20	UN1 4F	Nut for chaincase screw		4
21	TW-17	¼" plain washer		8
22	T2112	Screw, chaincase rear fixing		2
23	UN2 4F	Rear chain adjuster locknut		2
24	T2093	Rear chain adjuster		2
25	5775-56	Rubber grommet for rear chaincase		2
26	T2000 1	Rear chaincase, top half		1
27	T2000 2	Rear chaincase, bottom half		1
	T2000	Rear chaincase complete (two halves)		1
28	T74	Thrust washer for pivot bolt		1
29	T1074	Flexible bearing for pivoted rear forks		2
30	A8-103	Shim washer for pillion footrests (inter 344A-38)		2
31	UN5 14F	Bolt for pillion footrest		2
	UN2 5F	Nut for UN5 14F bolt		2
32	T1093	Distance washer for pivot bolt		2
33	TSW-5	⁷⁄₁₆" shakeproof washer		2
34	T1094	Distance piece for pivot bolt		1
35	T38	Pivot bolt for rear fork assembly		1
36	T102	Socket set screw for distance tube		1
37	T73	Distance tube		2
	T1114	Pivot bolt locking plate		1
		REAR MUDGUARD AND FITTINGS		
	T2113	Rear mudguard	Leader	1
	T2175 1	Rear mudguard (front section)	Arrow	1
	UN4 8F	Bolt for mudguard, bottom fixing		2
	UN1 4F	Nut for UN4 8F bolt and T2593 screw		2
	UN4 6F	Bolt for mudguard, top fixing		1
	T2204	Wing piping (frame—tail section)	Arrow	1
	T2174	Rear mudguard (tail section)	Arrow	1
	T2207	Screw, mudguard to frame	Arrow	2
	SN-32	Nut for T2207 screw	Arrow	2
	5647-55	Rear number plate	Arrow	1
	5650-53	Rubber beading for number plate	Arrow	1
	5672-56	Bolt for number plate (SSO/1723)	Arrow	2
		Nut (SNJ/1761/17/9) for 5672-56 bolt	Arrow	2
	5611-55	Mounting plate for rear lamp	Arrow	1
	T2596	Badge (Ariel)	Arrow	1
	T2606	Bezel for badge	Arrow	1
	T2195	Lifting handle	Arrow	2
	T2593	Screw for lifting handle	Arrow	2
	T2195/1	Lifting handle	Sports Arrow	2

PLATE 8 REAR SUSPENSION AND REAR CHAINCASE

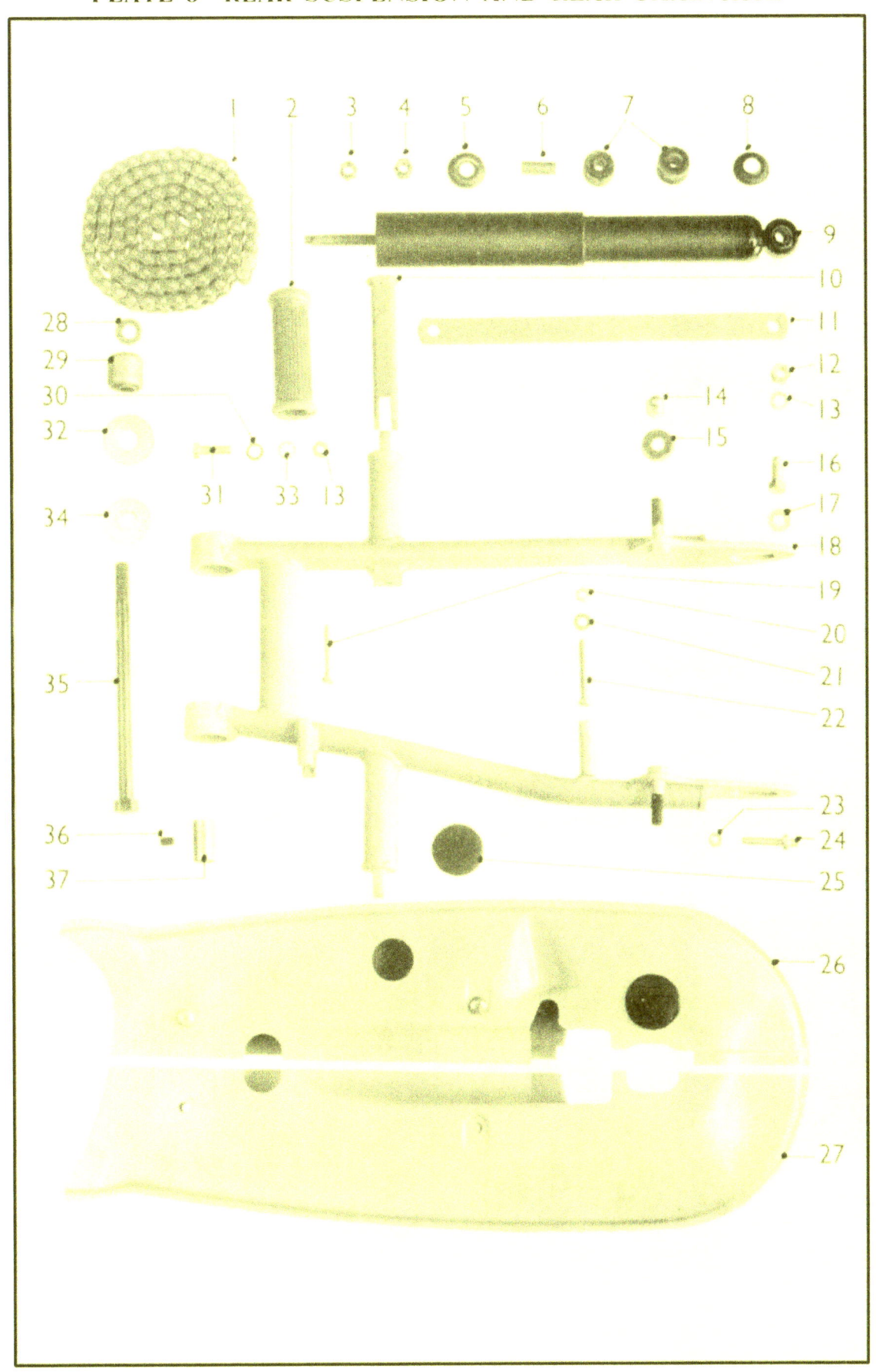

PLATE NO. 9 Ref. Nos.	PART NO.	DESCRIPTION OF PART		NO. PER SET
		EXHAUST PIPES AND SILENCERS		
1	T2114	Exhaust pipe, R/S	Leader	1
	T2165/1	Exhaust pipe, R/S	...Arrow	1
2	T2140	Nut for silencer		2
3	T2028	Silencer body, R/S	Leader	1
	T2117	Silencer body	...Arrow	2
	T2026	Silencer complete, R/S	Leader	1
	T2190	Silencer complete	...Arrow	2
4	T2037	Tube (silencer end)		2
5	T2160	Silencer baffle		2
6	T2029	Silencer body, L/S	Leader	1
	T2027	Silencer complete, L/S	Leader	1
	T2172 K	Silencer bracket, R/S	...Arrow	1
	T2173 K	Silencer bracket, L/S	...Arrow	1
7	T2046	Clip for silencer-exhaust pipe joint	Leader	2
	T2046 K	Clip for silencer-exhaust pipe joint	...Arrow	2
	T2593 K	Screw for silencer bracket to tail piece	...Arrow	4
8	T2115	Exhaust pipe, L/S	Leader	1
	T2166/1	Exhaust pipe, L/S	...Arrow	1
9	UN1 4F	Nut for T2101 pin and T2593 screw		4
10	E8-578	Swivel piece for T2046 clip (inter 6072-29)		2
11	T2101	Pin for T2046 clip		2
12	T2126	Sealing ring for silencer end cover		2
13	T2033	Silencer end cover		2
	T2033 F	Silencer end cover	...Arrow	2
14	T2035	Domed nut securing silencer end cover		2
15	T2034	End piece for end cover		2
16	T2038	Centre fixing rod for silencer		2
17	UN2 4F	Locknut securing silencer end piece		2
		FOOTREST, BRAKE PEDAL, CENTRE STAND AND FITTINGS		
1	T2551/1	Bracket, fixing side panels to crankcase	Leader	1
	UN5 10C	Bolt securing bracket to crankcase	Leader	2
2	T2060	Footrest rubber pad		2
3	T2170	Footrest, R/S		1
4	T2120	Split pin for brake rod		1
5	T2110	Plain washer for brake rod		1
6	T3010	Spring for stop lamp switch		1
7	T3018	Rear stop light switch		1
	T2194	Bracket for stoplight switch		1
8	T1081	Screw fixing stop lamp switch		2
9	SN-32	Nut for T1081 screw		2
10	T2098	Rear brake rod		1
11	UN1 4F	Nut for brake rod		1
12	T2119	Spring for rear brake rod		1
13	T2121	Swivel pin for rear brake lever		1
14	T2100	Rear brake rod adjusting nut		1
15	UN4 20F	Bolt for brake pedal lever		1
	UN1 4F	Nut for UN4 20F bolt		1
16	T2021	Lever for brake pedal		1
17	T2078	Rear brake pedal and spindle		1
18	T2080	Centre stand	Leader	1
	T2176	Centre stand	...Arrow	1
19	T2084	Rubber plug for centre stand		2
20	T2002	Connecting link		1
21	T2171	Footrest, L/S		1
22	T2085	Spring for centre stand		1
23	T2086	Connecting hook for centre stand spring		1
24	UN4 12F	Bolt for brake pedal stop plate		1
	UN1 4F	Nut for UN4 12F bolt		1
25	T1562	Grease nipple		1
26	T2104	Pivot tube for brake pedal spindle		1
27	T2087	Rubber stop for centre stand		1

PLATE 9 EXHAUST PIPES, SILENCERS, BRAKE PEDAL, FOOTREST & CENTRE STAND

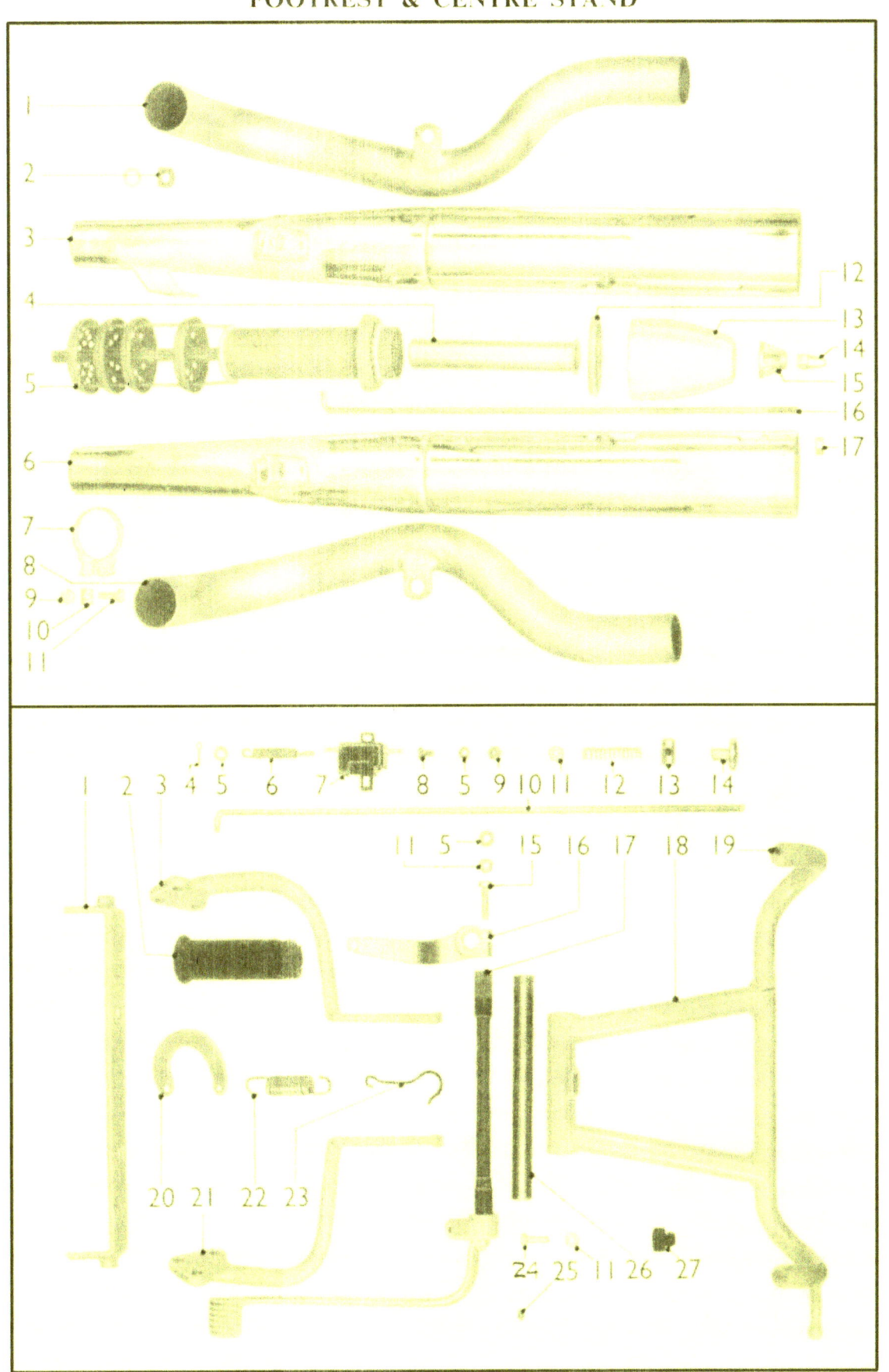

PLATE NO. 10 Ref. Nos.	PART NO.	DESCRIPTION OF PART		NO. PER SET
		FRAME AND FITTINGS		
1	T2066 1	Frame c w steering head cups	Leader	1
	T2164 1	Frame, c w steering head cups	Arrow	1
2	T2075	Bulkhead for frame		1
3	T2161 1	Petrol tank complete		1
	T2163	Rubber washer, petrol tank front fixing		1
	T2162	Bolt, petrol tank front fixing		1
4	T2010	Battery carrier	Leader	1
	T2167	Battery carrier	Arrow	1
5	T2138	Rubber covering tube for battery carrier (⅜" long)		2
	T2188	Fibre insulating plate for battery carrier	Arrow	1
6	UN4 8F	Bolt, securing battery carrier		2
	UN4 8F	Bolt, securing bulkhead		6
	UN4 8F	Bolt, securing rear mudguard		2
7	TSW-7	Shakeproof washer for UN4/8F washer		2
8	UN1 4F	Nut for battery carrier securing bolt		2
	UN1 4F	Nut for steering stop bolt	Leader	2
	UN4 8F	Bolt for steering stop and T2675 bracket		2
9	T2614 1	Bottom plate for steering lock bracket on Leader model, and support bracket on Arrow		1
10	TW-17	¼" plain washer		2
11	T2088	Pin for steering lock plunger	Leader	1
12	T2059	Steering lock bracket	Leader	1
13	T2089	Spring for steering lock plunger	Leader	1
14	T2092	Steering lock plunger	Leader	1
15		⅜" B.S.F. nut securing rectifier		1
16	TSW-5	Shakeproof washer		2
17	T3039	Electric horn	Leader	1
	T3058	Electric horn	Arrow	1
18	T2099	Tapped plate for horn bracket		1
	T2169	Horn bracket	Arrow	1
19	T2103	Bolt securing horn		2
20	T3016	Rectifier, complete		1
21		Plain washer		1
22		Shakeproof washer		1
23	T3001	Coil complete		2
	SS-6	Bolt securing coil to frame		4
	SN-47	Nut for SS-6 bolt		4
	TW-17	Washer for SS-6 bolt		4
	UN1 4F	Nut for T2059 bracket	Leader	2
24	T81	Stud, front engine mounting		1
25	A6-58	Fibre washer for petrol tap (inter 197-36)		1
26	T2096	Washer for petrol tap		as req
	T2208	Petrol tap with reserve	Arrow	1
27	T2094	Petrol tap	Leader	1
	T2191	Petrol tap	Arrow	1
	T2095	Petrol pipe complete		1
28	T2063 1	Petrol tank filler cap complete		1
29	T2108	Rubber mat for battery carrier		1
30	T2097	Rubber ring for petrol tank filler cap		2
	T2192	Washer for T2186 bracket	Arrow	4
31	T2077	Distance piece for rear suspension bracket		2
32	T2012	Bracket, R S securing rear of outer shell to frame	Leader	1
	T2186	Support bracket, frame to outer shell	Arrow	4
32	T2076	Bracket L S securing rear of outer shell to frame	Leader	1
33	UN4 18F	Bolt securing T2012 and T2076 to frame	Leader	4
34	SN-39	Nut for petrol tank fixing bolt (rear)		2
35	T2062	Rubber washer for petrol tank mounting		5
36	T108	Air cleaner rubber connection		1
37	TW-21	Plain washer for tank fixing bolt		3
38	T2061	Petrol tank fixing bolt (rear)		2
	T36 6	Air cleaner complete	Arrow	1

Continued

PLATE 10 FRAME AND FITTINGS

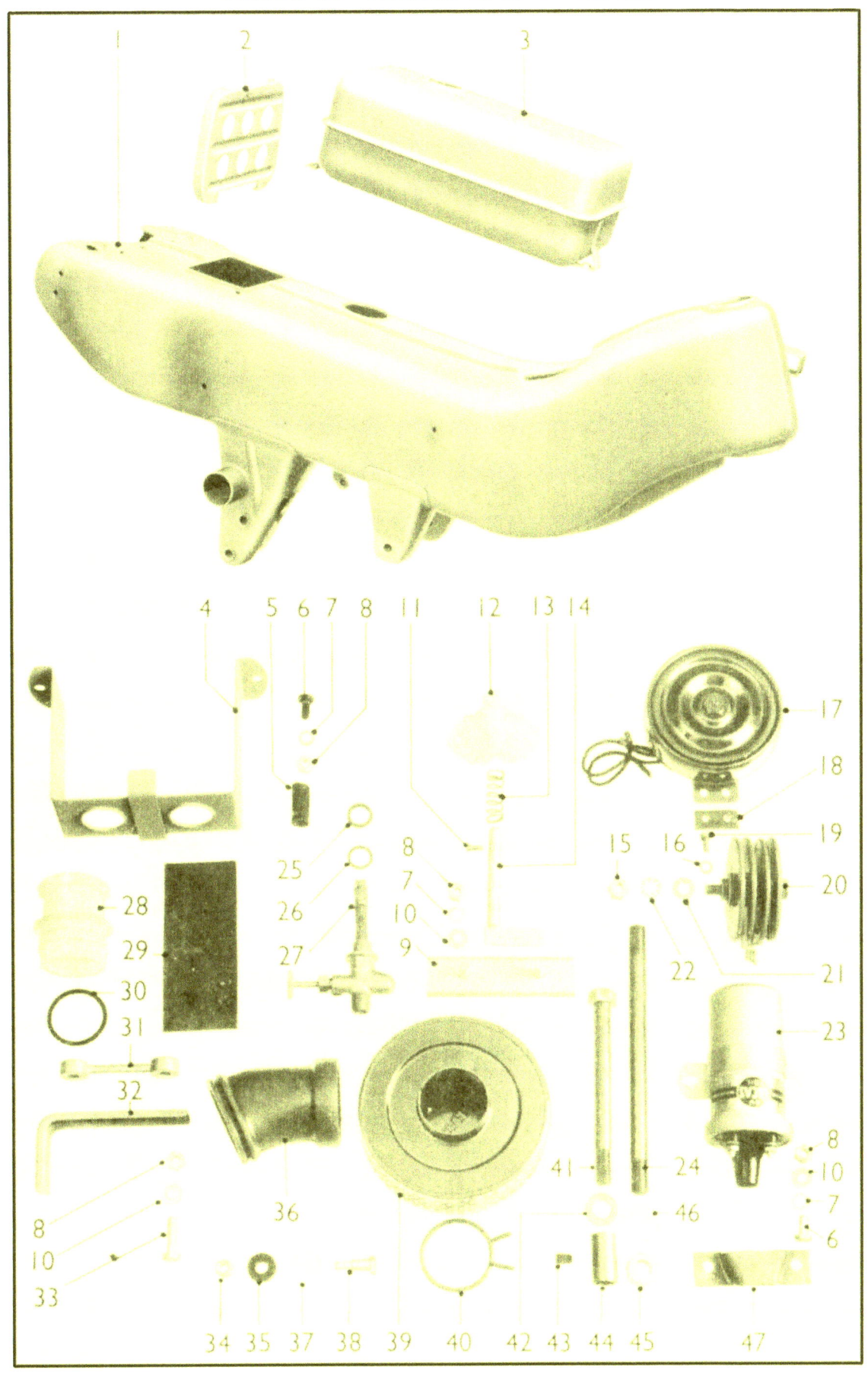

PLATE NO. 10 Ref. Nos.	PART NO.	DESCRIPTION OF PART		NO. PER SET
		FRAME AND FITTINGS		
39	T36	Air cleaner complete	Leader	1
	T36 7	Air cleaner complete	Sports Arrow	1
	T36 1	Element for air cleaner	Leader and Arrow	1
40	T119	Clip for air cleaner		1
41	T39	Bolt, for engine rear mounting		1
	T123	Spacer washer for **T39** bolt, 12, 13, 14 gauge (state gauge required)		1
42	T74	Thrust washer for **T38** bolt		1
43	T102	Socket set screw		2
44	T73	Distance tube for engine rear mounting bolt		2
45	UN1 8F	Nut for **T81** stud		2
46	TW-32	Plain washer for **T81** stud		2
	TSW-9	Shakeproof washer for **T81** stud		3
47	T2007	Steering head stop		1
	T2593	Screw, securing suspension bracket to frame on Leader and front shell to frame on Arrow		4
	T2203	Clip, securing cables to frame	Arrow	2
	T2136	Clip, securing cables to frame	Leader	3
	T2136	Clip, cable-footrest stud	Arrow	1
	T2141	Rubber for cable clip		3
	T2142	Clip, securing cables to frame	Leader	1
	T2011	Bracket for rear suspension		1
	UN4 8F	Bolt for **T2007** head stop	Leader	2
	UN4 8F	Bolt for **T2186** bracket	Arrow	4
	T2193	Nut for **UN4 8F** bolt	Arrow	4
	T2658	Cup washer for dual seat rubbers	Arrow	4
	T2110	Spacer for **T2658** cup washer	Arrow	3
	UN4 18F	Bolt, suspension bracket—cup washer	Arrow	4
	T2593	Screw, mudguard, bulkhead and lifting handles	Arrow	8
	T2672	Screw, lifting handle-suspension bracket	Arrow	2
	UN1 4F	Nut for **T2672** screw		2
		REAR CARRIER		
	T2607	Rear carrier complete	Leader only	1
	T3618 1	Rear carrier complete	Arrow only	1
	T2585	Screw, rear carrier mounting	Leader	4
	T2593	Screw, for carrier	Arrow	4
	TW-17	Plain washer for **T2585** screw		4
	TSW-4	Shakeproof washer for **T2585** screw		8
	UN1 4F	Nut for **T2585** screw and **T2593** screw		4
	T2644	Luggage strap c w hooks		2
		ACCESSORIES		
	T3534	Mirrors complete	Leader	1 pair
	T3534 1	Mirror complete R S	Leader	1
	T3534 2	Mirror complete, L S	Leader	1
	T1106	Smiths eight day clock	Leader	1
	T3626	Windscreen complete	Arrow only	1
	T3590C	Windscreen extension	Leader	1
	T2592	Nylon screw for extension	Leader	2
	T3609	Nylon nut for **T2592** screw	Leader	2
	T3611 1	Rear bumper bar complete	Leader	1
	T3571	Waterproof cover for dual seat		1

REAR LUGGAGE CONTAINERS

Part No.	Description	Model	Qty
5635-59	Pannier cases c/w fittings (state colour)	Leader	2
T3532	Holdall	Leader	2
T3502	Pannier case c/w lid, R/S	Leader	1
T3519	Bracket for R/S pannier	Leader	1
T3503	Pannier case c/w lid, L/S	Leader	1
T3520	Bracket for L/S pannier	Leader	1
T3517	Top bracket for **T3519** and **T3520** bracket	Leader	2
T3518	Bottom bracket for **T3519** and **T3520** bracket	Leader	2
T3533	Lock c/w key for pannier lid	Leader	2
T3610	Rivet for lock	Leader	4
T3538	Rubber beading for pannier lid	Leader	2
T2610	Rubber grommet for panniers	Leader	4
T2646/1	Beading for pannier (rear)	Leader	2
T2633	Grommet for pannier	Leader	4
UN4 10F	Bolt securing pannier brackets to outer shell	Leader	8
UN4 8F	Bolt securing pannier to tail cover	Leader	2
UN4 14F	Bolt securing pannier to tail cover, front fixing	Leader	2
UN4 16F	Bolt securing pannier to tail cover, centre fixing	Leader	2
E8-780	Distance piece for **UN4 16F** bolt	Leader	2
T3565	Distance piece for **UN4 14F** bolt	Leader	2
UN1 4F	Nut	Leader	14
UN5 8F	Bolt for bottom bracket fixing	Leader	2

FRONT STAND

Part No.	Description		Qty
T2151	Front stand complete		1

PROP STAND

Part No.	Description	Model	Qty
T2107	Prop stand complete	Leader	1
T2107/1	Prop stand complete	Arrow	1
E9-1375	Spring for stand (inter 2461-52)		1
T2197	Bracket for prop stand	Arrow	1
UN6 14F	Bolt securing prop stand to crankcase	Leader	2
UN6 14F	Bolt, bracket to stand and bracket to crankcase	Arrow	4
TSW-7	¼" Shakeproof washer		2
UN4 12F	Bolt, footrest—prop stand stop		1
UN1 4F	Nut for UN4 12F bolt		2
UN1 6F	Nut, prop stand-bracket	Arrow	2

PLATE NO. 11 Ref. Nos.	PART NO.	DESCRIPTION OF PART		NO. PER SET
1	T2577	Dual seat complete	Leader	1
	T2670	Dual seat complete	...Arrow	1
2	T2594	Grab handle complete for dual seat	...	1
	T2665	Rubber pad fixed to dual seat base	...Arrow	1
	5060-57	Dual seat mounting rubber	...Arrow	4
	T2659	Bracket for dual seat hinge	...Arrow	3
	T2662	Packing piece for T2659	...Arrow	2
	T2660	Link hinge	...Arrow	2
	T2510	Spring clip	...	2
	T2679	Screw, fixing grab handle	Leader	2
	T2183	Screw for tool box lid	...Arrow	1
	T2182	Spring retaining tool box lid	...Arrow	1
	T1116	Rubber washer for T2183 screw	...Arrow	1
	T2180	Lid for tool box (state colour)	...Arrow	1
	T2180 1	Lid for tool box	Sports Arrow	1
3	T2517	Lid for outer shell (state colour)	Leader	1
	SS-4	Screw for lid hinge	Leader	2
	SN-30	Spire nut for SS-4 screw	Leader	2
	T2562	Rubber beading for outer shell lid	Leader	1
	T2181	Rubber beading for tool box lid	...Arrow	1
	T2677	Stop strap for dual seat	...Arrow	1
4	T2500	Outer shell (state colour)	Leader	1
	T2178 1	Front shell (state colour)	...Arrow	1
	T2610	Rubber buffer, outer shell to dual seat base	Leader	6
	T2675	Support bracket (frame to shell)	...Arrow	2
	T2657	Badge for front shell	...Arrow	2
	T2603	Grommet for badge	...	2
5	T2611	Front shield	Leader	1
	T3516	Licence holder complete	Leader	1
	T3620	Licence holder complete	...Arrow	1
	T3515	Rubber ring for licence holder	...	1
	T2666	Beading for outer shell	...Arrow	2
	T3620 1	Rubber moulding for T3620 holder	...Arrow	1
6	T2531 1	Headlamp cowl	Leader	1
	T1081	Screw, cowl—bottom fixing	Leader	2
	SN-32	Nut for T1081	...	2
	SN-37	Nut for T2183 screw	...Arrow	1
7	T2505	Tail cover assembly	Leader	1
	T2588	Wing nut for tail cover bracket	Leader	2
8	T2519	Side panel, L S	Leader	1
9	T2518	Side panel, R S	Leader	1
10	T2549	Leg shield, R S	Leader	1
11	T2550	Leg shield, L S	Leader	1
	T2618	Badge (Leader) c w rivets	...	1
	T2610	Rubber grommet, tail cover-bridge	...	8
	T2610	Rubber grommet for front shield	Leader	2
	T2633	Rubber grommet for front shield	Leader	4
	T2620	Lining for glove box R S	Leader	1
	T2621	Lining for glove box L S	Leader	1
	T2137	Lining for glove box (centre)	Leader	1
	T2137	Lining for frame hatch	...Arrow	1
	T2152	Clip for T2137	...	2
	T2641	Support bracket, L S for outer shell	Leader	1
	T2642	Support bracket, R S for outer shell	Leader	1
	T2647	Striker plate for outer shell	Leader	1
	T1081	Screw for T2647	Leader	1
	TW-10	Plain washer	Leader	1
	SN-32	Nut for T1081 screw	Leader	1
	T2634	Latch assembly complete for dual seat	Leader	1
	T2637	Locking bracket for latch	Leader	1

SIDE PANELS, BODY AND DUAL SEAT

Continued

PLATE 11 SIDE PANELS, BODY, DUAL SEAT AND TOOL KIT

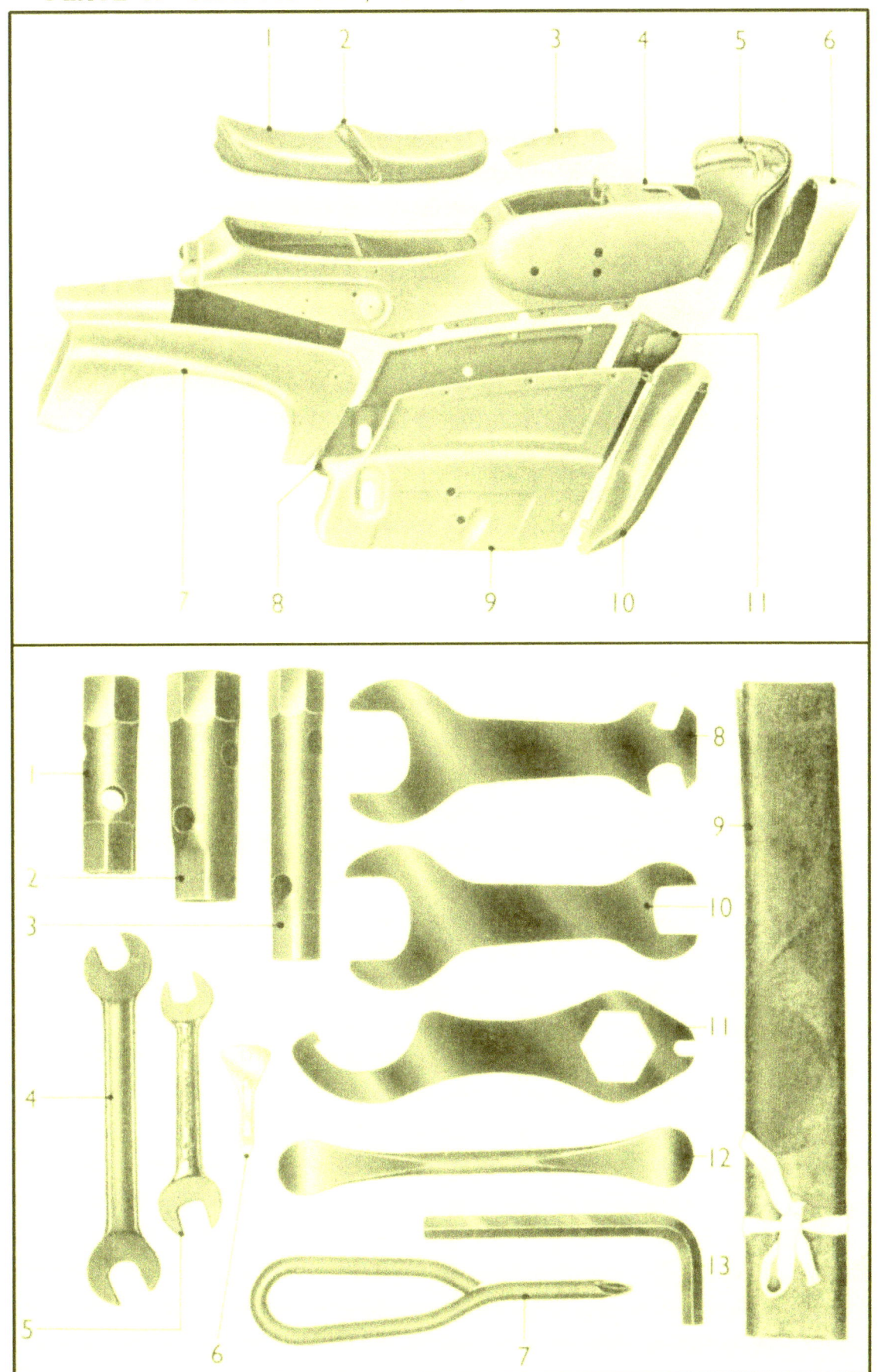

PLATE NO. 11 Ref. Nos.	PART NO.	DESCRIPTION OF PART		NO. PER SET

SIDE PANELS, BODY AND DUAL SEAT

	T2673	Screw for bracket	Leader	2
	T2638	Operating wire for latch	Leader	1
	T2648	Rubber grommet (fitted in outer shell for T2638 wire)	Leader	1
	T2109	Rubber grommet for clutch, brake and rear lamp cables	Leader	3
	UN4 8F	Bolt for tail cover bracket	Leader	2
	T77	Fibre washer for T2183 screw	Arrow	1

TOOL KIT

	T3529	Set of tools in tool bag	1
1	T3525	Double ended tube spanner	1
2	T3524	Double ended tube spanner	1
3	T3523	Double ended tube spanner	1
4	T3522	Double ended flat spanner	1
5	T3521	Double ended flat spanner	1
6	T3559	Screwdriver and feeler gauge	1
7	T3530	Screwdriver	1
8	T3526	Combination spanner	1
9	T3528	Tool bag	1
10	T3527	Double ended flat spanner	1
11	T3500	Combination spanner	1
12	6625-26	Tyre lever	1
13	T3501	Wrench for cylinder head bolt	1
	T3557	Peg for ignition timing	1
	T3558	Peg for front wheel removal	2
	T3562	Spanner for carburetter	1
	T3563	Spanner for petrol pipe nut and handlebar cover nut	1
	6636-54	Tyre inflator (12")	1
	T3624 1S	Front wheel spindle withdrawal tool complete	1

Note:—Set of tools does not include tyre inflator or T3624 1S withdrawal tool.

SERVICE TOOLS FOR WORKSHOP USE

T3569S	Engine service tool kit
T3572S	Bearing removal and replacement kit
T3592S	Oil seal and bush extractor and fitting kit

PLATE 11 SIDE PANELS, BODY, DUAL SEAT AND TOOL KIT

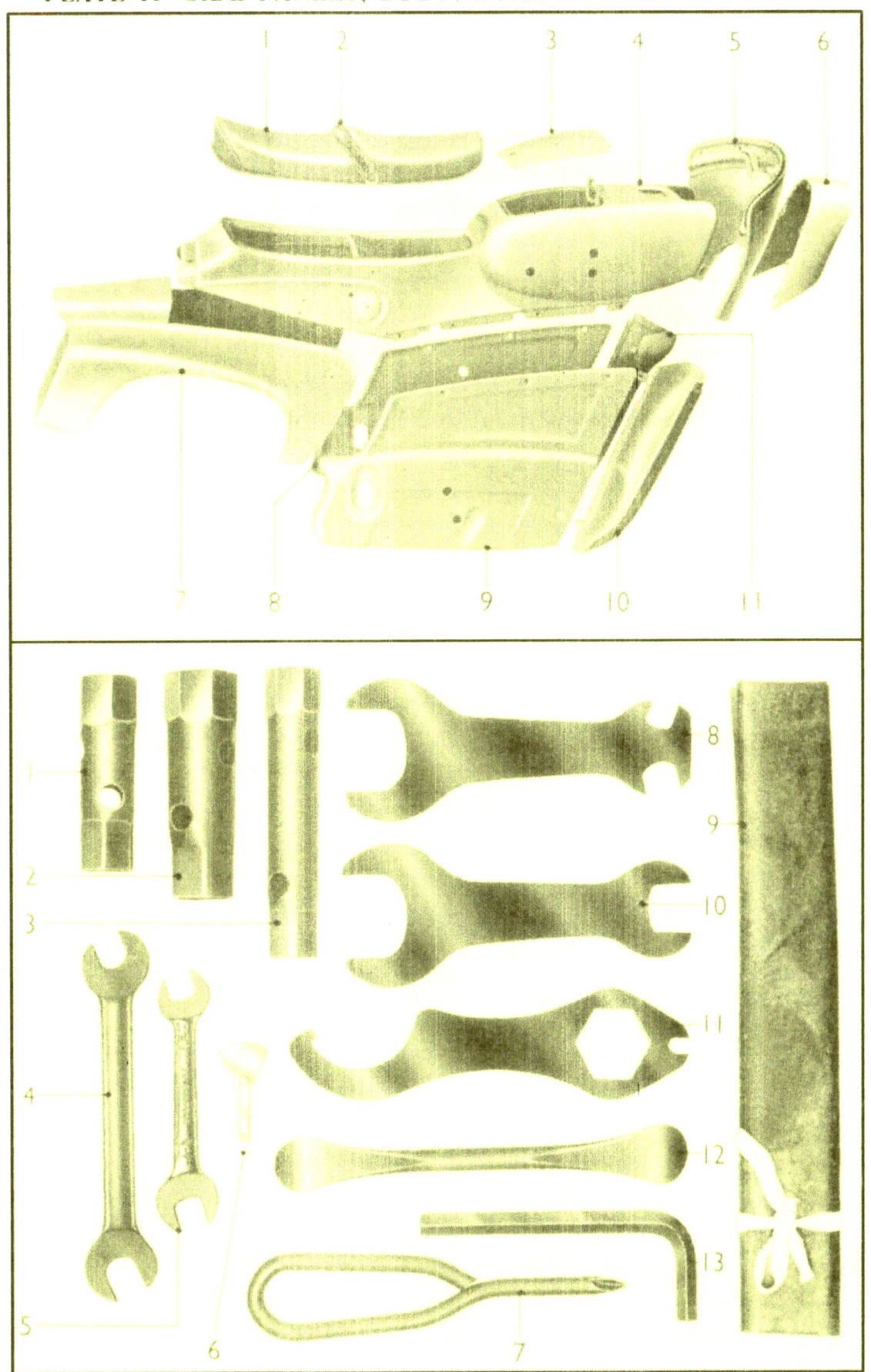

PLATE NO. 12 Ref. Nos.	PART NO.	DESCRIPTION OF PART		NO. PER SET
		HEADLAMP, WINDSCREEN AND INSTRUMENT PANEL		
1	T2601	Beading for headlamp cowl	Leader	1
2	516828	Light unit	Leader	1
3	54520003	Headlamp rim	Leader	1
4	T3000	Headlamp complete	Leader	1
	T3055	Headlamp (less speedometer and switches)	...Arrow	1
5	T3002	Ammeter		1
6	UN2 4F	Locknut for trimmer rod	Leader	2
7	T3003	Ignition switch (Lucas)		1
8	T2600 1	Trimmer rod complete	Leader	1
9	T3004	Lighting switch (Lucas)		1
10	T2556	Rubber grommet (fitted on instrument panel) for trimmer rod	Leader	1
11	T2554	Bolt for headlamp mounting	Leader	2
	T3059	Bolt for headlamp mounting	...Arrow	2
12	S6-6	Thackeray washer for T2554 bolt		2
13	T3051	Headlamp shell (Lucas 517527)	Leader	1
14	T2580	Windscreen stay	Leader	2
	T3626	Windscreen complete	...Arrow	1
	T2532	Windscreen	Leader	1
	T1171	Flyscreen	Sports Arrow	1
	T2587	Nylon bolt assembly, fixing windscreen to stay (top)	Leader	2
	T1172 1	Bracket and clip complete for flyscreen	Sports Arrow	1
15	T2589	Eye bolt for windscreen top fixing	Leader	2
16	T2590	Socket for eye bolt	Leader	2
17	T2592	Screw for eye bolt	Leader	2
18	T2603	Grommet for Ariel badge on instrument panel	Leader	1
19	T2602	Ariel badge on instrument panel	Leader	1
20	T2583	Nut for windscreen stay fixing joint	Leader	2
21	T2582	Fixing joint for windscreen stay	Leader	2
22	TW-25	Plain washer for fixing joint	Leader	2
23	UN1 6F	Nut for fixing joint	Leader	2
	T2617	Rubber corner piece for windscreen	Leader	2
	T2535	Rubber beading, windscreen-frontshield joint	Leader	1
24	T2646	Rubber beading for instrument panel	Leader	1
25	T2604	Badge (Leader)		1
	T2605	Rivet for badge		4
26	T2596	Badge (Ariel) for front shield	Leader	1
	T2606	Bezel for badge	Leader	1
27	T2585	Screw securing windscreen to front shield	Leader	6
28	T2586	Distance piece for T2585 screw		6
	T3054	Distance piece for headlamp	Arrow only	2
29	TW-17	Plain washer for T2585 screw		8
	TW-20	Plain washer for T3054 R S distance piece	Arrow only	1
	T3060	Plain washer for headlamp bolt T3059	...Arrow	2
30	SN-37	Nut for T2585 screw		4
	UN1 4F	Nut for instrument panel fixing screw	Leader	2
31	T2615	Dome nut for T2585 screw	Leader	2
	T2615	Dome nut for T2593 flyscreen screw	Sports Arrow	2
	T77	Fibre washer	Sports Arrow	4
32	T2610	Rubber grommet for instrument panel	Leader	2
33	T3008	Warning light—neutral indicator	Leader	1
34	T3007	Warning light—flasher (amber lens)	Leader	1
35	T2625	Bracket, R S, for instrument panel	Leader	1
	T2626	Bracket, L S, for instrument panel	Leader	1
	UN4 8F	Bolt securing bracket to outer shell	Leader	2
36	T2593	Screw, securing bracket to panel	Leader	4
	T2593	Screw, fixing flyscreen to handlebar	Sports Arrow	2
	T1148	Rubber grommet for speedometer head	...Arrow	1
37	T2597	Rubber grommet for speedometer head	Leader	1

Continued

PLATE 12 HEADLAMP AND INSTRUMENT PANEL

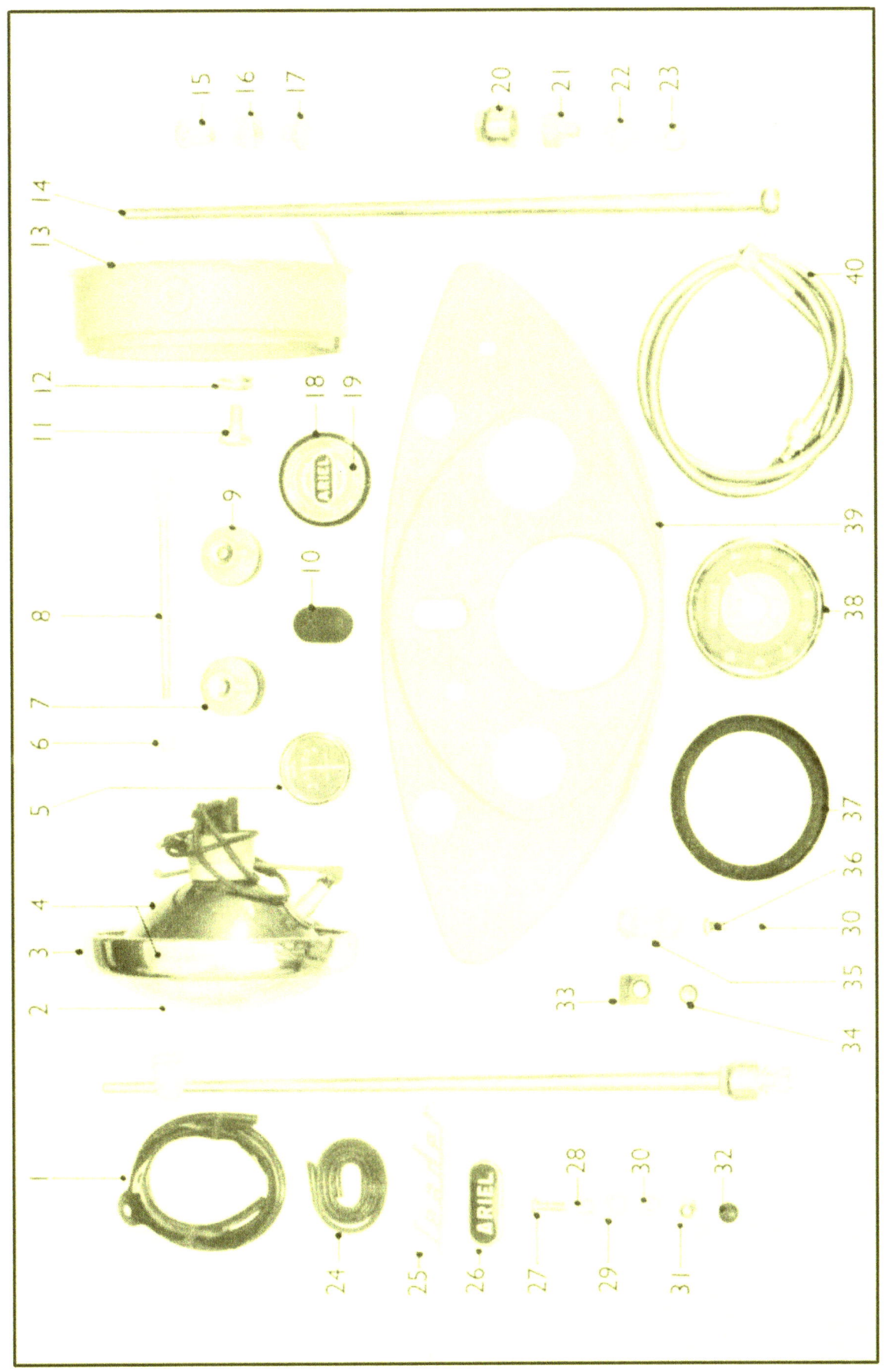

PLATE NO. 12 Ref. Nos.	PART NO.	DESCRIPTION OF PART		NO. PER SET

HEADLAMP, WINDSCREEN AND INSTRUMENT PANEL

38	T1109	Speedometer head (with trip) m.p.h.	Leader	1
38	T1110	Speedometer head (with trip) k.p.h.	Leader	1
	T1131	Speedometer head (m.p.h.)	...Arrow	1
	T1132	Speedometer head (k.p.h.)	...Arrow	1
39	T2530	Instrument panel only	Leader	1
40	T1105	Speedometer cable complete (37″ long)		1
	T2653	Grommet for windscreen	Leader	2

PLATE NO. 13 Ref. Nos.	PART NO.	DESCRIPTION OF PART		NO. PER SET

TOOL BOX, KNEE GRIPS, HANDLEBAR CONTROLS, ETC.

1	T2678	Screw for dual seat hinge	Leader	4
	T111	Washer for T2678 screw	Leader	4
2	T2566	Spacer for dual seat hinge	Leader	2
3	T2673	Screw for dual seat clip	Leader	4
4	T2510	Clip for dual seat	Leader	2
5	T1081	Screw for dual seat mounting plate	Leader	4
6	TW-10	Washer for T1081 screw		4
7	SN-32	Nut for mounting plate screw		4
8	T2512	Mounting plate for dual seat	Leader	2
9	T2506	Headed pin for link hinge	Leader	2
	T2650	Split pin		2
10	T2629	Spring for lifting handle	Leader	1
11	T2543	Knee grip motif L/S	Leader and Sports Arrow	1
11	T2544	Knee grip motif R/S	Leader and Sports Arrow	1
12	T2521	Knee grip rubber, R/S		1
12	T2522	Knee grip rubber L/S		1
	T2179	Tool box	...Arrow	1
13	T2122	Tool box	Leader	1
	T2125	Sponge rubber for inside tool box	Leader	1
14	T2539	Threaded plate for tail cover swivel	Leader	2
15	T2561	Backing plate for T2539 plate	Leader	2
16	T2545	Bolt for tail cover swivel	Leader	2
17	T2568	Washer for T2545 bolt	Leader	2
	T2652	Distance piece for tail pivot	Leader	2
	5058-55	Washer for distance piece	Leader	2
18	T2542	Screw, fixing side panels	Leader	8
	T2649	Screw, fixing side panels (bottom rear)	Leader	2
19	T2565	Rubber washer for side panel screw	Leader	10
20	UN1 4F	Nut for threaded plate screw	Leader	6
21	T2564	Circlip for panel screw T2542	Leader	8
22	T2573	Lock complete with 2 keys for outer shell lid	Leader	1
23	TW-17	Standard plain washer ¼″ i/dia × $\frac{9}{16}$″ o/dia × 20G		as req.
24	TSW-4	Standard ¼″ shakeproof washer		as req.
25		Key for T2573 lock (state key number when replacement required)	Leader	—
26	UN4 6F	Bolt securing outer shell to frame	Leader	4
	UN4 8F	Bolt fixing top legshield to outer shell and frame	Leader	2
27	T1164	Front brake cable complete	Leader	1
	T1165	Front brake cable complete	...Arrow	1
28	SS-4	Screw securing hinge to lid of outer shell	Leader	2
29	SN-30	Spire nut for SS-4 screw		2
	T1142	Clutch lever	...Arrow	1
	T1141	Front brake lever	...Arrow	1
30	T1083	Front brake lever	Leader	1
	T1167	Front brake lever	Sports Arrow only	1
30	T1083	Clutch lever	Leader	1
	T1168	Clutch lever	Sports Arrow	1
	T1152	Twist grip c/w lever, etc., complete	...Arrow	1
	T1163	Clutch lever assembly, complete	...Arrow	1

Continued

PLATE 13 TOOL BOX, KNEE GRIPS, HANDLEBAR CONTROLS, ETC.

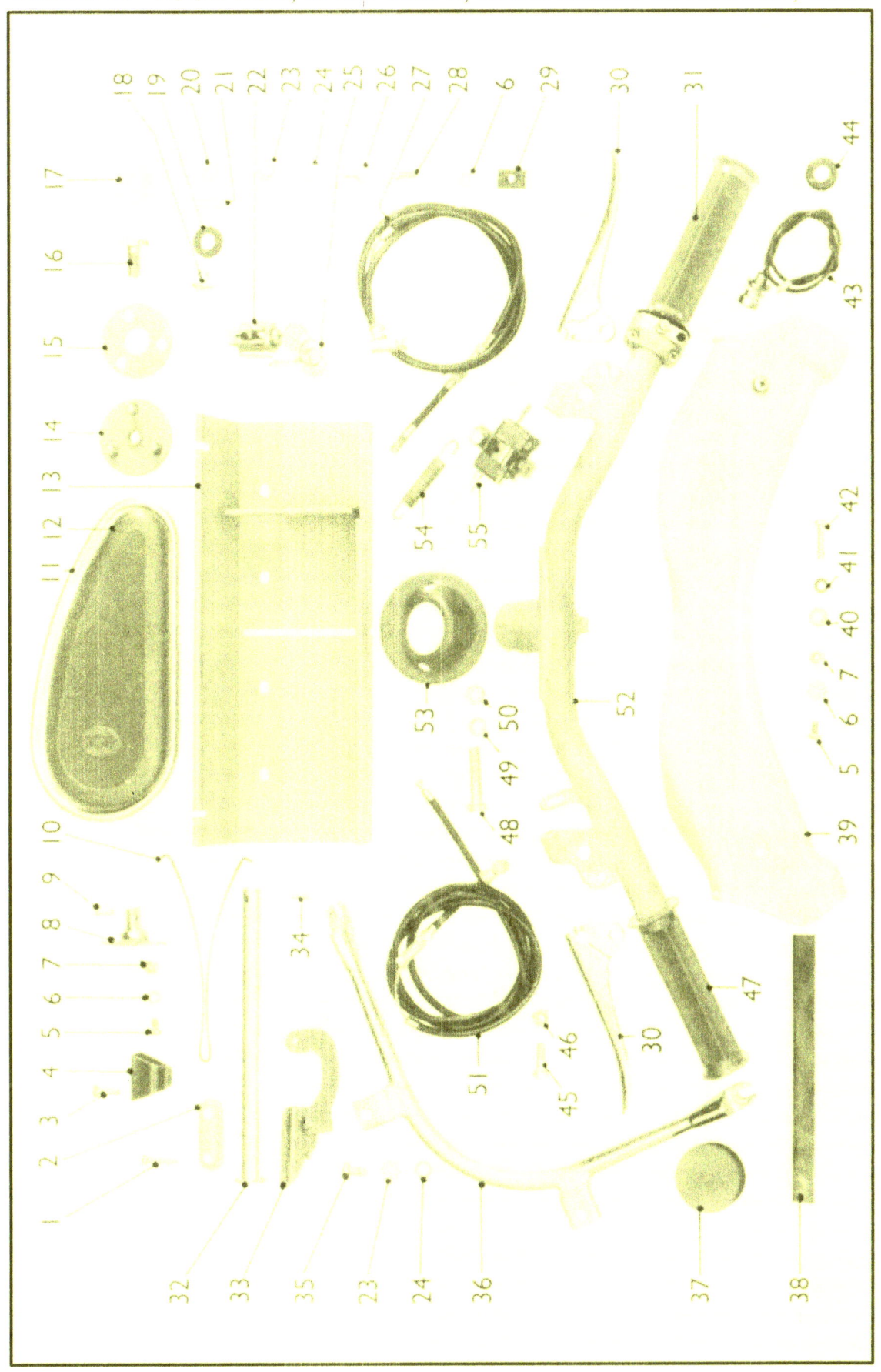

PLATE NO. 13 Ref. Nos.	PART NO.	DESCRIPTION OF PART		NO. PER SET

TOOL BOX, KNEE GRIPS, HANDLEBAR CONTROLS, ETC.

Ref.	Part No.	Description	Model	No.
31	T1113	Twist grip complete	Leader	1
	T1136	Twist grip	Arrow	1
	T1170	Twist grip rubber	Sports Arrow	1
32	T2627	Lifting handle	Leader	1
33	T2529	Link hinge for dual seat	Leader	2
34	T2632	Peg for lifting handle	Leader	1
	T2631	Spring for lifting handle (coil)	Leader	1
35	T2593	Screw for silencer support stay to tail cover	Leader	2
	UN1 4F	Nut for T2593 screw		2
36	T2042	Silencer support stay	Leader	1
37	T2574	Rubber pad fixed to dual seat base	Leader	1
38	T2536	Sealing strip (rubber) 6" long, for leg shield	Leader	2
39	T1077	Handlebar cover	Leader	1
40	T1080	Spacer for handlebar cover	Leader	2
41	T1082	Fibre washer for handlebar cover screw	Leader	3
42	T1091	Screw (long) for handlebar cover	Leader	2
	SN-32	Nut for handlebar cover screw		2
43	T3038	Horn push and harness (Lucas)		1
44	T2109	Rubber grommet		3
	T1144	Nut for T1143 screw	Arrow	2
	T1143	Pivot screw for clutch and brake lever	Arrow	2
45	T1088	Screw securing brake and clutch lever to handlebar	Leader	2
46	SN-39	Nut for T1088 screw	Leader	2
	T1137	Twist grip rubber	Arrow	1
47	T1107	Dummy grip		1
	T1169	Dummy grip	Sports Arrow	1
48	T1111	Bolt for handlebar mounting	Leader	1
	T1081	Screw for handle bar cover	Leader	1
	SN-32	Nut for T1081 screw		1
49	S5-3	Spring washer for T1111 bolt		1
50	UN2 5F	Locknut for T1111 bolt		1
51	T1085	Clutch cable complete	Leader	1
	T1133	Clutch cable complete	Arrow	1
	T1147	Handlebar (American type) export only	Arrow	1
52	T1042	Handlebar only	Leader	1
	T1166	Handlebar only	Sports Arrow only	1
	T1127	Handlebar only	Arrow	1
	H202	Split sleeve	Arrow	1
53	T2537	Rubber grommet (handlebar to outer shell)	Leader	1
54	T3010	Spring for front and rear stop lamp switch	Leader	2
55	T3019	Front stop lamp switch	Leader	1
	T3050	Bracket for switch	Leader	1
	T1081	Screw for stop lamp switches	Leader	2
	SN-32	Nut for T1081 screw		2
	T2610	Rubber grommet (tail cover—bridge)	Leader	8

PLATE 13 TOOL BOX, KNEE GRIPS, HANDLEBAR CONTROLS, ETC.

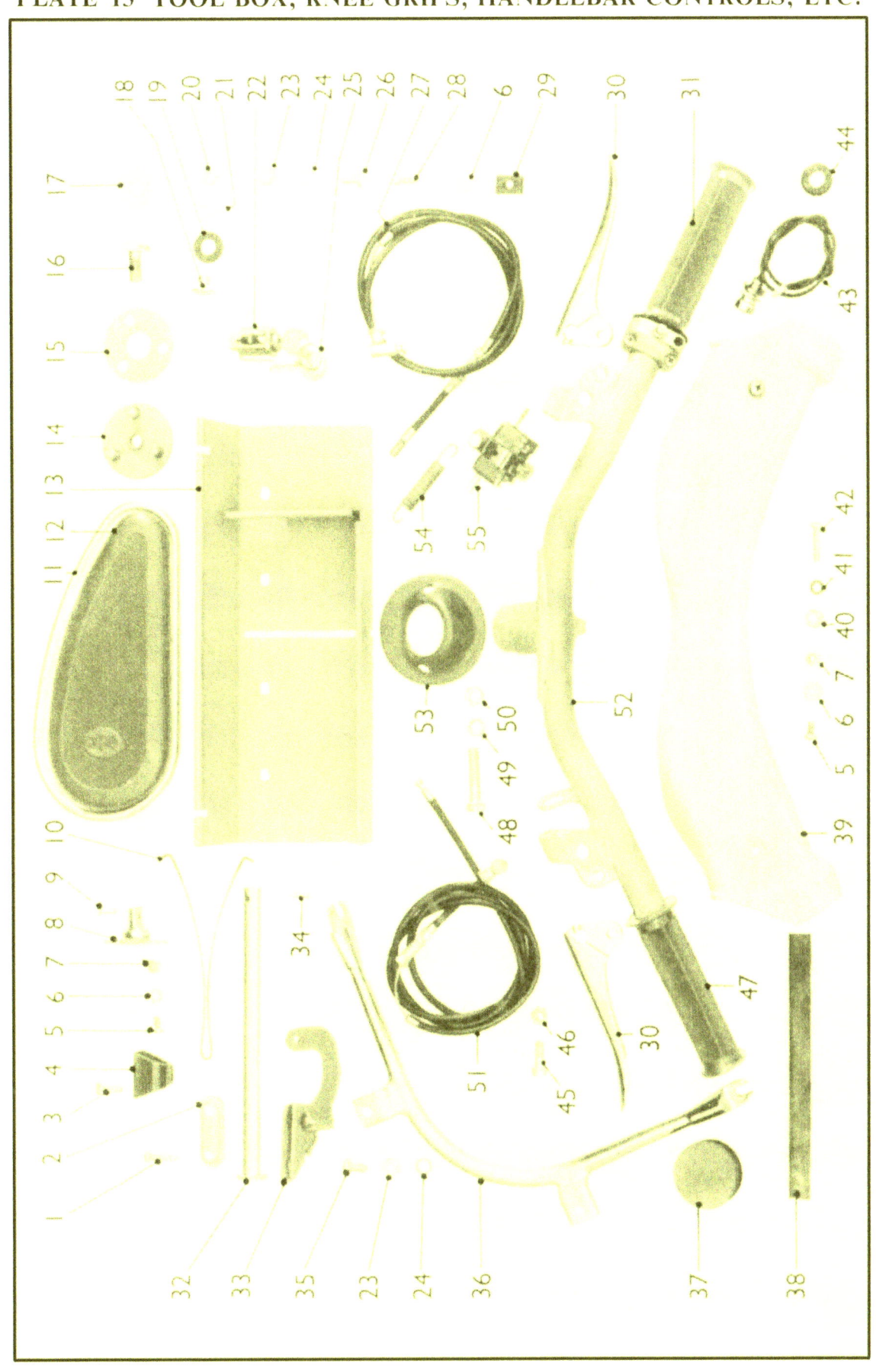

PLATE NO. 14 Ref. Nos.	PART NO.	DESCRIPTION OF PART	NO. PER SET
		CARBURETTER	
		Makers: AMAL LTD., Holdford Road, Witton, Birmingham 6	
	T131	Carburetter complete with cable, less controls (Amal 375 33) ... ... Except Sports Arrow	1
1	375/065	Mixing chamber cap	1
2	375/064	Mixing chamber top	1
3	375/090	Strangler complete	1
4	375/061	Throttle valve spring	1
5	375/089	Nut for strangler clamp screw	1
6	375/088	Strangler clamp screw	2
7	375/060	Throttle valve (3½)	1
8	244/765	Rubber seal for carburetter flange	1
9	375/027	Mixing chamber body	1
10	332/017	Air adjusting screw	1
11	4/148	Air adjusting screw spring	1
12	376/069	Throttle adjusting screw spring	1
13	376/068	Throttle adjusting screw	1
14	376/072	Needle jet (No. 105)	1
15	376/073	Jet holder	1
16	376/100	Main jet (No. 140)	1
17	376/075	Main jet cover	1
18	4/241	Mixing chamber cap spring screw	1
19	4/137A	Screw plug	1
20	4/035	Cable adjuster	1
21	4/235	Mixing chamber cap spring	1
22	4/230	Clip for needle	1
23	375/063	Taper needle	1
24	343/011	Tickler body	1
25	376/086	Tickler	1
26	376/087	Tickler spring	1
27	376/091	Banjo bolt	1
28	376/092	Washer for banjo bolt	1
29	376/130	Banjo	1
30	376/093	Filter gauze	1
31	376/088	Needle seating	1
32	376/089	Float needle	1
33	376/094	Float spindle bush	1
34	376/079	Float chamber cover screw	3
35	376/083	Float	1
36	376/077	Float chamber cover	1
37	376/078	Float chamber cover washer	1
38	T1084	Throttle cable complete	1
	375/059	Jet block complete	1
	376/070	Locating peg for jet block	1
	375/067	Jet block washer	1
	376/074	Jet holder washer	1
	376/076	Pilot jet (No. 30)	1
	376/095	Pilot jet cover nut	1
	116/162	Pilot jet cover nut washer	1
	T115/1	Rod for strangler ... ... Leader	1
	T132/1	Rod for strangler ... ... Arrow	1
	T133	Rubber grommet for strangler rod bracket ... Arrow	1

Continued

PLATE 14 CARBURETTER AND FITTINGS

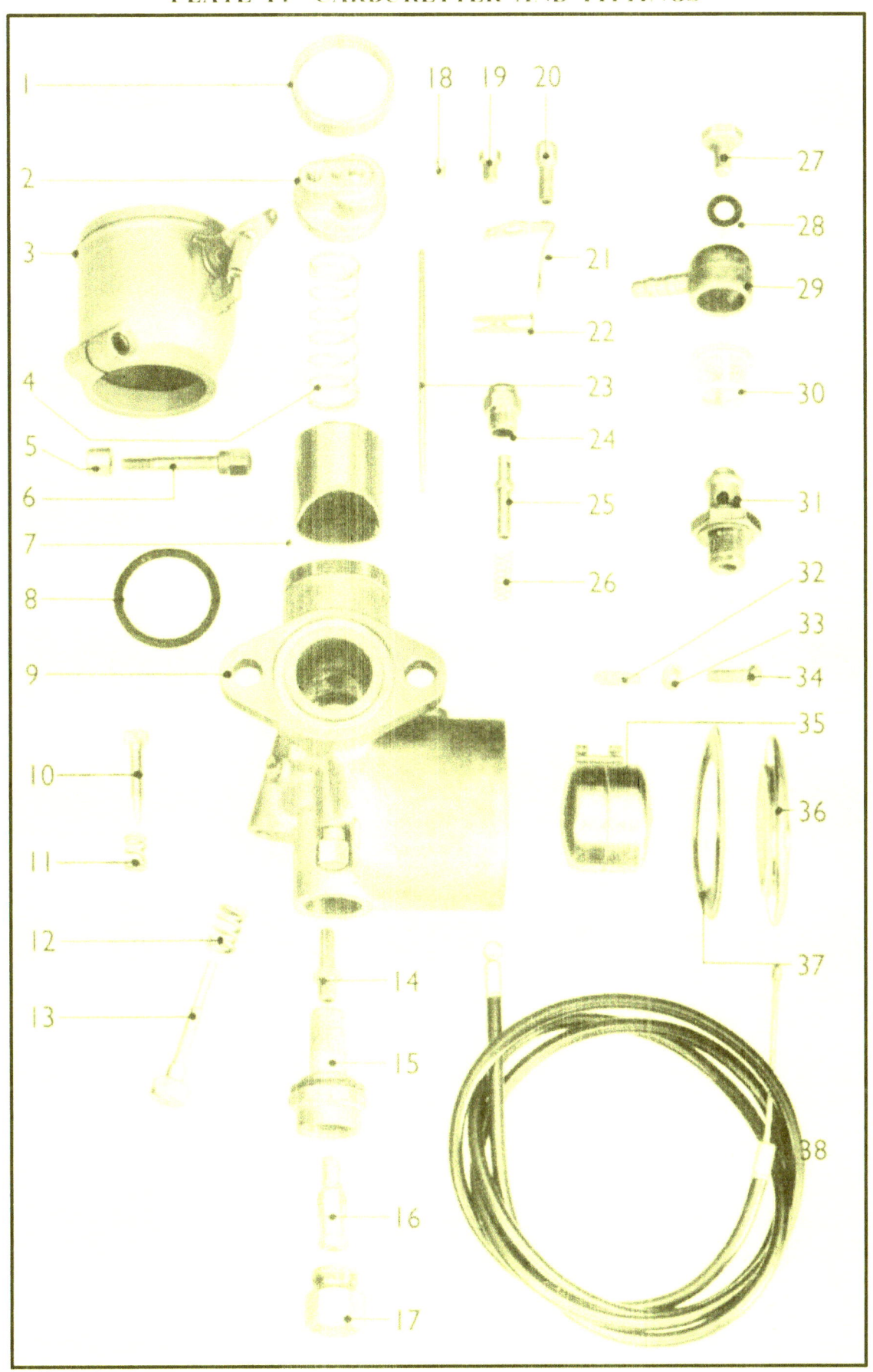

277

CARBURETTER

Makers: AMAL LTD., Holdford Road, Witton, Birmingham 6

Part No.	Description	Notes
T139	Carburetter complete with strangler (Amal 376/277)	Sports Arrow only
376/100	Main jet 230	Sports Arrow only
376/072	Needle jet 105	Sports Arrow only
376/076	Pilot jet 30	Sports Arrow only
376/060	Slide 3½	Sports Arrow only
376/015	Carburetter body	Sports Arrow only
376/064	Mixing chamber top	Sports Arrow only
376/065	Mixing chamber cap	Sports Arrow only
4/235	Mixing chamber cap spring	
4/241	Mixing chamber cap spring screw	
376/061	Throttle valve spring	Sports Arrow only
376/063	Jet needle	Sports Arrow only
4/230	Jet needle clip	
376/068	Throttle adjusting screw	
376/069	Throttle adjusting screw spring	
332/017	Pilot air adjusting screw	Sports Arrow only
4/148	Pilot air adjusting screw spring	
376/057	Jet block complete	Sports Arrow only
376/067	Jet block washer	Sports Arrow only
376/073	Jet holder	
376/074	Jet holder washer	
376/075	Main jet cover	
376/095	Pilot jet cover nut	
116/162	Pilot jet cover nut washer	
376/077	Side cover	
376/078	Side cover washer	
376/079	Side cover screw	
376/083	Float complete	
376/085	Float hinge spindle	Sports Arrow only
376/094	Float spindle bush	
376/086	Tickler	
376/011	Tickler body	Sports Arrow only
376/087	Tickler spring	
376/088	Needle seating	
376/089	Float needle	
376/130	Banjo	
376/091	Banjo bolt	
376/092	Banjo bolt washer	
376/093	Filter gauze	
244/1048	Sealing ring	Sports Arrow only
376/177	Strangler Assembly	Sports Arrow only
4/137A	Plug for m/ch top	

ELECTRICAL EQUIPMENT
Makers: MESSRS. JOSEPH LUCAS LTD.,
Great King Street, Birmingham 19

T3002	36084	**Ammeter (CZU27)**	
T3036	523986	Rubber beading for ammeter	
T3011	54021001	**Alternator** complete	
	423506	Rotor	
	468678	Stator	
	465918	Insulating pad	
	465717	Cable clip	
	186092	Screw for cable clip	
	128013	Washer for screw	
	465909	Nut	
	465910	Washer	
T3017	ML9E	**Battery**	
T3015	047539	**Cam and contact breaker** complete	
T3012		Cam c w bolt and circlip	
T3052		Circlip for contact breaker cam	
T3053		Bolt for fixing cam	
	169194	Nut, condenser and angle plate fixing	
	425382	Insulating plate	
	54410078	Contact set	
	425377	Condenser	
	425378	Lubricator felt	
	425370	Contact breaker base plate	
T3001	45077	**Coil (ignition) (Lucas MA6)** complete	
T3032	421554	Rubber grommet for coil connection	
T3031	421863	Clip, cable contact	
	166043	Terminal nut	
	188330	Shakeproof washer	
	131023	Plain washer	
T3039	70146	**Horn (HFI849)**	Leader
T3058	70157A	**Horn (HFI849)**	Arrow
	165498	Nut for tone disc	
T3038	076060	**Horn push (HP26)**	
T3005	303945	**Inspection lamp socket (red)**	Leader
T3006	303946	**Inspection lamp socket (black)**	Leader
T3000	58204	**Headlamp complete**	Leader
T3055	58587A	**Headlamp only** (less speedometer and switches)	Arrow
T3051	517527	Headlamp shell	Leader
	54520003	Rim	
	555911	Screw, rim fixing	
	534296	Plate, rim fixing screw	
	504665	Wire, light fixing unit	
	516828	Light unit	
	554602	Main bulb holder	
	188818	Sleeve, terminal	
	312	Main bulb	
	554710	Pilot bulb holder	
	553780	Interior, pilot	
	554354	Rubber ring bulb holder seating	
	988	Pilot bulb	
T3040	53394	**Tail lamp (564)**	
	573839	Lens	
	575200	Window	
	575219	Nut, barrel, lens fixing	
	575208	Gasket, lens seating	
	576002	Base assembly	
	575207	Grommet, bulb holder	
	575209	Bulb holder assembly, shell	
	573828	Interior, bulb holder	
	352	Bulb	
	573825	Cable grommet	
	166014	Nut, lamp fixing	
	188327	Washer	
	131023	Washer, fixing bolt spacer	
T3016	47111	**Rectifier (FSX1501)**	

T3037	038238	Dipper switch (99)		
	121964	Fixing screw		
	380427	Clip		
T3004		**Lighting switch**		
	54330642	Knob for lighting switch		
T3003		Ignition switch		
	54330641	Knob for ignition switch		
T3019	31384	Stop light switch for front brake	Leader	
T3018	31437	Stop light switch for rear brake		
	54940984	Cable harness	Leader	
T3041	54940988	Stop-tail lamp harness (not required when flashers or gear indicator fitted)	Leader	
T3061		Lead for stop-tail lamp	Arrow	
T3042	54940989	Lead for stop switch	Leader	
T3062		Lead for stop switch	Arrow	
T3043	54940990	Lead for inspection socket (not required when parking light fitted)	Leader	
T3044	54940991	Battery earth lead	Leader	
T3045	54940992	Rectifier earth lead	Leader	
T3046	54942616	Rectifier leads	Leader	
T3033	54940994	Lead, contact breaker		
T3063	54945879	Lead, coils—contact breaker	Arrow	
T3034		H.T. lead to spark plug	Leader	
T3034 1		H.T. lead to spark plug	Arrow	
T3035	038237	Wiring harness c w lighting and ignition switches	Leader	
T3057	54033090	Wiring harness c w switches	Arrow	
T2205		Sleeve for cables (frame to engine)	Arrow	

ELECTRICAL EQUIPMENT (Optional Extras)

8006-59		Flasher set complete (model fitted with panniers)	Leader	1
8007-60		Flasher set complete (model not fitted with panniers)	Leader	1
T3014C		Parking lamp complete	Leader	1
T3014		Parking lamp only	Leader	1
T1081		Screw for parking lamp	Leader	2
T2624		Flasher unit mounting bracket	Leader	1
T2585		Screw for T2624 bracket	Leader	1
T3007	38193	Flasher warning light (amber lens)	Leader	1
T3008	38194	Warning light (neutral indicator) (clear lens)	Leader	1
T3068		Inspection lamp complete	Leader	1
T3020		Rubber mat for flasher lamps	Leader	4
T3021	53733	Flasher lamp	Leader	4
T3022	031935	Switch for flasher lamp	Leader	1
T3023	031928	Flasher unit	Leader	1
T3024	54940996	Tail lamp and rear flasher leads	Leader	1
8003-59		Neutral gear indicator c w switch and harness	Leader	1
T3025	31820	Neutral indicator switch	Leader	1
T3026	54940997	Front flasher lead, L S	Leader	1
T3049		Parking lamp switch only	Leader	1
T46		Rubber grommet for flasher leads	Leader	6
T3027	54940998	Front flasher lead, R S	Leader	1
T3028	54940999	Flasher harness	Leader	1
T3029	54941000	Stop switch and gear indicator switch lead	Leader	1
T3030	54941001	Parking light and inspection socket leads	Leader	1
T3047		Flasher mounting bracket	Leader	4
T3047		Flasher mounting bracket (model not fitted with panniers)	Leader	2
T3048		Screw for flasher and bracket	Leader	12
T3048		Screw for flasher and bracket (model not fitted with panniers)	Leader	10
SN-39		Nut for T2585 screw		1
T3627		Flasher lamp mounting (rear) for model **not** fitted panniers	Leader	2
T2673		Screw	Leader	6
TW-10		Plain washer	Leader	6
T3628		Earthing wire	Leader	2
T3629		Support strip for flasher lamp (model not fitted panniers)	Leader	2

STANDARD PLAIN WASHERS

TW-10	Plain washer $\frac{3}{16}"$ i/dia., $\frac{7}{16}"$ o dia., 21 S.W.G.
TW-11	Plain washer $\frac{3}{32}"$ i/dia., $\frac{7}{16}"$ o dia., 21 S.W.G.
TW-15	Plain washer $\frac{7}{32}"$ i/dia., $\frac{1}{2}"$ o dia., 21 S.W.G.
TW-17	Plain washer $\frac{1}{4}"$ i/dia., $\frac{9}{16}"$ o dia., 20 S.W.G.
TW-20	Plain washer $\frac{5}{16}"$ i/dia., $\frac{3}{4}"$ o dia., 19 S.W.G.
TW-21	Plain washer $\frac{5}{16}"$ i/dia., $\frac{3}{4}"$ o dia., 18 S.W.G.
TW-22	Plain washer $\frac{5}{16}"$ i/dia., $1\frac{1}{4}"$ o dia., 16 S.W.G.
TW-25	Plain washer $\frac{3}{8}"$ i/dia., $\frac{3}{4}"$ o dia., 18 S.W.G.
TW-32	Plain washer $\frac{1}{2}"$ i/dia., $1"$ o dia., 17 S.W.G.
TW-33	Plain washer $\frac{1}{2}"$ i dia., $1\frac{1}{2}"$ o dia., 13 S.W.G.

STANDARD SHAKEPROOF WASHER WITH INTERNAL EARS

TSW-3	Shakeproof washer $\frac{3}{16}"$ i/dia.
TSW-4	Shakeproof washer $\frac{1}{4}"$ i/dia.
TSW-5	Shakeproof washer $\frac{5}{16}"$ i/dia.
TSW-7	Shakeproof washer $\frac{3}{8}"$ i/dia.
TSW-9	Shakeproof washer $\frac{1}{2}"$ i/dia.

STANDARD UNIFIED NUTS

UN1 4F	Standard nut
UN1 5F	Standard nut
UN1 6F	Standard nut
UN1 8F	Standard nut
UN2 4F	Locknut
UN2 5F	Locknut
UN2 6F	Locknut

STANDARD UNIFIED BOLTS

UN4 6F	Bolt $\frac{1}{4}"$ dia. length under head $\frac{3}{8}"$
UN4 8F	Bolt $\frac{1}{4}"$ dia. length under head $\frac{1}{2}"$
UN4 10C	Bolt $\frac{1}{4}"$ dia. length under head $\frac{5}{8}"$
UN4 10F	Bolt $\frac{1}{4}"$ dia. length under head $\frac{5}{8}"$
UN4 12F	Bolt $\frac{1}{4}"$ dia. length under head $\frac{3}{4}"$
UN4 14F	Bolt $\frac{1}{4}"$ dia. length under head $\frac{7}{8}"$
UN4 16F	Bolt $\frac{1}{4}"$ dia. length under head $1"$
UN4 18F	Bolt $\frac{1}{4}"$ dia. length under head $1\frac{1}{8}"$
UN4 28C	Bolt $\frac{1}{4}"$ dia. length under head $1\frac{3}{4}"$
UN5 8F	Bolt $\frac{5}{16}"$ dia. length under head $\frac{1}{2}"$
UN5 10C	Bolt $\frac{5}{16}"$ dia. length under head $\frac{5}{8}"$
UN5 10F	Bolt $\frac{5}{16}"$ dia. length under head $\frac{5}{8}"$
UN5 12C	Bolt $\frac{5}{16}"$ dia. length under head $\frac{3}{4}"$
UN5 14F	Bolt $\frac{5}{16}"$ dia. length under head $\frac{7}{8}"$
UN5 16F	Bolt $\frac{5}{16}"$ dia. length under head $1"$
UN6 14F	Bolt $\frac{3}{8}"$ dia. length under head $\frac{7}{8}"$

VELOCEPRESS MANUALS – MOTORCYCLE BY MAKE

AJS 1932-1948 SINGLES & TWINS 250cc THRU 1000cc (BOOK OF)
AJS 1945-1960 SINGLES 350cc & 500cc MODELS 16 & 18 (BOOK OF)
AJS 1955-1965 SINGLES 350cc & 500cc (BOOK OF)
AJS 1957-1966 FACTORY WSM - ALL SINGLES & TWINS
ARIEL UP TO 1932 (BOOK OF)
ARIEL 1932-1939 PREWAR MODELS (BOOK OF)
ARIEL 1933-1951 (WORKSHOP MANUAL)
ARIEL 1939-1960 4 STROKE SINGLES (BOOK OF)
ARIEL 1958-1964 LEADER & ARROW FACTORY WSM & PARTS LIST
ARIEL 1958-1964 LEADER & ARROW (BOOK OF)
BMW R26 R27 (1956-1967) FACTORY WORKSHOP MANUAL
BMW R50 R50S R60 R69S (1955-1969) FACTORY WORKSHOP MANUAL
BRIDGESTONE 90 SERIES FACTORY WSM & PARTS CATALOGUE
BRIDGESTONE 175 SERIES FACTORY WSM & PARTS CATALOGUE
BRIDGESTONE 350 SERIES FACTORY WSM & PARTS CATALOGUES
BSA SERVICE SHEETS MASTER CATALOGUE ALL MODELS 1945-1967
BSA BANTAM D1 TO D7 1948-1966 FACTORY SERVICE SHEETS MANUAL
BSA BANTAM ALL MODELS FROM 1948 ONWARDS (BOOK OF)
BSA DANDY FACTORY WORKSHOP MANUAL (COMPILATION)
BSA SINGLES & V-TWINS UP TO 1927 (BOOK OF)
BSA SINGLES & V-TWINS UP TO 1930 (BOOK OF)
BSA SINGLES & V-TWINS UP TO 1935 (BOOK OF)
BSA SINGLES & V-TWINS 1936-1939 (BOOK OF)
BSA C10, C11 & C12 1945-1958 FACTORY SERVICE SHEETS MANUAL
BSA OHV & SV SINGLES 250-600cc 1945-1959 (BOOK OF)
BSA C15 & B40 1958-1967 FACTORY SERVICE SHEETS MANUAL
BSA OHV & SV SINGLES 250cc (ONLY) 1954-1970 (BOOK OF)
BSA B31, B32, B33 & B34 1945-60 FACTORY SERVICE SHEETS MANUAL
BSA OHV SINGLES 350 & 500cc 1955-1967 (BOOK OF)
BSA M20, M21 & M33 1945-1963 FACTORY SERVICE SHEETS MANUAL
BSA TWINS A7 & A10 1948-1962 FACTORY SERVICE SHEETS MANUAL
BSA TWINS A7 & A10 1948-1962 (BOOK OF)
BSA TWINS A50 & A65 1962-1965 FACTORY WORKSHOP MANUAL
BSA TWINS A50 & A65 1962-1969 (SECOND BOOK OF)
DOUGLAS 1929-1939 PREWAR ALL MODELS (BOOK OF)
DOUGLAS 1948-1957 POSTWAR ALL MODELS FACTORY SHOP MANUAL
DUCATI 160cc, 250cc & 350cc OHC MODELS FACTORY SHOP MANUAL
HONDA 50cc ALL MODELS UP TO 1970 INC MONKEY & TRAIL (BOOK OF)
HONDA 90cc ALL MODELS UP TO 1966 (BOOK OF)
HONDA 50-65-70-90cc OHC SINGLES 1959-1983 FACTORY WSM
HONDA 100-125cc SINGLES CB/CD/CL/SL/TL 1970-1984 FACTORY WSM
HONDA 125-150cc TWINS C/CS/CB/CA FACTORY WORKSHOP MANUAL
HONDA 125-160-175-200cc TWINS 1965-1978 WORKSHOP MANUAL
HONDA 250-305cc TWINS C/CS/CB 1959-1967 FACTORY WSM
HOHDA 250-350cc TWINS CB/CL/SL 1968-1973 FACTORY WSM
HONDA 450cc TWINS CB/CL 1965-1974 K0 TO K7 WORKSHOP MANUAL
HONDA 500cc & 550cc 4CYL 1971-1978 FACTORY WORKSHOP MANUAL
HONDA 750cc SHOC 4 CYL 1969-1978 K0~K8 WORKSHOP MANUAL
HONDA C100 SUPER CUB FACTORY WORKSHOP MANUAL
HONDA C110 SPORT CUB 1962-1969 FACTORY WORKSHOP MANUAL
HONDA TWINS & SINGLES 50cc THRU 305cc 1960-1966 (BOOK OF)
HONDA TWINS ALL MODELS 125cc THRU 450cc UP TO 1968 (BOOK OF)
INDIAN PONYBIKE, BOY RACER & PAPOOSE ILL PARTS LIST & SALES LIT
J.A.P. ENGINES 1927-1952 & MOTORCYCLES 1934-1952 (BOOK OF)
MATCHLESS 1931-1939 ALL MODELS 250cc THRU 990cc (BOOK OF)
MATCHLESS 1945-1956 350 & 500cc SINGLES (BOOK OF)
MATCHLESS 1955-1966 350 & 500cc SINGLES (BOOK OF)
MATCHLESS 1957-1966 FACTORY WSM - ALL SINGLES & TWINS
NEW IMPERIAL ALL SV & OHV FROM 1935 ONWARDS (BOOK OF)
NORTON 1932-1939 PREWAR MODELS (BOOK OF)
NORTON 1932-1947 (BOOK OF)
NORTON 1938-1956 (BOOK OF)
NORTON 1955-1963 MODELS 19, 50 & ES2 (BOOK OF)
NORTON 1955-1965 DOMINATOR TWINS (BOOK OF)
NORTON 1960-1970 TWIN CYLINDER FACTORY WORKSHOP MANUAL
NORTON 1970-1975 COMMANDO 850 & 750cc FACTORY WSM
NORTON 1975-1978 MK 3 COMMANDO 850 cc FACTORY WSM
PANTHER 1932-1958 LIGHTWEIGHT MODELS 250 & 350cc (BOOK OF)
PANTHER 1938-1966 HEAVYWEIGHT MODELS 600 & 650cc (BOOK OF)
RALEIGH MOTORCYCLES 1919-1933 (BOOK OF)
ROYAL ENFIELD 1934-1946 SINGLES & V TWINS (BOOK OF)
ROYAL ENFIELD 1937-1953 SINGLES & V TWINS (BOOK OF)
ROYAL ENFIELD 1946-1962 SINGLES (BOOK OF)
ROYAL ENFIELD 1958-1966 250cc & 350cc SINGLES (SECOND BOOK OF)
ROYAL ENFIELD 1962-1970 INTERCEPTOR WSM'S & PARTS (Compilation)
RUDGE 1933-1939 (BOOK OF)
SUNBEAM 1928-1939 (BOOK OF)
SUNBEAM 1946-1957 S7 & S8 (BOOK OF)
SUZUKI 50cc & 80cc UP TO 1966 (BOOK OF)
SUZUKI T10 1963-1967 FACTORY WORKSHOP MANUAL
SUZUKI T20 & T200 1965-1969 FACTORY WORKSHOP MANUAL
SUZUKI TWINS 1962 ONWARDS 125-500cc WORKSHOP MANUAL
TRIUMPH 1935-1949 SINGLES & TWINS (BOOK OF)
TRIUMPH 1937-1951 (WORKSHOP MANUAL)
TRIUMPH 1945-1955 FACTORY WORKSHOP MANUAL
TRIUMPH 1945-1959 TWINS (BOOK OF)
TRIUMPH 1956-1969 TWINS (BOOK OF)
TRIUMPH 1963-1970 UNIT CONSTRUCTION 650cc FACTORY WSM
TRIUMPH 1963-1974 UNIT CONSTRUCTION 350-500cc FACTORY WSM
TRIUMPH 1968-1974 TRIDENT T150 & T150V FACTORY WSM
VELOCETTE 1925-1970 ALL SINGLES & TWINS (BOOK OF)
VELOCETTE 1933-1952 MOV-MAC-MSS RIGID FRAME FACTORY WSM
VELOCETTE 1954-1971 MSS-VENOM-THRUXTON-VIPER FACTORY WSM
VILLIERS ENGINE UP TO 1959 INC. 3 WHEELERS (BOOK OF)
VILLIERS ENGINE UP TO 1968 (BOOK OF)
VINCENT 1935-1955 (WORKSHOP MANUAL)
YAMAHA 1961-1967 YA5 & YA6 (WORKSHOP MANUAL & ILL PARTS LIST)
YAMAHA 1971-1972 JT1 & JT2 (WORKSHOP MANUAL & ILL PARTS LIST)

www.VelocePress.com

VELOCEPRESS TECHNICAL BOOKS – MOTORCYCLE

1930'S BRITISH MOTORCYCLE CARBS & ELEC COMPONENTS (BOOK OF)
1930'S BRITISH MOTORCYCLE ENGINES (OVERHAUL & MAINTENANCE)
1930'S BRITISH MOTORCYCLE GEARBOXES & CLUTCHES (BOOK OF)
CATALOG OF BRITISH MOTORCYCLES (1951 MODELS)
LUCAS ELECTRONICS BRITISH M/CYCLES REPAIR & PARTS (1950-1977)
MOTORCYCLE ENGINEERING (P.E. Irving)
MOTORCYCLE ROAD TESTS 1949-1953 (Motor Cycle Magazine UK)
SPEED AND HOW TO OBTAIN IT (Motor Cycle Magazine UK)
TUNING FOR SPEED (P.E. Irving)
WIPAC (COMBO) MANUAL NUMBER 3 + M/CYCLE & SCOOTER MANUAL

VELOCEPRESS MANUALS – SCOOTERS BY MAKE

BSA SUNBEAM SCOOTER WORKSHOP MANUAL 1959-1965
BSA SUNBEAM SCOOTER 1959-1965 (BOOK OF)
LAMBRETTA 1947-1957 ALL 125 & 150cc MODELS (BOOK OF)
LAMBRETTA 1957-1970 LI & TV MODELS (SECOND BOOK OF)
NSU PRIMA 1956-1964 ALL MODELS (BOOK OF)
TRIUMPH TIGRESS SCOOTER WORKSHOP MANUAL 1959-1965
TRIUMPH TIGRESS SCOOTER (BOOK OF)
VESPA 1951-1961 (BOOK OF)
VESPA 1955-1963 125 & 150cc & GS MODELS (SECOND BOOK OF)
VESPA 1955-1968 GS & SS (BOOK OF)
VESPA 1963-1972 90, 125 & 150cc (THIRD BOOK OF)

VELOCEPRESS MANUALS – MOPEDS & MOTORIZED BICYCLES

CYCLEMOTOR (BOOK OF)
NSU QUICKLY 1953-1963 ALL MODELS (BOOK OF)
PUCH MAXI N & S MAINTENANCE & REPAIR (3 MANUAL COMPILATION)
RALEIGH MOPEDS 1960-1969 (BOOK OF)

VELOCEPRESS MANUALS - THREE WHEELER'S

BOND MINICAR THREE WHEELER 1948-1967 (BOOK OF)
BMW ISETTA FACTORY WORKSHOP MANUAL
BSA THREE WHEELER (BOOK OF)
RELIANT REGAL THREE WHEELER 1952-1973 (BOOK OF)
VINTAGE MORGAN THREE WHEELER (BOOK OF)

VELOCEPRESS MANUALS – AUTOMOBILE BY MAKE

ALFA ROMEO GIULIA WORKSHOP MANUAL 1300 TO 2000cc 1962-1975
ALFA ROMEO GIULIA TECH MANUAL CARBURETED CARS FROM 1962
ALFA ROMEO GIULIA TECH MANUAL FUEL INJECTED CARS FROM 1969
ALFA ROMEO GIULIETTA & GIULIA 750 & 101 SERIES 1955-1965 WSM
AUSTIN-HEALEY SPRITE & MG MIDGET WORKSHOP MANUAL 1958-1971
BMW 600 LIMOUSINE FACTORY WORKSHOP MANUAL
BMW 600 LIMOUSINE OWNERS HAND BOOK & SERVICE MANUAL
BMW 2000 & 2002 1966-1976 WORKSHOP MANUAL
CORVAIR 1960-1969 WORKSHOP MANUAL
CORVETTE V8 1955-1962 WORKSHOP MANUAL
FERRARI HANDBOOK ROAD & RACE CARS (SERVICE/SPECS) 1948-1958
FERRARI 250/GT SERVICE & MAINTENANCE MANUAL 1956-1965
FIAT 500 FACTORY WORKSHOP MANUAL 1957-1973
FIAT 600, 600D & MULTIPLA FACTORY WORKSHOP MANUAL 1955-1969
JAGUAR E-TYPE 3.8 & 4.2 SERIES 1 & 2 WORKSHOP MANUAL
JAGUAR MK 7, 8, 9 & XK120, 140, 150 FACTORY WSM 1948-1961
METROPOLITAN FACTORY WORKSHOP MANUAL
MGA & MGB OWNERS HANDBOOK & WORKSHOP MANUAL
MG MIDGET TC, TD, TF & TF1500 WORKSHOP MANUAL
PORSCHE 356 1948-1965 WORKSHOP MANUAL
PORSCHE 911 2.0, 2.2, 2.4 LITRE 1964-1973 WORKSHOP MANUAL
PORSCHE 911 2.7, 3.0, 3.2 LITRE 1973-1989 WORKSHOP MANUAL
PORSCHE 912 WORKSHOP MANUAL
PORSCHE 914/4 & 914/6 1.7, 1.8, 2.0 LITRE 1970-1976 WSM
TRIUMPH TR2, TR3, TR4 1953-1965 WORKSHOP MANUAL
VOLKSWAGEN TRANSPORTER, TRUCKS & WAGONS 1950-1979 WSM
VOLVO 1944-1968 ALL MODELS WORKSHOP MANUAL

VELOCEPRESS TECHNICAL BOOKS - AUTOMOBILE

HOW TO BUILD A FIBERGLASS CAR
HOW TO BUILD A RACING CAR
HOW TO RESTORE THE MODEL 'A' FORD
MASERATI OWNER'S HANDBOOK
PERFORMANCE TUNING THE SUNBEAM TIGER
SOUPING THE VOLKSWAGEN
SOLEX CARBURETORS (EMPHASIS ON UK & EU AUTOMOBILES)
SU CARBURETORS (EMPHASIS ON UK AUTOMOBILES)
WEBER CARBURETORS (EMPHASIS ON ALFA & FIAT)

VELOCEPRESS BOOKS & GUIDES - AUTOMOBILE

COMPLETE CATALOG OF JAPANESE MOTOR VEHICLES
FERRARI 308 SERIES BUYER'S AND OWNER'S GUIDE
FERRARI BROCHURES AND SALES LITERATURE 1968-1989
FERRARI SERIAL NUMBERS PART I - ODD NUMBERS TO 21399
FERRARI SERIAL NUMBERS PART II - EVEN NUMBERS TO 1050
HENRY'S FABULOUS MODEL "A" FORD
MASERATI BROCHURES AND SALES LITERATURE

VELOCEPRESS BOOKS – RACING

CARRERA PANAMERICANA - MEXICAN ROAD RACE (BOOK OF)
DIALED IN - THE JAN OPPERMAN STORY
VEDA ORR'S NEW REVISED HOT ROD PICTORIAL

www.ingramcontent.com/pod-product-compliance
Lightning Source LLC
Chambersburg PA
CBHW060246240426
43673CB00047B/1883